A PEOPLE'S HISTORY OF
THE CIVIL WAR

ALSO BY DAVID WILLIAMS

Plain Folk in a Rich Man's War: Class and Dissent in Confederate Georgia
(with Teresa Crisp Williams and David Carlson)

Johnny Reb's War: Battlefield and Homefront

*Rich Man's War: Class, Caste, and Confederate Defeat in the Lower
Chattahoochee Valley*

The Georgia Gold Rush: Twenty-niners, Cherokees, and Gold Fever

Gold Fever: America's First Gold Rush
(with Ray C. Rensi)

A PEOPLE'S HISTORY OF THE CIVIL WAR

STRUGGLES FOR THE MEANING OF FREEDOM

DAVID WILLIAMS

THE NEW PRESS

NEW YORK
LONDON

© 2005 by David Williams
All rights reserved.
No part of this book may be reproduced, in any form, without written permission
from the publisher.

Requests for permission to reproduce selections from this book should be mailed to:
Permissions Department, The New Press, 38 Greene Street, New York, NY 10013

Published in the United States by The New Press, New York, 2005
Distributed by W. W. Norton & Company, Inc., New York

LIBRARY OF CONGRESS CATALOGING-IN-PUBLICATION DATA

Williams, David, 1959–
    A people's history of the Civil War : struggles for the meaning of freedom / David Williams.
        p. cm. — (A New Press people's history)
    Includes bibliographical references (p.).
    ISBN 1-59558-018-2
        1. United States—History—Civil War, 1861–1865—Social aspects.   2. United States—
History—Civil War, 1861–1865.   I. Title.   II. Series.

E468.9.W56 2005
973.7—dc22   2005043873

The New Press was established in 1990 as a not-for-profit alternative to the large, commercial
publishing houses currently dominating the book publishing industry. The New Press operates
in the public interest rather than for private gain, and is committed to publishing, in innovative
ways, works of educational, cultural, and community value that are often deemed
insufficiently profitable.

www.thenewpress.com

Composition by Westchester Book Composition

Printed in the United States of America

2   4   6   8   10   9   7   5   3   1

For Trish

Contents

Acknowledgments

Foremost among the many debts I owe in the making of this book is to Howard Zinn for encouraging me throughout the project and for his long years of dedication to the practice of people's history. I first read his *People's History of the United States* many years ago as a graduate student, and his point of view has inspired my work ever since. I hardly owe less of a debt to the many fine scholars upon whose work this book is based. The inquisitive perseverance and diligent research reflected in their works have made mine possible. For help with tracking down those works and making good use of them, I am indebted to Alan Bernstein, Denise Montgomery, and Rex DeVane of Valdosta State University's Odum Library.

Marc Favreau, senior editor at The New Press, deserves much appreciation for his suggestions on improving the manuscript and for shepherding it through the publishing works. Sarah Fan, my production editor, and David Allen, my copy editor, deserve much appreciation as well for their hard work in carrying the manuscript through its final paces toward print.

Though a small contribution to the literature of my field, this work is quite likely to be my magnum opus. So, on this occasion, I feel compelled, as I often do but fail in the follow-through, to say how grateful I am to those who contributed so much to the making of me and my career. First to my parents, Harold O. Williams and Anita D.

Williams, children of poverty and depression who made sure that their children knew the value of education. And to my younger brother, Scott, who often served more as an example to me than I did to him.

To my wife, Teresa Crisp Williams, I shall always be grateful for her many years of steadfast patience and loving encouragement. Her faith in me has been the foundation on which my efforts have been largely built. I am eternally grateful to her family as well for their patience, tolerance, and help with more moves than I care to remember.

I owe many thanks to a few professors from my undergraduate days at North Georgia College for their inspiration, insights, and personal efforts for me: John Csomor, who taught me that true patriotism is never blind; Frank Smith, who showed me that there are at least half-a-dozen reasons for everything; Brian Murphy, who gave me a broader view of what democracy should mean; and Ray Rensi, who showed me what I could be as a teacher.

I am especially grateful to my professors during my doctoral days at Auburn University for their exemplary lessons in what it is to be a scholar. Especially influential were Guy Beckwith, Donna Bohanan, Thomas Belser, John Cottier, Allen Cronenberg, Wayne Flynt, Larry Gerber, James Hansen, Joseph Harrison, Joe Kicklighter, David Lewis, Michael Melancon, Steve McFarland, and Bill Trimble. A special thanks goes to my dissertation adviser, Frank Lawrence Owsley Jr., who never kept the reins too tight.

I am grateful also to friends and fellow students along the way. Among those whose concern, companionship, and memories remain most treasured are Bob Patterson, Lisa Stepancic, Kay Ray, Tom Amsler, Joy Hartsfield, B.J. House, Beth McNeil, Kathy Yarbrough, Connie Dunbar, Renee Bruce, Debbie Brannon, Mark McDonough, Brian Phelps, Gene Smith, Jim Segrest, Bill Bryant, Johnny Dollar, Susan Dollar, Martha Viator, Karen Beckwith, Jack Bergstresser, Sandra Bergstresser, Mickey Crews, Hal Parker, Church Murdock, Kim Cantrell, Mary Lee Carter, Alice Pate, Lynne Rieff, Burt Rieff, Dottye Ricks, and Richard Porter.

Any number of fellow scholars have been supportive of my work over the years, read and commented on earlier manuscripts, or otherwise helped my career along the way. Among those who deserve special mention for their support are David Carlson, Lee Formwalt, John Inscoe, William Freehling, Wayne Durrill, Anne Bailey, Anastatia Sims, Mike Fitzgerald, Junius Rodriguez, Billy Winn, Victoria

Bynum, Jeff Jakeman, David Heidler, Jeanne Heidler, Emory Thomas, Nash Boney, Edmund Drago, Stanley Harrold, and Randall Miller.

Among friends and colleagues at Valdosta State University who have supported and encouraged me, my first nod of gratitude goes to Joe Tomberlin, professor emeritus and former history department chair, who placed his faith in me as a young scholar looking for an institutional home. For their help during my own time as department chair, I am grateful to Jay Rickman, director of the department's undergraduate studies program; Charles Johnson, who served as director of graduate studies; and Melanie Byrd, director of planning and program review. They carried much of the department's administrative burden while I was working on the early stages of this book.

Other friends and colleagues in Valdosta who deserve my sincere thanks are Tracy Meyers, Jacob Meyers, Mary Block, John Crowley, John Dunn, Paul Badura, Dixie Ray Haggard, Regina Haggard, Shirley Hardin, Pam Rickman, Okete Shiroya, Brian Adler, James La-Plant, Ernestine Clark, Catherine Schaeffer, Susan Eischeid, Patsy Howard, Patrick McElwain, Tommye Miller, Liz Rose, Martha Laughlin, Kate Warner, Allen DeVane, Deborah Davis, Sandra Walker, Susan Wehling, Willie Mincy, and Stan White. Most read parts of this or earlier incarnations of my work, and all have contributed mightily to making my environs a pleasant place to be. Particularly enjoyable has been my friendly banter with Chris Meyers, a fellow historian who remains grounded in the political-military history tradition despite my jestingly provocative efforts. No such difficulty with Cathy Badura, who is perhaps the most socially enlightened member of our department. I owe her a very special debt of gratitude for her comments on major portions of the manuscript and for her patience in tolerating her annoying friend from down the hall.

For their support in the form of encouragement and reassigned time to work on this project, I wish to thank Linda Calendrillo, dean of the College of Arts and Sciences; Sharon Gravett, assistant vice president for academic affairs; Louis Levy, vice president for academic affairs; and Ronald Zaccari, president of Valdosta State. I would especially like to thank my department chair and fellow guitar enthusiast, Paul Riggs, for the support and encouragement he has shown in more ways than I can say.

Finally, I wish to extend a very special thanks to Patricia Coleman Mincy, who has served for nearly twenty-five years as senior secretary of Valdosta State's Department of History. With infinite patience, inspirational pleasantness, and amazing grace, she has tolerated the quirky impositions of academia and the mindless minutiae of administration. Through it all she has remained the consummate professional and the department's central mainstay. And she has always made sure that the candy jar is full. It is to her that this book is dedicated with much appreciation and affection.

A PEOPLE'S HISTORY OF
THE CIVIL WAR

Introduction

"The People at War"

The Civil War years are among the most captivating of American history. Names of great leaders and great battles trip off the tongue like icons of ancient myth. Ghosts of the nineteenth century are daily resurrected to sanctify our past and justify our present. Yet for all the attention it receives, the Civil War as part of a larger and ongoing social conflict is still not generally acknowledged. But the people who lived through that time fought through everyday struggles whose collective meaning and results were ultimately much bigger than battles, much greater than leaders, and much broader than the Civil War itself. Laboring people, urban and rural, fought for economic justice. Women struggled for rights and opportunities and for their families' survival. Volunteers and conscripts demanded respect for themselves and their families, hundreds of thousands answering the call of a higher duty when their demands were not met. Dissenters constantly expanded the bounds of liberty and the rights of conscience. Native Americans struggled to hold their land and maintain their very existence. And African Americans fought in various ways for freedom and made the Civil War their own long before Lincoln drafted emancipation to the service of an embattled Union cause.[1]

Such struggles of people against power had been going on for decades. Fanny Wright—a Scottish-born crusader who spoke for human rights in Britain, organized for labor rights in New York, and campaigned for emancipation in Tennessee—wrote of those conflicts in her 1830 article, "The People at War."

> What distinguishes the present from every other struggle in which the human race has been engaged, is, that the present is, evidently, openly and acknowledgedly, a war of class, and that this war is universal. . . . It is the ridden people of the earth who are struggling to throw from their backs the "booted and spurred" riders whose legitimate title to starve as well as to work them to death will no longer pass current; it is labor rising up against idleness, industry against money, justice against law and against privilege.[2]

For over two centuries, the privileged men of colonial and early national America had worked to limit dissent, channel discontent, and secure wealth and power to themselves. They used the Bible and civil law to sanction Indian extermination or removal. They used God and natural law to argue for oppression of women and blacks. They used patriotism and bigotry to turn the native-born against immigrants and immigrants against each other. They used racism to unite whites across class lines and turn poor whites against blacks. They used nearly every conceivable strategy, appealing to the basest human vices at one turn and speaking for God himself at another, to keep the social underclasses divided and more easily controlled.

It was a precarious balancing act for power elites who had found it necessary to justify rebellion against Britain by proposing the radical idea that all men were created equal. Though the Founding Fathers rarely put that notion into practice, the Declaration of Independence served its immediate purpose of drawing at least some support for their rebellion.[3] Then, after the war, they tried largely to forget all their bluster about equality. But it was far from forgotten by less fortunate men who had fought for equality's promise and been betrayed by those who had promised it. Over the following decades—through action like Shays's Rebellion, the Whiskey Rebellion, Nat Turner's revolt, the abolitionist movement, the movement for women's rights—Americans fought a continuing revolution to make the Declaration of Independence a reality for themselves. Elite control was never easy or complete. Limited concessions, such as restricted voting rights, were often necessary. But control became even more difficult as deprived peoples continued resisting oppression—actively and passively, violently and nonviolently, individually and collectively—throughout the early nineteenth century into the Civil War era.

"Rich Man's War!"

In the South, many common whites like Hinton Rowan Helper began to see themselves as impoverished by the dominant slave system. Slaves themselves like Frederick Douglass were becoming increasingly resistant and more difficult to control. By 1860 most slaveholders worried that although Abraham Lincoln publicly opposed only slavery's expansion, not its continued existence, his election might give encouragement to dissenters and resisters, making control all the more difficult. Slaveholders were sure that with Lincoln in the White House, slaves would be even more prone "to insubordination, to poisoning, arson, pillage and murder." As for nonslaveholders, one planter asked nervously: "If the poor whites realized that slavery kept them poor, would they not vote it down?" Some feared that there might soon be "an Abolition party in the South, of Southern men." Another frankly admitted, "I mistrust our own people more than I fear all of the efforts of the Abolitionists."[4] Such fears led slaveholders to conclude that slavery's future would be more secure outside the Union than in it.

Up North, efforts of elites to channel economic and social discontent into the electoral process were beginning to fail as well. The anti-renter movement, an armed rebellion of tenant farmers in the Hudson River Valley, exemplified rural discontent. In urban areas, strikes by laboring men and women were increasingly common. Organizations like the Workingmen's Party in Lynn, Massachusetts, even threatened to wrest political control from the hands of elites.[5] During the early months of the secession crisis, working folk continued to show more interest in struggling against northern industrialists than against southern disunionists. In January 1861, as cotton states were seceding one by one, New York's *Rochester Union* wrote: "We hear a great deal of talk among the ardent platform Republicans about coercing the secessionists of the south by means of Northern soldiers, but the indications are that the fighting is to be done mostly with the tongue."[6]

Despite reluctance among the common folk, industrialists pressured Lincoln to hold the cotton states in the Union—by compromise if possible, by force if necessary. How else could they be guaranteed ongoing access to southern markets and cheap cotton? Some, like a writer in the *Boston Herald*, feared that an independent Confederacy would "impose a heavy tax upon the cotton used by northern manufacturers. In this way she would seek to cripple the North."[7] Such concerns carried little weight among the mass of working-class northerners. Only the Confederacy's firing on the Stars and Stripes at Fort Sumter sparked enough nationalism in the North to bring Lincoln the volunteers he needed for an army. That nationalism, along with brute force, would be used by northern elites over the next few years to divert worker hostility, suppress the labor movement, and, for a time at least, restore some measure of control.

Though there was some enthusiasm for the war early on, that the rich were profiting while others were dying led common people on both sides to question their respective causes. In the South, planters devoted far too much land to cotton and not enough to food. Spring of 1862 found one southwest Georgia man writing to Governor Joe Brown about planters growing too much cotton and begging him to "stop those internal enemies of the country, for they will whip us sooner than all Lincolndom combined could do it."[8] With cotton smuggled out by land and sea, some planters bragged that the longer the war went on the more money they made. The result was a severe food shortage for soldiers and civilians alike. Most of what food planters did produce was sold to speculators, who priced it far beyond the ability of common folk to pay.

Officials sought to compensate for the food shortage by imposing a tax-in-kind called impressment, taking what they needed for little or no pay. Impressment hit small farmers hardest, many of them women with husbands in the army. Planters often had the connections to avoid impressment. Much of the impressed food found its way to speculators through corrupt government officials, driving food prices even higher. Poor farm families struggling to survive increasingly had to sell what land they had, mostly to those who already had large land holdings. Urban workers fared little better. Industrial wages rose in the South, but so rampant were food shortages, speculation, and corruption that wages never kept pace with inflation.

The same was true of wages in the North. Corporate profits soared, and prices with them, but wages lagged far behind. Industrialists cut corners and provided shoddy goods to the military, killing soldiers in the process. They endangered workers back home as well, speeding up production with little thought of worker safety. Strikes for better wages and working conditions often followed. Railroad workers in New York, riggers in Boston, and coal miners in Pennsylvania were among the laboring multitudes who insisted on economic justice and safer working conditions. Capitalists struck back violently, often with the help of state, local, and federal authorities. In the interests of what we would today call "national security," ignoring worker security as if the two were separate and distinct, the army beat down strikers in Rutland, Vermont; St. Louis, Missouri; Cold Springs, New York; and Tioga County, Pennsylvania, among other places.

Women were likewise affected by difficulties on the home front. And they took action as well. Many participated in the struggle for economic justice and were beaten down just as their men were. There was the additional struggle to be accepted into professions typically occupied by men. In factories, in hospitals, in government offices, women insisted on their right to take on nontraditional roles. Though their services were needed, and in many cases appreciated, they still faced resentment from men and sometimes other women, constrained as they were by a "cult of domesticity" that placed strict boundaries on what women should and should not do. In army hospitals, male physicians frequently objected to the "petticoat government," as they put it, imposed by female matrons. One doctor was overheard complaining to a colleague "in a tone of ill-concealed disgust," as an army nurse recalled, "that 'one of *them* had come.' "[9]

Perhaps most difficult for women was the absence of their husbands. A northern preacher wrote: "Yesterday I saw the wife of one of our parishioners driving the team in a reaper; her husband is at Vicksburg. With what help she can secure and the assistance of her little children, she is carrying on the farm. In another field was a little boy of ten years, similarly employed; and in another a girl of about twelve, doing the same. Men cannot be found in sufficient numbers to secure the harvest."[10] Having their men in the army was especially hard on women in the South, where food shortages and impressment hit hard. Many urban women—from Richmond, Virginia, to Sherman, Texas— responded with riots and robberies to keep their families fed. So did those in rural areas. A southwest Georgia planter ran a notice in local papers warning poor soldiers' wives to stop stealing his livestock. Many such men were "bonded" planters who had signed agreements with the state to provide food for soldiers' families. But they grew too much cotton for export and sold what food they produced to speculators. In May 1863, a soldier from Harris County, Georgia, wrote home to his wife Sarah: "You spoke of a riot in Columbus . . . it is no more than I expected. I understand there was also one in Augusta. . . . What will become of the women and children with the food situation?"[11] Indeed, thousands of soldiers wondered how their families would get along in their absence. With hunger rampant and the planters unwilling to help, many began to question whether the Confederacy was worth preserving at all, much less fighting for. As the war lumbered on and conditions worsened, more and more soldiers decided it was not.

Hardships suffered by men and boys in the army were as bad as those on the home front and often worse. More than a fourth of all soldiers lost their lives. Disease struck most of them down; poor medical treatment condemned many of the rest. Dismal as standards of medicine were at the time, suffering was made even worse by government indifference to medical services. As one official noted, "the business of war is to tear the body, not mend it." Lincoln himself once referred to the Sanitary Commission, a civilian relief organization that provided free medical care for soldiers, as "the fifth wheel to the coach."[12]

Higher-ranking officers got the best of what treatment was available. One soldier complained that officers were the first to be taken to hospitals while more badly wounded enlisted men were left where they lay. It was but one example of the class disparities so prevalent in both armies. Officers got their pay when soldiers went without. Officers got furloughs when none were available to enlisted men. Punishment for soldiers ranged from beatings, to brandings, to executions, yet officers guilty of like offenses might suffer only confinement to quarters. As for quitting the army altogether, as one soldier put it: "A general could resign. That was honorable. A private could not resign . . . and if he deserted, it was death."[13]

Still, soldiers deserted by the hundreds of thousands. Desertion-rate estimates range as high as a third for the Federals and two-thirds for Confederates. Maltreatment and disillusionment played a part, but most left in response to pleas from their families to come home. "We have nothing in the house to eat but a little bit of meal," one southern woman penned to her soldier husband. If he did not come soon, she warned, " 'twont be no use to come, for we'll all hands of us be out there in the garden in the old grave yard with your ma and mine." As women near the edge of starvation saw it, for a man to look to his family's welfare could not be wrong. "Think the time past has sufficed for *public* service," a mother wrote to her boy in the army, "& that your own family require yr protection & help—as others are deciding."[14]

Some deserters allied themselves with a number of antiwar societies that operated in both the North and South. In the North, the most prominent "dark lantern" societies, such as the Order of American Knights and the Sons of Liberty, were connected with antiwar Democrats, or Copperheads. Responding to the threat of organized resistance, Lincoln suspended the writ of habeas corpus and moved to silence dissent where he could. Some newspapers were forced to shut down, and others were denied use of the postal service. Thousands of administration critics were jailed without warrant. Some were handcuffed and suspended by their wrists, while others were hosed down with painful jets of water. One man was subjected to this water torture for two hours until it finally broke his skin. Perhaps the most violent expressions of general dissent were the draft riots that broke out in Boston, Newark, Chicago, St. Paul, Milwaukee, and Toledo, among other northern cities. The most serious occurred in New York, where rioters rampaged through the streets shouting "Rich man's war!" More than 100 people lost their lives in a week of violence, suppressed only when federal troops, some straight from the Battle of Gettysburg, were sent into the city.

In the South, the "rich man's war" attitude and resistance to the draft was just as fierce, though more diffuse. Draft evaders simply refused to report for duty and hid out in southern swamps, pine barrens, and hill country. Some helped organize the Peace and Constitutional Society, which worked to undermine Confederate authority in Arkansas. Others formed the Order of the Heroes of America in the southern Appalachians. Perhaps the largest antiwar organization in the South was the Peace Society, which counted membership in Mississippi, Tennessee, Alabama, Georgia, and Florida. Historian Walter Fleming estimated that by 1863 at least half the white males in Alabama were associated with the Peace Society. Some deserters joined with draft dodgers and other anti-Confederates to organize guerrilla bands called "tory" or "layout" gangs. They attacked government supply trains, burned bridges, raided plantations, and harassed impressment agents and conscript officers. So violent did the South's internal civil war become by 1863 that one southern newspaper wrote, "We are fighting each other harder than we ever fought the enemy."[15]

If whites were often divided in their loyalties, blacks rarely were. As a group they were the most enthusiastic of anti-Confederates. The Confederacy's vice president, Alexander H. Stephens, had said in March 1861 that slavery was their natural condition and the cornerstone on which the new government was founded. With Lincoln's tentatively worded Emancipation Proclamation came at least a hope of freedom that enslaved southern blacks and their northern relatives eagerly embraced. But in fact, they were taking freedom for themselves long before the war or the Proclamation. More than a hundred thousand escaped to freedom in the years before the war.[16]

Others resisted in place by subtle and overt means. The war only quickened the pace of a wave of resistance that was already gaining strength. From the war's outset, in what historian W.E.B. Du Bois called a general strike against the Confederacy, enslaved blacks began to travel at will, demand wages for labor, gather freely, refuse instruction, and resist punishment. As early as 1861, an overseer complained to his employer that the slaves would not submit to physical punishment. One slave simply walked away when the overseer told him he was about to be whipped. Another slave drew a knife on an overseer who tried to whip him. A plantation mistress wrote concerning one of her slaves: "Nancy has been very impertinent.... She said she would not be hired out by the month, neither would she go out to get work." Another woman wrote to her husband: "We are doing as best we know, or as good as we can get the Servants to do; they learn to feel very independent."[17]

Slaves went so far as to strike out violently against slaveholders and local authorities, sometimes cooperating with anti-Confederate whites in the effort. Two slaves in Dale County, Alabama, helped John Ward, leader of a local deserter gang, kill their owner in his bed. In the spring of 1862, authorities arrested three white citizens of Calhoun County, Georgia, for supplying area slaves with firearms in preparation for a rebellion. Two years later, slaves in nearby Brooks County conspired with a local white man, John Vickery, to take the county and hold it for the Union.[18]

Tens of thousands of slaves freed themselves, fled North, and joined the Union army. But they were hardly welcomed with open arms. Blacks struggled for the right simply to be treated as soldiers instead of slaves. Most whites, wedded as they were to racist notions of white supremacy, argued that blacks were fit only for menial tasks and used that assumption to justify inadequate training and unequal pay. General William T. Sherman asked, "Can they improvise bridges, sorties, flank movements, etc., like the white man? I say no."[19] Few whites granted that blacks possessed the discipline for soldiering. In June 1863, blacks of the Union's 9th Louisiana proved them wrong at the Battle of Milliken's Bend. So did the 54th Massachusetts a month later at Fort Wagner. Time and time again black servicemen demonstrated their determination and capabilities, much more than whites generally were willing to acknowledge. Far from granting blacks their due, most northern whites remained hostile to blacks generally, and many to the goal of emancipation, throughout the war. Still, blacks continued their demand for freedom and pinned their hopes on a Union cause that at least held out the promise of freedom.

In Indian Territory (later Oklahoma) and other parts of the West, loyalties were often more difficult to settle upon. Some Native Americans sided with the United States, hoping to garner favor from Lincoln and avoid further land loss. Others allied themselves with the Confederacy, hoping that if the South could secure its independence, perhaps they could as well. The two camps formed secret societies, like the pro-Confederate Knights of the Golden Circle and the pro-Union Keetowahs, which sometimes came to blows. More cautious heads, like John Ross of the Cherokees, tried to remain neutral. But as it had been for centuries, events beyond their control tended to drive a wedge between the Indians. For the Territory nations, such divisions had deep roots and reflected much the same question that had divided them in the past—would cooperation with the United States or opposition to it bring the better result? Those divisions also reflected a class structure which broke down mainly along mixed-blood/full-blood lines. Slaveholding was more common among the dominant and affluent mixed-bloods, who tended to side with the Confederacy.

Further west, those natives who thought a show of support for the Union would secure tribal lands were wrong. The Treaty of Fort Wise in 1861 made that clear to Colorado's Cheyenne and Arapaho. Those who thought cooperation might offer at least some small protection

were equally mistaken. Western commanders used the war as an excuse to define all Indians as threats to national security regardless of
their posture toward the whites. In 1864, Cheyenne and Arapaho under Black Kettle negotiated peace, accepting settlement on the arid
wastes of Sand Creek in eastern Colorado. But at dawn on November
29, soldiers led by militia colonel and Methodist minister John Chivington attacked the Sand Creek settlement, killing every Indian they
could find, about 150 in all. Over half the dead were women and children. Black Kettle had tried to stop the massacre by tying a U.S. flag
and a white flag of truce to a lodge pole, telling his people to gather
around it. Those who did were cut down under the banners. It was but
a single instance of many in which Indians found themselves set upon
regardless of their actions or alliances. Simply being Indian was
enough to invite attack.

"It Does Not Tell the Truth"

Historians traditionally have paid little attention to the Civil War in
the West, failing to acknowledge the impact that Indian resistance had
on the larger course of events. That failure reflects a broader cultural
and scholarly tendency that until recently has ignored, and too often
still obscures, the efforts of common people in shaping American history. Fortunately, like the controls against which they have always
struggled, the historical tendency to ignore common folk has never
been complete. A few conscientious historians of the late nineteenth
and early twentieth centuries put their talents to work for a broader
view of history, among them Helen Hunt Jackson, with her work on
Indians; Philip Foner, famous for his studies of the early labor movement; Frank Owsley and Bell Wiley, who pioneered work on the
South's plain folk; W.E.B. Du Bois, with his groundbreaking studies
of African American history; Herbert Aptheker, whose work highlighted African American resistance to slavery; and Georgia Lee
Tatum, with her focus on dissent in the Confederacy.[20]

These and other scholarly voices called for a more comprehensive
treatment of American history, stressing that the mass of Americans,
not simply the power elites, made history. Yet it was mainly white
males of the power elite who had the means to attend college, become
professional historians, and shape a view of history that served their

own class, race, and gender interests at the expense of those not so fortunate—and quite literally to paper over aspects of history they found uncomfortable. "One is astonished in the study of history," wrote Du Bois in 1935, "at the recurrence of the idea that evil must be forgotten, distorted, skimmed over. . . . The difficulty, of course, with this philosophy is that history loses its value as an incentive and example; it paints perfect men and noble nations, but it does not tell the truth."[21]

The restrictive wall around higher education began to crumble after World War II, when veterans who had fought in the name of self-determination abroad demanded it for themselves at home. A compensatory GI bill funneled aid to hundreds of thousands of first-generation college students. The system of state four-year and community colleges that grew to take advantage of that aid further widened academic access across class lines, and across gender lines when young women insisted on their right to attend. And the civil rights movement, at great cost in pain and lives, forced open even more tightly shut doors to public higher education, as did AIM, the American Indian Movement. Those and other struggles of the post-war era clearly demonstrated the power of people's movements. For a new and more broadly representative generation of scholars, they also sparked an interest in the impact that people's struggles had on the nation's history.

Much of their interest has focused on people of the Civil War era. Through prolific research in original sources, they have expanded immensely our knowledge of how those left out of or marginalized in earlier histories helped shape their time and our own. The past few years have seen a proliferation of important and provocative works from new perspectives.[22] Yet compelling as they are, such works have had a depressingly small impact on popular views of the Civil War era. It is still too common to read that "Lincoln freed the slaves," as if African Americans themselves did not force the issue; to see commanding generals portrayed as having "won" or "lost" a battle, as if the men who fought, or refused to fight, had little to do with the outcome; to be told that the Civil War "created" opportunities for women, as if women did not insist upon and even create those opportunities for themselves; and to hear that "the North beat the South," as if the Union could have survived without the armed service of nearly half a million southerners, not to mention the anti-Confederate activities of many more.

Recent cinematic productions such as *Glory* and *Cold Mountain* have gone some way toward showing the public another side of the war. But they remain overshadowed in the public mind by films such as *Gone with the Wind* and *Gettysburg*, both of which foster traditional misconceptions of race, class, and general unity. One of the worst offenders is *Gods and Generals*, a much inferior prequel to the *Gettysburg* film. Professor Steven E. Woodworth, author of many scholarly books on the war, quite rightly notes that *Gods and Generals* "brings to the big screen the major themes of Lost Cause mythology that professional historians have been working for half a century to combat."[23]

Our misleading popular, and too often scholarly, image of Civil War America stems in large part from a general overemphasis on its military and political aspects. Such studies are certainly necessary to a complete understanding of the era. But focusing so much of our collective attention on battles and leaders tends to leave the misimpression that common folk simply drifted with the flow of events as their leaders directed. That misimpression persists largely because historians fail to shed light on the ways common folk influenced those events. In fact, what political leaders of the Civil War era did on the public stage reflected their reaction to popular forces as much as their desire to steer those forces in a given direction.

Such social tensions had deep roots in colonial and early-national America. They sprang from concentrations of power and wealth against which the people at large were constantly pressing in an effort to expand or protect their own rights and opportunities. The elites pressed back from their centers of power. Violent confrontations, large and small, were often the result. In that sense, civil wars were nothing new to nineteenth-century Americans. In many ways, the Civil War itself was an outgrowth of those earlier and ongoing struggles. And it was common people of all stripes who would largely shape the Civil War's course and outcome.

1

"All for the Benefit of the Wealthy"

But whoever waited for the common people when a great move
was to be made—We must make the move and force them to
follow.[1]

—ALFRED P. ALDRICH, SOUTH CAROLINA SECESSIONIST

There was an undoubted majority of the people who desired to
remain in the Union. . . . The election machinery was all in the
hands of the secessionists, who manipulated the election to suit
their end.[2]

—JOHN FRANCIS TENNEY, FLORIDA VOTER

"Shameless and Unconcealed Intimidation"

In November 1860, in the heart of Georgia's cotton belt, a large
crowd of local citizens gathered at Crawfordville to declare: "We do
not consider the election of Lincoln and Hamlin[3] as sufficient
cause for Disunion or Secession." A mass meeting in Walker County
expressed the same sentiment: "We are not of the opinion that the
election of any man in accordance with the prescribed forms of the

Constitution is sufficient cause to disrupt the ties which bind us to the Union." In Harris County, the newspaper editor stated firmly that "we are a Union loving people here, and will never forsake the old 'Star Spangled Banner.'" To stress the point, he printed the names of 175 local men, all pledged to "preserve the honor and rights of the South *in the Union*."[4]

Mechanics in Frederick County, Virginia, met to denounce the "folly and sinister selfishness of the demagogues of the South." Workers in Portsmouth were equally stirred: "We look upon any attempt to break up this Government or dissolve this Union as an attack upon the rights of the people of the whole country." A convention of laborers in Nashville, Tennessee, declared their "undying love for the Union" and called secessionist efforts "treason . . . by designing and mad politicians." At Lake Jackson Church near Tallahassee, Florida, there assembled a crowd of four hundred "whose heart beat time to the music of the Union." In the Confederacy's future Virginia capital, Union supporters organized a mass meeting of the "working men of Richmond" and called on the government to put secession down. All across the South, thousands of worried plain folk did their best to head off secession. While most had opposed Lincoln's candidacy, a similar majority saw no reason to destroy the country over his election. Three-fourths of southern whites held no slaves and tended to believe, as one of Georgia's plain folk put it, "that this fuss was all for the benefit of the wealthy."[5]

Still, secessionists pressed their advantage for all they could in the face of popular opposition. Alfred P. Aldrich, a South Carolina legislator and staunch secessionist, acknowledged that most southern plain folk opposed disunion. "But," he asked, "whoever waited for the common people when a great move was to be made—We must make the move and force them to follow."[6] Senator Robert Toombs of Georgia likewise expressed his determination to see the South out of the Union whether most southerners supported it or not. "Give me the sword!" he blustered. "But if you do not place it in my hands, before God *I will take it!*" When he learned of Toombs's threat, one Georgia newspaper editor wrote: "Let him take it, and, by way of doing his country a great service, let him run about six inches of it into his left breast."[7]

Secessionists employed more than words in pursuit of disunion.

One southerner recalled that secessionists "used the most shameless and unconcealed intimidation" to suppress their opponents. A secession meeting in Richmond turned violent when twenty or so "muscular young men" attacked several unionists who tried to disrupt a secessionist speech by whistling "Yankee Doodle." That was hardly the worst of it. In Mississippi's Panola County, a group of vigilantes announced their intention to "take notice of, and punish all and every persons who may . . . prove themselves untrue to the South, or Southern Rights, in any way whatever." There was no mistaking their meaning. In Tallahatchie County, a secessionist gang of "Minute Men" lynched seven local unionists. In Florida, secessionists formed armed bands of "Regulators" who ambushed Union men by night.[8] So the Civil War did not begin at Fort Sumter. It did not begin as a war between North and South. It began, and continued throughout, as a war between southerners themselves.

Animosities that tore the South apart from within had been building for decades and had much to do with a widening gap between rich and poor. On the Civil War's eve, nearly half the South's personal income went to just over a thousand families. The region's poorest half held only 5 percent of its agricultural wealth. Land and slave ownership dominated the South's economy, but most white southerners held no slaves and many owned no land. According to one antebellum resident, in southwest Georgia's Early County "there was a body of land east of Blakely . . . which made 216 square miles, and not one foot of it was owned by a poor man." John Welch, a poor farmer in western Tennessee, complained that the slaveholders of his district "owned nearly all the land and they wanted to keep it."[9]

Opportunities for upward mobility had not been so limited just a generation earlier. Land was relatively cheap in the 1820s and '30s after the Indians were forced into western exile. Wealthy men from crowded coastal regions bought much of the land, but small farmers too could get loans to buy land and slaves. Cotton prices were on the rise, and there was every reason to expect that loans could easily be repaid. Some yeoman farmers who were lucky enough to have good land and good weather became affluent slaveholders and even planters.[10]

But with a single act, Congress put an end to the hopes of millions. So did a resulting economic depression, the Panic of 1837. The year before, at the urging of Andrew Jackson—proclaimed friend of the common man—Congress passed the Specie Circular Act, which made it difficult for small farmers to buy land. No longer would the government accept bank notes in payment for the stolen Indian real estate it held. Only gold or silver would do. Few plain folk had the required "hard money" on hand, nor did they have the collateral with which to borrow it. Successful loan applications fell dramatically and small banks across the country began to fail. The resulting depression helped drive cotton prices under as well, and they continued falling into the 1840s. With their staple-crop income cut nearly in half, debt-ridden farmers found it impossible to keep up loan payments. Their land and slaves were repossessed and sold at auction, usually to already well-established slaveholders. The sheriff in Henry County, Alabama, auctioned off so many small farms that enraged plain folk demanded his resignation.[11]

Some farmers were able to keep a few acres and eke out a living as lesser yeomen. But many lost everything and fell into tenancy and sharecropping. When the cotton market finally recovered, affluent slaveholders held nearly all the South's best land. Most other farmers found themselves trapped in a system of poverty from which few could ever escape even with a move to cheaper lands toward the west. Historian Victoria Bynum recently noted that "most poor whites' geographic mobility grew out of class immobility rather than frontier opportunities. . . . Many moved time and again in search of elusive prosperity."[12]

"The slaveholders buy up all the fertile lands," recalled a disgruntled Mississippian who witnessed the process firsthand. "Hence the poor are crowded out, and if they remain in the vicinity of the place of their nativity, they must occupy the poor tracts whose sterility does not excite the cupidity of their rich neighbors." That gap between rich and poor continued to widen through the 1850s. Planters bought up more and more land, forcing a rise in land prices and making it nearly impossible for smaller farmers to increase their holdings or for tenant farmers to buy any land at all. Wealth in terms of slaveholding was also becoming concentrated in fewer hands. During the last decade of the antebellum period, the proportion of slaveholders in the free population dropped by 20 percent. Economic circumstances beyond their control forced many yeomen into landless tenancy—so many that some commentators predicted the complete disappearance of small independent farmers from the South. By 1860 at least 25 percent of southern farmers were tenants, and more were joining their landless ranks every day.[13]

"To Obtain the Liberty of My Countrymen"

At the bottom of the social scale in a caste of their own, separate and distinct from the white class structure, were free blacks and slaves. Numbering roughly four and a half million in 1860, they made up nearly a sixth of the nation's population and well over a third of that in the slave states. About four million were held in slavery.

Despite the social chasm between them, living and working conditions for slaves were not altogether different from those of many southern whites. In describing a typical day's labor, one slave remembered getting up every morning before sunrise to work in the fields. After a short dinner break at noon, it was back to the fields until dark. And the women, she said, worked just like the men.[14] The same was true among white tenant farmers, sharecroppers, and lesser yeomen of both genders. Similarly, neither slaves nor poor whites had much hope of ever improving their condition. Poor whites may have been free in the strictest sense, but freedom meant little without opportunities for economic improvement. On the other hand, African Americans held by law as property bore physical and psychological burdens from which poor whites were mercifully free. Threats of violence and forced separation from loved ones were constantly present in the slave's world.

Slaveholder claims to the contrary, the "wise master," as historian Kenneth Stampp put it, "did not take seriously the belief that Negroes were natural-born slaves. He knew better. He knew that Negroes freshly imported from Africa had to be broken into bondage; that each succeeding generation had to be carefully trained. This was no easy task, for the bondsman rarely submitted willingly. Moreover, he rarely submitted completely. In most cases there was no end to the need for control—at least not until old age reduced the slave to a condition of helplessness." Control of elderly slaves was hardly a concern in any case. Less than four in a hundred ever lived to see age sixty.[15]

Slave resistance took many forms, the most celebrated of which was the underground railroad. Harriet Tubman, perhaps the most successful of the railroad's "conductors," led hundreds of slaves to freedom. Rewards offered for her capture totaled upwards of $40,000, but she was never caught. Neither was Arnold Gragston, an enslaved Kentuckian who over several years ferried hundreds of fellow bondsmen and women across the Ohio River before making his own escape. Harry Smith helped escapees cross the river at Louisville, but never escaped himself because he did not want to leave his family. Thanks to Tubman, Gragston, Smith, and many others like them, by 1860 more than one hundred thousand enslaved people had escaped.[16]

Though most blacks remained in bondage, they still resisted. Slaves engineered work slowdowns. They feigned illness and ignorance. They sabotaged or destroyed equipment, or used the threat of it as a bargaining chip for better treatment. When they failed to get it, suicide was not uncommon. Some slaves were treated so badly that death was a welcomed relief. One Georgia slave took her own life by swallowing strychnine. In another case, two enslaved parents agreed to "send the souls of their children to Heaven rather than have them descend to the hell of slavery." After releasing their children's souls, they released their own. Another enslaved mother killed all thirteen of her children "rather than have them suffer slavery." Two boatloads of Africans newly arrived in Charleston committed mass suicide by starving themselves to death.[17]

Sometimes slaves killed their oppressors. Most famous for its violence was Nat Turner's 1831 Virginia rebellion in which well over fifty whites died. There were many others who fought back or conspired to do so. In 1800, over a thousand slaves marched on Richmond. The governor called out hundreds of armed militiamen to turn them back. When asked why he had rebelled, one slave calmly replied: "I have nothing more to offer than what General Washington would have had to offer, had he been taken by the British officers and put to trial by them. I have ventured my life in endeavoring to obtain the liberty of my countrymen, and am willing to sacrifice to their cause; and I beg, as a favour, that I may be immediately led to execution. I know that you have predetermined to shed my blood, why then all this mockery of a trial?"[18] There were similar efforts to obtain liberty in Petersburg and Norfolk.

In 1811, four hundred Louisiana slaves rose up for freedom. A year later, there was rebellion in New Orleans. In 1837, slaves near that city formed a rebel band and killed several whites before they were captured. Slaves fought back individually too. In 1849, a slave in Chambers

County, Alabama, shot his owner. In Macon County, a slave "violently attacked with a knife and cut to pieces" his overseer. A Florida slave killed his owner with an axe as the white man attempted to administer "punishment." When Edward Covey tried to bind and beat Frederick Douglass, Douglass fought Covey off. From that day forward, Douglass later wrote, "I did not hesitate to let it be known of me, that the white man who expected to succeed in whipping, must also succeed in killing me." Covey never touched him again.[19]

Douglass was fortunate to escape slavery before resistance cost him his life. Most others were not so lucky. Slaves were defined as property by slave-state courts and, in the Dred Scott case of 1857, by the United States Supreme Court. As personal property, slaves were subject to the absolute authority of slaveholders and to whatever controls they chose to employ. As one member of the Georgia Supreme Court insisted, "subordination can only be maintained by the right to give moderate correction—a right similar to that which exists in the father over his children."[20]

There were, however, laws limiting abusiveness of parents over their

On Christmas Eve 1855, a slave patrol closed in on escaping teenagers from Loudon County, Virginia. The self-emancipated blacks brandished their weapons and held their ground. Ann Wood, the group's leader, dared her pursuers to fire. The patrollers backed off and Ann led her friends on to Philadelphia. Rising resistance among slaves during the 1850s was a major force driving slaveholder demands for secession. (Still, *Underground Rail Road*)

children. Slaves enjoyed no such legal protection. And the definition of "moderate correction" was left entirely to the slaveholder. "Should death ensue by accident, while this slave is thus receiving moderate correction," recalled a British visitor, "the constitution of Georgia kindly denominates the offence justifiable homicide." The Reverend W.B. Allen, a former Alabama slave, personally knew those in bondage who were beaten to death for nothing more than being off the plantation without written permission. Other offenses that might result in extreme punishment were lying, loitering, stealing, and "talking back to—'sassing'—a white person."[21]

Because slaves had monetary value, death as a direct result of discipline was unusual. More often, the objective of physical punishment was to inflict as much pain as possible without doing permanent damage. Scarring or mutilation might decrease the slave's resale value or ability to work. In 1859, a student at East Alabama Male College (now Auburn University) wrote home advising his mother not to purchase a slave who obviously had "been very much abused."[22] Wide leather straps or perforated wooden paddles were more common than whips. They were just as painful but left no permanent marks that might identify the slave as a "troublemaker" to potential buyers.

Overseers frequently administered beatings to slaves in the "buck" or "rolling Jim" positions. In each case the slave was stripped naked and bound tight. One former slave remembered the buck as "making the Negro squat, running a stout stick under his bended knee, and then tying his hands firmly to the stick—between the knees. Then the lash was laid on his back parts." Another freedman recalled that with the rolling Jim the slave was "stretched on his stomach at full length on a large log, about eight feet long. Into holes bored in the end of this log, wooden pegs were driven. The feet were securely tied to one set of these pegs—one end of the log, and the hands to the pegs at the other end. The victim was then ready to be worked on."[23]

Another common torture was to hoist slaves up by their thumbs, with only their toes touching the ground, and beat them. The slave might be "further tormented by having his wounds 'doctored' with salt and red pepper." One former slave remembered that his owner's "favorite form of punishment was to take a man (or woman) to the edge of the plantation where a rail fence was located. His head was then placed between two rails so that escape was impossible and he was whipped until the overseer was exhausted. This was an almost daily occurrence, administered on the slightest provocation." After recall-ing the variety of tortures inflicted on slaves, one freedman told an interviewer in the 1930s: "Sir, you can never know what some slaves endured."[24]

Aside from the brutality they sanctioned, most state slave codes de-fined the limits of life for slaves far beyond their status as personal property. No slave could carry a gun, own property, travel without a written pass, testify against whites in a court of law, or learn to read or write. Slave gatherings, even for religious services, were forbidden without a white person present. Free blacks labored under similar le-gal restrictions. They had to have a white legal guardian and could not own property in their own names. In the words of historian James Oakes, "it was like turning the Bill of Rights upside down."[25]

Slave codes also forbade legal recognition of slave marriages. To permit it would have established a state-sanctioned bond between members of slave families, implicitly infringing on the "property rights" of slaveholders—specifically the right to deal with and dispose of his property as he saw fit. Nevertheless, slaveholders allowed and even encouraged slaves to marry at an early age and have lots of chil-dren. It not only increased the slaveholder's "property" holdings, but it also provided an additional means of control. Besides the constant threat of physical violence, the most effective means of keeping slaves under control was through the institution of the family. Any slave might be pushed to the point of disregard for his or her own safety and attempt to fight back or escape. But when slaveholders threatened family members, slaves were more likely to hold their anger in check. It was another way to drive home the point that even within the slave family, the slaveholder was still master. Some did not even allow par-ents to name their own children. Slaveholders usually reserved that privilege for themselves.[26]

In naming the children of slave women, many slaveholders were actually exercising their own parental rights. Some slaveholders viewed rape as another method of enforcing psychological dominance within the slave community. Others did it simply because they viewed slaves as property to be used at the slaveholder's pleasure. Frequently, the first sexual experience a planter's son had was with a female slave. Robert Ellet, held as a slave in King William County, Virginia, re-membered of the antebellum South: "In those days if you was a slave and had a good looking daughter, she was taken from you. They would put her in the big house where the young masters could have the run of her." Little wonder that slaves of light complexion were present on nearly every plantation. One former slave wrote after his escape that "slavery in America is not at all confined to persons of any particular complexion; there are a very large number of slaves as white as anyone."[27]

"Like the patriarchs of old," wrote Mary Chesnut, the wife of one of the largest planters in South Carolina, "our men live all in one house with their wives and their concubines, and the mulattoes one sees in every family exactly resemble the white children—and every lady tells you who is the father of all the mulatto children in everybody's household, but those in her own she seems to think drop from the clouds, or pretends so to think." Mary Chesnut's words carried the authority of experience. In referring to Harriet Beecher Stowe's *Uncle Tom's Cabin*, Chesnut suggested that the author "did not hit the sorest spot. She makes [Simon] Legree a bachelor."[28]

With the legal and political status of white women only marginally better than that of slaves, they had little choice but to endure their husbands' infidelity. For a woman to divorce or desert her husband meant risking scandal and poverty. When a Mississippi slave complained to her mistress about the master's sexual advances, she was advised to submit. To resist could mean death. The mistress admitted that her husband was a "dirty man," but told the slave, "I can't do a thing with him." Slaveholders' wives commonly insisted on selling off younger slaves who, sired by their own husbands, were often mistaken by visitors as children of the family. During the winter of 1831–32, women in Virginia took the unprecedented step of submitting petitions to the legislature calling for slavery's end. When slaves finally gained freedom more than three decades later, one relieved slaveholder's wife said of Lincoln, "He has freed us, too."[29]

No matter who the father, slaveholders usually encouraged slave women to have as many children as possible. More children meant more field hands, but they also gave the slaveholder an additional tool of control. Not only did slaves fear punishment for family members, there was the additional concern that they might be sold off at any time. As slaves well knew, a slaveholder's threat to sell spouses or children was no idle one. One observer wrote that "such separations as these are quite common, and appear to be no more thought of, by those who enforce them, than the separation of a calf from its brute parent."[30]

The slaves' monetary value made threats of selling family members even more menacing. In the 1850s, slave prices were on the rise. A field hand could cost over a thousand dollars. A skilled slave was much more. One ex-slave remembered slave traders driving groups of children to market "the same as they would a herd of cattle." Slaves constantly feared seeing their families, especially their children, put through such misery. That fear kept overt resistance in check to some degree. Slaves with families were also less likely to escape since that too would mean permanent separation from their loved ones. Of the tens of thousands who did escape bondage, most were young, unmarried, and childless.[31]

"Resentment of an Alien Race"

By the mid-nineteenth century, the tools of slave control seemed to have firmly secured perhaps the world's most rigid system of racial caste. It had not always been so. In early seventeenth-century British North America, there had been no distinctions in law or custom between whites and blacks. In fact, the term "slave" was often used in reference to all those laboring as indentured servants. Like white servants, blacks typically gained freedom after serving a given number of years, usually seven. The servants themselves were, as historian Kenneth Stampp put it, "remarkably unconcerned about their visible physical differences." They were very familiar with the confines of their class system, but rigid caste lines based on race were unknown. Black and white servants worked together, played together, lived together, and married each other. The brand of racism that would become all too familiar to later generations of Americans was absent through most of the seventeenth century.[32]

That began to change as colonial elites, fearing rebellion from below, took steps to divide poor whites and blacks both socially and economically. And the threat of rebellion was very real in a society where most people were servants, landless tenants, or small yeomen holding marginal lands that the gentry did not want. Few could vote or hold office. Those privileges were restricted by wealth throughout the colonies. As early as 1661, the Virginia assembly took a major step toward social division by defining blacks who had not already acquired freedom as "servants for life." It was not enough. In 1676, the underclasses of

Virginia, black and white, united against their oppressors in what came to be known as Bacon's Rebellion. They established fortifications all along the James River, marched against the colonial capital at Jamestown, and came close to seizing control of the colony before Crown forces put them down. Among the last to surrender was a band of eighty blacks and twenty whites.[33]

Bacon's Rebellion sent shock waves through the ranks of the ruling classes. Many feared that some future insurrection, perhaps larger and better organized, might succeed. What could be done to avert such a calamity? Their strategy became something akin to the military maxim "divide and conquer." In the words of historian Edmund Morgan: "For those with eyes to see, there was an obvious lesson in the rebellion. Resentment of an alien race might be more powerful than resentment of an upper class."[34] Creating a social distance between poor whites and blacks, assigning whites the superior social position, might make the two groups less likely to unite.

In the late seventeenth and early eighteenth centuries, colonial legislatures throughout British North America passed a series of laws designed to do just that. They outlawed interracial marriage. They amended criminal codes to deal more harshly with blacks than whites. They defined black servants as slaves outright, the absolute property of slaveholders. They mandated limited lands for whites on completing their term of indenture and restricted the practice of most skilled trades to whites only. None of this was enough to qualify lower-class whites for voting or office holding. That would not come for another century or more. But it did instill in whites of all classes a sense that they were somehow "better" than those with even a drop of African blood—though many had a few such drops in their own bloodlines whether they knew it or not.[35]

The strategy worked, and worked even better than elites had hoped. The new racism, they found, was a self-perpetuating thing passed on from generation to generation, keeping the poor divided and more easily controlled. Lower-class whites still resented their oppressors. There were any number of insurrections by poor whites in the eighteenth century—the Regulator movement, Shays's Rebellion, and the Whiskey Rebellion among them. Slaves too occasionally rose in rebellion. But never again did poor whites unite with blacks against their common oppressor to the extent that they had in 1676 Virginia.

Ironically, the eighteenth century was also a time of changing attitudes toward slavery. The Scientific Revolution had shown that there were natural laws governing the physical universe. Some reasoned that perhaps there were also natural laws governing human interaction. It may even be that people had natural rights. The most basic of these, as Thomas Jefferson wrote, would surely be "life, liberty, and the pursuit of happiness."[36] If so, was not slavery a violation of natural rights? The idea troubled many planters of Jefferson's generation, schooled as they were in Enlightenment philosophy. Most were not willing to give up slavery themselves, but they did see it as an unworthy institution. Some, like George Washington, freed their slaves in their wills. Even Virginia's archconservative John Randolph of Roanoke freed his slaves in his last will and testament.

Aside from the moral issues involved, most Americans of that era saw slavery as an economic dead end. The institution thrived only in the tobacco fields of the Chesapeake region and the rice country of coastal Carolina and Georgia. As the nation expanded, slavery would become proportionally less important to the nation's economy and would eventually die a natural death. But the development of an efficient cotton engine, or "gin," in the eighteenth century's last decade changed all that. The cotton gin became the vehicle by which slavery was carried across the South. Not surprisingly, attitudes toward slavery changed with the institution's growing economic importance.

That change did not occur overnight. Antislavery sentiment in the South remained open and active through the early 1830s. As of 1827, 106 of the country's 130 abolitionist societies were in the South. To discourage the use of slave labor, some of those societies paid above market prices for cotton produced without slave labor. North Carolina Quakers and Methodists repeatedly petitioned their state legislature for emancipation. In 1821, a leading Georgia newspaper insisted: "There is not a single editor in these States who dares advocate slavery as a principle." Far from advocating slavery, Alabama editor James G. Birney started an abolitionist newspaper. In 1827 the Alabama legislature passed a law prohibiting the importation of slaves from other states, and at every session throughout the decade members proposed legislation favoring gradual emancipation. As late as 1831, a proposal to end slavery was introduced in the Virginia state assembly.[37]

But the early nineteenth century was also the era of Indian removal. In 1827 Georgia forced out its few remaining Creeks. Nine years later Alabama did the same. The 1830s saw the Choctaws and

Chickasaws driven out of Mississippi. And Georgia annexed Cherokee land following the 1829 discovery of gold there. In an effort that carried the hopes of all Indian nations with it, the Cherokees fought to keep their land through the court system. The United States Supreme Court finally responded in 1832 with its *Worcester v. Georgia* decision: by treaty obligation, by prior act of Congress, and by the Constitution itself, the Indians held legal title to their land. But President Andrew Jackson refused to enforce the ruling, and Congress declined to intervene. Georgia ignored the court order, and the Cherokees were driven westward on the Trail of Tears. A quarter of them died on that brutal forced march. In 1842 Florida's Seminoles became the last of the southern nations to be violently relocated to land that they were promised would be theirs for "as long as grass grows or water runs." At the time it was called Indian Territory. Today it is called Oklahoma.[38]

Indian removal completed the transition in slaveholder attitudes begun a generation earlier by the cotton gin. Not only did they have the technology and labor force with which to make cotton king, they now had the land on which to do it. Slaveholders no longer viewed slavery as a temporary necessity but held it to be a positive good for both slaveholder and slave. The Founding Fathers' attitudes regarding slavery, they said, were completely erroneous. In the words of the pre-eminent Georgia planter-politician Alexander H. Stephens:

> The prevailing ideas entertained by . . . the leading statesmen at the time of the formation of the old Constitution were that the enslavement of the African was in violation of the laws of nature; that it was wrong in *principle*, socially, morally and politically. It was an evil they knew not well how to deal with, but the general opinion of the men of that day was that somehow or other in the order of Providence, the institution would be evanescent and pass away. . . . Those ideas, however, were fundamentally wrong.[39]

"Worthy of All Honor"

The slaveholders' new position presented them with an overriding difficulty. States north of the Mason-Dixon Line had long since ended slavery, and just a quarter of southern whites owned slaves. Outside the United States chattel slavery survived only in Brazil, Cuba, Puerto

Rico, Dutch Guiana, and parts of Africa.[40] How were they to guarantee the survival of slavery in a society where most held no slaves and in a world where slaveholders were a dying breed?

In the 1830s planters launched a campaign designed to educate their fellow Americans, and the world, on the virtues of slavery. In the first place, planters argued, the world could not do without southern cotton. English and northern mills depended too much upon it. Benjamin Hill of Troup County, Georgia, later a senator in the Confederate Congress, insisted that "the world can never give up slavery until it is ready to give up clothing."[41]

Besides, planters said, chattel slaves on southern plantations were much better off than "wage slaves" in northern factories. They were better housed, better clothed, and did lighter work than laborers in the North—indeed, than laborers anywhere in the world. They lived in cottages that were, in their humble way, as comfortable as the slaveholder's house. After the day's chores were done, the slaves ate a fine supper of meat and vegetables, sang and danced, played the banjo, and went to bed contented and happy. People of African descent were happy in slavery because it was their "natural and normal condition." They were, in the words of one slavery apologist, "utterly incapable of self-culture and self-government." No less a figure than the eminent Harvard geologist Louis Agassiz confirmed that Africans were a "degraded and degenerate race," lacking the intelligence necessary for independent thought and action.[42]

Dr. Samuel Cartwright of New Orleans attributed that lack of intelligence to small brains and a disease peculiar to those of African descent that he called *dysesthesia*. "It is the defective atmospherization of the blood," he said, "conjoined with a deficiency of cerebral matter in the cranium . . . that is the true cause of that debasement of mind which has rendered the people of Africa unable to take care of themselves." If slaves lacked intelligence, could not care for themselves, and were happy in slavery, why then did so many try to escape? Cartwright had an answer for that too—*drapetomania*, or "the insane desire to run away."[43]

Other supporters of slavery turned to a historical defense. The classical civilizations of Greece and Rome, the greatest the world had ever seen, had large slave populations. The institution must therefore necessarily be a hallmark of high culture. James Henry Hammond of South Carolina argued that the existence of slavery had always been necessary to make possible an upper class "which leads progress, civilization, and refinement."[44]

And, of course, there was the Biblical defense. How could slavery be an evil institution when the Hebrew patriarchs of the Old Testament had owned slaves? Were these not men ordained by God? Were their institutions, including slavery, not holy? Was not slavery the result of Noah's curse on his younger son Ham and all his descendants, whose skin was assumed to have been turned black as a sign of perpetual servitude? In the New Testament, did not both the apostles Paul and Peter make it clear that servants should be obedient to their masters? The Reverend Thornton Stringfellow, a Virginia Baptist, argued in 1856 that Christ himself "recognized this institution as one that was lawful among men." Stringfellow cited I Timothy 6 in which Paul, after counting masters "worthy of all honor," warned that "if any man teach otherwise, and consent not to wholesome words, even the words of our Lord Jesus Christ, and to the doctrine which is according to godliness, he is proud, knowing nothing, but doting about questions and strifes of words, whereof cometh envy, strife, railings, evil surmisings." There could be no question about it. Slavery was a hallowed institution ordained by God himself. All denouncements of it were nothing more than "evil surmisings."[45]

Throughout the South, clergymen emerged as some of the most eager and influential allies of the planter class in defending slavery. Those who held that scripture must be taken literally had been for some time disturbed by a strong opposing trend in Christianity. By the early nineteenth century, science had clearly shown that the Bible contained many factual errors and omissions. The sun did not revolve around the Earth as the story of Joshua suggested, and the Earth was much older than the Bible implied. Furthermore, plants and animals had not been created in their present form but had evolved. Many had become extinct. In the eighteenth century, influential clergymen and laity began to argue that the Bible must be understood symbolically, not literally. Thomas Jefferson even predicted that within a generation most southerners would abandon the literalist doctrines in favor of a more enlightened Unitarianism.[46]

But if the Bible was to be interpreted symbolically, what might that mean for its treatment of slavery? Was that to be taken symbolically as well? Could Paul have been using the relationship of servant to master as a metaphor for the relationship of humanity to God? No, such symbolism would not do—not for slaveholders and their ministerial allies. If the scriptures were to be used effectively as a moral defense of slavery, they must be taken literally—and not just in part but in their entirety. As the slaveholding South changed its attitude toward slavery's morality in the early nineteenth century, it became increasingly tied to a literalist view of the Bible.[47]

That literalism had a debilitating effect on the place of not only southern blacks but southern women too. From their pulpits every Sunday, many a preacher repeated St. Paul's instruction that wives submit themselves to their husbands "as to the Lord." In an atmosphere that stressed literalist doctrine, the message took a strong and lasting hold. The link between abolitionism and the movement for women's rights in the North further shackled southern women—in many ways to the point of practical slavery. George Fitzhugh, one of slavery's most prominent defenders, wrote that "wives and apprentices are slaves not in theory only, but often in fact." He referred to it approvingly as "family despotism."[48]

As much weight as Biblical argument carried, the most effective tactic adopted by slaveholders to secure their peculiar institution was encouraging racist fears. By playing on such fears, slavery's defenders hoped to make all whites feel they had a stake in preserving the slave system whether they owned slaves or not. Poor whites were encouraged to think of what slavery's demise in the South might mean for them. No longer would they be in a position of social superiority over slaves, or anyone else for that matter. Poor whites would occupy the bottom rung on the class ladder along with blacks, who would be their equals.

One Columbus, Georgia, man stated the case clearly: "It is African slavery that makes every white man in some sense a lord. . . . Here the division is between white free men and black slaves, and every white is, and feels that he is a MAN." At a political meeting in Colquitt, Georgia, during the 1856 presidential campaign, J.F.M. Caldwell delivered an hour-long speech in which he stressed the social importance of slavery for poor whites. According to a man who attended the meeting, "his arguments on the slavery question, and the reason why *poor* men at the South, above all others, ought to be enlisted under the banner of Southern Rights, were convincing."[49]

In many ways, planters argued, slavery was a good thing. Good not just for slaveholders, but for slaves, poor whites, the North, and the world. It was, after all, an institution ordained by God himself. "Whoever doubts that it is a blessing," wrote one apostle of slavery, "has no right to hold any opinion at all on the subject."[50] Other proslavery men said the same—and they meant it. By the 1830s it was becoming dangerous to express antislavery sentiments in the South. Those who opposed slavery either kept their views hidden or were driven out. The Grimké sisters of South Carolina, Sarah and Angelina, fled to the North where they were active in both the abolitionist and women's rights movements. James G. Birney followed from Alabama to form the Liberty Party, dedicated to slavery's abolition. In 1840 he became its first presidential candidate.

Intolerance had an especially chilling effect on southern institutions of higher learning. One southern newspaper editor boldly declared that "professorships should be sifted and weeded of those who may covertly circulate opinions not in sympathy with our social institutions." Slavery's defenders were happy to comply. Horace Holley, president of Kentucky's Transylvania University and a religious progressive, was removed from his post. The free-thinking president of South Carolina College, Thomas Cooper, was likewise driven from office. Professor Benjamin Hendrick lost the chair of agricultural chemistry at his own alma mater, the University of North Carolina, because he dared question slavery. The university's board justified Hendrick's removal on the grounds that his "political opinions . . . are not those entertained by any member of this body." Even the University of Virginia, founded by Thomas Jefferson as a haven of free thought and inquiry, introduced sectarian religious exercises.[51]

In less than a generation, southern academia lost many of its finest intellectuals. Those who remained dared not challenge the view that slavery was a positive good and that the King James Bible was God's literal word. To the contrary, men like Matthew Fontaine Maury—aristocratic Virginian, pioneer oceanographer, and father of the United States Weather Bureau—upheld the Bible as the greatest book of science there was. In responding to opponents who viewed the Bible as "no authority in matters of science," Maury proclaimed, "the Bible is authority for everything it touches." Joseph LeConte, a planter's son and professor at the University of Georgia, declared his own field of geology to be "the chief handmaid of religion among the sciences."[52]

Though religion, racism, pride, and fear were all used to bolster slavery at home and justify it abroad, the driving force behind planters' proslavery campaign was the same that caused their change of attitude in the first place—economic self-interest. Some planters, like Benjamin Hill, were candid enough to admit it: "In our early history the Southern statesmen were antislavery in feeling. So were Washington, Jefferson, Madison, Randolph, and many of that day who never studied the argument of the cotton gin, nor heard the eloquent productions of the great Mississippi Valley. Now our people not only see the justice of slavery, but its providence too."[53] It was cotton, along with tobacco, rice, and sugar, all cultivated by slave labor, that gave planters their economic power. And it was this power that gave planters the political strength with which to control the South's lower classes and silence or exile slavery's opponents.

"Those That Didn't Own Slaves Hated Those That Did"

Though most white males in the South could vote, and many did, there was not much for them to decide beyond the local level. Then as now, any successful bid for high political office depended as much on wealth as votes—and wealth went hand in hand with slavery. Both major parties, Whig and Democrat, centered more on personalities than issues, and both represented slaveholding interests. Fear of slave rebellion and abolitionism were always central campaign themes, with each candidate trying to "out-nigger" the other. But after the early 1830s, slavery's continued existence was never a topic of political debate in the South.[54]

The influence of planter wealth in politics was not lost on the plain folk. As one farmer noted, the planter "used money whenever he could. This fact usually elected him." A Tennessean noted that only slaveholders could afford "big barbecues during times of elections." In politics, said another, "it seemed that the slave holder had the firepower." Another nonslaveholder observed that the wealthy bought "votes, with liquor and cigars."[55] In Columbus, Georgia, a process of buying votes known as "penning" was so common that it came to be called "the peculiar institution of Muscogee County." On the day before an election, campaign workers would round up men off the streets, lodge them in local hotels, get them drunk, and then march them to the polls next morning. The party with the largest "pen" usually won the election.[56]

Obviously, these men felt that their right to vote meant little in the absence of real choices. Their interests would not be represented no matter who won. Donald Debats, in his study of the South's antebellum political culture, concluded that "far from encouraging citizen participation in the party system, the leaders of both parties discouraged grassroots politics. . . . Beyond the simple casting of a ballot, the role of the citizen in the party system was passive by design."[57] Moreover, poorer men in some states were kept entirely out of the political process by long-established property qualifications along with other such restrictive devices as the poll tax.[58]

Slaveholder control of southern politics, at least at the state level, was near absolute. One southerner complained that although a majority of qualified voters owned no slaves, "they have never yet had any part or lot in framing the laws under which they live. There is no legislation except for the benefit of slavery and slaveholders."[59] The predominance of slaveholders in politics helped insure that. During the 1850s, though the proportion of slaveholders in the South's general population was falling, their numbers in southern state legislatures were on the rise. In Mississippi, for example, state lawmakers who owned slaves rose from 61 percent to more than 80 percent.[60]

It seemed that slaveholder dominance of the South was assured and that slavery as an institution was secure. But even as slaveholders consolidated their political control, cracks appeared at the base of the South's social pyramid. They had always been there, suppressed and controlled. As wealth became concentrated in fewer hands and opportunities for economic advancement were increasingly closed to yeomen and poor whites, those cracks began to grow.

"A renter had no chance to save anything," complained a western Tennessee tenant farmer. "Slaveholders were the only men that could save enough money to do anything." Another agreed, saying that slaveholders "kept the poor class of people down as much as possible." The social gap was just as obvious as the economic. A North Carolina tenant said slaveholders "felt biggety and above poor folk who did not have slaves." A Tennessee commoner noted that slaveholders "thought because they owned slaves they were better than any body." Another complained that even "slave holder children . . . made fun of the non-slave holders." J.C. Keysaer, a yeoman farmer in Tennessee, insisted that "slave holders always acted as if they were of a better class and there was always an unpleasant feeling between slave holders and those working themselves." William Johnson, also of Tennessee, put it more bluntly: "Those that didn't own slaves hated those that did."[61]

Adding to slaveholder concerns was an undercurrent of antislavery sentiment among many whites that had never completely died out. Some nonslaveholders continued to view slavery as a moral evil. Others opposed it on economic grounds. Still others opposed slavery simply because they were too poor ever to own slaves themselves. Whatever the reasons, antislavery feeling was on the rise. In 1849, a Georgia carpenter openly declared his opposition to slavery. Competition with slave labor, he believed, kept his wages low. That same year, mechanics and workingmen in the slave state of Kentucky met at Lexington and drew up this statement: "Resolved, That the institution of slavery is prejudicial to every interest of the State . . . it degrades labor, enervates industry, interferes with the occupations of free laboring citizens, separates too widely the poor and the rich, shuts out the laboring classes from the blessings of education . . . and as slavery tends to the monopoly of as well as the degradation of labor, public and private right require its ultimate extinction."[62]

Experience suggested truth in that statement to southern laborers. Wage levels in the South were as much as 30 percent below those of the North. There was little southern workers could do about it, not when slave labor was so readily available. In 1830, out-of-work stone cutters in Norfolk, Virginia, asked the Navy Department to stop using slaves in construction of a dry dock. The Navy refused. When the workers appealed to Congress, they were ignored. In 1847, when employees at Richmond's Treadegar Iron Works went on strike to protest the use of slave labor, some were hauled into court and prosecuted. So were New Orleans longshoremen when they walked out for higher wages. One observer wrote: "I have seen free white mechanics obliged to stand aside while their families were suffering for the necessaries of life, when slave mechanics, owned by rich and influential men, could get plenty of work; and I have heard these same white mechanics breathe the most bitter curses against the institution of slavery and the slave aristocracy." That aristocracy, notes historian Roger Shugg, "was hardly of a mind to bargain with workers of one race when it owned so many of another."[63]

But there was danger in refusing to bargain, most of all to slavery's survival. If nonslaveholders were continually thwarted by the institution of slavery, how long could it last? In 1850, an editorial in the New

Orleans–based *De Bow's Review* pointed to the danger: "The great mass of our poor white population begin to understand that they have rights. . . . They are fast learning that there is an almost infinite world of industry opening before them, by which they can elevate themselves and their families from wretchedness and ignorance to competence and intelligence. *It is this great upbearing of our masses that we are to fear, so far as our institutions are concerned.*" The most endangerd institution to which the editor referred was slavery.[64]

Aside from their direct economic difficulties with it, some whites had a deeply personal stake in opposing slavery. A North Carolina planter's daughter, Tempie James, fell in love with the family's slave coachman, Squire James. When Tempie's father sold Squire to keep the two apart, Tempie followed him, bought and freed him, and changed his name. Because no white woman could legally marry a black man, Tempie drank whiskey laced with Squire's blood and "swore that she had Negro blood in her." The two were married and raised a large family together. They were both listed in the 1850 census as "mulatto." Others could not hide their racial identity, but lived as husband and wife just the same. One offspring of such a union recalled that "my mother [Mary] had two children by my [white] father. My father never married. He loved my mother, and he said if he could not marry Mary he did not want any other woman."[65]

Some whites sympathetic to the plight of slaves, like William Allen of Troup County, Georgia, wrote fake passes to help them escape on the underground railroad. Others gave them transportation. Some turned their homes into safe houses along the way. One grateful fugitive told of a white man named Thome in Augusta, Kentucky, who "would get out of his bed in the middle of the night to help runaway slaves out of the reach of their masters, would give them clothes and money and send them across the Ohio river." Another former slave recalled a white family in Mason County, Kentucky, that "hazarded everything for me," asking only "to remember them in my prayers." The hazards were very real. After Sam Fuller of North Carolina tried to help an escaping slave, he found a "crossbone and skull on a stick in front of his door." A short time later, he was kidnapped and killed by persons unknown.[66]

Even in the face of such dangers there were southern whites who worked against slavery in any way they could, up to and including rebellion. Four white South Carolinians were thrown in jail for encouraging

Denmark Vesey in his attempt to free the slaves around Charleston. In Mississippi, twenty-one "bleached and unbleached" men were hanged for plotting a slave revolt. A Virginia white man was hanged near Lynchburg for trying to help organize an uprising. So were several whites in Jefferson County, Georgia, for the same offense. And four "white abolition rascals" helped organize a slave insurrection at Iberville, Louisiana.[67]

Among the most outspoken southern opponents of slavery was Hinton Rowan Helper. Born the son of a yeoman farmer in North Carolina, Helper wrote what one historian has called "the most important single book, in terms of its political impact, that has ever been published in the United States. Even more perhaps than *Uncle Tom's Cabin*, it fed the fires of sectional controversy leading up to the Civil War."[68] In *The Impending Crisis of the South*, published in 1857, Helper argued vigorously that the "lords of the lash are not only absolute masters of the blacks . . . but they are also the oracles and arbiters of all non-slaveholding whites, whose freedom is merely nominal."[69] Slavery, Helper pointed out, existed for the benefit of only a very few. Its existence kept most white southerners in ignorance and poverty. The region's economic development was so retarded that it was little more than a colony of the North, providing raw materials and buying back manufactured goods:

> The North is the Mecca of our merchants, and to it they must and do make two pilgrimages per annum—one in the spring and one in the fall. All our commercial, mechanical, manufactural, and literary supplies come from there. We want Bibles, brooms, buckets and books, and we go to the North; we want pens, ink, paper, wafer and envelopes, and we go to the North; we want shoes, hats, handkerchiefs, umbrellas and pocket knives, and we go to the North; we want furniture, crockery, glassware and pianos, and we go to the North; we want toys, primers, school books, fashionable apparel, machinery, medicines, tombstones, and a thousand other things, and we go to the North for them all. Instead of keeping our money in circulation at home by patronizing our own mechanics, manufacturers, and laborers, we send it all away to the North, and there it remains; it never falls into our hands again. . . . Slavery, and nothing but slavery, has retarded the progress and prosperity of our portion of the Union . . . [and] made us a tributary to the North.[70]

Helper was not alone in pointing out the economic drawbacks of slavery. For those who looked beyond the Old South's plantation facade, the system's disadvantages were obvious enough. Like other visitors of his time, Englishman James Stirling, who passed through the South in the 1850s, asked why the region lagged behind in "development and prosperity." He could find only one answer—slavery. "When Southern statesmen count up the gains of slavery," warned Stirling, "let them not forget also to count its cost. They may depend upon it, there is a heavy 'per contra' to the profits of niggerdom."[71]

In 1855, in what one biographer called "one of the most succinct and pungent analyses of the racist component of the capitalistic labor system in our literature," Frederick Douglass, himself a former slave, reached out to oppressed whites.

> The slaveholders, with a craftiness peculiar to themselves, by encouraging the enmity of the poor, laboring white man against the blacks, succeeds in making the said white man almost as much a slave as the black slave himself. The difference between the white slave, and the black slave, is this: the latter belongs to *one* slaveholder, and the former belongs to *all* the slaveholders, collectively. The white slave has taken from him, by indirection, what the black slave has taken from him directly, and without ceremony. Both are plundered, and by the same plunderers. The slave is robbed, by his master, of all his earnings, above what is required for his bare physical necessities; and the white man is robbed by the slave system, of the just results of his labor, because he is flung into open competition with a class of laborers who work without wages.[72]

Not only did slaveholders hinder economic growth and enslave both blacks and whites, but their concentration on cotton and tobacco production forced the South into a state of dependency. Imports of manufacured goods had always been high, but food imports were also on the rise. During the 1850s, Georgia's comptroller-general lamented that with regard to food, the South was "every day becoming more dependent upon those 'not of us.'" In Georgia alone, livestock production was declining. The corn crop was stagnant. In just ten years, the oat crop had dropped by more than half. Hinton Helper calculated that the value of the North's food production outstripped that of the South by almost $45 million annually. In light of all this, he said, "the first and most sacred duty of every southerner who has the honor and the interest of his country at heart is to declare himself an unqualified and uncompromising abolitionist."[73]

"For the Spread of Slavery"

Growing discontent within the Cotton Kingdom, of little concern to slaveholders only a decade earlier, was by the 1850s causing panic among many of them. As if to confirm Helper's arguments, one planter asked, "If the poor whites realized that slavery kept them poor, would they not vote it down?" Many were beginning to think they might. How could support for slavery be maintained among lower-class whites if they owned no slaves and had no prospects of ever owning any? Some pushed for state laws mandating that each white family be given at least one slave. Others demanded a slave for every white person. Still others argued for reopening the slave trade from Africa to bring down the price of slaves. The African slave trade had been closed in 1808 with the backing of slaveholders who saw it as a opportunity to artificially inflate the price of their slaves.[74]

Slavery's supporters realized too that their difficulty stemmed not just from the expense of slaves but also the lack of land. There was only so much prime farmland to go around, and slaveholders already had most of it. The noted southern commentator J.D.B. De Bow wrote in 1853: "The non-slaveholders possess generally but very small means, and the land which they possess is almost universally poor and so sterile that a scanty subsistence is all that can be derived from its cultivation, and the more fertile soil being in the hands of the slaveholders." So long as the opportunity to acquire land was limited, support for slavery among poor whites would be uncertain. To slaveholders it was clear—slavery must expand or die.[75]

"There is not a slaveholder in this House or out of it," said Judge Warner in the Georgia House of Representatives, "but who knows perfectly well that whenever slavery is confined within certain specified limits, its future existence is doomed." And slaveholders were not inclined to limit their expansion demands to territories controlled by the United States. "I want Cuba," insisted Senator Albert Gallatin Brown of Misssissippi in 1858. "I want Tamaulipas, Potosí, and one or two other Mexican states. . . . And a footing in Central America will powerfully aid us in acquiring those other States. . . . Yes, I want these Countries for the spread of slavery. I would spread the blessings of slavery, like the religion of our Divine Master, to the uttermost ends of the earth."[76]

Brown's demand was not just rhetoric. Already the southern slavocracy was transforming its words into action. During the 1850s, ironically with support from some northern financiers, slaveholders backed efforts to annex Cuba and set up puppet dictatorships in Nicaragua and Honduras. Though all these attempts failed, they helped keep the dream of expansion alive. Indeed, some used the lure of Latin America as an argument for an independent South. As one pro-secession editor wrote: "In a Southern Confederacy, slave holders could have expansion. Soon all Mexico would be ours, and Cuba, the Queen of the Antilles; yes, and Central America, and some of the South American States. Then there would be a chance for us to get the Indian Territory, Utah, and New Mexico."[77]

Most white northerners, upper class and lower, were just as determined to keep slavery confined to the South. Industrialists viewed the West as a region ripe for exploitation of natural resources. Working folk saw in the West a chance to escape their dismal urban lives. Neither group wanted to compete with slaveholders for western lands. Nor did they want to live among blacks, either in the West or the North. There were a quarter-million blacks already in the North, and most whites wanted no more. If slavery could expand anywhere, they feared, it might expand northward too, bringing thousands of blacks with it.

A few years after his escape from southern slavery, Frederick Douglass said that "prejudice against color is stronger north than south." It was an impression many self-emancipated freedpeople gained through bitter experience. In July of 1834, when abolitionists tried to convene in New York City, a white mob broke up the meeting and went on a violent racist rampage. The mob grew to several thousand, and the rioting lasted for days. Hundreds of blacks lost their homes. Many lost their lives. Soon after, Philadelphia saw racist riots as well. So did Cincinnati and Utica. When William Lloyd Garrison called for immediate freedom for enslaved Americans in his new periodical, *The Liberator*, a gang of whites dragged him through the streets of Boston in chains. He barely escaped with his life. Elijah Lovejoy of Alton, Illinois, was not so lucky. A mob killed him and threw his printing press in the Ohio River.[78]

Though northern whites opposed slavery's expansion, they nevertheless tended to support its continued existence in the South. Working-class whites feared job competition from migrating southern blacks should they ever be freed. Those fears were flamed by northern industrialists, who encouraged whites to view blacks already in the North as the source of their economic woes. Industrialists themselves feared a sharp rise in the price of cotton should slavery ever end. In 1835, an assembly of businessmen in Boston pledged their complete support in defending slavery and expressed "regret and indignation at the conduct of the abolitionists." Slavery kept blacks in the South and in the fields, just where most white northerners wanted them. On a visit to America, the famed English journalist Charles Mackay observed that "Northern men, who talk so much of liberty and of the political equality of all men, turn up their scornful noses at the slightest possibility of contact with an African."[79]

"An Aristocracy of Wealth"

Northern elites were eager to keep racist and ethnic prejudice alive among the working classes. Not only did it encourage support for southern slavery, but bigotry also weakened the growing labor movement by keeping it divided and more easily repressed. Elitist concerns of a multiracial united front were not unfounded. In 1835, black and white carpenters and caulkers went on strike together at the Washington Navy Yard. Where the lower classes saw their common interests, they fought for them in a common effort. The trick for elites was to redefine those interests for white workers. Thus manufacturers and investors across the North launched an intense effort to convince them that freedom for blacks meant degradation for whites. Thus slaveholders, by keeping blacks enslaved and in the South, were the true friends of the northern working class. Abolitionists were their enemies.

There was more than a grain of truth in that warning. Ironically, some of the leading abolitionists were relatively well-to-do men who had little sympathy for, or understanding of, the difficulties of laboring whites. Some held investments directly threatened by labor strikes. William Lloyd Garrison denounced the labor movement as a misleading effort "to inflame the minds of our working class against the more opulent, and to persuade men that they are contemned and oppressed by a wealthy aristocracy." So did Wendell Phillips and Theodore Parker, both prominent abolitionists. To laboring folk who daily felt the weight of underpaid oppression, it seemed that they had few friends among the abolitionists.[80]

Northern working people, urban and rural alike, had little reason to feel that they had friends of any kind outside their own class. As in the South, the gap between rich and poor in the North was increasingly wide by the mid-nineteenth century. In Boston, the richest 1 percent's share of the city's collective wealth rose from 33 to 37 percent during the 1830s and '40s. At the same time, New York's top 1 percent increased its holdings from 29 to 40 percent. On the eve of the Civil War, that same small club in Philadelphia held fully half the city's riches. Across the North, the richest 5 percent held over half the wealth.[81]

And it was not simply industrial wealth. As in the South, landholding in the North was becoming concentrated in fewer hands. One New England farmer warned that "the number of land owners is diminishing and the number of dependent tenants and hired laborers is increasing." The result, another pointed out, was that "in many of our New England towns, two or three men own all the farms, or all the land worth having." Indeed, by the time of the Civil War, tenancy rates in the North were as great as—in some places much greater than—those in the South, ranging as high as 50 percent.[82]

In 1837, a workers' committee complained that although they lived under a system that portrayed itself as a representative government, "we are in reality subjected to the worst of all tyrannies—an aristocracy of wealth. Our actual government, our regulator of social rights and social intercourse, is *money*—the greater heaps ruling the less."[83] They had good reason to feel that way. Working and living conditions, especially in the cities, were abysmal even by standards of the day. From one textile town in the summer of 1833 came an Appeal of the Working People, which read:

> We are obliged by our employers to labor at this season from 5 o'clock in the morning until sunset, being fourteen hours and a half, with an intermission of half an hour for breakfast, and an hour for dinner, leaving thirteen hours of hard labor, at an unhealthy employment, where we never feel a refreshing breeze to cool us, over heated and suffocated as we are, and where we never behold the sun but through a

window, and an atmosphere thick with the dust and small particles of cotton, which we are constantly inhaling to the destruction of our health, our appetite, and strength.[84]

Housing was just as bad. The *Daily Tribune* in New York described typical family living conditions in the city as "a single room, or perhaps two, in the upper story of some poor, ill constructed, unventilated house in a filthy street. . . . In these rooms all the processes of cooking, eating, sleeping, washing and living are indiscriminately performed." Henry David Thoreau described New England workers as "living in sties, and all winter with an open door for the sake of light, without any visible, often imaginable, wood-pile, and the forms of both old and young are permanently contracted by the long habit of shrinking from cold and misery, and the development of all their limbs and faculties is checked." This picture of destitution against the backdrop of increasing national wealth was striking. One resident wrote that in "Our good city of New York . . . the two extremes of costly luxury and living, expensive establishments, and improvident waste are presented in daily and hourly contrast with squalid misery and hopeless destitution."[85]

That destitution sprang from an unregulated wage system which put workers entirely at the mercy of their employers. Few workers made as much as a dollar a day. Many were paid as little as twenty-five cents. Such wages, as one group of textile workers put it, were "barely sufficient to supply us with the necessaries of life. We cannot provide against sickness or difficulties of any kind, by laying by a single dollar, for our present wants consume the little we receive, and when we are confined to bed of sickness any length of time, we are plunged into the deepest distress, which often terminates in total ruin, poverty, and pauperism."[86] When that happened, local governments might hold a "pauper's auction" and sell entire families as virtual slaves to any bidder who had the means to feed, house, and clothe them.

Frequently, what wages a company might pay were forthcoming only in store orders or in scrip, which could be spent only at the company store. With the company setting both the workers' wages and the prices they paid, many workers' incomes never matched their cost of living. Week by week they owed the company more and more, trapping them in a debt slavery from which escape was nearly impossible. Looking for better work was rarely an option. Workers were legally bound to the company by debt. And under a "blacklist system," workers had to produce an "honorable discharge" from their previous employer before they could be hired by another.[87]

Children were especially vulnerable to the system's abuses. In order to learn a trade, children were frequently sent out to apprenticeships. Sometimes they did learn a trade. Often, however, they were simply used as slave labor. To avoid the miseries of pauperism for the entire family, many parents were forced to take that chance. In any case, there were few laws governing the system. Some states had none at all. Whether in apprenticeships or in factories, youth inspired little sympathy from employers. An 1835 report noted that in New York State, children typically labored "from twelve to fourteen hours each day, being several hours more daily labor than is exacted even from the convicts in our State Prisons."[88]

"All Men and Women Are Created Equal"

Young women faced a further exploitation. For some, wages were so low that they were "forced to abandon their virtue" to survive. For others, that force was literal. Managers at the textile mills in Lowell, Massachusetts, were especially notorious for sexually abusing young women who ran the spinning machines. It was a kind of sex slavery that was hardly uncommon throughout the factory system. So widespread was it that any young woman employed at the mills was tainted by a general assumption that she had been abused. For that reason, many found it difficult to marry into respectable families. Some never married at all. To this day, unmarried women are frequently referred to as "spinsters."[89]

The taint of premarital sex reflected a wider double standard that placed strict limits on women at every level of society. None could vote. Few could own property in their own names. Nearly all professions were closed to them. Those who labored for factory wages saw their wages paid to fathers, husbands, or nearest male relatives or guardians. For the same work, they were almost always paid less than men, who were themselves almost always dismally underpaid.[90]

Women's social position as near slaves themselves was especially clear to female activists in the abolition movement. Susan B. Anthony, Elizabeth Cady Stanton, and Lucretia Mott all took leading roles in demanding freedom both for slaves and for themselves. In 1848, they called the nation's first women's rights convention. That July, over two hundred women and about forty men gathered in the Wesleyan Chapel at Seneca Falls, New York, and drew up a Declaration of Women's Rights. Expanding on the country's founding declaration, it began: "We hold these truths to be self-evident, that all men and women are created equal." Pointing out that men in general had done all they could to destroy women's confidence, lessen their self-respect, and make them willing dependents of men, the declaration called for women's "immediate admission to all the rights and privileges which belong to them as citizens of the United States."[91]

The movement spread rapidly over the next few years, with hundreds of thousands of women taking action for equal pay, equal property rights, equal access to the professions, and an equal voice at the ballot box. And they began to have some success. Some women helped force more equitable pay. Others circulated successful petitions for state laws recognizing women's property rights. Still others, like Elizabeth Blackwell, demanded and got access to the professions. In 1849, Blackwell, the first woman to earn a medical degree in the United States, graduated from Geneva Medical College at the head of her class.[92]

"The Fruits of Their Own Toil"

Like women generally, working-class folk took direct action. They began to form consumer cooperatives such as the Mechanics and Laborers Association in Boston to develop direct worker ownership of production and distribution. "The direction and profits of industry," insisted the Boston organization, "must be kept in the hands of the producers. Laborers must own their own shops and factories, work their own stock, sell their own merchandise, and enjoy the fruits of their own toil." Workers also formed unions aimed at securing equitable pay and working conditions through collective bargaining. One of the first was the Female Labor Reform Association of Lowell, Massachusetts. Other such ventures included the Union Society of Journeymen Tailors and the National Trades Union based in New York City. When the city's bricklayers and plasterers formed a union, they insisted that "after years of comparative slavery to the will of the capitalists and employers, [the workers] deem it a duty they owe . . . to themselves and families, to unite together as an organized body for their mutual protection, for the purpose of obtaining fair remuneration for their labor." They even tried forming their own political parties such as the Equal Rights Party, whose members were called the Locofocos after the matches they used for illumination.[93]

Elites argued that such worker "combinations" were unnecessary, even sacrilegious. Labor unions were, said New York's *Journal of Commerce*, "at war with the order of things which the Creator has established for the general good, and therefore wicked." Ignoring the obvious, one group of industrialists insisted that "the law of Supply and Demand" would regulate the wage scale and "fix it on an equitable basis." Moreover, their efforts to control labor by such means as blacklisting demonstrated the hypocrisy of their "supply and demand" arguments. So did their efforts at control through the courts. When twenty blacklisted members of New York's Union Society of Journeymen Tailors went on strike, they were arrested on charges of "conspiracy to injure trade, riot, assault, battery." After a quick conviction and fines from $50 to $150 each, Judge Edwards told the "conspirators": "In this favored land of law and liberty, the road to advancement is open to all. . . . Every American knows that or ought to know that he has no better friend than the laws and that he needs no artificial combination for his protection."[94]

New York workers responded by circulating handbills which read in part:

> THE RICH AGAINST THE POOR!
>
> Judge Edwards, the tool of the aristocracy, against the people! Mechanics and workingmen! A deadly blow has been struck at your liberty! The prize for which your fathers fought has been robbed from you! The freemen of the North are now on a level with the slave of the South! . . . They have established the precedent that workingmen have no right to regulate the price of labor, or, in other words, the rich are the only judges of the wants of the poor man.[95]

Far from suppressing the labor movement, Edwards's ruling only made workers more determined in their struggle. Twenty-seven thousand people gathered at New York's City Hall Park to denounce Edwards and his view of workers as "mere tools to build up princely fortunes for men who grasp at all and produce nothing."[96] Across the country, more unions formed and more labor newspapers were founded. And workers organized political parties to extend their rights to the ballot box.

By taking action themselves, workers were beginning to succeed. There were hundreds of strikes for better wages and working conditions. Many were violently put down, but the workers kept pressing. They forced New Hampshire to set the industrial workday at ten hours. Rhode Island followed suit and further outlawed the employment of children under twelve. So did Connecticut. Ohio raised the industrial working age to fourteen. There were usually loopholes in the laws, such as allowing younger children to work "with their parents' permission" and allowing for longer workdays "with consent of the worker." Under threat of unemployment, that consent was not hard for employers to get. Still, that such laws could be passed demonstrated the rising anger of workers and the dangers it posed to absolute capitalist control. In some towns like Lynn, Massachusetts, strikes led to such activism among common folk that they took control of local government.[97] Could such a thing happen at the state or national level? Elites dreaded the thought.

"Fire-Eaters" and "Blatant Freedom Shriekers"

It was partly that dread that fueled the determination of northern politicians to keep slavery out of the western territories. Just as the lack of economic opportunity in the South spawned discontent, so it did in the North as well. Elites in both sections used the faint promise of western land in an effort to keep the hopes of common folk alive and dissension among them suppressed. During the Winnebago War of the 1820s and the Black Hawk War of the 1830s, the Kickapoos, Delawares, Shawnees, Sac, and Fox had all felt that painful reality as they were pushed from their northern homelands into Indian Territory.[98]

With factory conditions so dismal, few of the North's white industrial laborers saw any long-term opportunity in such work. Like many common folk, they saw their future in western land—land that they wanted free of competition from blacks and slavery. They made that clear with their demands both for free land grants and for antiblack legislation. Most politicians appeared happy to oblige. In 1848, nearly a hundred congressional candidates pledged their support for free land. By 1852, over half the North's congressmen had come to office promising "land reform." At the same time, Michigan, Ohio, Wisconsin, Illinois, Indiana, and Iowa all denied free blacks their right to vote. These and other states passed restrictive laws similar to the South's slave codes. Iowa, Indiana, Oregon, and Illinois even barred blacks from entering. One Ohio congressman insisted that the citizens of his state would never tolerate blacks settling there: "Three hundred thousand freemen of Ohio would . . . receive them on the points of their bayonets and drive them from [the] State." It was hardly an exaggeration. When a group of about 500 free blacks tried to settle in Ohio, they were quickly driven out. Northern whites were just as determined to keep blacks and slavery out of the West.[99]

Congress had reached a temporary settlement of the western slave question in 1820 with the Missouri Compromise. Missouri was admitted to the Union as a slave state and Maine as a free state, thus preserving the balance of free and slave states in the Senate. More significantly, a line extending from the southern border of Missouri to the Rocky Mountains (then the western boundary of the United States) established a dividing line between slavery and freedom. All future states created north of the line would be free. Those south of the line would be slave. That settled the issue as far as the federal government was concerned. There was even a "gag rule" forbidding any official discussion of slavery in Congress. But as the aggressively expansive United States pushed its way to the Pacific Ocean, politicians could not ignore the slavery question for long.

The issue again came to a head in 1848 after the United States took the upper half of Mexico following a two-year war of conquest. Mexico had abolished slavery two decades earlier. Would slavery now be reintroduced in the new U.S. territories? During the presidential campaign that year, Whigs ignored the issue, Democrats favored compromise, and a new party—the Free Soilers—took a strong stand for free land and against slavery's expansion. The successful Whig candidate, General Zachary Taylor, found slavery's status impossible to ignore when California, part of the Mexican cession, asked for admission to the Union as a free state in 1849. The next year California gained statehood under the Compromise of 1850. Though whites enslaving Indians was common in California, the free states now had a nominal two-seat advantage in the U.S. Senate.[100] As compensation, slaveholders got a fugitive slave law mandating the return of slaves who escaped to the North. As for the remaining territories of the Mexican cession, "popular sovereignty" would prevail. Voters in both the New Mexico and Utah territories, encompassing the modern states of New Mexico, Arizona, Nevada, Utah, and Colorado, would make the decision on slavery themselves.

Popular sovereignty's inherent complications became clear when Congress passed the Kansas-Nebraska Act in 1854. In exchange for southern congressional votes favoring organization of these territories through which northerners hoped to build the first transcontinental railroad, Kansas was opened to the possibility of slavery under popular sovereignty. Kansas actually lay north of the old Missouri Compromise line, which should have barred slavery from the area. But northern congressmen wanted their railroad and they needed southern votes to get it. Repeal of the Missouri Compromise was the price for those votes. It seemed at the time a small price to pay. Most northern legislators were certain there was no real danger of Kansas becoming a slave state since its geography was not suitable for large-scale cotton agriculture.

But Kansas was just west of Missouri, a slave state. Free Soilers and abolitionists rushed to get settlers into Kansas as quickly as possible. Proslavery men did the same. During elections for the legislature, thousands of "border ruffians" crossed over from Missouri to vote, giving the proslavery faction a victory. The territorial governor called the election a fraud but let the results stand anyway. The new proslavery legislature quickly expelled its few antislavery members and proposed a state constitution allowing slavery. Under the new government, to question the legality of slavery in Kansas was a felony. To aid or encourage an escaping slave was a capital offense. But antislavery men formed their own competing government and drew up a constitution excluding both slavery and free blacks from the territory. The controversy was by no means limited to political bickering. A proslavery raid on the town of Lawrence left one man dead. In retaliation, an antislavery band led by John Brown, later of Harper's Ferry fame, killed five proslavery men along Pottawatomie Creek. Violence spread quickly and by the end of 1856 more than two hundred people were dead.[101]

The Kansas-Nebraska Act and its resulting violence further polarized the politics of slavery's expansion. It drove a firm wedge between

the Democratic Party's northern and southern wings. It destroyed the
Whigs as a national force. And it gave rise to a political party that was
doggedly determined to keep slavery confined to the South. This new
Republican Party was composed mainly of former Free Soilers and
northern Whigs, with some northern Democrats and those abolitionists who could swallow their principles and ally themselves with men
who had no wish to see slavery ended, only limited. They ran their
first presidential candidate, John C. Frémont, in 1856. Though they
lost to Democrat James Buchanan, Republicans established a sectional
hold by capturing most of the free states. Southern Democrats added
fuel to the sectional fire by consistently painting opponents with the
broad brush of abolitionism, calling all who dared challenge them
"Black Republicans."

The U.S. Supreme Court's attempt to settle the slavery question
once and for all did little better. With its 1857 Dred Scott decision,
the high court cited the Fifth Amendment, which stated in part: "No
person shall . . . be deprived of life, liberty, or property without due
process of law." Slaves were not persons but property, claimed the justices, and could not be barred from the territories. By implication, neither could slaveholders be barred from taking their "property"
anywhere the Constitution held force, free states included. With its
ill-fated attempt to cool a heated atmosphere, the Court destroyed the
concept of free statehood and gave Republicans an issue on which
they could build.

John Brown's raid did the same for southern Democrats. In October 1859, Brown led an attempt to seize the federal arsenal at Harper's
Ferry, Virginia, and arm local slaves in rebellion. The effort failed and
a Virginia court sentenced Brown to hang for treason. Abolitionists
now had a martyr, but the South's secessionist "fire-eaters" had something even more valuable for their cause. In the aftermath of Brown's
raid, they easily played on southern white fears of northerners encouraging slave revolt. Fire-eaters pointed to Brown's black allies in the
Harper's Ferry raid and described them as organized and led by "bla-
tant freedom shriekers." Slavery's defenders warned their neighbors to
be on guard. The whole South, they said, was infested with "agents of
the Black Republican Party."[102]

This volatile atmosphere of panic and paranoia formed the backdrop of the presidential campaign in 1860. Democrats met in
Charleston, South Carolina, but could not agree on a policy regarding

slavery in the territories. Southern delegates insisted on adhering to the Dred Scott decision, which opened the territories to slavery. Northerners held to popular sovereignty, arguing that territorial legislatures could still effectively bar slavery simply by refusing to enact slave codes protecting the institution. Unable to find common ground in Charleston, the party reconvened in Baltimore later that year. Again it reached an impasse and most southerners walked out. The remaining delegates nominated Stephen A. Douglas of Illinois, who had championed popular sovereignty in the Senate for more than a decade. Southern Democrats held their own convention and nominated Vice President John C. Breckinridge of Kentucky for the presidency.

The Republicans met in Chicago and agreed on nearly everything but a candidate. Of the leading contenders, none had enough delegates to ensure nomination going into the convention. The party finally settled on a dark horse from Illinois who seemed to be everyone's second choice, Abraham Lincoln. As for slavery, their platform aimed to keep it confined to the South.

Some southerners, mainly Whigs concerned by the developing sectional nature of the campaign, formed the Constitutional Union Party. To represent their ticket, they nominated John Bell of Tennessee for president and Edward Everett of Massachusetts for vice president. The party's only platform was the "Constitution of the Country, the Union of the States, and the Enforcement of the Laws." Of the four candidates for president that year, none commanded a national following. Stephen Douglas was the only one who really tried.

Though often portrayed as such, the campaign was hardly a referendum on secession among southern whites. To the contrary, though Breckinridge was the most ardently "southern rights" candidate, he offered himself as the only man who could save the Union. Douglas had no real chance, and neither did Bell. If Lincoln came to office, argued Breckinridge and his supporters, the pressures for secession would be overwhelming. That, insisted Breckinridge, was something he never wanted to see. By playing both sides, he attracted votes from southern secessionists and unionists alike and carried eleven of the fifteen slave states.[103]

In the North, Democrats were as eager as their southern counterparts to paint Republicans with the broad brush of abolitionism and equality for blacks. Lincoln, though he personally found slavery distasteful, early and repeatedly insisted that he had no intention of ending slavery. Neither was he "in favor of bringing about in any way the social and political equality of the white and black races. . . . I as much as any other man am in favor of having the superior position assigned to the white race." Still, Lincoln's opponents warned that a Lincoln presidency would lead both to slavery's end and black equality. "If Lincoln is elected," wrote the Democratic *New York Herald* to the workers of that city, "you will have to compete with the labor of four million emancipated negroes." Besides that, "the normal state of the negro is barbarism," wrote the editor of Concord, New Hampshire's *Democratic Standard*. "Aided by the white man, and only through the medium of slavery, he becomes partially civilized and Christianized." Most northerners tended to agree. But unlike the Democrats, Lincoln and the Republicans pledged uncompromising opposition to slavery's expansion and support for free land in the West. That promise gained Lincoln 54 percent of the free states' popular vote and enough electoral votes to make him president-elect.[104]

"Nothing But Divisions Among Our People"

With Lincoln poised to enter the White House, secessionists felt that now was the time to push hard for disunion. Most slaveholders would certainly support such a move. If lesser yeomen and poor whites could be made to see Lincoln as a John Brown writ large, they too might support leaving the Union. Secessionist leaders had to act quickly before Lincoln took office or they might never have another chance.

"It is absolute submission to Black Republican Rule," insisted one fire-eating secessionist, "or absolute resistance." Another warned that Lincoln and his "Black Republican Party" intended to end slavery and hang all who supported it. The only way to avoid the "horrors of abolition" was immediate secession. "Why hesitate?" he asked. "The question is between life and death."[105]

Southern plain folk tended to be less certain. Those who held a few slaves certainly saw Lincoln as a potential threat despite his insistence to the contrary. For lesser yeomen and poor whites, though they owned no slaves, they still had their racist pride. Would Lincoln really try to free the slaves and grant them equality as secessionists claimed? Governor Joe Brown of Georgia, self-proclaimed friend of the common man, said it was true. He warned that poor whites would suffer more than planters if Lincoln ended slavery. Former slaves would, Brown insisted, "come into competition with [poor whites], associate with them and their children as equals—be allowed to testify in court against them—sit on juries with them, march to the ballot box by their sides, and participate in the choice of their rulers—claim social equality with them—and ask the hands of their children in marriage."[106]

Still, many plain folk were leery of secessionist motives. For years they had been told to think of themselves as the planter's equal. In 1860, Alabama planter and future Confederate senator William Lowndes Yancey called whites the "master race, and the white man is the equal of every other white man." Governor Brown of Georgia insisted that plain folk belonged "to the only true aristocracy, the race of *white men*."[107] But plain folk hardly lived as the planter's equal, nor did they have the economic opportunities that might make it possible for them to do so. Most blamed the planters themselves for that. It was just as clear to yeomen and poor whites that planters did not view them as equals no matter what they said in public.

Many planters had indeed come to view themselves as aristocrats and plain folk as little better than slaves. One planter, in a private letter to a friend, wrote of the poor whites: "Not one in ten is . . . a whit superior to a negro." Most planters tried to keep such opinions concealed lest their hypocrisy be exposed. Occasionally, though, suggestions of planter arrogance slipped into print. In his 1854 defense of slavery, *Sociology for the South; or, The Failure of Free Society*, George Fitzhugh not only insisted that slavery was "the best form of society yet devised for the masses" but also "that slavery, *black or white*, was right and necessary." Could white slavery be just around the corner? Some poor whites were beginning to think it might be. That so many slaves could "pass for white" was a worrisome fact to many free whites. It seemed to them that one way or the other, whether under Republican or planter rule, they might be condemned to occupy the lowest rung of the social ladder right along with slaves.[108]

In 1859, one poor Hancock County, Georgia, laborer confided to an acquaintance that if it came to a war over slavery he was going to "black himself" and fight to end it. Without slavery, perhaps he could get better wages. That same year, a farmer in Georgia's Taliaferro County was convicted of hiding a runaway slave for three months. Yet another in Greene County was found making fake passes for slaves and "teaching them to write and cipher." Some seemed prepared to go much further. In 1860, a large group of Alabama planters gathered to discuss ways to keep "low down poor whites" from plotting to free the slaves and redistribute land, resources, and wealth. An Alabamian confirmed slaveholder fears by pointing out that "slaves are constantly associating with low white men who are not slave owners. Such people are dangerous to the community." In Tennessee, police arrested a white man named Williams along with thirty slaves for plotting rebellion. Three Louisiana whites were charged with the same offense. Two in Mississippi were implicated in a slave conspiracy. Throughout the 1850s, with various means and motives, white southerners increasingly worked to undermine the slave system.[109]

It seemed obvious to most slaveholders that growing numbers of people like these were potential recruits for the Republican Party. With Lincoln in the White House and discontent among plain folk on the rise, a truly national Republican Party might become a reality. A writer in *De Bow's Review* reminded readers that many poor southern whites generally harbored "a feeling of deep-rooted jealousy and prejudice, of painful antagonism, if not hostility, to the institution of negro slavery, that threatens the most serious consequences, the moment Black-republicanism becomes triumphant in the Union." One secessionist warned that if the slaveholders did not take their states out of the Union, there would indeed soon be "an Abolition party in the South, of Southern men." Another frankly admitted, "I mistrust our own people more than I fear all of the efforts of the Abolitionists."[110]

And what of the slaves themselves? Though they argued otherwise, slaveholders knew very well that slavery did not come naturally to those of African descent. Slaves had to be controlled through fear and violence, though that control was never entirely effective. In 1850, a band of Missouri slaves rose up and fought to the death for their freedom. In 1856, a posse of North Carolina slaveholders succeeded only in getting one of their number killed when they attacked a settlement of black escapees hiding in a swamp. The former slaves yelled at their attackers to "come on, they were ready for them again." Two years later a Louisiana newspaper wrote that there were "more cases of insubordination among the negro population . . . than ever known before." A Mississippi paper noted that cases of slaves killing their owners were "alarmingly frequent."[111]

Throughout the 1850s, rebellion was on the rise. Slaves wanted to be set free, and by 1860 they believed Lincoln would do just that. How could they think otherwise with secessionists ranting throughout the South that Lincoln's ultimate goal was to free them? One freedman later remembered that slaves "hoped and prayed he would be elected. They wanted to be free and have a chance." When Lincoln won the presidency, most slaves took it as a sign that their prayers had been answered. Some did more than pray. They took action, expecting that Lincoln would back them up. One Mississippi slave roused his companions to rebellion with the promise that "Lincoln would set us free." In Virginia, Chesterfield County slaves planned an uprising, sure that Lincoln would come to their aid. Such plots were common in the weeks after Lincoln's election. Louisiana sugar planter Alexander Pugh wrote in his diary that "the negroes have got it into their heads they are going to be free [as] of the 4th of March [1861]," the day of Lincoln's inaugural. That thought made slaveholders' blood run cold.[112]

More than the abolitionists, more than Lincoln himself, slaveholders feared the South's slaves and nonslaveholding whites. Control of neither group had ever been easy. By the late 1850s it was getting harder. A Lincoln presidency would make control even more difficult, even if Lincoln himself was no direct threat. If the slave states remained in the Union, most slaveholders feared that their "peculiar institution" might collapse as much from internal as external pressures. Outside the Union, controlling the lower classes might be easier and slavery might be safer. Other factors certainly helped fuel the crisis. Overestimation of abolitionist strength in the North, the issue of slavery's expansion, and personal political ambitions all played their part. But slaveholders' fear of their fellow southerners was a primary, though publicly unacknowledged, force driving secession.

Even so, slaveholders were not entirely united behind the movement. Secession found its most enthusiastic support among the more numerous "new money" planters and lesser slaveholders. Their spokesmen tended to be young up-and-coming lawyer-politicians trying to carve out a niche for themselves at the expense of the older establishment. On the other side, wealthier and more conservative "old money" planters tended to view secession as much more risky than remaining in the Union. Some viewed themselves as having a greater stake in preserving the status quo. Others felt that even if slavery within the Union was in danger, they had enough capital and investments— much of it with the North—to ride out slavery's demise. Whatever their situation, more wealthy planters were generally more cautious than lesser slaveholders. Should withdrawal from the Union lead to civil war, business dealings with the North would certainly be disrupted. Furthermore, success for a southern confederacy would depend on widespread support from nonslaveholding whites. Many planters wondered how long that support could last. Secession might actually hasten the end of slavery rather than preserve it.[113]

That danger seemed clear enough to Texas governor Sam Houston. "The first gun fired in the war," he warned, "will be the knell of slavery." Georgians Alexander Stephens and Benjamin Hill, future Confederate vice president and Confederate senator, respectively, agreed with Houston. Stephens stressed that as dependent as a southern government would be on plain folk, slaveholders could lose their grip on the course of events: "The movement will before it ends I fear be beyond the control of those who started it." Hill was certain that a South divided by class could not survive a civil war. The southern government would fall and slavery with it.[114]

Many of Hill's colleagues had similar fears. Shortly after Lincoln's election, in what one contemporary called "a large meeting of the Members of the General Assembly" at the Georgia capitol, legislators called for thoughtful restraint. They appointed a committee of twenty-two, including Hill, to draft a resolution urging Georgia voters not to support secessionists in the upcoming election for convention delegates. Immediate secession would, they insisted, lead to "nothing but divisions among our people, confusion among the slaveholding States, strife around our firesides, and ultimate defeat to every movement for the effective redress of our grievances."[115]

"Covenants with Death and Agreements with Hell"

Such divisions set the stage for intense controversy at state secession conventions, at least in those states where secessionists had a strong voice. Though most slave state governments held elections for delegates to secession conventions, southern popular opinion ran so strongly against breaking up the Union that the upper South and border states, constituting over half the slave states, dismissed it out of hand. Only in the Deep South was secession an immediate threat. Even there voters were deeply divided. So worried were secessionist leaders over the possibility of secession being voted down that they used intimidation and violence in their efforts to control the ballot box wherever they could. Samuel Beaty, a farmer in Mississippi's Tippah County who was physically threatened because of his Union sentiments, dared not go to the polls. "It would," he said, "have been too dangerous." Secessionists threatened to hang James Cloud, a crippled farmer in Jackson County, Alabama, after he spoke up for the Union.[116]

There were many who resisted such antidemocratic pressure despite the dangers. In some cases, there was a resistance of only one. In south Alabama, sixty-four-year-old Middleton Martin came "pretty near getting into two or three cutting scrapes" as he pleaded with his neighbors to support the Union. "I said to the men 'Don't for God's sake vote that secession ticket.'" When one local secessionist told Martin to shut up or be run out of town, the old man gave better than he got. "Do you see this knife?" Martin asked the man who had threatened him. "If you don't get away from here right away I'll cut your guts out!" Many Union men showed the same kind of grit on election day. At one Mississippi polling place, a lone Methodist preacher summoned up the courage to defy local secessionists.

> Approaching the polls, I asked for a Union ticket, and was informed that none had been printed, and that it would be advisable to vote the secession ticket. I thought otherwise, and going to a desk, wrote out a Union ticket, and voted it amidst the frowns and suppressed murmurs of the judges and by-standers, and, as the result proved, I had the honour of depositing the only vote in favour of the Union which was polled in that precinct.

The preacher knew of many local men who opposed secession but were so frightened by threats to their lives that they stayed away from the polls.[117]

Due in large part to threat tactics, turnout in the popular vote for state convention delegates across the Deep South dropped by more than a third from the previous November's presidential election. Still, those opposing immediate secession gave a strong showing. They ran almost neck-and-neck with the secessionists in Alabama and Louisiana. Georgia's antisecessionists polled a likely majority of over a thousand. In Texas, two-thirds of voters opposed secession. Throughout the

A satirical, though not altogether inaccurate, view of how the South was voted out of the Union. During the winter of 1860–61, popular opinion in the slave states ran heavily against secession. Only in the Deep South was secession a serious threat. Even there voters were deeply divided. Secessionists forced disunion on a reluctant South mainly by using violence and intimidation to control the ballot box where they could. Samuel Beaty, a Mississippi farmer, was physically threatened because of his Union sentiments and dared not go to the polls. "It would," he said, "have been too dangerous." (*Harper's Weekly*)

Deep South official returns gave secession's opponents about 40 percent of the popular vote. However, fraud at the ballot box was so widespread that the returns cannot be trusted as a gauge of popular opinion. Most likely, antisecession sentiment was much stronger than the final vote suggests.[118]

In any case, the balloting for state convention delegates makes clear that the South was badly divided. It also suggests that those divisions were largely class related. North Carolina's vote declining even to hold a convention showed the state's electorate more clearly divided along class lines than ever before. In Louisiana, nonslaveholding voters left little doubt that they saw the whole secession movement as an effort simply to maintain "the peculiar rights of a privileged class." All seventeen counties in northern Alabama, where relatively few voters held slaves, sent delegates to the state convention with instructions to oppose secession. And in Texas, where 81 percent of slaveholders voted for secessionist delegates, only 32 percent of nonslaveholders did so. Slaveholders across the South, who constituted barely a fourth of the electorate, consistently demonstrated much greater support for secession than did their nonslaveholding neighbors.[119]

Nevertheless, slaveholders commanded the dominant voice at all the cotton state conventions. In Georgia, for example, while just over a third of qualified voters held slaves, 87 percent of the convention delegates were slaveholders.[120] Similar statistics at all the conventions virtually guaranteed secession regardless of the popular will. Beginning with South Carolina in December 1860, secessionists took, in order, Mississippi, Florida, Alabama, Georgia, and Louisiana out of the Union. Texas finally went on February 1, 1861. Three days later, representatives from the seceded states met in Montgomery, Alabama, to form the Confederate States of America with Jefferson Davis its appointed president.[121]

While many southerners welcomed the Confederacy's birth with wild enthusiastic celebrations, many others did not. Said one Georgia man of the merrymakers: "Poor fools! They may ring their bells now, but they will wring their hands—yes, and their hearts, too—before they are done with it." William Brownlow—a Tennessee preacher, newspaper editor, and leading unionist—called the secession ordinances "covenants with death and agreements with hell! They are so many decrees to carry out the behests of *madmen* and *traitors*."[122]

Some southerners continued to question the Confederacy's legitimacy and charged outright fraud. One furious Georgia voter accused Singleton Sisk, a Missionary Baptist preacher, of cheating Habersham County out of its antisecession vote. In an open letter to the *Athens Southern Watchman*, he told how this "[J]anus-faced expounder of the Gospel" had declared himself a Union man to gain the nomination of Habersham's antisecessionists. With their backing, he was elected to the state convention. "After the election, we find that he had privately promised the Secessionists that he would, in the Convention, support Secession." Sisk indeed betrayed his constituents and backed secession at the convention. Similar betrayals occurred among the representatives of at least twenty-eight other Georgia counties.[123]

So it was across the Deep South. John Powell, a Mississippi slaveholder, ran as the antisecession candidate in Jones County. When the state convention met on January 9, Powell deserted his constituents and voted to make Mississippi the second state to leave the Union. Such fraud was common in Florida and Alabama too. As one Florida resident complained: "The election machinery was all in the hands of the secessionists, who manipulated the election to suit their end." Jasper Harper, a disgusted voter from Marshall County, Alabama, complained bitterly: "I voted for those [delegates] who said the guns would have to be placed to their breast and the trigger pulled before they would vote for Alabama to go out of the Union, but they did not stick to what they said."[124]

Officials in Louisiana delayed releasing their questionable election returns for three months. So did Governor Joe Brown of Georgia, who did so only at the insistence of concerned voters. Even then he lied about the results. Brown falsely claimed that secessionist delegates had carried the state by over thirteen thousand votes. In fact, existing records from the time suggest that secession was defeated by just over a thousand votes.[125]

When Texas governor Sam Houston, in accordance with his state's two-thirds vote against secession, refused to call a convention, an unofficial cabal of secessionists in Austin organized one for themselves. Houston was able to get the convention's secession ordinance submitted to the voters for ratification in what was a "free election" in name only. But in the other six seceding states, ratification was never placed in the hands of voters. One Louisiana delegate told his colleagues that in "refusing to submit its action to [the voters] for their sanction . . . this Convention violates the great fundamental principle of American government, that the will of the people is supreme." In March, the *New Orleans Picayune* stated plainly that secessionist leaders across the South were giving "new and startling evidence of their distrust of the people, and thus furnished strong testimony . . . that the South was divided, and that the movement in which we are now engaged has not the sanction of the great body of the people."[126]

In his seminal study of the secession crisis, David Potter looked at the popular vote for state secession conventions throughout the South and concluded:

> At no time during the winter of 1860–1861 was secession desired by a majority of the people of the slave states. . . . Furthermore, secession was not basically desired even by a majority in the lower South, and the secessionists succeeded less because of the intrinsic popularity of their program than because of the extreme skill with which they utilized an emergency psychology, the promptness with which they invoked unilateral action by individual states, and the firmness with which they refused to submit the question of secession to popular referenda.[127]

Throughout the secession crisis, southerners had worried about what the results of secession might be. Some feared that the federal government might try to hold the cotton states in the Union by force. The *Vicksburg Whig* warned its readers that not only was it "treason to secede," but that such a move would bring "strife, discord, bloodshed, war, if not anarchy." It was a "blind and suicidal course." In an open letter, one southwest Georgia man was so sure civil war would come that he referred to secessionists as "the suicides." Others were just as certain that they were nothing of the sort. Georgia's *Albany Patriot* assured its readers that the Yankees would never dare make war on the South. "In all honesty we can say to our readers, be not afraid. We will insure the life of every southern man from being killed in war by the abolitionists for a postage stamp." The editor of Upson County's *Pilot* was not sure what the outcome of secession might be, but he was glad his county had voted against it: "If the demon of civil war is to ravage our fields only to fertilize them with blood—we know our Upson Delegates will be able, at the last dread account, to stand up with clean hands and pure hearts and exclaim through no chattering teeth from coward consciences:—'*Thou canst not say we did it!*'"[128]

"Is It Just That Creditors Should Go Unpaid?"

Uncertainty about the end result of secession in the South reflected a widespread reluctance for war, especially among common folk. Nor were common folk in the North eager to fight. All across the region people expressed strong antiwar sentiments. On January 16, four thousand attended a mass meeting in Philadelphia at which banners read NO CIVIL WAR. Bands played patriotic music, but there was a notable absence of American flags. Ten days later, another antiwar rally of Philadelphia workers drew a crowd of six thousand despite a snowstorm. The next month, a national workers' convention met in the city and resolved itself to be "utterly opposed to any measures that will evoke civil war." It seemed clear to the *New York Herald*'s editor that "the citizens of the free States are not prepared for civil war, nor will they consent to imbrue their hands in the blood of their brethren at the South."[129]

Just as northerners generally opposed war, they also tended to oppose compromise on slavery's expansion even if it meant letting the Deep South go. On January 3, 1861, Towanda, Pennsylvania's *Bradford Reporter* declared: "If South Carolina will not return unless 'conciliated,' let her go in peace. It will be less a loss than to lose our honor and self-respect." Some even expressed relief at seeing the Palmetto State cut its ties to the Union. The *Indianapolis Daily Journal* rejoiced: "We are well rid of South Carolina, if we are only wise enough to count it a riddance, and nothing more. . . . If all the South follows her, let it. . . . In God's name, and for humanity's sake, let them go in peace." The *Boston Advertiser* likewise supported peaceful separation. So did New York's *Albany Argus* and Maine's *Bangor Union*. Horace Greeley, one of Lincoln's staunchest supporters, wrote in the pages of his *New York Tribune* that if southerners were "satisfied that they can do better out of the Union than in it, we insist on letting them go in peace."[130]

But northern industrialists and financiers vigorously pressured the government to keep the cotton states in the Union—by compromise if possible, by force if necessary. How else could they guarantee continued access to southern markets and cheap cotton? It was a question that united most elites across party lines. The majority of them had direct business ties to the cotton South or investments in cotton textile industries. The *Boston Herald* warned that an independent South could "impose a heavy tax upon the manufactures of the North, and an export tax upon the cotton used by northern manufacturers." Such taxes would drive up both the price of cotton and the cost of doing business in the South, thus cutting into profits and reducing stock values. Under the threat of secession and civil war, the average price of stocks in forty-four northern textile mills had already dropped by over 40 percent. And secession would make it impossible for northern creditors to collect on the millions of dollars in debt southerners owed. Such upper-class concerns carried little weight among the North's common folk. "We hear a great deal of talk among the ardent platform republicans about coercing the secessionists of the South by means of Northern soldiers," wrote the editor of New York's *Rochester Union*, "but the indications are that the fighting is to be done mostly with the tongue."[131]

Corporate bosses in the North had other ideas. There was too much cash at stake to let southerners go. The South pumped $60 million annually into the pockets of Boston businessmen. For New York City, the figure was $200 million. Throughout the North, business leaders wrote letters, circulated petitions, and organized meetings to urge support for a compromise to keep the South in the Union and business ties with it secure. Congress responded with a plan, the Crittenden compromise, which would have extended the 1820 line between free and slave territory all the way to California. Most northern elites enthusiastically backed the effort as the only peaceful way to deal with disunion and get back to business as usual.[132]

Though it might have meant the end of secession, it would also have been fatal to the Republican Party. Republicans had carried the November elections on their pledge to hold slavery back. How could they now relent and sign on to a compromise extending slavery? To do so might destroy their constituent support and the party with it. Lincoln was silent on any possible intent to use force during those long weeks leading up to his March 4 inauguration, but on this issue he made his feelings clear: "Let there be no compromise on the question of extending slavery," he told fellow Republicans. "If there be, all our labor is lost." It would mean, he said, "the end of us." Compromise could get no Republican backing. Without it, the Crittenden plan had no chance to pass in Congress.[133]

Compromise or no, northern business elites were determined to hold the cotton states. How else could they get the $300 million in southern debts owed them? Reports from the South noted that planters and merchants "seemed to delight in the fancied release from their obligations secession gives them." Like so many others, one New York merchant "had not a word to say in condemnation of the South till they stopped paying him." When another New York supplier asked that merchandise be shipped back, his southern debtor replied, "I cannot return the goods, as you demand, for they are already sold, and the money invested in muskets to shoot you Yankees."[134]

And what of navigation on the Mississippi River? Millions of dollars in all sorts of goods traversed its muddy waters every year. Would access to the river be taxed or, worse yet, closed? When Mississippians placed artillery on the Vicksburg bluffs and began "amusing themselves by firing at steamboats passing down or up the river," Yankee businessmen stepped up their efforts to squash secession. Thirty of New York's most prominent business leaders visited outgoing president James Buchanan and insisted that he hold by force if necessary Fort Sumter at Charleston, South Carolina, Fort Pickens at Pensacola, Florida, and other federal posts in the South. A delegation of

Philadelphia businessmen did the same. Some even mailed letters directly to the secretary of war promising supplies for Fort Sumter whether Buchanan wanted them sent or not.[135]

Business elites put intense pressure on the incoming president and his party as well. "At present," wrote a group of New York merchants to Lincoln, "there are no means of collecting any portion of [southern] debts, nor can there be, until the authority of the United States government is re-established in the rebellious states." Many such men, like the Philadelphia banker Jay Cooke, had backed Republicans financially in the previous year's campaigns and now expected their payoff. When Crittenden's compromise efforts failed, Cooke began using his Republican contacts to lay the groundwork for wartime profits. So did a group of Boston manufacturers, who petitioned for contracts to supply military equipment.[136]

"Thus by March," as historian Kenneth Stampp wrote, "it was evident that northern businessmen had carefully measured the consequences of disunion and the collapse of central authority and decided that they were intolerable." So had Lincoln. Like other Republicans, he knew that to let secession stand and lose the support of financial backers would undermine the party as surely as would compromise on slavery's expansion. "I have no purpose, directly or indirectly, to interfere with slavery in the states where it exists," Lincoln said at his March 4 inauguration. "I have no lawful right to do so, and I have no inclination to do so." He had stressed the same point many times before. For the first time, however, he publicly made clear that like the North's businessmen and financiers, he too found disunion unacceptable. Under his administration, it would be "the declared purpose of the Union that it WILL Constitutionally defend and maintain itself." In a message to Congress justifying his stance and the war it would bring, Lincoln asked, "Is it just that creditors should go unpaid?"[137]

But how would Lincoln hold the cotton states and protect northern business interests? There was too little popular support for using force against the Confederacy. "It cannot be denied," wrote the *New York Times* on March 21, 1861, "that there is a growing sentiment throughout the North in favor of *letting the Gulf States go*." Though Lincoln, despite the popular will, was committed to holding the Deep South, he did not have the means to do so. His army was too small to mount a southern offensive, and few men were volunteering. A military draft, unpopular as it would be, was out of the question. Even if Congress approved it, such a move would enrage the populace and split the party. Lincoln needed men, willing men, to form an army large enough to retake the seceded states. To get them, he needed an incident.[138]

"The Design of the Administration Is Accomplished"

It was not hard to guess where and how Lincoln intended that incident to occur. After reading his inaugural speech, the editor of Iowa's *Dubuque Herald* was sure that Lincoln would try, or appear to try, to "re-enforce Fort Sumter, and thus aggravate the already excited ire of the South, and provoke a conflict." Lincoln would have to act soon, and he knew it. Even as he dispatched resupply ships to Fort Sumter, knowing the move would likely draw Confederate fire, Connecticut's *Hartford Daily Courant* reported: "Public opinion in the North seems to be gradually settling down in favor of recognition of the New Confederacy. . . . The thought of a bloody and protracted civil war . . . is abhorrent to all." The *New York Herald* agreed: "Nine out of ten of the people of the Northern and Central States repudiate [Lincoln's] coercive policy."[139]

That sentiment changed quickly when, on April 12, the Confederacy obliged Lincoln by firing on Fort Sumter and providing him with the incident he had sought when he threatened to run in supplies. Lincoln immediately called for seventy-five thousand volunteers and appealed "to all loyal citizens to favor, facilitate and aid this effort to maintain the honor, the integrity, and the existence of our National Union." Newspapers throughout the North echoed the refrain. "The Flag of Our Country—the glorious Stars and Stripes," reported the *Pittsburgh Post*, "has been fired into by American citizens disloyal to the government. . . . No American of true heart and brave soul will stand this. No American ought to stand it." Such words stirred thousands of young men with patriotic fervor as they rushed to uphold and redeem the national honor. Besides, the term of service was only ninety days. Hardly anyone thought it would take even that long to subdue the Rebels. Wrote the *Erie Weekly Gazette*: "The universal uprising of the Northern people in response to the President's appeal for volunteers to avenge the insult to our national flag and vindicate the honor of the National character, constitute the most remarkable event of this and probably any age." George Ticknor, an elderly witness to that transformation, wrote on April 21: "I never knew before what popular excitement can be. Holiday enthusiasm I have seen often enough, and anxious crowds I remember during the War of 1812, but never anything like this. Indeed, here at the North, at least, there was never anything like it."[140]

Lincoln knew well enough the passionate power of the North's nationalistic pride. That pride and its star-spangled symbol was attacked at Sumter, and many northerners responded as Lincoln was sure they would. A soldier from Lincoln's home state of Illinois recalled public meetings where "speakers blew the fife & beat the drum & exhorted the men to rally 'round the flag." This soldier and his comrades "left home burning with desire to wipe treason from the earth." Said one Brooklyn resident in the days after Sumter: "To talk of peace now would be to talk to the tempest and reason with the hurricane." A Wilkes-Barre, Pennsylvania, man agreed: "Blood has flown, madness rules the hour, the worst passions of human nature control the populace."[141]

But not the whole populace. Many remained as opposed to war as ever. Conscientious objectors refused to fight on grounds of religious principle. Others argued that Lincoln had no right to make war. "We are opposed to Secession and Coercion," wrote the editor of Pennsylvania's *Montrose Democrat*. "If the former is unconstitutional, so is the latter." Antiwar protestors in McKean County castigated southern fire-eaters and abolitionists alike for encouraging sectional tensions. On June 8, Washington County residents gathered at Cross Creek and stressed that to sustain "our beloved Union by fighting under present circumstances is simply preposterous." Pennsylvanian George McHenry went so far as to author a pamphlet entitled *Why Pennsylvania Should Become One of the Confederate States of America*. Of the state's sixty-five counties, twenty-seven formed no companies for military service. Eighteen others formed only one or two.[142]

Many citizens worried, despite Lincoln's assurance to the contrary, that the war might become a crusade against slavery. Though most white northerners seemed willing now to make war on southern secessionists, they had no desire to do so on behalf of slaves. The *New York Tribune*, a staunch pro-Lincoln paper, was quick to remind its readers that this conflict was "a War for the preservation of the Union, not for the destruction of Slavery." Congress also tried, with the Crittenden-Johnson resolutions, to assure whites North and South that this was a white man's war waged strictly against rebellion, not against slavery. Never would white soldiers be asked to put their lives on the line for blacks. But many remained unconvinced, or at least suspicious. Any hint of abolitionist talk was enough to prompt a raised eyebrow. In August 1861, a religious revival meeting in Centre County, Pennsylvania, ended sooner than planned because of unusually low turnout. Some of the preachers were rumored to be "hard Republicans." They were likely suspected of supporting abolition too. Most northerners wanted none of that.[143]

Among the soldiers themselves were those driven by other than patriotic motives. Many volunteered under family and community pressures. For others, the pressures were economic. Unemployed men were prominent among the volunteers. Good jobs were scarce, and the army offered at least some assurance of pay. "I could find nothing to do anywhere," wrote Edwin Worthington to his mother, "so . . . I went to New York and enlisted." Phinias Johnson volunteered "in a fit of dejection and discouragement at not being successful in getting steady work." Both young men were dead within a year. That prospect surely motivated some to quit before the war's first major battle. In May 1861, after learning of the Sumter bombardment, two Federal soldiers at Fort Pickens deserted.[144]

Still other northerners suspected Lincoln's motives and were critical of the way he had maneuvered a reluctant country into war. On the day of the Sumter attack, Jersey City's *American Standard* called Lincoln's strategy "a mere decoy to draw the first fire from the people of the South, which act by the pre-determination of the government is to be the pretext for letting loose the horrors of war." The entire affair was "a sham the most transparent, a mockery the most unsubstantial, an hypocrisy which is only more infamous than the low cunning with which it is commingled." Four days later, reflecting the agreement of many others, the *Buffalo Daily Courier* wrote: "With the facts before us we cannot believe that Mr. Lincoln intended that Sumter should be held. . . . War is inaugurated, and the design of the administration is accomplished."[145]

"My Father Fought for the Union and I Could Not Go Against It"

Lincoln helped accomplish Jefferson Davis's design as well. The certainty of invasion united white southerners behind the Confederacy like nothing else could. Within a few weeks, four more slave states—Arkansas, Tennessee, North Carolina, and Virginia—left the Union. So many men volunteered for service that the Confederacy was hard pressed to arm them all. "The Union feeling *was strong* up to [Lincoln's] recent proclamation," wrote a North Carolina congressman on April 26. "This War Manifest extinguishes it, and resistance is now on every mans lips and throbs in every bosom. . . . Union men are now such no longer."[146]

But that was not entirely the case. Despite the passionate post-Sumter excitement, there were large cracks in the facade of southern unity. Throughout the month of May, Unionists held antisecession rallies all across Tennessee. In Knoxville, William Brownlow continued to fly the U.S. flag at his home. That same month, there were reports from North Carolina that "Guilford, Randolph and adjoining counties are unshaken in their devotion to the Stars and Stripes." In Stanly County, on the day of the vote for convention delegates, a yeoman farmer named Elijah Hudson was hauled before a secessionist vigilante committee for "using language against the interest of the South." There was intimidation in Henderson County as well, where known Union men were kept from the polls "with threats that all such would be hung or shot."[147]

In Virginia, there was no popular vote for convention delegates after the firing on Fort Sumter. That state simply used the convention elected in February to oppose secession—which on April 17 voted to support it. Though there was a popular ratification in late May, that vote was just as rife with fraud and intimidation as the balloting in North Carolina had been. In Floyd County, tenant farmer Charles Huff recalled "leading Rebels" warning residents "that those who refused to vote for secession would be hung." Threats to their lives, their families, and their property convinced many unionists to vote the secession ticket. John Brunk did so "to protect himself and family from violence." So did David Rhodes for "fear of reprisal." Even so, there were those determined to have their say. Jacob Wenger was one of eleven known unionists in his Rockingham County precinct who went to the polls in the face of lynching threats. Such courage hardly made a difference. At Mount Crawford, armed secessionist vigilantes forced those who had cast Union ballots back to the polls at gunpoint and made them change their votes.[148]

Such tactics had characterized Virginia's secession process from the outset. Within days of the firing on Fort Sumter and Lincoln's call for volunteers, former Virginia governor Henry Wise and his secessionist allies demanded that the sitting governor, John Letcher, take hold of the federal arsenal at Harper's Ferry and the Gosport Navy Yard at Norfolk. Letcher refused and reminded his friends that Virginia's convention had not yet taken the state out of the Union. In what amounted to a coup d'état, secessionist leaders took control of volunteer troops and ordered assaults on the federal installations. Letcher reluctantly sanctioned the action a day later. When secessionists used mob tactics to intimidate the state convention, western Virginia threatened to split off and stay with the Union. So did eastern Tennessee, where only 30 percent of the fifty thousand votes cast favored ratifying the state's secession ordinance. And despite the Arkansas convention's near unanimous support for its secession ordinance, the vote, as one analyst observed, "did not reflect a similar enthusiasm among the people."[149]

Even among the volunteers, where enthusiasm was generally strongest, there were many reluctant warriors. As with their Union counterparts, family and community pressures held great influence over young southern men. One group of well-to-do young women in Columbus, Georgia, advertised the formation of a Ladies' Home Guard for the "special protection of young men who have concluded to remain at home during the existence of the war." A young belle in Selma, Alabama, put a halt to wedding plans when her fiancé refused to enlist. She sent him women's clothes along with a note reading "wear these or volunteer."[150]

Many of the reluctant still blamed slaveholders for instigating secession. One resident of Bedford County, Tennessee, who remembered the local gentry feeling "above those who did not own slaves," noted that class relations became increasingly strained as "the war clouds gathered." When war broke out, a Meigs County man confirmed that class interactions "became tense." A Hickman County colonel argued that any concerns about the conflict's origins were now irrelevant. They were certainly dangerous to men of his class. "To arms!" he demanded in a circulating recruitment broadside. "Our

Despite pressures to volunteer, North and South, many young men refused to enlist. To embarrass the reluctant, one group of well-to-do southern belles formed a Ladies' Home Guard for the "special protection of young men who have concluded to remain at home." Before the war was half over, however, women by the thousands would be writing to their men begging them to come home. (*Leslie's Illustrated Newspaper*)

Southern soil must be defended. We must not stop to ask who brought about the war, who is at fault, but let us go and do battle . . . and then settle the question who is to blame."[151]

The question of blame was beside the point for many poor southerners as well, but not because they were eager to defend southern soil—of which they owned little or none. Economic disruptions that appeared on the heels of secession threw thousands out of work and made taking a private's lowly pay of $11 a month the best option available to many poor laborers. When secession cut back the Mississippi's riverboat traffic, hundreds of Irish workers petitioned the British consulate in New Orleans for transport out of the South. Told that no funds were available, they had little alternative but to enlist. Many native southerners were in the same predicament. Paupers in the South's urban workhouses were released on the promise that they would volunteer. When the sheriff in Chatham County, North Carolina, arrested a poor transient for "refusing to do military duty and vagrancy," he was promised release if he would enlist.[152] That so many did so on account of economic necessity foreshadowed the increasingly central role class divisions would play in the wartime South.

Those divisions were made clear early on when commoners who went to the front lines quickly discovered that their personal sacrifice would be much greater than of those few elites who joined them. Lacking weapons enough for all its volunteers, the Confederacy mandated that those who could not properly arm themselves enlist for three years or the war's duration. Those who could enlisted for one year only. That meant purchasing the expensive .577-caliber Enfield rifle, which few common soldiers could afford. Most volunteers were not informed until they reached the front lines that their squirrel rifles would not do for military service. Many poor soldiers found that their one-year enlistments had suddenly turned into three. As historian Paul Escott put it: "The price of being a patriot was higher for the common man than for the rich man, three times higher to be exact."[153]

"Many of us here is anxious to serve our country if needed," wrote one recruit to the War Department. But they were "mostly men of familys and cannot leave our families for so long a term as three years." Neither could a company of Georgia volunteers who felt that "twelve months will be best for us & our families." The Mountain Rangers of Georgia's Meriwether County refused to enlist at all when they got word of the three-year rule. They abruptly disbanded in June 1861 before being mustered into service.[154]

Second thoughts became increasingly common as enthusiasm gave way to reality. Many of those early volunteers soon came to question their wisdom and reconsider their motives. Some acted on their doubts. In March 1861, four months before the war's first major battle at Manassas (Bull Run), two Georgia volunteers "took it into their heads to forego the honor and glory of serving the Confederate States upon the tented field, and without so much as saying to the officer in charge, 'By your leave,' took the back track from Griffin to Atlanta." In May, three men of Georgia's 2nd Infantry Regiment decided army life was not for them and headed home. A month later in Virginia, two members of the Macon Volunteers deserted to the Yankees. In June and July, five men of Virginia's own Floyd Guards deserted as well.[155]

What misgivings there were among the troops reflected even greater doubts on the home front. Some continued to express those doubts openly despite the growing danger of speaking one's mind. That danger was deadly real. At the height of post-Sumter excitement in May, a man living just west of Auburn, Alabama, spoke out against secession and was lynched for it. In southwest Georgia, George Martin was arrested on charges of "uttering treasonable sentiments against the Southern Confederacy." Perhaps fearing for his life, Martin nearly killed an army lieutenant while making his escape. Authorities offered a $250 reward for Martin's capture—dead or alive.[156]

Still, Union men in Georgia's Pickens County kept the Stars and Stripes flying at the county courthouse for weeks after secession. The old flag continued to fly for a time in northern Alabama as well. It was hard for many to forsake their ties to the Union, especially those who carried long memories of sacrifice. Alabama farmer Jacob Albright, whose father had fought in the Revolution, recalled after the war: "I told [the local pro-Confederate vigilance committee] that my father fought for the Union and I could not go against it . . . and that sooner than turn over [to the Confederacy] I would die right there." A fellow Alabamian, John Phillips, insisted that he "would never go back on 'Old Glory.' I had heard too much from my old grandparents about the sufferings and privation they had to endure during the Revolutionary War ever to engage against the 'Stars and Stripes.' "[157]

It was equally hard for large numbers of plain folk to forget that they had been cheated out of their vote. Had their voices been fairly represented there would have been no secession and no war. One South Carolina aristocrat expressed deep concern on hearing poor farmers in his area saying "this is a rich man's war." They were saying the same all across the South. "What the hell's it all about anyway?" asked an angry dissenter at the Texas state capitol. "The nigger!" came a reply. "I ain't got no nigger," yelled the speaker. "I ain't going to fight for somebody else's nigger." One Alabama farmer warned his son of the slaveholders: "All they want is to git you pupt up and go to fight for there infurnal negroes and after you do there fighting you may kiss there hine parts for o [all] they care."[158]

A month after the firing on Sumter, William Brooks, who presided at Alabama's secession convention, wrote a worried letter to Jefferson Davis. Brooks feared the sentiment among commoners that "nothing is now in peril in the prevailing war but the title of the master to his slaves." Already some had openly "declared that they will 'fight for no rich man's slaves.'" More and more, plain folk were beginning to express their class resentment. If this trend continued, Brooks told the president, "I leave you to imagine the consequences."[159]

Those consequences were already becoming manifest. In May of 1861, a "vigilance committee" in Greene County, Mississippi, was on the lookout for a band of local unionists "who openly declare that they will fight for Lincoln when an opportunity offers." By June, the committee had information that the McLeod brothers, all nonslaveholding yeoman farmers, were leading the unionists. When hauled in for questioning, Allen McLeod called Jefferson Davis "a murdering scamp & traitor." His brother Peter told the committee not only of his own forces, but also that there were 700 to 800 men in nearby Choctaw County, Alabama, who "would fight against the South & slave owners." From Fannin County, Georgia, came word that "quite a number" were prepared to defend the old flag and help "whip Georgia and the South back into the Union."[160]

In June a North Carolina man warned that Randolph County unionists had as many men under arms as the secessionist home guard, and that anti-Confederates were "holding secret meetings in several places and have a roll or list of names of persons pledged to the support of the Union." On June 7 in Bradley County, Tennessee, word spread that Confederates were on their way to disarm local Union men. Though the rumor proved false, within twelve hours a thousand armed unionists were assembled and ready to turn them back. In Blount County, Alabama, there was a similar number prepared to resist Confederate authority by force. Among the anti-Confederates of Walker County, Georgia, there was talk of forming a company "to defend the glorious Union."[161]

Even more disaffected than many nonslaveholding whites were southern blacks, the vast majority of them enslaved. Comprising a third of the Confederacy's population, they could hardly be counted on to support a government whose "cornerstone" was, as Vice President Alexander Stephens put it in March 1861, "the great truth that the negro is not the equal of the white man" and that slavery was their "natural and normal condition." But Stephens knew better. The fear that he and other slaveholders had of slave rebellion demonstrated that most clearly—and those fears were not unfounded. In April, slaves rose up in Charleston, South Carolina. The next month, so did slaves in Kentucky's Owen and Gallatin counties. At the same time, Georgia's Decatur County, Mississippi's Jefferson County, Virginia's Charles City County, and Monroe, Arkansas, saw enslaved people developing plans for similar uprisings. Not all the conspirators were black. Five local whites were implicated in the Jefferson County conspiracy. In Columbia, South Carolina, a white stonecutter helped slaves plan their uprising. Two white men were found assisting escaped slaves along Louisiana's Comite River.[162]

At the height of the secession crisis a newspaper editor in Augusta, Georgia, wrote an ominous warning to his fellow southerners: "The greatest danger to the new Confederacy arises not from without, not from the North, but from our own people." Virginia's *Richmond Examiner* agreed, admitting that the South was "more rife with treason to her own independence and honour than any community that ever engaged before in a struggle with an adversary."[163] It was clear even in its early days that the disunited Confederacy was in for a three-front war: one against the North, another against white dissenters, and yet another against black resisters. If it could not win the second or third, it could hardly expect to win the first.

2

"The Brunt Is Thrown upon the Working Classes"

The war is based on the principle and *fact* of the inequality of mankind—for policy we say races, in reality, as all history shows it as the *truth* is *classes*.[1]

—JAMES HENRY HAMMOND, SOUTH CAROLINA PLANTER

These abolitionists have strange notions of justice and right. They seem to think that only poor men are fit food for gunpowder.[2]

— *QUINCY HERALD,* ILLINOIS NEWSPAPER

"Such Is Patriotism—the Love of Dirt"

As the excitement of summer faded into fall, home front opposition continued to undermine the Confederate war effort. Unionists in Walker County, Alabama, organized armed anti-Confederate companies and vowed to fight for Lincoln. Anti-Confederates were doing the same in Fayette, Randolph, Winston, and Limestone counties. One citizen in Georgia's Cass (later Bartow) County wrote directly to Lincoln saying that he and other local Union men were "ready to sholder our guns" against secession. Joseph Cooper, a Tennessee farmer and

Mexican War veteran, trained and drilled five hundred Union men in the Campbell County region. In Tennessee's Carter and Johnson counties, anti-Confederates killed two secessionists and ran others out of the area. When authorities jailed the Reverend William Brownlow of Knoxville on charges of treason, he was offered release if he would swear allegiance to the Confederacy. Said Brownlow: "I would lie here until I died with old age before I would take such an oath."[3]

Most southerners were not quite that stubborn, but many continued to question service in the cause of a rich man's war. The price of that service for many was simply too high. Interdependent as most women and children were on their menfolk, how would they survive without them? Who would work small farmers' land with husbands and sons at the front? Planters had few worries there. Aside from the fact that few were enlisting, their plantations were worked by slaves. As for taxes, they were going up on everything except slaves. As the fall 1861 state elections approached, issues such as the war, enlistment, taxes, and even slavery were uppermost in the minds of plain folk. In September, Georgia voters who signed themselves "Many Anxious to Hear" addressed an open letter to their legislative candidates through state newspapers.

> Please give your views concerning our present condition—about the war, and the cause of the war . . . and our present condition of taxation for the support of the war. Is it right that the poor man should be taxed for the support of the war, when the war was brought about on the slave question, and the slave at home accumulating for the benefit of his master, and the poor man's farm left uncultivated, and a chance for his wife to be a widow, and his children orphans? Now, in justice, would it not be right to levy a direct tax on the species of property that brought about the war, to support it?

A week later, an editor apologized for printing the letter, saying that this kind of talk might cause class division.[4] In fact, the letter simply expressed an underlying class resentment that had long been there and was growing every day.

That those few planters who had joined the army as officers could resign at will simply added to class resentment. Just a week after the firing on Fort Sumter, one observer noticed that "there has been a withdrawing from the volunteer companies of men who have done their best to destroy this Union." An Arkansas man noted in his diary, "Most of those who were so willing to shed the last drop of blood in the contest for a separate Government, are entirely unwilling to shed the first." In October 1861, one soldier wrote home from the Virginia front that "a great many of our commissioned officers are resigning and going home."[5]

For enlisted men, most of them nonslaveholders, resignation was forbidden. Such class distinctions were not lost on the men in the ranks, and the uneven treatment took its toll on morale. "The temper of the army is not good," wrote one Rebel soldier from Virginia during the winter of 1861–62. "The troops widely feel the unjust oppression and partial hand that is laid upon them, and in my opinion the spirit of the army is dying." Corporal James Atkins of the 12th Georgia Regiment, also stationed in Virginia, clearly reflected the army's declining morale. He wrote in December 1861 that "reflection has modified my expressed view of patriotism." Atkins had come to feel that it was "a strange virtue that clings to mere soil and in its defense will take the life of the dearest relatives; yet such is patriotism—*the love of dirt.*" A few months after penning those lines Atkins deserted.[6]

"Rich Man's War, Poor Man's Fight"

Thousands of men like Atkins abandoned the army that fall and winter, but few were coming forward to take their places. In October came word from Greene County, Georgia, to the governor's office that "our people don't seem to be inclined to offer their services." That same month an officer in Columbus reported that it was almost impossible to find volunteers. In February 1862, an Augusta man wrote that he had been trying for two weeks to raise a company in what he called "this 'Yankee City,' but I regret to say every effort has failed." That failure could not be blamed on a lack of potential recruits. The *Augusta Chronicle and Sentinel* noted a week earlier that "one who walks Broad street and sees the number of young men, would come to the conclusion that no war . . . was now waging." From rural Brooks County in south Georgia, C.S. Gaulden reported that "several large families of young men in this county have not sent out soldiers." Another concerned southerner wondered "how are the men to be got? . . . I have within a few days heard men say they would not go to the war; they had nothing to fight for and they would not go."[7]

Whether they had anything to fight for was beside the point as far as the government was concerned. Willing or not, the army had to have more men. In April 1862 the Confederate Congress passed its first Conscription Act, giving the president authority to force young men into the military with or without their consent. Under the terms of this act, commonly known as the draft, white males between the ages of eighteen and thirty-five became subject to involuntary military service. As an inducement to enlist before the draft went into effect, the government offered a cash bonus to those who volunteered and allowed them to serve with units of their choice. Fearing they would be drafted in any case, thousands of reluctant men volunteered in March and early April. The Confederate War Department estimated that three-fourths of those who volunteered did so to avoid being drafted.[8]

One late-coming volunteer was John Joseph Kirkland, the author's great-great-grandfather. A slaveless yeoman farmer in Early County, Georgia, Kirkland had a wife and five children with another on the way when he enlisted as first corporal with the Early Volunteers in March 1862. He was thirty-three, only two years short of exemption. His younger brother Jacob joined the Early Volunteers too. A few weeks later Jacob died in Virginia. John Joseph had the heartbreaking duty of escorting the body home to their mother. A year after that, having fought through the Peninsula Campaign, Second Manassas, Sharpsburg, and Fredericksburg, he was nearly killed himself when his right leg was shattered at the Battle of Chancellorsville. The leg was amputated just below the knee.[9]

To plain folk, the most offensive provisions of conscription were those allowing the wealthy to avoid service. Under the act, monied men could simply pay an expensive commutation fee to the government in lieu of service. Or they could hire a substitute, which was also very expensive. Five hundred dollars was the going rate soon after the draft began. By late 1863 it ranged into the thousands—as high as $10,000 in some parts of the South. An advertisement for a substitute in one newspaper offered to pay "in cash, land, or negro property." Another offered a 230-acre farm. At least fifty thousand southern gentlemen politely sidestepped military service by hiring substitutes. So few men of means served that soldiers in Richmond jokingly said it was easier for a camel to go through the eye of a needle than for a rich man to enter Camp Lee.[10]

Wealthy and well-connected men could avoid service in any number of ways, legal or otherwise. Some found bribing the local conscript officer to be cheaper than hiring a substitute. Colonel Carey Styles of southeastern Georgia sold exemptions for a thousand dollars to anyone who could afford to pay. Army surgeons got in on the action as well by selling medical exemptions. Other officers offered fraudulent substitute papers for sale. The Bureau of Conscription's superintendent cited abundant evidence of actions "grossly criminal and mischievous, in the conduct of the officers of the army respecting substitutes."[11]

Elites could also use their influence with local judges like Richard Henry Clark of southwest Georgia, who granted exemptions to well-connected men on a regular basis. Such exemptions did not always come cheap. In Crawfordville, Georgia, several men paid one court official a $1,500 bribe in exchange for exemptions. Those with influence in government could also have themselves appointed to exempted positions. Sometimes it took more than influence. Appointments to such positions as postmaster, clerk, bailiff, or coroner could cost $500 or more. In North Carolina alone, Governor Zebulon Vance declared nearly fifteen thousand state employees, most with "above average connections," exempt from the draft. In Georgia, Governor Joe Brown did the same, extending protection to state militia officers as well. Those posts, noted one state paper, were "sought and obtained by young gentlemen." General Howell Cobb wrote to Brown complaining of able-bodied young men holding state militia commissions "to the exclusion of old men competent to fill the places. . . . This class I fear is large." "It is a notorious fact," wrote an anonymous southerner to the War Department, "if a man has influential friends—or a little money to spare he will never be enrolled."[12]

Then there was the infamous twenty-slave law, which virtually excused planters outright from the draft. Though few in high office seemed to realize it at the time, this single law defined the entire nature of the war for southerners outside the planter class. "It gave us the blues," wrote Tennessee private Sam Watkins. "We wanted twenty negroes. Negro property suddenly became very valuable, and there was raised the howl of 'rich man's war, poor man's fight.'" Watkins later recalled that "from this time on till the end of the war, a soldier was simply a machine. We cursed the war . . . we cursed the Southern Confederacy. All our pride and valor was gone." A soldier from North

Shielded from the draft in various ways, planters who wished to avoid military service had little trouble doing so. "Their negroes must make cotton," complained one Confederate soldier, and "the poor men must be taken from their families and put in the Army to protect their negroes. Was ever a greater wrong, or a more damning sin, perpetrated by men or devils?" (*Harper's Weekly*)

Carolina wrote to Governor Vance complaining of the law's "distinction between the rich man (who had something to fight for) and the poor man who fights for that he never will have. The exemption of the owners of 20 negroes & the allowing of substitutes clearly proves it."[13]

Reaction to the draft in general, and the twenty-slave exemption in particular, was just as vicious on the home front. A Lafayette, Alabama, man warned his senator that the twenty-slave law was "considered class legislation & has given more dissatisfaction than any thing else Congress has done." A.W. Millican of Dirt Town, Georgia, wrote a biting letter to Governor Joe Brown demanding that the governor more firmly oppose "the centralized military despotism at Richmond" and asking, "Why didn't you hang the first minion of Richmond that called himself a Conscription officer for treason against the Government [of] Georgia?" Millican insisted that if Brown were not going to defend his people from Confederate tyranny, he should tell them how they might do it themselves. "You will very much oblige many men in Georgia if you will assist them in finding out whether they are *citizens* or *slaves*." Someone in the governor's office scribbled on the back of the letter "Impertinent and disrespectful. No answer."[14]

Many draft officials themselves were hardly enthusiastic about having to force men into service. Aside from finding the cruel nature of their work distasteful, some suspected that dragging unwilling men from their dependent families ultimately did the Confederate cause more harm than good. A North Carolina lieutenant, assigned to enforce the draft, wrote of the forays he made:

> While performing my duty as enrolling officer I witnessed scenes & compelled compliance with orders which God grant I may never do again. To ride up to a man's door, whose hospitable kindess makes you feel welcome & tell him, in the presence of his faithful & loving wife & sunny-faced children, that he must be ready in 10 minutes to go with you, and see the very looks of sadness and dispair seize the wife & a cloud of apprehension cover the smiling faces of his children—their imploring looks and glances—the tears of sorrow—the Solemn silence—the affectionate clasping of hands—the fervent kisses—the sad & bitter Goodbye—the longing glance at the place most dear to him on earth, as he slowly moves out of sight—this is indeed a sad & unplesant task. When we left doors on the road crowded with the faces of frightened & crying & helpless women with the question, "For God's sake are you going to leave us at the mercy of the Yankees" made me ask often what have we gained by this trip?[15]

"They've got me in this war at last," complained a poor Georgia farmer to a neighbor after he was drafted. "I didn't want to have any thing to do with it any how. *I* didn't vote for Secession—but them are the ones who have to go & fight now—and those who were so fast for war stay out." And so it was all across the South. "The brunt is thrown upon the working classes while the rich live at home in ease and pleasure," wrote one exasperated woman. That was evident on the draft rolls. Among conscripts in one regiment from eastern North Carolina, average personal property was under $100 and average real estate held was almost nothing.[16]

Pressured to rush men into service, draft officers took not only the poor but the sick, lame, and nearly blind as well. One distraught woman wrote that her conscripted husband could not see clearly enough to tell a black man from a white. Another man was hauled off despite a hacking cough and heart palpitations. One young conscript, described as "a helpless cripple . . . afflicted with epilepsy," was abandoned on the streets of Savannah after it became obvious to draft officers that he was incapable of military service. His father was fortunate enough to find the boy.[17]

Army nurse Kate Cumming wrote in her journal of two Alabama women wandering through the camps looking for their young sons, one of whom suffered with a facial cancer that had already eaten an eye out of its socket. "How can our people be guilty of such outrages?" Cumming wondered. "There is no punishment too severe for those thus guilty. But," she continued, "I have known conscript officers to take men from their homes whom the surgeons had discharged many times, and sent them to camp. We have had them die in our hospital before reaching the army."[18]

"It is strange to us," wrote the editor of southwest Georgia's *Early County News*, "that the Government allows its officers to conscript poor men who have the appearance of *dead men*, while they turn loose rich ones who are *young, hale and hearty*." That seemed strange to many others too. In a letter to the *Savannah Republican*, a resident of Valdosta, Georgia, wrote that "several healthy looking individuals have come home in Lowndes and Brooks counties, discharged as diseased" and that "most if not all of them *happened* to be men of means and influence, which looked strange." J.M. Radford of Virginia wrote to the War Department about the impact of such practices: "It is impossible to make *poor* people comprehend the policy of putting ablebodied, healthy, Mr. A. in such light service as collecting tithes and money *at home*, when the well known feeble & delicate Mr. B.—who is a poor man with a large family of children depending on him for bread—is sent to the front. . . . I beseech you to be warned of the coming storm—the people will not *always* submit to this *unequal, unjust* and partial distribution of favor and wholesale conscription of the *poor* while the able-bodied & healthy men of property are all occupying *soft places*." Such angry letters also went to elected officials. So many poured into the office of Senator James Phelan of Mississippi that he wrote to Jefferson Davis: "Never did a law meet with more universal odium than the exemption of slave owners. . . . Its influence upon the poor is most calamitous. . . . It has aroused a spirit of rebellion . . . and bodies of men have banded together to resist."[19]

It hardly helped attitudes among common folk that wealthy men flaunted privileges in the faces of their less fortunate neighbors. One young member of southwest Georgia's gentry ran an ad in a local newspaper reading "WIFE WANTED—by a young man of good habits, plenty of money, good looking and legally exempt from Confederate Service."[20]

"A Never Ending Stream of Cotton"

Well-connected southerners held jealously to their exemption privileges. By their reasoning, it protected those to whom the Confederacy looked for economic and political leadership. Planters in particular stressed their special role as food producers. The soldiers would need vast stores of food and so would their families back home. With their huge reserves of slave labor, who better to supply that food than the planters? Many agreed to bonding contracts that obligated them to contribute food or sell it below market rates to soldiers' families and the army. As soldiers left for the front, they were assured that they need have no worries. They and their families would be well fed.[21]

But common folk quickly learned that planter patriotism was more apparent than real. Though as a proportion of total agricultural output the South's food production did increase during the war, it never came close to meeting demand because planters devoted far too much acreage to cotton and tobacco. Though the Confederacy imposed a ban on cotton exports in an effort to force recognition from Britain and France, planters and their agents simply smuggled it out through, or with cooperation from, the Federal blockade fleet or stockpiled it for future sale. There was big money in cotton, as the planters well knew—much more than in food products. In April 1861, southern newspapers announced that raw cotton was going for "the enormous price of 12½ cents per pound. It has not been so high for years." Prices continued to rise as the war went on, reaching over a dollar a pound by 1864.[22]

"Plant corn! Plant corn!" demanded Georgia's *Macon Telegraph* editor. "We must have large supplies, or poverty and suffering will come upon us like a strong man armed." The *Richmond Examiner* agreed: "If all citizens were intelligent and patriotic, not another leaf of tobacco or pod of cotton would be seen in the fields of the South until peace is declared." In letters to southern papers, concerned citizens repeatedly called on planters to plow up their cotton and replace it with corn. "Yes, plow it up," agreed one editor. "Look out for corn first, last and all the time." Another warned planters who continued to grow cotton and tobacco: "Look out, Gentlemen, the public eye is upon you, as will the public scorn unless you desist."[23]

Such warnings fell on deaf ears. During a land-buying trip to Alabama in February 1863, Mississippi planter James Alcorn wrote back home instructing his wife to "put in as much cotton as possible. You need not listen to what others say, plant corn to do you and the balance in cotton." Alcorn was sure that when the war was over, no matter which side won, cotton would be "worth a dollar a pound in good money." By "good money," Alcorn meant Yankee greenbacks.[24]

Among the most reluctant to hold back on cotton production was General Robert Toombs of Georgia. Some reports from the summer of 1862 had Toombs planting between 800 and 900 acres in cotton. Citizens' committees of public safety near the Toombs plantation issued resolutions condemning Toombs and half a dozen local planters for contributing to the South's food shortage. But condemnation could not compete with profits, and the resolutions had little impact. "My property," responded Toombs, "as long as I live, shall never be subject to the orders of those cowardly miscreants, the Committees of Public Safety. . . . You cannot intimidate me."

Ironically, just a year earlier General Winfield Scott, a southerner who had remained loyal to the Union, wrote Toombs asking him "to quit his rebel nonsense." Scott predicted that if the South continued on its imprudent course, it would eventually be starved to death. In reply, Toombs sent an ear of corn by express to his old friend. Said one southern editor, "We consider this one of Bob's best letters." But a year later, unable to shake his addiction to cotton, Toombs was among the thousands of planters helping Scott's prediction come true.[25]

By fall 1862, southern planters were growing so much cotton that the warehouses could not hold it all. In September, the firm of Dillard, Powell, and Company in Columbus, Georgia, ran this announcement in a local paper: "TO PLANTERS: Our Warehouse being full, Planters will please stop consignments of Cotton to our care until further notice." A worried Georgia citizen wrote to the governor begging him to force planters to grow more food or "they will whip us sooner that all Lincolndom combined could do it." One disgusted editor wrote that if southerners refused to devote more land to food production, then they were "not only a blockaded but a block-headed people."[26]

Government response to cotton and tobacco overproduction was cursory and ineffective, often by design. After all, many legislators were themselves planters who were making huge profits from cotton and tobacco. Using the "state rights" dodge, Congress did no more than approve a nonbinding resolution asking planters to grow more food. For appearance's sake, some states did pass acts limiting production of nonfood items. Alabama placed a 10 percent tax on excess cotton. Georgia limited it to three acres for every slave owned or laborer employed. Other states made the limit four acres. Virginia set tobacco production at no more than 2,500 plants per hand. Such acts were barely enforced and almost completely ignored.[27]

"Lynchburg has gone mad," wrote one exasperated Virginian, "stark mad . . . all tobacco—tobacco—from morning till night from night till morning. It's still rising." Out in Texas, one teamster recalled that throughout the war there was "a never ending stream of cotton pouring into Brownsville." Along the Mississippi River, cotton flowed as fast as the river could carry it and moved easily between Union and Confederate lines.[28]

In the southeast, river systems like the Chattahoochee-Flint-Apalachicola, the Ocmulgee-Oconee-Alatamaha, and the Savannah all served as avenues of cotton smuggling. In March of 1862, two men from Fort Gaines, Georgia, a port town on the Chattahoochee, told Governor Joe Brown that cotton smuggling was rife along the river. Steamboats typically made their way upriver, loading cotton as they went, with Columbus their supposed destination. But much of the cotton somehow found its way down to Apalachicola on the Gulf Coast where it was transferred to vessels that took "pleasure excursions" out to see the Union blockading fleet. The vessels always returned with empty cargo holds. As late as March 1865, the steamboat *Comet* was caught on Georgia's Ocmulgee River with "a cargo of cotton designed for traffic with the enemy." General Howell Cobb, commanding reserve forces in Georgia, was implicated in the affair.[29]

Cotton moved along rail lines too, sometimes choking off transport of vital food supplies. In Albany, Georgia, there were one hundred thousand bushels of corn rotting in city warehouses while outbound trains loaded with cotton clogged the rails. "Is the Southwestern Railroad leaning to *favorites*, or speculating in the article themselves?" asked the *Albany Patriot*. Even wounded soldiers took a back seat to cotton. In November 1864, with Sherman's army bearing

Despite the Confederacy's cotton embargo, southern cotton merchants regularly smuggled their product out to eager northern buyers. The *Shamrock*, built in Columbus, Georgia, during the war, hauled cotton downriver to the Gulf port of Apalachicola. There it was transferred to oceangoing vessels for transport to Europe and the North. With cotton prices at an all-time high, some planters bragged openly that the longer the war went on, the more money they made. (Florida State Archives)

down, officers telegraphed Governor Brown from Macon about a state-owned train loaded with cotton: "We need the train to remove our sick from hospitals. I request your authority to use this train for the sick. . . . Please answer at once."[30]

Much of the Deep South's cotton traveled along rail lines into Tennessee and from there to points north. On March 12, 1862, a report was sent to Georgia's governor about two suspicious Tennessee men buying cotton in Macon. "It is believed they intend to let the Federals have it," read the communication. Two weeks later an Atlanta newspaper published a letter warning that "uncompromising adherents to the Northern Government have been, for weeks, shipping cotton to East Tennessee. . . . Don't sell them your cotton. They are your enemies." It was not only Tennesseans who were engaged in the business. The paper's Chattanooga correspondent reported that "a few traitorous Georgians have a finger in the pie." Based on the amount of cotton smuggled out during the war, the "traitors" numbered far more than a few.[31]

In direct violation of state law and Confederate policy, "planters insisted," as one historian put it, "on their right to grow unlimited amounts of cotton; to retain it for sale whenever they chose; and to sell it whenever, and to whomever, they chose." And it did not matter who the buyers were. Of the one and a half million bales that left the

South during the war, two-thirds went to the North. Blockade runners carried much of it to Nassau in the Bahamas, where they sold it to
buyers from New York, Liverpool, and other import centers. But a
good portion made its way north by more direct routes, with government officials on both sides, civil and military, accepting bribes along
the way. Some producers reaped such profits from the cotton trade
that they were not eager to see the conflict end. In a private letter, one
planter wrote that he feared a "terrific fall" in cotton prices if the war
ended. Others bragged openly that the longer the war went on, the
more money they made.[32]

The result was predictable. And it was obvious for anyone who
cared to look. Concerned about the families of his men, Colonel J.L.
Sheffield of the 48th Alabama wrote to the governor:

> I have, sir, made it my business to go through the country to ascertain
> the condition of families of *poor men* who are in the service. I find *hun-
> dreds* of them entirely destitute of everything upon which to live, not
> even *Bread*. Nor is it to be had in the Country. . . . Something should
> be done else they are bound to suffer. All they ask for is *Bread*.[33]

"Hellish Greed for Gold"

Planters' reluctance to devote themselves more to food production
contributed not only to hunger, but also to an inflationary spiral that
began to spin out of control soon after the war started. During the
war's first year, the South suffered a 300 percent inflation rate. It
would only get worse as the war continued. Butter went from twelve
cents a pound in 1861 to seventy-five cents two years later. By the end
of the war it was five dollars or more. Corn that was two dollars a
bushel in 1863 sold for fourteen by February 1865. Bacon went from
twelve cents to fifty cents a pound in the war's first year. By the end of
the war a pound of bacon was four dollars. Flour that sold for nine
dollars a barrel before the war was going for four hundred by war's
end. Coffee went to thirty dollars a pound shortly after the war began
and from there to sixty and seventy dollars.[34]

Though the Union naval blockade contributed to rising prices,
even more damaging to the economy was profiteering and speculation
by planters and merchants. In his study of Columbus, Georgia, during

the war, historian Diffee Standard concluded that the blockade was more an excuse than a reason for most price increases. So did Harriet Amos in her study of wartime Mobile, noting "the relative ease with which ships passed the Federal fleet." Contemporary accounts support those conclusions. One southern editor boldly entitled a news commentary "The Blockade No Excuse." For months he had heard merchants blaming the blockade for high prices. But he and many others observed that there were "dry goods alone within our southern limits sufficient to supply the wants of the people of the Confederate States for the next ten years to come. The blockade therefore is no excuse." In a private letter to a friend, one planter admitted as much. For years, southerners had been "abusing the Yankees for extortion and speculation, but [we are] quite as bad ourselves."[35]

The inflation that hit so many so hard sprang largely from inducements of the market. Merchants kept a tight grip on food and clothing resources, selling only to those who could pay top dollar or holding out for even higher prices. Planters continued to focus far too much on increasingly profitable cotton and tobacco, leaving the South short of the food production it needed. What edibles they did produce went not to support soldiers' families as promised, but to speculators who scoured the countryside buying up the scarce foodstuffs. Planters and merchants both took the same self-interested path that had served them so well before the war, following the dollar wherever it led. But in so doing, they left the interests of the soldiers, their families, and ultimately the Confederacy itself far behind.

As early as November 1861, one Georgian complained in a letter to Vice President Alexander Stephens that he and other "common farmers" were finding it difficult "to keep our heads above the flood of destruction" brought on by "the money thieves, those Speculators." Dependent as the Confederacy was on the support of plain folk, if speculation forced them down, the government would go down with them. That danger was clear to James Bethune of Columbus, Georgia. In a letter to the *Columbus Daily Sun*, Bethune warned that the avarice of southern elites was the Yankees' most powerful ally. He urged the well-off to contrast their own inconveniences with the hardships of poor soldiers and their families who were suffering and dying. "And now you complain of making sacrifices if you furnish bread for him at less than you might get for it from somebody else." E.H. Grouby, editor of Georgia's *Early County News*, saw the danger as well. He publicly denounced speculators as "home Yankees" who were "by far greater enemies to the South and do more to injure her cause than ten times their number of Yankees in the field."[36]

In a vein of religious bigotry and scapegoating, some editors openly associated speculation with southern Jews. Grouby's own *Early County News* carried on its masthead: DEATH ON SPECULATORS, JEWS, RASCALLY GOVERNMENT OFFICIALS. Other editors, though just as bigoted, were more broad with their criticism. The *Mobile News* observed that politicians, planters, and merchants generally had "out-Jewed Jews, out-traded the sharp Yankee trader, and descended from that exalted position known on earth—Southern gentlemen—to become nothing better than common hucksters." The *Richmond Examiner* agreed: "Southern merchants have outdone Yankees and Jews. . . . The whole South stinks with the lust of extortion."[37]

Nowhere was that more obvious than in Atlanta. As the Confederacy's rail hub it became the South's commercial capital. Inevitably, it was soon swarming with a class of speculating industrialists and merchants whose "ruling passion," wrote one city editor, "is a lust for gain; their sordid souls care naught for the miseries of their fellow mortals, and [they] have no interest in the good of the country, if its ruin would advance their own personal aggrandizement." It seemed to this editor the height of hypocrisy for men who had, for the most part, supported secession to now benefit handsomely from the war they had brought on. And then to buy exemptions for themselves while preying on soldiers' families, keeping their wages low and cost of living high, was more than the editor could stomach. "Is it right that the war . . . with its carnage and woe, should work an absolute benefit to one class, while it ruins the rest? Shall those who are permitted to . . . be exempt from service on account of these employments out of which they are making such fortunes, amassing such wealth and splendor, in full view of want, poverty and destitution . . . not be required to contribute a portion of these gains for the benefit of the sufferers by the war?"[38]

A writer signing as "One of the People" in the *Lynchburg Virginian* demanded court-ordered price fixing to rein in speculators. He warned that if the courts did not take action, "the people would take the subject of redress into their own hands." There were similar warnings in Burke County, North Carolina, where "capitalists" were "defrauding the helpless." One Texas man went a step further with a bold call: "Men of Austin, Arise!!!" He urged that they "mark forever with a brand of infamy" those extortioners "who no longer crawl like the slimy reptiles that they are, but boldly stalk through your streets, grinding at every step with their iron heels, deeper and deeper down, the poor man, the widow and the orphan." Some did take direct action. Nelson Tift, the founder of Albany, Georgia, was such a notorious speculator that a local court imposed pricing restrictions on him. Tift simply ignored the order. His neighbors sued him, then threatened him, and finally set fire to his Flint River bridge house.[39]

Speculation by southern planters and merchants marked the starting point of what became a vicious encircling trap for the common people. Planters fed a lucrative market for cotton, devoting not nearly enough acreage to food production. Scarcity forced food prices up and speculating merchants drove them even higher. Rampant inflation inevitably followed, making planters and merchants even less willing to exchange what food they had for the Confederacy's increasingly worthless currency. Lydia Brassfield of North Carolina's Orange County, a soldier's wife left with three children to care for, walked for five days in the winter of 1863 to buy corn only to have merchants tell her that they would not sell for Confederate notes. In Georgia's Early County, a soldier's wife wrote to the local paper complaining of planters hoarding food and refusing to take paper currency. They would, however, take what little the poor had, if they had anything worth trading. "This is the only way many Soldiers' families in the county can get anything to eat," wrote this distraught woman. "Love nor Confederate money won't do it."[40]

Planters and merchants would also take gold or silver coin, which common folk rarely held. From Paulding County, Georgia, came a letter from J.B. Adair to the governor telling of local planters hoarding "considerable quantities" of corn. He singled out one for special censure: "Bennett Cooper of this County has about fifteen hundred bushels, more than sufficient to answer his purposes and refuses to sell a grain for anything except gold or silver." A Virginia soldier wrote that the planters' "hellish greed for gold" was throwing common folk into ruin.[41]

The editor of Georgia's *Athens Southern Watchman* felt the same way: "Some hard cases have come to our knowledge recently of men who were very active in bringing on the war, and who now vehemently urge its prosecution, and yet refuse to receive Confederate money in payment of notes given by poor men." An Alabama grand jury pointed

Kate Cumming, a nurse from Mobile, Alabama, criticized speculators for "making *piles* of money out of the misfortunes of their country." She expressed the feeling of many, North and South, when she wrote that speculators were surely destined to burn in hell. "If they only suffer one half the pangs of which they have been the cause, their case will be sad indeed." (Cumming, *Gleanings from Southland*)

out that "the man who refused to take this money is doing more damage to our cause, more injury to our soldiers and their families than if he were in the ranks of the enemy." And that was where some urged they be sent. One Georgia editor wrote that such men "should be drummed out of every respectable community, and sent heels over head to Yankeedoodledum, where they properly belong."[42]

Perhaps more infuriating was that planters and speculators would take Federal greenbacks, which smugglers who traded with the Yankees brought in across the lines. Such trade was so common in Vicksburg, Mississippi, that Confederate general Earl Van Dorn declared martial law and threatened those demanding Yankee money with fines and imprisonment. But such was the influence of Mississippi elites that they successfully pressured the Davis administration to revoke Van Dorn's order.[43] In so doing, Davis undermined his own treasury. If suppliers would not take paper currency from common folk, neither would they take it from the government.

"If He Were a Poor Man He Would Be Hanged"

In 1863 the Confederacy determined that what it could not buy, it would take by force. That summer Congress passed a series of taxes, the most far-reaching of which was a 10 percent levy on such agricultural products as livestock, wheat, corn, oats, hay, fodder, potatoes, peas, beans, and peanuts. Even this tax-in-kind did not provide enough food to meet the army's needs. So officers began to "impress" produce, and anything else they wanted, far beyond the 10 percent level. Though no member of any class held impressment in high regard, its weight fell heaviest on the plain folk. Only when their farms were stripped bare did impressment officers turn to the plantations. Even then, planters paid a proportionally lighter tax or used political connections to avoid impressment entirely. When Robert Toombs used his influence to dodge impressment, one newspaper editor lashed out: "We believe Toombs, because he is rich, does pretty much what he wants . . . if he were a poor man he would be hanged." The editor concluded that "a *poor* man in this world has no more showing than a blind dog in a meat house with a dozen starving Yankees after him."[44]

Some impressment agents could be ruthless. One seventy-year-old Georgia man who had sent five sons to Confederate service, two of them already dead, was threatened with a beating if he did not hand over his horse. Another was killed when he refused to give up his cattle. When an impressment officer took two cows from a South Carolina farmer, the man thundered that "the sooner this damned Government fell to pieces the better it would be for us." Governor John Milton of Florida wrote to the War Department complaining of impressment agents' "lawless and wicked conduct." So did Governor Joe Brown of Georgia, who warned that impressment's "baneful operations" were producing an "evil spirit, bordering already in many cases on open disloyalty." And he was right. The *Atlanta Southern*

Confederacy wrote of impressment officers, "We advise the people to resist them." So did the editor of Georgia's *Early County News*. Otherwise "our military officers will soon think they own the whole country." Judge James Bush, the author's great-great-great-grandfather, headed an assembly of Early County citizens who drafted a petition warning that impressment officers were so numerous that they threatened to "alienate the affections of the people from the government."[45] As the war went on, enforcing impressment laws became more and more dangerous, with agents beaten up, shot at, and sometimes killed.

What angered impressment's victims most, often to the point of violence, were the corrupt activities in which impressment agents frequently engaged. May Lane of Wilkes County, Georgia, complained that William Sneed, the local impressment agent, was feeding confiscated produce to his slaves. Other agents, civil and military, sold impressed produce on the open market and kept the money for themselves. Illicit trade in clothing occurred as well. Uniforms made by women in Augusta, Georgia, for donation to soldiers were "charged against the soldiers at full prices." An Augusta man wrote Governor Brown that army quartermaster officers in the city were "involved and complicated" with speculators. J.B. Jones, a clerk in the Confederacy's capital at Richmond, accused quartermaster officers there of the same. They were getting rich by passing army rations to speculators and bringing the Confederacy to ruin in the process.[46]

As early as the fall of 1861, a Georgia farmer wrote to the *Athens Southern Watchman*: "I have never entertained the shadow of a doubt as to our success—our whipping out all the Yankees that can be produced—but God knows how we shall escape the *corruptions* of our own Government, and the *leeches and sharks* of our own people." In reflecting on the extent of speculation and corruption, an Atlanta newspaper commented in the summer of 1862: "If we are defeated, it will be by the people at home."[47]

Scandal rocked the War Department that year when quartermaster officers were caught selling army rations to speculators. Congress responded by making it illegal for the public to buy military supplies from enlisted men but said nothing of officers. Small wonder that the act did little to stop corruption. It served only to emphasize the

South's pervasive class divisions, and Georgia's *Early County News* denounced the legislation for its elitist overtones.

> Why is it not also against the law to buy any of these articles from Quarter Masters, Commissaries, &c., when it is a well known fact that many of these swoll head gentry steal a great deal of this kind of Government property which they have in their possession, to be distributed among the needy Soldiers, sell them, and pocket the money? There is more rascality, according to the number, among officers than privates. Why are not officers bound up as tight as privates? There is altogether too much *favoritism* shown to little jackass officers by Congress.[48]

Corruption among quartermasters and commissary officers was even more obvious to soldiers in the field. An officer of the 4th Alabama wrote anonymously to one of his senators suggesting that "*every one of them* be beheaded at the expiration of their first 12 months in office. *Any man* who remains in either position longer will *steal.*" Another exasperated southerner thought it would take more than that to stop the corruption. He added his voice to a swelling chorus when he urged of his governor: "Do for God's sake put an end to this unrighteous war. We shall be eaten up by Confederate Office holders and Speculators."[49]

If common folk were being "eaten up" by officeholders, speculators, and other well-to-do southerners, then elites ate well indeed despite the food shortage. A Virginia belle recalled feeling "intensely patriotic and self-sacrificing" when she gave up ice cream and cake. She called it "putting our tables on a war footing." Many would not do even that. In Eufaula, Alabama, a guest of one upper-crust family described "a very nice table indeed, meats of various kinds, cakes, fruits, custards, floats and plenty of pure coffee." Coffee was one of the rarest commodities in the wartime South, but the rich could get it any time. Blockade runners had long since reduced imports of basic necessities and even war material, preferring to smuggle in goods they knew would bring top dollar from rich southerners in gold, silver, or Yankee greenbacks. In the spring of 1863 Florida governor John Milton made that point when he wrote to Jefferson Davis of the "villainous traffic" by smugglers and speculators who brought in rum and gin "but no arms or munitions of war." They were in it for the money, not the Confederacy.[50]

"Gaunt Starvation"

While southern elites sacrificed ice cream and cake, Confederate soldiers were going hungry. In September 1862, during the Army of Northern Virginia's campaign into Maryland, a Sharpsburg woman recalled that Lee's soldiers "were half famished. . . . They nearly worried us to death asking for something to eat." Another woman felt that words were inadequate to express the soldiers' sad condition: "When I say that they were hungry, I convey no impression of the gaunt starvation that looked from their cavernous eyes."[51]

Starvation was also stalking their families back home. A North Carolina soldier wrote to Governor Vance from Fayetteville in February 1863:

> Now Govr. Do tell me how we poor soldiers who are fighting for the "rich mans Negro" can support our families at $11 per month? How can the poor live? I dread to see summer as I am fearful there will be much suffering and probably many deaths from starvation. They are suffering now. A poor little factory girl begged for a piece of bread the other day & said she had not had anything to eat since the day before when she eat a small piece of Bread for her Breakfast.[52]

In the spring of 1864 South Carolina's governor Milledge Bonham asked the War Department to suspend conscription in one nonslaveholding region of his state for fear that it would cause "great suffering next year, and possible starvation." That same year, a Confederate official wrote to Jefferson Davis that in Alabama "deaths from starvation have absolutely occurred." A Lynchburg, Virginia, newspaper stated the obvious: "The Masses cannot starve and yet maintain the spirit that is necessary to uphold this great cause, and fight through this bloody war."[53]

As hunger grew worse, there were more and more calls in southern newspapers for the rich to "Give to the Poor!" as many a headline read. In February 1862, Georgia's *Milledgeville Confederate Union* called on wealthy men of Baldwin County to "COME UP WITH YOUR MONEY!" Soldiers' families were suffering, and the editor reminded planters that they were obliged to help: "It is for you and your property that tens of thousands of poor men are now fighting. . . . What are the rich men of Baldwin doing? Nothing. Wake up from your slumber." A year later, the situation had not changed. As the *Union* editor wrote: "There are many men, in every county in the state, who have fallen short of their duty. . . . When called on to make subscriptions to aid a poor disabled soldier, or help a soldier's suffering family, they have turned the back of their hands." The same was true across the South. From Virginia's Spotsylvania County came a letter from a poor woman to Jefferson Davis telling of widespread starvation and complaining that "it is folly for a poor mother to call on the rich people about here[.] [T]here hearts are of steel[.] [T]hey would sooner th[r]ow what they have to spare to their dogs than give it to a starving child." In May 1863 one southern editor openly and boldly expressed doubt that the southern gentry would ever change its self-serving ways: "To expect such miserable abortions of humanity, who have been living a lie for more than two years, to give in their property at anything like its value in Confederate money is to expect heat from ice or light from darkness."[54]

Officials at the state and local levels tried to do what the wealthy would not, but relief efforts were frequently half-hearted and nearly always ineffective. All too often, funds slated for poor relief wound up in the pockets of corrupt officials. In Marion County, Alabama, the probate judge was found misappropriating money from a fund set aside for indigent families of soldiers. George Cleveland of Miller County, Georgia, wrote to the governor accusing relief agents of "swindling." The state assembly had allocated $2.5 million in aid to soldiers' families but none was getting through. In Valdosta, Thomas and Joshua Griffin, assigned to distribute government salt, sold it at more than twice what the state allowed and pocketed the difference.[55]

To keep their heads above the flood tide of corruption and speculation, many soldiers' families and other commoners were forced deep into debt to local merchants and planters at extortion prices for what little food was available. Often the debt could not be repaid. Then, wrote a group of angry North Carolinians to their governor, creditors could "take there land & every thing they hav." A seventy-two-year-old widow with her only supporting son in the army wrote to Governor Vance for help when her small farm went on the auction block to cover a $50 debt. "It is with and aking hart and tremelous hand I seat my self this morning to inform you of my condition. . . . [T]he Specerlators will prove too hard for us . . . those that can assist the nedy will not do so . . . pleas excuse bad speling and writing and help me if you pleas." She was hardly alone. Thousands of such letters poured into government offices during the war.[56]

Reacting to the outcry, some southern states passed "stay laws" to prevent confiscation of soldiers' property in their absence or postpone it until after the war. But creditors would have none of it. Alabama planter John Horry Dent called indebted farm families "worthless and unprincipled" and called stay laws unconstitutional. Jonathan Worth—a North Carolina slaveholder, cotton planter, mill owner, and speculator—complained that the stay law "disorganized Civilized society." A fellow North Carolina elite, B.F. Moore, called it "radical, unwise, demoralizing, disgraceful." Many such men simply used their influence with local magistrates to ignore the stay law and continue taking land. In North Carolina, they succeeded in having the stay law repealed after only four months. The result was that tens of thousands of Confederate soldiers returned home to find their families destitute and their land gone.[57]

Some states also tried to relieve suffering by contracting with employers who promised to provide jobs for the poor at prescribed wages. But it was all too easy for government contractors to skim wages. In November 1862, a Georgia woman wrote of the wives of government contractors bragging that they would be millionaires if the war went on much longer. Some paid their workers barely half the contracted wages, keeping the rest for themselves.[58] The practice was so common that citizens lashed out in editorials such as this one from an April 1863 issue of Georgia's *Columbus Sun* telling how local seamstresses were mistreated.

Only think of it. A sleek speculator growing rich by the labor of the poor half-famished needle woman, who gave up her husband as a sacrifice on the altar of our country! A man who forcibly wrests from the hands of starving children that which is to make him rich! A man who will deliberately rob the widow and orphan of their daily bread, that he may add to his opulence. A man who professes not only to be a patriot, but also a Christian, who would deliberately drive the poor sewing woman to choose between a life of shame or an ignominious death by starvation! How dare such a monster look his fellow man in the face without cowering in very shame? The milder forms of villainy, such as treachery and counterfeiting, sink into insignificance when compared with such enormities.[59]

But the Confederacy refused to interfere with industrial operations on workers' behalf. Within a year of the war's outbreak, southern manufacturers were cranking out arms and supporting material at an astonishing rate. The Ordnance Bureau under Josiah Gorgas was especially efficient in producing and funneling military accouterments to the field. So much was manufactured and transported that no Confederate army ever lost a major battle for lack of munitions. The Confederate government was prepared to pay well for their delivery, and was not particular about where the money went.[60]

"God Help the Poor Day-Laborers"

Despite enormous profits flowing into the pockets of southern industrialists, wages were generally low from the war's outset. In October 1861, a "poor mechanic" in Georgia wrote the *Athens Southern Watchman* complaining that he could not find work that paid nearly what he got before the war. With prices on the rise, he wondered how he was going to support his family. He was not alone. The paper's editor knew that many local workers faced similar hardships. The only thing he could add to the man's "words of truth and soberness" was "God help the poor day-laborers."[61]

Working conditions were just as appalling as wages. In some cases, they were deadly. Few industrialists saw much point in spending money on worker safety. The result was that throughout the war, the South's urban newspapers were filled with reports of fatal industrial accidents. One of the worst occurred at Augusta's Confederate States Laboratory where gunpowder was made. In August 1864, eighteen thousand pounds of powder exploded at the granulating mill, killing nine employees. The concussion stripped leaves from neighborhood trees and broke window panes in all the surrounding buildings. According to one report, the victims were "blown to atoms. Hardly a vestige of them remaining. Portions of the bodies were found hanging on the trees—a most shocking spectacle."[62]

Children in the labor force were even more imperiled. Because they were usually unskilled and economically less valuable, they often performed the most hazardous jobs. One factory in Augusta, Georgia, had a special storeroom filled with caskets for its workers, most of them small. Young Martin Reilly, who worked at a Savannah foundry to support his widowed mother, was blinded in one eye when molten lead splattered his face. A falling timber killed John Henry, a boy of fifteen, at Oglesby's Mill near Augusta. His father had died earlier working at the same mill. Jack McElrath and John Madden, aged twelve and fifteen respectively, were horribly mangled when an artillery shell they were working on exploded at the Naval Iron Works in Columbus, Georgia. Both suffered through more than an hour of agony before they mercifully died.[63]

Facing dangerous conditions and low wages from the war's early days, workers often went on strike. In the fall of 1861, employees at Richmond's Tredegar Iron Works struck for more equitable pay, setting off a series of industrial strikes across the South. Influential manufacturers pressed the government for help. Such pressure, along with a lack of volunteers for the army, contributed to passage of the Conscription Act in early 1862. Under the legislation, certain categories of workers were declared exempt from the draft as long as they were employed. If they went on strike and lost their jobs, they could be hauled off to combat. Factory owners found in the act an effective tool to keep workers in line and wages low. In one of the measure's first tests, Lynchburg machinists went on strike for a living wage. They were fired, then drafted. Telegraph operators in Augusta struck as well, with the same result.

Still, consumer prices outstripped wages so far and fast that workers frequently had to take action. In 1863, postal clerks in Richmond struck for a wage increase. The next year, gravediggers at the city's Shockoe Cemetery did the same. With the draft act in force, they risked more than just a loss of their jobs. When lithographers in Richmond went on strike, they were locked up in a military prison and threatened with conscription unless they returned to work. Managers at the Virginia and Tennessee Railroad used the same tactic when their workers went on strike. They contacted the local enrolling officer and had the strikers sent to the guardhouse. There was little legal recourse for the detainees. With the writ of habeas corpus suspended, government officials could imprison almost anyone without warrant, charge, or trial.[64]

Such obvious extortion of labor, coercing men to live poor or risk death in battle, infuriated plain folk. As some had feared even before the war, white slavery had arrived in force and was backed by the Confederate government. Still, workers continued to resist. In early 1864, angry workers at the Mississippi Manufacturing Company in Bankston struck for better treatment, but were thwarted when Confederate cavalry arrived to disperse them. Reacting to similar heavy-handed actions, one enraged citizen wrote to a Georgia newspaper: "When this war broke out our people thought they had something to fight for, but now they have nothing, but to keep the Yankees checked, so that our own Government may oppress them more." The paper's editor was in full agreement. "Our freedom is now gone!" he declared. "May the devil get the whole of the old Congress!" One commoner spoke for many when he wrote that "freemen . . . are to day slaves—nay, worse than slaves." And in a way they were. Since a free man represented no investment, to the elites nothing was lost by his death either in the factory or on the battlefield. One disgusted southerner called the whole system of labor extortion "a criminal sort of economy."[65]

Common folk reserved their most intense scorn for those who brought on the war yet refused to serve in it or grow enough food to support it. "The crime is with the planters," wrote an angry Georgian to the *Savannah Morning News*. "As a class, they have yielded their patriotism, if they ever had any, to covetousness . . . for the sake of money, they are pursuing a course to destroy or demoralize our army—to starve out the other class dependent on them for provisions." Another asked: "What class has most interest in the war and has made the most money by it, *and sacrificed the least to maintain it?* . . . It is the class known as the planters."[66] One soldier called the planters

> the most contemptible of all our public enemies. . . . These fellows talk loudly about *their* constitutional rights—that no body has a right to say how much cotton they shall plant and intend to put at defiance the law and the authorities. But listen again and you will hear them loud for the enforcement of the Conscript Law. Oh, yes! Their negroes must make cotton and whilst doing it the poor men must be taken from their families and put in the Army to protect their negroes. Was ever a greater wrong, or a more damning sin, perpetrated by men or devils?[67]

"Many Voters Who Are Not Planters"

Such attitudes produced a class-based political consciousness among plain folk that made itself felt in the 1863–64 elections. Not all those who threatened to vote against incumbents were anti-Confederate, nor did they do so for entirely class-related reasons. That most of Tennessee and Arkansas, and much of Mississippi and Louisiana, were already in Union hands—together with the losses at Gettysburg and Vicksburg that summer—also eroded support for the Confederacy. Yet among those discouraged by Confederate military failures, there were also clear signs of class resentment. In September 1863, just before fall elections, this broadside circulated in Texas:

Common Sense
It is high time for the people of Texas to determine whether they will invite the fate of Louisiana and Mississippi, and allow a few men more distinguished for shallow brains and loud talk, than other capacity, and who have little stomach for the suffering they prepare for others, to drag them down to inevitable ruin.

The author signed himself "One who was at Vicksburg."[68]

Some plain folk were even more direct with their expressions of class antagonism. On the eve of Georgia's October 1863 elections, in an open letter to the *Savannah Morning News*, southeast Georgia commoners called on two of their state assemblymen to make public their positions on a recent state tax hike: "There was a tax act passed at the last session for the support of indigent widows and orphans of deceased soldiers, *from which the planters were specially exempted*. Did you, or either of you, vote *for that exemption*, or oppose it? And how did you manifest your opposition to that gross and palpable injustice?" They signed themselves "Many Voters Who are not Planters."[69]

Planters and their allies increasingly became worried that their political control might be slipping away. "The poor hate the rich," wrote South Carolina planter James Henry Hammond, "& make war on them everywhere & here especially with universal suffrage." So great were elitist fears of rising voter disaffection that they began calls to reinstate class-based restrictions on voting rights. Some demanded an increase in the poll tax to discourage poor citizens from casting ballots. Others suggested banning them from politics entirely with property qualifications for voting and office holding. As early as November 1861, a committee assigned to consider revising Virginia's state constitution called for more restricted suffrage and fewer popularly elected offices. In May 1863, the Reverend H.W. Hilliard, a former member of Congress from Georgia, spoke out publicly for a more restricted suffrage. When word of Hilliard's remarks reached Athens, a local paper raved that "the most unfeeling, unjust and cruel wrong we have ever witnessed, is this effort of designing politicians and juggling priests who are lying about home doing nothing, and worse than nothing, to disfranchise the brave and noble poor men who are fighting the battles of the country."[70]

Such efforts on the part of elites served only to inflame the plain folk and further undermine Confederate support. By 1863 many were openly demanding peace. In North Carolina there were peace rallies throughout the mountain regions. In Georgia, the editor of Griffin's *Southern Union* called for an end to the war and reconstruction of the old Union. Several candidates for Georgia's General Assembly from Gilmer and surrounding counties ran on the "Union" ticket. So did candidates in northern Alabama. In parts of Mississippi, so numerous were Union men that cavalry units were posted to keep them away from the polls. Still, armed bands of deserters showed up at Mississippi polling places defying arrest and demanding their right to vote. In Floyd County, Virginia, Confederates guarded every precinct to prevent deserters from voting. Nevertheless, so many local deserters' relatives went to the polls that they elected a pro-Union sheriff, Ferdinand Winston, and several other county officials. In Mississippi's Tishomingo County, Confederate officials were so worried about a Union victory at the polls that they suspended elections entirely.[71]

Fear, intimidation, and despondency kept many alienated voters away from the polls. And because the Confederate Constitution gave presidents a six-year term, Jefferson Davis was in no danger of losing his office. Even so, the election returns brought discouraging news for the Davis administration. In North Carolina, candidates for the Conservative Party, composed mainly of longtime secession opponents, won nine of ten congressional seats—eight of them "reported to be in favor of peace." George Logan of the tenth district was nominated at a peace rally. Both of the state's gubernatorial candidates were Conservative Party men.

In Texas, half the incumbent congressmen lost their seats. Of Georgia's ten congressional representatives, only one was reelected. The state's 90 percent freshman rate was the highest in the Confederacy. Eight of Georgia's new representatives ran on an anti-Davis platform.

Alabama voted out its staunchly pro-Davis governor. Four of the state's new congressmen were suspected of being outright unionists. One north Alabamian wrote that the election results showed a "decided wish amongst the people for peace." In all, nearly half the old Congress was turned out. Two-thirds of the newly elected members had long opposed secession. The congressional freshman rate would likely have been much greater had it not been for the large block of returning members representing districts under Federal occupation who were "elected" by refugees, by soldiers, or by general ticket in a given state's districts still held by the Confederacy.[72]

Plain folk had an impact on local elections as well, especially in urban areas, where turnout tended to be higher. Some plain folk even formed their own political alliances. In Columbus, Georgia, they organized and offered a slate of candidates for city office on the "Mechanics' and Working Men's Ticket." According to the *Enquirer,* the new party "prevailed by a very large majority." Its success sent shock waves through the ranks of the city's political establishment. The *Enquirer's* editor voiced upper-class fears just two days after the vote when he chastised plain folk for their "antagonistic" attitude and condemned the "causeless divisions of our citizens into classes." The *Enquirer* conceded that because of their numbers the city's plain folk could control any election in which they were united. But he insisted that this fact alone was among the strongest reasons why they should not unite. "Nothing can be more mischievous in any society," he warned, "than antagonistic organizations of its classes. Such divisions are more bitter in their alienations than any other political parties, and are far more apt to produce hurtful collisions."[73]

Reaction to the *Enquirer's* criticism was swift and direct. On October 13, a competing city paper, the *Daily Sun,* ran a letter it received from a local man signing himself "Mechanic." He argued that mischief had already been done by the elites. Common folk were trying only to protect themselves from further harm.

Voting by Classes

Editor Daily Sun:—I notice in the Enquirer, of Friday evining, an article complaining bitterly of the people voting by classes, in which both classes are accused of clannishness, but the burden of his complaint seems to rest on mechanics and working men. He says, "there is certainly no ground for any antagonism in the city." In this the Enquirer is mistaken; for any man, woman or child can see that the people are dividing into two classes, just as fast as the pressure of the times can force them on. As for example: class No. 1, in their thirst for gain, in their worship of Mammon, and in their mighty efforts to appropriate every dollar on earth to their own account, have lost sight of every principle of humanity, patriotism, and virtue itself, and seem to have forgotten that the very treasures they are now heaping up are the price of blood, and unless this mania ceases, will be the price of liberty itself; for we know something of the feeling which now exists in the army, as well as in our work-shops at home. The men know well enough that their helpless families are not cared for, as they were promised at the beginning of the war. . . . They know, too, that every day they remain from home, reduces them more and more in circumstances, and that by the close of the war a large majority of the soldiery will be unable to live; in fact, many of them are ruined now, as many of their homes and other effects are passing into the hands of speculators and extortioners, for subsistence to their families. Thus you see, that all the capital, both in money and property, in the South, is passing into the hands of class No. 1, while class No. 2 are traveling down, soon to take their station among the descendants of Ham. You can easily see who are class No. 2. The soldiery, the mechanics, and the workingmen, not only of Columbus, but of all the Confederate States. In view of these things, is it not time that our class should awake to a sense of their danger, and in the mildest possible manner begin the work of self-defense, and endeavor to escape a bondage more servile than that imposed by the aristocracy of England on their poor peasantry? Then we claim the right, as the first alternative, to try and avert the great calamity, by electing such men to the councils of the nation as we think will best represent our interests. If this should fail, we must then try more potent remedies.[74]

Efforts to find "more potent remedies" had already resulted in the formation of peace organizations and anti-Confederate partisan bands throughout the South. Many of them were composed of deserters who abandoned the army because they were hungry, because their families were suffering, or because they were tired of fighting a rich man's war. By 1864, President Davis publicly lamented that two-thirds of Confederate soldiers were absent, most of them without leave. The new Congress reacted by addressing at least one class-related concern in rescinding the substitute law. It hardly mattered. Ninety percent of substitutes never reported for duty anyway. Some congressmen also tried to end or limit conscription and impressment but were constantly thwarted, mainly by representatives of Federally occupied districts where Confederate law held no force.[75]

All such efforts, successful or not, were too little and too late. Voters had expressed considerable opposition to Confederate policy, and to some extent the Confederacy itself, in the 1863 elections. They might have done so even more clearly in 1865 had the war not ended before they had the chance. Frank L. Owsley Sr., the leading authority of his generation on the Old South's plain folk, believed that "the Confederacy, even had it not suffered military defeat at the hands of the North in 1865, would have been defeated in the next state and congressional elections, which would have disintegrated its armies and brought peace." In fact, most common soldiers had already sealed the Confederacy's fate by voting with their feet and going home.[76]

"A Political and Mercantile Operation to Be Exploited for Personal Advantage"

By contrast, the United States was never in danger of being voted out of existence. No amount of desertion and no turn at the ballot box would mean the government's collapse. In that regard, the United States enjoyed its greatest advantage over the Confederate States. But Lincoln enjoyed no immunity from being voted out of office, and he faced many of the same difficulties that plagued Jefferson Davis—and for much the same reasons. Enthusiasm for the war was declining in the fall and winter of 1861–62. Lack of volunteering reflected the popular mood. Military setbacks of spring and summer further deflated public resolve. Lincoln's reluctant solution to his manpower problem—the Emancipation Proclamation—sparked a backlash of anger among white northerners, most of whom had no desire to make the war a crusade against slavery. But even more infuriating to poor and middling whites were lagging wages, corruption in government, profiteering by speculators and industrialists, and a draft that the rich could buy their way out of—all of which fostered, just as they had in the South, a pervasive "rich man's war" attitude.

It was clear to common folk at home and in service that their sacrifices were making the rich even more wealthy, often through graft and other forms of corruption. In New York's notorious Customs House frauds, civil officials regularly took bribes to undervalue imports and thus lower taxes on incoming merchandise. Military officers lined their pockets as well. Colonel William Fish of the 1st Connecticut Cavalry misappropriated nearly $4,000 in gold on a sale of horses. Such corruption was so widespread that a single congressional committee discovered up to $50 million in losses to the public treasury from government contract frauds.[77]

Those contracts frequently went to suppliers who cut costs by delivering poor quality goods. "You can sell anything to the government at almost any price you've got the guts to ask," bragged war profiteer Jim Fisk. An inferior type of wool called "shoddy," which fell apart after minimal wear, was so common that the term soon came to describe any defective equipment. One manufacturer, Charles C. Roberts, delivered 50,000 haversacks and 50,000 knapsacks, all of which were, said one contemporary, "a fraud upon the Government, for they were not linen; they were shoddy." In a fraud involving Cornelius Vanderbilt, troops were sent to sea in transport ships with timbers so rotten that they hardly had, wrote one witness, "the slightest capacity to hold a nail."[78]

The Albany Contractors who have "influence" at Washington, and   Their Victim.

Driven by bribes and other illicit dealings, government contracts often went to suppliers who cut costs by delivering poor quality goods. "You can sell anything to the government at almost any price you've got the guts to ask," bragged war profiteer Jim Fisk. An inferior type of wool called "shoddy," which fell apart after minimal wear, was so common that the term soon came to describe any defective equipment. And it led the *New York Herald* to dub the era "the age of shoddy." (*Harper's Weekly*)

"The world has seen its iron age, its silver age, its golden age and its brazen age," proclaimed a writer in the *New York Herald*. "This is the age of shoddy." Ruling the age were "shoddy brokers in Wall Street," "shoddy manufacturers of shoddy goods," and "shoddy contractors for shoddy articles." On Sundays, wrote the *Herald*, these men showed up at church as "shoddy Christians."[79]

During the war's first year, the *Herald*'s "shoddy Christians" delivered to the army $3 million in shoes so poorly made that they could not be sold on the open market. The government also bought tents "which were valueless." Soldiers testified that they "could better keep dry out of them than under." Blankets that were "rotten and condemned" went to the army as well, along with uniforms that disintegrated in the rain. Foodstuffs could be just as worthless. One commissary officer described a delivery of coffee as "a compound of roasted peas, of licorice, and a variety of other substances, with just coffee enough to give it a taste and aroma of coffee." One shipment of bags marked "sugar" turned out to be little use in sweetening anything. All they contained was sand.[80]

In the war's early months, speculators bought old surplus weapons from Europe and bribed U.S. government inspectors to purchase them for the army. Most if not all were unserviceable. In 1862, a congressional commission reported that "a large proportion of our troops are armed with guns of a very inferior quality, and tens of thousands of the refuse arms of Europe are at this moment in our arsenals, and thousands more are still to arrive, all unfit." American industrialists too were guilty of delivering unfit weapons. Phillip S. Justice, a Philadelphia gun manufacturer, sent the army four thousand rifles described by an ordnance officer as "unserviceable and irreparable." The officer noted that "many of them are made up of parts of muskets to which the stamp of condemnation has been affixed by an inspecting officer." Another testified that "at target practice so many burst that the men became afraid to fire them." In one of the greatest scandals of the war, a group of profiteers that included J. Pierpont Morgan Sr. bought five thousand condemned Hall's carbines from the government at $3.50 each, then sold them back to the army at $22.00 apiece. A congressional committee investigating the affair reported that the guns were so dangerous that they had a tendency to blow the thumbs off soldiers firing them.[81]

Even the United States Sanitary Commission, a private soldier relief organization, was sometimes found cheating the troops rather than aiding them. Though the commission had many volunteers, money given in offering frequently went into the pockets of employees, often in the form of self-determined compensation. Commission officials set their own salaries at between $1,500 and $4,000 annually at a time when working families were lucky to see $300 a year and a soldier's pay was only $13 a month. Salary was not their only compensation. Food donated to the commission was sometimes sold to speculators. Clothing intended as gifts to wounded soldiers in commission hospitals were offered to them only at a price. One woman complained that a returning soldier "says that *every thing* is *sold* by the Commission to the patients." Walt Whitman, who often did volunteer work in soldiers' hospitals, wrote of the salaried commission employees: "They seem to me always a set of foxes & wolves."[82]

Northern merchants displayed the same disregard for the soldiers and the Union cause in their eagerness to trade with the South. The blockade was little deterrent to them or anyone else. There was so much traffic in and out of southern ports that in September 1863 the *London Times* called the blockade a "veriest farce." So much of that traffic was carried on by Yankee traders that the judge advocate of the South Atlantic Blockading Squadron was sure that they promoted more southern commerce than "all the merchants of Europe."[83]

If Yankee traders had few scruples about who they traded with, they had just as few about what they traded. Even war matériel was not out of bounds. One congressional investigation made clear that "supplies have not only gone in, but bullets and powder." Slaves too were part of their traffic. In June 1861, U.S. Marshal Robert Murry seized a ship outfitted for slave transport just as it was about to slip out of New York harbor. A group of northern capitalists led by Appleton Oakes Smith was financing the venture. To Murry's astonishment, New York's federal district attorney let the vessel go. Murry was sure there had been some deal between the slavers and the district attorney's office. Though he reported the incident to his superiors, there was no investigation. Two years later, in a letter to British minister to the United States Lord Lyons, Secretary of State William Seward admitted that "very prominent and wealthy persons" in the North were still engaged in the illicit slave trade.[84]

In pursuing their trade with the South, cotton was what northern

capitalists wanted most. Access to cotton was, after all, the main reason they had pressed Lincoln to fight secession in the first place. Their
motives had not changed. Such men as Edward Atkinson, an influential promoter of textile interests in New England, had a direct line to
the White House and used it to their advantage. In conversation with
Lincoln, Atkinson pointed out that the South was making tons of
money selling cotton to Europe. He argued that the cotton should
stay in the country. Such trade might bolster the Confederacy, but
whatever impact trade might have internally was irrelevant since the
United States did not recognize the Confederacy as a sovereign nation. Under pressure from the textile lobby, Lincoln approved licenses
to traders operating between the lines. Over the course of the war,
nearly a million bales of southern cotton reached the North by both
legal and illegal means.[85]

Officers of the armed services profited from the southern trade as
well. So common was army profiteering that one New Jersey congressman lamented: "I am greatly afraid that in some quarters the movements of our armies have been conducted more with a view to carry on
trade . . . than to strike down the rebels." Among the most notorious
for self-enrichment was General Benjamin F. Butler, whose name was
synonymous with illicit trade. According to historian Ludwell Johnson,
who researched Butler's nefarious trade practices: "Wherever Butler
was, whether New Orleans or Norfolk, business boomed, and much of
it was in the hands of his friends and relatives." Butler was from the
heart of cotton textile country—Lowell, Massachusetts—and held
stock in the Middlesex mills. Funneling cotton to New England made
both money and friends in high places. "To Butler," wrote Johnson,
the war "was a political and mercantile operation to be exploited for
personal advantage."[86]

Funneling Yankee supplies and currency to the Confederacy enabled it to attain an economic vitality greater than it otherwise could
and enabled it to survive longer than it otherwise would. That was obvious to many at the time. Critics were sure that Yankee traders had
"prolonged the rebellion, and strengthened the arm of traitors." That
would hardly have surprised the Reverend Theodore Parker, a Boston
theologian who before the war had warned of the capitalist's increasing tendency both to control government and disregard it as he
pleased: "He cheats in his trade; sometimes against the law, commonly
with it. . . . In politics he wants a Government that will ensure his

dividends; so asks what is good for him, but ill for the rest. He knows no right, only power; no man but self; no God but his calf of gold."[87]

The dividends that capitalists worked to secure were well protected by fiscal policy within Lincoln's government "for the people." At the behest of investors, Congress and the president made sure that Federal greenbacks, worth only forty cents on the dollar in currency markets, were taken at full face value in the purchase of government bonds. While soldiers and government workers were paid currency worth less than half its face value, those with the excess wealth to purchase bonds were assured valuation at 100 percent. The government assured even greater profits for investors, and at the same time less revenue for the public treasury by raising import taxes nearly 50 percent over the course of the war. Such taxes discouraged importation, depressed competition, raised the price of foreign goods, promoted inflation, and further devalued the currency—all to the short-term benefit of domestic investors. It also meant that at the same time they were sending soldiers into battle, Lincoln and Congress were undercutting the government's ability to support them. The first three months after Congress passed, and Lincoln signed, the Morrill Tariff Act, import tax revenues dropped by nearly half from the previous three months. Nevertheless, under pressure from politically influential investors, import taxes continued to rise during the war and import revenues continued to fall—to the detriment of war aims that investors themselves had urged. The entire affair was a fine example of unenlightened self-interest at work.[88]

The immediate financial benefits of political influence went to a relative few. Small manufacturers had neither the capital to gear up for increased government orders nor the influence in Washington to secure contracts for those orders. Throughout the war, countless small establishments were driven out of business under the weight of economic conditions promoted by corporations large enough to survive and prosper in such conditions. The result was that enormous wealth became increasingly concentrated in fewer hands. The Vanderbilt fortune alone increased fivefold during the Civil War. In New York City, the number of millionaires tripled.[89]

The rise of such vast fortunes certainly reflected a substantial altering of the economy. But, though some texts still suggest otherwise, they did not reflect a substantial rise of industrial output despite increased wartime government orders. In his study of the war's economic patterns, historian Stanley Engerman argues that the Civil War represented an interruption of industrial growth rather than a stimulus for it. Robert Gallman gives evidence supporting Engerman's conclusion, noting that from 1840 to 1860 commodity output grew at an annual rate of 4.6 percent and at 4.4 percent annually from 1870 to 1890. Between 1860 and 1870, the growth rate averaged only 2 percent annually.[90]

The growing concentration of wealth during the Civil War years came largely through speculation, which produced nothing, employed no one, and financially benefited only the speculator. And that wealth frequently came with government aid, especially for those who already had a good deal of wealth and influence. Under the Homestead Act, government aid came in the guise of free western land for the poor. In 1862, stolen Indian lands defined as "public domain" went in 160-acre plots free of charge to any white man who would cultivate his land grant for five consecutive years. The loophole was that after six months the land could be purchased at $1.25 an acre, which few real settlers could afford. "Dummy settlers" employed by land speculation companies headed west in droves, crowded out poorer folk, staked their claims, and bought up most of the homestead plots after six months. Over the next few decades, more of the West's "public domain" went for little or no charge to mining corporations, lumber companies, cattle barons, railroads, and other business concerns. Many of the transactions were arranged with bribes up front or the promise of future kickback payments. Left out in all this were those whom the Homestead Act had supposedly been intended to help. By 1890, only 3.5 percent of western land was held by genuine homesteaders.[91]

"I Would Not Serve My Country with Niggers"

As cheated as commoners felt at the vast fortunes being made at their expense, many were even more angry that the war had become what they were promised that it would never be—a crusade to free the slaves. Lincoln himself was hardly eager to make the war anything other than an effort to hold the South in the Union, but by the summer of 1862 he had little choice. Desertion was up, volunteering was down, and Confederate armies were on the move. Lee's Army of Northern Virginia drove George McClellan's Army of the Potomac off the

Yorktown Peninsula in June, routed John Pope's Army of Virginia at Second Manassas in August, and on September 17 fought the Army of the Potomac to a standstill at Antietam. That month in Kentucky, Braxton Bragg's Confederate army beat the Federals at Munfordville, captured Lexington, and installed a Confederate government at Frankfort. It was clear to Lincoln that the Union needed more soldiers. But with the November midterm elections approaching he feared popular reaction to a military draft. The only alternative was to recruit blacks and give them something to fight for. And the slaves themselves had forced the issue by flocking to Union armies at every opportunity.

On September 22, Lincoln issued a preliminary Emancipation Proclamation. It announced that as of January 1, 1863, all persons held in bondage in areas then in rebellion against the United States would forever be free. Though far-reaching in concept, it was a limited measure designed mainly to recruit blacks and ward off European recognition of the Confederacy. It freed no one in the border slave states of Delaware, Maryland, Kentucky, and Missouri. It did not even free slaves in the Federally occupied regions in western Virginia, southern Louisiana, and most of Tennessee and Arkansas. And it held only the hope of freedom, not its certainty, for slaves in Confederate territory. Still, it made freedom for at least some slaves a Union war aim. That was enough to spark a firestorm of criticism across the North.

Democrats took full advantage of antiemancipation sentiment in the fall 1862 elections. It was no easy task, despite racial apprehensions among northern whites. The nation was at war and Republicans blasted any criticism of the administration as "unpatriotic." Democrats shot back with emotionally charged rhetoric of their own. In New York, supporters of Democratic gubernatorial candidate Horatio Seymour told the electorate that "a vote for Seymour is a vote to protect our white laborers against the association and competition of Southern negroes." Others warned that "every white man in the North who does not want to be swapped off for a free Nigger, should vote the Democratic ticket." Though Republicans had done their best to gerrymander opponents out of office, and succeeded in some cases, the Democrats managed a net gain of thirty-two seats in the House of Representatives. They also took back the governor's seats in New York and New Jersey, and regained control of the Illinois and Indiana legislatures. Their victories would surely have been even greater had not the Pennsylvania and Ohio state elections been scheduled for odd years and had the governors of Indiana and Illinois not been holding four-year terms that began in 1861.[92]

Perhaps emancipation's most devastating blow to the administration came with its impact on the soldiers. One soldier who had voted for Lincoln in 1860 threatened to desert so that "the negro worshippers might fight it out themselves." "Loyal as I am," wrote a Pennsylvania solider, "I would not serve my country with niggers for my companions." Thousands of soldiers felt the same way—and they deserted in droves. All but thirty-five men of an Illinois regiment went home, saying that they would "lie in the woods until moss grew on their backs rather than help free the slaves." A group of Kentucky women whose sons were serving in the Union army urged them to desert as well. Comparing Lincoln to the devil, they said his Emancipation Proclamation showed "the cloven foot." A Midwestern father wrote to his son in the army: "I am sorry you are engaged in this unholy, unconstitutional and hellish war . . . which has no other purpose but to free the negroes and enslave the whites. Come home. If you have to desert, you will be protected."[93]

Refusing to fight for emancipation, thousands of soldiers deserted in the winter of 1862–63. By January 26, when Joe Hooker took command of the Army of the Potomac, hundreds were deserting every day. His rolls showed 25 percent of his men had left. It was the same everywhere. February's compiled reports for all Union armies showed that a third of the troops were absent. Private Adam Pickel of Pennsylvania wrote that month: "If it were not treason to tell the truth I would say that the whole army would run home if they had the chance." With the November election behind him, Lincoln reacted to the wave of desertion by calling on Congress to institute a national draft. Congress had authorized militia drafts the previous summer, and Lincoln himself had imposed recruitment quotas on the states. Neither measure was very effective in bringing new recruits to replace losses from death and desertion. So on March 3, 1863, Congress enacted compulsory military service.[94]

"A Poor Man's Life Is as Dear as a Rich Man's"

The Conscript Act provided outright exemptions only for ill health and hardship. But like its Confederate counterpart, anyone with enough ready cash could avoid the federal draft. Men with $300 in spare change could simply pay a commutation fee and be excused. Or the draftee might hire a substitute for a little less. Neither of these options was viable for common folk, who were fortunate to have an annual income of as much as $300. But it was no trouble for men like John D. Rockefeller, James Mellon, Andrew Carnegie, J.P. Morgan, Philip Armour, and Jay Gould, all of whom bought their way out of the draft while building fortunes from the war. Rockefeller made money by inflating food prices, then used his gains to enter the oil business. Jay Gould had a government operative inform him of Union victories or defeats before the news became public. With that advanced notice, he anticipated stock-market reaction and raked in huge profits. Such men as Rockefeller and Gould thought no less of themselves for having other men die to make them rich. Indeed, so rare was it for wealthy capitalists or their sons to serve in the military that those who did were sometimes treated by their peers as social outcasts. James Mellon's father told his son that he could be a patriot without lowering himself to don a uniform and risk his own life. There were, said the elder Mellon, plenty of other lives worth much less.[95]

Abraham Lincoln felt the same way about his son, Robert Todd Lincoln. The president would send hundreds of thousands of other men's sons to die in the war. But neither the cause of Union nor emancipation was worth the risk of his own offspring. Though Robert turned eighteen in 1861, he spent almost the entire war enrolled at Harvard. Stung by accusations of cowardice and by jabs at his father's hypocrisy, Robert begged Lincoln to make some arrangement for him after graduation. Finally in January 1865, with the war winding down, Lincoln wrote to Grant asking a favor. The president was willing to have his son serve, but insisted, "I do not wish to put him in the ranks." Grant obligingly gave Robert a captain's commission, placed him on his personal staff, and kept him out of harm's way.[96]

Even men of moderate means could sometimes avoid service if they had the right connections. In Pennsylvania, provost marshals withdrew the names of known war-supporting Republicans from their draft rolls. In Wisconsin, a mob ransacked one Masonic meeting hall when Masons on the local draft board exempted several healthy brother members. Outright bribes for such exemptions were not uncommon. The governor of Ohio wrote that draft officers were somehow "manifesting outward tokens of worldly means not derived from salaries." He was sure that at least half of them were on the take. From Dayton came complaints that the local provost marshal was striking names from draft rolls for $150. John Bennett Free, enrollment officer for Philadelphia's First Ward, was court-martialed for taking bribes in the form of both gifts and money. Physicians too could often be bribed for medical exemptions. The draft board examining surgeon in Kalamazoo, Michigan, made extra money by giving "private" examinations. So did an Ohio doctor, whose earnings from such examinations totaled about $1,500. Dr. Stephen Morris of Indianapolis received a visit from a draftee who had two bandages on his leg. When Morris removed them for examination, he found $50 hidden beneath each. He slipped the money in his pocket and pronounced the man unfit for duty.[97]

The genuinely unfit who could afford to pay were sometimes targets for extortion. In New York's Allegany County, the draft board was subject to a storm of criticism when physically unfit draftees from Angelica were forced to pay $100 and up to draft agents for release from service. For those who could not or would not pay, ill health sometimes offered little protection. Jacob Moon of Chenango County, New York, complained that the local enrolling physician conducted "shame examinations": "Harry Duncan, Morris Brown, and H. Warner Duncan, three as able-bodied men as there are in the district, have been rejected by the surgeon. George Negus, a lame man, has been accepted. William Calvert, with a cancer, has been accepted; a man by the name of Paw, who has fits, has been accepted and Andrew Thompson, with a lame knee, also accepted." When five New Englanders, all unfit for duty and unable to buy their way out, were drafted to fill a local quota, one astonished citizen commented that "another such a haul could not be made outside a graveyard."[98]

Many enrolling officials would go to almost any lengths to meet the army's demand. So would substitute brokers who, as dealers in human flesh, were held in as low a regard in the North as slave traders were in the South. Kidnaping was a common practice among such men. It was not unusual for some poor drunk to awaken from his stupor only to find himself on a troop train or ship headed for the front lines. In September 1863, an employee of the mental asylum at Troy, New York, sold a young patient to a substitute broker. The boy's mother spent months searching for her only son but never found him. His last known post was in Virginia with the 52nd New York Regiment in February 1864.[99]

Conscript officials in New York City arrested Antonio Cutormini, an Italian seaman, on charges of desertion and forced him into the 39th New York. His protests were ignored because he could not speak English. Foreigners who could sometimes fared little better. William Whitehead of Manchester, England, was drugged and enlisted by a recruiting officer in New York while attempting to return home after visiting his brother in Ohio. Canadians were victimized as well. Recruiters and substitute brokers lured men across the border with promises of good jobs, then forced them into service. They even made armed raids into Canada, returning with kidnaped recruits for the army. They lured men across the Atlantic as well. Recruiting contractors traveled through Europe promising good jobs and good wages in America. When the immigrants arrived, they were herded to the nearest enrolling office where the contractor collected their bounty.[100]

That wealthy and well-connected men could avoid the draft while the poor and sick were victimized by it spawned resentment and more throughout the North. Ohio editor Samuel Medary wrote of conscription: "The distinction it makes between the rich and the poor is a scandal to a government boasting that 'all men are created equal.'" The editor of Pennsylvania's *Johnstown Democrat* took the following jab at the draft's classism:

> *Q:* Why does Abe with his Conscription Act differ from the butchers that drive bullocks to the slaughter house?
> *A:* Because butchers drive the fat of the land to the slaughter pen, but Abe drives none but the poor.[101]

Another Pennsylvania paper, the *Wayne County Herald*, suggested that the best way to get recruits would be for "our prominent, influential, and wealthy men . . . [to] shoulder their muskets and say 'come with us.' They take the lead in receiving benefits from the government and why not in its defense?" But the rich and their political puppets would have none of that. When Congress came under pressure to repeal the draft's substitute provision, Senator Henry Wilson of Massachusetts argued strenuously against it: "We have got the business interests of the country to take care of as well as the military interests."[102]

Soldiers were among the most offended at such upper-class attitudes.

"I believe that a *poor* man's life is as dear as a rich man's," wrote Illinois soldier Levi Ross. Private Joseph Osborn of New Jersey expressed his view that "allowing men to pay $300 for their exemption is a imposition on the poor people. And I hope they will resist it."[103]

Resist it they did. The cry of "rich man's war" swept the North that summer, and the nation faced the worst riots in its history. Mobs of working-class New Yorkers, men and women, roamed the streets shouting "kill the niggers." They went after well-dressed gentlemen too, calling them "$300 men." They torched the draft office, razed pro-Lincoln newspapers, looted and destroyed the homes of prominent Republicans and abolitionists, burned a home for orphaned children, and lynched at least a dozen blacks. In all, more than one hundred people lost their lives during the furious rampage. Federal troops straight from the Battle of Gettysburg rushed in to stop the carnage. There were similar riots in Boston, Newark, Toledo, Chicago, St. Paul, Milwaukee, and numerous other towns.[104]

"Absolute Want in Many Families"

Reaction to the draft reflected a broad discontent brought on not only by draft inequities but also by speculation, corruption, and government policies that helped make the rich richer. At the same time, those policies were making the poor poorer. The draft robbed them of any chance for more gainful employment. Loopholes in the Homestead Act robbed them of opportunities in the West. The Morrill Tariff contributed to inflation. The result was rising prices and lagging wages. In New York City the price of eggs rose by 67 percent during the first two years of the war. The price of potatoes increased 50 percent; cheese went up 125 percent. By 1864, milk was up by almost 600 percent and so was butter. The overall cost of living had nearly doubled. But wages had not. The *New York Tribune* reported that they were "only from 12 to 20 percent higher than they were before the war, and there is absolute want in many families, while thousands of young children who should be at school are shut up at work that they may earn something to eke out the scant supplies at home."[105]

The war's impact on children was indeed heartrending. Hundreds of thousands were left fatherless, temporarily or permanently, in households that could not afford the lost income, little as it was. There was hardly any choice but for children to work or starve. They swept the street for what money passersby would throw their way. They sold newspapers, matches, and apples for what they could get. Some lived by gathering manure in the streets and selling it as fuel. Many found meager earnings at the textile mills, where in Massachusetts they made up 13 percent of the wartime labor force. In Pennsylvania's mills, their labor-force percentage was nearly one-fourth.[106]

Those were the fortunate ones. Many could find no work at all and wandered the streets as homeless beggars, sleeping in alleys and competing with dogs and each other in digging through trash piles for food. By 1863, there were as many as six thousand vagrant children in Boston. Estimates of those in New York City ranged as high as thirty thousand. As living conditions for children went down, crime rates went up. Petty theft, mostly of food, was the only thing keeping many children from starvation. And theft frequently led to arrest. At New York City's "House of Refuge," a children's prison, the occupancy rate was up by 68 percent two years into the war. By 1865 it had nearly doubled. A Massachusetts inspector of prisons was well aware of the war's connection to the juvenile crime rate: "I have talked with many boys in Jails and Houses of Correction who were either sons or brothers of soldiers or sailors in the service."[107]

The impact on young girls was even more degrading, as many were

FRANK, FREDERICK & ALICE.

The war left tens of thousands of children fatherless. This image showing three of them was the only identification found on the body of a slain Union soldier after Gettysburg. Copies of the image were made and described in newspapers that circulated throughout the North in an effort to locate the man's family. In November 1863 a woman whose husband, Sergeant Amos Humiston of the 154th New York, was missing in action identified the photo as one she had sent to him just prior to the battle. (Special Collections Library, Pennsylvania State University)

forced onto the streets and sometimes into the brothels. Every city of any size, not just those along the battle lines, saw a startling rise in prostitution during the war. And the practitioners were getting younger all the time. As George Templeton Strong of New York observed: "No one can walk the length of Broadway without meeting some hideous troop of ragged girls, from twelve years old down, brutalized already almost beyond redemption by premature vice, clad in filthy refuse of the rag pickers' collections, obscene of speech, the stamp of childhood gone from their faces, hurrying along with harsh laughter and foulness on their lips that some of them have learned by rote, yet too young to understand it; with thief written on their cunning eyes and whore on their depraved faces."[108]

Under the guise of offering assistance to such children, agents of newly consolidated corporate farms rounded them up and hauled them off to work as virtual slave laborers. Child snatching was lucrative business owing to the rapid rate at which corporate farms were being established. Rising export demand, farm mechanization, higher land prices, and an accompanying rise in property taxes during the war made farming so expensive that many small farmers were driven out of business, bought out at low prices by the new corporate farms. It was a trend that had begun even before the war. The *Rural New Yorker* wrote in 1860: "We doubt very much whether any man could take a farm at present prices . . . and pay for it from the proceeds after pay for the help, stock and machinery necessary to carry it on properly. On the contrary, we know many persons who have paid from one third to one half of the value of their farm, who can barely raise the annual interest money on their debts, and in bad years not even that."[109]

In robbing family farms of their menfolk, the war accelerated that trend. "I am left all a lone," wrote a desperate farm woman to the Lincoln administration. "I have a small plase and don't want to be taxed to death. . . . [B]y good rights you should pass a law to exemt such as I am from heavey taxes. . . . [I]t is unjust and cruel to tax a poor woman to death." But taxes on small farmers kept going up, as did their debts. Maria Swett had borrowed money to buy a little land and livestock, assuming at the time that her son would help work the farm and pay off the debt. When he went off to war, Swett wrote to Secretary of War Edwin Stanton demanding restitution. She simply could not do all the labor herself. She needed her son. "I require that you send him home," she insisted, "if he is willing to come *and* pay me for his time." War or no war, Swett had serious business at hand. She had a farm to run and bills to pay.[110]

Few such requests were ever answered, much less granted. And it showed in rural areas. A wartime missionary wrote home from Iowa that he "met more women driving teams on the road and saw more at work in the fields than men." Another wrote from Kansas: "If the war continues, the next year will be a very trying one for Kansas, especially in the back counties, where in many cases the women must harvest the corn and take care of the stock, in addition to their ordinary work." The war continued. And the longer it did, the more farm families went under. Many a soldier returned home only to find that his farm had been sold because his family could not keep up with mortgage or tax payments—or both—in his absence.[111]

Life was little better for women in urban areas left trying to hold their families together. The soldier's pay of $13 per month hardly began to cover living expenses, even if he sent it all home. With the mother working longer hours to make ends meet, young children were left unsupervised for long periods and lived almost as orphans. Many did become de facto orphans when, unable to feed their families on meager earnings, soldiers' wives resorted to theft and were thrown in prison. The occurrence was all too common. In Massachusetts, women made up 20 percent of county jail inmates when the war began. By war's end that figure had tripled to 60 percent. In New York's Sing Sing prison, the percentage of women inmates doubled during the war. And in the Detroit House of Corrections by 1865, nearly half the prisoners were women. Those who bothered to pay attention to the trend were astonished that so many of the women were related to soldiers.[112]

For those families not separated by arrest or the war, living conditions could still be dismal. One report on New York's tenement houses described a single twelve-by-twelve room housing twenty people of all ages and both sexes who lived as traders in dung at four cents a basket. In another room lived a family of five who supplemented their income by allowing prostitutes to entertain there for a percentage of the earnings. In a third room was a blind man sitting over a bucket of burning charcoal, the room's only source of heat. Nearby were several children lying on a pile of rags next to the body of their recently deceased mother. At least thirty thousand people were living in Manhattan cellars "literally buried alive, huddled together like cattle in a pen." Disabled and unemployed veterans constituted many of the urban poor. A Boston relief worker reported: "We have found dwellings where there are sick, shivering, hungry soldiers; more destitute, perhaps, than on the fields of Gettysburg."[113]

Relief efforts for the poor did increase in the North during the war. Contributions to the New York Children's Aid Society went up significantly. And the New York Society for the Improvement of the Condition of the Poor was able to cut its list of relief recipients in half by war's end. Attempts to establish subsistence aid to soldiers' families produced allowances ranging from as much as five dollars a week in New York to four dollars a month in some rural areas. But those funds could be cut off if a soldier was discharged or killed. Blaming the poor for their poverty, some upper-crust socialites argued that any degree of aid was too much, calling it "profuse and injurious" to the development of a work ethic. Those who complained most loudly were often the same men who worked their employees ten or more hours a day and paid them wages so low that poverty was guaranteed.[114]

Low wages were only one of many ways in which employers sought to keep wealth concentrated in their own hands and workers in virtual slavery. Factory, mill, and mine employees frequently had to live in company housing, pay rent to the company, and take wages in "store-orders" instead of cash, keeping them in constant debt to their employers. As one miner complained: "Every article sold in White and Brown's store . . . can be purchased at least one-third cheaper at any respectable store unconnected with the coal business." Pennsylvania's *St. Clair Sentinel* wrote that prices generally ranged between 25 and 30 percent more at company stores. Some mine owners even charged employees for work-related goods, such as blasting powder. Any word of complaint might get a worker fired. And because of the blacklist system, it was difficult to find other work.[115]

In dealing with employers, working folk were almost always on their own. Less than 10 percent of industrial workers held union membership. Labor organizations had been on the rise through 1860, but the outbreak of war brought that progress to a standstill. Though most workers had initially opposed war, attitudes changed when Rebels fired on the flag at Fort Sumter. Responding to Lincoln's nationalist call, tens of thousands of workers volunteered for service and labor union rolls were drastically depleted. In some small and middling towns, the war destroyed unions entirely. Every trade union in

Minneapolis and St. Paul was shut down by enlistments. Though peripheral to their purpose, industrialists surely knew that war could weaken organized labor as they pressured Lincoln to hold the cotton states by force. In turning the anger of common people against the South and away from themselves, northern capitalists dealt a staggering blow to the labor union movement.[116]

"Each Trade Must Organize"

As the war went on, labor's worsening condition and the obvious advantage industrialists were taking from the war gave new life to organizing efforts. In November 1863, Philadelphia shoemakers declared: "The time has now arrived when it is absolutely necessary that an organization should be formed in our trade, for the regulation of our wages and the protection of our rights in general. The high prices of provisions, fuel, clothing, etc., render it imperative that we should have an advance in our present wages . . . and this cannot be done without organization." The previous summer had seen a rise in union membership all across the North, and the movement developed increased momentum, with new unions forming almost every week.[117]

Labor newspapers like *Fincher's Trades' Review* of Philadelphia, the *Workingman's Advocate* of Chicago, Boston's *Daily Evening Voice*, St. Louis's *Daily Press*, and the *Weekly Miner* of Belleville, Illinois, spread the word of labor organizing and gave the movement voices of mass communication. "Not until their advent," said labor leader William H. Sylvis, "did we make the slightest advance." Due in large part to the encouragement these papers gave, union membership was estimated at about 200,000 by 1864 and was still on the rise. Those in the labor press made little money from their efforts. To maintain his independence from corporate influence, Jonathan Fincher accepted no commercial advertising in his *Trades' Review*. But making money was hardly the point. Fincher wrote in 1865 that "the *Review*, in a financial point of view, is a failure, yet, as a progressive movement in the cause of right and justice, it has been an unquestioned success, as a glance at the Labor movement of today, as compared with it three years ago, will amply demonstrate."[118]

Many local unions combined and enhanced their strength by forming citywide trades assemblies designed to offer mutual support.

"To find protection," declared a speaker in New York, "each trade must organize itself and then come into a central organization." That they did, not only in New York but in other cities like Buffalo, Albany, Rochester, Boston, Philadelphia, Pittsburgh, Chicago, Louisville, St. Louis, and far to the west in San Francisco. Every major city in the Union and many other smaller industrial towns saw trades assemblies cobbled together. The weight of their numbers frequently had the intended effect. When printers went on strike in Philadelphia, the city's trades assembly pressured local politicians to intervene. They did, and worked out an arrangement with employers favoring the printers' demands. In San Francisco, the trades assembly went into action when employers tried to bring in strikebreakers by ship from the east to thwart the local iron molders' union in its call for higher wages. Assembly representatives met the incoming workers in Panama and explained the importance of the strike and its significance for all the city's workers, themselves included. When the strikebreakers arrived at the San Francisco docks, they refused to scab and joined the union. Employers had little choice but to grant the union's wage requests.[119]

To offset the effects of inflation and speculation, many trades assemblies opened cooperative stores for their members where goods were sold at cost. Such stores were set up in at least thirty-six cities and towns from Biddeford, Maine, to San Francisco. Some assemblies organized boycotts when local merchants tried to charge speculation prices. They also established funds to assist striking workers. When machinists in New York went on strike, assembly agents collected $5,000 in supporting donations from all over the country. Philadelphia alone sent $2,000. Workers in New York and other cities returned the favor when Philadelphia's iron molders went on strike, sending a total of $5,000.[120]

Industrialists countered labor organizing efforts with their own employers' associations. They set wage caps, blacklisted union members, and pressured government for antilabor laws. That pressure was not always initially successful. Labor blocked efforts by employers to pass antistrike laws in Massachusetts and New York, and got legislation abolishing store-order and scrip wage payments in New York, New Jersey, and Pennsylvania. But, as *Fincher's Trades' Review* pointed out, enforcement was almost nonexistent and the store-order system continued to operate openly.[121]

Through the efforts of employers' associations, several state legislatures did pass acts making strikes illegal. And, unlike prolabor laws, antilabor laws were almost always enforced. Among the most notorious were Illinois's LaSalle Black Laws, which outlawed union efforts to influence workers "by threats, suggestions of danger, or other means." The definition of "other means" was left entirely open, and any effort to organize a union or initiate a strike could be interpreted as a violation of state law. Ohio had a similar law restricting trade-union efforts. In Minnesota, union members could be slapped with fines of up to $100 or six months in prison for resisting strikebreakers. The Pennsylvania legislature officially authorized railroad and mining companies to use their own private police forces against the unions. Some states virtually outlawed unions altogether by defining them as "conspiracies to restrain trade," which gave employers a green light to go after unions through the courts.[122]

The federal government also helped employers fight the unions by providing them with easy access to scabs and strikebreakers. Army officers at southern posts regularly funneled newly freed blacks to northern industrialists for use against strikers. Such efforts frequently led white workers to conclude that the war was designed mainly "to enable abolitionist Capitalists to transport Negroes into the northern cities to replace . . . workers who were striking for higher wages." It solidly entrenched the "rich man's war" attitude and led to animosities with blacks as well. Violence often broke out when employers tried to replace striking white workers with blacks. In Boston, Chicago, Cleveland, Buffalo, Cincinnati, Albany, Detroit, New York, Brooklyn, and many other cities race riots occurred as working-class whites tried to fight off blacks brought in to take their jobs. Using blacks as strikebreakers had an added benefit for employers—it fomented racism, which fostered deeply entrenched divisions among the working classes and further weakened the labor movement.[123]

Employers fostered ethnic divisions as well, also with government help. The Contract Labor Law, signed and sanctioned by both Lincoln and Congress, made it possible for business to import strikebreakers from Europe as indentured servants. In exchange for the privilege of immigrating, workers forfeited their first year's salary to their employers. The law further stated that imported contract workers could not be drafted into military service. Native workers enjoyed no such immunity. Even before the law went into effect, the American

Emigrant Company, chartered by the Connecticut state legislature and capitalized at $1 million, sent agents throughout Europe promising good work at good wages. What immigrants usually found when they arrived were dangerous working conditions, no pay for the first year, and violent opposition from workers striking for better wages. Such violence between native and immigrant workers created wounds within the labor movement that took decades to heal.[124]

Government at all levels frequently intervened on the side of employers in more direct and violent ways. When miners around Pottsville struck for higher wages in May 1862, Pennsylvania's governor, Andrew Curtin, sent two hundred troopers against the striking workers. At Cold Spring, New York, just across the Hudson River from West Point, federal troops imposed martial law when employees of the Parrot Shot and Shell Works went on strike. Officers jailed four strike leaders without charge or trial, held them for seven weeks, then drove them and their families out of town. In Tioga County, Pennsylvania, a combined force of six hundred federal soldiers and local police raided the homes of striking miners, arrested their leaders, and forced the rest back to work at half pay. The state legislature supported the action with its Tioga County Law, which sanctioned immediate and unannounced eviction of striking miners' families from company towns.[125]

In the spring of 1864, the tailors' union and the machinists' and blacksmiths' union of St. Louis, Missouri, went on strike. In response, at the urging of employers, General William S. Rosecrans issued his broadly antilabor General Order No. 65, which outlawed unions in war-related industries. Almost any trade could be defined directly or indirectly as war related. It made strikes in those industries illegal, offered military protection to strikebreakers, and was used repeatedly to thwart union organizing efforts among coal miners, tailors, printers, and machinists. The order made virtual slaves of industrial workers, who were at times prevented from striking at gunpoint. Roscrans called it securing "the military power of the nation." Military commanders in other areas took similar heavy-handed action against the labor movement. General W.D. Whipple put his troops at the service of management during a strike at the Gorrell Mine in Pennsylvania's Columbia County. General Stephen Burbridge, in collusion with employers, used troops to break a machinists' strike in Louisville. When mechanics at the U.S. arsenal in Nashville went on strike after promised overtime wages were not paid, General George Thomas exiled two hundred of the most "untrustworthy" among them. He forced the rest back to work at the point of a bayonet for half their regular wages.[126]

Newspaper bosses of the for-profit press, many of them holding financial ties to the larger corporate world, usually supported both the employers' associations and the government's use of force to back them up. Countless editors smeared union members as "disloyal" and labor leaders as "traitors." At the same time, they praised employers' associations as patriotic organizations protecting American workers from "foreign agitators," who, they insisted, spearheaded the labor movement and threatened free labor with forced unionization. By 1864, many labor leaders had caved in to accusations of disloyalty by calling for strikes less frequently and backing away from the aggressiveness that had carried the movement to that point. In early 1861 many unions, such as the iron molders', had resolved themselves to be "utterly opposed to any measures that will evoke civil war." But more than their leaders detested civil war and capitalist corruption, they feared the taint of being called unpatriotic. Rather than fight it head on, they usually ran from it and let the threat of name calling drive them straight into bed with those who worked against labor interests. Many labor leaders became strong supporters of the war and backed prowar candidates at the expense of smaller workingmen's parties.[127]

Lincoln himself encouraged the trend with carefully directed rhetoric designed to make himself appear sympathetic to labor while doing little to support it. "I myself was a hired laborer," he told a number of receptive audiences. "I know the trials and woes of workingmen. I have always felt for them." When a delegation of machinists and blacksmiths visited Lincoln to air their grievances, he responded: "I know in almost every case of strike the men have just cause for complaint." He even directed Rosecrans to make sure that General Order No. 65 did not interfere with the "legitimate demands of labor." But that was as far as he would go. For all Lincoln's willingness to use his army to support the cause of national union, the cause of labor union was more likely to have Lincoln's army used against it.[128]

The racial and ethnic hatreds that business encouraged among workers, the mixed messages workers got from government and many labor leaders, and workers' own fears of being called unpatriotic made it difficult for the labor movement to present a united front. What victories it had were limited state by state and were often themselves divisive. Employers frequently made concessions to some groups and not others, or did so only if workers agreed to abandon their unions.[129]

"The Curse of Workingmen"

The well-financed two-party system further widened labor's divisions as candidates courted workers' votes with appeals that had little to do with labor's economic interests. Republicans defined patriotism as supporting the war and votes against them as unpatriotic. Many Democrats followed suit, wrapped themselves in the flag, and supported the war. Others opposed it and appealed to racism by calling the war effort nothing more than an attempt to free the slaves and put them in competition with whites. Other Democrats, critical of the draft and Lincoln's attacks on civil liberties, called the conflict a war to enslave the free. Still others appealed to the immigrant vote, particularly Irish Catholics, calling Republicans an offshoot of the anti-Catholic, anti-immigrant, nativist American (or "Know-Nothing") Party of a decade earlier. Many Republicans were in fact just that. Some openly confirmed it with attacks on "dangerous foreign influences" and "Popish plots." Both parties insisted that they represented the working class, though neither could show much evidence for the claim.[130]

This complex and confusing mix of racism, nativism, patriotism, and prejudice divided labor like never before. Lacking aggressive leadership strong enough to fight the "unpatriotic" label and to stress labor's common interests, workers tended to be swayed by whatever emotionally charged issue dominated their neighborhood, ethnic group, religion, or region. In areas with diverse constituencies, workers in the same factory or trade union might be on opposite sides of the political fence. In areas of less diversity, worker strength could be overwhelmed by a single party accusing any opponent of disloyalty to the religion, the race, or the country. In Pennsylvania's Irish-Catholic anthracite coal regions, Democrats built a stronghold. In Anglo-Protestant New England, Republicans established a firm grip. Lynn, Massachusetts, where the Workingmen's Party had been so strong before the war, saw Republicans in control of city government by 1863. A similar trend could be seen throughout the industrial North. Almost everywhere, labor issues were being subsumed in one way or another by party politics. Little wonder that one prominent labor newspaper called political parties "the curse of workingmen."[131]

But the divisions that worked against labor proved to be a double-edged sword that could also cut against Lincoln and threaten business's ultimate aim of holding southern states in the Union. So divided were voters as the 1864 elections approached that Lincoln was unsure of his hold on the presidency. He was not even sure that he could regain his own party's nomination at its June convention in Baltimore. Home-front divisions had weakened the war effort to such an extent that although Ulysses S. Grant's spring campaign against Richmond was pressing forward, victory seemed distant and hardly assured. Union casualties were mounting so high that many northern papers called Grant a "butcher." And they did not know the worst of it. Throughout the conflict's final year, the War Department under-reported casualty figures in an effort to keep up what support there was for the war and to secure Lincoln's renomination and reelection. General Joshua Lawrence Chamberlain, the Union's hero of Little Round Top, later admitted that "we were not called upon or permitted to report our casualties during that whole campaign from the Rapidan Rappahannock to the James and Appomatox, for fear that the country could not stand the disclosure."[132]

At no time was the practice of withholding accurate casualty reports more obvious than after Grant's attack at Cold Harbor in spring 1864. The only message he ever sent to Secretary of War Stanton about Cold Harbor reported that "our loss was not severe." A figure of 3,000 killed and wounded floated through the northern press, but that was less than a third of the actual losses from May 31 to June 3. During Grant's final attack, 7,000 Union soldiers fell in less than half an hour. The heavily entrenched Confederate defenders lost about 1,500. With rumors of mass casualties filtering back through unofficial channels, many on the home front knew that the War Department was hiding something. On June 9 the *Philadelphia Age* wrote: "We think Mr. Stanton might be a little more explicit in his telegrams about the condition of affairs in Virginia. . . . From his dispatches we can scarcely find out that there was fought one of the bloodiest battles of the war . . . they have lost all significance as candid reports of military operations." But with the Baltimore convention only days away and Lincoln's nomination hanging in the balance, his administration kept the death toll hidden from public view. It would continue to do so through the November elections and for the rest of the war.[133]

To further strengthen their position, Lincoln and the Republicans also formed an alliance with Democrats who supported the war. Together they met at the Baltimore convention and formed the National Union Party, nominating Lincoln for a second term and Democrat Andrew Johnson of Tennessee as his running mate. Then they tapped into the voting block of soldiers who had stayed with the war and were considered likely to support Lincoln. In states where Republicans held sway, legislatures passed laws allowing soldiers to vote from the field. For those who could not, Lincoln granted furloughs so they could go home to vote. To draw some of those votes from Lincoln, the Democrats nominated George McClellan, former commander of the Army of the Potomac, who was thought to be still much-beloved among the troops. But in so doing, they sent mixed signals on their plans to end the war. The platform called for an armistice, then negotiations leading to reunion. McClellan insisted that reunion was his ultimate goal, but he never answered the question of what might happen if negotiations did not produce that result. Most northerners concluded that a McClellan victory would likely mean peace with or without reunion.[134]

Lincoln's reelection bid got a boost in September when Atlanta fell and the Union seemed to be a major step closer to victory. In the days leading up to the election, Lincoln's suspension of habeas corpus came in handy as well. Republican officials arrested hundreds of potential Democratic voters in key areas to keep them away from the polls. In Pennsylvania's Luzerne and Columbia counties, Democrats by the score were thrown in jail and held without charge. In Philadelphia, Democrats alleged that thousands of Lincoln ballots were fraudulent, and the surprisingly large vote total supported their claim. McClellan's backers were sure that the arrests and election frauds gave the state to Lincoln.[135]

True or not, the soldier vote almost certainly swung Pennsylvania to Lincoln—at least by the official figures. Fraud and intimidation were so rife in the entire soldier-vote system that there is no way to tell how accurate those figures were. Union party operatives in Connecticut succeeded in keeping known Democrats off the rolls of soldiers registered to vote. The Union officer corps, by that time purged of nearly all but pro-Lincoln men, also exerted its influence over the voting process. Some sent false figures up the line. Others allowed no secret balloting. A disgusted Illinois soldier wrote home that he had been forced to vote for Lincoln against his will. On election day, his company was ordered to form up and the commanding officer called on those who favored McClellan to take one step backward. No one dared move.[136]

Democrats were not above election fraud themselves, but they could hardly compete with Republicans on that field. When election day came, the War Department sent thousands of federal troops into cities throughout the North on the pretext of guarding against disruptions by Confederate agents. The result was predictable. Complaints of soldiers intimidating voters and stuffing ballot boxes were rampant. But even with the backing of War Democrats, confusion among the Peace Democrats, Atlanta's fall, election fraud, and the duplicity of false casualty figures, officials recorded Lincoln's margin of victory in the popular vote at no more than 10 percent.[137]

It is difficult to say whether the election's outcome, or that of the war itself, might have been different without the administration's heavy-handed influence. A slightly more than 5 percent shift in the official total would have robbed Lincoln of a popular majority, but he might still have carried enough states for victory in the electoral college. As for the war, the Confederacy's home-front divisions and resulting battlefield defeats had weakened it to such an extent that it would almost certainly have collapsed even without Lincoln's November 1864 reelection. Lincoln would still have held office until March 1865 in any case, by which time the Confederacy would be nearly finished.

What can be said with certainty is that the election reflected no consensus on the war or the issues surrounding it. Nor did the election reflect majority will one way or the other since a majority could not vote. Jailed and intimidated Lincoln opponents were not the only northerners barred from voting. Women constituted the largest disfranchised group of potential voters, many of whom would surely have voted to oust Lincoln, end the war on whatever terms, and bring their men home. Most southern women by that time would have voted to end the war as well, victory or no. Many had long since encouraged their men to vote with their feet and head back home. By summer 1864, almost two-thirds of Confederate soldiers had done just that. It was but one area in which women had a major influence on the war's course and conclusion despite their second-class legal status. Through their own efforts, women made the war a turning point for themselves individually and collectively as they fought their own battles for respect, opportunity, and simple survival.

3

"The Women Rising"

The care of sick and wounded in war is not a feminine business. It must have a masculine discipline, or as a system, as a sustained and "normal" arrangement, it must have a bad tendency.[1]

— FREDERICK LAW OLMSTED, SANITARY COMMISSION

I'll go to Cairo [Illinois], and I'll clean things up there. You don't need to worry about that, neither. Them generals and all ain't going to stop me. This is the Lord's work you're calling me to do.[2]

— MARY ANN BICKERDYKE, HOSPITAL VOLUNTEER

"Like a Pent-Up Volcano"

From the war's outset, attitudes among white women, North and South, varied widely with their regional, religious, economic, and family circumstances. While these factors were not absolute determinants of support for or opposition to the war, they certainly influenced the way women viewed the world and reacted to it. Women's worldview was influenced as well by the fact that whatever their circumstances, they were females in a society that assigned predominant roles to males at most levels of society. Except for interactions with male

servants or slaves and those of a lower class, white women were restricted by custom and law to subordinate status in nearly all their contacts with men. In some cases, particularly in the professions, the
opportunities for those contacts were almost entirely closed to them.
And while lower-class white males could vote when they were not
priced out of it by a poll tax, no woman of any class could express her
opinion at the ballot box. Whatever their attitudes, to a greater degree than men, women at least initially experienced feelings of helplessness about the war: helplessness to prevent it or to advance it, to
take some active role in it or to shield themselves and their families
from its ravages.

Women's journals and letters, most from early in the war, are
replete with expressions of vulnerability and uselessness. For Emma
Holmes, the coming of war brought a feeling of "aimless existence."
Wrote another woman to a friend, "If only I could be of some use to
our poor stricken country." Sarah Wadley wrote in her diary, "We
young ladies are all so . . . useless." Julia LeGrand felt "like a pent-up
volcano. I wish I had a field for my energies."[3] But through a process
of self-empowerment women would take a hand in their fate and that
of their country, expanding their existing spheres of activity or pressing outside traditional roles altogether. That expansion, however, was
hardly one of upward mobility. Social position mattered, and women's
routes of empowerment were usually limited more by class than by
gender. Under the worst of circumstances, well-connected women
could use their connections to feed themselves through employment
or empathy. Occasionally some found it necessary to bestow selective
sexual favors. Lower-class women were often forced into outright, indiscriminate prostitution. In many cases, they simply stole or rioted
for food.

If women found it all but impossible to expand opportunities upward, simply to expand opportunities outward was difficult enough.
For upper-class women already at or near the top of the social ladder,
the push out was considerably easier. They tended to be more steeped
in social conventions of the day and were more inclined to self-restrict
their efforts within socially acceptable bounds. Philanthropic activity
was an area in which upper-class women traditionally took a role, and
it was in that role that they had their greatest impact. They staged
benefits to raise money for troops, organized soldiers' aid societies to
help with food and clothing, set up wayside rest stops for soldiers in

transit, and established hospital associations to assist the wounded. The Ladies Aiken Relief Association of South Carolina sent medicine to the army. The Women's Central Relief Association of New York City did the same. In Portsmouth, Virginia, well-to-do women raised money to transform an abandoned hotel into a hospital. Society women in Georgia formed the Atlanta Hospital Association and sent all sorts of supplies to hospitals on the Virginia front.[4]

As much good as upper-class women tried to do, elitist attitudes could limit the benefit of their efforts. Supplies sent to the field were sometimes earmarked for " 'gentlemen' from the 'best families.' " Sidney Harding of Louisiana could barely conceal her disgust at disabled soldiers who asked for food, writing in her diary that "Two wounded came up—ugly, common, not much wounded." At times the class gap got in the way of good intentions, as when a Richmond lady offered delicacies to a backwoods Carolina soldier who obviously needed more hearty food. Some upper-crust do-gooders enjoyed making a show of their status and proved to be little more than a nuisance to hospital staff. "If I owned a hospital no philanthropist should ever enter," wrote Caroline Woolsey, a young worker at Beverly Hospital near Philadelphia. "I could have pounded two benevolent old ladies yesterday on a tour of 'inspection' through my ward."[5]

Perhaps just as debilitating to the efforts of well-intentioned upper-class women was the assumption on the part of men, and some women, that they could not handle those efforts for themselves. When the Woman's Central Association of Relief formed in April 1861, half of those on the twenty-four-member governing board were men. In the summer of 1861 Frederick Law Olmsted wrote to Henry Bellows that "the care of sick and wounded in war is not a feminine business. It must have a masculine discipline, or as a system, as a sustained and 'normal' arrangement, it must have a bad tendency." Shortly thereafter, Olmsted and Bellows took the lead in forming the United States Sanitary Commission, a male-dominated body through which they intended that all local women's relief organizations across the North would funnel contributions.[6]

Independently minded middle- and upper-class women balked at the commission's attempt to control their efforts, especially since many were themselves well organized. The New England Women's Auxiliary Association represented a network of 750 local soldier-aid societies. The association kept in touch with Washington and informed its member societies of army needs so that "not one unneeded stitch may be set." The Sanitary Commission seemed to many a duplication of an already well-organized effort. Even so, some women's groups, like the Soldiers' Aid Society of Bridgeport, Connecticut, sent donations to the commission but held it strictly accountable, demanding to know the exact use of all their contributions. Others gave limited gifts but supervised most of their own relief activities. Disturbed by reports of high salaries and corruption within the commission ranks, many women's groups refused to deal with the organization at all. The ladies of Lynn, Massachusetts, sent their aid directly to a trusted woman at Washington's Finley Hospital who supervised and reported on the distribution.[7]

"Petticoat Government"

Foremost among those women who stuck to an independent course was Clara Barton. She became a relief worker in 1861 and by the late summer campaigns of 1862 she was serving as a volunteer nurse on the front lines. At Antietam, she performed surgical procedures herself and was so close to the firing line that a bullet passed through her sleeve and killed the man she was tending. She appealed to friends and to the public for direct contributions, refusing to have money or supplies funneled through the hands of Sanitary Commission men who held neither her respect nor her trust. Barton knew what the soldiers needs were, she knew where they were, and she made sure all contributions got there. Explaining her independent stance to an acquaintance in 1864, Barton wrote: "If, by practice, I have acquired any skill, it belongs to me to use discretionary, and I might not work as efficiently, or labor as happily, under the direction of those of less experience than myself."[8]

Tens of thousands of women like Barton who took up nursing during the Civil War essentially created the profession and made it their own. Dr. Elizabeth Blackwell, the first woman to earn a degree from a U.S. medical school, led the Women's Central Relief Association in founding an institute to train female nurses for the army. Young women who entered nursing most often did so over the objections of family, friends, and society at large. The notion that any woman would actively seek such close contact with strangers of the opposite sex was scandalous. In the minds of many it implied sexual promiscuity. To others the impropriety lay in the chance that women might assume authority over men. The *Confederate Baptist* acknowledged that women might be "most valuable auxiliaries" in the hospitals, but only so long as they kept "in their proper sphere" and made no attempt to "direct or control the physician."[9]

What work they did and what authority they assumed over men often had more to do with class than sex. Well-to-do women like Emma Crutcher of Mississippi, though eager to serve, set their own boundaries in keeping with social status. "I shall never take on myself," wrote Crutcher, "anything that a servant can do as well, and never do anything that a lady may not with perfect propriety do. I shall not talk familiarly with the patients. . . . I shall maintain every particle of the dignity which belongs to my sex and position, and at the same time I think I can be kind and useful." Phoebe Pember and Kate Cumming, who wrote extensively of their "nursing" experience in Confederate hospitals, actually functioned in their role of ward matrons more as administrators than nurses. Cumming did not dress a wound until two years after she began her service. "It is as much as we can do," she wrote, "to see that the nurses [mostly male orderlies, slaves, or lower-class women] do their duty."[10]

Still, administrative and other duties in a Civil War hospital took considerable stamina. Some of the more "delicately bred" ladies simply were not up to the task. Early in her career, Cumming was taken aback at the sight of "a stream of blood running off an operating table into a tub, which also held the patient's recently severed arm." Harriet Douglas Whetten of Philadelphia complained in a letter home of a colleague who was "too fine a lady to make a good nurse, [she] touches things somewhat too much with the tips of her fingers, so that the actual nursing in our ward falls chiefly to me." But she also noted that "there are men nurses and orderlies detailed, so that we volunteer ladies have nothing disagreeable to do."[11]

That was hardly the case for women of the lower classes. Many took hospital nursing jobs for what little support they offered and did everything from laundry and mopping floors to changing linen and bed pans. And they did all the other "disagreeable" chores of actual nursing. Upper-class ward matrons tended to treat them with little more regard than they would a servant or slave. Phoebe Pember referred to them with contempt as "uneducated women, hardly above the laboring classes." There was little they could afford to be above in caring for themselves and their children. Some were army wives whose husbands had not been paid in months. Others were army widows who had received no compensation for the loss of their husbands. Little wonder that some nurses were on the lookout for a replacement. Kate Cumming overheard one widow say how much she liked being a nurse because of the opportunity it offered to find a second husband. So many young women were drawn to the hospitals on the chance of finding a man that the Union's superintendent of women nurses Dorothea Dix, widely know as "Dragon Dix" for her stern ways, set the minimum age for women nurses at thirty and accepted applications only from women who were "plain in appearance."[12]

Regardless of class or motive, Civil War nursing was dangerous business. At least twenty female nurses died in service and many others suffered permanent ill effects. More than 10 percent experienced physical breakdowns. Several were deafened by exploding shells. Others never fully recovered from diseases they encountered on duty. Elida Fowle contracted an infection that left scars on her face for life. Still they came, and many stayed for the war's duration. In all there were at least 3,200 women who held paid nursing positions during the war. Many more served as volunteers.[13]

Despite the need for their services, most army physicians saw ward matrons as a threat to their authority and resented their "petticoat government." One doctor was overheard complaining to a colleague "in a tone of ill-concealed disgust, that 'one of *them* had come.'" Sophronia Bucklin was sure that the doctors "were determined by a systematic course of ill-treatment . . . to drive women from the service." Georgeanna Woolsey felt the same way. The surgeons did all they could "to make their lives so unbearable that they should be forced in self-defense to leave." Woolsey wrote that no one knew "how much opposition, how much ill-will, how much unfeeling want of thought these women nurses endured. Hardly a surgeon of whom I can think, received or treated them with even common courtesy."[14]

Not all men were so unalterably opposed to women serving in the wards. Some expressed great appreciation for their efforts and gave them whole-hearted support. When U.S. Surgeon General William A. Hammond got word of an intended boycott of women by the physicians, he ordered that at least a third of all army nursing positions be held by females. Amanda Sterns, a nurse at Washington's Armory

Square Hospital, wrote home of a ward master named "Jobes" who did all he could for her in the face of disapproval from the head surgeon. When the chief surgeon ignored Sterns, Jobes made a point of introducing her as "the lady who is to have charge of the ward." The surgeon responded with a gruff "Humph!" Sadly, wrote Sterns, "[i]t is not every nurse here that has a Jobes." Nor was it every nurse that needed a Jobes. When Annie Wittenmeyer found the directing physician of her hospital "reeling drunk" and criticized him for it, he ordered her out of the hospital, yelling "I'm the boss here." Wittenmeyer quietly arranged to have the man dismissed. She found another surgeon stealing coffee intended for the patients. He too was soon fired.[15]

The soldiers very much appreciated women's efforts on their behalf, even if the surgeons did not. Among the most beloved was Mary Ann Bickerdyke, called "Mother" Bickerdyke by the grateful troops. She meant more to the army, insisted one soldier, "than the Madonna to Catholics." Astonished at her conviction and energy, one colleague wrote: "She talks bad grammar, jaws at us all . . . and is not afraid of anybody . . . but Lord, how she works!" When asked in 1861 to accompany medical supplies from her home in Galesburg, Illinois, to the troops in Cairo, Illinois, she promised to do more than that: "I'll go to Cairo, and I'll clean things up there. You don't need to worry about that, neither. Them generals and all ain't going to stop me. This is the Lord's work you're calling me to do." And the Lord was always on Mother Bickerdyke's side.[16]

Through little more than sheer force of will, she transformed Cairo's military hospitals from filthy wrecks to models of cleanliness and efficiency. She had the buildings cleaned top to bottom, ordered bathtubs made from barrels, set up decent kitchens, and had anyone who stood in her way dismissed or disciplined. After she caught an officer pilfering clothes slated for distribution to the patients, Bickerdyke stripped the man in public "leaving him nude save his pantaloons." When an officer complained of her tactics to William T. Sherman, the general brushed him aside with the reply, "She ranks me." Ulysses S. Grant told a surgeon who balked after she accused him of some impropriety: "My God, man, Mother Bickerdyke outranks everybody, even Lincoln. If you have run amuck of her I advise you to get out quickly before she has you under arrest."[17]

With their emphasis on cleanliness and proper diet, aspects of recovery so often ignored by the medical profession, women like

MRS. MARY A. BICKERDYKE.

Mary Ann Bickerdyke meant more to the army, said one soldier, "than the Madonna to Catholics." Ulysses S. Grant told a surgeon who balked after she accused him of some impropriety: "My God, man, Mother Bickerdyke outranks everybody, even Lincoln. If you have run amuck of her I advise you to get out quickly before she has you under arrest." (Abraham Lincoln Presidential Library)

Mother Bickerdyke saved thousands of lives. They sometimes saved lives too by direct intervention in treatment. Amputation was the most commonly overused procedure among Civil War doctors, and women charged with patient recovery often saw its ill effects more clearly than the surgeons. Sophronia Bucklin challenged one operation that she knew was unnecessary. The soldier's wound, she wrote, "was only that of a bullet through the fleshy part of the arm, and it seemed to be doing as well as could be expected. After the amputation, which did not discharge properly, his symptoms grew fatal." Mary Newcomb stood down a group of surgeons preparing to take a young soldier's arm off. She had seen the procedure used too many times as a first rather than a last resort, and she had seen the sad consequences. When she protested that the operation was premature, one old doctor reminded her that she was only a nurse. "I am well aware of that fact," Newcomb replied, "but I persist that that boy's arm shall not come off. I don't care who sent you nor what authority you work under. . . . I wear no shoulder-straps, but that boy's arm shall not come off while I am here." The surgeons moved on.[18]

Mary Walker, the only female doctor commissioned during the war, also cautioned against the overuse of amputation.

I made it my business, whenever I found that there were contemplated operations, and a complaint from a soldier that a decision had been made to remove a limb, I casually asked to see it, and in almost every instance I saw amputation was not only unnecessary, but to me it seemed wickedly cruel. I would then swear the soldier not to repeat anything that I told him, and then I would tell him that no one was obliged to submit to an amputation unless he chose to do so, that his limbs belonged to himself. I then instructed him to protest against amputation, and that if the physicians insisted upon it that if he had never used a swearing word to swear and declare that if they forced him to have an operation that he would never rest after his recovery until he had shot them dead. I need not say that secrecy regarding what I had told to the soldier was kept and that my advice was followed and that many a man today has for it the perfect and good use of his limbs who would not have had but for my advice, to say nothing about the millions of dollars in pensions that would have been paid without all the suffering, had I not decided in my solemn duty to the soldiers instead of carrying out etiquette towards my medical and surgical brothers.[19]

Walker, one of the first women in the United States to hold a medical degree, applied for a position as military surgeon in 1861 but was turned away by the U.S. Surgeon General's Office. Refusing a nurse's post, she informally volunteered her services until 1864, when General George Thomas, over strenuous objections from an examining board of surgeons, rewarded her sacrifice with a commission as assistant surgeon to the 52nd Ohio. Walker also served Thomas's Army of the Cumberland as a spy, which led to her capture by Confederates. One Rebel captain was astonished to find a female doctor among the prisoners. He wrote to his wife expressing amusement "at the sight of a *thing* that nothing but the debased and depraved Yankee nation could produce." Walker was sent to Castle Thunder prison in Richmond, though the captain thought she should have gone to "a lunatic asylum." Four months later, both sides implicitly recognized Walker's position when she was traded for a Confederate surgeon during a prisoner exchange.[20]

"So I Took the Major"

Social conventions of the day that downplayed women's capabilities also made them some of the war's most effective spies. Any notion of women engaging in such intrigue was so unthinkable, at least early in the war, that it was less likely they would be caught. For those who were, convention also offered some protection; no female spy faced execution during the war. But the opposing side's press was merciless toward them, hurling accusations of everything from prostitution to insanity. Newspaper editors on the other side were just as quick to hail them as heroines and avenging angels.[21]

Among the Confederacy's most renowned heroines was Rose O'Neal Greenhow, a Washington socialite with extensive political connections. It was Greenhow who sent warning to Confederates of the Union army's approach just before First Manassas. Even after her capture and confinement in the Old Capitol Prison, she continued funneling information south. In an effort to cut Greenhow off from her sources, officials finally banished her to the Confederacy. They did the same with Maria Isabella "Belle" Boyd of Matinsburg, Virginia (later West Virginia), who served as a spy for Stonewall Jackson during his Shenandoah Valley campaign in 1862. Information she sent to Jackson on Union strength at Front Royal was key to a Confederate victory there. Federals finally caught Boyd delivering dispatches in July and sent her to the Old Capitol Prison. She was released, arrested again, then fell in love with a Union officer, whom she married in October 1864. Antonia Ford, a Confederate spy from Virginia's Fairfax County who was instrumental in John Singleton Mosby's capture of Union General Edwin Stoughton, also married a union officer, Major Joseph Williard, after her capture. When a relative asked why she had married a northerner, Ford wrote, "I knew I could not revenge myself on the whole nation, but felt very capable of tormenting one yankee to death, so I took the Major."[22]

On the other side, ironically, most women who spied *for* the North were not *from* the North. With most military action occurring in the South and divisions running so deep among southerners, it should hardly be surprising that, like their men, so many southern women acted on their antisecession sentiments. Mary Gordon and Carrie King spied for the Union army in Georgia. Anna Campbell in northern Alabama rode seventy miles in thirty-six hours with intelligence for the Federals. In Tennessee, Lucy Williams rode through heavy rain to warn the Yankees of General John Hunt Morgan's planned attack. Acting on her word, they struck first and killed Morgan in the fray.[23]

Pauline Cushman, a New Orleans–born actress, established a

reputation as a staunch secessionist by toasting Jefferson Davis on stage in Louisville, Kentucky, then set out on a campaign of counterespionage. Working with the Union's Army of the Cumberland, Cushman wormed her way into the confidence of Nashville secessionists, all the while reporting their activities to the Yankees. She acted as a Federal courier too, and her exploits ranged from Kentucky and Tennessee through the northern tiers of Mississippi, Alabama, and Georgia. She was finally caught in the spring of 1863 near Shelbyville, Tennessee, with drawings she had taken from a Rebel army engineer. Cushman escaped, was recaptured, then rescued in a Union surprise attack. The Federals gave her an honorary commission, and she spent the rest of the war touring the North and lecturing on her exploits as the "Little Major."[24]

One of the most effective spies on either side was a middle-aged spinster named Elizabeth Van Lew, or "Crazy Bet" as she was known locally in Richmond. A member of one of Virginia's wealthiest families, Van Lew cultivated her reputation for mental instability by dressing strangely and wandering city streets singing nonsense songs. At one point she was seen in an outfit of "buckskin leggings, a one-piece skirt and waist of cotton, topped off with a huge calico sunbonnet." Adding to her unorthodox reputation were her long-standing antislavery views. She had freed the family slaves, made sure they were reunited with their spouses, and made her home a station on the underground railroad. But her unaware neighbors saw her as a harmless eccentric, gracious but too unbalanced to be a threat.

As one of the richest women in town, Van Lew played hostess in her palatial home to some of the Confederacy's most prominent figures. She relayed by secret code any information she gathered to the Federals, using slaves and free blacks eager to help as couriers. It was a nerve-wracking existence. As one report put it: "There was not a moment during those four years when Lizzie Van Lew could hear a step behind her on the street without expecting to have somebody tap her on the shoulder and say 'You are my prisoner.'" But no one ever did. When the Union army finally entered Richmond, her home was among the first to display the Stars and Stripes.[25]

Among northern women who spied for the Union, Sarah Emma Edmonds of Michigan was one of the most enthusiastic. So caught up in the excitement of post-Sumter patriotism was Edmonds that she enlisted as a man under the name "Franklin Thompson" and went to the Virginia front. Edmonds's first mission found her disguised not only as a man but a slave. Told to gather information on Confederate fortifications, she shaved her head nearly bald, rubbed on silver nitrate to temporarily darken her skin, and slipped through the picket lines. Edmonds soon fell in with a group of slaves headed for work on fortifications. If they found anything amiss with her, no one said a word. On the contrary, when it became obvious that she was having trouble with the heavy labor, she was, as she put it, "often helped by some good natured darkie." When she could, Edmonds made notes of conversations she overheard and drew diagrams of the Rebel works. When a Confederate officer sent her forward with food for the pickets, she secreted some of it to the slaves, delivered the rest as ordered to avoid suspicion, then took her opportunity to get back across the lines.[26]

"A Father Giving Birth to a Child"

Edmonds was but one of several hundred women known to have donned uniforms and posed as men during the war. Some estimates range as high as four hundred. In the most thorough treatment of the subject, *They Fought Like Demons: Women Soldiers in the American Civil War*, authors DeAnne Blanton and Lauren Cook document about two hundred and fifty. But, as Blanton and Cook point out, we will never know for sure how many there were. Some had their sex discovered only after they were wounded or died in battle. A Brooklyn girl of nineteen known only as "Emily" enlisted with a Michigan regiment while visiting an aunt. Her comrades learned her secret only after she was mortally wounded at Chickamauga. A Yankee burial detail at Gettysburg found an unnamed "female (private) in rebel uniform" among the dead.[27]

Sometimes pregnancy gave the soldier away. Union general William Rosecrans recorded that a sergeant under his command *"was delivered of a baby,"* which, he felt compelled to state, was "in violation of all military law and of the army regulation." In December 1864, a Confederate officer held at Johnson's Island as a prisoner of war gave birth to a "bouncing baby boy." The *Commercial Register* in nearby Sandusky, Ohio, wryly noted: "This is the first instance of a father giving birth to a child we have heard of." One woman in a

New York regiment was promoted for gallantry at the Battle of Fredericksburg shortly before she gave birth. Others like Jennie Hodges, who enlisted as Albert Cashier, held on to their male identities after the war. Hodges kept her secret until 1911 when she was carried to a veteran's hospital for treatment of injuries she suffered in an auto accident. Some took their secrets to the grave. In 1934, a man living near the Shiloh battlefield found the bones of nine soldiers while digging in his flower bed. All were shrouded in tattered bits of uniform. Investigators discovered that one set of remains was that of a woman.[28]

That women could become soldiers in the first place was relatively easy owing to lax medical exams. According to one report, physical fitness tests for the volunteers were rarely "more rigorous than holding out his hands to demonstrate that he had a working trigger finger, or perhaps opening his mouth to show that his teeth were strong enough to rip open a minié ball cartridge." When Sarah Edmonds signed up, the examiner simply took her hand and asked "Well, what sort of a living has this hand earned?" Mainly in getting an education, Edmonds replied. With that, the doctor passed her on and "Franklin Thompson" was sent off to war. When "Albert Cashier" enlisted, all she was required to display were her hands and feet.[29]

Why some women wanted to become soldiers is an altogether more involved question. For those who were discovered, the popular press often labeled them prostitutes. Perhaps some were, though it was easy enough to practice the trade without enduring a soldier's burdens. Most were probably driven by a taste for what they saw as adventure beyond the confines of convention. Such women saw enlistment as a chance to step beyond the restrictive roles in which society had placed them. Nellie Williams, when she was discovered, said that she volunteered simply because she enjoyed the soldier's life. Some poor women, like Sarah Wakeman of New York, were attracted by financial incentives. Ties of love drew some to the field when parting from an enlisted husband or lover was too painful for either partner. Malinda Blalock of North Carolina volunteered under the name "Sam," posing as her husband's brother. Another female Confederate soldier, Amy Clarke, enlisted to be with her husband and continued to serve after he was killed at Shiloh. So did Mary Owens of Pennsylvania, whose husband was killed in battle at her side. Owens was wounded three times before her comrades learned that she was a woman.[30]

"Teachers of the Young"

For women with some degree of formal education, expanded teaching opportunities offered more respectable and generally desirable employment than soldiering. The war helped create those opportunities, but they still often had to be forced. Though women had already made some limited inroads in the teaching profession before the war, there remained a general preference for male teachers. But many of the male teachers were going off to fight and taking their older students with them. Other men who tried to fill the gap frequently did so to dodge the draft and were hardly suited by qualification or temperament to be teachers. Seizing their chance, many women eagerly offered themselves as more desirable alternatives. Besides, they could be paid less than men, which was no small consideration in financially strapped communities that wanted a school. Most states at the time neither required nor supported public education.[31]

Many women encountered considerable family as well as societal opposition to their taking on teaching positions. Emma Holmes, a young South Carolina teacher, wrote in her diary of a friend's family opposition when she took up teaching at a local school. Holmes herself had similar family difficulties. Elizabeth Gimball's mother was "terribly mortified" at her daughter's desire to teach. Margaret Gillis enjoyed teaching at a plantation school, though her soldier husband was "very much hurt at my perversity." He returned home on furlough and pressured her to quit, but shortly after his departure she was teaching again.[32]

For Cora Benton of Albion, New York, teaching became not only her means of support but also of independence. Pregnant with their second child when her husband went off to war, Cora at first hardly knew what to do. There were bills and taxes to be paid, children to feed, and not nearly enough income with which to do it. She finally decided to start her own boarding school and made it a great success. Before her husband returned, Cora felt so self-assured that she wrote to him: "There will be two heads after this do you understand, darling?"[33]

Independence was a constant motivating theme among those women who went into teaching. "My restless desire for independence is quite as strong as ever," wrote one young woman who took up teaching to free herself of reliance on her father. The profession had little choice but to give in to such determined women. *"Our females must engage in the work of teaching,"* wrote the president of North Carolina's Davidson College in 1864, "for there is no other alternative." As Georgia's *Augusta Daily Constitutionalist* put it, the war had "swallowed up" most of the young men bound for the teaching profession. "We are left with no resource then but to have female teachers." It was just as well, wrote the paper, since women were better "fitted, naturally and morally, for teachers of the young."[34]

Some women did take naturally to teaching. "I had rather teach than do anything else in the world," wrote one women enthusiastically. But even for the best of them it was no easy task. Shortages of nearly every type of school supply, especially in the South, proved to be a constant source of frustration. So did the unruly nature of many students. Some women found that their love of the academic disciplines left them little patience for students who did not share that love. Nor did it prepare them to dispense discipline effectively in the classroom. Low salaries offered little consolation for the disenchanted, though most had little choice but to persevere. A Vermont woman admitted that she "despised" teaching, but in her town there were only two occupations open to women. They could work as domestics from "dawn till nine P.M." for two dollars a week or teach five months a year for three dollars a week. Teaching was, for her, the lesser of two evils. Some married out of teaching as soon as they could. Others sought alternative employment. Elizabeth Richmond of North Carolina was by 1864 so "worn out" with the "duties and privations" of teaching that she wrote to Governor Vance hoping for "a place of employment that will not require as much energy of mind and body, and yet, will give me a comfortable support." Specifically, she wanted to know if he had a position for her as a clerk in some government office.[35]

"Government Girls"

As with teachers, the war created a shortage of literate men able to staff expanding posts in state and national offices. In 1861, Treasurer of the United States Francis Spinner hired the first "government girls," presenting the action as both a necessity and an economy measure—women were more plentiful and could be paid less. The same was true in the Confederacy, where Secretary of the Treasury

Christopher Memminger noted that each vacancy announcement brought a hundred applications from women in dire need of employment. North and South, most women had to take the leftovers as well-connected men scrambling to avoid conscription got the choice positions. And class was a factor too, especially in the South, where so many well-to-do ladies were falling on hard times. Of the government jobs women could get, the best went to the best connected. In such offices as the War Department, the Commissary General, the Quartermaster Department, and the Treasury Department, coveted government clerkships were generally offered to those women with letters of reference from the most prominent society folk. And their salaries reflected it. In 1863, a Confederate private received $11 a month. Female clerks got $65. A year later they were making $3,000 to account for inflation.[36]

Still, the thought of any society woman working a salaried job outside the home remained scandalous in higher circles. One southern belle wrote scornfully of a friend employed by the Treasury Department who had to walk home "in the broiling sun. See what this dreadful war has brought delicate ladies to." Mary Chesnut and a friend, Mrs. John Preston, agreed that neither could give themselves over to such humiliation: "Survive or perish—we will not go into one of the departments. We will not stand up all day and cut notes apart, ordered round by a department clerk. We will live at home with our families and starve in a body. Any homework we will do. Any menial service— under the shadow of our own rooftree. Department—never!"[37] Actually, there was little danger that either Chesnut or Preston, wives of a senator and general respectively and both mistresses of large plantations, would ever have to do much heavy labor themselves in or out of the home. But the comment reflected a strong upper-crust assumption that the dividing line of class was as much a matter of appearance as economic circumstance and had to be maintained at all costs. Those who failed to do so could expect little sympathy from women who had not yet been forced to chose between starvation and the degradation of work.

That presumed degradation was not simply one of class but also of a sexual double standard. Unlike men, any respectable society woman who sought outside work carried with her a suspicion of less than virtuous motives, especially if that work brought her into regular contact with men outside her close circle of family and friends. Long held by the middle and upper classes was an assumption of loose sexuality among working-class women generally. Having pointed the finger of disdain for so long, many society women in dire straits now saw that finger turned against them. During the war's last year a group of female government workers were transferred from Virginia to Columbia, South Carolina. Without knowing anything of their backgrounds, high born or low, the local gentry disparaged them all as "fast" women.[38]

Such broad disparagement was just as common in the North, where newspapers accused "government girls" of everything from distracting male colleagues to "corrupting public morals." "Guilty until proven innocent" was the prevailing view, and the sentence could sometimes be death. In April 1864 Congressman James Brooks of New York demanded an investigation of the Treasury Department, which he called "a house for orgies." A congressional committee chaired by James A. Garfield investigated charges that Spencer Clark, a Treasury official, was having illicit relations with three young women in his office. It appointed as lead investigator Lafayette Baker, provost marshal of the War Department, who threw himself into the witch hunt with all the moral fervor and certitude of a zealot.

Sidestepping a direct attack on Clark, Baker went after the women. He broke into their rooms, confiscated their property, placed them under arrest, told each that the others had admitted to the charges, and forced them to sign confessions or face confinement in the Old Capitol Prison. When one of the women, Laura Duvall, died during the first week of committee hearings, Baker claimed that her death was the result of a botched abortion. So eager was Baker to prove his point that he had Duvall's casket taken from the hearse on its way to the cemetery and ordered three doctors to do a thorough autopsy. To Baker's disappointment and embarrassment, all three agreed that Duvall's body showed "incontestable evidence of unsullied virtue." She had died a virgin. What killed her was pneumonia, aggravated by, if not resulting from, the stress of Baker's inquisition. The committee chastised Baker, calling his treatment of Duvall's remains "a barbarity rarely surpassed," but he apparently suffered no further repercussions.[39]

As cruel as professional circumstances could be for women in government offices, salaries and working conditions were generally far worse for lower-class women employed in public or private industry.

Harper's Weekly published this rendering of women assembling rifle cartridges at an arsenal in Watertown, Massachusetts. Such work was hazardous. Nineteen female employees died in an explosion at the Washington Arsenal. A cartridge factory in Virginia blew up, "scattering workers like confetti." The accident killed thirty-two women and injured thirty others.

For many of them, unlike their higher-class counterparts, work outside the home was nothing new. By 1860 women held 25 percent of the nation's manufacturing jobs. In New England they made up 65 percent of the industrial workforce. The war brought even more women into the factories, but hardly to their benefit. They found themselves increasingly at the mercy of corrupt government contractors, who skimmed their wages for everything from the cost of thread to the time spent at meals.

Much of the work was increasingly hazardous. Nineteen female employees died in an explosion at the Washington Arsenal. Another such accident in Jackson, Mississippi, took the lives of fifteen. Women were killed in similar explosions at Pennsylvania's Allegheny Arsenal and Connecticut's Waterbury Flask and Cask Company. A cartridge factory in Virginia blew up, "scattering workers like confetti." The mishap killed thirty-two women and injured thirty others. After nearly fifty Richmond women died in an ordnance factory explosion, a city newspaper asked why "poor women engaged in a perilous and hazardous occupation . . . are denied a living compensation for their labour, when so many of the departments are filled with *young ladies* . . . at salaries equal to and in some cases better than the best male clerks in the different departments."[40]

Though women's pay for the same work was on average less than half that of men, it was true that well-connected *"young ladies"* holding government clerkships were often paid lucrative salaries while poor seamstresses in the Quartermaster Department were making barely enough to survive. In private industry, North and South, salaries for working-class women were even more dismal. "How shall women, dependent on their own exertions for a livelihood, find remunerative employment?" asked Mary Livermore of the Sanitary Commission. "There is sewing," she wrote, "which is another name for suicide or starvation." One New York seamstress who made eleven cents a day sewing underwear felt fortunate if she was able to "get to bed about daylight, and sleep two or three hours." Some women got no wage at all. Businesses often held newly employed women to a six-month "training" term during which they received no pay. After that, they might get two or three dollars a week but were often fired to make room for a new crop of unpaid "trainees." On the whole, wages for working folk never kept pace with inflation during the war. In many jobs held by women, mostly in the clothing industry, salaries had actually declined by the war's midpoint.[41]

"More Just Compensation of Female Labor"

Late in 1863, "A Needy Soldier's Wife" of Montgomery, Alabama, wrote in a letter to the city press that she and her children simply could not survive on the twelve dollars a week she got as a government seamstress. The cost of beef and other basic commodities was much too high. With winter coming on, she wondered how Montgomery's well-to-do could "enjoy their warm houses and comfortable beds" when so many poor women and children were in such dire straits. In a petition to President Davis, Montgomery women wrote that they were willing to "work to support ourselves and little ones" but they had to get more for their labors or perish. From Cincinnati came a petition to President Lincoln signed by the working "wives, widows, sisters, and friends of the soldiers." They were "willing and anxious to do the work required by the Government for clothing and equipping the armies of the United States," but pleaded that they were "unable to sustain life for the price offered by contractors, who fatten on their contracts by grinding immense profits out of the labor of their operatives." A delegation representing over 10,000 Philadelphia seamstresses called on Lincoln at the White House "to inform him of the relation that existed between themselves and the contractors of the Government." They begged for his help in getting them a living wage. Lincoln asked the Quartermaster Department to make sure they got "the wages ordinarily paid," but the wages women ordinarily got hardly provided a living.[42]

Lacking substantive help under either government, Union or Confederate, self-help was the order of the day for workingwomen. In Detroit, they established a Sewing Women's Protective Association, set up their own sewing machines in the association hall, and bypassed the contractors by contracting with the government themselves. Few such women's unions could provide enough machines for all their members, but the competition they offered sometimes gave women leverage enough to force better wages from regular contractors. Similar workingwomen's unions were formed in Boston, Philadelphia, Baltimore, Chicago, Buffalo, Worcester, and Brooklyn.

In Providence, a women's union organized to boycott employers who had used strikebreakers. The Working Women's Protective Union of New York City trained women for new jobs and set up a placement service for its members to discourage overcrowding in particular trades. It also helped combat one of the most underhanded practices of the garment industry—that of employers withholding pay for so-called imperfect work. It was the employers who decided how "imperfect" was defined, and they always defined it to their own advantage. For some employers, little if any work was good enough. It was in large part through the efforts of the Women's Protective Union that legislation was enacted penalizing those contractors who refused to pay women for their work. So persistent was the organization in pressing for enforcement that a threat of legal action was sometimes enough to force employer cooperation. An 1880 treasurer's report listed 27,292 disputes settled, over 20,000 of them out of court, since the organization's founding in 1864.[43]

Women encountered stiff resistance to their organizing efforts not only from employers but also from men who saw workingwomen as a drag on their own employment and wages. The Journeymen's Tailors' Association of St. Louis vowed to "resist any attempt to introduce female apprentices" and condemned women "mixing with men in a workshop from morning to night." *Fincher's Trades' Review* warned that returning soldiers would "esteem it a poor reward for all their sacrifice to find every avenue choked up by their wives and daughters at half paying prices." But realities of the labor market and the determination of women themselves made clear that they were becoming a permanent part of the general workforce. The more farsighted among male labor leaders soon realized that the best way to get fair wages for men was to demand the same for women. Several influential male labor leaders spoke at a meeting of the New York Working Women's Union promising their full support. By the fall of 1863, even *Fincher's Review* was campaigning for "more just compensation of female labor." It encouraged women to organize for fair wages and pressed men to help them do so, "for no person claiming to be a *man* would shrink from any duty assigned him in such a cause."[44]

With or without men's help, women were taking action for fair pay and working conditions. In October 1863 a union of one thousand female umbrella sewers in New York City and Brooklyn went on strike. The women, who worked eighteen hours a day for six to eight cents per umbrella and had to furnish their own needles and thread, were asking for an extra two cents on the umbrella covers. Some employers gave in; others did not. When women at the city's Miller Shoe Company went on strike, they got the requested 12.5 percent wage increase. Another New York employer fired all his striking seamstresses and brought in strikebreakers. The *New York Herald* expressed sympathy for the strikers, acknowledging that "no class in the community has greater claim to the sympathies than our sewing girls who work for inadequate wages."[45]

The same could be said for female workers in southern industries, who were just as determined to get pay equity. Facing dangerous conditions and low wages, women at Augusta's gunpowder works staged a walkout in October 1864 after being refused a raise to supplement a salary eaten away by rampant inflation. Management replaced them with strikebreakers at a barely living wage. One local paper called it "criminal" to offer "a schedule of pay upon calculation of the minimum amount of food it requires to sustain a human life." Women at Richmond's government arsenal, the Confederate States Laboratory, met with little more success. They went on strike for higher pay and got it, but on a sliding scale whereby after ten months married women were making 40 percent more than those who were unmarried. In October 1864, all three hundred of the laboratory's female employees went on strike to have all their salaries set to the higher level, with married women already at that level supporting the move. Management reacted by putting out a call for three hundred strikebreakers, much to the women's astonished disappointment. The *Richmond Examiner* was appalled. Its editor reminded readers that these women "engaged in a perilous and hazardous occupation" for much less pay than the well-to-do female "pets" employed at government offices.[46]

Such class disparity was just as prevalent among women of the rural South. As historian Laura Edwards notes: "Everything about the Civil War was far worse for white women from yeoman and propertyless families than it was for their wealthier white neighbors. Instead of making do with less, they went without. Their clothes went to rags, their farms went to weeds, their livestock went to the Confederate army, and they went hungry. When their husbands and fathers were killed, they lost their land, were evicted from their homes, and were expected to make ends meet on their own."[47]

"I Can Only Dream of Being with You"

Though more privileged than their poorer neighbors, women of the slaveholding classes were hardly free from worry. Chief among their concerns was that they held slaves at all. In areas of the black belt from which most white males had gone off to war, slaves became increasingly defiant. Despite their public insistence that slaves were generally content, slaveholders knew better than anyone besides the slaves themselves that discontent was the norm. That was certainly clear to Jane Eubanks of Columbia County, Georgia, who wrote to Governor Brown about needing men assigned to control local slaves. There were four hundred slaves in her vicinity and few white men to keep them subdued. In December 1863, Mrs. John Green of Burke County wrote to Brown about the lack of white men in her area, called away by the draft. She urged the governor to create a police force for the protection of Georgia's "planting interest." Green insisted that Brown must "see to it, that [the planter] class of citizens are protected."[48]

Eubanks and Green were hardly alone in worrying about the possibility of slave rebellion. "It is dreadful to dwell on insurrections," wrote a South Carolina slaveholding widow. Still, she could not ignore the risk. "Many an hour have I laid awake in my life thinking of our danger . . . we know not what moment we may be hacked to death in the most cruel manner by our slaves." Though such fears were most often unfounded, the danger for some slaveholders was real enough. Early in the war, another widowed Carolina slaveholder was smothered to death by her slaves. When she heard of the murder, Ada Bacot wrote of her own slaves: "I fear twould take very little to make them put me out of the way." Mrs. A. Ingraham of Vicksburg shared Bacot's concerns: "I fear the blacks more than I do the Yankees." A Virginia woman felt that having slaves was like having "enemies in our own households."[49]

Some slaveholding women used both connections and the threat of slave rebellion to get their husbands out of military service. Mrs. Richard B. Hill of Early County, Georgia, penned a letter to the governor requesting an exemption for her husband. She wrote that he had charge of his mother's and sister's plantations and had just sold his own to purchase other lands. Of course, he would need to remain home to take care of the transaction. Hill pointed out that "only the enrolling officers need know of your exemption," suggesting that the matter be kept confidential. Brown responded that it was not in his power to grant her request since he had no control over the enrolling officers of the Confederacy. However, if her husband joined a state company, Brown could detail him at home as an overseer where he could conveniently take care of his pending purchase and ease his family's fear of being left alone with the slaves.

Mrs. Mitchell Jones of Brooks County, whose husband was already in the army, wrote to Brown asking his release. A slave conspiracy organized by a local white man had been discovered, and one of her slaves was involved. She asked that her husband be allowed to come home and administer proper punishment even though the Quitman jailer had already thoroughly beaten the slave and thrown him in the county jail. But Jones feared more slave unrest. "I believe," she wrote, "I would rather fall into the hands of the Yankees than the Negroes."[50]

From early in the war, some nonslaveholders had suggested that one way to head off insurrection might be to put slaves in the army, especially those held by "speculating" planters. Mrs. C.J. Owen of Georgia's Putnam County, upset that local planters were "heaping up money on sufferings of the poor," insisted that those "rich speculators and extortioners should be compelled to send a part of their negros to fight." As it stood, slaves were being used only to "uphold their aristocratic owners who are nothing but Vampires."[51]

Such class resentment reflected not only disgust at the war profits slaveholders were reaping but also that those profits came at the expense of poor farming folk. Planters' cotton overproduction meant food was harder to buy. The draft meant fewer men at home and less labor to grow food. What food women could grow was frequently carried off by impressment officers, leaving them little to eat or sell. It all meant that women had to work more and more for less and less. When a soldier "saw two women each with a yoke of oxen plowing a field by the roadside" in southern Missouri, he lamented that the draft had taken away almost all the male farmers. The same was true in North Carolina, where Nancy Jordan wrote to the governor: "There are many others besides myself who have neither brother husband nor Father at home to cut our wheat and no slave labor to depend on."[52]

Northern farm women too were feeling the pressure of absent men. After a day of hoeing potatoes, a Michigan wife wrote to her husband of having "lameness in my arms and a pair of hands pretty badly blistered. . . . It takes me a good while for I cannot work very fast." On one New York farm, a woman and her seven daughters plowed, dragged, sowed, and rolled 100 acres of wheat. They also kept twenty-two cows milked, and made butter and cheese. A Wisconsin farm wife wrote of women in her region planting and hoeing corn, harrowing with oxen, and binding grain. Many farm women and children had done all these things before the war. But with so many of their men taken by the army, the burdens of farm work were now entirely on their shoulders. And like southern women, they worked more for less—so much more that the farm production rate per worker rose 1.35 percent per year during the 1860s, faster than at any other time during the nineteenth century. As historians Lee Craig and Thomas Weiss discovered, that increase was due not so much to farm mechanization, as has been the traditional interpretation, but to "increased labor inputs of women and children, in numbers, effort, and—especially—time."[53]

Letters from soldiers to their wives were filled with advice on how to get along until they returned home. In November 1863, William Asbell wrote to his wife Sarah: "I have received both of your letters and was glad to hear Through Them that you are all alive but sorry to know that the children are sick on your hands when I cannot be there to assist you with Them." William told Sarah to feed their hogs corn once a day and potatoes the rest of the time. "If the children are not able to dig the potatoes," he said, "fence off a portion of the patch for [the hogs]." As the weather grew colder and food ran low, William wrote his wife, "You had better try and sell one or other of the horses . . . as you are scarce of Provisions. You will have to do the best you can."[54]

Separation from male loved ones was not simply an economic hardship but a severely emotional one as well. Mary Livermore, a nurse with the Sanitary Commission, had seen men wounded in every imaginable way. Yet she wrote that their pain was hardly worse than that of their women who had to watch them march off to war "knowing full well the risks they run—this involves exquisite suffering, and calls for another kind of courage." Melissa Wells of Michigan wrote to her husband Ben in late 1863:

I have spent many gloomy and unhappy hours since you have been in the South. I hope I may never experience such feelings again for it is suffering indeed. Many times have I received a letter from you and would think that perhaps it was the last I would receive. . . . Many such times have I seen during the past two years, for instance when you were sick last winter and all communications cut off from Nashville . . . and then again last spring when you relapsed and was sick with the fever at Murfreesboro. . . . I often think I never knew what trouble was until since the commencement of this horrid rebellion, but how many others there are who have learned the same by bitter experience.[55]

Most bolstered their courage with faith that the future held better times. "I believe thare is happy days on earth for us yet," wrote Malinda Taylor of Alabama to her husband Grant. "Trust in God. He is the only helper." Until those happier days arrived, she found comfort living in her dreams. She closed one of her letters to Grant: "I dreamed of sleeping with you last night." Jennie Thompson of Iowa wrote to her husband: "Oh, how I wish I could sleep with you tonight. . . . But I can only dream of being with you and that is very pleasant for I see you every night in my dreams."[56]

Sallie Lovett of Troup County, Georgia, also wrote in moving terms of how the days dragged by as she waited for her husband Billie's return.

My dearest husband:

It is with a sad and heavy heart I take my pen in hand to write you a few lines. I received your very welcome letter last evening, glad indeed to hear from you and hear you was getting along so well. For it is more than I am. Billie, I am in so much trouble this evening. I have looked for you so hard today. I thought you would be sure to come. . . . Every time I hear a train I go to the door. I say, well, I do hope Billie [will] come down on that train. I wait and look until dinner. Then I say, well, I do hope he will come this evening. I wait until dark. No Billie yet. Then I bring a long sigh, perhaps a tear and say, well, I don't know why he don't come. Every time I hear a noise towards the gate I run to the door, but what do I see: nothing but trees and bushes. I strain my eyes almost out of their sockets but no Billie can I see. I turn 'round with a sigh. To think he has forgotten me! . . . I am not living any now, only breathing. It is true I am well in body but not at heart. My heart is grieved, the worst of all diseases. Honey, why don't you come home?[57]

Melissa Wells asked the same of her Ben in December 1863: "How I wish you could come home soon—by Christmas anyhow. . . . I have paid but little attention to the holidays for the last two years for I felt that I could not enjoy them very well as long as my companion was in the army, but if he will only come home now I think I can enjoy myself as well as the rest." Ben did get a furlough, his only one of the war. The time it gave him and Melissa was all too brief. After his departure, Melissa wrote to Ben that the "ten short days were soon past and they did not seem more than half as long as any other ten days. Time always passes swiftly away when we enjoy ourselves the best. It is one week ago tomorrow since we parted; that was a sad parting indeed."[58]

Such sad partings were repeated hundreds of thousands of times. Few were more poignant than when Malinda Taylor and her young son Leonard took Grant to Demopolis, Alabama, for transport to Mobile after his furlough. A few days later Malinda wrote to Grant: "The day I left you I knew that you was looking after us. Leonard cried for several Miles before we got out of sight of you. He would say poor Pa is standing there yet. I thought I would venture to look back. I looked back just as you turned to go back. Your being at home seems like a dream to me. Grant, I don't think I can feel any wors when you are dead than I did when I got home and opend the doors and saw your coat and hat and the rest of you[r] things that you had wore while you was at home."[59]

"To Risk a Certain Event"

As eager as soldiers' wives were to see their husbands home, if only for a short time, their joy could be tempered not only by the sadness of parting but also by the fear of an unplanned pregnancy. When she learned that her husband was coming home, one woman called the possibility of becoming pregnant a "*horrible* nightmare which would always frighten away any little happiness that might occasionally cross my path." Most soldiers' wives were having a hard enough time caring for themselves and what children they had. The last thing they needed was a debilitating pregnancy and another mouth to feed. After her husband's furlough, Amanda Bullock wrote to him of her relief that their time together had not resulted in pregnancy, "for none but myself can tell my dread of such suffering." Still, she wrote, "I would not have you stay a way from me for any thing in the world[.] just to be with you a little while will compensate me for a great deal, and I will hope that the something will not happen."[60]

Some women might have risked pregnancy out of fear that if their husbands could not get full satisfaction at home they might look for it elsewhere. Soldiers far from home found opportunities enough for extramarital sex. When prostitutes began making regular visits to his camp, Jesse Reid of the 4th South Carolina wrote to his wife: "If you could be here on those occasions you would think that there was not a married man in the regiment but me. A great many of them are married men." Reid was quick to distance himself from the proceedings, but the subtle message of available sex could not have been missed. Others, teasingly or not, were hardly so subtle. A Yankee officer wrote to his wife: "I now have two very pretty rebel girls on my hands as prisoners and what the devil to do with them I don't know, as I don't like to put them in the guard house. I expect I will have to take them into my room and let them sleep with me."[61]

James Simpson, on station in Virginia, wrote home to his wife Addie in Montgomery, Alabama, of his plan to visit a local belle "who they say lets almost any body make love [i.e., flirt] and talk poetry to her." Addie took the jibe as a titillating jest, but others were not so certain that their husbands' intentions were simply to tease. Even if they were, some still resented the implication. When Dorsey Pender wrote to his wife, Fanny, of his casual attentions to some attractive Virginia ladies, she replied with indignation: "I did not think you would trifle with my feelings in that way.... Nothing you have ever said this whole of our married life every pained me so acutely or grieved me so deeply. I know you are sorry for it now, for you must feel it to be unjust, but it is enough to know that you could, in any mood, say so much to pain me." One Louisiana wife was pained as well when she received a letter from her husband that had been intended for another woman—one he had recently married in Virginia. He had placed the letter in the wrong envelope.[62]

Despite the possibility of their husbands' infidelity, such was their overriding fear of pregnancy that some women took every precaution they could to prevent it. Lizzie Neblett of Texas wrote to her husband Will before he came home: "I had rather meet a woods full of bare than meet you after a long absence, when I feared the love I bare you would ... make me willing for your sake to risk a certain event happening." But Lizzie had given birth to her fifth and unplanned child just two months after he left home. She would take no chances on a sixth. "If you cant comply with my orders ... about the preventatives to come in your pocket home—you may come without, but must submit, to my laws after reaching home & you need not fear that they will not be made strict enough to ensure my safety."[63]

Women's efforts to avoid pregnancy were not always successful. Sometimes the cause was faulty contraception. Often pregnancy resulted from men neglecting to hold themselves in check. All too often, men simply forced themselves upon unwilling women. Rape, in or out of marriage, was hardly uncommon. When unplanned pregnancy occurred, especially under violent circumstances, abortion was a frequently sought option—increasingly so during the Civil War. In 1860, Dr. Edwin M. Hale of Chicago wrote in his *On the Homeopathic Treatment of Abortion* that 20 percent of all pregnancies ended with abortion. By war's end, his research showed the abortion rate at 25 percent.[64]

Most women had little enthusiasm for childbearing in wartime not only for the burdens more children imposed but also for the impact war had on the children themselves. One woman called it "sorrowful" to see young children playing at war—sometimes violently. They built small forts, fired toy guns at each other, pretended to amputate limbs, and fought over who was to be the prisoner of whom. "It is sad indeed," she lamented, "that they must learn such things in their very infancy." Even sadder was that so many children barely out of their infancy were not playing war but participating in the real thing. Tens of thousands of youngsters not yet eighteen served in the military. Tens of thousands more were caught up in partisan warfare in the border states and across the South's pine barrens and hill country. Youth offered little protection against injury or death. At thirteen years of age, John Mather Sloan of the 9th Texas lost a leg in combat near Farmington, West Virginia. Fourteen-year-old Orion Howe of the 55th Illinois was "severely wounded" while serving as a courier at Vicksburg. Confederate troopers summarily shot and killed David Shelton, a boy of thirteen, along with his father and older brothers over a few sacks of salt. The Sheltons were North Carolina unionists suspected of involvement with a raid on hoarded salt supplies at the town of Marshall.[65]

"O, They Have Killed My Darling"

Countless mothers across the country felt the crushing loss of beloved sons as the war ground on. Eliza Upchurch of Illinois lost three of her boys to the war. Nancy Rhodes of Maine lost four. So did Ora Palmer of North Carolina, all of them killed at Gettysburg. Polly Ray, also of North Carolina, had seven of her sons killed. In Dale County, Alabama, Sarah McDonald walked the yard and cried all day when her youngest son James enlisted. "He returned home a corpse," recalled one of James's siblings, "and then the climax came. My father sent for Dr. Plant. . . . He attended Mother all during the night, she fainting away and giving up at the death of her precious boy."[66]

Mary Chesnut wrote of a South Carolina mother who "heard her son was killed—had hardly taken in the horror of it" when she got word that it had all been a mistake. Someone had confused her son's name with that of another soldier. "She fell on her knees with a shout of joy. . . . The household was totally upset. The swing back of the pendulum from the scene of weeping and wailing of a few moments

Barbara McCoy Howell had five sons who fought in the war. Three did not survive the conflict. One of her neighbors lamented that "this inhuman war is putting our whole country in mourning." (Georgia Department of Archives and History)

before was very exciting." But the family's relief was short lived. There had been no mistake. A few moments later, up drove a hearse with her dead boy in his coffin. This shock put the poor woman "at the point of death with brain fever; the sudden changes from joy to grief were more than she could bear."[67]

After being told that her husband had been killed and her son was wounded and captured, one woman covered herself with a shawl and sat motionless. Someone finally lifted the shawl and found that the woman was dead. "Does anybody wonder so many women die?" asked Mary Chesnut. "Grief and constant anxiety kill nearly as many women as men die on the battlefield." Trying to calm his wife's fears, James Curtright of Troup County, Georgia, wrote home on October 6, 1862: "My heart is fuller than ever of love to you. . . . Knowing the uneasiness you constantly feel about me, nothing I can write will keep you from feeling so, but I do desire you to try & look on the bright side of the Picture. I know you will say that there is no bright side, but I think there is, & from past protections & safteys we can with confidence ask for a continuation of these." But past protection held no guarantees for the future. Two days later Curtright died in the Battle of Perryville and was buried near the battlefield. It was years after the war before a nephew found Curtright's grave and had his remains moved home to rest beside those of his wife.[68]

It was hardly uncommon for soldiers' remains to be lost for years if not forever. Even getting timely word of a soldier's death was difficult enough. In her study of women and the war, Mary Massey wrote of how "women often waited months before hearing of their husbands' death and some never received official confirmation. Those living near telegraph lines and railroads might make it a habit to meet the trains and scan the casualty lists posted outside the telegraph or newspaper offices, but others tucked away in isolated areas could only wait, pray, and hope." She wrote of one scene in South Carolina where " 'poor country women with babes in their arms' converged on the Spartanburg depot hours before a train was due to arrive so that they might hear the casualty lists read. The tense silence was broken only by the calling of names until a penetrating 'shriek' informed the crowd that 'some poor woman' had lost a loved one."[69]

When women got the sad news of a family member's death, they sometimes set out to retrieve the body if they could. One mother journeyed 450 miles to claim her son's remains. She spent the train ride back home waving flies away from his corpse. For women who could not make such a trip right away or learned of a loved one's death weeks or months later, they found only bones to be carried back in a satchel if they found any remains at all.[70] The chances of a successful search were better, though no less heartrending, if it were conducted in a battle's immediate aftermath. Private Sam Watkins recalled one search among the dead after the Battle of Chickamauga.

> While a detail of us were passing over the field of death and blood, with a dim lantern, looking for our wounded soldiers to carry to the hospital, we came across a group of ladies, looking among the killed and wounded for their relatives, when I heard one of the ladies say, "There they come with their lanterns." I approached the ladies and asked them for whom they were looking. They told me the name, but I have forgotten it. We passed on, and coming to a pile of our slain, we had turned over several of our dead, when one of the ladies screamed out, "O, there he is! Poor fellow! Dead, dead, dead!" She ran to the pile of slain and raised the dead man's head and placed it on her lap and began kissing him and saying, "O, O, they have killed my darling, my darling, my darling! O, mother, mother, what must I do! My poor, poor darling! O, they have killed him, they have killed him!" I could witness the scene no longer. I turned and walked away, and William A.

Hughes was crying, and remarked, "O, law me; this war is a terrible thing."[71]

Women reacted to the loss of their men with indignation as well as grief. Some blamed the enemy for their misery. After an Arkansas woman found the bodies of her husband and two brothers on the Prairie Grove battlefield, she let go a volley of curses on the "God-damned Federals" and wished them all "in hell." Others ranted against their own government. "What do I care for patriotism," asked one distraught soldier's wife. "My husband is my country. What is country to me if he be killed?" When Margaret Preston heard that her stepson was dead, she asked defiantly, "Who thinks or cares for victory now!" Many women simply blamed war itself for the ever-present reality of death. After searching the field for her wounded cousin at Seven Pines and seeing men "in every stage of mutilation," Constance Cary Harrison declared herself "permanently convinced that nothing is worth war!"[72]

"Resisting His Violence"

Women's fears of physical danger as a direct result of war were not confined to their men. That was especially true across vast stretches of the South where partisan conflict and invading armies posed a constant threat to women's safety. In Madison County, North Carolina, Confederate cavalry tortured the wives and mothers of suspected unionist, or "tory," gang members. In an effort to get information on their men's hideout, the horsemen tied up and beat several women, an eighty-five-year-old and a seventy-year-old among them. In neighboring Montgomery County, Rebel home guards regularly harassed and assaulted Union women. Adam Brewer of nearby Moore County, leader of one such home guard unit, ordered his men to shoot down three women who had thwarted his attempt to capture a seventeen-year-old deserter. They were saved only by the refusal of Brewer's men to fire.[73]

Some women were not so fortunate. Pro-Confederates in Cooke County, Texas, lynched a soldier's wife in front of her three young children. Her crime had been to publicly express hope that the Federals would soon overrun the state so her husband could stay home with

his family. In the vicinity of Cleveland, Tennessee, Confederate guerrillas shot a woman for holding similar views. Near Bull's Gap, Confederate soldiers hanged several Union women who refused to reveal
their husbands' whereabouts. They shot another for no more than
"making a too free use of her tongue."[74]

Southern women were just as abused by rampaging Union troops,
though dangers to food and valuables were usually greater than threats
of physical violence. When such threats were made, they were often
met with daring defiance. After a Yankee soldier exposed himself to
one Arkansas woman, she grabbed her gun and fired twice at him.
When a Yankee officer made a veiled threat toward Evelyn Smith, informing her that "we sometimes divest Southern women of their
clothes," she warned him that if he laid a hand on her, he would never
again be able to ride a horse. But resistance could prove dangerous and
sadly futile. Private Frederick Wells of New York, according to court
records, "did enter the house of one Mary Harvey of Winchester, Virginia, and did then and there attempt to commit a rape . . . striking her
on the face and head for resisting his violence and attempting to defend herself." Near Tullahoma, Tennessee, Lieutenant Harvey John
of the 49th Ohio beat and raped Catherine Farmer. In Tennessee's
Shelby County, three armed privates of the 2nd New Jersey Cavalry—
Thomas Johnson, John Callahan, and Jacob Snover—broke into the
home of Margaret Brooks and took turns raping her. Most soldiers got
light jail terms for such assaults when they were punished at all. In a
rare exception, Johnson, Callahan, and Snover were executed by firing
squad.[75]

Relations between southern women and Union troops were not always so antagonistic. In Federally occupied cities where loneliness and
poverty had stalked so many for so long, some women welcomed the
soldiers' company and their greenbacks—much to the disgust of die-
hard Rebels. A Nashville belle wrote to her brother in the Confederate
army that the city's women were "dropping off into the arms of the
ruthless invader." One was his own sweetheart, who was now singing
"Rally Round the Flag Boys" and "The Union Forever" with Federal
officers who visited her each evening. Another women who had slept
"with the Bonnie Blue Flag under her pillow and looked pistols and
daggers at the invaders" was now keeping company with them. One
had "gone the way of all flesh and married an officer with that de-
testable eagle on his shoulder." "Marry who you can" was the theme

among local women. She warned her brother that there would be few if any unwed girls left by the time he and his friends got back home.[76]

"To Extend Their Gentle Favors"

Soldiers could not always be taken at their word, especially when it came to promises of marriage. Sixteen-year-old Mary French was by all accounts "a very respectable young girl" when she took up with Lieutenant William Henry. The Union officer led Mary to believe that his intentions were honorable and had been sleeping with her for a month when a sergeant of Henry's acquaintance recorded the truth in his diary: "Alas she is unaware that disgrace and disappointment are in store. She fondly hopes some day to be his wife. She does not know that Henry has a family at home." The sergeant blamed Henry for the deception, but took no steps to warn Mary. He viewed her now as a soiled woman for whom there could be but one fate: "She will soon be added to the no. of prostitutes that throng our cities and towns and hang around the camps of our soldiers."[77]

Thousands of women met that fate in increasing numbers as the war went on. One reporter wrote that "Boston absolutely swarms with strumpets" and that New York had "at least two hundred and fifty supper and concert saloons, which are dins of prostitution." One observer estimated that Richmond had more prostitutes than New Orleans and Paris put together. Memphis too was a haven for prostitutes, where they virtually ruled Beale Street. In Washington, D.C., the number of prostitutes rose during the war from 500 at its start to more than 5,000 by its end. That figure does not include hundreds more in the bawdy houses of neighboring Alexandria and Georgetown.[78]

The more mobile "camp followers," as those who trailed after armies in the field were called, could be found in the vicinity of almost any sizeable encampment. To maintain some degree of respectability, many claimed to be widows in need of aid. There can be little doubt that some indeed were. Widows or not, few women became camp followers by choice. Most were driven to it as the lesser of many unfortunate circumstances of their lives. Once in the profession, they tended to make the most of it. In 1862 when the Rebels abandoned their Mississippi River stronghold on Island No. 10, Federal troops found what one called "a bevy of nymphs . . . disheveled and rumpled . . . but as

much at home as though they had campaigned all their lives." As rampant inflation began eating away at Confederate currency, southern
prostitutes increasingly welcomed the arrival of Union forces and
their Yankee dollars. One northern correspondent wrote of twenty
Tennessee prostitutes who, after their Confederate customers fell
back in retreat, waited patiently for the arrival of the Federals, "as
willing to extend their gentle favors to the National officers as to their
late Rebel protectors."[79]

As a general rule, officers made a show of discouraging their men
from enlisting the services of prostitutes. As a matter of practicality,
they tried simply to keep prostitution socially and medically controlled. Sexually transmitted disease became such a problem in Nashville that the occupying Federals began licensing prostitutes. Every
woman in the trade was registered at the provost marshal's office,
given a weekly medical examination, certified to be in good health, and
taxed at a rate of fifty cents a week to fund a hospital for those found
to be in need of medical treatment. Furthermore, officials mandated
that "all public women found plying their vocation without license and
certificate be at once arrested and incarcerated in the workhouse for a
period of not less than 30 days." The system seems to have worked
well. One officer noted that "a marked improvement was speedily noticed in the manner and appearance of the women," not to mention
their health and that of the soldiers. So well did the system control
venereal disease that the "better class of prostitutes" flocked to
Nashville from cities across the country. Memphis, where similar licensing was required, also became a Mecca for "hookers," as they were
called.[80]

Though the term "hooker" was in limited use as a reference to
prostitutes before the war, General Joseph "Fighting Joe" Hooker
gave it a boost and forever linked it to himself when he ordered Washington's prostitutes to be concentrated around Murder Bay (now the
Federal Triangle), stretching from Capitol Hill to the White House.
The area quickly became known as "Hooker's Division." According to
one source, Hooker went out of his way to provide sexual recreation
"to bolster the morale of his men." The general himself was said to
frequent Constitution Avenue's bordellos. Other high-ranking officers
did the same. Many kept personal mistresses, sometimes trying to pass
them off as their wives.[81] Such women often used their charms to elevate their social standing, sometimes competing with other women or

playing one officer against another in the process. It was a dangerous game that could quickly backfire, as "Major" Annie Jones discovered when she was drawn into the trap.

Orphaned in Massachusetts as a young girl and taken in by a minister and his wife, Annie left home against her guardians' wishes in 1861 when she was only seventeen. She headed straight for the Virginia front, traveling with the 135th New York Infantry as a "Daughter of the Regiment." By her own account, she applied for an army nursing post but was turned down by Dorothea Dix because of her youth. Annie then set out on a four-year odyssey that took her from camp to prison to the White House and back. It began when Annie, as she told it, "procured a pass from General [John E.] Wool to visit the different camps in and around Baltimore. I had no particular object or business in the Army, but went out of curiosity. I spent some months in this way. In the various camps, I was furnished by the commanding officer with a tent and sometimes occupied quarters with the officers."

By the fall of 1862 Annie was living as a "guest" of General Franz Sigel. She next attached herself to General Julius Stahel, who conferred on her the honorary rank of major. Annie soon became intimate with General Judson Kilpatrick, who was enraged when she just as quickly left him for General George Armstrong Custer. Kilpatrick accused Annie of being a Confederate spy, a charge that landed her in the Old Capitol Prison. Because so many prominent officers were implicated, Lincoln himself became involved with the investigation. He asked Annie her side of the story, and she freely admitted to spending time as "a guest of different officers who kept her supplied with her own tent, horses, orderlies, escorts, sentinels . . . rations, etc." She even confessed to an affair with John L. Lockwood, a guard at the Old Capitol Prison. Lockwood was afterward fired by William Wood, the prison superintendent, whom Annie accused of paying her for sex. All the while she insisted that she was entirely loyal to the Union cause. In early 1864, officials finally agreed. They concluded that the spy charges were groundless and released Annie on the condition that she keep away from Washington and the Army of the Potomac.

Three weeks later, Annie was back in Washington on a pass she managed to wrangle from a Major Wybert of the Treasury Department. She was arrested for parole violation and sent to the House of Correction in Barnstable, Massachusetts. Soon after, Annie wrote to Lincoln protesting that "I have never violated my parole," arguing that the pass from Wybert overrode her parole terms. "I am an orphan and an unprotected girl . . . the victim of the fiendish malice of . . . the Superintendent of Capitol Prison and of Colonel [Lafayette] Baker," a jilted federal investigator with whom Annie had been involved. She also wrote to Congressman Fernando Wood, a Democrat and former mayor of New York City. Why she approached Wood is unclear since there seems to have been no prior connection between the two. But Annie's escapades had been so covered, and almost certainly embellished, by the press that Wood must surely have heard of her. She told him her situation and asked for money, clothes, and books, lamenting that she had no money and was down to her "last copy of Shakespeare." Wood sent her fifty dollars and wrote to Secretary of War Stanton asking that she be released into his custody. Hoping to finally be rid of her, Stanton complied and wrote to Wood: "I hope you may be able to exercise sufficient influence to keep her away from the Army."

Stanton later received a bill for her upkeep from the Massachusetts judge advocate general's office and wondered why she had not already been released. Stanton was told that the state's Republican governor, John Andrew, intervened to keep Annie out of the hands of Wood and the Democrats for fear that they would use her to embarrass the Republican Party. "We were unwilling," wrote the judge advocate general, "that she should be used as a political tool . . . and left to commence [law] suits under the direction of her new advisers." So in prison Annie remained for the rest of the war.[82]

Besides the war itself, it is impossible to say for certain what compelled Annie to embark on her escapades. Perhaps she sought the attention she had missed as a child. She was hardly more than a child when the war broke out. But once labeled a camp follower she was a marked young woman, even if it was generals who passed her from one tent to the next. And like so many other women, it was Annie, not her older male consorts, who carried the burden of societal scorn.

Tens of thousands of women found themselves carrying a similar burden as a direct consequence of the war. Some were young girls left with no other means of support than to sell sexual favors. Some were widows with hungry children to feed. Others who heard no word of their husbands for months hardly knew whether they were widows or not. Low wages and inflation contributed to the problem as well,

North and South. Boston police picked up a young woman for "soliciting on the street." She was a seamstress, her mother's only support, whose employment did not provide a living wage. And she was only sixteen. In New York, another girl found herself a soldier's widow at seventeen. Unable to find a job, she took up with a man who promised her support. But he treated her so brutally that, in desperation, she tried to take her own life. When hauled into court on charges of attempted suicide, the only regret she expressed was that her attempt had failed. There was no report of the man who abused her facing any charge for his crimes.[83]

Female suicide increased dramatically during the war. In the Victorian era, it was often viewed as the only honorable recourse for any woman revealed to be a "soiled dove." When police in Chicago raided a house of prostitution in 1864, five of the women killed themselves. Two others tried unsuccessfully to do so. But many women had little choice but to chance discovery and possible suicide. In an open letter to a local paper, a man from Columbus, Georgia, outlined in graphic detail the hopeless sufferings of soldiers' wives and widows. He noted with regret that they were frequently offered help only "at the sacrifice of their honor, and that by men who occupy high places in church and State."[84]

"If You Cud Hear the Crys of My Little Children"

The choice of risking death by suicide on the one hand or by starvation on the other was a very real one for poorer women. Hunger became so rampant in the South's eastern hill country that one North Carolinian suggested ordering soldiers to "knock the women and children of the mountains in the head, to put them out of their misery." In the North Carolina coastal town of Wilmington, a mother and her child were reduced to living in an outhouse, where they soon died of starvation. The father had been jailed simply for criticizing the Confederate government.[85] But jailed, drafted, or killed in battle, the family's fate might have been the same. Death stemming from malnutrition was common enough among soldiers' families.

In the spring of 1863, southern newspapers circulated this heartwrenching verse. It was a direct reminder of women's sacrifices. And it was a general cry for help.

The Widow's Appeal

Stranger, have you corn?
Can you my wants supply?
My infant, early born,
Needs succor, else 'twill die.

At Crampton,[86] where the skies
With bullets were o'ercast—
There my loved Charlie lies,
And sadly breathed his last.
I cannot, will not steal,
Me loved one to supply.
Will you my sorrows heal?
Refuse me and I die.

The days are sad and drear,
Since Charlie left me alone,
I'm a stranger, pilgrim here,
To Heaven I make my moan.[87]

Appeals to heaven were the best women could do for all the impact they had on the southern gentry. One South Carolina woman expressed general class resentment when she wrote to Jefferson Davis: "I wish you would have all the big leguslater men and big men about towns ordered in to confederate serviz. They [are] no serviz to us at home." Planters were a special target of the plain folks' scorn. Many were obligated by law to assist needy soldiers' families when called upon to do so. But it was all too easy for planters to ignore the stipulations of their bonding contracts.[88]

"It is folly for a poor mother to call on the rich people about here," wrote one hungry mother of three in an 1862 letter to Jefferson Davis. "There hearts are of steel [and] they would sooner throw what they have to spare to their dogs than give it to a starving child." One group of Georgia women wrote to their governor that the planters "don't care what becomes of the poor class of people" as long as "they can save there niggroes."[89]

Thousands of letters from all across the South telling of starvation flooded into state and Confederate offices. Most were from soldiers'

While poor families with absent fathers and husbands daily faced the threat of starvation, the wealthy enjoyed a lifestyle hardly touched by the war, even in the South. As late as March 1865, one visitor wrote of a meal at a posh Columbus, Georgia, inn where the table was so heavy with food that it "actually groaned." (*Leslie's Illustrated Newspaper*)

families asking for their discharge. A North Carolina soldier's wife wrote to Governor Zebulon Vance:

> I set down to rite you a few lins and pray to god that you will oblige me I ame apore woman with a posel of little children and I wil hav to starv or go neked me and my little children if my husban is kep a way from home much longer . . . I beg you to let him come . . . if you cud hear the crys of my little children I think you wod fell for us I am pore in this world but I trust rich in heven I trust in god . . . and hope he will Cos you to have compashion on the pore.[90]

Ida Wilkom of New Iberia, Louisiana, wrote to Secretary of War Judah Benjamin imploring him to let her husband come home. Her baby was dying, and her three other children were in dire need. She had done all she could to eke out a living but death was now at the door: "I have tried every thing to submit to the will of God in tranquil resignation; but I find, a human being can suffer only according to his human strength."[91]

With her husband at the front, Almira Acors bluntly wrote North Carolina's Governor Vance: "I do not see how God can give the South a victory when the cries of so many suffering mothers and little children are constantly ascending up to him." After asking for her husband to be sent home, another soldier's wife demanded of Vance: "I would like to know what he is fighting for." To her, the answer seemed clear: "I don't think that he is fighting for anything only for his family to starve." In northern Georgia, Marcella League and Ruth Nicholson, neither of whom could write even their names, had a neighbor draw up a letter on their behalf to both the president and secretary of war threatening to sue the Confederacy if their husbands were not immediately discharged. Both women signed the letter by marking "X."[92]

With hunger rampant and the elites refusing help, their families' survival was much more important to southern women than the Confederacy's fate. In September 1863 came a letter to Davis from soldiers' wives and widows in Miller County, Georgia.

> Our crops is limited and so short . . . cannot reach the first day of march next. . . . But little [food] of any sort to Rescue us and our children from a unanamus starveation. . . . We can seldom find [bacon] for non has got But those that are exzempt from service . . . and they have no humane feeling nor patraotic prinsables. . . . An allwise god ho is slow to anger and full of grace and murcy and without Respect of persons and full of love and charity that he will send down his fury and judgement in a very grate manar [on] all those our leading men and those that are in power ef thare is no more favors shone to those the mothers and wives. . . . I tell you that with out som grate and speadly alterating in the conduckting of afares in this our little nation god will frown on it and that speadly.[93]

Another woman was just as direct in her letter to Davis: "If I and my little children suffer [and] die while there Father is in service I invoke God Almighty that our blood rest upon the South."[94]

"Bread or Blood"

Southern women were appealing not only to God and the state for help. They were also helping themselves. As early as July 1861, a crowd of New Orleans soldiers' families numbering ten thousand gathered outside the mayor's office insisting on aid with food and rent. Some were taking more direct action. In June 1862, a group of soldiers' wives in Bartow County, Georgia, descended on Cass Depot and demanded cotton to make clothes for their families at home and their husbands in the field. They needed only a small amount and intended to pay, but the agent refused to deal with them. That would not be the end of it. Returning later that day, the women "called for the Agent as a witness of their doings, and cut the rope from one bale, took what they needed, and marched very quietly home with it." In November, a "party of Ladies . . . driven by necessity" raided a store in nearby Cartersville. The next month, twenty women shouting "Salt or blood!" marched on the depot in Greenville, Alabama, and took what they needed. With desperate times calling for desperate measures, others across the South soon followed their example.[95]

In February 1863, as the war's second winter was depleting private food stocks, a band of "regulators" in North Carolina's Bladen County sent their governor an ominous warning.

> The time has come that we the common people has to hav bread or blood & we are bound booth men & women to hav it or die in the attempt. . . . the common people is drove of in the ware to fight for the big mans negro & he at home making nearly all the corn that is made, & then becaus he has the play in his own fingers he puts the price on his courn so as to take all the Solders wages for a fiew bushels & then . . . [extend credit] until the debt will about take there land & every thing they hav & then they will stop all & if not they will hav to Rent there lands of there lords Sir we hoos sons brothers & husbands is now fighting for the big man's negros are determined to hav bread out of there barns & that at a price that we can pay or we will slaughter as we go.[96]

It was no idle threat. Shortly after the letter was sent, hungry women attacked a government depot in Bladenboro taking six sacks of corn and one sack of rice.[97]

Women's riots were breaking out all over the Confederacy during the spring of 1863. In late March, a crowd of at least fifty axe-wielding North Carolina women appeared at the government supply depot in Salisbury demanding food. When an agent tried to send them away, they stormed the building and stole ten barrels of flour. A few weeks later in Guilford County, as Nancy Mangum reported, "a crowd of we Poor wemen went to Greensborough yesterday for something to eat as we had not a mouthful [of] meet nor bread in my house[.] what did they do but put us in gail. . . . they threatened to shoot us and drawed their pistols over us." Such threats did nothing to address the problem of hunger. Nor did they deter North Carolina women. A short time later, women were again rioting in nearby High Point.[98]

The largest of the women's riots took place in the Confederacy's capital city of Richmond, Virginia. Like so many of the South's urban areas, the city was thronged with soldiers' wives and widows left on their own and barely surviving. With planters growing too much to-bacco and cotton, there was never enough food on the shelves. The re-sulting high prices were driven even higher by speculation. And the paltry wages paid to those women fortunate enough to find work were falling further behind rising prices every day. After two years of war-time suffering and little or no help from elites in the public or private sector, poor women were at the breaking point. When Richmond's city council refused even a slight increase in funding for poor relief that spring, it was the last straw. On April 1, several hundred women gath-ered at Oregon Hill Baptist Church to discuss how they were going to feed themselves and their children. One fiery speaker named Mary Jackson said out loud what they were all thinking. They needed food, and they needed it now. If merchants would not sell at prices the women could afford, they would have to take what they needed—by force if necessary.

The next morning, hundreds of women assembled at Capitol Square and headed for the business district. Hundreds more joined their ranks and they went. Soon the surging crowd of women, and some men, numbered over a thousand. They hit the clustered shops like a human hurricane, smashing down doors, looting stock, and sending terrified merchants running for their lives. Governor John Lechter called out the city battalion and threatened to shoot the riot-ers if they refused to turn back. They ignored him and continued their rampage. City officials turned fire hoses on the looters. Still they pushed ahead. Finally, Jefferson Davis himself appeared on the scene. Mounting a drayman's cart, he threw what money he had to the crowd but also threatened to order them shot if they did not disperse. Many of the rioters, with all they could carry, were beginning to scatter in any case. The police hurried after them, arresting a few who later re-ceived jail time ranging from weeks to months. Among them was

Mary Duke, a poor soldier's wife who was sentenced to six months in prison. Her young son Andrew begged for his mother's release in this undated letter addressed to Governor John Letcher.

I am a poor boy, the oldest of four children & I am only 15 years old. My father is in Genl Lee's army & my mother is in prison—and we are left to ourselves, dependent on my labor to support us. When my mother was first put in prison, a lady came to stay with us but she says that she cannot stay no longer—and these little children will be left alone.

Our poor Mother did very wrong, but she has suffered greatly—all the rioters that have been tried have been discharged from the prison but her—she is in a decline and suffers in mind & body.

Four little children appeal to you clemency and ask you for their sake & for their father's sake who is fighting for the country, to pardon our sick mother and let her come back to our humble home. My little sisters are 10, 7 and 2 years old.

I sell news papers to feed us & try to save a little to help pay her fine which by the help of friends I can do if you will show us mercy.

Do good Governor, and four little hearts will rise up and call you "blessed." I served 10 mos [months] under the good Jackson in Co. C, Irish batt. [battery—as drummer].

Don't be angry that a poor boy troubles you to read this. He asks most respectfully mercy for his mother, Mary Duke who was imprisoned 12 May last.

Letcher quietly pardoned Duke on July 1, 1863.[99]

The day after the riot, soldiers patrolled Richmond's business district and artillery guarded its streets. Hoping to keep news of the riot suppressed, government officials ordered telegraph operators and newspaper editors not to mention it in their communications. Obligingly, the *Richmond Dispatch* entitled the next day's lead editorial "Sufferings in the North." But word of rioting in the capital quickly leaked out and filtered through southern newspapers over the next few weeks. It would have made little difference even if the news could have been contained. Widespread as hunger was that spring, the Richmond riot was but one of many that broke out almost simultaneously across the South.[100]

In April, when speculators drove the price of bacon up in Mobile, Alabama, dozens of women marched through the city with banners reading "Bread or Blood" and "Bread and Peace." One witness reported that this "army of women" carried "axes, hatchets, hammers and brooms." And they were prepared to use them. As they reached each grocery store, if the doors were not already open they tore them down and helped themselves to ham, flour, and any other supplies. Army officers sent in Confederate troops, but they refused to level their rifles at the women. According to one merchant who witnessed the scene: "The military was withdrawn from the field as soon as possible—for there were unmistakable signs of fraternizing with the mob." By the time Mobile's mayor arrived to appeal for calm, women with armloads of booty were making their way home.

Elsewhere in Alabama, women were banding together both to take what they needed and to send a strong message. Barefooted women in Talladega stormed a local store and ransacked its supply of shoes. In Lafayette, fourteen women armed with "guns, pistols, knives and tongues" marched on a grist mill and took what flour they wanted. Knowing that cotton overproduction was a major cause of food shortage and high prices, a band of about forty enraged women in Calhoun County attacked local plantations and destroyed the cotton fields.[101]

Georgia was a hotbed of women's riots that spring. On March 16 about a dozen women raided a store on White Hall Street in Atlanta. Their leader, "a tall lady on whose countenance rested care and determination," asked about the price of bacon. When she heard it was a dollar a pound, she said that the women in her group were wives and daughters of soldiers and could not afford to pay such prices. To demonstrate her seriousness, "this tall lady proceeded to draw from her bosom a long navy repeater, and at the same time ordered the others in the crowd to help themselves to what they liked." They cleared the room and made off with nearly $200 worth of bacon. A few weeks later in Cobb County, just north of Atlanta, a black man driving a wagonload of goods to Marietta was robbed of several bales of yarn by a "gang of women" who forcibly took three to six bunches of yarn each.

On April 10, women entered a store near Augusta's Upper Market and asked about prices for shoes and calico. The proprietor sensed mischief afoot, so he closed his store due to "pressing business" elsewhere. The women moved to another store, but took nothing and dispersed after authorities came on the scene. They arrested one man for "telling the women they did perfectly right." One Augusta newspaper labeled the women "Amazonian warriors" even though the mob never turned violent. A few days later, Columbus newspapers gave accounts of that city's "seizing party." On April 11, a group of women numbering about sixty-five rallied at the intersection of Broad Street and Franklin Street (now Fourteenth Street) and marched down Broad Street "to raid the stores of speculators." Armed with knives and pistols, the rioters shouted curses as they went. They first struck George A. Norris's dry goods store and "commenced helping themselves to whatever they wanted." Police arrived in time to disperse the mob before it could reach other stores. A man named "Shanghai Brooks," described by the press as a vagabond, was arrested for encouraging the women. Seven months later, Columbus women warned the governor by letter that they would again organize a mob and take provisions if they received no relief. Brown forwarded the letter to Muscogee County's inferior court justices, "requesting them to take such action in the premises as the court might think proper."

Women in Georgia's state capital of Milledgeville seized items from a dry goods store on the morning of April 14, 1863. They dispersed only when a city magistrate promised immediate relief. The women agreed and were issued funds directly from the city treasury. Macon saw its women rioting that same month as well. In what one editor called "The Women Rising," a crowd armed with pistols and knives attacked "Rosenwald & Bro." store on Second Street to seize calico and other supplies. The proprietor grabbed one of his assailants, wrestled a Bowie knife from her, and retrieved two bolts of calico. The other women escaped with their loot.

Later in April, a band of twenty-eight women, most of them armed with pistols and knives, robbed a freight wagon headed from a factory in Butts County to the rail depot at Forsyth. The editor of the *Macon Telegraph* called on officials "to nip this dangerous business in the bud." Sensing class animosities reflected in the riots, the editor emphasized that protection of private property for both elites and commoners was at stake. "The rich can better afford to be robbed than the poor, and when that game is set afoot the poor will be the greatest sufferers." But from a plain-folk perspective, the rich had robbed them through speculation and impressment. They saw themselves as taking back only what was, in a general sense, theirs by right.[102]

At the height of the spring riots, Congress passed a joint resolution urging that planters, "instead of planting cotton and tobacco, shall direct their agricultural labor mainly to the production of such crops as will insure a sufficiency of food for all classes, and for every emergency, thereby with true patriotism subordinating the hope of gain to the certain good of the country." The resolution was merely a suggestion. It carried no force in law. Nor did efforts on the part of cities like Richmond to set up "free markets" for the destitute. Such markets did ward off further riots in some urban areas, but they were usually underfunded and often relied more on private charity than public finance. Predictably, most wealthy folk ignored government pleas and continued, as one Georgia editor wrote, to "carry their patriotism in the *pocket-book*."[103]

Later that year, eleven women in Georgia's Pickens County stormed the tanyard at Talking Rock. According to one report, they "helped themselves to as much leather as they could well carry off." They boasted of having protection from menfolk home as paroled prisoners of war, and threatened to raid other businesses. One local merchant wrote to Governor Brown begging him to stop the riots and to protect the community from those "who have not our cause at heart." But the riots did not stop. Food was too scarce and hunger too rampant.[104]

In the late fall of 1863, starving women rampaged through Thomasville, Georgia, for the "purpose of supplying themselves with goods." Threats of further violence caused such fear among city officials that they called for help from as far away as Lowndes County, fifty miles to the east. Thannie Wisenbaker, a Valdosta resident, later remembered when the town's home guard

> was ordered to Thomasville where some great excitement was reported. My! Such preparation in getting ready for the trip! Everything that they imagined they might need was gotten ready. Old muskets, used in the war with the Indians, shotguns and such old pistols that they had on hand, were readied. . . . The men rushed hurriedly from place to place, pressing into use every horse and mule available, until at last they rode off to Thomasville. But alas! For their hopes and dreams of meeting and subduing the enemy. When they arrived in Thomasville, they learned, to their utter chagrin, that some soldiers' wives had threatened to break into the government commissary to obtain food for their hungry children.[105]

It was the only time Valdosta's gallant home guard was ever called to service.

At its December session, the Thomas County Superior Court called the riot a "disgraceful act," and warned that "all such misguided females" should refrain from "unlawful demonstrations in the future." Driven by continuing hunger, women did not always heed such warnings. Some months later, six Thomas County women armed with rifles stopped a wagon and stole its cargo of corn.

"I Did Not Blame the Women"

Another wave of rioting struck Georgia in the spring of 1864, this time focused on the state's southern half. In April, newspapers reported a "daring robbery" in Savannah. A number of women entered the stores of A.F. Mira on Whitaker Street, John Gilliland on Congress Street, W. and R. McIntire on Saint Julian Street, and a Mr. Stroup's store on Bryan Street, helping themselves to bacon and other items. Mira was preparing to sell the women bacon, but was forced into a corner while they helped themselves. One of the McIntires offered the women rice and sugar free of charge, hoping to avoid a general ransacking. His gesture appeased the women. They moved on to Gilliland's store, where they stole all his bacon. Gilliland tried forcibly to retrieve some of his pork, but most of the women escaped with their plunder. Sheriff Cole of Chatham County arrested three women and placed them in jail. Mary Welsh, charged with taking bacon from Gilliland's store, was turned over to the magistrate for prosecution. Anne McGlin and Julia McLane were charged with disorderly conduct. In the end, none of the women was prosecuted. There was too much popular sympathy for them, especially since they were soldiers' wives.

On April 19, E. Yulee of Stockton wrote Governor Brown that "thirteen women made their appearance here armed with pistols and knives and demanded admittance to the depot containing the provisions collected as tax in kind." Three guards at the depot tried without success to "pacify" the women. They shoved the guards aside, broke open the door, and took over one hundred pounds of bacon. Yulee believed that these women would steal more supplies now that they knew they could "seize them with impunity." He suggested that the civil courts might offer a remedy, but "unfortunately these are now silent in the middle of our troubles." Most of the governor's incoming correspondence was read by clerks who wrote a short description on the outside of envelopes or letters for faster processing. Yulee's letter was marked "women outrages."

Just to the west of Stockton, Lowndes County saw more female lawlessness that month. A group of Valdosta women marched on a local store and tried to buy cotton yarn, but the proprietor refused to take Confederate money. He would, however, trade for bacon. Having no bacon to exchange, the women "forcibly took all the yarns in the store." In the same neighborhood, a dozen or more women, at least one armed with a pistol, broke into a government warehouse and stole a wagonload of bacon. At about the same time, the small Lowndes County settlement of Naylor had troubles of its own. A mob went on a rampage "for the purpos of taking of spun yarn cloth and bacon." Among the participants were three members of Union Primitive Baptist Church. Hetta Peters, Rachel Chitty, and W.S. Peters came under the "displeasure" of the congregation for their role in the riot. According to church minutes, "W.S. Peters cleared himself; Hetta Peters confessed and was forgiven with joy." Chitty, apparently unrepentant, refused to answer the church summons and was turned out of the congregation.

Campbell County Justice of the Peace B.D. Smith found himself in an uncomfortable situation in May over the issue of women taking impressment into their own hands. In a letter to Governor Brown, Smith outlined the circumstances which led two men to accuse him of "up holding the women presying provisions." The men in question were trying to avoid conscription by having Smith call bailiff elections and running for the positions themselves. Once elected, they would not have to report for duty. To force the issue, they had tried to frighten a sixty-one-year-old bailiff into quitting his post. But neither Smith nor the bailiff would be intimidated. In retaliation, the two men accused Smith of supporting women who forcibly took what they needed. He denied the accusation but wrote, "I did not blame the women." Smith told of a gentleman who was "staying at home" only to profit from a war in which he refused to fight. Though the man was well aware of how badly soldiers' wives needed provisions and had "a right smart to spair, he would not let them have it neither for money nor work but was speculating on it." Careful not to alarm the governor, Smith noted

Southern planters grew so much cotton and tobacco that food shortages and widespread hunger inevitably followed. Women in Miller County, Georgia, wrote to Jefferson Davis warning that God would "send down his fury and judgement in a very grate manar [on] all those our leading men and those that are in power ef thare is no more favors shone to those the mothers and wives." But they were not waiting for God. With a fury of their own, women from Virginia to Texas—including those in Miller County—rioted for food. (*Leslie's Illustrated Newspaper*)

that the women's actions were peaceful. He refused to call the impressment a raid, insisting that no such incident, with all its violent connotations, had ever taken place in Campbell County.

Destruction of property was usually not a part of the women's plans for justice. But there was at least one raid that resulted in severe property damage. In June 1864, a number of armed Pierce County women broke into a storehouse, "carried off several wagon-loads of bacon, and burned some houses." These women boasted that they had plenty of men, including deserters hiding in the Okefenokee Swamp, who would back them up should they meet resistance. According to one source, "the people of property were much alarmed"—so much so that one "prominent citizen" took the train from Blackshear to Savannah and personally reported the attack to authorities.[106]

It was the same all over the South. About a dozen women in Floyd County, Virginia, ransacked a Confederate supply depot and stole a large supply of bacon. Fifty miles to the west, a dozen mountain women brandishing pistols and knives descended on Abingdon and looted the town. The raid's success inspired a second band of women, who shortly afterward swept through Abingdon taking what was left. In Raleigh, North Carolina, about twenty soldiers' wives fell on the Confederate impressment depot and took all the flour and grain they could carry. In the state's port city of Wilmington, women were involved with an attack on a blockade runner in which most of the cargo was stolen. When authorities ordered members of the home guard to fire into the crowd, they refused. There were more riots in Barnwell, South Carolina, Archer, Florida, and Waco, Texas. On the Texas coast, Galveston citizens assembled at the local Confederate commander's home demanding access to commissary provisions. And in the north Texas town of Sherman, 125 armed women ransacked town stores for what provisions they needed.[107]

As the war entered its final months, the plight of the South's women grew even more desperate as they continued their robberies and raids. During the winter of 1864–65, soldiers' wives and children were regularly seen stealing livestock in Georgia's Early and Miller counties. One man who signed himself "A Stock Raiser" placed a notice in Blakely's *Early County News* demanding that the thievery stop. He insisted that he had already given generously to local relief efforts, and was sorely disappointed in the women. He threatened to publish their names in a later issue of the *Early County News* if they did not stop their criminal ways. "What would your husbands and fathers think if they should see your names in a public print as *stock stealers?*" John Davis of Miller County, a well-to-do slaveholder and stock raiser, complained about women stealing his sheep's wool. The sheep were being caught, sheared, then released back into the woods. He too warned that unless the women stopped their "nefarious business," he would have their names published in the local paper. Besides, Davis insisted, these apparently desperate women were not needy at all. It was simply, he said, their nature to steal. "They are now acting as they always would have done, had they the same opportunity."[108]

Such attitudes were common among the upper classes. Godfrey

Barnsley, a wealthy Georgia planter, complained that "the character of the population here . . . is growing worse." "Thieving," he said, "in no small way" was among their character flaws. J.A. Turner, who published Georgia's *Turnwold Countryman* on his Putnam County plantation, held females who resorted to theft in particularly low regard. "Women do not transgress the bounds of decorum so often as men, but, when they do, they go [to] greater lengths." The editor continued: "For with reason, somewhat weaker, they have to contend with passions somewhat stronger. Besides, a female by *one* transgression forfeits her place in society forever." According to Turner, a woman's modesty was her greatest asset; if she engaged in stealing and rioting, she forfeited her heavenly "ornament" forever. Turner ended his condemnation of such women by saying that "if an angel falls, the transition must be to a demon."[109]

Newspapers all over the South were quick to brand destitute women in such unflattering ways, some denying they were destitute at all. Wrote an Alabama editor: "The class composing the mobs are of the lowest—prostitutes, plug uglies . . . and those who have always been a nuisance to the community, and who are not in a perishing, or even suffering condition, for want of food." A Georgia editor insisted that the rioters were little more than loafers, vagrants, and loose women who used the pretense of necessity to justify their theft. Virginia's *Richmond Examiner* suggested that many were not even southerners, calling them "prostitutes, professional thieves, Irish and Yankee hags, gallows-birds from all lands but our own." Few were bold enough to acknowledge the obvious link between desperate circumstances and desperate acts.[110]

One brave soul who did was the editor of Georgia's *Athens Southern Watchman*. In a painstaking editorial, he looked for the root cause of the riots and concluded that ultimate blame lay not with the women but with self-interested money men, especially planters and speculators, who cared more for profit than patriotism. He begged the wealthy to change their ways while there was still time: "In the name of our beloved country—in the name of outraged humanity—in the name of that religion they profess to reverence—in the name of the God they pretend to fear—we call upon these men to change their policy before it shall be too late!" But his plea fell on deaf ears, relief never came, and rioting went on.[111]

In February 1865, fifty women raided the government depot in Colquitt, Georgia, the seat of Miller County. Armed with axes, they broke open the doors and took close to fifty sacks of government corn, or about one hundred bushels. It was reported that the women were soldiers' wives and that the judges of Miller County's inferior court, responsible for poor relief, were to blame for their condition. In an open letter, one local resident accused the judges of being more focused on their own concerns than the well-being of the destitute women and children. The accusations of callousness did not stop with local officials. State officials, including Governor Brown, were also at fault. Singling out the governor, the writer had always thought of Brown as a "complete demagogue" and an "out and out humbug." The *Augusta Chronicle and Sentinel* shared the writer's sentiments, especially about the lack of proper administration of poor relief. Commenting on the Colquitt raid, the editor wrote: "The Government has lost the corn. Would it not have been much better to have given it freely to the sufferers? We think so." Those who were the women's staunchest supporters—their husbands and sons—very much agreed. Shortly after the Colquitt raid, Georgia soldiers from Hart County arrived home and were appalled at the destitution they found among their families. Realizing that no help was coming from the county's inferior court justices, these men raided a grist mill and distributed sacks of flour to local women.[112]

"Unless You Come Home, We Must Die"

Help from their men was something southern women needed more and more as the war continued. Rural women might have been able to get along well enough had it not been for government impressment agents taking much of what they had. Urban women might have fended for themselves if not for rampant hoarding and speculation. Perhaps neither impressment nor speculation would have been so widespread and devastating had the planters grown more food and less tobacco and cotton. But impressment, speculation, and cash-crop overproduction were facts of the wartime southern economy, much to the despair of workingwomen. To them it was clear that the war was little more than a profit-making enterprise for speculators in money crops and other commodities. One southern woman wrote her soldier husband: "I do believe every soldier on each side ought to run away and go home and let them that wants it carried on for the purpose of speculation carry it on themselves. I hear some saying they would not have it stopped for know price. I do think hanging would be too good for such men."[113]

Tens of thousands of women wrote such letters begging their men to come home. "We have nothing in the house to eat but a little bit of meal," one southern wife penned to her soldier husband. If he did not come soon, she warned, " 'twont be no use to come, for we'll all hands of us be out there in the garden in the old grave yard with your ma and mine." Another woman wrote of similar dire straits: "Last night I was aroused by little Eddie's crying. I called and said, 'What is the matter, Eddie?' and he said, 'O, mama, I am so hungry!' And Lucy, Edward, your darling Lucy, is growing thinner every day. . . . I would not have you do anything wrong for the world, but before God, Edward, unless you come home, we must die." To women with families nearing starvation, it could not be wrong for a man to look to his family's survival. One southern mother encouraged her soldier son to "think the time past has sufficed for *public* service, & that your own family require yr protection & help—as others are deciding."[114]

Northern women too were demanding that their men come home. To many, it was a rich man's war in which their poor husbands had no stake. Wrote one Connecticut wife to her husband: "They have got you all into the scrape & that is all they care for." For her beloved to risk his life only to secure profits for men who would not risk theirs was a much greater mark of shame than to be called unpatriotic. "I don't think it will be half as much disgrace to you to have you come home as it will be to stay . . . don't stay for . . . a minute nor an hour if you see a chance."[115]

Thousands of soldiers' families were determined to see that their men got that chance. A New Hampshire officer wrote that desertion was commonly "encouraged and aided by letters and citizens' clothing from relatives or acquaintances at home." A lieutenant colonel of the 132nd Pennsylvania noted that many of his men received civilian clothes from home along with letters telling them to desert. So common was the practice that the adjutant general's office ordered all packages to be labeled with an invoice of their contents and certified by the receiving officer. Those containing "citizens' clothing" were not to be delivered to any soldier. One woman got around the order by smuggling in a suit of civilian clothes to her husband, which he soon used to desert.[116]

The support did not end there. When deserters made it home, they could usually count on help from sympathetic neighbors, especially female relatives. James Hummel, a deserter from Union County, Pennsylvania, was attending his sister's funeral when an army detachment rushed in to arrest him. Hummel wounded one soldier before being fatally shot himself. Enraged women in the congregation set on the man Hummel had injured and forced him to flee the church. It reflected not only their anger at the thought of soldiers invading a church but also how enrolling officials were generally viewed. Pennsylvania's *Easton Argus* wrote that conscription was as unpopular as a plague of smallpox and conscript officers as welcome as "a pack of mad dogs." Mad dogs could not have been treated much worse. When an armed conscript company rode into the Luzerne County mining town of Archbald, a mob of angry women drove it out. In Mauch Chunk, twenty-five women stoned two conscript officers. A Berks County woman threw boiling water on an enrolling officer when he tried to arrest her half-blind husband.[117]

All across the North, women took whatever steps necessary to protect their men. In Boone County, Indiana, they pelted enrollment officials with eggs. Others had more deadly intentions. In Scott County, Illinois, two women fired on troopers coming to take their father and brother. Because of female opposition, officials in Milwaukee, Wisconsin, found it impossible to carry out the draft without a large detachment of armed guards. Milwaukee's provost marshal wrote to his superiors that the city was "thoroughly disloyal, and is controlled by mobs." He hastened to add that "nearly all the trouble thus far has been brought about by women and children, the former threatening to make use of hot water, and the latter throwing stones."[118]

On conscription day at the courthouse in Port Washington, Wisconsin, women leading a crowd of a thousand protesters carried a huge banner reading NO DRAFT. When William Pors, the local draft commissioner, tried to turn them back some of the men and several women attacked him. According to Pors's testimony, "I was pushed, kicked, my hair torn, my clothes ripped and myself knocked on the head." They might have killed him, but as the assailants turned their energies to breaking up the draft box, Pors ran off and hid in the post office basement. From there, Pors could hear the rioters "howling" for his death.[119]

Women in Chicago formed part of a mob numbering several hundred that attacked enrolling officers when they arrested two men for protesting conscription. After being pummeled with stones, bricks, and any other missiles the crowd found convenient, the officers released their prisoners and made a hasty retreat. Women also took an active role in the worst of the draft riots in New York City. Some assaulted the police by grabbing stones and using their stockings as slingshots. Boston's draft riot began when a conscript officer tried to arrest a woman who had slapped him. She screamed for help, and neighbors quickly came to her aid. Soon hundreds of citizens were rampaging through the city, attacking any enrollment officer they could find. When police tried to intervene, the crowds attacked them as well. One policeman was chased home by a group of women and children yelling, "Kill the damned Yankee son-of-a-bitch!"[120]

On the other side of the Mason-Dixon Line, there were plenty of southern women prepared to kill anyone who tried to take their men. One contemporary recalled a Missouri woman who "stood between her husband and a Secesh with a loaded gun." When it came to protecting their families, he wrote, "the gentler sex are anything but gentle."[121] A group of Florida women made that plain when Confederate horsemen came after their deserter husbands. In a letter to his wife, their commanding officer told of general antiwar sentiment, organized resistance, and women rising in defense of their men.[122]

> Corpl Smith returned from the East side of the St Johns [River] last night and gives a gloomy picture of affairs on that side, and an incident happened to him, that will illustrate the feelings on that side. He rode up to the house of one of my Deserters about daylight but the man was not at home, he then went on a few miles to another's home and there they saw both the men at work in the field, but the deserters saw them when they were about ¼ mile from them and ran for the swamp close by, Corpl Smith and party charged their horses as fast as they could, and the women (about a dozen) came out with hoes and axes and tryed to cut Smith off, but all the party were good horsemen but Smith and passed safely but his horse took fright and threw him in a bunch of palmettoes and the women shouted theres one of the d——d rascals off. Smith got up and the women blew the horn to let others

know and told Smith if he would stay 15 minutes they would catch
h—l, using all the time the most profane language they could think of.
Some of the party would have gotten the deserters but they . . . got to
the swamp before they could be overtaken, some of the party fired at
them but missed. Smith says they have regular spies and that no party
can go through the country without being found out by these persons
on the watch.

Popular support and plenty of hiding places made it almost impossible for Confederate authorities to bring in deserters. One deserter
band set up camp on an island in the Chattahoochee River just north
of Columbus, Georgia. Family and friends kept them supplied until
the end of the war. In North Carolina's Montgomery County, two sisters, Sarah Moore and Caroline Hulin, took food and supplies to their
husbands who were hiding in the surrounding woods dodging the
draft. In Dale County, Alabama, two deserters lived in a cave near
their homes during the war's last two years. Said one local resident,
they "were peaceable, and did not disturb any one." At one point, a
military patrol discovered their hideout and found cotton cards and
spinning wheels that they used to help clothe their families. The deserters themselves were never found. Few ever were. When patrols
were nearby, women had various ways of calling for help or warning
their husbands to stay in hiding—blowing horns or whistles, ringing
bells, or hanging out quilts of different colors or patterns to warn of
danger.[123]

Sometimes desertion and draft dodging could be just as dangerous
for women as for men. Phebe Cook of North Carolina complained to
Governor Vance of the treatment state militia troops meted out to
women suspected of helping their men avoid service. She wrote of officials rounding up women and "boxing their jaws and knocking them
about as if they ware Bruts" in an effort to force confessions from
them and information on their men's whereabouts. Caroline Hulin
and Sarah Moore had their hands held under a fence rail while a soldier sat with his full weight on it.

The wife of William Owen, leader of a North Carolina deserter
band, experienced a similar torture. When she refused to tell a Rebel
home guard where her husband was, its commander, Colonel Alfred
Pike, slapped her. According to Pike, his men then "tied her thumbs
together behind her back & suspended her with a cord tied to her two

thumbs thus fastened behind her to a limb so that her toes could just touch the ground. . . . I think [then] she told some truth, but after a while, I thought she commenced lying again & I . . . put her thumbs under a corner of a fence, [and] she soon became quiet and behaved very respectfully." When criticized for his behavior, this southern gentleman was unashamed and unrepentant. Pike insisted that he would go into exile "before I will live in country in which I cannot treat such people in this manner." In spite of the dangers, southern women continued to stand up for their abused menfolk. Tabitha Brown and Adeline Bolin of Randolph County, North Carolina, told Captain W.R. McMasters that his place would be torched if he did not release James and Joseph Brown. McMasters brushed their warning aside as an idle threat. That night, "unknown persons" torched his barn.[124]

In the spring of 1863, Daniel Snell of Harris County, Georgia, wrote home to his wife Sarah: "You spoke of a riot in Columbus . . . it is no more than I expected. I understand there was also one in Augusta. . . . What will become of the women and children with the food situation?" More and more soldiers were wondering how their families would get along in their absence. Others knew all too well. Said one man serving in the Army of Tennessee:

> I have been in all the battles of the West, and wounded more than once, and my family, driven from their home, and stript of everything, are struggling in Georgia to get a shelter and something to eat. . . . little sympathy is shown my suffering wife and children—they are charged three prices for what scanty accommodation they get, and often are nigh starvation. We might as well be under Lincoln's despotism as to endure such treatment.

Like so many others, he was ready to give up the fight and go home.[125]

Soldiers on both sides faced the dilemma of whether to allow their families to suffer and die at home or risk death themselves by deserting. In the end, hundreds of thousands decided to desert. Presenting their rifles as furloughs to anyone who dared challenge them, they made their way over hundreds of rugged miles to help their needy families. Some never made it. Many of those who did were dragged back to the army in chains. Sergeant William Andrews of Lee's Army of Northern Virginia wrote that it was "an everyday occurrence for men to get letters from home stating that their families are on the point of starvation. Many a poor soldier has deserted and gone home in answer to that appeal, to be brought back and shot for desertion."[126]

The way the soldiers saw it, they had very little choice. If society could not care for their families, they had to. Their first duty was to their wives and children. Even soldiers with no families languishing at home had great sympathy for those who did. Sergeant William Andrews, a bachelor, insisted that he too, faced with the same choice, would desert. "Thank God," he wrote, "I have no wife and children to suffer on account of an ungrateful government."[127]

4

"We Poor Soldiers"

War is not the fine adventure it is represented to be by novelists and historians, but a dirty bloody mess, unworthy of people who claim to be civilized.[1]

—GEORGE A. GIBBS, PRIVATE, 18TH MISSISSIPPI INFANTRY

Will God forgive men for such work is a question I often ask myself, but I receive a silent reply and utter my own prayer for the safety of my poor soul and my country.[2]

—HAMLIN A. COE, SERGEANT, 19TH MICHIGAN INFANTRY

"Glorious and Holy"

In the war's early days, few soldiers had wives or children to leave behind. Most were barely out of childhood themselves, and many thousands were children still. Walt Whitman, who served as a hospital nurse in Washington, told of meeting a fifteen-year-old east Tennessee soldier carrying a musket as tall as he was. The boy had been in the Union army for a year and fought through several major battles. His father was dead. His mother had been driven from their home, and the boy was not sure where she was. The next day Whitman caught sight of a Tennessee regiment marching along Pennsylvania Avenue. "My boy was stepping along with the rest," Whitman wrote. "There were many boys no older. There did not appear to be a man over thirty years of age, and a large proportion were from 15 to 22 or 23. They all had the look of veterans, stain'd, impassive, and a certain unbent, lounging gait."[3]

As many as seventy-six thousand children not yet eighteen years old served in Civil War armies. The actual figure may have been higher since so many lied about their age, especially during the post-Sumter excitement of spring 1861. Boys often placed small scraps of paper on which they had scribbled "18" in their shoes so they could truthfully state that they were "over eighteen." Some began army life as musicians, later trading their instruments for weapons, but most were front-line soldiers from the start. Eighteen-year-olds were the largest single age group among the soldiers of '61, and most of the more than six hundred thousand who died in the war barely lived to see their mid-twenties. Rarely has any nation so widely and willfully slaughtered its own youth.[4]

For most young men, that their elders told them it was honorable to fight was reason enough to do so. It was their patriotic duty, said those who were older and seemingly wiser. It was their sacred obligation to kill and be killed in the name of God and country. For both Yanks and Rebs, the eyes of community and family were upon them. The country, whatever their country, was in peril. Duty had to be done and family honor upheld. Cephas Walton, age twenty-two, wrote home to his folks in Virginia that he had "volenteered to fight for my cuntry and my wife and my father and my mother and my brothers and friends." For young men to do otherwise, they were told, was to bring shame and disgrace upon themselves and their loved ones.[5]

There was more at stake than duty and honor for these young men; nearly every preacher told them so. The Reverend A.L. Stone of Boston's Park Street Congregational Church insisted that war was a Christian duty, "as sacred as prayer—as solemn as sacraments." For Union soldiers, they were commissioned by God to save the great American republic, his favored nation, his "New Israel," as the preachers called it. The fate of their religion itself was at stake. Most "holy war" rhetoric came from mainline Protestant clergy. But Catholics as well, stung by years of nativist persecution and accusations of popish plots, generally came to support the war. Many Jews too, long victims of similar suspicion and bigotry, were eager to demonstrate their patriotism, however it was defined. Whatever their doctrinal differences, most religious leaders seemed sure that their America was the world's political messiah. God's "redeemer nation" had to be preserved, in whole and not in part, else all humanity was beyond redemption.[6]

Not all men of conscience were so sure that God, whose kingdom was manifestly not of this earth, favored earthly war of any kind for any reason. Had God not commanded of his followers "Thou shalt not kill"? Had Christ not taught people to love their enemies and do good to them? To Adin Ballou, a Massachusetts religious reformer, these tenants seemed clear enough. "How long," he asked, "will men in the sacred name of Jesus Christ disgrace his religion, stultify themselves, and obfuscate the minds of the multitude, with this absurd twaddle, that Christians, under proper circumstances, ought to smite, kill, slay and destroy their offenders, enemies, and even fellow saints." Ezra Heywood, though a committed abolitionist, wrote simply that it was a more damnable sin to kill a man than to enslave him.[7]

Some northern promoters of holy war overlaid religious sentiment with antislavery fervor. Most did not. But whatever their feelings on slavery, they instilled in soldiers the certainty that a divine plan was at work through them. "God is using our actions, with that of our rulers, the citizens, leaders, soldiers, of the land, as elements in the great result to come." That was what the Reverend Cyrus Bartol preached from his pulpit soon after the war began. "Let us offer all we are or have of thought or word, deed or sacrificial blood." The Union cause was a holy crusade to save God's "city on a hill" and mankind's last best hope. "His truth" would march on, even if it was over a mountain of corpses.[8]

If northern boys believed themselves enlisted in the army of God, young Confederates were taught to believe the same divine truth about themselves. It was in some ways a more difficult task. The South of 1861 was not yet the "Bible Belt" that later generations would call it. At the time, religious zealotry was associated more with New England than any other part of the country. What religion southerners had was much more individualistic, when they had any religion at all. As historian Steve Woodworth points out: "Christianity had traditionally been less dominant there and had proliferated only in more recent decades. Some enclaves of the South, and some strata of southern society, were therefore relatively untouched by its influences." Woodworth tells the story of one southern missionary "who in 1861 encountered three companies—then close to 300 men—among whom he could find only seven who professed to have saving faith in Christ." That number was unusually low, but it does give some sense of what soldiers like Thomas Boatright went through. He wrote of his discomfort at being "thrown among men in my tent that seem to care but little about spiritual things. . . . If I mention [religion] some one will bear it off as if it were unpleasant so I have to remain silent on that subject but if I bring up any other subject all is right, all take part."[9]

Though many southern soldiers were associated with no particular religious denomination, most did have a sense that in taking up arms to defend their homes they were doing their duty to God and country. Theirs was a "holy cause of liberty and independence," wrote a Texas cavalryman to his sister. A young Virginian wrote to his father of "the holy cause of Southern freedom." A Louisiana corporal wrote to a friend that this "struggle for liberty" was "a glorious and holy one," while an Alabama farmer wrote of his "duty to my country and to my God." To men such as these, their cause was God's as well, and southern liberty was at its heart. A twenty-year-old Alabamian recorded in his diary: "I am engaged in the glorious cause of liberty and justice, fighting for the rights of man—fighting for all that we of the South hold dear."[10]

What many southerners held dear was the institution of slavery, which they had little difficulty reconciling with a war for liberty. To them, it was in fact slavery for blacks that insured liberty for whites, distinguishing all whites as members of the "master race." A Carolina soldier could write of the South as "the land of liberty and freemen" though he held men in bondage himself. When his brother was killed at Cold Harbor, a Mississippi soldier and slaveholder assured their mother that "he died that we might live free."[11]

That slavery was supported by holy scripture made the Confederacy's cause a holy crusade—a crusade against that hated government in Washington controlled by vile abolitionists who would overturn God's natural order. The argument that slavery was a positive good ordained by God, little used in earlier generations, was one to which most southern preachers now held fast and proselytized at every opportunity—much to the disgust of more conservative southerners. Among them was John Wood, a Virginia-born resident of Mississippi. Though he held a few slaves himself, Wood saw nothing holy in the practice. He was appalled that men of the cloth would use God not only to justify slavery but also a war to perpetuate it.

> Within the last few years a set of political parsons have seized upon the subject of slavery as a Divine institution, and have rivaled the most fanatical enthusiasts of the North in their extreme views and zealous exertions. Should a Southern man dare to express the opinions of the framers of the Constitution of the United States, with whom slavery was considered an irremediable evil, he was a fit subject for the end of a rope. . . . The evil produced by these political preachers illustrates the wisdom of our ancestors in drawing a line of separation between Church and State, for whenever they have meddled with the affairs of our Government . . . the result has been marked by the bloody footprints of their deluded followers.[12]

What southern soldiers seemed most deluded about was the attitude of northerners toward slavery. Though secessionist preachers and politicians told their audiences otherwise, most northerners at the war's outset had no designs against slavery, only its expansion. In his March 1861 inaugural address, weeks before the firing on Fort Sumter, Lincoln made clear that the North had "no purpose, directly or indirectly, to interfere with slavery in the States where it exists." Congress passed a resolution declaring the same. Still, to drum up support for secession, even those secessionists who knew better took pains to portray all northerners as abolitionists. Their lies had the desired effect. Wrote one Kentucky infantryman as he marched off to war in April 1861: "We are fighting for our liberty, against tyrants of the North . . . who are determined to destroy slavery."[13]

The belief that slavery was in danger stirred up even white southerners who held no slaves, such was the depth of their racism and their fear of what freedom for blacks might mean. "There are too many free niggers . . . now to suit me, let alone having four millions," wrote one Louisiana soldier in 1862. A farmer from Virginia's Shenandoah Valley told his fiancée that he was fighting so he could live under "a white man's government instead of living under a black republican government." A young North Carolina soldier was sure that the Yankees were "trying to force us to live as the colored race."[14]

Early in the war, a resident of Knoxville recorded his impressions of east Tennessee's nonslaveholding volunteers and their reasons for enlisting.

> It was a common thing to hear men of this class, dressed in uniform, and under the influence of mean whiskey, swearing upon the streets that they intended to have their rights, or kill the last Lincolnite north of Mason & Dixon's line! Ask one of them what rights he had lost and was so vehemently contending for, and the reply would be, the right to carry his negroes into the Territories. At the same time, the man never owned a negro in his life, and never was related, by consanguinity or affinity, to any one who did own a negro! Nay, I have heard captains of Rebel companies bluster in this way, who could not get credit in a Secession store for a pair of shoes or a pound of coffee.[15]

The expressed motives of some nonslaveholders for their anti-Union stance was just as perplexing to the Yankees. One astonished private from Wisconsin wrote home after men of his unit spoke with Confederate prisoners: "Some of the boys asked them what they were fighting for, and they answered, 'You Yanks want us to marry our daughters to the niggers.' "[16]

"Put Your Trust in the Lord"

Whether driven to battle by patriotism, "God's will," support for slavery or opposition to it, enthusiasm was tough for soldiers on both sides to maintain in the face of war's harsh realities. "How I wish this war was over," wrote one Rebel private. "There ain't a bit of fun in it." A Yankee private remembered feeling the same way at Shiloh: "As we lay there and the shells were flying over us, my thoughts went back to my home, and I thought what a foolish boy I was to run away and to get into such a mess I was in." Like most of the rank and file on both sides, Private Sam Watkins of Tennessee concluded that "the glory of war was at home among the ladies and not upon the field of blood and carnage . . . where our comrades were mutilated and torn by shot and shell."[17]

Horrible though it was, battle was but a small part of a soldier's life. The misery of camp life and campaigning made up the rest. Disease was rampant, food was poor, clothing was ill suited to extremes of heat and cold, and the soldiers felt helpless to do much about it. "You can compare the Soldier to a mule," wrote one disgusted northerner. "He has to go when he is told to and never knows when he will stop until his driver tells him, it makes no difference how the roads is or how hard it rains nor whether it is light or dark and he eats what is given him without the power to get any better." Elias Register, an Alabama farmer, was no stranger to hardship or hard work. Still, after only a few weeks in the army, he wrote home to his wife, "I never knew what a hard life was before but I know now what it is."[18]

Thousands of men and boys had second thoughts about enlisting as a realization of what they had done began to set in. Confederate Private Thomas Warrick wrote back home: "Martha . . . I can inform you that I have seen the Monkey Show at last, and I don't Waunt to see it no more. . . . Martha I Cant tell you how many ded I did see." Many soldiers advised their friends and relatives to stay out of the army if they could. In 1863 Union soldier Tom Magee wrote to his brother Harvey—just turned sixteen and eager to enlist—warning him of soldiers' hardships and telling him to stay on the farm. A Georgia soldier urged his brother not to let recruiting officers "persuade you off. They may tell you great tails . . . and how well we are fixed up here . . . but do not let them excite you into it." An Alabamian did the same. "I still advise you," he wrote to his brother, "to not come to the war. I tell you you will repent it if you do I do believe. You have no idea of what it is to be a soldier . . . and be you assure[d] that if I had your chance to stay out of it I would."[19]

Such men no longer seemed sure that it was God's will that they fight. Even those who had been most certain about God's hand in the war at its beginning expressed doubt before it was over. Joshua Lawrence Chamberlain of Maine, who had trained at Bangor Theological Seminary as a Congregational missionary, went to war convinced that he was an instrument in the hands of the Lord. Chamberlain later wondered whether he and his comrades, in killing their fellow men, were really answering God's call or whether they should all beg His forgiveness for their murderous sins. Hamlin Coe of the 19th Michigan had gone into the conflict proclaiming his "trust in Him who wields the destiny of all." "God protect the right" was his creed, and Coe had no doubt that his cause was the right one. To his mind, that cause—God's cause—must prevail if it cost the life of every Rebel in the South. But by the summer of 1864, Coe's unquestioning conviction that he was doing God's will had vanished. After viewing the carnage of a Georgia battlefield, Coe wrote: "Will God forgive men for such work is a question I often ask myself, but I receive a silent reply and utter my own prayer for the safety of my poor soul and my country."[20]

Few men lost their faith completely as a result of the war. Indeed, the experience of combat seems to have bolstered the faith of many, in the short term at least. Many soldiers facing the prospect of battle promised God that they would give up gambling, drinking, profanity, or fornication, and lead more moral lives if only He would see them through the fight. Some even promised to enter the ministry. Religious revivals swept through the Union armies in the winter of 1862–63 and through the Confederate armies a year later. But, like Coe and Chamberlain, soldiers on both sides increasingly came to see a distinction between God's will and man's. And they were less certain which was which. "Many of the officers and men," wrote Confederate soldier Alfred Fielder, "deny the special providence of God or that prayers will avail in temporal affairs."[21] For some, God became a more distant figure, one in whom they placed a far off hope but who was little involved in their daily lives. For others God became closer in a sense—more personal, less political—a God for whom outward displays of religious piety were unnecessary. In either case, God's role in the war became less certain and expressions of organized religion less common.

Even the Army of Northern Virginia lost the religious zeal that many of its commanders had tried to instill. Alexander Hunter, one of "Lee's Miserables,"[22] wrote that "religious fervor soon changed to indifference; and I certainly saw nothing or heard nothing of an outdoor prayer-meeting or a conversion among the cavalry during the last year of the war." It was the same among northern troops. Sundays "seemed but little like the Sabbath," wrote one Yankee soldier. Said another of Christmas, "we know it only in name."[23]

Army chaplains usually tried to give aid and comfort where they could. They consoled men in need of hope, wrote letters for those who could not write, and interceded on behalf of the men when they felt compelled to do so. Some faced enemy fire as they ministered to the men. But such courage was not universal among chaplains and became increasingly rare as the war continued. That so many ministers came to lack the kind of fortitude they preached hardly inspired the troops. Abner Small witnessed that hypocrisy among the chaplains of his brigade during a worship service in spring 1863 just before the Battle of Chancellorsville: "They were eloquent in their appeals to patriotism, and pictured in glowing colors the glory that would crown the dead and blazons of promotion that would decorate the surviving heroes. They besought us all to stand firm, to be brave; God being our shield, we had nothing to fear." Suddenly Rebel cannons opened fire. "'Whoosh!' . . . 'Crash!' . . . The explosions . . . the screams of horses and the shouted commands of officers were almost drowned out by the yells and laughter of the men as the brave chaplains, hatless and bookless, their coattails streaming in the wind, fled madly to the rear over stone walls and hedges and ditches, followed by gleefully shouted counsel: 'Stand firm; put your trust in the Lord!' "[24]

Chaplains who fled under fire found no respect among the soldiers. Nor did those who took advantage of the social distance between themselves and the troops. Though there were those who remained true to their calling, far too many clergymen spent more time among the officers and local civilians than they did ministering to the men. The influence they wielded over those men declined in proportion. When weary soldiers of the Union's Sherman Brigade began tossing their testaments aside on the march, their chaplain railed against them. But as "Bibles and blisters didn't go well together," the soldiers ignored the chaplain's protest. Besides, wrote one of the men, "he had a horse to ride." When chaplains displayed so little empathy for the troops, it was noted and resented. Thomas Galwey of the 8th Ohio complained that "the chaplain of our regiment continued sitting idly in his saddle with one of his saddle bags full of bottles of Jamaica ginger while men were prostrated and dying of sunstroke." And when clergymen had enough of army life, they simply went home. The soldiers had no such freedom. To them, such faint-hearted holy men were no better than "those ignoble sons [of the wealthy] who have remained at the rear and reaped the home harvest."[25]

"To Make Fortunes for Others"

Soldiers deeply resented wealthy men who dodged the draft and "reaped the home harvest" when the only thing poor men were reaping was a harvest of death. One Alabama soldier complained of the rich: "They think all you are fit for is to stop bullets for them, your betters, who call you poor white trash." It often seemed to soldiers that they were little more than cogs in a money-making war machine. Nowhere was that more clear than in Union-occupied New Orleans. When the city fell in 1862, cotton smugglers hardly missed a beat. So open was the illicit trade, helped along with bribes and kickbacks, that enraged Union soldiers threatened mutiny. One Yankee officer wrote that his men were all ready to quit the army, "not wishing to risk their lives to make fortunes for others." Rebel troops felt the same way. Lambasting planters and speculators, one disgusted southerner wrote: "Those of our people who are living at home in comfort have no conception of the hardships which our soldiers are enduring. And I think they manifest very little interest in it. They are disposed to get rich from the troubles of the country, and exact from the Government the highest prices for everything needed for the army."[26]

Jesse Ried, a poor South Carolina soldier, was among those who held his high-born neighbors in low esteem: "I have come here and left everything that is dear to me on earth to fight and suffer all manner of hardships to protect property, not my own, whilst many of them who have property are still at home with their families—in fact they are the ones as a general rule that stay at home. . . . Will we poor soldiers ever be recompensed for what we are doing? I fear not."[27]

Few soldiers expected that they would ever reap a just reward for all their misery. Certainly their pay was little reward. Long after the war, one southerner recalled with some bitterness, "The private's pay was eleven dollars per month, if he got it; the general's pay was three hundred dollars per month, and he always got his." Few Union privates got their $13-per-month pay regularly either. Some refused to serve without it. A Confederate sergeant reported several Union deserters coming into camp who told of widespread discontent in the Federal ranks. "They have not been paid for some time," wrote the sergeant, "& are getting as tired of the war as ourselves." After not being paid for fourteen months, seamen on the USS *Cincinnati* threw down their mops and pails, refusing to work until their pay arrived.[28]

On the Confederate side, one Alabama soldier wrote home about how the officers in his regiment received their pay while the privates

The most difficult hardship most soldiers faced was separation from loved ones. And they resented wealthy men who suffered no such pain. Jesse Ried, a poor South Carolina soldier, wrote: "I have come here and left everything that is dear to me on earth to fight and suffer all manner of hardships to protect property, not my own, whilst many of them who have property are still at home with their families—in fact they are the ones as a general rule that stay at home." (*Harper's Weekly*)

got none. In response, he and his comrades laid down their arms until the payroll came through. "Our officers said that we were rebelling against our country but," the soldier protested, "we deny the charge it was not so. We were only rebelling against those haughty officers, for not giving us our rights—and other tyranizeing over us."[29]

Many others did the same. A Confederate regiment in South Carolina refused to obey orders sending it to Tennessee until the payroll arrived. Two Mississippi companies went on strike, saying they would perform no further military duty until they got their pay. In late 1862, word reached Houston of rampant dissatisfaction in the 2nd Texas Infantry Regiment. Though the officers were getting their wages, the soldiers had not been paid for months. "When we ask why the privates are not paid," read an open letter to Houston's *Tri-Weekly Telegraph*, "all the satisfaction we get is, 'No money for the soldiers yet.' Yes, the poor soldier, who finds himself far away from home and friends, who risks his life for his country, is neglected, he falls sick, is sent to the hospital with not a dime in his pocket to buy any of the luxuries that a sick man requires. Vegetables are paraded before him; No, money, he says, and turns over and suffers. Week after week he lingers, and then fills an unmarked grave."[30]

"Salt Junk and Hard Bread"

Tens of thousands of men on both sides died of malnutrition. Those who did not suffered much of the time from an unbalanced diet. Vegetables were an unusual treat. Even in the hospitals, as one worker for the Union's Sanitary Commission admonished, government issues of "potatoes and onions . . . are doled out with parsimonious hand, on semi-occasional periods, and green vegetables are totally ignored." For troops in the field, pickled beef and salt pork were the common fare, supplemented with hardtack (a large unleavened wheat cracker) among the Federals and, more rarely, cornbread among the Rebels.[31]

Meat was usually so bad that it could be taken only in small portions. "Much of it was musty and rancid," wrote one Yank, "and much more was flabby, stringy, 'sow-belly.'" On the outside "it was black as a shoe; on the inside, often yellow with putrefacion." A New Jersey private recalled that "maggots had to be scraped off before it was put into the pot. . . . The salt junk as we called our pork was sometimes alive with worms." So was the hardtack, which the soldiers called "worm castles." On the march, soldiers sometimes killed their own meat but frequently had no time to cook it. A member of the 34th Massachusetts wrote that meat was "eaten, in many cases, raw and quivering." One North Carolinian recalled, "I learned to eat fat bacon raw, and to like it."[32]

Officers usually ate much better than their men. And the higher their rank, the better they ate. That was especially true on naval vessels, which carried livestock to ensure that the officers got fresh meat. It was quite a chore for common seamen to care for the animals on top of their regular duties. It was a chore from which they themselves would rarely benefit. Seaman James Henneberry, assigned to clean up after cows and chickens roaming the decks of his gunboat, wrote grudgingly in his journal: "All the chickens and roast beef that I will get for dinner will be salt junk and hard bread."[33]

Consumption of meat poorly preserved or improperly prepared kept seamen and soldiers alike in a nearly constant state of digestive distress. After one meat ration issue, a private wrote: "Every man who had eaton the stuf was laid up, and what with the heaving up and the back door trot, we had a sorry time of it." To kill the worms and the taste of rot, soldiers fried almost everything they ate when they had the time. But the stomach cramps that resulted from consuming so much grease could sometimes kill a man. "Death from the frying pan," as one medical officer called it, was all too common.[34]

Even when higher command took steps to address dietary deficiencies, corruption in the officer corps often hampered the effort. During the winter of 1862–63, when scurvy threatened to destroy his Army of the Cumberland, General William Rosecrans saw to it that one hundred barrels of vegetables a day were issued. Still the army's health continued to deteriorate. Rosecrans ordered an investigation, which found "that one fourth in amount of this issue went to the staff officers and their families at Head-Quarters, and that of the remaining three-fourths, the Commissaries of the various Corps, Divisions and Brigades obtained the larger portions, so that the Regimental Commissaries who supplied the wants of the private soldiers were left almost unprovided." A further inquiry by medical officials revealed that during one twelve-month period from 1862 to 1863, though regimental records showed almost daily distributions of vegetables, the men actually received such issues only three times.[35]

Most soldiers placed primary blame for their miserable rations, as John Billings of the Army of the Potomac made clear, on "rascally, thieving contractors who supplied them, for which they received the price of good rations." Neither were they blind to corruption among "inspectors, who were in league with the contractors." Billings expressed enduring outrage among common folk when, years after the war, he wrote: "No language can be too strong to express the contempt every patriotic man, woman, and child must feel for such small-souled creatures, many of whom are to-day rolling in the riches acquired in this way and other ways equally disreputable and dishonorable."[36]

Still, expressing more generosity than many of his comrades might have, Billings was quick to add that "the government did well, under the circumstances, to furnish the soldiers with so good a quality of food as they averaged to receive." "Unwholesome rations," he thought, "were not the rule, but were the exception." Few ex-Confederates could have made such a claim. According to one postwar report, the Confederacy "was barely able to scrape together, week by week, the stinted rations of bacon indispensable to keep life in the soldiers." Often it could not even do that. Cotton and tobacco overproduction, along with indifference among planters and their political allies, combined to keep Confederate soldiers in a state of near starvation.[37]

Lack of adequate transportation also contributed to the Confederacy's food problem. The rail system was almost constantly in need of repair, and it was difficult to get replacement parts. In the summer of 1863, Captain A.M. Allen of Columbus, Georgia, wrote that he had 300,000 bushels of corn ready for shipment to Lee's Army of Northern Virginia, but he was having trouble getting the corn to Richmond. "The corn is ready," he wrote. "Transportation is the great difficulty." But even had there been no problem with the rail system, the underproduction of food would have remained. By Allen's own calculations, his corn would have met the demands of Lee's army for barely a month. And in an earlier letter to the War Department, Allen complained that the corn crop in southwest Georgia was nearly exhausted.[38]

The Confederacy's inability to feed its army was especially obvious on campaign. In the spring of 1862, just after their retreat from Yorktown to Richmond, one Confederate wrote that he "came nearer starving than I ever did before." During their September march into Maryland, one woman said of the Rebels who passed by, "When I say they were hungry, I convey no impression of the gaunt starvation that looked from their cavernous eyes." A Sharpsburg woman recalled that "they were half famished and they looked like tramps. They nearly worried us to death asking for something to eat." Most of the time, despite orders to the contrary, the soldiers did not ask. Living off the land, they gave in to the law of survival and took what they needed. It was the same wherever Confederate armies went, and it got worse as the war dragged on. By September 1864 one soldier wrote that the Army of Tennessee would "steal and plunder indiscriminately regardless of age or sex." Said another: "They talk about the ravages of the enemy in their marches through the country, but I do not think the Yankees are any worse than our own army."[39]

The food situation was nearly as bad when the army was encamped. What little food they had was constantly under attack by rats. It seemed that they infested every camp. Like the Pied Piper of Hamlin, where soldiers went, rats were sure to follow. At Whitmarsh Island, Georgia, wharf rats were so numerous that rations had to be protected constantly. When food ran low, the rats became the rations. William Andrews told in his diary how each morning "rat details" would form, armed with sticks and shovels prepared to do battle with the rodents. "The rats burrow under a row of cedars near the camps and the boys will dig them out and then let them run for their lives. They don't get far before they are knocked on the head. After the boys kill about 50, they turn too and dress them, each man cooking to suit his taste. Some fry, some stew, while others bake them, and the boys say they eat as well as a cat squirrel."[40]

Higher-ranking officers who had easier access to what commissary stores there were rarely experienced the kind of hunger that was so common in the ranks. The soldiers knew that and sometimes did more than simply complain about it. In the spring of 1863, General Braxton Bragg cut the Army of Tennessee's daily ration to corn meal and water only. In protest, a number of his men refused to fall in for drill. Worse was to come. Some months later, soldiers in the Army of Tennessee intercepted one of their own supply trains and made off with all its cargo of bacon, meal, and flour. At Galveston, the entire 3rd Texas Infantry mutinied when their officers tried to feed them corn meal that was "sour, dirty, weevel-eaten, and filled with ants and worms." Near Richmond, members of the 31st North Carolina Regiment, led by several of their noncommissioned officers, stormed the commissary. Two hundred men of a Georgia brigade raided their post commissary, making off with seventy-five sacks of flour, seven hundred pounds of bacon, and ten casks of brandy. A similar riot occurred among soldiers in Danville, Virginia.[41]

"We Were Uniformly Ragged"

Like rations, clothing was also a mark of rank and social distinction. When Yankees captured a Confederate baggage train at Perryville, Kentucky, one of the Rebel army's more affluent members laid out hundreds of dollars to buy a fine new uniform. Few among the rank and file could afford to do the same. "Our uniforms were uniform in one respect only," recalled one Tennessee soldier. "We were uniformly ragged!" When Lee's Army of Northern Virginia set out for Maryland in August of 1862, a Virginian said of the men's uniforms, "There is not a scarecrow in our cornfields that would not scorn to exchange clothes with them."[42]

Some Confederates tried to make light of their inadequate clothing. When a Yankee yelled across the lines to a poorly clad private, "Hant you got no better clothes than those?" the Reb replied, "Do you suppose we put on our good clothes to go out to kill damned dogs?" But when they got the chance, Confederate troops would not hesitate to trade their rags for the clothes off a dead Yankee. A soldier in the Army of Northern Virginia confessed that it was "nothing unusual to see yankee clothing in our camps, which was stripped off the dead on the battlefield. Saw Sgt. Alex Clemency of Company G wearing an officer's cap with a slot of his brains sticking to it. Sgt. Bridges of Company M wears a frock coat with a ball hole in the waist of it, and the tails covered in blood where the fellow was shot in the back." In some Rebel units, there were more blue uniforms than gray.[43]

Shoes were among the Confederate soldiers' most sought-after articles of clothing. Southerners had been used to buying leather goods from northern factories before secession. After that, the main sources of leather were the fledgling tanneries of Tennessee. But the Union advances in that state in the spring of 1862 had cut off even this meager source. Hard campaigning in the summer of 1862 wore out most of the Confederate army's shoes, and the government found it difficult to procure new ones. During the Army of Northern Virginia's Antietam campaign early that fall, as many as 80 percent of its soldiers were without shoes. Many of what shoes the army did have had been scavenged from dead bodies on the battlefield of Second Manassas less than a month earlier. One southerner wrote that of the hundreds of dead Yankees he saw after the battle, not one had a pair of shoes. On those occasions when Confederates were forced from the field, which was the case more often than not, there was no opportunity to plunder shoes from the dead. In late 1862, during the Army of Tennessee's retreat from Kentucky after the Battle of Perryville, one soldier recalled that the entire army could be tracked by the blood from the soldiers' bare feet.[44]

For the soldiers to have proper clothing was often a matter of life or death, especially during winter campaigns. Private Sam Watkins told of an incident, one of many like it, that illustrates the point.

Our regiment was ordered to go to a little stream called St. John's Run, to relieve the 14th Georgia Regiment and the 3rd Arkansas. I cannot tell the facts as I desire to. In fact, my hand trembles so, and my feelings are so overcome, that it is hard for me to write at all. But we went to the place that we were ordered to go to, and when we arrived there we found the guard sure enough. If I remember correctly, there were just eleven of them. Some were sitting down and some were lying down; but each and every one was as cold and as hard frozen as the icicles that hung from their hands and faces and clothing—dead! They had died at their post of duty. Two of them, a little in advance of the others, were standing with their guns in their hands, as cold and as hard frozen as a monument of marble—standing sentinel with loaded guns in their frozen hands![45]

There were times when men refused to be driven to such lengths. Long after the war, Watkins wrote of rampant frostbite among Stonewall Jackson's men during their January 1862 march from Winchester, Virginia, to Romney (later in West Virginia). "My feet peeled off like a peeled onion on that march," he recalled, "and I have not recovered from its effects to this day. . . . The soldiers in the whole army got rebellious—almost mutinous—and would curse and abuse Stonewall Jackson; in fact, they called him 'Fool Tom Jackson.' . . . Soldiers from all commands would fall out of ranks and stop by the road side and swear that they would not follow such a leader any longer." When Jackson reached Romney with the soldiers who remained, he drew up plans to strike nearby Federal forces. But his men refused to go any farther. Jackson, widely known as a commander who "would have a man shot at the drop of a hat, and drop it himself," had little choice but to fall back to Winchester or shoot all his men for mutiny. He fell back to Winchester.[46]

Union troops were generally better clothed than the Confederates, but there were still serious deficiencies in the Federal ranks. During the war's first year, the government purchased thousands of cheap shoddy uniforms that fell apart after a few days of wear. Some troops refused to accept them in spite of the dangers of not doing so. The 2nd Wisconsin went into battle at First Manassas wearing their gray militia uniforms and were shot at by other Federal units who thought they were Confederates. At Cheat Mountain, several members of the 13th Indiana were killed and wounded by friendly fire when they were mistaken for Rebels. Still, many clung to their gray militia uniforms. In April 1862, just three days before Shiloh, Grant reported that some of his units were still clad in gray. Even after the shoddy uniforms began to be phased out, hard campaigning took its toll. After an intensive campaign in northern Alabama, one Ohio soldier wrote to a friend: "Our reg[iment] is purty naked they look moor like a reg of secesh than northern troops soom barfooted, soom with out coats soom with a citizens soot on. . . . I have ben barfooted evry sens we got back from brig porte." As this Ohioan suggests, such an appearance was much more common among the Rebs than the Yanks.[47]

"These Damn Quacks"

Still, men on both sides suffered terribly from exposure to the elements. On the march, wrote one soldier, "we were exposed to such weather as came." At night they slept in the rain, in the mud, in the snow, or on the frozen ground. Soldiers often awakened to find that they were covered with snow or drenched with rain. Along with the lack of proper diet, such exposure made the men susceptible to all sorts of deadly illnesses. Disease, in fact, killed twice as many men as died from combat. Pneumonia and pleurisy were among the most frequent killers. So was malaria, which accounted for 20 percent of all reported illness on both sides.[48]

Crowded conditions contributed to a major outbreak of measles early in the war. In one Union regiment, over half the men were stricken with it. In some units, most died from it. From the vicinity of Vicksburg, Union private John McMeekin wrote home to his mother: "We burred Simon Groves yestery he dide with the mesels that is what kilde the moste of our boys thay wod take the measels and haft to lay out in the rane and storm and the wod only laste a bot 2 days." So many died from a combination of measles and exposure that commanders frequently refused to accept men for active duty until they had been "put through the measles." Still, the need for soldiers, especially among the Confederates, meant that sick men were often rushed to duty. One southerner wrote of five or six ill men in his company: "They all had the measles, & were getting well & they turn out to drill too soon after it and they all have relapsed. . . . Piercy and . . . Evans . . . died . . . both were hollering and dying at the same time."[49]

Poor sanitation and lack of clean drinking water, two problems often linked, were a constant source of illness in the ranks. On a tour through the Union camps outside Washington, one inspector noted: "In most cases the only sink is merely a straight trench some thirty feet long, unprovided with pole or rail; the edges are filthy, and the stench exceedingly offensive; the easy expedient of daily turning fresh earth into the trench being often neglected. . . . From the ammoniacal odor frequently perceptible in some camps it is obvious that men are allowed to void their urine, during the night, at least, wherever convenient." The result was often an infestation of flies and other vermin that transported bacteria from human waste to food stores. Very often, indiscriminate urination contaminated drinking water as well. The resulting diarrhea, dysentery, and typhoid fever were among the most feared killers throughout the war. Clean drinking water was especially hard to come by when an army was on the move. Water from mudholes in barnyards was sometimes all that was available to drink. The bowel cramps that followed could be deadly. During the campaign for Atlanta, one Michigan soldier grumbled, "I expect to be as tough as a knot as soon as I get over the Georgia shitts." Tens of thousands never did get over such ailments. More soldiers died of diarrhea and dysentery alone than were killed in battle.[50]

Syphilis and gonorrhea took a horrible toll as well. As early as July 1861 an Alabama regiment of roughly one thousand men stationed in Richmond reported sixty-two new cases of gonorrhea and six of syphilis. Neither disease could be treated effectively, and for many they eventually proved fatal. In his study of sexual activity during the Civil War, Thomas Lowry notes that one-third of the men who died in Union and Confederate veterans' homes were killed by the later stages of venereal disease, during which the infection ate away at their brains, blood vessels, and vital organs. Just as poignantly he adds: "No one knows how many Union and Confederate wives and widows went to their graves, rotted and ravaged by the pox that their men brought home, or how many veterans' children were blinded by gonorrhea or stunted by syphilis. Like ripples in some Stygian pond, the wounds of war spread long after the shooting died away."[51]

Doctors of the mid-nineteenth century knew virtually nothing of what caused disease, how it spread, or how to treat it. The germ theory was not widely known or accepted until the turn of the century. Antibiotics were not available for nearly half a century after that. Most Civil War army doctors simply tried to keep the bowels and kidneys regulated, and the patients quiet, using uncertain combinations of expectorants, purgatives, and narcotics. Opinions on procedure ranged so widely that there were few standard treatments for any ailment. The result was confusion for the physicians and misery for the soldiers.

"The Damed Surgeons are not worth a Curse," wrote Henry Bear of the 116th Illinois to his wife. A soldier of the 4th Louisiana agreed: "It is astonishing what an amount of ignorance there is amongst the Medical fraternity. The most of them will administer a large dose of calomel [a purgative] to the patient, it doesn't matter what the disease may be, without caring how much the constitution may be injured. Then comes dose after dose of quinine and other strong medicines until they either kill the individual or ruin his constitution for life." When Private Theodore Mandeville of the 5th Louisiana came down with what was thought to be a liver ailment, he wrote to a friend: "I believe these damn quacks they have got for Drs. in this regt. are doing me more harm than good. They know nothing but Calomel & Quinine. . . . Yesterday they dosed me with Elixor of Vitriol and to day, intend giving me Iodine of Potash & paint me in the region of the liver with Iodine which burns like the devil." Many soldiers simply refused the treatments. One went to his regimental physician "suffering violently" with bowel cramps and was given pills of calomel, quinine, and opium. The soldier returned to his quarters, threw the pills away, and finally got well "by dieting myself."[52]

Most doctors did the best they knew how for their patients, which caused suffering enough. Suffering was sometimes made much worse by carelessness and neglect. Addiction to alcohol and other narcotics was common among the doctors. Some were dismissed for "habitual drunkenness." Some were not. Others were doctors in name only, having secured their posts through pretense or patronage. A Pennsylvania infantryman recalled, "Many of these fellows, if compelled to depend upon their profession in civil life, would have starved, but having, through the influence of political friends, been appointed army surgeons . . . helped fill many graves where our army marched."[53]

All too often, callousness was a trait soldiers attributed to their doctors. "Our Regimental doctor has no more respect for a sick soldier than I would have for a good dog," wrote one Tennessean in his diary, and added, "no not near so much, for if my dog was sick or wounded I would spend some little time in relieving him. Our doctor will not." After the death of a friend, one Massachusetts soldier complained, "He never received humane treatment from the doctors & I believe they thought no more of his death than they would of that of a sheep."[54]

"Our Poppycock Generals"

If the soldiers felt ill treated, they noticed that the officers were not. What care was available, officers got the best of it. Sergeant William Andrews of the 1st Georgia made note of that in his diary: "There has been a great deal of sickness in camps and many deaths, especially among the rank and file. . . . The officers always manage to get home or to a hospital. Have never known one to die in camps." After all the officers in his unit went on sick call, a disgusted Texan complained: "If one of them has the *Belly Ache* for a day or two he is posted off to the hospital. While the poor private who has all of the burden to bear, has to stay and tough it out." It was the same among the Yankees. When a group of women from Utica, New York, went to see for themselves how their contributions to the soldiers' care were handled, they were outraged to find that "only the officers' hospitals secure any of the delicacies forwarded" while the enlisted men "suffer from want of care." From another New Yorker came complaints that "articles sent to the sick soldiers never reach the privates, but are appropriated by the officers."[55]

That rank had its privileges was commonly accepted among professional military men, but it was a hard pill to swallow for the democratically minded citizen-soldiers who made up Civil War armies. That officers got more and suffered less simply because they were officers smacked of aristocracy to the men in the ranks. Daniel Crotty complained that Union officers lived "like princes" compared to him and his comrades. Of Confederate officers, Alexander Hunter wrote: "They had their black cooks, who were out foraging all the time, and they filled their masters' bellies if there was fish or fowl to be had. The regimental wagons carried the officers' clothes, and they were never half-naked, lousy, or dirty. They never had to sleep upon the bare ground nor carry forty rounds of cartridges strapped around their galled hips; the officers were never unshod or felt the torture of stone-bruise."[56]

Rank in Civil War armies, Union and Confederate, usually reflected social standing in civilian life. Well-to-do and well-connected men made up most of the officer corps while commoners were generally restricted to the enlisted ranks. In one regiment, the 1st North Carolina, the average wealth of colonels and majors was $114,000. Among captains and lieutenants it was $88,500. Sergeants, corporals, and privates averaged just $760. The wealth gap was not so great in all units, but the pattern of rank and social standing held true. What men experienced in the army by way of social hierarchy was little different from what they saw in society at large.[57]

Still, the soldiers saw themselves as suffering for a cause. Should not the officers suffer equally for that cause? To see officers' needs met while their own were so often neglected was galling to the soldiers. It led not only to, as one enlisted man put it, a "loss of personal devotion," but it showed officers as lacking in their responsibility to the men. "Who is it that has the hardships to under go?" asked Confederate private T.W. Hall; "It is the privates." "Who is it that has bacon to eat, Sugar to put in their coffee and all luxuries of this kind?" he asked; "the officers." Union private Charles A. Barker complained: "The officers consider themselves as made of a different material from the low fellows in the ranks. . . . They get all the glory and most of the pay and don't *earn* [emphasis added] ten cents apiece on the average, the drunken rascals."[58]

Some officers grabbed at that glory much too obviously. "Our Gen Reub Davis goes by the name of 'Henry of Navarre' among the boys," wrote one Rebel private, "from the long white plume he wears in his hat. . . . He is a vain, stuck-up illiterate ass, and I don't believe there is a man in the regiment who would willingly go into battle with him." So many of their officers had so little military experience that soldiers often felt little but contempt for them. "He is a man of but little Military capacity," wrote an Alabama soldier of his newly assigned colonel, "consequently a great many of the [officers] . . . are resigning . . . we poor privates have to stick it out. . . . I don't want to be lead into Battle by an ignoramus, Col. Henry is fit for nothing higher than the cultivation of corn." Some viewed their officers as even less worthy. A Florida soldier wrote of his regimental officers: "Our major is a fine man, the rest are not fit to tote guts to a Bear."[59]

Lack of military skill on the part of their officers, many of whom were appointed through political connections, was glaringly obvious to the men—never more so than in the case of Colonel William C. Scott, commander of the 44th Virginia. Shortly after his appointment, Scott received word that Union cavalry was headed toward him down a road that his regiment held. Scott hastily prepared for an ambush. As one of Scott's soldiers wrote of the incident, the colonel "placed the men on each side of the road facing each other. . . . The folly of the thing was so apparent that such a peal of laughter went up that he had to command silence lest the enemy should discover our whereabouts."[60]

It was vitally important to morale that soldiers have confidence in the judgment of their officers. The soldiers' lives, after all, were in their officers' hands. Trusted or not, it was the soldiers who paid in blood for the misjudgments of their superiors. In the words of a Massachusetts soldier: "Our poppycock generals kill men as Herod killed the innocents." Ambrose Burnside's order to advance across open ground at Fredericksburg was just such a pointless slaughter. So was Robert E. Lee's order for Pickett's Charge at Gettysburg. The same can be said of Ulysses S. Grant at Cold Harbor, William T. Sherman at Kennesaw Mountain, and John Bell Hood at Franklin. Some of their men never forgave them for it. Long after the war, George Pickett held a grudge against Lee for having his division "massacred." Of Hood's fiasco, an outraged Texan wrote: "The wails and cries of widows and orphans made at Franklin will heat up the fires of the bottomless pit to burn the soul of Gen J B Hood for Murdering their husbands and fathers at that place that day."[61]

Frequently when soldiers felt they had been ill treated or disrespected, they were not shy about getting their satisfaction. A North Carolina trooper wrote of his captain: "He put me in the gard house one time & he got drunk agoin from Wilmington to Golesboro on the train and we put him in the Sh-t House so we are even." Privates of the 53rd Georgia rode their colonel on a rail until he promised them better treatment. When guards dutifully challenged a drunken captain riding along their picket line, he responded by insulting the men. They dragged the officer from his horse, gave him a sound beating, and sent him back to camp without his horse. The Union XX Corps's inspector general got the same treatment when he chastised a group of soldiers eating breakfast and threatened to beat them with his sword. The men gave him a bloody nose and black eyes before making their retreat.[62]

Confederate General Allison Nelson, by all accounts an "arrogant" West Pointer, ordered two men strung up by their thumbs overnight with only their toes touching the ground—unjustly so as their comrades saw it. While Nelson slept, some of them fired a volley into his tent just over his head. The two men were quickly released. General Thomas Williams of the 6th New Hampshire was, according to the unit historian, universally hated by his men. And they made their displeasure with him clear: "They would shoot at him as he rode through the bushes, and when he was in his tent, they put the balls into his bedpost."[63]

Some men did not stop with simple warnings. Private Francis Gillespie, a twenty-three-year-old New York farmer, had a service record showing no history of undisciplined behavior. Yet in July of 1864 he picked up a revolver and blew a lieutenant's brains out. Private John Lanahan of the 46th Pennsylvania also murdered one of his officers. So did Private Francis Scott of the 1st Louisiana. When an Illinois sergeant killed a captain who had, in the sergeant's view, ordered him punished unjustly, he said of the incident: "I killed him. The company wanted him killed." More commonly soldiers would, individually or collectively, take their revenge during combat. General Charles Sidney Winder, who commanded the Stonewall Brigade, was, as one of his soldiers put it, "very severe, and very tyrannical"—too much so for his own good. "We could hear it remarked near every day that the next fight . . . would be the last for Winder." Union artillery saved Winder's men the trouble of killing him. During the opening moments of the Battle of Cedar Mountain, a Federal shell cut Winder nearly in half.[64]

"Sentence Approved. A. Lincoln"

Opposing tyrannical officers in violent ways was dangerous; they too had the power of life and death. Moreover, they had the authority to wield it. Soldiers could be executed for no more than sleeping on duty or being away from their post. Death for such infractions could come instantly and arbitrarily without trial or court-martial. Lieutenant Ira Gibbs of the 2nd Kentucky (U.S.) shot and killed a sergeant for not taking his men on a work detail. When a group of 200 soldiers from the 2nd Rhode Island Cavalry refused to be transferred to his unit, Lieutenant Colonel H. Robinson of the 1st Louisiana Cavalry (U.S.) selected two of the men and, as a warning to the rest, had them executed. An officers' board of inquiry not only exonerated Robinson but praised him for the "prompt and efficient manner" in which he handled the affair.[65]

In November 1862, an apprehended deserter from Company K of the 1st California again got away. Colonel Joseph Rodman West suspected that the sergeant of the guard and some of the men had assisted with the escape. When he placed the sergeant and three privates in irons, all the privates of Company K were so enraged that they refused to fall out for duty. Corporal Charles Smith, acting as spokesman for the enlisted men, told West that neither he nor any of the men would return to duty until their comrades were released. West had Smith shot on the spot. When the escapee was recaptured later that day, West questioned him and realized that the sergeant and his men had nothing to do with the escape. In a letter of explanation to his commanding general, West wrote that "the whole affair is deeply to be regretted." A court of inquiry convened on the case, but West, by then a general himself, had no action taken against him.[66]

Desertion was the most common offense for which execution was prescribed, though many accused of it were guilty of nothing more than straggling from their ranks looking for food, clothing, or medical care that the army would not provide. So common was desertion and straggling in the Army of Northern Virginia that Robert E. Lee began ritual executions soon after he took command in the summer of 1862. It was hardly welcome news for the soldiers. Just before the Battle of Second Manassas in August, three members of the 10th Virginia and one from the 15th Virginia became, as Private John Casler recalled, "the first that had been sentenced to be shot for desertion in our division." One made his escape during the night. The other three were shot to death the next day. When all three officers who had sat on their court-martial were killed or mortally wounded in battle a few days later, "most of the soldiers," wrote Casler, "looked upon it as a judgment."[67]

Such judgments could fall on the mightiest of men. Private William H. Howe of the 116th Pennsylvania was in the forefront of combat during the Battle of Fredericksburg. When his unit's flag fell at the heaviest fighting near the stone wall, he made himself a target by picking it up and was lauded as a hero. Shortly afterward, Howe came down with a severe case of dysentery. He went to the regimental hospital, but it was full and he was sent away. He tried a second hospital, but it too was full. So he took his doctor's advice to go home. While at home recuperating, Howe's name appeared on a list of deserters for whose capture the government offered a cash reward. Three armed bounty hunters went after Howe. As they approached his house in the dark, shots rang out and one of the bounty hunters was killed.

Howe stood accused now both of desertion and murder. A court-martial presided over by Lieutenant Colonel Henry Fink of the 11th Pennsylvania found Howe guilty on all counts, but the sentence of death was overturned on appeal due to the trial's "informality." Another court-martial was ordered, Fink again presiding, and Howe was sentenced to death for a second time. This despite evidence that the testimony of the only other eyewitnesses, the two surviving bounty hunters, was highly suspect. Their companion was killed with a revolver; Howe had defended himself with a rifle. An additional oddity was that a defense witness at the first trial, after a promotion to captain, became a witness for the prosecution at the second trial.

Howe's impending execution outraged his comrades in the 116th Pennsylvania. From the regiment's colonel on down, they petitioned Lincoln to commute Howe's sentence. The president simply wrote across the petition: "Sentence approved. A. Lincoln." A few weeks later, after being forced to witness the building of his own gallows, William Howe finally faced execution. When Lincoln himself was murdered in April 1865, some members of the 116th Pennsylvania likely viewed it as a judgment.[68]

Military executions were not always conducted with military precision. Union soldier John Billings remembered one hanging, witnessed by upwards of twenty-seven thousand men, in which, as he wrote,

> the provost-marshal made a dreadful botch of the job, for the rope was too long, and when the drop fell the man's feet touched the ground. This obliged the provost-marshal to seize the rope, and by main strength to hold him clear of the ground till death ensued. It is quite probable that strangulation instead of a broken neck ended his life. His body was so light and emaciated that it is doubtful if, even under more favorable circumstances, his fall could have broken his neck.[69]

In another hanging attempt, the rope broke when the trap fell and the poor soldier crashed to the ground. As the condemned man cried out "Shoot me! Shoot me!" his executioners hauled him back onto the gallows and dropped him again, this time to his death.[70]

Execution by firing squad was hardly more humane. Sometimes those assigned to execution detail aimed high, refusing to kill a comrade, but that only prolonged the condemned's torture. Even when a firing squad aimed to kill, several volleys were often required to complete the job. One soldier recalled that during the execution of five privates, as the echoes of the first volley died away,

> to our astonishment each man yet remained standing, showing conclusively that the detail had fired high. The second or reserve detail was at once marched into position . . . and at the same signal the smoke puffed from their carbines, and their fire proved more accurate, but not entirely effective. The prisoners all fell. Three were dead, while two were trying hard to rise again, and one of them even got up to his knees when a bullet from the revolver of the provost marshal sent him down. Again he attempted to rise, getting upon his elbow and raising his body nearly to a sitting posture, when a second bullet in the head from the marshal's revolver suddenly extinguished what little life was left and a third shot put out the life of the second prisoner.[71]

Execution, though the most extreme of punishments, was only one of many painful, debilitating, and humiliating ways in which officers sought to establish their authority over the enlisted men. A soldier could be whipped, bucked and gagged, suspended by his thumbs, forced to carry a log or some other heavy object, or shackled with leg irons depending on the severity of the offense or the inclination of the officer. One man was hung up by his wrists for four hours just for swearing. A soldier accused of cowardice could be branded on the cheek, palm, shoulder, or hip with the letter C. A deserter, if he was fortunate enough to escape execution, could be branded with the letter D.[72]

Officers themselves were mercifully spared these tortures. An offense that might mean mutilation or death for an enlisted man would bring much lighter punishment for an officer. In Baltimore, when a private was called to testify at a court-martial and showed up drunk, the court made him wear a ball and chain for a month. An officer appearing before the court in the same condition was excused from testifying and no disciplinary action was taken against him. In 1864, a court-martial in the Army of the Potomac found a soldier guilty of abandoning his post during combat and sentenced him to be shot. At about the same time, another court-martial found an officer guilty of the same offense. His only punishment was to be discharged from the army.[73]

Some officers were quicker to inflict pain than others. There were those, as John Billings recalled, who "had no desire to torture the erring, but aimed to combine a reasonable form of punishment with utility to the camp and to the better behaved class of soldier." But in an era when punishment through pain was the rule rather than the exception, so was the officer who was likely to inflict it. Some took a perverse pleasure in doing so. When one soldier talked back to a lieutenant, the officer had him gagged with a rope and suspended by his thumbs. The soldier assigned guard duty over the unfortunate sufferer later wrote: "It was a cold day & the blood running down from his hands and arms & the tight cord cutting through the skin made the man groan so that I was strongly tempted to cut him down myself. . . . The Lieut. [ordered] . . . me if he Struggled to release himself to put my Bayonet through him. Once in a while the said Brute would come & visit him & seemed to enjoy his torture exceedingly."[74]

Some men simply could not stand by and see their comrades put through such misery despite the risk to themselves. Alfred Bellard and a few of his friends in the 5th New Jersey tried to cut down two privates who had been strung up by their captain. The officer caught them in the act and wounded one of the men with his sword before they could get away. When word of the incident got out and the camp erupted in a near riot, the captain took the hint and resigned. Had he not done so, he may not have lived much longer. "It was such officers as that," Bellard later wrote, "who received a stray ball occasionally on the field of battle."[75]

"I Do Not Want Any Man's Blood on My Hands"

If it often seemed to enlisted men that officers were the enemy, it sometimes seemed as if the enemy was not. Seldom have such cordial relations existed informally between men of opposing armies during any war. A Union soldier wrote from his post near Georgia's Kennesaw Mountain: "Under cover of night our lines were pushed close to theirs. We made a bargain with them that we would not fire on them if they would not fire on us, and they were as good as their word." He went on to lament: "It seems too bad that we have to fight men that we like. Now these southern soldiers seem just like our own boys, only they are on the other side."[76]

Not all soldiers held such cordial feelings for those on the other side. The war inevitably fomented a hatred in some that seemed to consume them. When two of his tentmates were wounded, one Yankee soldier recalled: "I acted like a madman. . . . The feeling uppermost in my mind was a desire to kill as many rebels as I could." When he got word of enemy troops wreaking havoc back home, a Mississippi private said of the Yankees: "I intend to fight them as long as I live and after this war stops. . . . I intend to kill Every one that crosses my path."

But such blood lust was by far the exception rather than the rule, as soldiers so often demonstrated in word and deed. Rebel and Yankee picket lines, which were sometimes only a few yards apart, often appeared more like social gatherings than military operations. The boys would meet between the lines to trade southern tobacco for northern coffee, pick blackberries, exchange newspapers, or simply have a conversation. If a creek separated the lines and the weather permitted, they would take a swim together. "The keenest sense of honor existed among the enlisted men of each side," recalled a Pennsylvania soldier. "It was no uncommon sight, when visiting the picket posts, to see an equal number of 'graybacks' and 'bluebellies,' as they facetiously termed each other, enjoying a social game of euchre or seven-up and sometimes the great national game of draw poker, with army rations and sutler's delicacies as the stakes."[77]

Sometimes men from one army would visit the camps of the other. A Wisconsin private wrote of one such visit in a letter to his sweetheart.

> We had two visitors day before yesterday. They were Johnny Rebs. They came over and took dinner with us and brought over some corn bread and tobacco and we made some coffee and all sat down on the ground together and had a good chat as well as a good dinner. . . . They were real smart fellows both of them. You must not think up there that we fight down here because we are mad, for it is not the case . . . but we fight for fun, or rather because we can't help ourselves.[78]

Officers frowned on their men's fraternization across the lines, and discouraged it by giving orders to shoot enemy soldiers on sight. But disobedience of those orders was so widespread that they could not be enforced. Unless their units were on the attack or under attack, the men displayed no eager wish to kill. They were soldiers, not murderers. To fire on the enemy in battle was a matter of duty; to do so otherwise was murder, no matter what their officers said. James Dinkins of the Army of Northern Virginia made that clear when he and his comrades were posted opposite the Army of the Potomac across the Rappahannock River.

> It was but a short time after the battle of Fredericksburg, where the two armies had been arrayed against each other with all the ferocity of wolves, and yet the men on both sides were perfectly friendly as individuals. "The Yanks" sent us newspapers, coffee and other things they could get, and we sent them tobacco. We had nothing else they wanted. The neighborly feeling was growing, till the officers thought it was going too far, and ordered us to stop all communications, and to shoot at every man we saw. But all the bitterness was forgotten, and it was impossible to stop us from being friendly toward each other.

When the armies were not arrayed in battle, according to Dinkins, "the kindest feeling prevailed, and I venture to assert . . . that the war could have been settled in ten days if the question had been left to the soldiers." The boys on the other side felt the same way. Whatever their differences, they all agreed "perfectly on one thing," as a Wisconsin soldier put it: "If the settlement of this war was left to the Enlisted men on both sides we would soon go home."[79]

When officers' orders to fire became too insistent to ignore, the boys had their way of maintaining good relations across the lines. Warning yells of "Look out, Johnny!" or "Hunt your holes, Billy, I'm going to shoot!" were common. After firing a few volleys to keep the officers happy, said one eyewitness, "the boys from both sides would walk around us as leisurely as if there was not an enemy in a thousand miles."[80]

Though most tried to avoid it when they could, killing was an inevitable part of war and that fact weighed heavily on the men. God's commandment that "Thou shalt not kill" accepted no excuses and offered no exceptions, even for the enemy. On the contrary, their Bibles instructed them to love their enemies and do good to them. After being issued his first rounds of ammunition, one Confederate soldier looked at the cartridges in his hand and wondered silently, "Is it possible that we are actually to *kill men? Human beings?*" The thought was too much for many of the men to bear. Like thousands of other soldiers who fired volleys in the direction of opposing troops during battle without aiming very carefully, Union soldier Numa Barned insisted: "I don't know that I ever shot any one. . . . I do not want any man's blood on my hands." Others simply shifted the burden of sin to whichever government they served. John Holahan reasoned that as a soldier in the Union army he belonged to "Uncle Sam, mentally, morally, and physically." Therefore, he concluded, any blame for his actions rested on the government's shoulders, not on his: "My virtues and vices must correspond to that of my fellows; I must *lie* to rebels, *steal* from rebels and *kill* rebels;—Uncle Sam making vicarious atonement for these sins."[81]

"Terrors of the Battlefield"

The reluctance of soldiers to kill, or to accept responsibility for it when they did, reflected concerns not only for their fellow men but for their own mortality. Death was all around them all the time, and no one wanted to be its next victim. The wounded and diseased prayed for recovery. Men going into battle prayed for deliverance. Some threw away their playing cards and promised never to gamble again. Others promised to dedicate their lives to the ministry should they be spared. Still, the righteous fell with the unrighteous. There was no way to know who's number would be drawn next in war's lottery of death. When Bill Blevins of the 21st Georgia could no longer take the strain, he asked his captain to make him the company cook. "I can't stand the shooting," he said, "and I'm afraid I might run,—and disgrace my name."[82]

For some, the "call of nature" provided a convenient excuse to absent themselves as their lines formed for battle. Others took refuge in sudden illness. One Union officer wrote that his regiment "turned out to a man and were in line of Battle in 7 minutes, and ready for the enemy. Yet there was a number who were suddenly taken with a *'pain in the stomach'* and felt like going back to their tents." As the Peninsula campaign got underway in the spring of 1862, Confederate general D.H. Hill reported that "several thousand soldiers . . . have fled to Richmond under pretext of sickness. They have even thrown away their arms that their flight might not be impeded."[83]

Those who wanted not only to avoid combat but to get out of the army altogether sometimes resorted to self-mutilation. Like many others on both sides, one Illinois soldier shot off his trigger finger. Another from Vermont shot off three fingers using a stick to fire his rifle. When he failed to shoot off his toe, a Massachusetts private tried the same on his trigger finger. It was not blown completely off, but it was mangled so badly that it had to be amputated. William Andrews of the 1st Georgia recalled one man who was so desperate to get out of the army that he shot off his entire left hand. "That," wrote Andrews, "ended his soldiering."[84]

It is hardly surprising that so many were so desperate to avoid trial by fire. Civil War combat was a murderous affair directed largely by unimaginative commanders using outdated tactics. The practice of massing infantry and advancing over open ground was a relic of earlier wars, when soldiers faced smoothbore cannon and musket of relatively short range. Civil War battlefields were ruled by the new rifled muzzle-loaders with an effective range of hundreds of yards, not to mention rifled artillery that could accurately target infantry from more than a mile away. But military minds lagged far behind military technology. The nation's best-trained West Pointers, in accordance with the doctrines of the time, repeatedly sent line after line of massed infantry over exposed terrain against distant positions. By the time the attacking forced reached its objective, if it got there at all, it was usually bled too weak to make a successful assault. Casualty rates of over 50 percent were common. Some units suffered losses of 80 percent and more.

On those occasions when attackers succeeded in reaching the opposing line, a breakthrough was rare. Even so, such a clash was devastating for both sides. In recalling the unsuccessful Yankee assault on his position north of Atlanta at Kennesaw Mountain, where "column after column of Federal soldiers were crowded upon that line," Private Sam Watkins wrote of

> a solid line of blazing fire right from the muzzles of the Yankee guns being poured right into our very faces, singeing our hair and clothes, the hot blood of our dead and wounded spurting on us, the blinding smoke and stifling atmosphere filling our eyes and mouths, and the awful concussion causing the blood to gush out of our noses and ears, and above all, the roar of battle, made it a perfect pandemonium. Afterward I heard a soldier express himself by saying that he thought "Hell had broke loose in Georgia, sure enough."[85]

Little wonder that so many soldiers found themselves unnerved at the sight of mass slaughter. And exposure to it did not diminish the fear of it. As one Confederate wrote of his own experience:

I must confess that the terrors of the battlefield grew not less as we advanced in the war, for I felt far less fear in the second battle of Manassas than at South Mountain or even at Fredericksburg; and I believe that soldiers generally do not fear death less because of their repeated escape from its jaws. For, in every battle they see so many new forms of death, see so many frightful and novel kinds of mutilation, see such varying fortunes in the tide of strife, and appreciate so highly their deliverance from destruction, that their dread of incurring the like fearful perils unnerves them for each succeeding conflict, quite as much as their confidence in their oft tried courage sustains them and stimulates them to gain new laurels at the cannon's mouth.[86]

Many was the soldier who, in the thick of battle, felt certain that his next breath would be his last. A Texan who survived Gettysburg wrote home to his young son that "one poor fellow had his head knocked off in a few feet of me, and I felt all the time as if I would never see you and little sister again." He nearly did not. As his regiment advanced through the mass of boulders at Devil's Den, a bullet passed through his beard and shattered on a rock just a half inch from his head. At Antietam, Private Edward Spangler of Pennsylvania was sure he had seen his last sunrise. "The bullets flew thicker than bees and the shells exploded with a deafening roar," he wrote after the battle. "I thought of home and friends, and felt that I surely would be killed, and how I didn't want to be!"[87]

Avoiding the killing fields could be difficult for men in the ranks when their officers were nearby. When one Yankee soldier turned to run in the heat of battle, a general caught sight of the man and forced him to turn around at gunpoint, vowing to "kill him on the spot" if he refused. The soldier went back to the line and was promptly killed by enemy fire. The general, Rutherford B. Hayes, went on to become president of the United States. Hayes said he was gratified to have been able to insure a hero's death for the soldier instead of a coward's. He assumed the soldier's eternal gratitude as well. But there is no record of soldiers expressing the sort of gratitude that generals like Hayes seemed to expect. On the contrary, when Confederate general W.J. Hardee tried to force one reluctant regiment into battle, the men shot at him. When another officer threatened to report a group of fugitives from battle as "a pack of cowards," they replied that "they did not care a damn" what he called them.[88]

For the soldiers, it was much more difficult to say who among them were cowards than it seemed to be for the generals. Robert Burdette of Illinois wrote of one of his comrades as a fine soldier in nearly every respect. He never faked an illness, never requested light duty, never stumbled or stopped to tie his shoes as the regiment moved forward in battle. But at the first sight of blood, he turned and ran. "He was beaten in every fight," said Burdette, but at every fight "he went in." "This man was a coward," but "a good coward." It was a fine line to draw, and it led Burdette to wonder if there was such a line at all: "Who are the cowards? And how do we distinguish them from heroes? How does God tell?"[89]

During their attack at Fredericksburg, when one of his fellow soldiers of the 16th Maine fell to the ground uninjured, Abner Small called him a coward and dragged him back up. But after the man, with a look of tortured confusion on his face, said that "his legs would not obey him," Small apologized. After thinking on the incident, Small finally decided that men "were heroes or cowards in spite of themselves."[90] Both Burdette's and Small's thoughts reflected an unspoken fear harbored by every man—that he too might reach a breaking point and falter in battle.

Still, such was the bond of loyalty and sense of obligation the soldiers had for each other that most soldiers held fast on the firing line unless ordered to withdraw or compelled by force to do so. For a soldier to break and run on his own meant abandoning and further endangering men whom he had lived with, marched with, suffered with, and often grew up with—men that he had come to love as brothers and often more than himself. Whatever the cause for which they fought as an army, in combat their cause was each other and each man depended on the next to cover his flank. At Shiloh, Private Samuel Evans was hit by a ball that ripped through his mouth—in one cheek and out the other. But he stayed with his comrades "and fought for a considerable length of time, cheering on the men and loading and shooting as fast as he could." Stunned by the concussion of an exploding shell and wounded by a bullet in the thigh at Chickamauga, Private Mayfield was being carried to the rear by litter bearers when he recovered from his stupor. Mayfield yelled, "This will not do for me," jumped off the litter, and limped back to join his comrades on the line. O.W. Norton wrote that when he saw two of his friends wounded at

Gaines's Mill, "a kind of desperation" came over him and he fought like a demon. "The loss of comrades maddened me."[91]

Yet even in the heat of battle, when to kill or be killed was the order of the day, some soldiers were able to retain their humanity and display compassion not only for their comrades but for those on the other side too. As the Federals attacked at Fredericksburg, rising above the sound of gunfire came the cries of thousands of wounded men. Too weak to move, they lay there begging for water. When Sergeant Richard Kirkland of South Carolina could listen to their pleading no longer he gathered as many canteens as he could carry, leaped from behind the safety of a stone wall, and moved among the wounded Yankees giving water and comfort where he could. When the soldiers saw what he was doing, both sides stopped firing as Kirkland, forever after hailed as the Angel of Marye's Heights, continued on his merciful errand. Such scenes were witnessed on other battlefields, including Vicksburg and Cold Harbor. At Gettysburg, Patrick McNeil of Virginia jumped into the line of fire when he saw a wounded Yankee unable to move. Just as he finished pulling the man to safety, a cannonball tore off both his legs. McNeil cried out, "Oh, my poor wife and children," as he fell to the ground and died.[92]

Amid the slaughter at Kennesaw Mountain, there was another act of compassion. Powder sparks had ignited the underbrush in front of the 1st Arkansas's entrenchments, and flames threatened to engulf dozens of wounded Federals. William Martin, commanding the 1st Arkansas, mounted the top of his earthworks, exposing himself to a hail of bullets, and, waving a white handkerchief tied to a ramrod, called for a truce. The crack of musketry died away and the helpless men were carried from danger—some by Rebels who only moments before had been shooting at them. This done, a Union officer presented Martin with his own pistols as a gesture of appreciation.[93]

At other times the wounded were not so fortunate. One of the more horrible forms of death suffered at Antietam involved the many haystacks that dotted the landscape. Throughout the day's battle, wounded men of both armies crawled into the hay for shelter. As fighting around them continued, some of the haystacks were set ablaze by bursting shells. Helpless men, too badly injured to crawl away, were roasted alive. So were many at the Wilderness battlefield after the woods caught fire.[94]

"For What Had These Young Lives Been Sacrificed?"

After every major Civil War battle, mutilated bodies lay, as one soldier put it, "thick as autumn leaves" over the field. One man described the aftermath of Chancellorsville as "the most revolting scene I had ever witnessed."

> Our line of battle extended over some eight miles and for that distance you see the dead bodies of the enemy lying in every direction, some with their heads shot off, some with their brains oozing out, some pierced through the head with musket balls, some with their noses shot away, some with their mouths smashed, some wounded in the neck, some with broken arms or legs, some shot through the breast and some cut in two with shells.[95]

Some men became hardened to such sights after a time. Surveying the bloody fields around Sharpsburg, one Union soldier wrote: "We don't mind the sight of dead men no more than if they was dead Hogs." "That is what less than a year has done to us," said another of the men's growing insensitivity to death. "At that rate two years more and we will be murdering in cold blood." Others found it more difficult to push the meaning and impact of death out of their minds. Private David Thompson of the 9th New York wrote after one battle: "Before the sunlight faded, I walked over the narrow field. All around lay the Confederate dead, clad in butternut. As I looked down on the poor pinched faces all enmity died out. There was no 'secession' in those rigid forms nor in those fixed eyes staring at the sky. Clearly, it was not *their* war."[96] As his comrades overran a Confederate position at Shiloh, John Cockerill later recalled:

> I passed . . . the corpse of a beautiful boy in gray who lay with his blond curls scattered about his face and his hand folded peacefully across his breast. He was clad in a bright and neat uniform, well garnished with gold, which seemed to tell the story of a loving mother and sisters who had sent their household pet to the field of war. His neat little hat lying beside him bore the number of a Georgia regiment. . . . He was about my age. . . . At the sight of the poor boy's corpse, I burst into a regular boo-hoo and started on.[97]

Even as the war neared its end, there were still plenty of war-weary veterans who remained deeply affected by death. "I saw fifteen unburied Confederate soldiers lying where they had fallen," wrote Rice Bull late in the war. "It was not a pleasant sight to me, even though these men had been our enemies. I thought when I saw them, of the sorrow and grief there would be in fifteen homes somewhere; and for what had these young lives been sacrificed?" Like so many others who had seen too much of death, Bull concluded: "There should be some way to settle political differences without slaughtering human beings and wearing out the bodies and sapping the strength of those who may be fortunate enough to escape the death penalty."[98]

For those fortunate enough to avoid death or injury in battle came the inevitable task of burying the dead. It was crucial to get the job done as soon as possible, especially when the opposing lines remained intact. After the Union's unsuccessful attack at Kennesaw Mountain, both armies, each fearing an assault from the other, stayed on their

Soldiers killed in battle were often hastily buried in shallow graves. Some, like these poor souls found near Chancellorsville, were simply covered over with a thin layer of soil. Wind, rain, and hungry scavengers soon exposed the remains. Raw recruits of the 15th Alabama visited Manassas a few weeks after the first battle there and were astonished to find skeletal body parts protruding from the ground and hogs feeding on the dead. (United States Army Military History Institute)

battle lines. Three days later, the two sides were forced to call a truce and begin burial details, "not for any respect either army had for the dead," recalled Sam Watkins, "but to get rid of the sickening stench." Theodore Upson wrote that men from both armies gathered the dead, wrapped them in their blankets, and laid them in mass graves side by side. A chaplain from either army—it did not matter which—said a prayer before the men began filling in each pit. That done, the soldiers "parted with expressions of good will such as: 'I hope to miss you, Yank, if I happen to shoot in your direction,' or 'May I never hit you Johnny if we fight again.' "[99]

Aside from the sickening smell, another incentive to bury the dead quickly was that a fresh corpse could be handled more easily than a rotting one. After a few days it was difficult to lift the deceased because flesh simply tore away from bone and the body fell apart. At Gettysburg, a battle that lasted three days, there was no choice but to wait. By the time the Yankee victors and captured Rebels could get to them, some of the bodies had been lying in the summer heat for more than a week. Hogs, buzzards, and other critters had to be chased away before what remained could be collected. It was literally a sickening task. A Confederate prisoner on burial detail after Gettysburg wrote:

> The sights and smells that assailed us were simply indescribable—corpses swollen to twice their original size, some of them actually burst asunder with the pressure of foul gases and vapors.... The odors were nauseating and so deadly that in a short time we all sickened and were lying with our mouths close to the ground, most of us vomiting profusely.[100]

"Wounded in Every Manner Possible"

There were times when soldiers were too quick to bury the apparently dead. Care had to be taken not to bury someone alive. The danger was common enough in the nineteenth century, even more so in the hurried aftermath of battle. During Sherman's march through Georgia, as Union troops were moving Confederate dead after the Battle of Griswoldville, they heard a groan from under the pile. "We moved a few bodies," recalled one soldier, "and there was a boy with a broken arm and leg—just a boy 14 years old." That was not the worst of it. "Beside him, cold in death, lay his Father, two Brothers, and an Uncle. It was a harvest of death. We brought the poor fellow up to the fire. Our surgeons made him as comfortable as they could."[101] Not all of the barely living were recognized as such, scattered as they were among the dead. It will never be known how many men awoke from the shock of an injury to find themselves entombed. The more fortunate suffocated to death before they could regain consciousness.

Not all soldiers were entirely opposed to becoming battlefield casualties as long as the wound was relatively minor. It could mean a short rest at an army hospital followed perhaps by a furlough. Leave was tough to get, and nearly any opportunity for time away from the war was welcomed. The trick was to incur a wound just serious enough to warrant hospitalization. Not all were, as Union private Jimmie McMillian discovered much to his disappointment. During the siege of Kennesaw Mountain, the young soldier was hit and fell to the ground screaming, "Jasus, I'm kilt. I'm dead." Friends rushed to his aid and found, much to their relief, that a bullet had passed through the fleshy part of his arm doing no major damage. A jubilant McMillian jumped to his feet, his happiness multiplied by the prospect of a recuperative furlough. As he raised his arms with joy, however, the others noticed a slight stream of blood trickling through a small hole in his shirt. Informed of this discovery, McMillian again fell to the ground, certain that his end was near. His friends removed the shirt and found a minié ball lodged between two ribs just under the skin. But the wound was not serious enough to get him sent home. "Jimmie turned mad as fire," said one of his comrades. "He got no furlough and did not even go to the hospital. Instead, he was given the company mule to lead."[102]

Private McMillian was lucky that the bullet's force was spent before it hit his chest. Had it penetrated much more deeply, he would almost certainly have died. Effective surgical techniques for repair of internal wounds to the abdominal and chest cavities were nearly nonexistent. Even a wound to the extremities could be fatal if shock or infection set in. The Civil War's typical .58 caliber soft lead bullet, over half an inch in diameter, spread out on impact at full velocity, its distorted edges carrying dirty clothing and skin into the body. The wound, wrote one student of Civil War medicine, "presented a violently lacerated appearance and a track enlarged out of all proportion to the caliber of the projectile."[103] And if a bullet hit bone, the bone was usually shattered several inches on either side of the impact point.

Among the first difficulties wounded men faced was stopping the flow of blood. Soldiers were issued no emergency field dressings, so they used anything at hand. Usually a dirty handkerchief or sweaty piece of shirt would have to do. If a soldier was able to avoid bleeding to death, getting to a field hospital was his next task. It could take some time. Troops had orders not to stop during combat to aid wounded friends, so the injured had to wait for help or help themselves. At Sharpsburg, one poor Confederate with a leg blown off had to haul himself to the rear using two rifles as crutches.[104]

Once at a field hospital, usually in a barn or simply out in the open, the soldier faced horrors like none he had ever seen. One soldier visited a field hospital during the Atlanta campaign and later wrote:

> It was the only field hospital that I saw during the whole war, and I have no desire to see another. Those hollow-eyed and sunken-cheeked sufferers, shot in every conceivable part of the body; some shrieking, and calling upon their mothers; some laughing the hard, cackling laugh of the sufferer without hope, and some cursing like troopers, and some writhing and groaning as their wounds were being bandaged and dressed. I saw a man . . . who had lost his right hand, another his leg, then another whose head was laid open, and I could see his brain thump, and another with his under jaw shot off; in fact, wounded in every manner possible.[105]

At Fredericksburg, there were so many wounded and so few surgeons that it took at least twenty-four hours for a soldier to be examined after arriving at a field hospital. If he did not die waiting for it, the examination itself could kill a man. One soldier who suffered an upper arm wound at Antietam remembered that "the young surgeon thrust his finger into the hole where the bullet had entered, and with his other forefinger plunged into the place of its exit, he rummaged around for broken bones, splinters, etc., until I swooned away."[106]

With limited time and a seemingly endless line of wounded men, amputation was among the most common surgical procedures. For an arm or leg wound where the bone was shattered, amputation was considered the quickest and safest treatment. Speed was essential not only because of the large number of wounded but also to limit the patients' exposure to the knife. A good surgeon could complete the operation in less than thirty seconds. Since there was seldom enough ether or chloroform to go around, amputations were most often performed with the soldier wide awake. The lucky ones quickly loss consciousness from the extreme pain. Even when some form of anesthesia was available, applications were so crude and some doctors so poorly trained in its use that the patient could die of an overdose. Still, the fortunate part for the soldiers was that with so much practice their surgeons became very good at doing amputations. Though the death rate among Civil War amputees was a chilling one in four, it was much better than average. Civilian surgeons of the day lost fully half their amputee patients.[107]

Wounded men were moved on and off the cutting tables so fast that surgeons became, as one witness recalled, "literally covered from head to foot with the blood of the sufferers." Another wrote that they looked like "a bevy of butchers."[108] One officer had much the same impression when he visited an open-air field hospital at Gettysburg.

> There stood the surgeons, their sleeves rolled up to their elbows, their bare arms as well as their linen aprons smeared with blood, their knives not seldom held between their teeth, while they were helping a patient on or off the table. . . . As a wounded man was lifted on the table, often shrieking with pain as the attendants handled him, the surgeon quickly examined the wound and resolved upon cutting off the injured limb. Some ether was administered and the body was put in position in a moment. The surgeon snatched his knife from between his teeth . . . wiped it rapidly once or twice across his bloodstained apron, and the cutting began. The operation accomplished, the surgeon would look around with a deep sigh, and then—"Next!"[109]

The body parts accumulated rapidly. One soldier recalled late in life that nothing ever filled him with "more horror than that pile of legs and arms that had been cut off our soldiers."[110]

It was tough on the surgeons as well. In a brief letter to his wife, one physician wrote from Fredericksburg:

> We are almost worked to death. My feet are terribly swollen; yet we cannot rest for there are so many poor fellows who are suffering. All day yesterday I worked at those terrible operations since the battle

commenced, and I have also worked at the tables two whole nights and a part of another. Oh! it is awful. It does not seem as though I could take a knife in my hand to-day, yet there are a hundred cases of amputation waiting for me. Poor fellows come and beg almost on their knees for the first chance to have an arm taken off. It is a scene of horror such as I never saw. God forbid that I should see another.[111]

At Antietam, a disgruntled surgeon fumed: "I am tired of this inhuman incompetence, this neglect and folly, which leave me alone with all these soldiers on my hands, five hundred of whom will die before daybreak unless they have attention and I with no light but a five-inch candle."[112]

Neglect of care for the wounded started at the top. The prevailing view among high-ranking government and military officials on both sides was that, as one noted, "the business of war is to tear the body,

Amputation was among the most common surgical procedures. Since there was seldom enough ether or chloroform to go around, amputations were most often performed with the soldier wide awake. The lucky ones quickly lost consciousness from the extreme pain. Shown here are wounded soldiers, amputees among them. (National Archives)

not mend it." Lincoln himself referred to the Sanitary Commission as the "fifth wheel to the coach." That attitude filtered down through the officer corps. There were never enough attendants assigned to help all the wounded, and never enough ambulance wagons to carry them. Despite complaints from the doctors, what ambulances they had were often diverted to carry the personal baggage of high-ranking officers. As a result, after nearly every battle many of the wounded had to be left behind. "Why not take away some of this transportation from these three-starred gentry," complained an officer of the 4th Alabama, "and use it for the benefit of the bone and sinew of the army. It certainly is *very hard, very unjust,* and *very* discouraging to even brave men to have to fight when they know that they will be left (if wounded) in the hands of the enemy."[113]

Those not left behind were little better off. On the Confederate retreat from Gettysburg, one officer wrote of the misery he witnessed among the wounded.

The column moved rapidly . . . and from almost every wagon for many miles issued heart-rending wails of agony. For four hours I hurried forward on my way to the front, and in all that time I was never out of hearing of the groans and cries of the wounded and dying. Scarcely one in a hundred had received adequate surgical aid. . . . Many of the wounded in the wagons had been without food for thirty-six hours. Their torn and bloody clothing, matted and hardened, was rasping the tender, inflamed, and still oozing wounds. Very few of the wagons had even a layer of straw in them, and all were without springs. The road was rough and rocky. . . . The jolting was enough to have killed strong men, if long exposed to it. From nearly every wagon as the teams trotted on, urged by whip and shout, came such cries and shrieks as these:

"Oh God! why can't I die?"

"My God, will no one have mercy and kill me?"

"Stop! Oh! for God's sake, stop just for one minute; take me out and leave me to die on the roadside."

"I am dying! I am dying! My poor wife, my dear children, what will become of you?" . . .

No heed could be given to any of their appeals. . . . On! on! We *must* move on. . . . During this one night I realized more of the horrors of war than I had in all the two preceding years.[114]

"We Knew Nothing About Antiseptics"

Those who survived evacuation from the battlefield were carried to military hospitals where, if their injuries did not kill them, disease and infection likely would. Louisa May Alcott, author of *Little Women*, wrote of a military hospital in Washington where she served as a nurse: "A more perfect pestilence box than this I never saw—cold, damp, dirty, full of vile odors from wounds, kitchens, and stables."[115] After only a few weeks work, the twenty-seven-year-old Alcott came down with typhoid fever. It left her a semi-invalid for the rest of her life. Unless soldiers were fortunate enough to have a ward matron like Mother Bickerdyke with the energy, will, and continuing good health to enforce strict cleanliness, poor sanitation was an ever-present fact of hospital life.

Malnutrition was another killer that stalked the wards. Lack of proper diet was especially severe in Confederate hospitals. The Southern army could barely feed healthy soldiers, much less the sick and injured. "In the hospital," recalled survivor Harrison Farrell, "our allowance was [designed] to starve one to Death." All he got was one cracker, two spoonfuls of "chicken water," and a little coffee per day. "It was awful," he wrote, "to See [the sick] Begging for something to eat [and] Die hungry." A friend, David Brooks, saved Farrell's life by smuggling in some sweet potatoes. After a few visits, Brooks caught fever and died. Weak and paralyzed in one arm, Farrell asked for and was granted a furlough to escort Brooks's body home. Farrell never went back.[116]

Water was often in short supply at hospitals North and South, so clothes and bedding were almost never washed as often as they should have been. Neither was tableware. At St. Mary's Hospital in Dalton, Georgia, attendants did not wash plates until they had been used by at least two patients. The most serious problem lack of water caused was difficulty in disposing of urine and defecation. One inspector described the toilet facilities at Savannah's General Hospital No. 1 as "unclean and offensive." Conditions were even worse at Richmond's Jackson Hospital, where toiletry floors and seats were "smeared with excrement." At Central Park Hospital in New York City, water pressure was not strong enough to serve toilets on the upper floors. In Philadelphia, hospitals were equipped with long zinc troughs covered by a row of seat holes. A faucet was supposed to supply water constantly at one end, washing all waste matter to a drain pipe at the other. But to conserve water, the tap was opened only occasionally after a number of patients had relieved themselves.[117]

Ignorant of how diseases spread and ill supplied by the government, even the Sanitary Commission encouraged such unsanitary measures as using old dressings on new patients after a cursory washing.[118] One Federal surgeon, who lived to see medical science transformed by the germ theory, wrote in 1918 about general hospital and surgical practices during the Civil War era:

> We operated in old blood-stained and often pus-stained coats, the veterans of a hundred fights. . . . We used undisinfected instruments from undisinfected plush-lined cases, and still worse, used marine sponges which had been used in prior pus cases and had been only washed in tap water. If a sponge or an instrument fell on the floor it was washed and squeezed in a basin of tap water and used as if it were clean. Our silk to tie blood vessels was undisinfected. . . . The silk with which we sewed up all wounds was undisinfected. If there was any difficulty in threading the needle we moistened it with . . . bacteria-laden saliva, and rolled it between bacteria-infected fingers. We dressed the wounds with clean but undisinfected sheets, shirts, tablecloths, or other old soft linen rescued from the family ragbag. We had no sterilized gauze dressing, no gauze sponges. . . . We knew nothing about antiseptics and therefore used none.[119]

The result was rampant infection throughout the wards. Ailments nearly unknown in modern hospitals were the scourge of Civil War patients. A blood infection called pyemia, known as bacteremia today, was fatal in almost 97.4 percent of all cases. Tetanus was only slightly less deadly, with a mortality rate of 89 percent. The most common postoperational complication was gangrene. If the blood flow to healing tissue was not sufficient or if bacterial infection set in, the flesh began to die. If gangrene struck an arm or leg, the only way to stop its spread was amputation—sometimes on a limb that had only recently undergone the operation.[120]

If gangrene appeared in a chest or abdominal wound there was no known way to stop it, at least not at the war's outset. But at a Chattanooga stockade, Confederate surgeons held as prisoners of war discovered a cure. When they were denied bandages by Union doctors hoarding their own short supplies, injured Rebels were left to suffer with wounds left unbound. The wounds became maggot infested within days. But the captured physicians found that the tiny creatures ate away only dead flesh and left a clean and heathy wound. The recovery rate among their men was much greater than that of the Federal wounded. After their release, the Confederate doctors continued to leave wounds exposed, encouraging the development of maggots, and spread the word among their colleagues. Union doctors continued to bind wounds with unsterilized bandages, encouraging the development of infection, and watched their patients die by the thousands.[121]

"Hell on Earth"

Perhaps the only institution more miserable for its inmates than Civil War hospitals were Civil War prisons—at least those occupied by enlisted men. Both sides housed captured officers in their own quarters, which were generally more comfortable. But prisons for the rank and file were crowded, filthy, and infested with vermin and disease. In the words of prisoner Sam Boggs, they were "the closest existence to hell on earth."[122]

Soldiers captured early in the war were mercifully spared the misery of long imprisonment. Prisoners were typically exchanged or paroled as soon as they could be processed, usually within days or weeks. There were few military prisons to speak of. That changed in 1863 after the Union army began enlisting black troops and the Confederate government refused to recognize them as legitimate combatants. By order of the Davis administration, black soldiers were to be treated as rebellious chattel, subject to enslavement. Their white officers were to be viewed as leaders of slave insurrection and subject to execution. Neither blacks nor whites serving in any regiment of the United States Colored Troops, as such units were designated, would be exchanged or paroled by the Confederacy.

Lincoln responded by halting the practice of exchange and parole altogether. The move sent a message, North and South, that there was no turning back on the controversial issue of using black troops. Lincoln saw the move as a military benefit as well. Since he could replace his own combat losses more easily than could the Confederates, doing away with exchange and parole could only work in favor of the Union war effort. But from the perspective of most men in the ranks, it was hardly a favorable development. Both sides quickly began throwing together makeshift prisons which by the middle of 1864 held over one hundred thousand men in overcrowded confinement.[123]

Neither side gave much thought to providing adequate housing, food, or clothing for prisoners. That was particularly hard on southern prisoners suffering through northern winters. The shivering voice of captured Confederates came through clearly in Fred Bailey's study of *Class and Tennessee's Confederate Generation.*

> At Camp Morton, J. R. Cox wrote, he was not issued a blanket in spite of temperatures as cold as ten degrees below zero; John Hinkle complained that, at Camp Douglas, he had little more than a "piece of oil cloth for cover in very Severe winter weather"; at Rock Island, John Chisum "had to trot the Burricks day and night in cold spells to keep from freezing." Ford Adams and his comrades fought the intense chill at Camp Chase "by piling up to gether," and at Fort Delaware, Carter Upchurch often slept on the frozen ground "hungry and nearly naked." As far as James Gold was concerned, Confederate prisoners "suffered more from cold than anything else."[124]

Such suffering was not entirely a matter of poor planning. It was also a matter of policy. "So long as a prisoner has clothing upon him, however much torn," wrote the Union's commissary general, Colonel William H. Hoffman, to a subordinate, "issue nothing to him."[125]

Both Union and Confederate prisoners suffered from hunger as well. Photographs of former inmates taken just after the war testify to the effect of malnutrition on the men. Many coming out of the South's Andersonville and Belle Isle prisons looked like walking skeletons. So did many released from the North. After two years in a Yankee prison, William Morelock weighed only seventy pounds. Joseph Wall was slightly better off at 102. Among the most pathetic was A.M. Bruce, whose hip bones actually protruded from his skin.[126]

Withholding rations was a common means of prisoner control. Food allocations for prisoners of war on both sides nearly always fell short of what was needed, especially in the South. But many officials, Major Henry Wirz of Andersonville among them, made the situation incalculably worse by withholding food from prisoners for all sorts of infractions real or imagined. In a retaliatory tit-for-tat move, William

One out of five Confederate prisoners died of exposure and disease at Camp Morton near Indianapolis. U.S. surgeon Charles Kipp wrote that the problem of disease was "undoubtedly caused by overcrowding in the barracks and by the exhalations from the ground, which has served as a receptacle for the excreta of thousands of men." August Clark, a Union medical inspector, reported: "The camp is a disgrace to the name of military prison." (Hargrett Library, University of Georgia)

Hoffman reduced prison rations even more when he got word of hunger among Union prisoners in the South. On top of that, as a matter of War Department policy, northern prisons held back a portion of their food budget to establish a fund for lump-sum purchases of vegetables for the prisoners. But Hoffman never gave authorization to use the fund. At war's end, he was pleased to be able to return $1.8 million to the War Department. He could have returned much more had it not been for the untold amounts from the fund that found its way into the pockets of corrupt prison officials.[127]

Many captives supplemented their diet with anything in the form of nutrition they could get their hands on, cats and dogs included. Some were strays, but others were pets of the guards or officers. Hungry Confederates at New York's Elmira prison caught the camp baker's dog and ate it, saying that it "tasted like mutton." To be caught eating

someone's pet could result in severe punishment, so rats were more often the targets of hungry soldiers. Besides, they were much more
abundant. Joseph Riley made a small crossbow with which to shoot
them. He was so successful that he invited fellow inmates to join him
in dining on "rat boiled, rat stew and once rat and dumplings." Long
after the war, Riley spoke of his satisfaction at being able to provide for
his friends: "These feasts are pleasant memories to me yet. They . . .
broke the monotony of prison life, and to play host to a rat dinner
[which relieved] your comrades of that awful torture of gnawing
hunger gave you the consciousness of having done well."[128]

For thousands of hungry men, such efforts were not quite well
enough. Of more than four hundred thousand Civil War soldiers held
as prisoners of war at one time or another, fifty-six thousand of them
died in captivity. The mortality rate in Union prisons generally was
about 12 percent. The rate in Confederate prisons was slightly higher
at 15.5 percent. Most deadly of the Union camps was Elmira, with a
death rate of over 24 percent. By far the worst, North or South, with
a death rate of 35 percent, was Andersonville. Of the forty-one thousand men imprisoned at the stockade, nearly fifteen thousand never
came out alive. One Georgia woman wrote of the suffering prisoners:
"My heart aches for these poor wretches, Yankees though they are, and
I am afraid God will suffer some terrible retribution to fall upon us for
letting such things happen. If the Yankees should ever come to South-
West Georgia, and go to Anderson and see the graves there, God have
mercy on the land!" The Yankees did eventually see Andersonville's
many graves. They heard the gruesome tales of the prisoners who
lived to tell them. And they had no mercy on the prison's commandant, Henry Wirz. Convicted of war crimes, he was hanged at Washington's Old Capitol Prison in November 1865.[129]

"Anxiety on Account of My Family"

Prisoners endured not only the physical agony of ill-treated confinement, but also suffered the emotional anguish of being out of touch
with their families. Hartford's *Connecticut Courant* wrote in July 1864
that "the greatest trial of captivity is having nothing from home." It
was little less of a trial for soldiers in the field for whom an unreliable
postal service was the only link to home. When mail did get through,

each letter was treated almost as a sacred relic. Harvey Hightower wrote to his sister, "I had rather have letters now than clothes." In a note to his wife, Benjamin Franklin Jackson wrote, "I hope I shall get an answer before long, for it makes me so proud when I get a letter from you. I have to read it over two or three times before I can stop." One Alabama soldier risked his life dodging rifle fire to retrieve a letter from his wife. A Georgia man told his wife, "I want you to write me 20 letters (in one envelope) each letter twenty pages long." Many a letter home closed with the words "write soon."[130]

If soldiers felt great joy on receiving a cherished letter, they also experienced deep depression when no word came. As young Thomas Lightfoot wrote to his cousin Hennie: "You cant imagine how bad it makes one feel to see all the boys eagerly seizing on their letters from home—while he is standing by intently gazing on the package as it gradually grows smaller—expecting every minute to hear his name—but the last one is gone and his name has not ben called. He reluctantly turns away with a sad heart while 'Forgotten' 'Forgotten' rings in his ears." Thomas Daniel felt that way and told his family to write more often. "I have riten a bout twenty leters to you all and have got the hole a mount of thre I think you all have forgoten me I wont you all to write to me and let me no how you all are a geten a long."[131]

Soldiers rarely got as much mail as they would have liked, but seldom was it because they had been forgotten. Many soldiers' wives were illiterate and had to rely on family or friends for contact with their husbands. Even among those who could read and write, some could not afford to buy paper. In other cases, the burdens of farming, factory work, and child rearing left little time for letter writing.

Sometimes letters were simply lost. With armies frequently on the move, it was not uncommon for letters to go missing in transit. Few of Sallie Lovett's letters ever seemed to reach her husband. "Honey, what in the world do you reckon is the reason my letters don't go to you?" she asked in May 1862. "This is the fourth or fifth one I have written to you since you have received one. I don't know what can be the matter. I have directed some to Chattanooga, some to Corinth and one to Bethel Springs. I wrote you a letter only four days ago." She let Billie know that he was by no means forgotten. "Now, honey don't you think I don't never write to you, for I do write and put the letters in the office and what more can I do, though I wish it was so I could go and put them in your sweet hand, which so oft I have held in mine."[132]

Along with expressions of love and loneliness, letters from home invariably brought news of hardship and deprivation. Most of the home folks tried not to burden their soldiers with bad news, but for many families bad news was the only news. As early as July 1861, before the war's first major battle, Alabama's *Opelika Southern Republic* urged its readers not to write "gloomy" letters. Such letters were inevitable even from the war's outset. They became increasingly frequent as the war went on.[133]

Mary Brooks was left with three young children, a baby not yet weaned, and a farm to run near Greenville, Georgia. She wrote to her husband, Rhodam, "I never get any rest night or day, and I don't think I will last much longer." She was running low on bacon and salt as well as money with which to purchase them. "It is money for everything," she said, "so you may know it is getting low with me." Most soldiers had little or no money to send home. Enlisted men's pay was next to nothing even by the standards of the time. And some went for months without being paid their meager salary. When payrolls did arrive, they often contained only a fraction of what the soldiers were owed. Benjamin Franklin Jackson of Alabama told his wife, "I have not received any money yet and don't know when I shall." A Federal soldier, John N. Henry, wrote home to his wife, "I have suffered more anxiety on account of my family for several weeks past than for the whole year. Six months pay behind . . ." Thousands of common soldiers were constantly in that predicament.[134]

Soldiers paid so little and so infrequently could hardly be expected to meet their financial obligations. Yet their creditors did expect prompt payment and threatened their families when payment could not be made. In Pontiac, Michigan, John Pierson's family was constantly hounded by one creditor for some small amount. The angry soldier wrote back: "Those left at home in the quiet pursuit of their business can well afford to wait. The business I am engaged in is a game of heads and I may lose mine and his is in no danger." When the pressure from creditors continued, Pierson told his wife: "If I get killed they may come where I am and collect." Another Union soldier, Samuel Cormany, had a wife and baby girl threatened with eviction and starvation. His wife wrote to him of their landlord, "He has been treating me more like a dog than a human being with human feelings."[135]

In Lee's Army of Northern Virginia, a group of angry North Carolina soldiers wrote to their governor insisting that he make good on his promise that their families would be cared for: "Very many of our wives were dependent on our labor for support before the war when articles of food and clothing could be obtained easier than now. At this time they are alone, without a protector, and cannot by hard and honest labor, obtain enough money to purchase the necessaries of life." The letter contained a veiled and portentous threat: "We cannot hear the cries of our little ones, and stand." A young soldier from Columbus, Georgia, was more blunt in a letter to a friend: "I don't want mother to suffer for anything as long as I live. I am willing for her to work and I know she will do it; but when I hear she is in want of provisions and cant get them, I am going home. . . . The last two letters I received from her don't suit me."[136]

Knowing that their families were suffering made soldiers' own suffering that much worse. They were constantly requesting furloughs to help needy home folk and were bitterly disappointed when they could get none. One Federal officer wrote to his commanding general that the volunteers, "if not allowed to go home and see their families . . . droop and die. . . . I have watched this." Confederate soldier George Hancock asked to "go home to prepare some land for to sow some wheat for the use of my family." Another asked for a furlough to harvest his family's grain. But furloughs were hard to come by, North or South. And when restrictions were enforced, they applied only to the enlisted men. One despondent Virginia soldier wrote to his wife that "no furloughs are granted at this time to Privates or *non commissioned officers*, only to those that support the gold lace."[137]

To raise money for destitute soldiers' families, two brigades in the Army of Northern Virginia formed a theatrical troupe, wrote their own plays, and performed for area audiences at a dollar admission. One of their most popular shows, entitled "Medical Board," was not only a "burlesque on the surgeons" but also highlighted the difficulty soldiers had getting furloughs. As one soldier wrote of it:

> The characters were a number of surgeons sitting around a table playing cards, with a bottle of brandy on the table, which was passed around quite frequently, until one doctor inquired how they came to get such good brandy.
>
> "Oh! this is some that was sent down from Augusta County for the sick soldiers, but the poor devils don't need it, so we'll drink it."

Then a courier would come in and inform them that there was a soldier outside badly wounded.

"Bring him in! bring him in!" said the chief surgeon. When brought in an examination would take place with the result that his arm would have to be amputated. The poor fellow wanted to know if when that was done he could not have a furlough.

"Oh! no," replied the surgeon. A further examination developed that his leg would have to amputated.

"Then can I have a furlough?" said the soldier.

"By no means," replied the surgeon, "for you can drive an ambulance when you get well."

It was finally determined by the medical board, as he was wounded in the head, that his head would have to come off.

"Then," says the soldier, "I *know* I can have a furlough."

"No, indeed," replied the surgeon, "we are so scarce of men that your body will have to be set up in the breastworks to fool the enemy."[138]

Though the chances were low and the risks high, soldiers by the thousands continued to seek medical furloughs and discharges. Self-mutilation was hardly an option for men with families to support. They had to be able to work when they got home. Their injuries had to be only temporarily debilitating; often they were nonexistent. John Billings recalled one soldier in Burnside's corps who tried "the *rheumatic dodge*" to get a discharge: "He responded daily to sick call, pitifully warped out of shape, was prescribed for, but all to no avail. One leg was drawn up so that, apparently, he could not use it, and groans indicative of excruciating agony escaped him at studied intervals and on suitable occasions. So his case went on for six weeks, till at last the surgeon recommended his discharge." His discharge was making its way through channels when the soldier and his comrades came into possession of a whiskey barrel. The apparently lame man took his turn at the tap, got as drunk as the rest, and in his inebriated state "was soon as sprightly on both legs as ever." The regiment's commander, who had just approved the supposed invalid's discharge, found him stumbling around on two healthy legs. "Of course," wrote Billings, "his discharge was recalled from corps headquarters, and the way of this transgressor was made hard for months afterwards."[139]

William Lloyd of New Jersey nearly poisoned himself to death trying to get home. In October 1863, he wrote to his wife:

> I want to get out of this thing some way if I can, but I don't know how I will do it Hardley. There is no chance for deserting. I will have to work some plan to get my discharge. I have been stuffing medicine in myself since I been out here. I have been taking Pulsotil, Bryvina, Beladona, Acoute, Nuy Pom . . . Mucurins And Arsnic Poison when you write I wish you would send me some Arsnic or some other kind of stuff so as to make me look pale . . . find out at the druggist what will make you look pale and sickly . . . and send a small quantity in every letter.

Perhaps fearing for her husband's life, Lloyd's wife never sent any arsenic. Lloyd never got his discharge.[140]

Worry over their family's well-being was not the only motive men had for wanting out of the army. But William Fuller, second assistant surgeon with the 1st Michigan during the Chancellorsville and Gettysburg campaigns, felt sure that family concerns were the main reason soldiers played sick. In a "Thesis on Malingering" done in 1864 at the University of Michigan Medical School, Fuller wrote that among soldiers who "try to assimilate diseases, we generally find the greater proportion to be married men . . . who have families at home." He added that their "desire to procure a discharge from service . . . quite frequently depends upon the reception of despondent letters from home." A Confederate officer agreed, saying that "the source of all the present evils of Toryism & desertion in our country is letter writing to . . . the army." He suggested that the War Department begin censoring mail to keep despondent letters from home out of the soldiers' hands.[141]

"Desert, Jake! Desert Agin, Jake!"

Such letters often told of the rich getting richer and the poor getting poorer, while the soldiers, unwell and unwealthy, died by the hundreds of thousands. "I believe that a *poor* man's life is as dear as a rich man's," wrote Union soldier Levi Ross to his father in 1863. "The blood of a poor man is as precious as that of the wealthy." Such class sentiment was widespread in the ranks, North and South. And tens of thousands of soldiers acted on their resentment. "My men are deserting fast," wrote a Rebel captain to his wife in January 1864. "The laws that have been passed generally protect the rich, and the poor begin to say it is the rich mans war and the poor mans fight, and they will not stand it." Private James Zimmerman of North Carolina wrote home in October 1863: "If you will show me a man that is trying to compel soldiers to stay in the army he is a speculator or a slave holder, or has an interest in slaves." To Jasper Collins of Mississippi, the twenty-slave law exposed the Confederacy's struggle as a "rich man's war and poor man's fight." Soon after its enactment, he deserted.[142]

Angry as they were that the financially well-off could avoid service, most galling to soldiers was what the rich were doing to their families back home. A Virginia soldier wrote home in 1862: "I begin to hear a good deal of murmuring & complaint among the soldiers & reproaches thrown at 'the rich' who have no mercy in grinding every cent out of the poor." With prices high and wages low, it seemed to the soldiers that they were fighting mainly to protect the ability of the rich to grow richer at their expense. One Union soldier complained that it was the rich who "should sacrifice more in suppressing this infernal Rebellion and in restoring the Union and thereby save their property, homes and liberty."[143] The rich did not see it that way on either side of the Mason-Dixon Line. To them, their property bestowed the liberty to do as they pleased. Those with little or no property had liberty to do only what pleased the rich.

Soldiers with suffering families were anything but pleased with such an arrangement. That was especially true among Confederate soldiers for whom slave property had for decades been an obvious mark of class distinction. In February 1863, Private O. Goddin of the 51st North Carolina wrote to Governor Vance:

> Now Govr. do tell me how we poor soldiers who are fighting for the "rich mans negro" can support our families at $11 per month? How can the poor live? I dread to see summer as I am fearful there will be much suffering and probably many deaths from starvation. They are suffering now. . . .
>
> I am fearful we will have a revolution unless something is done as the majority of our soldiers are poor men with families who say they are tired of the rich mans war & poor mans fight, they wish to get to their families & fully believe some settlement could be made were it not that our authorities have made up their minds to prosecute the war regardless of all suffering. . . . A man's first duty is to provide for his own household the soldiers wont be imposed upon much longer.[144]

To men in the ranks with destitute families, their higher duty was clear. Their loved ones came first. "My family are nearer and dearer to me than any Confederacy could be," wrote Private Edwin Hedge Fay. "My first allegiance is to my family." Asked another Confederate soldier, "If I lose all that life holds dear to me, what is my country or any country to me?"[145]

To Lieutenant A.H. Burch of Alabama, such attitudes were hardly surprising. Late in the war, in a letter to Governor Thomas Watts, he stressed the obvious connection between suffering among soldiers' families, the class-based root of that suffering, and desertion.

> Is it any wonder that our armies are decimated by desertion and dissatisfaction prevails throughout the poor classes when such nefarious practices (i.e. buying up corn in middle Alabama and selling it at eight dollars a bushel) are allowed to be carried on at home by wealthy men and officers . . . how many families who have not means to purchase . . . and are suffering while Messrs. ——— and ——— wealthy citizens and one of them a Government official of conscript age, hiding in a bomb-proof behind a miserable little tax collector's office, are speculating upon the bread that ought to go into the mouths of poor women and children, many of whom have husbands and sons now for four years defending the lives, liberty and property of these miserable, avaricious and cold blooded speculators.[146]

Attitudes were much the same up North. Governor Oliver Morton of Indiana, in his petition to Congress requesting a increase in the soldiers' pay, was more circumspect than Burch in drawing connections between class, destitution, and desertion. But his message was clear.

> Desertion is becoming frequent, and threatens the demoralization and destruction of the army unless it can be promptly arrested. The most potent cause . . . is the condition of the soldier's family at home. He receives letters from his wife, children, or parents, announcing that they are destitute of food, fuel, clothing, or are about to be turned out of doors for nonpayment of rent, and that their neighbors are failing to provide for them, as they are able and ought to do. He becomes maddened and desperate, and finding a furlough impossible, desertion is frequently the result.[147]

To any careful reader of the time, there could be no mistaking the class status of the "neighbors" to whom Morton referred. His comments were an indictment of those who were inflating prices, depressing wages, and growing richer, while the soldiers and their families grew poorer.

With most of the burden of family suffering borne on the shoulders of wives and mothers, it was their letters that directly or indirectly brought their men home. So clear was the connection between bad news from home and men leaving the army that many, especially among the upper crust, ignored the roots of family destitution and placed blame for desertion squarely on women. In February 1864, a North Carolina government official wrote to his sister, "Desertion takes place because desertion is encouraged. . . . And though the ladies may not be willing to concede the fact, they are nevertheless responsible."[148]

Many women were not at all reluctant to concede that they encouraged desertion. Like thousands of others, one woman told her husband in no uncertain terms to come home. The children were barefooted and cold, and there was almost nothing in the house to eat. "My dear, if you put off a-coming, 'twont be any use to come, for we'll all hands of us be out there in the garden in the old grave yard with your ma and mine." Another woman not only conceded her encouragement of desertion, she made it publicly clear. At the rail depot in Charlotte, North Carolina, she called to her deserter husband, who was being dragged back to the army: "Take it easy, Jake—you desert agin, quick as you kin—come back to your wife and children." As the distance between them grew, she yelled even louder. "Desert, Jake! desert agin, Jake!"[149]

Desertion was a dangerous act for soldiers to undertake. Of those sentenced to death by court-martial during the war, two-thirds were tried as deserters. Many did not get even the formality of a trial. Samuel Henderson Frier of Irwin County, Georgia, like the rest of his family, had opposed secession. Too poor to hire a substitute, he joined the Confederate army under threat of conscription in May 1862. Frier deserted later that year in Virginia and made his way back home, telling his family that he had never been able to reconcile himself to killing. "Thou shalt not kill" was the Good Book's teaching. It was a creed he would follow for the rest of his life. He would not have long to hold it. A few months later, Frier was ambushed by Confederate home guards who shot him dead without warning. Frier's widow, two young children, and other family and friends laid him to rest in Irwin County's Brushy Creek Primitive Baptist cemetery.[150]

Bob Anderson of Louisiana was another unfortunate deserter for whom a hearing was denied. Jack Maddox, at the time a neighborhood slave, recalled Anderson's gruesome murder decades after the war.

> Goin' home I stopped by Mrs. Anderson's place. She had a boy named Bob who deserted and was hidin' at home. Some 'federate soldiers come and say they'll burn the house down lessen he comes out. So he came out and they tied him with a rope and the other end to a saddle and went off with him trottin' 'hind the hoss. His mammy s[e]nt me followin' in the wagon. I followed thirteen mile. After a few miles I seen where he fell down and the drag signs on the ground. Then when I come to Hornage Creek I seen they'd gone through the water. I went across and after a while I found him. But you couldn't tell any of the front side of him. They'd drug the face off him. I took him home.[151]

For hundreds of thousands, the pull from home was too strong to ignore despite the dangers. After witnessing the execution of an Indiana deserter, John Billings concluded that the death penalty was useless: "I do not believe that the shooting of a deserter had any great deterring influence on the rank and file." And he was right. Over half a million men were listed as deserters from the Union army, nearly a third of its total force. Some turned themselves over to opposing Confederates and went home as paroled prisoners of war. When both sides stopped paroling prisoners, some took furloughs or sick leave and never returned. Many others simply went home without leave of any kind. Their comrades understood why. One member of the 4th Rhode Island wrote that "no blame was attached to any one who was smart enough to get away."[152]

Desertion rates were even higher in the Confederate army. By late 1863, close to half its soldiers had abandoned their ranks. Less than a year later, President Jefferson Davis publicly admitted that "two-thirds of our men are absent . . . most of them without leave." As early as April 1863, a brigade commander in the Army of Northern Virginia told General Lee that his regiments "were being depleted by desertion far more rapidly than they had ever been in battle." A Virginia colonel

The execution of deserter William Johnson as depicted in *Harper's Weekly*. Despite the risk of facing a firing squad, men on both sides deserted by the hundreds of thousands, most in response to family needs back home. After witnessing the execution of an Indiana deserter, soldier John Billings concluded that the death penalty was useless: "I do not believe that the shooting of a deserter had any great deterring influence on the rank and file."

tried to stop desertion in his regiment by posting guards around the men. When that failed, he went "into a perfect rage." He cancelled furloughs, got drunk, and yelled at his troops that they could "go to hell for all he cared."[153]

If higher-ranking officers had cared a little more, perhaps desertion might not have been so rampant. Better fed, better clothed, and better paid, it seemed to the men that the army's upper crust shared few of their hardships. That disparity was especially hard to bear when military elites acted toward those under them in ways the men found humiliating. Confederate soldiers were especially sensitive to ill treatment by officers, many of whom were slaveholders, equating such treatment to the way those officers might handle their slaves. One planter's son made his attitudes clear when he wrote home that "most of the common soldiers have to be treated like negroes . . . they are a very low set of men being composed of these low Irish and the scum of creation." As historian Armstead Robinson observed, "If there was anything the Southern yeomanry would resent more deeply than slurs about its Celtic origins it would be that they needed to be 'treated like negroes.'" One Johnny Reb told the folks back home that "the tiranny of officers is as great as can be." The army's "numerous desertions," he wrote, "is mainly caused by the tyranny of officers with their high pay they enjoy themselves no matter how high prices while the poor soldier suffers."[154]

Most deserters slipped away individually or in small groups. Sometimes whole units deserted en masse, as when "a regiment of Arkansas Confederates went over to the enemy." The 3rd Alabama did the same. In June 1864, as Yankee forces advanced on Atlanta, Company D of the 54th Virginia broke ranks and headed back home. For the 58th North Carolina, almost the entire regiment melted away when it was stationed near Jacksboro, Tennessee, just 150 miles from the men's Ashe County homes. When Lee detailed a fifty-man detachment of the 25th North Carolina to return home and track down deserters, every one of them deserted as well. Members of the 62nd and 64th North Carolina regiments did the same. North Carolina was the destination for its deserting native sons, but it was also a waypoint for deserters from the Army of Northern Virginia traveling south and those from the Army of Tennessee going north. One state resident observed that "a good many deserters are passing the various roads daily." If challenged—and they rarely were—"they just pat their guns and defiantly say, 'This is my furlough.'"[155]

Once home, southern deserters found plenty of neighbors willing to help them avoid further entanglements with the Confederacy. That was obvious even from distant Richmond. A disgusted head of the Bureau of Conscription complained that desertion had "in popular estimation, lost the stigma that justly pertains to it, and therefore the criminals are everywhere shielded by their families and by the sympathies of many communities." There was abundant evidence to support that view. A resident of Bibb County, Georgia, wrote that the area around Macon was "full of deserters and almost every man in the community will feed them and keep them from being arrested." From Marshall County, Mississippi, came word that "many deserters have been for months in this place without molestation. . . . Conscripts and deserters are daily seen on the streets of the town." When deserters were arrested in Alabama's Randolph County, an armed mob stormed the jail and set them free.[156]

Northern deserters also found ready sympathizers. When authorities threatened to arrest deserters in Jay County, Indiana, the fugitives' supporters promised to burn the town of Portland and take revenge against all local "Union men." In Pennsylvania's Monroe County, when a posse of ten arrested one deserter, an armed band intervened and forced his release. Gunfire broke out in Woodsfield, Ohio, when locals freed a deserter. In Anna, Illinois, a mob of enraged citizens set several deserters free and killed the man who arrested them.[157]

On both sides of the Mason-Dixon Line, opposition sentiment was so strong that deserters usually had all the allies they needed. If each deserter received help from only two or three people, then those Americans actively involved in civil disobedience numbered into the millions. That dissenting spirit found many other outlets among common folk as well. From simple objectors of conscience to more active draft rioters and even more active—and armed—bands of deserters and draft evaders, dissenters were major thorns in the sides of both the Federal and Confederate governments throughout the war. Though Lincoln, Davis, and their allies took great pains to suppress dissent and violently beat it back, millions of Americans insisted and acted upon the right of a free people to live in accord with their own values. What was patriotic or treasonous, what was wisdom or intemperance, which was the greater or lesser evil were questions that no preacher, no politician, and no wealthy profiteer would define for them. They would do that for themselves.

5

"Come In Out of the Draft"

The people here are nearly all unanimously against [the] war holding on any longer. There is no dificulty now in staying at home [and] no opposition from the citizens. I can tell you if you can only get here with out being took up it is all right—for in the place of opposition you will have protection.[1]

—JOHN HOPPER, GEORGIA DESERTER

A large number of persons have held meetings to consider measures for resisting the draft. They have procured a large number of guns and revolvers and meet frequently to drill. They rang the bells when news of the New York riot came and threaten to burn the buildings of the Union men.[2]

—CHESTER PIKE, NEW HAMPSHIRE PROVOST MARSHAL

"Sure to Help the Enemy"

That so many people, North and South, were prepared to protect draft evaders and deserters reflected a broad disenchantment with the war and "the cause," be it union or disunion, abolitionism or the preservation of slavery. Whichever cause prevailed, it seemed increasingly obvious that the main beneficiaries would be the ruling elites on either side. That the war made rich people richer and poor people poorer was the daily experience of common folk. If war should end with the Union intact or not, with slavery preserved or abolished, would the gap between rich and poor be less? Would a system emerge whereby laboring classes, urban and rural, could be assured the benefit of their labor? Neither government, North nor South, promised anything of the sort. Indeed, while they did not hesitate to help the rich become richer with land grants, tax loopholes, lucrative contracts, and corrupt bargains, politicians rejected the notion that government might intervene on behalf of working folk in a "free market" economy. Stressing a self-reliance they were loath to practice, elites proclaimed that government legislation designed to aid anyone but themselves was downright un-American.

Common people had their own ways of defining what was un-American and what was not. For tens of thousands of them, forcing men to fight in a war they did not support was un-American. Never before had an American national government instituted a draft. The very idea ran counter to the inalienable right of liberty. So did arrest without charge and imprisonment without trial, protected against by the constitutions of both the United States and the Confederate States. Yet both governments repeatedly violated the spirit of their traditions and the letter of their laws, generally to the benefit of the wealthy and well connected. In so doing they encouraged class antagonism and dissent, undermining support for the very war efforts they sought to promote.

The Lincoln administration's first violations of civil liberties came soon after the war began. In several regions, mainly in the border states, Lincoln suspended the writ of habeas corpus which, at least until the Civil War, had been the legal mechanism of constitutional protection against imprisonment without charge or trial. In Maryland a number of pro-Confederates, including archsecessionist John Merryman, were arrested without warrant in May 1861. Chief Justice Roger Taney of the United States Supreme Court, responding to the arrests in *Ex parte Merryman*, ruled that Lincoln had no constitutional authority to suspend the writ. Lincoln ignored the decision and continued threatening arrest of anyone who openly denounced his policies. Even silence was no protection for dissenters. Adopting a stridently preemptive "with or against us" attitude, Lincoln wrote: "The man who stands by and says nothing when the peril of his government is discussed cannot be misunderstood. If not hindered he is sure to help the enemy."[3]

By late 1862, he had extended suspension of habeas corpus to the point that the entire country was under martial law. Authorities arrested Daniel Cory of Somerset County, New Jersey, for calling Lincoln a Tory and a traitor. Cory added that he would just as soon see the president shot, and would be happy to pull the trigger himself. Moses Stannard of Madison, Connecticut, was thrown in jail for hoisting a Confederate flag over his home, telling anyone who complained that he hoped the Rebel army would capture Washington and kill Lincoln and his whole cabinet. In St. Louis, George J. Jones was arrested for printing handbills containing what authorities called "treasonous" reprints from British newspapers.[4]

As much as Lincoln claimed to be fighting the war to protect constitution law, he demonstrated little concern for its freedom of the press guarantee. Newspapers critical of his administration, such as the *New York World* and the *Philadelphia Evening Journal*, were forced to suspend operations. Others, like the German-language antiwar paper *National Zeitung*, were denied use of the postal service.[5] Lincoln and his Republican allies went after individual newspapermen as well. In his book *The Fate of Liberty*, historian Mark Neely lists among those arrested: "Daniel Deckar, publisher of the Hagerstown (Maryland) *Mail*; Reuben T. Durrett, acting editor of the Louisville *Courier*; Francis D. and Joseph R. Flanders, owners and editors of the Franklin *Gazette*, of Malone, Franklin County, New York; F. Key Howard and W. W. Glenn, editors of the Baltimore *Exchange*; Thomas W. Hall, Jr., and Thomas H. Piggott, editors, and Samuel Sands Mills, publisher and proprietor, of the *South*, published in Baltimore; James A. McMaster, editor of New York's *Freeman's Appeal*; Henry A. Reeves, editor of the *Republican Watchman*, published on Long Island; James W. Wall, a contributor of columns to the New York *News*; and several Missouri editors."[6]

Neely is quick to add that it was Republican political and military operatives, not Lincoln himself, who initiated most of the arrests. And there were times when Lincoln chastised those under him for overzealousness, writing to one subordinate after the arbitrary arrest of a

St. Louis editor and antiwar Democrat, "Please spare me the trouble this is likely to bring."[7] But Lincoln brought much of the trouble upon himself. He continued to support and defend anticonstitutional measures, becoming in large part personally responsible for generating much of the dissent he tried to suppress.

To hold the threat of arbitrary arrest over the heads of opponents was a temptation few politicians could resist. Certainly it was clear to contemporaries that, in suppressing dissent, Lincoln and other Republicans were often motivated more by politics than patriotism. They tended to paint any opposition with a broad brush of treason, and people suffered prolonged imprisonment and worse for no other crime than being a Democrat. The antiwar or Peace Democrats were special Republican targets. As a sign of protest against Lincoln's suppression of civil liberties, Peace Democrats wore copper pennies with the head of "Lady Liberty" emblazoned on them. This practice gave rise to the term "Copperheads," though Republicans equated it with the poisonous snake of that name.

The Union officer corps, almost entirely prowar, proved an especially reliable Republican ally. In November 1861, General Joseph Hooker arrested Perry Davis, a candidate for the Maryland legislature, and accused him of making "treasonous" comments during the campaign. Hooker released Davis only after he promised not to vote for a secession ordinance should one be presented. In 1862, when Democrats won control of the Illinois legislature, officers in fifty-five of the state's infantry regiments, four cavalry regiments, and four artillery batteries offered to forcefully oust the duly elected representatives and install a Republican regime. Governor Richard Yates, himself a Republican, declined the offer and simply declared the legislature out of session. State courts ruled that Yates had no such authority, but no one dared challenge the governor. For nearly two years, Yates governed as a virtual dictator in Illinois. So did Indiana's Republican governor, Oliver P. Morton. After Democrats carried the legislature, Morton robbed that body of its quorum by instructing Republican legislators not to take their seats. Despite outraged protests, Lincoln endorsed Yates's and Morton's actions. But both governorships were up for grabs in 1864 and the dictators might be forced out. Still, to Republicans, the army's offer of support for Republican dictatorship suggested ways in which opponents might be intimidated and power maintained.[8]

"Pretty Damned Warm Times"

As Illinois entered another election year in 1864, the attack on Peace Democrats got underway. Members of the 54th Illinois while home on leave began randomly forcing citizens on the streets of Mattoon to recite a "loyal oath." When a Democrat refused and tried to run, the soldiers shot him dead. A month later, Illinois troops killed two Democrats in the town of Paris. One of the most violent incidents came on March 28 when Democrats, most of them local farmers, assembled on the Charleston, Illinois, town square to hear an address by John Rice Eden, the district's Democratic congressman. The 54th Illinois was there too. Tempers began to flare and Eden cancelled the rally, moving through the square urging his constituents to disperse peaceably. As the crowd began to melt away, a fight broke out between David Nelson Wells, a young Democrat, and a soldier named Oliver Sallee. Suddenly shots rang out and both men fell mortally wounded. The startled farmers grabbed pistols from under their coats and rifles from their wagons and began firing on the soldiers. The soldiers quickly returned fire. In the brief battle that followed, bullets flew so thick that they cleaned the bark off trees in the square. Moments later, Sheriff John O'Hair, a Democrat, restored order by taking command of the civilians, rallying them on the square's southeast corner away from the soldiers, and leading them in an orderly march down Jackson Street and out of town. The soldiers captured one lone Democrat who lingered too long and shot him to death when he tried to break loose. The shots also killed a Republican storekeeper standing nearby. Nine men died in the Charleston riot that day—six soldiers, two Democrats, and one Republican bystander. Twelve more were wounded. One witness remembered it all as "pretty damned warm times."[9]

Charleston made clear that Democrats could not always be cowed by threats of armed force, but Republicans had other ways of advancing their agenda. Though they could not capture all elective offices, they did control federal appointments. And they used them to Republican advantage. In Ohio's gubernatorial election of 1863, the state's postmasters—all of them Republicans—made sure that the Republican State Central Committee had up-to-date mailing lists. And they dutifully delivered Republican pamphlets to potential voters. They offered no mailing lists to Democrats, and the party's literature was prone to being lost in transit.

Republicans held the country under martial law as well. In the spring of 1863, with Lincoln's blessing, General Ambrose Burnside issued General Order No. 38. Burnside commanded a U.S. military district covering the states of Ohio, Indiana, Illinois, Michigan, and eastern Kentucky. His order stated that anyone who so much as implied treasonable sentiments would be hauled before a military tribunal. Though the order was far-reaching, it was aimed mainly at Clement L. Vallandingham, a candidate for the Democratic nomination to the Ohio governor's office and the nation's leading Peace Democrat.[10]

Vallandingham was an Ohio congressman when the war broke out, and opposed every war measure Republicans put forward. He was especially critical of Lincoln's record on civil liberties. That criticism became vehement as Vallandingham geared up for the Ohio governor's race. On May 1, 1863, he delivered a hard-driving antiwar speech at Mt. Vernon, Ohio, in direct violation of General Order No. 38, calling the order itself unconstitutional. Vallandingham was arrested a few days later and hauled before a military board on charges of treason. There was little evidence to support such a charge. Even prosecution witnesses admitted that Vallandingham had denounced violent resistance to the law, stressing that voters should use the ballot box to bring about change. He was nevertheless convicted and sentenced to imprisonment for the remainder of the war. Fearing that Vallandingham would be an opposition lightning rod as long as he remained in Federal custody, Lincoln banished him to the Confederacy. No Confederate sympathizer, Vallandingham quickly moved to Canada and continued his antiwar efforts from exile.

Reaction to the Vallandingham case was more critical than Republicans had expected. In some cases it was violent. The day after Vallandingham's arrest, a mob of outraged Democrats in Dayton attacked the Republican newspaper office and burned it to the ground. There were Republicans too who thought the administration went too far in bringing charges of treason against Vallandingham. Horace Greeley, a New York editor, while supporting some limits on freedom of speech and the press, saw more loyal dissent than treason in Vallandingham. George William Curtis, editor of *Harper's Weekly* and a Lincoln supporter from the war's outset, also opposed the arrest. And Joel Parker, the Harvard law professor who had written a strong defense of Lincoln's suspension of habeas corpus in the *Merryman* case, now called Lincoln a despot.[11]

Stung by the Vallandingham backlash and the rising tide of anti-administration sentiment, Lincoln and the Republicans sought closer ties with Democrats who supported the war, largely subsuming them within the Republican camp. Civil liberties still suffered, but victims tended to be lower profile and more vulnerable. And their liberties were not all that suffered. In direct violation of constitutional guarantees against self-incrimination and cruel and unusual punishment, torture became an increasingly common way for federal officials to drag confessions from suspects or to take revenge for suspected dissent. J.W. Nash had "a hose of water directed with full and powerful action against his naked person." So did James Buckley, who was subjected to the torture for two hours until the force of the water split his skin. John Crozier Lloyd was tied up by his thumbs and suspended in midair for eleven hours. William Rodgers, arrested in Baltimore on charges of desertion, had a gag rammed into his mouth, and was subjected to physical abuse until he finally confessed to being a deserter just to stop the painful treatment. Luke Riley, also charged with desertion, nearly froze to death when he was drenched with cold water nine times a day in zero-degree weather. Members of Lincoln's cabinet, and probably Lincoln himself, knew of the torture. But no directives against such treatment ever came from the administration.[12]

"Persons Having Conscientious Scruples"

That men could be forced to serve against their will, much less tortured for declining the honor, was of at least questionable constitutionality. But the U.S. Supreme Court never touched the issue, and lower courts could never agree. With Lincoln and Congress controlling appointments, federal judges tended to support the draft. State courts could be more hostile to conscription, especially in those states where Democrats held sway. In the *Kneedler v. Lane* case of November 1863, Pennsylvania's Supreme Court declared the federal Enrollment Act unconstitutional, upheld the writ of habeas corpus, and issued an injunction barring federal officials from drafting Pennsylvania citizens. The administration instructed its Provost Marshal General's Bureau, which oversaw conscription, to ignore the court's ruling. Lincoln meant to press ahead with the draft whether it was constitutional or not.[13]

For common folk, the draft question was more a personal than constitutional issue. Many were already on the brink of poverty and wondered how their families would survive if a father, brother, or son were drafted. Few could pay three hundred dollars to buy their way out of the draft. Nor could they afford to hire a substitute. And a paltry thirteen dollars per month, made even more meager by wartime inflation, was hardly an inducement for them to risk their lives in what many saw as a rich man's war.

Not all those who opposed conscription did so for economic rea-

> How are you, Conscript?
> How are you, I say?
> Have you got "three hundred greenbacks"
> To "pony up" and pay?
> If not you are "a goner"
> Now don't you fret and cry,
> For you're only going to Dixie
> To fight and "mind your eye"

Verse from a popular wartime song by Frank Wilder about a northern conscript who could not buy his way out of the draft. (*Harper's Weekly*)

sons. For some, military service was in direct conflict with their moral and religious convictions. Clearly, God's commandment "Thou shalt not kill" and Christ's directive to do good to one's enemies was taken more to heart by some believers than others. Nonviolence, or "nonresistance" as they called it, was a central tenant of several religious sects, among them the Society of Friends (Quakers), the Mennonite Church, the Church of the German Baptist Brethren (Dunkers or Dunkards), and the United Society of Believers in Christ's Second Appearing (Shakers). A few members of these sects did serve in the military, but the vast majority found bearing arms against their fellow men utterly at odds with Holy Scripture. To the government, their views mattered little one way or the other.

In August 1863, Colonel Joseph Holt, judge advocate general of the army, made clear that "persons having conscientious scruples in regard to bearing arms are not on that account exempt." He added, however, that "the Society of Friends, and others entertaining similar sentiments, if drafted, may find relief from their scruples in the employment of substitutes, or in the payment of the $300." Most could afford neither. Those who could often refused to do so. To support the war even through substitution or commutation was against their pacifist principles. The government was faced with either letting them go, a dangerous precedent with antidraft sentiment running so high, or placing some of its most devout citizens in jail for treason.[14]

Congress tried to settle the delicate issue with legislation stating that "members of religious denominations, who shall by oath or affirmation declare that they are conscientiously opposed to the bearing of arms . . . shall when drafted into the military service, be considered non-combatants, and shall be assigned by the Secretary of War to duty in the hospitals, or to care for freedmen, or shall pay the sum of three hundred dollars to such person as the Secretary of War shall designate."[15] According to an editorial in *The Friend*, a Quaker newspaper, Congress had missed the point entirely.

> While, therefore, we fully appreciate the good motives which, we doubt not, prompted the adoption of the section above quoted, and hail it as a cheering indication of the advance of correct views upon this important subject, we do not see how it can relieve our members, or they consistently avail themselves of its provisions. . . . It matters not whether the commutation for military service is money or personal service in some

other department; in either case it is an assumption on the part of the government of a right to oblige the subject to violate his conscience, or to exact a penalty if he elects to obey God rather than man.[16]

Alfred Love, a Philadelphia woolens merchant, was among those determined to obey God. In the summer of 1863, Love was drafted and called before an enrollment board. He stated up front that he had no intention of doing military service and asked what punishment he could expect for his refusal. "Obey the laws or be shot," replied one member of the board. Love responded that he could be "ready in 5 min[utes] in yonder lot if that be the penalty of standing up for conscience." Fortunately for Love, a physical examination revealed that he was unfit for duty, and he escaped both the service and execution. But Love remained true to his antiwar principles. While other merchants made fortunes from the war, Love consistently refused to deal with the government or its contractors. At one point, Love refused a government contract to provide flannels to the army. When Love's business partner, who was also his brother-in-law, tried to do business with the government behind his back, Love cut all financial ties with him. Love insisted that he would rather "go barefoot through the streets" than make money from the war.[17]

Other conscientious objectors were not as fortunate as Love. Dragged into the army by force, some were subjected to horrendous treatment for their passive refusal to fight. John Wesley Pratt, an abolitionist and pacifist from Quincy, Massachusetts, was hauled off to the Army of the Potomac, but he declined to drill or carry a weapon. As punishment, he was thrown in prison, subjected to physical abuse, threatened with execution, and nearly starved to death.[18] Cyrus Pringle, along with two other Quakers from Charlotte, Vermont, were drafted and sent to the front in July 1863. By Pringle's account, when he made it clear that he refused to do military service,

> Two sergeants soon called for me and taking me a little aside, bid me lie down on my back, and stretching my limbs apart tied cords to my wrists and ankles and these to four stakes driven in the ground somewhat in the form of an X. I was very quiet in my mind as I lay there on the ground [soaked] with the rain of the previous day, exposed to the heat of the sun, and suffering keenly from the cords binding my wrists and straining my muscles.[19]

Pringle still refused take up arms. So determined were people like Pringle and Pratt and so troublesome did they become for the army that Provost Marshal General James Fry finally issued a directive instructing his subordinates to parole and send home all draftees belonging to pacifist religious sects.[20]

Rights of conscience were not open to all those who wanted to avoid killing. Fry's directive applied only to long-standing members of pacifist denominations. All the pleading of postdraft converts fell on deaf ears, especially when there was no pacifist church within a hundred miles. Indeed, it was often hard to find any ordained servant of the Prince of Peace who did not support the war. If His kingdom was not of this earth, theirs certainly was. To them, America was the world's new messiah, its city on a hill, and it had to be preserved intact. The god they professed was an activist, interventionist deity who bent human affairs to his will—which happened also to be their own.

Most of the North's Protestant clergymen were especially insistent that opposing Lincoln and his war was opposing God himself. And woe betide any minister who dared disagree. Though an avowed Union supporter, the Reverend Samuel Chamberlain of Indiana opposed the war on religious grounds. His state conference defrocked him. In 1863, Ohio's Methodist Conference revoked the licenses of all its ministers who refused to openly back the Republican gubernatorial candidate that year. In Illinois, a church tribunal composed of Republicans expelled a deacon "for his opposition to the pollution of the pulpit and religious press with politics." The Reverend William Blundell, along with several other Illinois preachers, lost his license for refusing to join a Union League and "failing to pray in public for the President or Armies of the United States."[21] One of the defrocked ministers complained:

> We could not remain silent and be in peace; we could not speak without censure and vile abuse following. If we used moderation, we showed treason; if we condemned unjust arrests in private, the same were published on the house tops. Our very whispers appeared to be watched, and we suffered more from what we did not do than for what we did.[22]

With most pulpits occupied by war-supporting zealots, it was not long before some began linking political leaning with spiritual salvation.

There were those who warned their listeners: "He who does not adopt, maintain and defend a correct theory relative to 'matters of state' . . . will 'certainly lose his soul.'"[23] Their message was clear—back the war or burn in hell.

"Bent on Avoiding the Draft"

Despite threats of damnation in the next world from stay-at-home preachers, most northern men seemed more concerned about their fate in this world. As one newspaper poetically summed it up:

> Fathers and sons, and old bachelors too,
> Are sweating their brains to know what to do,
> But 'mid hope, fear, and a good deal of craft,
> They all seem bent on avoiding the draft.[24]

Some mistakenly thought the draft law excused all married men. In fact, married men over age thirty-five were on secondary draft status, but they were not excused. Nevertheless, untold numbers of bachelors hurriedly sought to tie the matrimonial knot. Others thought family hardships would save them, and the more the better. One young man swore that he was the only son of a widowed mother, that his father was too sick to find employment, and that two of his brothers were already soldiers—all at once. In Auburn, New York, a father went with his drafted son to the provost office, family Bible in hand, to prove that the boy was below draft age. All his children's names, he insisted, had been written down in the book at the time they were born. When the enrolling officer looked at the Bible's publication date, he saw that it was ten years after the young draftee's claimed date of birth.[25]

In 1863, as draft-dodging fever gripped the North, Ednor Rossiter and B. Frank Walthers wrote what became one of the war's most popular songs, "Come In Out of the Draft, or How Are You Conscript?" It was "respectfully dedicated to all disconsolate conscripts."

> As it was rather warm, I thought the other day,
> I'd find some cooler place, the summer months to stay;
> I had not long been gone when a paper to me came,
> And in the list of conscripts I chanced to see my name.

I showed it to my friends, and at me they all laughed,
They said "How are you conscript? Come in out of the draft."

Oh, soon I hurried home, for I felt rather blue;
I thought I'd ask my dad what I had better do;
Says he, "You are not young,—you're over thirty-five;
The best thing you can do, sir, is—go and take a bride."
My mother on me smiled, my brother at me laughed,
And said, "How are you conscript? Come in out of the draft."

I soon made up my mind that I would take a wife;
For she could save my cash, and I could save my life.
I called upon a friend, I offered her my hand,
But she said she couldn't see it, for she loved another man.
She told it to her man, and at me they both laughed,
And said, "How are you conscript? Come in out of the draft."

So next I advertised, and soon a chap I found
Who said that he would go for just two hundred down.
I took him home to sleep. Says I, "Now I'm all right."
But, when I woke, I found that he'd robbed me in the night!
I went and told the mayor: the people round me laughed,
And said, "How are you conscript? Come in out of the draft."

I've tried to get a wife, I've tried to get a "sub,"
But what I next shall do, now, really, is the "rub."
My money's almost gone, and I am nearly daft;
Will some one tell me what to do to get out of the draft?
I've asked my friends all round, but at me they all laughed,
And said, "How are you conscript? Come in out of the draft."[26]

Many got out of the draft simply by ignoring it. In Pennsylvania's Tenth District, an officer wrote that "nearly all the men fail to report." In total, more than two hundred thousand Union conscripts simply did not show up at their local enrolling office. Of those who did, some gave false identities and slipped through the conscription net. Others headed west hoping to get beyond Uncle Sam's reach. The western territories were especially attractive since only residents of states were subject to the draft. John Taylor found sanctuary in Nebraska Territory, which he called the true land of liberty. David Viars went all the way to California, getting paid in the process when he found work driving for a mule train. Though California had been a state since 1850, it was still a good place to hide. One officer charged with tracking down deserters and draft dodgers complained that California's large population of drifters, the state's tremendous size, and the indifference of its people to the war made his job almost impossible. It was even more difficult for the government to get its hands on fugitives who had taken the "skedaddle quickstep" to Canada. Close to ninety thousand young Americans took refuge from the Union draft among their neighbors to the north.[27]

With the government offering close to a hundred dollars bounty for enlisting, some did so—then deserted—repeatedly, making good money for their efforts. One bounty jumper enlisted and reenlisted thirty-two times before he was finally caught and sentenced to four years in New York's Albany penitentiary. For most conscripts, it was not so easy to give a fake name, take the cash, then disappear. Men who were too well established simply to run off but not well enough to buy their way out of the draft by paying the commutation fee or hiring a substitute seemed trapped. August Ebner of New York City became so desperate to stay out of the war that he attempted suicide by slashing his jugular vein. Though he suffered a terrible wound, Ebner survived. When they learned that a soldier had to have enough teeth to bite the end off a paper bullet cartridge, some draftees had their teeth pulled. One man nearly bled to death when he had sixteen removed. Another had every one of his teeth taken out—then learned that the neighbor who told him he had been drafted was only joking.[28]

Medical exemptions for missing teeth or other physical disqualifications were among the most sought-after dodges for reluctant draftees. And they were willing to pay for such exemptions. Some bribed physicians directly. Others tried to fool them with prefabricated debilities. Among the latter were those who used the services of a lawyer in New York's Orleans County who advertised that for a ten-dollar fee he could give any draftee a set of hemorrhoids guaranteed to keep them out of service. It seems that he used mercury to induce the appearance of hemorrhoids. In another case he produced a fifteen-page affidavit attesting to some fictitious ailment. He had one draftee spin on his heels to produce blisters, then claimed the man was too disabled to march. The lawyer raked in a hefty sum from medical fraud until he was finally caught.[29]

Some draftees pretended to be deaf. Others feigned blindness. Many disabilities such as rheumatism, lameness, and hernias suddenly afflicted men who had seemed perfectly healthy before Uncle Sam came calling. It was hard not to notice that the poor conscripts were being struck down with mysterious diseases to which their undrafted neighbors seemed immune. In Ohio's state militia draft of 1862, half the men in Marietta asked for medical exemption. With suspicion running high, it was not always easy to fool examining physicians. When one conscript asked for exemption on account of a stiff right knee, the doctor gave him chloroform. Under its intoxicating influence, the stiffness moved to his left knee. Those claiming hernias were forced to go without a truss for at least a day to see if any settling occurred. One doctor set up an obstacle course for conscripts claiming problems with eyesight. For claims of deafness, a Kentucky surgeon held the conscript's nostrils closed, told him to puff out his cheeks, and checked for escaping air through the ear drums. Some doctors began to think of themselves as miracle workers. Like never before, wrote one, "the blind have been made to see, the deaf to hear, and the lame to walk." Even so, nearly one hundred and sixty thousand men across the North, 31 percent of all draftees, got medical exemptions, legitimately or not. An Ohio newspaper editor found it hard to believe "that not one-third of the present generation of the male persuasion" was fit for military duty.[30]

In the summer of 1863, just as conscription was beginning to gear up in Philadelphia, the *Public Ledger* was among the first public organs to suggest what became a popular and relatively inexpensive draft dodge. The newspaper pointed out that men might "club together" to form a draft insurance society, each contributing $10 or $20 to be used in hiring a substitute or paying the commutation fee should any of them be drafted. Within a week Philadelphia's draft-age men were taking the hint. So were many thousands of others across the North in such cities as Boston, New York, Milwaukee, and Indianapolis. The amount of an individual's contribution depended on the number of men in his draft insurance society and the number of members actually drafted. In one Philadelphia society with a membership of twelve, four were drafted. So each member paid $100 to cover commutation for the four. Most societies had larger memberships and lower dues. In one Chicago club, members paid $25. In another, the dues were $15. In Ashtabula County, Ohio, a club of 165 members paid $25 each. When only one of their members was drafted and his commutation fee paid, each of the other members got a $23.32 refund.[31]

"No Enrolling Officer Could Go Through the Towns Alive"

Cheap as it was, most potential conscripts from the working classes, urban or rural, could not afford draft insurance even if the bulk of their dues came back. They simply did not have the cash to put up front. But the support they got from fellow resisters and the community at large frequently meant that they did not have to. In Utica, New York, the provost marshal reported that antiwar meetings were being held every night, and told of "a desperate and powerful organization in opposition to the draft." Citizens in Washington County, Wisconsin, tried to protect local draftees by stealing the draft rolls. The enrolling agent barely escaped with his rolls and his life. A draft officer in Olney, Illinois, made a similar narrow escape. In Illinois's Hancock County, a gang of men forced their way into the homes of draft agents and demanded the conscript rolls at gunpoint.

In Indiana's Owen and Clay counties, parties unknown stole the draft rolls and let it be known that no such lists would ever make it out of the district. Draft resisters in Fulton County attacked an enrolling officer and took his draft lists. In Putnam County, according to an Indianapolis newspaper, a number of enrolling officers "were waited on either by committee, or by mob, and the books demanded, or the officers notified that any further work by them in enrolling would imperil their lives."[32]

Threats of violence against draft officers were hardly uncommon. When an enrolling officer showed up in Bucks County, Pennsylvania, locals called him a "d——n dirty rascal," threw rocks at him, and shot up his wagon. Enrollers in Carbon and Schuylkill counties met with similar threats. In Davistown, a crowd carrying a rope warned their draft officer to get out of town within three minutes or he would be hanged. Cambria County men told their draft agent to stop his enrolling efforts or "make peace with his God." In Rome, Iowa, locals drove their enrolling officer out of town. The same happened in Hartford, Indiana. In Delaware and Maryland anonymous citizens sent enrolling officers threatening letters and fired at their homes. Conscript officers were shot at in Wisconsin's Calumet and Manitowoc counties and were run out of Outagamie, Oconto, Door, and Brown counties.[33] Of conscription efforts in the towns of Holland and Morrison, both in Brown County, Provost Marshal Curtis R. Merrill wrote:

> Three delegations of the most capable and determined men I could find, one under the sheriff of the county, were sent, but the hostility was so great and the country being heavily timbered, the roads and by-paths obscure, a party of two or three could accomplish nothing. It was publicly announced that no enrolling officer could go through the towns alive and after repeated threats and warnings, they were all obliged to return unsuccessful. Thinking an example of the determination and power of the authorities would be beneficial to all other hostile localities as well as these, I sent for 20 soldiers dividing them into four squads and sent them with a guide and the enrolling officer to every house in town, but the women and children being on watch, the men would fly to the woods on the approach of the party.[34]

Milwaukee's women and children did more than give warning. They drove off enrollment officers with rocks and hot water. In Pennsylvania, enrollment officers from nearly every district reported women and children hurling hot water, stones, sticks, and any other convenient projectile at them. An enrolling officer in Whitestown, Indiana, fled town after being accosted by an angry crowd, the female participants hurling eggs at him. It was the same in Chicago. When a draft officer showed up at the home of a conscript who had failed to report, the man's wife set their dog on him and went after him herself with a knife. Officials sent in a second draft officer who got the same treatment. The woman was finally arrested and put on trial, but the jury refused to convict her.[35]

In some areas, intimidation was such that no one could be found who was willing to round up conscripts. Peter Kutz of Pennsylvania's Hegins Township relinquished his enrolling duties when local residents "put him in such fear of his life or bodily harm that he was obliged to desist . . . and go home." Henry Ikes of St. Clair Township stepped down after his sawmill was torched and he was threatened with murder. An enrolling officer in Know County, Ohio, resigned after similar warnings. Threats against draft officers in Wisconsin's Kewaunee, Manitowoc, Calumet, Outagamie, and Oconto counties became so frequent that no one would take an enrollment job.[36]

Caution among draft officers was well advised. Many of the threats made against them had real teeth. In June 1863, an enrolling agent was assassinated in Pennsylvania's Napier Township. On June 11, a deputy provost marshal died in Rush County, Indiana, after being ambushed by men hidden in a wheat field. Another enrolling officer was murdered in Dodge County, Wisconsin. Four died in Union County, Illinois, trying to make arrests. When a deputy provost marshal was killed in DeKalb County, Indiana, a local paper made its support for the act clear when it labeled the story "Murderer at Heart Himself Murdered." That kind of community support made it difficult to catch killers or to convict them if they were caught. A Pennsylvania mine owner was murdered after he held a party for soldiers sent to enforce the draft. Locals knew who the killers were but no one was ever prosecuted.[37]

"Stones, Brick-Bats, and Other Missiles"

Violent draft resistance was not limited to small groups or individuals. Draft riots involving crowds of hundreds, even thousands, of enraged protestors swept the North in the summer of 1863. They would continue sporadically for the rest of the war. When draft officers showed up in Troy, New York, three hundred employees of the Albany Nail Works and the Rensselaer Iron Works went on a rampage. They destroyed a pro-Lincoln newspaper office, threatened to torch the African Church, and sacked the town jail. There was trouble too in Hastings, Tarrytown, and Rye. Draft resistance in New York emboldened draft resisters in Detroit as well. In Rutland, Vermont, a thousand marble quarrymen wielding clubs and stones attacked soldiers sent to enforce the draft. Draft rioters in New Jersey's Fifth District stoned the provost marshal's home, attacked a newspaper office, and for a time ruled the streets of Newark. Similar riots broke out in Jersey City; Portsmouth, New Hampshire; St. Paul, Minnesota; Blackford County, Indiana; Hartford, Connecticut; and in Wooster and Toledo, Ohio. In Cleveland, a mob of draft protesters broke up the enrolling officer's box from which he was to draw names of new conscripts. Mansfield was also a center of antiwar, anti-Lincoln sentiment. Draft rioters in the neighboring counties of Crawford, Morrow, and Knox were so violent that federal troops were sent in to suppress them.[38]

Draft resistance was rampant throughout Illinois during the summer of 1863. So many of the state's enrolling agents were shot that it seemed Lincoln had more to fear from residents of his home state than from the Rebels. In DuQuoin, a mob four hundred strong assaulted the provost marshal and released several deserters. Chicago was one of the most dangerous cities in the country for draft agents, especially the city's Third Ward. In an elitist dig at the area's poor residents and at its rival newspaper, the *Chicago Times*, the *Weekly Tribune* wrote that residents of the Third Ward were "the lowest, most ignorant, depraved and besotted rabble that can be found in the city. Fights, rows, and even murders are not infrequent among them, and after nightfall it is unsafe for any person to pass through the locality unless armed to the teeth. The natives of this neighborhood are all Copperheads. They read the Chicago *Times*, and they pursue its teachings to the letter."[39]

If the *Tribune's* view of Chicago's Third Ward was a politically motivated exaggeration, enrolling agents certainly found it to be a danger zone. A.H. Carter and J.A. Bailey, two draft officers for the Third Ward, were so frightened that they refused to do their jobs without a police escort. But that was no guarantee against violence. When Carter and Bailey, along with their escort, tried to arrest two conscripts near the Rock Island Railroad machine shops, a mob of three to four hundred attacked the agents and the police, forcing them to release their captives. Carter was hit with a brick during the melee, his skull crushed so badly that doctors did not expect him to recover.[40]

Wisconsin too was dangerous ground for draft agents. An armed crowd of between one and two hundred stood down enrolling officers in Green Bay. A mob in Kewaunee County drove off their draft commissioner. Some of the state's worst violence occurred at Port Washington. Trouble began when the governor appointed two local Freemasons as conscript commissioner and examining surgeon. Their first act was to exempt their Masonic brethren from the draft, much to the dismay of other potential draftees. On draft day, an angry crowd of one thousand, nearly half the town's population, assembled at the courthouse armed with "stones, brick-bats and other missiles." When the commissioner tried to draw names, the crowd threw him down the courthouse steps and destroyed his draft box. After sacking the courthouse, they marched through town and, said one eyewitness, "wreaked their vengeance upon several eminent citizens who had been counseling obedience to the laws." They destroyed homes of the draft commissioner and local elites who were known draft supporters. They broke open and looted a well-stocked warehouse. And, to hardly anyone's surprise, they ransacked the Masonic meeting hall. The governor had to send nearly eight hundred soldiers to put down the rebellion. After viewing its aftermath, one reporter wrote that "the village looks as though a tornado had swept through some portions of it, completely gutting several fine mansions, and devastating the grounds around them."[41]

Another riot was narrowly averted in Milwaukee. When a notice appeared of the approaching draft, protesters marched through the streets playing music and carrying banners which read NO DRAFT. A few days later when the draft was to take place, conscription opponents assembled in force at the courthouse but found no draft commissioner there as scheduled. When they got word that he had taken refuge in the sheriff's office, they marched there and called for the commissioner to come out. He did—and immediately told the crowd that he had resigned and that the governor had suspended conscription in Milwaukee.[42]

Draft officials found the Pennsylvania coal country to be just as unwelcoming. Some of the worst rioting occurred in Bradford and Wyoming counties. Draft opposition was stiff as well in Schuylkill, Luzerne, and Carbon counties, where the governor called organized resistance "very formidable." Near Tremont, a thousand miners stopped one train loaded with new conscripts to keep it from leaving Schuylkill County. One of the most violent outbreaks of draft rioting took place in the small mining town of Archbald in Luzerne County. The trouble started when an enrolling officer was taunted by women and children trailing after him as he made his way through town. After the crowd grew to several hundred, protestors "commenced a violent assault with stones, clubs, etc." and drove the man out of town. He was back a week later, this time with a military escort and—hoping to dissuade the predominantly Irish-Catholic miners—a priest in tow. Even so, a running battle broke out between townsfolk and the soldiers lasting into the night. One man was killed and several others wounded.[43]

One of the most serious draft riots took place in Boston, Massachusetts. For nearly twelve hours, from around noon until near midnight on July 14, 1863, much of the city was an urban war zone. It started after a woman slapped draft agent David Howe, who was searching for conscripts in the city's North End. When Howe tried to arrest her, the woman's screams brought neighbors to her rescue. Howe sought protection from a nearby policeman, but the rioters shoved the officer aside and gave Howe a severe beating from he barely escaped with his life. Police reinforcements soon arrived, but the crowd of at least two hundred drove them off by hurling bricks and bottles. Three policemen were seriously injured in the fray. Flush with their victory, rioters marched on the District One police station where they believed Howe was hiding. By the time they arrived around two o'clock, they were five hundred strong. Still, they did not attack the building. The mob simply milled around for most of the afternoon taunting any officers who dared to come out.

The trouble might have died away at that point, but local military officers feared that rioters might seize the North End armory and sent in troops to occupy it. Crowds of agitated residents followed after the soldiers and surrounded the armory, shouting insults and pro-Confederate slogans at the soldiers trapped inside. By 7:30 that evening there were up to a thousand angry Bostonians at the scene. When two officers came out and warned the assembly to disperse, they were pelted with rocks and more insults, forcing them to retreat back into the armory.

The crowd also attacked a tardy lieutenant trying to report for duty. According to one witness, he was "actually trampled upon by women, a large number of whom was in the crowd, and added to its fury by their demonic yells." Soldiers from the armory rushed out to rescue the man, firing into the air as they dragged him back in. The gun fire sent the mob into a violent rage—men, women, and children alike. They began tearing up sidewalk bricks and hurling them at the armory. A witness recalled "one Amazonian woman, shouting and screaming, and urging the assailants on in their desperate work. . . . [W]ith hair streaming, arms swinging, and her face the picture of phrenzy she rushed again and again to the assault." As the armory door began to give way, the soldiers inside fired a cannon blast into the crowd that killed perhaps twenty people, at least four young children among them.

Though the explosion sent rioters running, they were not yet ready to give up the fight. What they needed were guns, and they knew where to get them. They headed for the gun shops of nearby Dock Square and Faneuil Hall Square. As they approached the shops, Major

Charles Wilder intercepted them with two companies of infantry and a battalion of mounted dragoons. Wilder warned the crowd to disperse but was ignored. Boston's Mayor Frederick Walker Lincoln tried to read the riot act, but was shouted down. Wilder then ordered his men to attack. Backed up by infantry, the dragoons with sabers drawn rode into the crowd and sent it flying in all directions. Though sporadic incidents continued, the troops were back in control by midnight. They continued to patrol the volatile North End for several days.[44]

"Furious as Demons"

By far the most deadly riot of the Civil War, or in all of U.S. history, broke out in New York City on Monday, July 13, 1863, and lasted for nearly a week. The city had long been a center of both antidraft and antiwar sentiment. Just over a month before the draft riot broke out, Peace Democrats held a "Great Peace Convention" in New York City. Appealing to a receptive hometown crowd was featured speaker and former city mayor Fernando Wood, now serving in the U.S. House of Representatives. Since his election to Congress, Wood had consistently advocated peace. At one point he asked Lincoln to send a peace commission to Richmond with Wood at its head. In his speech at the Peace Convention, Wood called both "war and hate the children of Satan" and chastised ministers of the gospel who preached that there was any good in it. He denounced the war and urged people of good will everywhere, North and South, to "raise the Banner of Peace." For many of Wood's listeners, if they could not have peace, they were determined at least not to have a draft.[45]

Draft lottery drawings began on Saturday, July 11, in the city's Ninth District, populated mainly by poor Irish immigrants whose shouts of "a rich man's war" grew more threatening with each name called. Draft protesters distributed "Song of the Conscripts," a parody of the patriotic recruiting song by New Yorker James Sloan Gibbon, "We Are Coming Father Abraham." One verse went:

> We're coming Father Abraham, three hundred thousand more,
> We leave our homes and firesides with bleeding hearts and sore,
> Since poverty has been our crime, we bow to thy decree,
> We are the poor who have no wealth to purchase liberty.[46]

One name drawn belonged to a member of the Black Joke Fire Company Number Thirty-three, whose men had assumed they were exempt from any federal draft just as they had been from previous state drafts. When the lottery started up again on that Monday, the firemen decided to shut it down. Urged on by angry onlookers, they stormed the draft office, destroyed the lottery wheel, and set fire to the building. Word of the incident spread quickly through uptown wards, sending the whole region into an uproar. According to one report, by noon crowds on the Upper East Side had grown to a "concourse of over twelve thousand." Some turned out just to see the excitement. Others joined the rioters who roamed the streets in a violent frenzy. One man wrote: "Taking the 4th Av. I found the streets full of people, and when I reached the terminus (now 34th St.) I found the whole road way and sidewalks filled with rough fellows (and some equally rough women) who were tearing up rails, cutting down telegraph poles, and setting fire to buildings."

Women were among the riot's leading participants, especially in the factory districts where their families labored at menial jobs for dismal pay. That the government now tried to take their husbands, sons, and fathers away from what little employment they had and leave the women to fend for themselves was unthinkable. That the owners in whose shops they labored could buy out of the draft was maddening. One observer in the industrial Eleventh Ward wrote that local women "vow vengeance on all enrolling officers and provost marshals."[47]

Over the next several days, crowds of enraged working-class whites, immigrant and native-born alike, torched the draft headquarters and razed pro-Lincoln newspaper offices, including Horace Greeley's *New York Tribune*. In some cases, employees turned on employers, burning their shops and factories. Worker rage against the rich did not stop there. They looted and destroyed homes of prominent businessmen, Republicans, and abolitionists, including that of James Sloan Gibbon. And they went after well-dressed gentlemen on the streets, calling them "three-hundred-dollar men."

Mobs hit the posh mansions of Lexington Avenue with particular ferocity, stealing or smashing "pictures with gilt frames, elegant pier glasses, sofas, chairs, clocks, furniture of every kind, wearing apparel, bed clothes." Some of the more well-to-do were able to save their homes by convincing the angry crowds that they were not Republicans. On Monday evening just before dark, one city resident "took a

Armed draft resisters fight off militiamen on First Avenue during the New York draft riot, the largest riot in U.S. history. Raising a cry of "rich man's war," rioters torched the draft office, razed pro-Lincoln newspaper offices, and burned the homes of prominent war supporters. Similar riots broke out in Boston, Hartford, Jersey City, Newark, Detroit, Cleveland, Toledo, St. Paul, Green Bay, and Chicago. (*Illustrated London News*)

walk down 5th Avenue, and seeing a group of rowdies in the grounds of Dr. Ward's large and superb mansion, I found they had gone there with the intention of setting fire to the building, which is filled with costly art! The family were all out, entreating the scamps to desist, as 'they were all Breckenridge democrats and opposed to the *draft*.'" The family's denunciation of Lincoln appeased the crowd, which soon drifted away.[48]

It proved tougher for local authorities to control the crowds. Their forces were simply too few and the riots too widespread. Even to try was a dangerous risk. A mob caught John A. Kennedy, the police superintendent, and beat him so badly that he was lucky to survive. Colonel Henry O'Brien of the 11th New York was not so fortunate. Early in the week, O'Brien led his men against rioters marching up Second Avenue. He ordered his men to fire over their heads to frighten them off, but the gunfire hit two children watching the scene from nearby windows. One, a two-year-old girl named Ellen Kirk, was killed. The mob retreated, but then attacked O'Brien's nearby home and burned it to the ground. The next day when O'Brien brought a wagon to collect what was left, neighbors enraged over the little girl's killing fell on O'Brien and beat him to death.[49]

Blacks were special targets of the rioters. A reporter from the Eleventh Ward wrote that "the laboring classes there appear to be of the opinion that the negroes are the sole cause of all their trouble, and many even say that were it not for the negroes there would be no war and no necessity for a draft." Some hoped to drive blacks entirely out of the city. All across town, blacks were beaten, lynched, and burned out of their homes. Some were forced to jump from upper floors of tenement buildings to escape approaching flames or pursuing rioters. The mob even burned a charity home for black orphans. A resident of the Nineteenth Ward wrote a short time after witnessing the attack that "towards evening the mob, furious as demons, went yelling over to the Colored-Orphan Asylum in 5th Avenue a little below where we live—and rolling a barrel of kerosine in it, the whole structure was soon in a blaze, and is now a smoking ruin. What has become of the 300 poor innocent orphans I could not learn. They must have had some warning of what the rioters intended; and I trust the children were removed in time to escape a cruel death." The children did barely make it out, rushing through the back door as rioters screaming "burn the niggers" broke down the front door.[50]

Rioting continued through Friday, July 17, when Federal troops straight from the Battle of Gettysburg rushed in to reestablish order. By that time, at least a hundred people had lost their lives and hundreds more had been injured. Some estimates of the casualty count ranged to more than a thousand. Whatever the figure, in the eyes of white lower-class New Yorkers, the effort had not been in vain. So frightened was the city government of another such riot that it passed an ordinance laying out city funds to pay the commutation fee for every drafted resident. Other towns in New York, such as Brooklyn, Yonkers, Albany, Buffalo, Utica, Syracuse, Troy, and Tarrytown, did the same.

All across the North, local governments increased the enlistment bounties in an effort to meet their enrollment quotas and avoid the draft requirement. At the federal level, draft protesters eventually claimed at least a minor victory as well. So stinging was the charge of "rich man's war" and so worried were Republicans about its impact on upcoming elections that the most blatantly elitist of the Conscription Act's provisions—the commutation fee—was abolished July 1864. Still, the substitute clause remained in place, and New York City hired them for any draftee who did not want to serve. In New York and elsewhere, some companies hired substitutes for their drafted employees (paid for by withheld wages) not only to stabilize their workforce but also to head off the possibility of a draft riot that might be turned back on the company.[51]

Small employers could afford no such protection for their workers, and local officials sometimes found it difficult, even dangerous, to try raising enough cash to do so. The recruiting committee in Stow Corners, Ohio, just northeast of Akron, discovered that to be true when it fell short of its enrollment quota. The committee decided to impose a fee on area property holders and offer the money as a recruitment bounty to encourage volunteering. It could thereby meet its quota and avoid the need for a draft. Most citizens paid up, but William Graham refused. Graham was a local farmer who held strong antiwar views. He had opposed the war from its start and would pay no fee to support it now. And he was prepared to defend his right to dissent at the point of a gun. Graham proved that when twenty members of Stow's recruiting committee decided to pay him a visit and convince him to pay his fee. They caught sight of Graham at work in his field, and probably saw the rifle next to him as well. The committee decided it would be safest to send one of its members to talk to Graham while the rest waited at the road. As a lone committeeman approached, Graham shouted for the man to get off his land and fired a single shot. The man turned and fled back toward his comrades, but Graham was hot in pursuit. As Graham neared the committee, he stopped, leveled his rifle, and fired two shots. They both found their mark. Two committeemen lay dead on the road.[52]

"Well Organized to Resist the Enrollment"

There were tens of thousands like Graham demanding to be left alone and ready to kill if they were not. But unlike Graham, most did not act alone. Men subject to the draft often banded together in mutual protection societies or associations. Some were made up mainly of deserters or conscripts dodging the draft. Others formed to head off conscription just in case they were drafted or to prevent a draft from being held in the first place. These organizations varied in background and in size from a handful to hundreds. What they all had in common was an opposition to the war and a determination to stay out of it by armed resistance if necessary.

In Pennsylvania, coal miners formed an organization called the "Buckshots," with membership throughout Carbon and Luzerne counties. They refused to fight the Rebels, but they were fully prepared to defend themselves against Lincoln's forces. So too were the Molly Maguires in Schuylkill County. Enrollment officers had planned to hold a draft there, but the Molly Maguires who "ruled the mines," as one draft officer put it, were so well organized that they thought better of it. There were troops waiting at Pottsville for orders to proceed along the rail line to Cass, but miners were posted all along the tracks to give plenty of warning. With the Molly Maguires armed and ready for a fight, a small war was sure to break out if the troops were sent in. Pennsylvania's state draft administrator, Alexander McClure, telegraphed Lincoln that he was hesitant to bring on such a bloody affair. Cautiously, Lincoln ordered McClure to "see the law enforced or at least appear to have been enforced." McClure took the hint. He ordered the local draft commissioner to doctor his books. At least on paper, Cass Township would meet its conscript quota. And McClure would never again consider sending state draft agents after the Molly Maguires.[53]

In Clearfield and Cambria counties, there were up to 1,800 deserters openly working the timber fields. They built a fort at the head of Clearfield River in case they had to fight off federal or state troops. And military units did go after deserter gangs in the mountain regions of north-central Pennsylvania. They killed the leader of one band and captured his men, but there were so many others in the region that the effort had little impact. Nor was force any more effective in the Pennsylvania farm country. In April 1863, when authorities in Reading arrested four men for organizing an antiwar meeting, three hundred enraged farmers marched on the town. Less than a month later, locals defiantly staged a huge antiwar rally in Reading. Organizers did not deny the existence of secret antiwar societies in the area, but insisted that they had been formed "for no other purpose than the protection of their rights." One speaker called "resistance by force to an invasion of personal freedom a virtue."[54]

Residents of Monroe County agreed. So hostile were they to the draft that no one would take a post there as draft agent. When authorities sent in a small force of ten to arrest a deserter, a band of local men ambushed the party and released the prisoner. "The people in that district," wrote one provost marshal, "are defiant—so much so as to frighten any who feel disposed to undertake [a draft agent's job]." He called the band that attacked his men "part of an organized society in the county to resist the conscript act." It was even worse for draft officials in Columbia County. That area was home to one of the state's most active antiwar bands, a force of well-armed and organized deserters numbering about five hundred. Antiwar factions generally exercised such control in Columbia that some called it the "Fishingcreek Confederacy" after a stream that ran through the county. The local draft had to be suspended temporarily when someone stole the draft books. Those who were later drafted felt perfectly safe if they chose not to report for duty. The assistant district provost marshal finally went into Columbia County hunting for draft dodgers—and he died there at the hands of parties unknown.[55]

Antiwar and antidraft societies were spread far and wide across the northern and border states. A provost marshal in New Jersey reported that "organizations are formed or forming in nearly all the districts in New Jersey to resist the draft." From New Hampshire came word of "intense hostility in this State to the present Administration, amounting almost to open rebellion in some localities." From New Hampshire's Third District, Provost Marshal Chester Pike wrote that in Sullivan County, "a large number of persons have held meetings to consider measures for resisting the draft. They have procured a large number of guns and revolvers and meet frequently to drill. They rang the bells when news of the New York riot came and threatened to burn the buildings of the Union men."[56]

In Minnesota, armed and organized antiwar bands controlled entire counties. The same was true in Holmes County, Ohio, where a small army of about a thousand men armed itself with four howitzers and prepared to fight off draft officials. In Ohio's Coshocton County, bands of deserters attacked government forces on a regular basis. When one hundred mounted infantrymen rode into Morgan County, Kentucky, to enforce the draft, they "were bushwhacked from the time they entered the county till they returned." In Iowa, an antiwar gang ambushed and killed two draft officers in Poweshiek County.

When "a large body of armed men" organized in Keokuk County, Iowa's governor wrote to Secretary of War Stanton begging for help.[57]

Indiana seemed to have more than its share of violent antiwar activists. One official reported that draft resisters across the state were collecting "large quantities of arms and ammunition." Provost Marshal James Parks discovered that the Eighth District was infested with secret societies committed to draft resistance. "The people," wrote Parks, "were urged by the disloyal portions of the press and every crossroads politician to arouse and prepare themselves to resist the enrollment of this 'tyrannical Administration.' These appeals were met with a hearty response." Anyone who wore a Federal uniform was called a "Lincoln dog." In the Seventh District, a provost marshal attempted to stop all arms sales after draft resisters tried to buy fifty sabers. The Second District was home to a band of five hundred antiwar men prepared to fight off troops sent after them. Usually, a fight was not necessary. When a company of infantry was sent after draft resisters in New Castle Township it found "the enemies of the government so thoroughly organized as to prevent our getting sufficient information to warrant the arrest and retention of any parties that we could then find."[58]

Antiwar organizations pervaded Illinois as well. Governor Richard Yates wrote Secretary of War Stanton warning that "companies and battalions" of antiwar men all over the state were drilling "by night and day, threatening opposition to the government." A provost marshal in Illinois's Ninth District reported organized and violent draft resistance in his area, encouraged by news of the "riotous conduct of the same classes in New York City." In Williamson County, according to one contemporary, "inhabitants one and all [were] . . . opposed to the Conscription Act in all its forms and were . . . well organized to resist the enrollment." Over one hundred deserters in the county built a fort on Muddy River and vowed to fight any attempts to force them back into the army. In Fulton County, there was a camp of deserters numbering about four hundred. One antiwar band established itself in Brown County near LaGrange and put out the word that it was ready to fight the draft in any form. Deserter bands in Fayette and Effingham counties did the same, attacking any government forces they came across.[59]

Though rumors circulated of northern conspiracies to overthrow the federal government by force of arms, few were ever substantiated and none proved to be any real threat. Such conspiracy theories were often concocted or exaggerated by prowar politicians for political gain or by newspapers to increase circulation. Still, armed and organized mutual protection societies were loosely and locally associated with the Peace Democrats if only because they shared supporters and sometimes actual membership. That alone was enough to worry federal authorities. In Iowa, members of an antiwar band known as the "Democrat Rangers" were suspected of killing two provost marshals. Republicans in Pennsylvania accused members of the antiwar society "Democratic Castle" of plotting revolution. The provost marshal in Terre Haute, Indiana, frantically reported that large numbers of Copperheads throughout the state had armed themselves and were meeting every day to draw up their "infernal schemes."[60]

When the state provost marshal in Indianapolis got word of an upcoming Democratic barbeque in Vigo County, he sent news back to Washington straining to draw connections between the Democratic Party, violent draft resistance, and a secret society known as the "Knights of the Golden Circle."

> The disloyal element, under the name of "Democracy," are holding large mass-meetings in different parts of the State, at which the people are urged to arm and drill, which they are doing in many places in large numbers. Large quantities of arms and ammunition are being purchased and distributed, especially in the Seventh District and adjoining counties in Illinois. I inclose you a poster advertising one of these meetings to come off on Saturday next. The watchword given on the bill is, I am assured, the watchword of the Knights of the Golden Circle.[61]

The Knights of the Golden Circle was one of several secret or semisecret antiwar societies promoting antiwar activities in the North, including the Sons of Liberty and the Order of American Knights. The Knights of the Golden Circle was perhaps the largest, with membership stretching from Pennsylvania to Iowa and chapters active in such cities as Detroit, Cincinnati, and Des Moines. In southern Illinois, rumor held that the Knights were encouraging men to join the Confederate army. Members of the order in Iowa were suspected of running guns to pro-Confederate guerrillas in Missouri. In Sullivan County, Indiana, the Knights were accused of murdering an enrollment officer. The Sons of Liberty, of which Clement Vallandingham was a leading member, had even more serious charges leveled against it. According to one exposé, the organization's objectives included not only ending the war but also establishing an independent midwestern confederacy. The Sons of Liberty had signs and grips that members used to identify each other. There was also an oath in which members promised to "if need be, take up arms in the cause of the oppressed—*in my country first of all*—against any Monarch, Prince, Potentate, Power or Government usurper."[62]

Such politically oriented secret societies certainly existed, but their influence and organization was much more limited than either pro- or antiwar partisans claimed. When state representatives of the Sons of Liberty came together to form a national organization with Vallandingham at its head, they argued so intensely among themselves about what their objectives should be that the meeting broke up with nothing accomplished. There were divisions at the state level as well. When Harrison Dodd, a midlevel Democratic functionary in Indianapolis, hatched a plot to consolidate various mutual protection associations and use them to overthrow state governments in the Midwest by force, Indiana's Democratic leaders ordered a halt to any such plans. Already stung by accusations of disloyalty, the party hierarchy wanted to give their opponents no grounds on which to confirm the charge.[63]

Though Peace Democrats gave Lincoln no end of trouble, their function as a loyal opposition party goes far toward explaining why violent resistance to Lincoln's policies in the North was never well organized beyond the local level. Democrats generally absorbed much of the anger common folk directed at the "rich man's war" and funneled it into an electoral process controlled by rich men. Even so, most northerners who wanted nothing to do with the war between elections found ways of avoiding government entanglements through active or passive resistance. Such resistance certainly delayed Union victory, but it was never a direct threat to the central government's existence.[64]

"I Aint Mad with Nobody"

That was not the case for the Confederacy. Whether actively working against it or withholding support for it, southern plain folk who refused to back the Confederacy's war effort—an effort upon which the new government depended for its survival—were contributing to its downfall. In Georgia, Augusta's *Chronicle and Sentinel* made that point when it warned in June 1863 that the South contained "a large number of persons who not only sympathize with the Federals, but who are doing all in their power to injure us in every possible manner." Samuel Knight of southwest Georgia wrote to Governor Brown with a similar warning in February 1864. After three months of "mingling freely with the common people," Knight reported that "among that class generally there is a strong union feeling."[65]

From Russell County, Virginia, came word in March 1862 that there were "plenty of Union men here." There were plenty in Arkansas too. A former Confederate general declared in an 1863 address: "The loyalty to Jeff. Davis in Arkansas does not extend practically beyond the shadow of his army, while the hatred of him is as widespread as it is intense. The Union sentiment is manifesting itself on all sides and by every indication—in Union meetings—in desertions from the Confederate army—in taking the oath of allegiance [to the United States] unsolicited—in organizing for home defense, and enlisting in the Federal army."[66]

When the Confederacy's "Ole Stonewall" succumbed to complications from wounds received at Chancellorsville in May 1863, a young North Carolina woman wrote that "some of the people about here actually rejoiced at the death of Genl Jackson!" That same year, an exile from Mississippi told a northern audience: "The question has been asked, is there any Union sentiment in the South? I reply that there is strong Union sentiment, even in Mississippi. . . . I make this statement without fear of successful contradiction, that the majority of the white inhabitants of the South are Union-loving men." Though most southern whites were hardly outright unionists, it was "a certain fact," as one Georgian wrote in a letter to Governor Brown, "that the Southern people are fast becoming as bitterly divided against each other as the Southern and Northern people ever has been." The man concluded his observation by insisting that "I have not written this letter to exaggerate these things. I only write such as I know to be true."[67]

The writer did not need to exaggerate in making his point. Brown could find abundant evidence of dissent simply by reading the newspapers in his own state capital of Milledgeville. Letters to the editor were filled with near constant criticism of Brown, Davis, the war, and the Confederacy. Some wrapped their dissent in humorous parody. In the summer of 1864, with a Shakespearean-like expression of his feelings on the war, one farmer gave voice to many rural men through a Milledgeville paper.

To Go or Not to Go

To go or not to go, that is the question:
Whether it pays best to suffer pestering
By idle girls and garrulous old women,
Or to take up arms against a host of Yankees,
And by opposing get killed—To die, to sleep,
(Git eout) and in this sleep to say we "sink
To rest by all our Country's wishes blest"
And live forever—(that's a consummation
Just what I'm after). To march, to fight—
To fight! perchance to die, aye there's the rub!
For while I'm sleep, who'll take care Mary
and the babes—when Billy's in the low ground,
Who'll feed 'em, hey! There's the respect
I have for *them* that makes life sweet;
For who would bear the bag to mill,
Plough Dobbin,[68] cut the wheat, dig taters,
Kill hogs, and do all sorts of drudgery
If I am fool enough to get a Yankee
Bullet on my brain! Who'll cry for me!
Would patriotism pay my debts, when dead?
But oh! The dread of something after death—
That undiscovered fellow who'll court Mary,
And do my huggin—that's agony,
And makes me want to stay home,
Specially as I aint mad with nobody.
Shells and bullets make cowards of us all,
And blam'd my skin if snortin steeds,
And pomp and circumstance of War
Are to be compared with feather beds,
And Mary by my side.[69]

"In Hell Where All Secessionists Ought to Be"

Southern plain folk were rarely eager to fight. Had they been so, no draft would have been needed to encourage them. Most simply wanted to be left alone. A majority of them had opposed secession to begin with. Even those who lent support to the cause of southern independence early on found ample cause to disown the Confederacy as the war continued. That seemed obvious to John Wood of Mississippi, who wrote that "the power which wealth always gives has been brought to bear most heavily upon the poorer classes, producing a degree of suffering almost incredible in a country professing to be free." It was producing disaffection as well. South Carolina's commandant of conscripts reported that the state's hill folk were "little identified with our struggle."[70]

Sam Scott found the same to be true in southwestern Arkansas, attributing antiwar sentiment at least in part to the twenty-slave law. He reported that "the old cry of poor men being obliged to fight for the rich may be heard on all sides." Mississippian James Phelan warned Jefferson Davis that "never did a law meet with more universal odium" than the Conscription Act and its exemption of planters from the draft. "Its influence upon the poor is most calamitous, and has awakened a spirit and elicited a discussion of which we may safely predict the most unfortunate results."[71]

Privileges for planters made disaffection among plain folk predictable enough. Just as predictable were the results of speculative profiteering. Cotton and tobacco overproduction, along with speculation on what foodstuffs there were, led plain folk to conclude that the Confederacy's ongoing bid for independence held nothing for them. An army officer in South Carolina wrote to his superiors after a failed attempt to talk a group of deserters back into service that they were outraged over "speculations and extortions so rampant throughout the land. . . . They swear by all they hold sacred that they will die at home before they will ever be dragged forth again to do battle for such a cause." With prices high and food scarce across the South, small wonder that one North Carolinian wrote to his brother in the field telling him not only to desert but desert to the Yankees: "I would advise you to . . . go to the other side whear you can get plenty and not stay in this one horse barefooted naked and famine striken Southern Confederacy."[72]

Planters had promised to provide food for soldiers and their families but instead usually sold it to speculators, giving plain folk little reason to view the conflict as anything but a rich man's war. At the same time, it gave plain folk reason to hate both the planters and the government that sustained them. Georgia's *Early County News*, after reflecting on planter indifference to starving soldiers' families, asked, "Ain't it a pity but what the Yankees would take every thing such men have, and leave them without a single mouthful of anything? We hope to live to see the day." When told that a Union fleet was on its way downriver to support an invasion of Mississippi, a non-slaveholder from Jefferson County publicly proclaimed that he "wished the Gun Boats would shell every God Damn plantation on the River."[73]

Such language could be dangerous. One resident wrote to her mother that there were many unionists in Randolph County, North Carolina, "some of which have had to leave for their large talking in favor of Lincoln. Others keep quiet and are let alone." But silence was not always a sure safeguard. F.A.P. Barnard, chancellor of the University of Mississippi, revealed his support of the Union only in private correspondence, but local secessionists got wind of his sentiments. They made life in Oxford so unpleasant for Barnard that he resigned and fled the state, finally settling in Virginia.[74]

Barnard was lucky to escape with his life. Many other unionists did not. A Mississippi minister noted that "the rebels punished with death any who declared himself in favor of the Union. . . . at Tupelo, they were taken out daily and shot for expression of sentiments adverse to the rebellion." The slightest hint of abolition sentiment, past or present, could put one's life in danger—even those of two decades earlier. Wrote the minister:

An old gentleman in Winston county was arrested for an act committed twenty years before, which was construed as proof of his abolition proclivities. The old gentleman had several daughters, and his mother-in-law had given him a negro girl. Observing that his daughters were becoming lazy, and were imposing all the labour upon the slave, he sent her back to the donor, with a statement of the cause of returning her. This was now the ground for his arrest, but escaping from their clutches, a precipitate flight alone saved his life.[75]

In Floyd County, Virginia, unionist Hyram Dulany told neighbors that he was "glad to hear of the death of Henry Lane in the Battle of Cedar Run [and] that he hoped he was in Hell where all secessionists ought to be." Local secessionists heard of the remark and shot him for it.[76] In Mississippi, secessionists raided the home of a suspected unionist and decided to execute him on the spot when he refused to recite a Confederate loyalty oath. According to one account of the murder,

> He had a large family of small children, who, together with his wife, begged that his life might be spared. He himself had no favours to ask of the secessionists. Among his foes, the only point of dispute was, as to the mode of his death. Some favoured shooting, some hanging; but the prevailing majority were in favour of scalding him to death. And there, in the presence of his weeping and helpless family, these fiends in human form *deliberately heated water, with which they scalded to death their chained and defenceless victim.* Thus perished a patriot of whom the State was not worthy. The corpse was then suspended from a tree, with a label on the breast, stating that whoever cut him down and buried him, should suffer the same fate.

Defying the threat, some of his neighbors took the body down that night and secretly buried it deep in the woods to prevent further desecration.[77]

"Lord, Forgive Them"

Even ministers of the gospel were afforded little protection if they expressed, or were suspected of harboring, Union sentiments. In southeast Alabama's Dale County, rumor had it that the Reverend Bill Sketoe was somehow involved with a gang of unionist raiders. For Captain Joseph Breare of the local home guard, that was all the evidence necessary to convict Sketoe. In December 1864, Breare's men dragged Sketoe from his home in Newton and hauled him just north of town near the Choctawhatchee River bridge. There they prepared to hang him.

Just as the rope was being tied off, Captain Wesley Dowling, a Confederate soldier at home recuperating from a wound, came riding across the bridge and tried to stop the lynching. Breare warned Dowling off, saying that if he did not move on he would "get the same medicine." Breare then turned to Sketoe and asked if he had any last words. The preacher began to pray aloud, not for himself but for his murderers. "Forgive them, Lord, forgive them." Sketoe's pious pleading so enraged the guardsmen that they threw the noose around his neck before he had finished his prayer. They shoved him onto a buggy, pulled the rope tight over a tree limb, and slapped the horse, jerking the buggy from under Sketoe. But in their haste to lynch him, the guardsmen had tied the rope over a weak branch. When it caught Sketoe's full weight, it bent down just low enough for the preacher's toes to touch the ground. One of Breare's men, George Echols, rushed over and dug a hole under his feet. Now swinging freely, Sketoe strangled to death within a few minutes. His body was cut down next morning, and he was laid to rest at Mt. Carmel Church cemetery on the outskirts of Newton.

Bill Sketoe's fate became grist for one of Alabama's most famous ghost stories. As the tale went, all the men connected with his lynching died violent and mysterious deaths shortly after the war. Lightning struck one man. Another was found dead in a swamp. Still another was killed when a mule ran off with him. George Echols was shot in a raid on a local unionist's home, and Breare was killed when a falling limb knocked him from his horse during a thunderstorm. As for the hole George Echols dug, legend says that it can never remain filled. Whenever leaves or dirt cover the spot, so the story goes, it is miraculously cleared out again by Bill Sketoe's ghost. Mary Edwards Fleming, who grew up in Dale County after the war and saw the hole many times herself, had a more logical explanation. By her account, the hole "was kept raked out by the dead man's friends who pretended that it was something supernatural." Wash Reynolds, a friend of Sketoe's, was suspected of keeping the hole clear, though he always insisted that he knew no more about the mystery than anyone else.[78]

Like Sketoe, the Reverend James Pelan, pastor of the Presbyterian Church in Macon, Mississippi, was hardly outspoken about his unionist sentiments. Nevertheless, his refusal to preach secession brought close scrutiny and eventually attempts on his life. One night while on his way home, hidden bushwhackers shot and nearly killed him. As he was recovering, three men showed up at his door and asked if he and his wife could spare some food for supper. As was the custom, the Pelans invited them to sit at their table. When Pelan's wife left the room to see to preparations for the meal, the three men stood up and yelled at Pelan, "All the supper we want is to kill you, you infernal Unionist and abolitionist." A blast of gunfire brought Pelan's wife rushing back to the dining room. As she cradled her dying husband in her arms, Pelan managed to whisper, "Father, forgive them, they know not what they do."[79]

A fellow Mississippi Presbyterian, the Reverend John Aughey, nearly suffered the same fate for his own unionism. A gang of armed secessionists attacked the Aughey home one night, but were foiled when several of them fell into an unfinished well. On a later evening, an assassin named Smith approaching the Aughey home caught sight of a minister and drew his pistol. He fired a single shot which killed the man—the wrong man. Lying dead on the ground was a local Methodist preacher whom Smith had mistaken for Aughey.

Where assassins had failed, Confederate authorities nearly succeeded. They arrested Aughey, imprisoned him at Tupelo, and were about to execute him for treason when, with the help of sympathetic friends, he escaped and made his way to Federal lines. From there he traveled north and in 1863 published a book recounting his experiences entitled *The Iron Furnace: or, Slavery and Secession*. In its preface, Aughey wrote with sympathy of the "many loyal men in the southern States, who to avoid martyrdom, conceal their opinions. . . . they now 'bide their time,' in prayerful trust that God will, in his own good time, subvert rebellion, and overthrow anarchy, by a restoration of the supremacy of constitutional law. By these, and their name is legion, my book will be warmly approved."[80]

Among those who did *not* approve was Jefferson Davis. Still, he knew Aughey was right about one thing at least—that by the hundreds of thousands, southerners worked against or were indifferent to the Confederate cause. Davis's reaction to dissent was much the same as Lincoln's. Though both professed to be fighting for liberty, both took steps to undermine personal liberties guaranteed by their respective constitutions. In January 1862, Congress authorized Davis to declare martial law and suspend the writ of habeas corpus. Civilians could now be arrested and held without charge. Even if they were charged, they could be tried by military courts in areas where martial law had been declared.

Davis wasted no time in identifying hotbeds of dissent, beginning with Richmond itself. The Confederate capital was so rife with anti-Confederates that it was one of the first cities to have martial law imposed upon it. Its military governor, General John H. Winder, was soon rounding up civilians he considered dangerous. Among them was the Reverend Alden Bosserman, who had publicly prayed for Confederate defeat. Winder also went after John Minor Botts, a former U.S. congressman from Virginia, when word got out that Botts was working on a manuscript exposing the secession movement as a conspiracy of southern Democrats. Winder arrested so many Richmond civilians that they took up the entire second floor of Castle Thunder military prison.[81]

It was the same across much of the South. One witness recalled that among the inmates of a Columbus, Mississippi, prison were "a number of political prisoners. . . . about one hundred and fifty Mississippi citizens, such as were suspected of Union sentiments." The prisoners included "three clergymen—one a Presbyterian, one a 'United Brother,' and the other a Methodist." Without the ear of some sympathetic judge, such men were beyond the reach of any legal remedy. Even to seek legal redress could be dangerous. William Hyman, a young defense attorney in Alexandria, Louisiana, was arrested in January 1864. Though there was no evidence of his holding unionist sentiments, he had tried to secure the release of several "illegally conscribed persons" by applying for writs of habeas corpus. In doing so, he had made himself "obnoxious to the authorities," and quickly found himself lodged in jail with his former clients.[82]

It was hardly unusual for questions to be raised about the legality under which "conscribed persons" were drafted. According to one account from Alabama, conscript officers went "sweeping through the country with little deference either to the law or the regulations designed to temper its unavoidable rigor." A man in Troup County, Georgia, wrote to General Howell Cobb, commander of the Confederate military district that included Georgia, complaining that "the poppinjays employed as enrolling officers . . . delight in harassing and putting to expense everybody." A resident of Georgia's Clay County wrote that conscript officers were everywhere, "watching for some poor devil who is trying to keep out of the army." He told of conscript companies running men down with hounds and dragging them off to the army in chains. One draft dodger was caught in Albany, Georgia, disguised as a woman. The man was chained and delivered to his company wearing the dress in which he was captured.[83]

Not all men of military age were necessarily subject to the draft. Beyond those who held twenty slaves or who could afford to buy their way out, the Confederacy, unlike the Union, exempted any number of occupational positions. Government employees and officeholders, those engaged in river, rail, or marine transportation, workers in certain military support industries, mail carriers, telegraph operators, hospital staff, druggists, ministers, college professors, and teachers with at least twenty pupils were all legally excused from the draft. Still, in their zeal to reach enrollment quotas, draft officials frequently rounded up such men and herded them off to conscript camps. In August 1863, sixty people from the small community of Attapulgus in Decatur County, Georgia, signed a petition urging Governor Brown to have their postmaster discharged from the army. "If our Post office is permitted to go down for the want of a P.M.," they insisted, "our nearest office will be Bainbridge distant—12½ miles."[84]

Though they were not always a guaranteed draft dodge, exempted positions became the most sought after, and among the most corrupt, in the Confederacy. Schools were suddenly opened all over the South by men with little formal education or none at all. Their founders were often willing to teach for free if only they could get twenty students to enroll. Drug stores sprang up too, run by druggists who, according to one southern editor, "could not analyze the simplest compound or put the plainest prescription in a satisfactory manner if his life depended upon it." In Early County, Georgia, thirty-seven candidates vied for five seats on the Inferior Court. "But there was no politics in the race," said one county resident. "The candidate just wanted the office to keep him out of the war." So did candidates in Randolph County, Alabama, where office holding was "more sought after than Heaven." In Florida's fall 1863 elections, most of those winning county offices were Confederate soldiers, some of them already deserters, looking for a legal way to keep out of the army.[85]

One of the most common ways of dodging the draft was to join a home guard or militia company. Nearly every town and county had such units, which were supposed to be manned primarily by old men, young boys, and the physically disabled. There were a few home guard companies, like the Nancy Harts of LaGrange, Georgia, made up entirely of women. Invariably, there were also many healthy men of draft age in home guards claiming exemption from conscription on that basis. In January 1864, four young men from Columbus, Georgia, who had just reached draft age organized a home guard company of younger boys for the alleged purpose of "guarding bridges" and performing other light duty. According to one local citizen, their action was prompted only by fear of being sent to the front lines. John Smith of Cherokee County, Alabama, said derisively of the local home guard, "Their business was to gather up conscripts and deserters from the Confederate army, but their main business was to keep from going to the front themselves and to do as little as possible and stay about home."[86]

"We Don't Shoot People"

Those who objected to the war on grounds of conscience refused to do military service of any kind. Like their northern brethren, among the most confirmed objectors were members of pacifist sects such as the Dunkards, Mennonites, and Quakers. In Virginia's Floyd County, one unsympathetic man wrote that local Dunkards refused to "bear arms in the defense of their country's rights . . . alleging that it is not right to fight." They paid a high price to secure the rights of conscience. According to county resident Willis Reed, who had friends among the Dunkards, area secessionists saw no difference between pacifists and unionists: "All that class of people were persecuted and abused as rebels to the Confederacy during the war."[87]

Richmond at first refused exemptions for religious objectors. But, like anyone, they could buy their way out of the draft if they could afford to do so.[88] Even those who could often refused on religious grounds. They would not support the war directly or indirectly, even when forced to serve. Christian Good, a Mennonite ordered into the 146th Virginia Militia, made it clear that even when placed on the firing line, he would not kill his fellow men. As he related the story to a friend,

> Over and over he was forced into battle but he would not shoot anybody. At the first battle the captain came up and asked him if he shot. He said, "No, I did not shoot." Sometime afterward he got into another

battle. After it was over the captain came to him and asked him whether he shot. He said, "No, I didn't see anything to shoot at." The captain asked, "Why, didn't you see all those Yankees over there?" "No, they're people; we don't shoot people."[89]

Resistance among members of pacifist sects was so persistent and troublesome that in June 1864 the Confederacy finally exempted them from the draft. However, the act applied only to men who had been members as of October 11, 1862, when the Second Conscription Act took effect. Viewing their religion as a sanctuary for anyone who wished to join, North Carolina Quakers petitioned Congress to exempt all their adherents regardless of when they joined. Their request was ignored, but they and other pacifists continued to resist the draft as best they could.[90]

But how to resist the conscript law? That was the question dissenters faced throughout the war. Many of those who could do so simply left the Confederacy. Most headed north, but escaping dissenters in the western Confederacy often went south. A thriving anti-Confederate community of exiled Texans, Hispanic and Anglo alike, sprang up just across the Rio Grande from Brownsville in Matamoros, Mexico. Immigrant Germans too were among the exiles. They had come to the United States escaping Europe's turbulent revolutions of 1848, and now wanted nothing to do with any rebellion. When Confederate officials tried to conscript them, hundreds struck out for Mexico. In August 1862 one group of families totaling sixty-one individuals assembled west of Kerrville and headed for the border. On August 10, just a day's ride from Mexico, they were ambushed in Kinney County near the Nueces River by pursuing Rebel cavalrymen. About half were killed on the spot, some after they had been wounded and taken prisoner. Of those who escaped the Nueces massacre, six were later shot trying to cross the Rio Grande.[91]

Those dissenters for whom exile was not an option were no less determined to escape conscription. In January 1863, at a conscript camp in Magnolia, Arkansas, a group of draftees numbering perhaps fifty lined up on the parade ground, announced their refusal to be inducted, then marched out of camp. One observer reported that the conscript law was "making Union people fast" in Arkansas. Hardly pacifists, such men were prepared to defend their right of dissent by force if necessary. It was the same all across the South. In Clay

When Confederate officials tried to conscript antiwar men in Texas, hundreds struck out for Mexico. In August 1862 one group of families assembled west of Kerrville and headed for the border. Most never made it. On August 10, just a day's ride from Mexico, they were ambushed near the Nueces River by pursuing Rebel cavalry. About half were killed on the spot, some after they had been wounded and taken prisoner. Of those who escaped the Nueces massacre, several were later shot trying to cross the Rio Grande. (*Harper's New Monthly Magazine*)

County, Georgia, a conscript officer was nearly killed when he tried to enforce the draft. Threats to his life became so serious that he fled the state. In Oak Hill, West Virginia, local unionists posted a notice on the courthouse door warning the Confederate conscript officer and his guard to get out of town. The Dial brothers of North Carolina wrote to Captain Quill Hunter, telling him that "if yo Ever hut for us a gin I will put lead in yo god dam your hell fired Sole. . . . If this don't give yo warning enough the next warning we will give yo with powder and lead. take the hint."[92]

The wise draft officer did not take such threats lightly. Putting the word of resisters to the test could be plenty dangerous. In the No-lichucky Valley of North Carolina, when conscript officials went after a professed unionist and draft dodger, the man and his three daughters stood them down. "Old Yank," as he was later known, told a visitor, "I just reached 'round the door and pulled out my Henry rifle, an' my gals understood it an' got their double-barreled shotguns, an' I just told them boys I had lived too long in the mountains to be scared that way, an' if they . . . laid hand on an ole man like me they'd never do it agin, fur my gals had the bead on 'em." They left Old Yank alone. In

Rapides Parish, Louisiana, two draft officers were fired on, and one was badly wounded. Draft resisters in Jones County, Alabama, killed their enrolling officer and captured his entire guard. In Virginia, officer John R. Payton went after draft dodgers on Bent Mountain and was shot dead from his horse.[93]

Stories of such violent draft resistance survive in southern family traditions to this day. Descendants of Newton Knight, a Confederate deserter from Jones County, Mississippi, still tell of how he killed Major Amos McLemore for hunting conscripts. As Ethel Knight tells the story, McLemore was a "hot-headed young fellow" who was "warned that he was treading on dangerous ground but he refused to heed the warning." A similar tale has been passed down in the author's own family. His great-great-grandfather Frank Williams was born to a nonslaveholding farm family in Dooly County, Georgia. He reached draft age in 1862 but never served in the Confederate army. When Frank's father Asa stabbed a man, perhaps a draft officer trying to conscript Frank, the family fled Dooly County and settled in Miller County a hundred miles to the southwest.[94]

Large areas of the Confederacy became so dangerous for conscript companies that no one could be found to fill their ranks. Even where such companies could be formed, the troops often displayed more sympathy for their neighbors than for the Confederacy. That was the case in Austin County, Texas, where authorities could not trust the local militia to enforce conscription. In southeast Georgia, when Colonel Duncan Clinch sent the 4th Georgia Cavalry to round up deserters and draft evaders, some of his men themselves deserted and joined the resistance. So did members of the 16th South Carolina Infantry in Greenville, Pickens, and Spartanburg counties. One disgusted officer wrote in 1863 that in those and surrounding counties, it was "no longer a reproach to be known as a deserter."[95]

For deserters and draft dodgers who were captured, punishment was not guaranteed. When a conscript company in Franklin County, Georgia, rounded up several deserters, the local jailor refused to lodge them. In White County, a band of over twenty men broke into the Cleveland jail and released a draft dodger. So strong was antiwar feeling in some parts of the South that judges could not hold court on antiwar men without a military escort. Even when trials were held, convictions were rare. Juries consistently refused to return guilty verdicts against those who opposed the war. Georgia's General Howell Cobb conceded in August of 1863 that to drag antiwar men into court was "simply to provide for a farcical trial." Later that year two Lumpkin County men, John Woody and John A. Wimpy, were tried on charges of treason. In the face of strong evidence against them, and after Woody confessed his opposition to the war, a local jury acquitted both men.[96]

In September 1863, from north Georgia's Fannin County, deserter John Hopper wrote assuring his brother who was still in the army, "There is no dificulty now in staying at home [and] no opposition from the citizens. I can tell you if you can only get here with out being took up it is all right—for in the place of opposition you will have protection." Augusta County, Virginia, was another place where deserters could find protection. Confederate authorities advertised the names of 181 area deserters in a local paper, offering thirty dollars reward each to anyone turning them in. After five months hardly any names had been stricken from the list. In Madison County, North Carolina, when enrollment companies came around, draft dodgers took to the hills while friends and family kept them informed of their pursuer's movements. Farmers like Willis Bone of Irwin County, Georgia, and David Weddle of Floyd County, Virginia, offered havens on their property for deserters and draft dodgers who worked the land in exchange for lodging. The resister community on Weddle's lands numbered as many as 150 men. Other Floyd County unionists, like Tilman Overstreet and Eli Epperly, offered help for deserters because doing so would also help "brake up the war."[97]

"Making War on Women and Children"

Offering help to layouts could be a dangerous undertaking. By law, anyone who fed, harbored, or aided the escape of a deserter could be fined a thousand dollars or imprisoned for up to two years. In practice, penalties could be much worse since those charged with enforcing the law often paid little attention to it. In the hill country around Fredericksburg, Texas, Confederates took whole families and their farms. Patrols roamed the countryside gathering up deserters' wives and children, confiscating their property in the process. "It was a pitiable sight," wrote a sympathetic Rebel soldier in Fredericksburg, "to see all these poor folks stripped of their property, such as it was, earned by hard toil and exposure to a dangerous frontier."[98]

In April 1863, Isaac Miller, a War of 1812 veteran, offered the following testimony after the home guard of Randolph County, North Carolina, murdered his son, a draft resister: "Then they come and taken me and put me in Jale and kep me thare twenty four days and then turned me out and made me pay for my Board and I am a man About Eighty Eight years old and I was A soldier in the jackson wars." Another North Carolina man told of "one old helpless bed-ridden mother, with 3 sons in the army (C.S.A.) and 3 in the bushes" who had been "dispoiled of her property" by Confederate soldiers, part of a force sent down from the Army of Northern Virginia by Robert E. Lee to hunt for deserters. "Many deserters families have been deprived of all means of subsistence & left to starve this winter," complained the writer. "Is this not making war on women & children?"[99]

In Virginia, Floyd County home guard members were just as callous in rooting out resistance. They kidnaped the nine-year-old son of a deserter when the family refused to reveal the father's whereabouts. They looted the farm of an old couple named Wilson when they refused to turn over their three deserter sons. Guardsmen threatened to hang Jacob Moses for harboring his brother Jefferson and son-in-law David Spangler. They threatened to shoot William Dillon for aiding deserters among his family and friends. Dillon called their bluff, proclaiming that "he would [as] soon die that way as any way." The guardsmen backed down.[100]

Dillon was lucky. Confederate home guards did not always bluff. One man who learned that the hard way was George M. Kierce, a sixty-year-old farmer in south Georgia's Worth County. Kierce often allowed deserters and layouts to hide on his property. In November 1862, he and his thirteen-year-old son John disappeared. Some locals said they had fled to the North. Others thought they had gone to Florida. Most, however, were sure they had been murdered. According to Worth County court records, Justice of the Peace Hudson Tabor had issued warrants against George and John Kierce the day before they vanished. Deputy Sheriff Lewis Simmons arrested Kierce and his son and was escorting them to Judge Tabor when they were stopped by George Green, the local conscript officer, and a band of thirteen riders. Green took custody of the Kierces, then told his men to "continue their search for said deserters as it would be a more easy matter now to take them." That was the last time anyone admitted to seeing Kierce and his son alive. Weeks later, a family member finally discovered their bodies sunken in nearby Abram's Creek. Their throats had been cut, the boy's almost to the point of decapitation, and their clothes were filled with gravel to weigh them down.[101]

In the winter of 1862–63, authorities in Madison County, North Carolina, determined to draw local deserters out of hiding by cutting their families off from the state's salt distribution. The move amounted to a sentence of death by starvation since meat could not be cured or preserved without salt. So on January 8 a band of fifty deserters and other antiwar men from Shelton Laurel raided the county seat of Marshall and took what salt and other provisions they needed. Within days, hundreds of Confederate soldiers were scouring through the Laurel Valley. As historian Phillip Shaw Paludan put it in his book about the incident, aptly entitled *Victims: A True Story of the Civil War,* "it was the fortunate women and old people who had their men taken from them."

> Those unfortunate enough to be relatives of suspects that the troops could not find were whipped and tortured and hanged until almost dead and then let down again for more questioning. Eighty-five-year-old Mrs. Unus Riddle was whipped, hanged temporarily, and robbed. Seventy-year-old Sally Moore was whipped with hickory rods until the blood ran down her back. Another woman, the mother of an infant child, was tied in the snow to a tree and her baby placed in the doorway of their cabin. Unless she talked, the soldiers told her, they would leave them both there. Sarah and Mary Shelton, wives of two suspected Marshall raiders, were whipped and suspended by ropes around their necks. A young mentally retarded girl named Martha White was beaten and tied by the neck all day to a tree.

The soldiers rounded up fifteen men and boys, no more than five of whom had participated in the Marshall raid. Two managed to escape during their first night of captivity. The remaining prisoners, ranging in age from thirteen to sixty-five, were marched out of Shelton Laurel the next morning, presumably to imprisonment with or without trial. They had gone only a short distance when their captors led them off the road and ordered five to their knees. The prisoners quickly realized that they were about to be murdered. As they begged for their lives, some of the soldiers refused to fire. "Fire or you will take their place," warned the detachment commander. They fired—or at least enough of them did so to complete the executions. Then five more captives were forced to the ground. A volley exploded and four of the five lay dead. The fifth, a thirteen-year-old boy named David Shelton, had enough life left in him to plead for mercy. "You have killed my old father and my three brothers; you have shot me in both arms—I forgive you all this—I can get well. Let me go home to my mother and sisters." Hardly had David spoken before another volley rang out and he was shot dead. Moments later, the remaining three prisoners followed him to eternity. A day later, relatives found the victims buried in a shallow mass grave. Wild hogs had rooted up one of the bodies and eaten much of its head away.[102]

Despite the dangers, anti-Confederate southerners continued helping each other when they could. Such help was most often local. But if Confederate pressure got too intense, and if there was time enough, there were underground railroads out of the South with guides and safe houses along the way. The Reverend John Aughey, a confirmed unionist, wrote that many men "who would not muster nor be enrolled as conscripts resolved to escape to the Federal lines." He recalled "skillful guides who could course it from point to point through the densest forests, with the unerring instinct of the panther."[103] He knew what he was talking about. Aughey himself used such guides and safe houses during his escape from Tupelo, Mississippi, in 1862. Great care had to be used in identifying those willing to help. A few days after his jailbreak—tired, hungry, and still wearing his prison leg irons—Aughey spotted a likely looking farmhouse.

> I remained near it till I was satisfied there were no negroes held by that family. I then went boldly up, knocked, gained admittance, and asked for some water, which was given to me. The lady of the house, scrutinizing me closely, asked me if I were from Tupelo. I replied in the affirmative. She then inquired my name. I gave her my Christian name, John Hill, suppressing the surname. Her husband was sitting near, a man of Herculean frame; and as the wife's inquisitiveness was beginning to alarm me, I turned to him and said: "My friend, you are a man of great physical powers, and at this time you ought to be in the army. The Yankees are overrunning all our country, and the service of every

man is needed." His wife replied that he was not in the army, nor would he go into it, unless he was forced to go. They had been told that the cavalry would be after him in a few days, to take him as a conscript; but she considered the conscript law base and tyrannical. Overjoyed at the utterance of such sentiments as these, I then revealed my true character. I told them that I had recently made my escape from Tupelo, where I was doomed to execution on the gallows, and that I was now flying from prison and from death. I then exhibited the iron bands upon my ankles. Both promised all the aid in their power.

The couple fed Aughey, gave him a new suit of clothes, helped remove his leg irons, and led him to a Union friend's home a half mile away. Aughey was passed from one safe house to another, escorted by sympathizers from point to point, until he finally reached Union army pickets at Rienzi, Mississippi, just south of Corinth.[104]

Aughey mentioned few names in his 1863 memoir, writing that he did not want to "compromise the safety of my Union friends who

Family and friends regularly supplied groups of deserters and draft dodgers hiding out across the countryside. It was dangerous work. Home guard units hunting for men evading service could be brutal, even deadly. One woman wrote to North Carolina's governor complaining of guardsmen rounding up women and "boxing their jaws and knocking them about as if they ware Bruts" in an effort to force information from them. Two women had their hands held under a fence rail while a soldier sat on it. Some who refused to talk were killed. (Drake, *Fast and Loose in Dixie*)

rendered me assistance, and who are still within the rebel lines." Nor did he want to put in danger friends with whom he had conspired to resist Confederate authority. There were plenty of them to be concerned about. Soon after the Confederate Congress adopted conscription, he and other like-minded neighbors had banded together for mutual advise and support.

> Knowing that in a multitude of counsellors there is wisdom, we held secret meetings, in order to devise the best method of resisting the law. We met at night, and had our counter-signs to prevent detection. Often our wives, sisters, and daughters met with us. Our meeting-place was some ravine, or secluded glen, as far as possible from the haunts of the secessionists; all were armed; even the ladies had revolvers, and could use them too. The crime of treason [against the United States] we were resolved not to commit.[105]

"The Secrets of This Order"

Aughey's group was but one of many secret societies—large and small, active and passive—that sprang up across the South to oppose the war. Another was the city of Montgomery's Closet Fellowship, which held secret meetings on Commerce Street at Israel Robert's hardware store and George Cowles's dry goods store on Market Street. They passed around northern newspapers, talked about the war's progress, and condemned the treason of pro-Confederate neighbors. There was also Atlanta's Union Circle, whose members worked to undermine Confederate authority and sometimes aided escaping Federal prisoners of war. Also assisting Federal escapees was a Union Association in Charleston, South Carolina, said to be fourteen hundred strong. Two Union officers imprisoned in the city who made good their escape later wrote that they could not have done so without help from Association members.[106]

The first such society known to be sizeable and well organized was the Peace and Constitutional Society, founded in the fall of 1861 in Arkansas's Ozark Mountains. By the end of that year the society numbered seventeen hundred. It had secret signs and passwords to identify members, each of whom took an oath to encourage desertion from the Confederate army and enlistment in the Union army. A piece of yellow cloth posted on or near a cabin marked the residents as society members. They identified each other at night with the call of a wolf's howl answered by a hooting sound like that of an owl. Examining a sample of nearly two hundred members, historian Ted Worley discovered that the vast majority were native southerners and relatively poor. None held any slaves.

The society's effectiveness as an organized resistance movement was at least partially diminished within months of its founding when Confederates arrested over one hundred of the society's leading members. Under threat of execution, some revealed its secrets and divulged the names of other members. Still, the strength of anti-Confederate sympathies among Ozark residents insured that the Peace and Constitutional Society's mission would continue in spite of its organizational breakdown.[107]

The same was true for the Peace Party, or Union League, in Texas. Centered around Cooke County in the northern part of the state, it had secret signs, handshakes, and passwords. And its members swore allegiance to the Union. There were also accusations that its members, said to number in the thousands, were stockpiling arms and ammunition. In October 1862 local officials began rounding up suspected Union men in and around Gainesville, the county seat. They quickly threw together a vigilante "citizens court" to give their proceedings at least the appearance of judicial decorum. But there was no question that executions would soon follow. The court was comprised mainly of men who followed or feared James G. Bourland, the local provost marshal.

Bourland was a rabid anti-Union man described by those who knew him as "a good fighter and a good hater." But at age sixty-one, he had no stomach for fighting on the battlefield. When conscription came, this planter and former state senator had himself appointed as local provost marshal. It was a job he relished. Bourland's aggressive conscription efforts accounted at least in part for the strong membership of the Peace Party. Now Bourland held the fate of Peace Party members in his hands through his "citizens court." Over the next few days, on weak or trumped-up evidence, the court ordered at least forty-four men executed in what came to be known as the "Great Hanging at Gainesville." Bourland was later called "the Hangman of Texas."[108]

Among his victims was John M. Crisp, a Cooke County blacksmith and deacon in the Church of Christ. Crisp admitted that he was an initiated member of the Peace Party and that he had initiated others. But he insisted that he had never committed any act of aggression against the Confederacy. There was no evidence that he had. Still, the vigilantes found him guilty and sentenced him to hang. Crisp barely had time to scribble down a will leaving his modest possessions to his wife and three children before he was hauled out to the hanging tree.[109]

Gainesville was not the end of Texas-style justice. In February 1863, pro-Confederates slaughtered 180 peace men in central Texas for no other crime, wrote one Texan, than "loving the flag of Washington." A Hays County refugee recalled that vigilantes would shoot "Union men to see which way they would fall," slice open the throats "of loyal men, that they might listen to the music of the death rattle," and lynch "crowds of faithful citizens just to observe the varieties of the death gasp." The man compared what he had witnessed to France's Reign of Terror after the French Revolution.[110]

Persecution of Texas dissenters continued throughout the war. Very often, it was a persecution based on class. Such was the split between slaveholders and nonslaveholders in parts of the state that the violence amounted to open class warfare. In *Brushmen and Vigilantes*, authors David Pickering and Judy Falls point out that in the Sulphur Forks region of northeast Texas, "many of the vigilantes were wealthy men or their middle-class followers while records for the victims show that most of them had little wealth."[111]

The most widespread of the South's antiwar organizations was the Peace Society, dedicated to ending the conflict with or without southern independence. Little is known of the Society's early days. It probably formed in northern Alabama or eastern Tennessee in early 1862. From there its influence spread throughout the Deep South. For Alabama alone, historian Walter Fleming estimated that by 1863 at least half the state's men were associated with or supporters of the Peace Society.[112]

Though its membership numbered in the thousands and it counted many more as sympathizers, the Peace Society was only loosely organized. One contemporary wrote from Opelika, Alabama, that the Peace Society had "no regular times or places of meeting, and has no organized 'lodges' or 'communities.' Men who have studied the obligations, signs, &c., and who can communicate them well are styled 'eminent,' and pass through the country giving the 'degree' to all whom they regard as fit subjects." Those inducted into the society promised always to aid other members and their families. They also promised never to "cut, carve, mark, scratch, show, &c., upon anything, movable or immovable, under the whole canopy of heaven, whereby any of the secrets of this order might become legible or intelligible." Finally, the inductee concluded with this statement: "I bind myself under no less penalty than that of having my head cut open, my brains taken from thence and strewn over the ground, my body cast to the beasts of the field or to the vultures of the air should I be so vile as to reveal any of the secrets of this order."[113]

Members recognized each other by a variety of complicated signs, which differed from one region to another. One of the most complex was a handshake and greeting popular in central Alabama. It was, according to one report, "given by taking hold of the hand as usual in shaking hands, only the thumb is turned with the side instead of the ball to the back of the hand." The following dialogue, which each member committed to memory, would then commence.

> What is that?
> A grip.
> A grip of what?
> A constitutional peace grip.
> Has it a name?
> It has.
> Will you give it to me?
> I did not so receive it, neither can I so impart it.
> How will you impart it?
> I will letter it to you.
> Letter it and begin.
> Begin you.
> No, you begin.
> Begin you.

Then, starting with any letter but the first, they spelled the word "peace" by calling out letters alternately to each other.[114] Other signs of recognition included a salute with the right hand closed and the thumb pointed backward over the shoulder, throwing a stick to the right using both hands, and tapping on the toe of the right foot three times with a stick or switch, then waving it to the right. In a crowd, a society member made himself known by three slaps on the right leg. One might also use the phrase, "I dreamed that the boys are all coming home." A distress signal was given by using the expression "Oh! Washington!" or "by extending the right hand horizontally and then bringing it down by three distinct motions." Repeating the word "Washington" four times could get a member of the Peace Society released from jail within twenty-four hours if his guard happened to be a brother member.[115]

The society's activities included spreading dissent among soldiers as well as civilians. Apparently the organization met with considerable success. James Longstreet, Lee's senior corps commander, said that "the large and increasing number of desertions, particularly amongst the Georgia troops, induces me to believe that some such outside influence must be operating upon our men." In October 1863, a Savannah man wrote that troops in southeast Georgia were demanding peace and would soon turn to mutiny or desertion if they did not get it. A few months later, an insurrection plot was discovered among troops at the Rose Dew Island batteries south of Savannah. Encouraged by local citizens connected with the Peace Society, the soldiers took an oath never to fight the Yankees, to desert at the earliest opportunity, and encourage others to do the same. Members of the Peace Society claimed credit for mass desertions that contributed to Confederate defeats at Vicksburg and Missionary Ridge.[116]

Another peace organiztion, the Order of the Heroes of America, actively encouraged desertions as well by writing soldiers in the field, urging them to come home, and promising protection if they would. The Heroes of America, also called the Heroes of 1776 or the Red Strings after the identification they wore, formed in the north-central section of North Carolina and spread through the western part of the state and into the hill country of South Carolina, eastern Tennessee, and southwestern Virginia. Like its counterparts elsewhere, the Heroes had secret passwords, handshakes, obligations, and oaths. Its members swore to protect deserters and prisoners of war, to aid Federal spy operations, and to do whatever they could to undermine the Confederacy.[117]

The Heroes of America began holding peace rallies in earnest shortly after the July 1863 Rebel defeats at Gettysburg and Vicksburg. In Wake County, North Carolina, they held two that summer condemning Jefferson Davis and demanding an end to the war. A Heroes meeting in Surry County called for maintaining "the Constitution as it is and the Union as it was." By fall the Heroes of America were pressing for peace throughout the southern Appalachians and adjacent regions. Their message was especially well received in southwestern Virginia. No more than a quarter of the region's voters had favored secession in the first place. A Confederate officer sent there to hunt deserters lamented that southwest Virginians, most of them slaveless farmers, had "little knowledge and less sympathy with the troubles of the slaveholders, and as a class were opposed to secession." That was certainly the case in Wise County, where local unionists were in regular contact with Federal troops at nearby Pikeville, Kentucky. They kept their Union allies informed of Rebel movements through the mountains and provided them with lists of area pro-Confederates. Beside each name was a note on how they were to be treated, based on their secessionist activities, when the Federals eventually took control of the region. Some were to take an oath to the United States and be released. Some were slated for imprisonment. Others were marked for execution.[118]

In addition to acting as informants for Union forces, the Heroes of America organized an underground railroad to shuttle escaping unionists through the mountains to Federal lines. Some had run afoul of Confederate authorities. Others simply wanted to get out of the South and away from the war. All across the mountain South, antiwar activists assisted southern dissenters heading for Union territory. They guided refugees from Alabama, Georgia, and the Carolinas safely through the hills to the Federals in Tennessee. One such guide, Daniel Ellis, was said to have piloted ten thousand people out of the Confederacy. In western Virginia's Shenandoah Valley, antiwar Mennonites set up their own underground railroad. Using their church and the homes of church members as safe houses, they ferried hundreds of refugees and deserters out of the Confederacy. In north Georgia's Union County, Austin Mason organized a chain of safe houses to shelter prisoners and deserters as they fled north through the Georgia mountains.[119]

"Union Men to the Core"

Men like Mason were hardly unusual. Anti-Confederate activists throughout the South established an extensive network of safe houses, guides, and secret signals to aid refugees, deserters, draft dodgers, and escaped Federal prisoners. In southeast Alabama and southwest Georgia, residents of the Wiregrass region helped deserters and draft dodgers make their way south to the Federals in Florida. They even helped Union prisoners of war make their escapes. One day in late 1864, J.B. Norman of southwest Georgia's Colquitt County came across two Yankee escapees from Andersonville on his property. He fed the men and put them up for the night. The next morning he served them steak, then pointed them toward Florida.[120]

Those requiring the services of the South's unionists and antiwar activists were most grateful. A Wisconsin colonel trying to reach Sherman's army in Chattanooga later wrote that they were "generous, hospitable, brave, and Union men to the core; men who would suffer privations, and death itself, rather than array themselves in strife against the Stars and Stripes, the emblem of the country they loved. . . . under their homespun jackets beat hearts pure as gold, and stout as oaks."[121]

Union men were not alone in their efforts to help escaping prisoners. Some of the most daring allies captured Yankees had were the South's Union women. In Atlanta, Emily Farnsworth, Cyrena Stone, and other women of the city's Union Circle slipped prisoners cash and other contraband to ease their escape. In the southern Appalachians, women gave escaping Yankees room and board, pointed them toward safe routes through the mountains, and served as guides to Union lines. Escaping Union Captain Madison Drake encountered one such woman in North Carolina who found him and several companions hidden in a ravine. She "boldly advanced" toward the group and demanded to know who they were. She warned them, "you must not use deceit or you will be shot down where you stand. A dozen true rifles are now leveled at you, and if I raise my hand you will fall dead at my feet." The woman was relieved to learn that they were Yankee soldiers trying to make it to the Union lines in Tennessee, and that they were no threat to her husband, a deserter from the Confederate army. She took the men to her cabin, fed them, and gave them directions to Federal forces. Drake later recalled they they had "never met such a woman . . . certainly the bravest of her sex."[122]

Like other Union escapees, Drake and his comrades found themselves beholden to former enemies as well. Gangs of deserters and layouts that were common in the mountains occasionally shared their hideouts, their knowledge of the landscape, and what rations they had with Yankees on the run. Drake's admiration and appreciation of such men came through clearly in his recollections: "Here we were, four Yankee officers, in the heart of the enemy's country, in a mountain fastness, surrounded by some of the men whom we had encountered in battle's stern array at Bull Run, Roanoke, Newbern, Fredericksburg, and on other ensanguined fields, who now were keeping watch and ward over our lives, which they regarded as precious in their sight—willing to shed their blood in our defense."[123]

Much to his surprise, Drake also discovered friends among Rebel soldiers still on duty. At one point during their journey, Drake's startled group came across a Confederate officer who accused them of being "d——n Yankees." But before they could bolt, he assured the fugitives that they had nothing to fear from him. The officer told of having three sons killed in battle and a fourth dying of fever in a Delaware prison. He was sick of war and wanted nothing more to do with it. The officer wished Drake and his companions well, then continued on his way.[124]

Even in the Confederacy's capital city of Richmond, Virginia, there was a thriving network of unionists active in helping Yankee captives get out of prison and slip through the lines. They also functioned as a spy ring, giving escapees valuable military and political intelligence to take with them. To the west in the Virginia mountains there were spies, or scouts as they were called, giving aid and comfort to the Federals. In the spring of 1862, Confederates at Lebanon in Russell County were attacked by Federal troops guided through the mountains by local unionists. Around the same time in northeastern Mississippi, authorities caught three women carrying important documents to the Union army at Shiloh. Levi Naron of Mississippi's Chickasaw County joined the Union Secret Service that year and, wrote one appreciative Federal officer, "rendered valuable services in that capacity." Union General Grenville Dodge made Naron, or "Chickasaw" as he was covertly known, his chief of scouts, a position he held for over a year. Dodge wrote of Naron: "Daring, bold, and shrewd, he rendered me most valuable services by keeping me informed of the movements of the enemy in Tennessee, Alabama, Mississippi and Georgia, and by operating against the enemies' outposts."[125]

In Georgia, James George Brown of Murray County led a network of native pro-Union spies who operated throughout the northern part of the state. Further south in late 1864, James C. McBurney of Macon, who had previously guided a Federal raid through Alabama and Georgia, now provided William T. Sherman with information on resources and railroads during his March to the Sea. Georgians spying for the Union was hardly the worst of it. Earlier that year, Governor Joe Brown had issued a call to all militia members and government employees ordering them to rally in Atlanta and help fight off the Yankees. Soon after, word came from Dawson County that the local surveyor, Elias Darnel, "instead of obeying your proclamation went about organizing a federal home guard to assist the enemy."[126]

In Georgia's Pickens County, 125 men formed a Union home guard to protect themselves from Confederate militia, to raid pro-Confederate plantations, and to assist the advancing Federals. One Yankee officer was sure that several hundred more men in neighboring counties could be called to arms for the Union. In August 1864, the Federals did just that. Hoping to form not simply a home guard but a regular fighting force, they recruited about 300 northeast Georgia men. Some were sent directly to the 5th Tennessee Mounted Infantry. Others formed an independent company operating in Fannin County attached to the 5th Tennessee. The rest were enrolled as the 1st Georgia State Troops Volunteer Battalion. Though well armed, the 1st Georgia was ill trained and never much use to the Federals in regular combat. But the men of the 1st Georgia fought a running guerrilla war that kept Confederate loyalists busy who might otherwise have been put into battle against the Yankees.[127]

"Not a Braver Man Than He"

There were other Georgians better trained and willing to put their training to use for the Union. Thomas A. Watson of Fannin County, William Fife of Harris County, Cornelius Dawson of Clinch County, and Andrew T. Harris of Murray County—all Confederate deserters—were among thousands of white Georgians who joined Federal units. In total, about three hundred thousand southern whites joined the Union armies, a number equaling almost all of the Federals killed during the war. Among them were forty-four-year-old farmer Wesley Cornutt and his teenage son David of Ashe County, North Carolina, who served with the Union's 13th Tennessee Cavalry. Another was

One North Carolinian, disgusted with government ineptitude, advised his brother in the field to "go to the other side whear you can get plenty and not stay in this one horse barefooted naked and famine striken Southern Confederacy." Thomas A. Watson of Fannin County, Georgia, was among thousands who did just that. A poor farm laborer before the war, Watson deserted from the 65th Georgia Infantry Regiment in June 1863 and joined the Union army. He is pictured here in his federal uniform. (Georgia Department of Archives and History)

Aaron Phillips, a farmhand who deserted from the 42nd Virginia. Others included survivors of the Nueces Massacre in Texas.[128]

David R. Snelling of Baldwin County, Georgia, had deeply personal reasons for his Union stand. David's father William, a man of modest means, died of fever when David was five. His mother Elizabeth Lester Snelling, whose wealthy family had never approved of her marrying a poor man, was given only a small plot of land adjoining large plantations her brothers owned. When Elizabeth died a few years later, young David was taken in by his uncle, David Lester. While Lester sent his own sons off to school, he put David to work in the fields along with the slaves. Treated much as a slave himself, David came to detest slavery and to hold an abiding compassion for the enslaved. Threatened with conscription in the spring of 1862, David joined the Confederate army. But he deserted that summer and joined the Federals. Two years later, as a lieutenant in Sherman's cavalry escort during the March to the Sea, David went out of his way to lead a raid against his uncle's plantation a few miles from the state capital of Milledgeville. His troops seized as many provisions as they could carry and destroyed the cotton gin.[129]

Though most Confederate soldiers were nonslaveholders and poorer than their slaveholding neighbors, white southerners who served the Union were most often poorer still. In the North Fork district of western North Carolina's Ashe County, a comparison of thirty-four Union and forty-two Confederate volunteers shows that holdings in real and personal property among Confederates was more than twice that of their Union counterparts. In eastern North Carolina, the difference was even more dramatic. In Washington County, which supplied nearly an equal number of troops to the Union and the Confederacy, Union soldiers were fourteen times poorer than those in the Confederate army. Such figures reflect a class-based unionism that made itself felt all across the South. It was reflected too among members of the Union's 1st Alabama Cavalry, recruited from poor farmers in the northern part of the state who relished the opportunity to sack plantations during Sherman's March to the Sea.[130]

"The poor hate the rich," wrote James Henry Hammond to a friend, "& make war on them every where." Many were happy to do so under the Stars and Stripes. Operating out of Mexico, the 1st Regiment of Union Troops plundered Texas ranches all along the Rio Grande. Cotton was the special target of Union raiders in Nueces County. Many were Hispanics who, like their Anglo comrades, saw the war as a chance to right old political and economic wrongs done them by wealthy Texans, most of whom supported the Confederacy. Back east, the 1st North Carolina Union Volunteers raided plantations along the state's tidewater region and fought back local Confederate troops sent to stop them. In one engagement, wrote a Federal officer, the "loyal North Carolinians were fast and fierce in the pursuit of their rebel neighbors. The chase was given up only when the enemy was completely put to flight." Just as fierce were the Mississippi Mounted Rifles, all natives of the state, who aided Federal raids into northern Mississippi and helped beat back Confederate General Nathan Bedford Forrest's April 1864 attack on Memphis.[131]

In Florida, the Union's East Gulf Blockading Squadron recruited native anti-Confederates for service in the 2nd Florida Cavalry based at Cedar Key. One of the unit's first members was Milledge Brannen. Born in Columbia County and living in the Tampa Bay area when the war broke out, Brannen was a former Confederate soldier who had become disillusioned with the Confederate cause. Brannen deserted and went home, became active among anti-Confederate refugees, then joined the Union's 2nd Florida Cavalry. From their coastal base, the men raided inland against plantations, railroads, and Confederate supplies. In May 1864, the 2nd Florida was instrumental to the Federal occupation of Tampa.[132]

Like Brannen, Joseph Sanders of Dale County, Alabama, was a former Confederate who had deserted. Early in the war, Sanders enlisted with Company C of the 31st Georgia, a company composed largely of men from the southeast Alabama counties of Barbour, Henry, Dale, and Coffee. Sanders was so admired by his comrades that they elected him as one of their company sergeants. He fought with the 31st Georgia, part of Stonewall Jackson's corps, through the early Virginia campaigns. By all accounts "there was not a braver man than he in the unit." Still, Sanders at length decided that the Confederate cause was not his. He fled south to Florida's Gulf Coast and sought refuge with Union forces. Soon after, the Federals granted him a lieutenant's commission in their 1st Florida Cavalry.

One of Sanders's first missions found him leading the advance guard of a Federal raid into southern Alabama. With Lieutenant Colonel Andrew B. Spurling in command, 450 men of the 2nd Maine and 1st Florida cavalries headed north following the rail line that led from Pensacola to Montgomery. Only eleven miles out of camp, they began picking up sentries from a Confederate cavalry unit. By the time their raid was over, the Federals had captured thirty-eight prisoners, forty-seven horses, three mules, and seventy-five rifles. In his report on the expedition, Spurling spoke highly of Sanders's performance: "It would hardly be doing justice did I not make special mention of Lieut. Joseph G. Sanders, Company F, First Florida Cavalry. He is a worthy officer, and deserves high praise for his meritorious conduct. He was at all times in command of the advance guard, and much of the success is due to the prompt and faithful manner in which all orders were executed."

Not long after this raid, Sanders was placed on detached duty and took charge of a force composed mainly of local Union men from the Wiregrass. For the rest of the war Sanders and his men conducted a series of raids throughout southeast Alabama. They seized horses and military supplies, plundered well-stocked plantations, and skirmished with Confederate forces. At one point, they raided the town of Elba in Coffee County and burned down the courthouse.[133]

In Arkansas and Missouri, the Ozark uplands were prime recruiting ground for Union companies of "mountain Feds." Among the most active was Williams's Raiders, formed around the Williams clan of Arkansas's Conway and Van Buren counties and led by fifty-one-year-old Thomas Jefferson (Jeff) Williams. Williams and his neighbors were small farmers who at first wanted nothing to do with the war. But when Confederate draft officers came calling, Williams—along with his four sons, three sons-in-law, two brothers, a brother-in-law, four nephews, and twenty-five other men—struck out for Federal lines in Missouri. They formed the heart of Company B, 1st Arkansas Infantry Battalion, electing Jeff Williams their captain and his son Nathan a second lieutenant.

In 1863 after the Federals entered northern Arkansas, they authorized Williams to form an independent company of local unionists to fight back Confederate home guards in the region. For the next two years Williams's Raiders fought with considerable success against Confederates trying to regain control in their corner of the Ozarks. But on February 12, 1865, Rebel guerrillas surrounded the Williams cabin, killed Jeff Williams with a volley of buckshot, and beat the Williams women. Williams's pregnant daughter-in-law, Sarah Jane, lost her baby after the Rebels hit her in the belly with their gun stocks. That night Sarah Jane's husband Leroy, enraged at the killing of his father and unborn child, hunted down the Rebels and shot eight of them to death. The next day, joined by other Williams men and about seventy soldiers of the 3rd Arkansas Cavalry (U.S.), Leroy went after the rest. They tracked the Rebel gang to Clinton, twenty miles to the north, where they killed at least one of its members. Five more were taken prisoner in Quitman. Before the killing stopped, Leroy alone shot as many as sixteen men.[134]

"Deserters, Disaffected, and Turbulent Characters"

Unlike Jeff Williams, Joseph Sanders, and their comrades, the vast majority of active dissidents and deserters never attached themselves to the Union army. Instead, they formed hundreds of armed guerilla bands, often called "layout" or "tory" gangs, to fight off Confederate authority. Some were committed unionists. Others simply struggled to keep conscript and impressment companies at bay. Most were non-slaveholders who wanted no part of a rich man's war. But they were prepared to fight back when the Confederacy forced war upon them.

One such group of men in southern Mississippi's Jones County was led by Newton Knight, a slaveless farmer who deserted the Confederate army soon after conscription began. Upset that wealthy men could avoid the draft, Knight went home and took up with others of his community who had done the same. "We stayed out in the woods minding our own business," Knight said, "until the Confederate Army began sending raiders after us with bloodhounds. . . . Then we saw we had to fight." And fight they did. For the rest of the war Knight and his men, numbering around five hundred, drove off Confederate agents, ambushed army patrols, looted government depots, and distributed the food stored there to the poor. So successfully did they subvert Confederate control of the county that some called it "The Free State of Jones."[135]

It was the same all across the South. Most famous are the partisan struggles in Kentucky and Missouri, but the Deep South was almost as violently divided against itself. By the summer of 1863 there were ten thousand deserters and conscripts in the Alabama hill country formed into armed bands. Some had killed officers sent to arrest them. In Louisiana, James Madison Wells denounced the Confederacy as a rich man's government and organized a guerrilla campaign against it. From his Bear Wallow stronghold in Rapides Parish, Wells led deserters and other resisters in raids against Confederate supply lines and depots. Further south in the state's Acadian parishes, bands of anti-Confederates did the same. One group commanded by a Cajun named Carrier numbered more than three hundred.[136]

A Shiloh veteran went home to Decatur, Mississippi, and refused to return to the army unless it paid him for the mule he had lost in the battle. No funds were forthcoming. So he formed a band of area deserters and draft dodgers that became, as one resident complained, "so strong that the community in which they live have to submit to any demand they make." They organized a warning system of horns and trumpets, and dodged or fought off anyone sent to capture them. "Unless something is done soon," wrote a frightened pro-Confederate, "we will be in as bad or worse condition than Jones County."[137]

In Texas's Rio Grande county of Zapata, local Hispanics denounced the Confederacy, formed a band of pro-Union partisans, and plundered the property of loyal Confederates. In Bandera County, just west of San Antonio, residents became so upset with the inequitable tax system that they formed a pro-Union militia, declined to pay their taxes, and swore to kill anyone who tried to make them do so. At the state's northern extreme near Bonham, several hundred anti-Confederates established three large camps close enough so that the entire force could assemble within two hours. They patrolled the region so effectively that no one could approach without their knowing of it. In the central Texas county of Bell, deserters led by Lige Bivens fortified themselves in a cave known as Camp Safety. From there they mounted raids against the area's pro-Confederates. According to an 1863 report, two thousand other Texas deserters "fortified themselves near the Red River, and defied the Confederacy. At last account they had been established . . . eight months, and were constantly receiving accession of discontented rebels and desperadoes."[138]

An Arkansas band of anti-Confederates operated out of Greasy Cove, a mountain pass at the head of the Little Missouri River. Made up of "deserters, disaffected, and turbulent characters," as one newspaper called them, they swept through the countryside harassing Confederate loyalists and challenging Confederate authority. So did

Troopers sent to round up deserters and "layouts" often ran into stiff resistance, especially in the South. Hundreds of layout gangs went on the offensive, attacking government supply wagons, raiding local plantations, and harassing draft officials. They eliminated Confederate authority in large parts of the South. So violent did the South's inner civil war become by 1863 that one southern newspaper editor wrote, "We are fighting each other harder than we ever fought the enemy." (Devens, *Pictorial Book of Anecdotes and Incidents of the War of the Rebellion*)

anti-Confederates in east Tennessee, a region where open rebellion against the Confederacy was common from the start. As early as the fall of 1861, bands of native unionists disrupted Confederate operations by spying for the Federals, cutting telegraph lines, and burning railroad bridges. The next spring unionists in Scott and Morgan counties staged a coup. They forcibly took control of all county offices, disbanded the Confederate home guard, and put in its place a force made up of local Union men.[139]

After pro-Confederates from neighboring North Carolina mounted a series of raids against unionists in and around the Smoky Mountain town of Cades Cove, Tennessee, the area's Union men formed their own militia. Led by Russell Gregory, pastor of a local Primitive Baptist church, they established a network of sentries along the roads to warn of approaching danger. In the spring of 1864, raiders invaded Cades Cove once again to steal livestock and provisions. They plundered several farms, taking all they could carry, but never made it back to North Carolina with their loot. Near the state line, Gregory's militiamen felled trees across the roads and ambushed the Rebel partisans, forcing them to scatter and leave their loot behind.[140]

Anti-Confederates, deserters, and resisters alike in the South Carolina hill country also formed defensive militias and set up warning networks. Centered in Greenville, Pickens, and Spartanburg counties, they had designated assembly areas and a "well-arranged system of signals" to warn of trouble on the way. "Every woman and child," according to one report, was "a watch and a guard for them." The same was true in the southwestern Virginia counties of Montgomery, Floyd, and Giles, which were "infested by armed bands of deserters." Local unionists too, aroused by Confederate home guard depredations, formed armed militias. One such unit, headed by "Captain" Charles Huff of Floyd County, regularly backed up local deserters and ambushed home guard patrols. The job was made easier by Joseph Phares, a double agent who kept Huff informed of the guard's plans while feeding its officers disinformation.[141]

Though their motives were not always the same, the one thing nearly all armed resisters had in common was that they were nonslaveholders of modest means. The rise of such class warfare was the very thing that slaveholders had tried to avoid for so long and what had, in large part, led them to push for secession in the first place. "Ironically," as historian Charles Bolton points out, "by engineering disunion, slaveowners fostered the growth of the kind of organizations they had long feared: class-based groups that pitted nonslaveholders against the interests of slaveowners."[142]

Nowhere was that more evident than in the lowcountry of North Carolina. Planters in the region were terrified to learn that, as one wrote, unionists among the lower classes had "gone so far as to declare [that they] will take the property from the rich men & divide it among the poor men."[143] It was no idle threat. From near the war's beginning, bands of unionists had been raiding coastal plantations. Formed initially to protect themselves from conscription and Confederate raiders, their objectives eventually expanded to include driving planters from their land and dividing it among themselves.

In the spring and summer of 1862, a pro-Union newspaper in New Bern reported the formation of unionist militias in Washington, Tyrrell, Martin, Bertie, Hertford, Gates, Chowan, Perquimans, Pasquotank, and Camden counties "not only for self-protection against rebel guerillas, but for the purpose of expatriating all the rebel families from their limits." Further west in the central piedmont region of North Carolina, class antagonism was also a strong motive for resistance. Many members of the Heroes of America were poor men who, as one contemporary recalled, were "induced to join the organization by the promise of a division here after among them of the property of the loyal Southern citizens."[144]

Plantations were also the targets of deserter and layout gangs in Georgia's cotton belt. "These scoundrels," as a Milledgeville paper called them, "seek the fairest, fattest and most quiet portion of our territory for the theatre of their depredations. They pounce suddenly upon the prosperous plantations, and sweep them of their best laboring stock, and such stores of meat, grain and forage as they can carry off."[145] In south Georgia's Coffee County, a band of layouts headed by "Old Man" Bill Wall plundered livestock and produce on lands belonging to Ben Pearson. When Pearson threatened retaliation, he found a grave dug outside his front door. He finally offered Wall a reward and amnesty if the "Old Man" would help local authorities lay a trap for his men. Something of a poor man's poet, Wall could not resist poking fun at Pearson's assumption that he might do such a thing.

> If it is my choice to stay at home,
> and the woods in beauty roam;

Pluck the flowers in early spring,
and hear the little songsters sing!
Why, then, should I, for the sake of gain,
leave my conscience with a stain.
A traitor! who could hear the name
with no respect for age or fame;

Who, for the sake of a little gold,
would have his friends in bondage sold?
I would rather take the lash
than betray them for Confederate trash.

You say they kill your sheep and cows,
You say they take your hoss and your plows,
You say they took your potatoes away,
You say they dug your grave one day.
All this may be true;
It makes me sorry for you.

Yet, sir, if I, these men betray
and they were all taken away,
And they did not in the battlefield fall,
They would then come back and kill
"Old Man Bill Wall."[146]

"Fighting Each Other Harder Than We Ever Fought the Enemy"

The Confederacy's keystone state of Georgia was one of the most divided in the South. Anti-Confederate gangs like Bill Wall's operated in every part of the state. They raided plantations, attacked army supply depots, and drove off impressment and conscript officers. Some areas were so hostile to the Confederacy that army patrols dared not enter them. The pine barrens tract of southeast Georgia was a favorite hideout for those trying to avoid Confederate entanglements. Soldier Camp Island in the region's Okefenokee Swamp was home to as many as a thousand deserters. In southwest Georgia, a Fort Gaines man begged Governor Brown to send cavalry for protection against deserters and layout gangs. So did pro-Confederates in northwest Georgia's

Dade and Walker counties. All across the state, from the mountains to the Piedmont to the Wiregrass, there raged an inner civil war so violent that the editor of Milledgeville's *Confederate Union* wrote, "We are fighting each other harder than we ever fought the enemy."[147]

From the upland county of Gilmer came news in July 1862 of "tories and traitors who have taken up their abode in the mountains." That same month, a letter arrived on the governor's desk from Fannin County, just north of Gilmer, warning that "a very large majority of the people now here perhaps two thirds are disloyal." Anti-Confederates became so aggressive in Fannin that one man called it a "general uprising among our Torys of this County." September 1862 found Lumpkin County overrun by tories and deserters, robbing pro-Confederates of guns, money, clothes, and provisions. One Confederate sympathizer wrote that "the Union men—Tories—are very abusive indeed and says they will do as they please." The *Dahlonega Signal* estimated that one of Lumpkin County's tory bands, led by "the notorious Jeff Anderson," numbered between one and two hundred.[148]

One of the earliest formed and most active bands of Union men in north Georgia was led by Horatio Hennion. A northerner by birth, Hennion moved to White County's Mossy Creek community in his early twenties and married a local girl. The other men in his band of at least two dozen were natives of Georgia and the Carolinas. All were nonslaveholders. Some were tenants or day laborers who owned no land. Those who did own land held no more than a few hundred dollars' worth of real estate and personal property.

Hennion was working as a wagon maker in Gainesville when secession came. From the start, he made no secret of his support for the Union. Even after war broke out, Hennion remained openly anti-Confederate even as other local unionists were falling silent. Threats to his life forced him and his family back to Mossy Creek. There he hoped to live in peace. Then, in the summer of 1861, pro-Confederates tired to kill him. He fled to North Carolina but soon returned and organized a band of anti-Confederates that included men from White County and neighboring Hall County. They fought running battles with Confederate conscript companies, rescuing one of their members from the White County jail after a draft officer arrested him. Hennion's band became even more effective when he signed "an agreement of mutual protection" with deserters hiding out in the region.[149]

Soon after he got word of events in the mountains, Governor Brown issued a proclamation aimed at the "very considerable number of deserters and stragglers" and those who aided them. Brown knew "that numbers of these deserters, encouraged by disloyal citizens in the mountains of Northeastern Georgia, have associated themselves together with arms in their hands and are now in rebellion against the authority of this State and the Confederate States." He issued a proclamation "commanding all persons . . . to return to their respective commands immediately." Brown also warned "all disloyal citizens to cease to harbor deserters or encourage desertion . . . as the law against treason will be strictly enforced against all who subject themselves to its penalties."

Brown's warning had little effect, and in late January 1863 he took action. He sent a mounted force under Colonel George Washington Lee, commandant of Atlanta, and Captain E. M. Galt to Dahlonega with orders to "secure the arrest of deserters and restore the public tranquility." By early February, around six hundred deserters had been rounded up and marched back to the army. Fifty-three civilian unionists were arrested and sent to Atlanta, among them the tory leader Jeff Anderson. But only a month later, Confederate loyalists in Lumpkin County were begging Governor Brown for more troops. In June, the *Athens Southern Watchman* reported that "some of those who were forced into the army by the cavalry last winter have returned with Government arms and ammunition in their hands and are creating serious apprehensions of future troubles." Already anti-Confederates led by a Hall County man calling himself Major Finger had attacked a small iron works in White County. They burned the coal, stole the tools, and broke the forge hammer. In Fannin County, tories attacked a group of Confederates sent to arrest deserters, killing one man and wounding several others.

Fannin County was hit again in August 1863 when tories led by Soloman Bryan disarmed county residents loyal to the Confederacy. According to one pro-Confederate, they "robbed our people of every single gun and all the ammunition." Similar confrontations took place all over the Georgia upcountry. A Union County man informed the governor that the "mountains are filling with deserters and disloyal men," and begged him to send arms and ammunition. Brown sought help from the Richmond government, telling Jefferson Davis that "tories and deserters in North Eastern Georgia are now disarming the loyal people and committing many outrages." He got no response. Brown finally sent a state force that arrested "quite a number of deserters, stragglers, marauders," but the effort did little to combat the rise of anti-Confederate resistance. One Gilmer County Confederate wrote that "the Tories with their squirrel rifles, pick off our men from behind rocks and trees and all manner of hiding places. In this way they have killed six or eight of our soldiers." J.J. Findley of Dahlonega reported that "the District is overrun with Deserters, Tories, and Rogues . . . and that the condition of things is worse in that region than ever."[150]

Resistance was just as fierce in the lower part of the state. In September 1862, forty men of southwest Georgia's Marion County "secured and provisioned a house and arranged it in the manner of a military castle." Armed and provisioned for the long haul, they swore not only to prevent their own capture but to protect anyone who sought sanctuary in their fortress. Though Confederate and state military officials tried repeatedly to force them out, they had little success against these men, determined as they were to "resist to the last extremity." Captain Caleb Camfield, stationed at Bainbridge with a detachment of cavalrymen, had no better luck . He finally retreated after fierce battles with layout gangs in south Georgia and north Florida.[151]

Anti-Confederates in the region were often backed by Federal forces operating along the Florida coast. In February 1863 John Harvey, representing a group of five hundred Wiregrass deserters and draft evaders, met with Lieutenant George Welch of the USS *Amanda* to discuss placing his friends under Federal protection. Armed only with shotguns, they had been skirmishing with conscript companies for some time and their ammunition was running low. They preferred to be taken into protective custody as refugees, and, reported Welch, said "that they would follow me or any other leader to any peril they are ordered to rather than leave their families." Welch was sympathetic but declined, saying he did not have enough manpower to guarantee safe passage for the men and their families from that deep in enemy territory. However, as unionist strength in the region increased, the Federals did begin running ammunition and other supplies to the area's anti-Confederate partisans.[152]

William Strickland's band of Wiregrass anti-Confederates was among the most active. Born in south Georgia's Lowndes County around 1835, Strickland migrated to Florida's Big Bend county of

Taylor where he began raising cattle. A year after the war broke out, he enlisted with the Confederacy's 2nd Florida Cavalry. In December of 1862, Strickland got word that his wife was seriously ill. Though his unit was stationed in Jefferson County, just across the Aucilla River from his home in Taylor, Strickland's superiors refused to grant him a furlough. He went home anyway and stayed for four months. When he returned in the spring, he was court-martialed as a deserter.

Strickland deserted again and joined with other deserters and draft evaders living on Snyder's Island in the relative safety of Taylor County's Gulf Coast marshlands. There they raised crops, tended cattle, and visited family from time to time. Unable to mount an assault through the marshes, Confederate forces rounded up the men's families and imprisoned them at Camp Smith near Tallahassee. Enraged at the arrests, Strickland and his comrades went on the offensive. They drew up an organizational constitution, established an alliance with the Federal Gulf Coast naval squadron, and went to war against the Confederacy as the Independent Union Rangers of Taylor County.[153]

"Union Men, Deserters, and Negroes"

Among the most eager and effective allies men like Strickland had were local slaves. They hid deserters and draft evaders traveling through the region, funneled plantation supplies to their bands, and often joined with them in their war against the planters and the Confederacy. A worried Confederate officer wrote in August 1864 that "many deserters . . . are collected in the swamps and fastnesses of Taylor, LaFayette, Levy and other counties, and have organized, with runaway negroes, bands for the purpose of committing depredations upon the plantations and crops of loyal citizens and running off their slaves. These depredatory bands have even threatened the cities of Tallahassee, Madison, and Marianna." That same month came word that a band of "500 Union men, deserters, and negroes were . . . raiding towards Gainesville."[154]

Such alliances had been forming for some time. As early as April 1862, a Confederate general urged Florida's governor to declare martial law in Nassau, Duval, Clay, Putnam, St. John's, and Volusia counties "as a measure of absolute necessity, as they contain a nest of traitors and lawless negroes." So did many other parts of the South. In

North Carolina, a Randolph County woman wrote that "our negroes are nearly all in league with the deserters." From Wilmington came warnings of interracial bands raiding between Fayetteville and Lumberton. In north Georgia, former slaves who had liberated themselves joined with Jeff Anderson's band of raiders operating in the mountains around Dahlonega.[155]

So numerous were interracial bands of resisters in the Wiregrass region of southeast Alabama that the governor called it "the common retreat of deserters from our army, tories, and runaway negroes." Even slaves who did not run away could be just as dangerous to slaveholders as those who did. Those belonging to Columbus Holley of Dale County, in the heart of Alabama's Wiregrass country, made that clear. Holley was known to pass any knowledge he had of area deserters on to authorities. John Ward, leader of a local deserter gang, hatched a plan to kill him for it. Holley's slaves were eager to help. On the designated evening, two of them met Ward at a rendezvous point not far from the plantation, lifted him from his horse, and carried him on their shoulders to Holley's bedroom window. With one shot Ward killed Holley as he slept. The slaves then carried Ward back to his horse, and he made a clean getaway. Because Ward's feet never touched the ground there was no scent for the bloodhounds to follow. The only tracks near the house were those of the slaves, but no one thought of that as unusual. Their footprints were all over the plantation. Besides, the slaves owned no guns. And they kept the secret to themselves. The mystery of Holley's murder remained unsolved until years after the war when Ward finally confessed on his death bed.[156]

Slaveholder fears of lower-class cooperation across racial lines had been on the rise throughout the late antebellum era. Their fears were well founded and in large part drove them to establish a Confederate slaveholder's republic in which they hoped resistance to slavery and slaveholder rule might be more easily controlled. Far from making control easier, though, secession gave rise to new opportunities for resistance, especially among the slaves.

6

"My God! Are We Free?"

You cannot make soldiers of slaves. . . . If slaves will make good
soldiers, our whole theory of slavery is wrong.[1]

—HOWELL COBB, CONFEDERATE GENERAL

Jess put de guns into our hans, and you'll soon see dat we not
only knows *how* to shoot, but *who* to shoot. *My* master wouldn't
be wuff much ef I was a soldier.[2]

—TOM, ENSLAVED VIRGINIAN

"Yes, We All Shall Be Free"

"I can just barely remember my mother." That was what Tom Robinson, born into slavery on a North Carolina plantation, told an interviewer for the 1930s Federal Writers Project. He was only ten years
old when sold away from his mother shortly before the war started.
"But I do remember how she used to take us children and kneel down
in front of the fireplace and pray. She'd pray that the time would come
when everybody could worship the Lord under their own vine and fig
tree—all of them free. It's come to me lots of time since. There she

was a'praying, and on other plantations women was a'praying. All over the country the same prayer was being prayed."[3]

Secession and war served only to make such prayers more expectant and intense—and to make slaves more rebellious. Despite efforts to conceal the war's implications from them, slaves had many ways of learning about what its outcome could mean for them. Years after the war, Hattie Nettles of Opelika, Alabama, remembered climbing a fence as a young girl to watch Confederate soldiers pass by. She did not know where they were going at first, but it was not long before she found out. Mary Gladdy, a Georgia freedwoman, recalled "the whisperings among the slaves—their talking of the possibility of freedom." Anne Maddox heard a great deal of talk about Abraham Lincoln from older slaves on her Alabama plantation. So did Louis Meadows, who was well aware that Jefferson Davis intended to keep him and his friends enslaved. "That was why," Meadows said, "everybody hoped Master Lincoln would conquer."

Throughout the war, slaves met in secret to hold prayer meetings for freedom. According to Mary Gladdy, those on her plantation gathered in their cabins two or three nights a week for such meetings. They placed large pots against the doors to keep their voices muffled. "Then," she said, "the slaves would sing, pray, and relate experiences all night long. Their great, soul-hungering desire was freedom." Those few slaves who could read kept up with events through pilfered newspapers and spread the word to their neighbors. As news of Confederate reversals became more frequent, excitement among the slaves grew. Young Ella Hawkins of Georgia heard the older slaves whispering among themselves, "Us is gonna be free! Jes as sho's anything. God has heard our prayers; us is gonna be free!" When a white minister preached that slavery was ordained by God and prayed aloud for Him to drive the Yankees back, one Georgia slave prayed silently to herself, "Oh, Lord, please send the Yankees on."[4]

In her reminiscences of the war years, Susie King Taylor wrote vividly of the excitement among her Savannah neighbors: "Oh, how those people prayed for freedom! I remember, one night, my grandmother went out into the suburbs of the city to a church meeting, and they were fervently singing this old hymn,—"

Yes, we all shall be free,
Yes, we all shall be free,

Yes, we all shall be free,
When the Lord shall appear.

Suddenly local lawmen burst in and arrested the entire congregation for "planning freedom." They further accused the slaves of singing "the Lord" instead of "Yankee," as King recalled, "to blind any one who might be listening."[5]

"Doing as They Please"

Enslaved blacks were not simply waiting for either God or the Yankees to give them freedom. They were taking it for themselves. Though Lincoln's Emancipation Proclamation is often cited as having "freed the slaves," it only grudgingly recognized what blacks had themselves already forced on Lincoln's government. The document, as Ira Berlin points out, "heralded not the dawn of universal liberty but the compromised and piecemeal arrival of an undefined freedom. Indeed, the Proclamation's flat prose, ridiculed as having the moral grandeur of a bill of lading, suggests that the true authorship of African American freedom lies elsewhere—not at the top of American society but at the bottom."[6]

Slaveholder Laura Comer illustrated Berlin's point when she wrote in her diary: "The servants are so indolent and obstinate it is a trial to have anything to do with them." Slaves resisted slavery by feigning ignorance or illness, sabotaging plantation equipment, and roaming freely in defiance of the law. One disturbed white passenger on a southwest Georgia rail line was astonished to see "crowds of slaves in gayest attire" getting on and off the trains "at every country stopping place." In Houston, Texas, a newspaper editor wrote with worried amazement that blacks were refusing to step aside for whites on city streets and sidewalks. As for forced labor, what work slaves did was done with measured effort. Some refused to work at all. A plantation mistress wrote of one of her slaves, "Nancy has been very impertinent. . . . She said she would not be hired out by the month, neither would she go out to get work." Another woman wrote to her husband, "We are doing as best we know, or as good as we can get the Servants to do; they learn to feel very independent."[7]

If slaves were increasingly reluctant to work for their owners, they werè always eager to work for themselves. In southwest Georgia a member of the local gentry complained that blacks were "doing as they please, hiring out their time which the law of Georgia forbids." To seek work for wages had long been a hallmark of freedom, and southern blacks were asserting that freedom long before Federal troops arrived. As early as April 1862, a slaveholder visiting Columbus, Georgia, found one of his runaways working at a mechanic's shop. In Russell County, Alabama, a slave hired himself out as a blacksmith and by war's end had a trunk full of money, albeit in worthless Confederate bills.[8]

Southern labor shortages brought new opportunities for hundreds of blacks as they moved into occupations previously closed to them. Nearly a third of the Columbus Factory Company's workforce was black as early as the spring of 1861. Any number of highly skilled black workers held jobs at the Columbus Naval Iron Works as well as the city's sword and pistol factories. The Grant Factory of Columbus, which had previously hired only white workers, quickly began building a force of black labor. So did the city's giant Eagle Manufacturing Company, which advertised for free black workers at "good wages and steady employment." In 1862, the Manchester Company of Richmond, Virginia, employed blacks at double the rates of a year earlier. Throughout the Confederacy, blacks began entering the industrial workforce in unprecedented numbers depite legal restrictions and resistance from white workers. They also became clerks and bookkeepers, which would have been almost unthinkable before the war.[9]

Many blacks saw industrial and clerical work as a way to achieve greater social and economic status. Perhaps a few saw such employment as a chance to prove themselves to whites—an opportunity to destroy justifications that supported oppression for all blacks and slavery for most. A major pillar of the proslavery argument had been that people of African descent were capable of performing only menial tasks. However, such was the skill and efficiency of black bookkeepers, clerks, and mechanics that one southern editor, long a vocal opponent of free blacks in the labor force, felt compelled to call their performance "laudable."[10]

Despite such praise, there were no corresponding calls for better treatment of blacks. If any expected it, they were very disappointed. The dynamics of a caste system based on race simply would not allow it. Those blacks who thought hard work alone was the path to civil and economic freedom failed to understand that the problem was not with themselves but rather with the class-related self-image of whites and how they used blacks to bolster that image. No amount of dedicated hard work on the part of blacks could overcome that. Most were probably under no illusion that it would. Years after the war, one former slave said of the freedman: "You can't fool him about a white man! And you couldn't fool him when he was a slave! He knows a white man for what he is, and he knew him the same way in slavery times."[11]

That knowledge carried with it a stark realization of the risks blacks ran in trying to carve out better lives for themselves. Resistance could lead to beating, dismemberment, or death. When one slave refused to accompany his master to the army, he was beaten so badly that his sister later wrote, "You couldn't tell what he looked like." Slaves in Williamson County, Texas, received a "whippin' at de stake" if they were caught off the plantation. Sometimes they received much worse. Freedman Lee McGillery recalled that "a few slaves try to run away to the north after the war started and when the white folks of the south find them they would most of the time jest shoot them." In Arkansas, one planter told his slaves that if they wanted their freedom, he would line them up on the banks of Bois d'Arc Creek and free them with his shotgun.[12]

Faced with such threats, some blacks decided early on that cooperation with their pro-Confederate neighbors might be the safest, perhaps the quickest, way to achieve some measure of freedom. Besides, Lincoln made clear at least initially that he had no intention of ending slavery or granting the rights of citizenship to blacks. If the Confederacy needed the support of blacks badly enough, perhaps Richmond would consider doing so. There were at least a few willing to test the possibility. In early 1861, seventy free blacks in Lynchburg, Virginia, tried to join the militia. So did sixty in Richmond, who marched to the enrollment office carrying a Confederate flag. Charles Tinsley, spokesman for a group of blacks in Petersburg, said that he and his comrades were "willing to aid Virginia's cause to the utmost extent of our ability." Another company of blacks offered their services in Nashville. The biracial Creoles of Mobile promised to form an entire regiment if called upon. In New Orleans, Creoles put together two regiments that were made part of the Louisiana state militia.[13]

There was a fine line to walk for those who tried to straddle the social divide. Blacks who appeared too eager to help white Confederates ran the risk of alienating their fellows. When a black Baptist preacher offered his services and those of his sons to Virginia, his parishioners began to avoid him. Afraid of losing his congregation entirely, the man insisted that he was trying only to do what was best for his flock. He finally apologized, but church members turned him a deaf ear. Nor did his or any offer of military service from blacks get much of a positive hearing from whites. Except for the New Orleans state regiments, which were barred from Confederate service, along with those few who were light skinned enough to "pass" for white, few offers from blacks to bear arms were accepted early in the war. The very notion seemed ridiculous to most whites. In the words of Vice President Alexander Stephens, the Confederacy's very "cornerstone" rested upon the "great truth" that the black man was not the equal of the white. Slavery, insisted Stephens, not soldiery, was the "natural and normal condition" of blacks.[14]

Military service, especially in local militias, had long been a mark of American citizenship. Proslavery doctrine held that only white men could be citizens because only white men possessed the qualities of duty and fortitude necessary to stand in the face of battle. How then could blacks possibly make good soldiers? Howell Cobb, president of the Confederacy's provisional congress and later a general, warned that "if slaves will make good soldiers our whole theory of slavery is wrong." Men like Cobb did not want to risk being proven wrong. When told by a white general that they could not be sent to the front, one New Orleans Creole reminded him, "Our fathers were brought here as slaves because they were captured in war, and in hand-to-hand fights, too. Pardon me, General, but the only cowardly blood we have got in our veins is the white blood."[15]

Though they were reluctant to admit it, slaveholders knew that blacks would fight. They were much less certain about *whom* blacks would fight. Ill treated as they had been for so long, armed southern blacks might turn their rifles against slaveholders. Freedom and equality was what blacks wanted. If neither side would grant it, blacks would take it when and where they could. In the spring of 1862, months before Lincoln made even limited emancipation a war aim, when Federal troops captured New Orleans, a free black resident told Union officers: "No matter where I fight, I only wish to spend what I have, and fight as long as I can, if only my boy may stand in the street equal to a white boy when the war is over."[16]

Despite their refusal to arm blacks, slaveholders continued to insist that slaves loved their masters and would remain faithful to them come what may. "I know they says dese tings," said a Virginia slave named Tom, "but dey lies. Our masters may talk now all dey choose; but one ting's sartin,—*dey don't dare to try us.* Jess put de guns into our hans, and you'll soon see dat we not only knows *how* to shoot, but *who* to shoot. *My* master wouldn't be wuff much ef I was a soldier." One man who had escaped slavery after more than twenty years in its grip wrote of the wartime slaveholder: "When he lies down at night, he knows not but that ere another morning shall dawn, he may be left mangled and bleeding, and at the mercy of those maddened slaves whom he has so long ruled with an iron rod." Such images hardly squared with the "faithful slave" myth, though slaveholders continued to press it publicly. But what they dared not say in public, they did sometimes whisper among themselves. In a private letter to a friend, one Alabama slaveholder frankly admitted, "the 'faithful slave' is about played out."[17]

"To Keep Them Down"

Tension between slaves and slaveholders hung over the South like a storm cloud whose lightning could strike anywhere at any time—and slaveholders knew it. Sensing a rise in violent tendencies among her slaves, Addie Harris of Alabama wrote: "I lay down at night & do not know what hour . . . my house may [be] broken open & myself & children murdered." In Georgia, a plantation mistress fearing slave rebellion wrote the governor asking for more slave patrols. The state assembly responded to such fears by reinforcing laws forbidding slaves to travel without a pass. It further canceled all exemptions from patrol duty. In August 1862, C.F. Howell of Jackson County, Mississippi, told his governor that no more men could be spared for military service. Those remaining were all needed to ride patrol over the local slaves. If the army drafted any more men from Jackson County, warned Howell, "we may as well give it to the negroes . . . now we have to patrol every night to keep them down."[18]

But slaves would not be kept down. Such was the force of slave resistance that patrols were losing their power of intimidation. One slave boy who outran patrollers made fun of them after he was safely behind his owner's fence. Some slaves went so far as to fight back. They tied ropes or vines neck-high across a dark stretch of road just before the patrollers passed by. These traps were guaranteed to un-horse at least one rider. When a group of patrollers broke in on a prayer meeting near Columbus, Georgia, one slave stuck a shovel in the fireplace and threw hot coals all over them. Instantly the room "filled with smoke and the smell of burning clothes and white flesh." In the confusion, every slave got away.[19]

A Georgia plantation overseer complained by letter to his absentee employer that his slaves would not submit to physical punishment. One slave simply walked away when the overseer told him he was about to be whipped. "I wish you would . . . come down and let the matter be settle," the overseer wrote, "as I do not feel wiling to be run over by him." In Texas, a slave threatened with beating by his owner "cursed the old man all to pieces, and walked off in the woods." He re-fused to come back until he was promised there would be no punish-ment. Another slave drew a knife on an overseer who tried to whip him. His owner locked him up and placed him on a bread-and-water diet. Such punishment did little to suppress rebellion. It tended only to make slaves press even more persistently for freedom. "I am satis-fied that his imprisonment has only tended to harden him," one over-seer wrote soon after releasing an unruly slave. "I don't think he will ever reform."[20]

Besides being terribly painful, whipping was for slaves a key symbol of their lowly social status. It is hardly surprising then that resistance to whipping became one of the main ways slaves sought to demon-strate a measure of independence. Such resistance could be very dan-gerous. Some planters were known to turn their dogs on slaves who refused to be whipped. Others, like a slave on the Hines Holt planta-tion in Georgia, were shot for it. The slave had beaten off six men who tried to hold him down.[21]

Despite such dangers, slaves continued to resist. One day while hoeing in the fields, a Georgia slave named Sylvia was told by an over-seer to take her clothes off when she got to the end of a fence row. She was going to be whipped for not working fast enough. When the over-seer reached for her, she grabbed a wooden rail and broke it across the man's arms. An enslaved Virginian, Clary Ann, choked her mistress to death when the woman tried to whip her. Another slave named Crecie, described as "a grown young woman and big and strong," was tied to a

stump by an overseer named Sanders in preparation for whipping. He
had two dogs with him in case Crecie resisted. When the first lick hit
Crecie's back, she pulled up the stump and whipped Sanders and his
dogs.[22]

Sanders was fortunate to escape Crecie's wrath with his life. Some
were not so lucky. When one overseer began beating a young slave
girl with a sapling tree, another slave grabbed an axe and killed him. It
was with good reason that, as a Texas slaveholder wrote, "a great many
of the people are actually afraid to whip the negroes." When one overseer whipped a slave in the summer of 1862, the victim's enslaved
comrades made a rope from their cotton suspenders and hanged the
overseer. In September, an issue of the *Mobile Advertiser and Register*
told of a slave who had poisoned his owner. In Virginia, a band of
slaves armed with shotguns killed two planters returning to their
homes after a Federal raid. After Mississippi slaveholder Jim Rankin
returned from the army "meaner than before," as one of his chattel
told it, a slave "sneaked up in the darkness an' shot him three times."
Rankin lingered in agony the rest of the night before he died the next
morning. "He never knowed who done it," one slave recalled. "I was
glad they shot him down."[23]

From the beginning of the war, whites feared that individual acts of
insubordination might lead to a general slave uprising. As early as May
of 1861 an Alabama planter urged the men in his district to stay
at home and save their families "from the horrors of insurrection."
Southwest Georgia's *Albany Patriot* complained that area blacks would
"congregate together contrary to law, *exhibit their weapons*, and no
doubt devise their secret, but destructive plans."[24]

During the late spring and early summer of 1861 a rebellion hyste-
ria swept across large parts of the South's plantation belt, southwest
Georgia included. Slaveholders in the large plantation districts along
the region's Chattahoochee and Flint rivers were especially distraught.
Panic spread through Decatur County in June when one of the local
slave patrols caught a slave named Israel away from his plantation
without a pass. Somehow Israel led the patrollers to believe that a general slave revolt involving slaves from plantations all over the county
was about to break out. Rumors spread that blacks in the county seat
of Bainbridge were collecting firearms and planning to "kill all of the
men and old women and children and take the younger ones for their
wives." Two suspected insurrection leaders were arrested. Local

whites swore that they would be killed if they ever got out of jail. By midsummer insurrection mania had died down, but slaveholder fears of rebellion remained strong. William Mansfield wrote Governor Brown that slaveholders in Stewart County were terrified of their slaves, fearing that local militiamen were not "prepared to quell any riots that might begin." A Fort Gaines man asked the governor for a company of cavalry to protect slaveholders in southwest Georgia from the general slave rebellion that he felt sure was coming.[25]

Throughout the war, rebellions and rumors of rebellions kept slaveholders constantly on alert. In Richmond, a black saloon waiter named Bob Richardson was thrown in Castle Thunder for plotting a slave uprising. In the area around Natchez, slaves on a number of plantations laid plans to kill their owners and set themselves free. When word leaked out, local whites hanged at least forty blacks and tortured many more. Sometimes authorities did not move quickly enough. Slaves in Yazoo City, Mississippi, did rise up, setting a fire that destroyed the courthouse and fourteen other buildings. A similarly dangerous plot was discovered near Troy, Alabama, in which a number of whites were implicated.[26]

"They Will Help the Negroes"

It was not uncommon to find whites involved with rebellious slaves. From the war's early months, so strong was anti-Confederate sentiment among southern whites that many were perfectly willing to work with blacks in undermining the government. December 1861 brought word from north Georgia's Gordon County to the governor's office of local unionists holding secret meetings and organizing a military force to protect themselves from Confederate authorities. They swore to resist attempts to draft them into the Confederate army. And they swore to aid the Yankees should they reach that far south. Most troubling was that the unionists "say in case of an insurrection they will help the Negroes."[27]

In July 1861 the *Columbus Sun* reported that a vigilance committee in southwest Georgia's Mitchell County had uncovered plans for a slave uprising to be led by several local whites. James Patillo, William McLendon, Samuel Edwards, Romulus Weeks, Stephen G.W. Wood, John C. Morgan, and Ephraim McLeod were all named as conspirators.

According to the *Sun*, Patillo was to supply the slaves "with as much ammunition as he possibly could to butcher the good citizens of the county." Patillo, McLendon, Weeks, Morgan, and McLeod all got the lash for their crimes and were expelled from the county. Edwards and Wood escaped a whipping, but were ordered never to set foot in Mitchell County again "under the penalty of death."[28]

In the spring of 1862, three white men in neighboring Calhoun County tried a similar scheme. Mindful of the previous year's failed attempt in Mitchell County, Harvell Scaggs, William Scaggs, and Giles Shoots, all citizens of Calhoun County, sought out Federal help to back the venture. Traveling down to the Gulf Coast under pretense of making salt, the trio contacted Union blockaders. Soon they were running "superior new guns" to slaves in Calhoun County. The plot came to light in June, and the three men were sentenced "to receive a sound whipping, to be tarred all over, and then ordered to quit the State." Some thought the punishment much too light. One local editor asked, "Is it safe to the community to suffer such inhuman wretches, such dangerous animals, to go at large?" He suggested changing the sentence to life in prison or, better yet, execution.[29]

John Vickery and three slaves got just that when they tried to instigate a slave uprising in south Georgia's Brooks County. Vickery was a local white man of modest means for whom no evidence can be found of prior trouble with the law. In fact, Vickery is found on Brooks County jury lists in 1863. However, he next appears in county records on August 23, 1864, at the end of a hangman's rope. Details of events leading to his execution vary, but all sources agree that Vickery, with the assistance of local slaves, organized a small insurrectionary force that intended to murder some of the county's wealthier planters.

After killing the planters and stealing whatever weapons they could find, the conspirators next planned to set the county seat of Quitman afire and seize the local rail depot. From there they would head south toward Madison, Florida, then seize and burn that town. Hoping to be reinforced by deserters and Union troops on the Gulf Coast, the men would return to Quitman from where they could control the region. On the eve of the planned uprising, local authorities learn of its details from a slave arrested for theft. After forcing information out of other slaves, the Brooks County police patrol arrested Vickery and three of the leading slave co-conspirators.

It is hardly surprising that Vickery's plan involved Confederate deserters and Union troops from Florida. As early as January 1863, Confederates were warned that Dead Man's Bay on the Gulf Coast of Florida should be considered a prime target for a Union invasion. Dead Man's Bay was in Taylor County, a stronghold of unionists and deserters who would be willing to help Union troops. The ground was firm, no natural obstructions blocked the roads between the bay and the interior, and there was a direct route from the bay to Madison, Florida. Just such a landing occurred one week prior to the planned Vickery uprising. Eight hundred Union troops disembarked at the mouth of the Aucilla River with another five hundred at Dead Man's Bay. It is possible these were the men that Vickery and his allies were to meet at Madison and lead back into south Georgia.

After Vickery's arrest, the Brooks County home guard took steps to use the conspirators as warning examples against further such plots. A home guard court convened to try the case, although it had no authority to do so. Governor Brown had specified that either county inferior courts or state militia courts would try all cases resulting from police patrol arrests. But Brooks County, for that day at least, was controlled by the home guard. Vickery and his three slave co-conspirators stood little chance of acquittal. After a mock trial, the court presented its findings: John Vickery—guilty of arson, inciting slaves to insurrection, and aiding slaves to flee to the Yankees; the slave Sam—guilty of insurrection and inducing slaves to insurrection; the slave Nelson— guilty of insurrection; the slave George—guilty of insurrection. All were condemned to death by hanging. At six o'clock that evening the sentence was carried out on the courthouse square.[30]

Despite the dangers, many white southerners continued to help blacks when they could—some for pity's sake, others for profit, still others because they would take any chance to undermine planter rule. Robert Bezley of Atlanta was arrested in December 1862 for giving fraudulent passes to slaves. In Shelby, North Carolina, a white man was hanged for the same crime. Some white farmers gave escaped slaves safe haven in exchange for work on their lands. Others gave them cash for stolen plantation supplies, no questions asked. A white merchant in Plymouth, North Carolina, worked out a deal with local slaves to buy goods stolen from their owners' plantations; the deal fell through when word of it leaked out. In some cases, blacks were such valuable trading partners that whites would take great risks to preserve the connections. In Granville County, North Carolina, two whites helped a black man named Kearsey break out of jail so he could maintain the extensive trading network he controlled.[31]

Such cooperation, however, was by far the exception. Though most whites never wanted secession and eventually turned against the Confederacy, they remained committed to keeping the South, and America, a white man's country and to keeping blacks "in their place." That some whites were willing to help slaves escape usually said more about how they felt toward slaveholders than slaves. Southern blacks were more often left to help each other or help themselves.[32]

One slave who had learned his letters forged a pass and made his way from Richmond north to Federal lines. Another slave journeyed 500 miles writing his own passes along the way. Some slaves did not have quite that far to go. In northern Missouri, the free state of Iowa was right next door. So common was it for slaves to cross the border during the war that many slaveholders either moved south or had their slaves "sold down the river." Joe Johnson was a Missouri slave who feared that fate. So he hid his family in a wagon, slipped past the slave patrols, and kept going until he reached the Iowa border. For slaves in Texas, the route to freedom most often led south to the Mexican border. "In Mexico you could be free," recalled a former Texas slave. "They didn't care what color you was, black, white, yellow, or blue. Hundreds of slaves did go to Mexico and got on all right." Another freedman remembered that slave patrols constantly rode the Rio Grande during the war, but hundreds of slaves got through their lines and crossed the river.[33]

Slaves trapped deeper in the heart of Dixie had a much harder time making their way to free territory. That had always been true but was even more so during the war. With whites using greater vigilance, escaping slaves had to take greater risks. In South Carolina, William and Anne Summerson risked suffocation by having themselves packed in rice casks and shipped out of Charleston. In March 1864, several slaves struck out from Floyd County, Georgia, headed for Union lines in Tennessee. Within days, slave catchers cornered two of the fugitives just short of the state line. Both were suffering from exposure and frostbite. One later died from the ordeal.[34]

Many escaping slaves found it simpler and safer to stay close to home. After a severe beating, one Georgia slave ran away and dug out a sizeable cave in which he took up residence. A short time later, under cover of night, he crept back to his old plantation, packed up his wife and two children, and took them back to his cave where they all lived until the war's end. In most cases, fugitives banded together for mutual support and protection. They sustained themselves by living off the land and making raids against local plantations—often the very plantations on which they had labored without pay for years. In their view, it was time for back pay. S.S. Massey of Chattahoochee County, Georgia, complained to the governor that runaway slaves were "killing up the stock and stealing ever thing they can put their hands on." In Blakely, Georgia, the *Early County News* reported in March 1864 that there had been "more *stealing*, and *rascality generally*, going on in Blakely and Early County, for the past few months, than has ever been known . . . negroes are doing a great deal of this stealing, burning, &c."[35]

The Okefenokee Swamp served as a runaway haven in southeast Georgia. For slaves in the tidewater regions of North Carolina and Virginia, the Great Dismal Swamp offered a refuge. In the North Carolina swamp counties of Camden and Currituck, there was a band of fugitives numbering between five and six hundred who made frequent raids on area plantations and Confederate supply depots. Frightened planters urged authorities to stop the raiders, but rooting them out of their well-defended hideouts was dangerous work. Sometimes it was fatal. In October 1862, a patrol of three armed whites went into the backwoods of Surry County, Virginia, looking for an encampment of about one hundred fugitives. They found the camp, but surely wished they had not. None were ever again seen alive.[36]

"Ready to Help Anybody Opposed to the Rebels"

Those slaves who did not escape gave aid and comfort to those who did. They funneled food and supplies to their fugitive friends and relatives, passed information to them, and provided a much needed support network. It would have been difficult if not impossible for many fugitive bands to operate effectively without such support. The same was true for bands of white deserters, draft evaders, and their families who also depended on local slaves for support. Like so many other enslaved blacks, Jeff Rayford did whatever he could to help deserters hiding in the Pearl River swamp of Mississippi. As he told an interviewer years after the war, "I cooked and carried many a pan of food to these men." Another Mississippi freedman recalled carrying food to hideouts where women and children had taken up residence. In Jones County, Rachel Knight, a slave of both white and black ancestry, was a key ally of the deserter gang led by Newton Knight, her owner's grandson. She supplied food for the men and served as a spy in their operations against local Confederates.[37]

Any number of slaves helped their owners and owners' relatives avoid Confederate service. Riley Tirey, one of twelve slaves owned by Robert Guttery of Walker County, Alabama, told how he carried blankets and other supplies to Guttery, who was hiding in the woods, "to help him keep out of the way of the Rebel cavalry." Another Alabama slave, Benjamin Haynes, took provisions to his owner's son who was "hid out to prevent his being conscripted." Though slaves' motives for rendering such aid were varied, among them was the knowledge that every effort made to help keep anyone out of Confederate service put them a step closer to freedom.[38]

Slaves welcomed strangers too who were trying to avoid Confederate service. Deserters traveling home through the plantation belt knew that slave cabins were their safest bet for food, shelter, and support. One deserter killed Georgia planter William McDonald when the slaveholder discovered him hiding in his slave quarters. The slaves did not intervene. Nancy Johnson, enslaved on a Georgia plantation during the war, told how "some of the rebel soldiers deserted & came to our house & we fed them. They were opposed to the war & didn't own slaves & said they would die rather than fight. Those who were poor white people, who didn't own slaves were some of them Union people. I befriended them because they were on our side."[39]

Defining supporters of the Union as being on "our side" became easier for southern blacks as word of the Emancipation Proclamation, effective January 1, 1863, began to spread. Though it did not free all slaves, it did make eventual freedom a direct Union war aim. Like never before, blacks came to identify with the Union cause, with white southern unionists, and with Union soldiers. But taught from birth to deal cautiously with whites, blacks did not always know what to make of their new allies' motives nor did they trust them entirely. Still, with freedom and Union joined together, blacks were ready to join with

Southern blacks operated as a fifth column, undermining the Confederate war effort when-ever they could. They worked with white anti-Confederates, carried food to deserter gangs and fugitive slaves, and spied for the Union army. And they aided those headed for Union lines. As a grateful former Union prisoner of war later wrote: "They were always ready to help anybody opposed to the Rebels. Union refugees, Confederate deserters, escaped pris-oners—all received from them the same prompt and invariable kindness." (Browne, *Four Years in Secessia*)

whites in whatever effort might serve the interests of both. As an escaping Union prisoner of war put it: "They were always ready to help anybody opposed to the Rebels. Union refugees, Confederate de-serters, escaped prisoners—all received from them the same prompt and invariable kindness."[40]

Once word of emancipation spread, most southern blacks went out of their way to help the Federals every chance they got. Black women in Savannah secreted food to Union prisoners. Susie King Taylor, a black Savannah native, wrote of the city's prison stockade as "an awful place. The Union soldiers were in it, worse than pigs, without any shelter from sun or storm, and the colored women would take food there at night and pass it to them through the holes in the fence. The soldiers were starving, and these women did all they could towards re-lieving those men, although they knew the penalty should they be caught giving them aid."[41]

Blacks also helped imprisoned anti-Confederates escape. Robert Webster, a mulatto barber in Atlanta, helped an aging Tennessee unionist named William Clift break out of the city's military prison in December 1863. Clift had served as a courier for the Federals in his home state until he was arrested by his own son, Moses Clift, a Confederate cavalry officer. Webster supplied the old man with a rope to use in making his escape. Along their routes of escape, people like Clift could expect to find safe haven and escorts among the slaves. Nancy Johnson told of a Yankee fugitive who showed up at her doorstep one evening. After keeping him hidden through the next day, she recalled, "my husband slipped him over to a man named Joel Hodges & he conveyed him off so that he got home."[42]

John Kellogg, a Union prisoner escaping through the Georgia mountains with the help of local blacks, was impressed by what he called the slave "telegraph line." Slaves near Carnesville told Kellogg and his comrades of Union troop movements, some at a distance of 150 miles, between Chattanooga and Atlanta. The information was essential to planning the safest route back to Federal lines. Union prisoner James Gilmore, who slipped out of Richmond's Libby Prison and made it back to safety with the help of Virginia blacks, made his gratitude clear in a manuscript he authored shortly after the war. Gilmore's publisher, Edmund Kirke, was eager to get it into print. "It tells," Kirke said, "what the North does not as yet fully realize—the fact that in the very heart of the South are four millions of people—of strong, able-bodied, true-hearted people,—whose loyalty led them, while the heel of the 'chivalry' was on their necks, and a halter dangling before their eyes, to give their last crust, and their only suit of Sunday homespun, to the fleeing fugitive, simply because he wore the livery and fought the battles of the Union."[43]

On July 18, 1864, as a Union raiding party approached the outskirts of Auburn, Alabama, a group of local blacks hurried out to warn its commander, Colonel William Hamilton, of Rebels hidden among the thickets ahead. In a charge that "could be better heard than seen," Hamilton and his men rushed the surprised Confederates, who, as Hamilton reported, "broke on our first fire and scattered in every direction."[44] "It is a matter of notoriety," lamented one high-ranking Confederate official, "in sections of the Confederacy where raids are frequent that the guides of the enemy are nearly always free negroes and slaves." Jim Williams, an escaped former slave from Carroll Parish, Louisiana, led Federal troops through the canebrakes of his old haunts to ambush a small Confederate force.[45] In North Carolina, Colonel S.H. Mix of the 3rd New York Cavalry expressed appreciation to his guide in the form of a certificate which read:

Samuel Williams, colored man, served the United States Government, as guide to my regiment out of Newbern, N. C., in the direction of Trenton, on the morning of the 15th of May, and performed effective service for us at the imminent risk and peril of his life, guiding my men faithfully until his horse was shot down under him, and he was compelled to take refuge in a swamp.[46]

Harriet Tubman, famous for her prewar service on the underground railroad, headed a ring of spies and scouts who operated along the South Carolina coast. Mary Louveste, an employee at Virginia's Gosport Navy Yard where the Confederacy's ironclad warship *Virginia* was under construction, smuggled out plans and other documents related to the new secret weapon. She carried the material to Washington, D.C., where she placed it in the hands of Secretary of the Navy Gideon Welles. "Mrs. Louveste encountered no small risk in bringing this information . . . and other facts," Welles recalled years later in support of her pension application. "I am aware of none more meritorious than this poor colored woman whose zeal and fidelity I remember and acknowledge with gratitude." There was even a black Union spy in the Confederate White House. Mary Elizabeth Bowser, an associate of unionist Richmond socialite Elizabeth Van Lew, worked as a maid at the presidential residence. She funneled anything worthy of note to Van Lew, who passed the information on to the Federals at City Point.[47]

A black Virginia couple named Dabney proved to be one of the most innovative spy teams of the war. In early 1863, as Union and Confederate armies eyed each other across the Rappahannock River, they escaped slavery, and the husband found work as a cook for the Federals stationed at the river. He became interested in the army's telegraph system and asked some of the soldiers how it worked. Soon after, his wife went back across the lines to get a job doing laundry for a Confederate general. Within a short time, the husband began updating Union officers on Rebel troop movements. The officers were astonished at how accurate the information seemed to be and asked the man how he knew such things. He took them to a hill overlooking the river and pointed across to the headquarters of General Robert E. Lee.

That clothes-line tells me in half an hour just what goes on at Lee's headquarters. You see my wife over there; she washes for the officers, and cooks, and waits around, and as soon as she hears about any movement or anything going on, she comes down and moves the clothes on that line so I can understand it in a minute. That there gray shirt is Longstreet; and when she takes it off, it means he's gone down about Richmond. That white shirt means Hill; and when she moves it up to the west end of the line, Hill's corps has moved upstream. That red one is Stonewall. He's down on the right now, and if he moves, she will move that red shirt.[48]

During the weeks leading up to the Battle of Chancellorsville, thanks to the Dabneys' clothesline telegraph, Confederates could not make a move without the Federals knowing about it.

"Gone to the Yankees"

Very often intelligence came from escaping slaves who related news of fortifications, military movements, and Confederate troop strength. One evening near Fortress Monroe, six Virginia slaves arrived behind Federal lines with detailed information on Confederate deployments in the region. There were two earthworks guarding approaches to the Nansemond River "about one-half mile apart—the first about four miles from the mouth—both on the left bank. . . . Each mounts four guns, about 24-pounders. . . . The first is garrisoned by forty men of the Isle of Wight regiment, the second by eight. One gun in each fort will traverse; the chassis of the others are immovable." The men went on to give valuable information on major troop deployments: "The Isle of Wight regiment is at Smithfield. The Petersburg Cavalry Company is at Chuckatuck. There are thirteen regiments of South Carolina troops at the old brick church near Smithfield. . . . At Suffolk there are 10,000 Georgia troops."[49]

Sometimes escaping slaves brought more than information. In May 1862, Robert Smalls ran the side-wheel steamer *Planter* with its cargo of ammunition and artillery out of Charleston harbor and turned it over to the blockading Federals. Smalls was a skilled seaman whose owner had hired him out as assistant pilot on the ship. When he learned that General David Hunter, commanding the Federals at Beaufort, had effectively freed all the slaves in his area of operations, Smalls laid plans to escape. On the night of May 12, after his captain and white shipmates went ashore, Smalls and a few other black crewmen fired up the boilers and headed for a nearby wharf where they picked up family members. They then headed down the harbor and past Fort Sumter. Guards at outposts along the way, and even those at Sumter, suspected nothing because Smalls knew all the proper signals. And in the darkness, no one ashore could tell that the crewmen waving to them were all black.

Once past Sumter, Smalls ordered full steam and made for the Federals, hoping they would see the old sheet he had hoisted as a white flag of truce. As Smalls approached the first Union vessel he sighted, someone yelled "All hand to quarters!" and the startled Yankees brought their guns to bear on the *Planter*. A member of the Federal crew later recalled:

> Just as No. 3 port gun was being elevated, some one cried out, "I see something that looks like a white flag;" and true enough there was something flying on the steamer that would have been *white* by application of soap and water. As she neared us, we looked in vain for the face of a white man. When they discovered that we would not fire on them, there was a rush of contrabands out on her deck, some dancing, some singing, whistling, jumping; and others stood looking towards Fort Sumter, and muttering all sorts of maledictions against it, and *"de heart of de Souf,"* generally.

As the *Planter* came alongside, Smalls stepped forward, took off his hat, and called out, "Good morning, sir! I've brought you some of the old United States guns, sir!"[50]

More and more, in groups large and small, slaves made their way to Union lines. In what historian W.E.B. Du Bois called a general strike against the Confederacy, slaves by the tens of thousands simply threw down their tools, packed up their meager belongings, and walked off the plantations. Depriving the Confederacy of much-needed labor, escaping slaves made clear how devastating an impact their attitudes had on the Confederate war effort. Mary Chesnut reflected the dread of many planters when she confided to her diary: "If anything can reconcile me to the idea of a horrid failure after all to make good our independence of Yankees, it is Mr. Lincoln's proclamation freeing the negroes. . . . Three hundred of Mr. Walter Blake's negroes have gone to the Yankees." As early as summer of 1861, at least fifteen thousand slaves escaped to the Federals. A year later, in North Carolina alone, one Confederate general estimated that slaves worth at least a million dollars had run off. By late summer 1862, Georgia slaves numbering twenty thousand had fled to the Union forces occupying the state's coastal regions. And the further south Union armies advanced, the more slaves sought their promise of freedom. In December 1864 when Sherman's army moved through Georgia, a single column reported seventeen thousand blacks trailing behind.[51]

That so many bondsmen and women took flight to follow Sherman was more a reflection of their desire for freedom than of any love they had for Union troops. Few were under any illusion that "Uncle Billy," as Sherman's men affectionately called him, held any great affection for them. If any did, they were quickly disappointed. On December 3, 1864, with Confederate cavalry hot on their heels, Sherman's men pulled up their pontoon bridges after crossing Ebenezer Creek near Savannah, leaving over five hundred terrified refugees stranded on the opposite bank. Some were shot down by pursuing Rebels. Others, with children clinging to their backs, jumped into the swollen creek and drowned. Survivors were rounded up and carried back to their owners. Reflecting on the callousness of his army's role in the affair, one appalled Union soldier asked, "Where can you find in all the annals of plantation cruelty anything more completely inhuman and fiendish than this?"[52]

Such expressions of sympathy were hardly common among white Union soldiers. Most blamed not just slavery but slaves themselves for the war. The weight of that resentment could fall hard on blacks who sought refuge with the Yankees. For some it could be deadly. When a black man showed up in the camps of the 4th New York Heavy Artillery, he was met with the cry "Kill him!"; the soldiers almost clubbed him to death. For black women, there was the additional danger of rape. Sexual assault was perhaps the most underreported crime of the Civil War, especially when black women were the victims. Even so, one survey accounting for less than 5 percent of all Union courts-martial showed over thirty trials for rape. In one case, a "woman of color" named Susan was raped by Private Adolph Bork of the 183rd Ohio. When she refused his advances, as Susan testified, Bork "took out his revolver and said, 'God damn you, I will force you to do it.' He said he would blow me to pieces if I didn't let him do it." Bork was eventually executed by firing squad, not for the crime of rape but for shooting another soldier. Raping a woman with any degree of African ancestry was hardly considered a crime at all. After Private Patrick Manning of the 8th New Hampshire assaulted a quadroon named Clara Grier, he was tried and found not guilty of attempted rape.[53]

In most cases, Yankee mistreatment of blacks was more casual, though no less cruel. Drunken Federals occupying Alexandria, Virginia, shot blacks in the streets just for amusement. Some Indiana soldiers entertained themselves by shoving a black child into a large cask of molasses. The boy nearly suffocated before he could clear the sticky substance from his nose and mouth. One Union company set up camp on a plantation and found entertainment locking the terrified black children in a dark storeroom. A bemused sergeant recalled that "such a yell of terror as they set up, Pandemonium never heard! They shrieked, groaned, yelled, prayed, and pulled their wool!"[54]

"We Are Oppressed Everywhere in This Slavery-Cursed Land"

Such cruelty among white northern soldiers fighting in the South reflected attitudes that were just as common back home. The *Christian Recorder* noted that in wartime Philadelphia it was "almost impossible for a respectable colored person to walk the streets without being insulted." The same was true for public transportation. Even a soldier's pass offered Harriet Tubman no protection from abuse. On a train heading home to Auburn, New York, from the Virginia front, she encountered a conductor in New Jersey who was sure her pass was forged or stolen. He could not conceive that a black woman might get such a pass any other way. When Tubman refused to vacate her seat, four men grabbed her up, dumped her in the baggage car, and there she was held until the train reached Auburn.[55]

Legal ground for blacks in the Midwest was even more shaky. Illinois voters, by a majority of two to one, amended their constitution in 1862 to keep blacks from settling there. The next year, when Indiana passed a law barring blacks from entering the state at all, Sojourner Truth set out on an Indiana speaking tour. Authorities arrested her several times but she kept to her mission. After a crowd at Angola threatened to burn down the hall in which she was scheduled to speak, she defiantly proclaimed, "Then I will speak upon the ashes."[56]

I SELL THE SHADOW TO SUPPORT THE
SUBSTANCE
SOJOURNER TRUTH.

Northern whites rarely welcomed escaping slaves. Even John Andrew, the abolitionist governor of Massachusetts, refused to allow his state to become a haven for southern blacks.
But there were blacks who fought back. When Indiana barred blacks from entering the
state in 1863, Sojourner Truth set out on an Indiana speaking tour. She was arrested several
times but kept to her mission. After a crowd at Angola threatened to burn down the hall in
which she was scheduled to speak, she defiantly proclaimed, "Then I will speak upon the
ashes." (Library of Congress)

In Iowa's Wapello and Johnson counties, whites declared their intention to "resist the introduction of free negroes into Iowa; first by
lawful means, and when that fails, we will drive them, together with
such whites as may be engaged in bringing them in, out of the State or
afford them 'hospitable graves.'" Farmers in Page County who had
hired "colored girls" as house servants were warned "that they must
send those 'niggers' back" or see their farms burned to the ground. In
Muscatine County, twenty whites visited a local farmer who had hired
a former slave boy. "By threats of personal violence," they intended to
"convince" the farmer of "his error."[57]

White mobs sometimes made good on their threats of violence. In
July 1862, spurred by reports of whites being thrown out of employment and wages being reduced, gangs of Irish workers attacked black
laborers at the Cincinnati docks. "No d——d niggers," yelled the

Irishmen, "should work on the levee." Some of the blacks, wrote one city newspaper, turned on their attackers, "the result being several Irishmen pretty well whaled." But being far outnumbered, most of the victims took refuge on boats lining the wharves. It did little good. "On went the mob from boat to boat, in pursuit of every negro they could find. One poor 'contraband' . . . was finally over taken and pelted with boulders. His teeth were knocked out, or down his throat, while his jaw bone was fractured, eight or ten rowdies having pounced on him at once." Those who could get away headed for the city's black tenements. Police never responded to calls for help, reported the paper, "as is usual in such cases."[58]

Even when police did respond, it was as often to help the mobs as to hinder them. One morning in September 1862, an angry crowd of thirty to forty whites in Brooklyn, New York, gathered outside a tobacco factory where a handful of blacks were employed. Soon they began hurling bricks and pavement stones at the building. Before long the crowd numbered more than a thousand whites, many of them screaming "Down with the nagers" and "Turn out the nagers." Two police officers walking their beat happened on the scene, but, wrote the *Brooklyn Eagle*, "instead of attacking the white rioters they struck at the negros with their clubs." The trapped blacks, five men and fifteen women, barricaded themselves on the top floor and threw anything they could find down on rioters who tried to come up the stairway. Police finally arrived in force and dispersed the mob, but not before the building was nearly gutted. Though it was only a twenty-minute walk from city hall, police took two hours to respond.[59]

There was little blacks could do to protect themselves through the political process or the judicial system. In most free states, it was illegal for blacks to testify in court against whites or to serve on juries. Even where it was not against the law, blacks were rarely called. Only in the five states of New England, where blacks made up only a small percent of the population, did they have unrestricted voting rights. Some blacks could vote in New York, but needed substantial property holdings to qualify. Things were much the same for blacks in the social realm as well. Schools, hospitals, theaters, and churches normally denied access to blacks or pushed them off to inferior segregated areas labeled "Colored."[60]

Even in Massachusetts, where black men could vote and black children could attend public schools, there was rampant and debilitating discrimination. In an open letter to Boston's antislavery newspaper, *The Liberator*, John Rock wrote in August 1862 that "the whole nation seems to have entered into a conspiracy to crush" African Americans.

The masses seem to think that we are oppressed only in the South. This is a mistake; we are oppressed everywhere in this slavery-cursed land. Massachusetts has a great name, and deserves much credit for what she has done, but the position of the colored people in Massachusetts is far from being an enviable one. . . . We have the right of suffrage, the free schools and colleges are open to our children, and from them have come forth young men capable of filling any post of profit or honor. But there is no field for these young men. . . . You can hardly imagine the humiliation and contempt a colored lad must feel by graduating the first in his class, and then being rejected everywhere else because of his color. . . . Even in Boston, which has a great reputation for being anti-slavery, he has no field for his talent. . . . It is five times as difficult to get a house in a good location in Boston as it is in Philadelphia, and it is ten times more difficult for a colored mechanic to get employment than in Charleston. Colored men in business in Massachusetts receive more respect, and less patronage than in any place that I know of. In Boston we are proscribed in some of the eating-houses, many of the hotels, and all the theaters but one. . . . You know that the colored man is proscribed in some of the churches, and that this proscription is carried even to the grave-yards. This is Boston—by far the best, or at least the most liberal large city in the United States.[61]

The editor of a local Unitarian weekly confirmed such observations and condemned "the disdain and abhorrence here manifested toward these unfortunate creatures of God. No where on God's earth is found the inconsistency so glaring as in educated, moral, religious New England."[62]

"Shedding the First Blood"

Though denied the rights of full citizenship, Boston's black population was ready to assume what was generally held to be one of the ultimate responsibilities of any citizen. When Lincoln called for volunteers in April 1861, blacks held a mass meeting at the Twelfth Baptist Church and announced their willingness to "stand by and defend the Government with 'our lives, our fortunes, and our sacred honor.'" Even the women were ready to take the field "as nurses, seamstresses, and warriors if need be." Similar offers came from blacks all over the North. Some formed a company in Providence and asked to be attached to the 1st Rhode Island Regiment. In Philadelphia, blacks organized two regiments and waited for orders on where to report. A letter arrived on the secretary of war's desk from New York announcing that "a black regiment from this city could be put into the field in thirty days." In Washington itself, three hundred free blacks petitioned the War Department to "enter the service for the defence of the City."[63]

Blacks had compelling reasons to answer Lincoln's call to arms. Some associated military service with citizenship, and meant to get a uniform on as a further means of demanding their full rights. Others saw in the call an opportunity to strike out against slaveholders. Even if the struggle was not yet a war against slavery, it was at least a war against slave states. For most northern blacks, many of whom had family members still enslaved in the South, that was enough for the time being. To be handed a weapon and marched south would do for the moment. All they needed was the order to do it.

Nicholas Biddle did not wait for orders. Two days after Lincoln called for volunteers, the sixty-five-year-old escaped former slave stepped off with his white neighbors of Pottsville, Pennsylvania's Washington Artillerists when they were ordered south to the nation's capital. Though not officially enlisted, Biddle was given a uniform and expressed his readiness to serve in whatever way he could. Along with four other Pennsylvania companies, the men arrived by train in Baltimore on April 18. As they marched past a jeering pro-Confederate mob, shouts of "Nigger in uniform" were heard. Then someone yelled "Kill that ——ed brother of Abe Lincoln." Suddenly Biddle was hit in the face "with a missile" that cut through his skin and exposed the bone. Lieutenant James Russell caught Biddle as he stumbled, and the troops hurried on to their waiting train bound for Washington. Nothing is known of Biddle's service after the Baltimore incident, but years later his Pottsville friends engraved these words on Biddle's tombstone:

He has the proud distinction of shedding the first blood in the late war for the Union, being wounded while marching through Baltimore with the first volunteers from Schuylkill County, 18 April 1861.[64]

Few northern whites were so generous in acknowledging the efforts of their black neighbors. For the most part, they meant to keep the United States a white man's country and were determined to keep their conflict with the South a white man's war. Neither rights for blacks nor emancipation for slaves were issues that most whites cared to touch. Police officials in Providence ordered local blacks to stop holding military drills, calling them "disorderly gatherings." In New York City, the chief of police warned black companies to stop drilling or he would offer them no protection against white mobs. Ohio's adjutant general told blacks that the state constitution prohibited their enlistment.[65]

Lincoln was no more eager for their services. Though differing with Confederates on the issue of disunion, Lincoln was united with them in his racist views. Blacks, he said, simply could not make good soldiers. "If we were to arm them," Lincoln said, "I fear that in a few weeks the arms would be in the hands of the rebels." Nor did he want to make slavery a war issue. In his first inaugural address, Lincoln stated flatly that he had "no purpose, directly or indirectly, to interfere with slavery in the States where it exists." Congress agreed. In a near unanimous vote, it passed the Crittenden-Johnson resolution, assuring the nation that the war was being fought not to overthrow or interfere "with the rights or established institutions" of the slave states but only "to defend and maintain the supremacy of the Constitution and to preserve the Union."[66]

Northern upper classes had wanted the war primarily to maintain easy access to cotton state resources. With the aid of middle- and lower-class nationalism, that was all they set out to do. Since slave labor produced most of the cotton, some feared that the end of slavery might mean the end of cheap cotton. So Lincoln and Congress promised that this war would be a white man's war, fought by and for white men. As far as the federal government was concerned, neither slavery nor blacks had any business in the affair. That suited the soldiers just fine, and they were not shy about letting their superiors know it. Within earshot of the White House, they marched into Virginia singing:

> To the flag we are pledged, all its foes we abhor.
> And we ain't for the nigger, but we are for the war.[67]

Army commanders got the message both from the troops and from Lincoln. In the fall of 1861, as escaping slaves began filtering into Union camps, Major General Henry Halleck issued orders barring them from Federal lines. It was not the army's role, Halleck wrote, "to decide upon the relation of master to man." As far as he and Lincoln were concerned, slaves, like stray cattle, were private property and were to be returned to their legal owners. General William Harney, commanding the Department of the West, dutifully ordered his troops to return runaways. So did Colonel D.S. Miles in Virginia, who ordered one of his subordinates to make sure that any escaped slaves were sent "back to the farm."[68]

"Save a Little Strip for Yourself"

Despite Lincoln's efforts not to make slavery a war issue, blacks themselves forced the question by refusing to stay put. The further south Lincoln's army advanced, the more self-emancipated blacks flooded Union lines. And it was impossible to reenslave them. They simply would not submit to it. By the war's second year, it became clear to Lincoln that Union victory would inevitably mean the end of slavery. Blacks were seeing to that whether whites wanted it or not. So Lincoln tried to get in front of the issue by calling for gradual emancipation, government compensation for slaveholders, and—in a vein of racial cleansing—the deportation of African Americans to Africa, or to the Caribbean, or to Central America, or almost anywhere as long as it was out of the United States.[69]

Like so many other white northerners, Lincoln was as quick to blame the victims as the perpetrators of slavery for the nation's troubles. In the summer of 1862, reflecting on the issue of slavery's expansion that precipitated the conflict, he told a delegation of leading African Americans: "But for your race among us there could not be war, although many men engaged on either side do not care for you one way or the other." That being the case, he insisted, "we should be separated." Congress agreed. In its *Report on Emancipation and Colonization,* the U.S. House of Representatives plainly stated that "the highest interests of the white race, whether Anglo-Saxon, Celt, or Scandinavian, require that the whole country should be held and occupied by these races alone." As a first step toward that goal, Congress allocated $600,000 to transport and colonize blacks "in some tropical country."[70]

Lincoln wasted no time in following through. By the end of 1862 he had contracted with a shady promoter named Bernard Kock to employ almost five hundred deported blacks as timber cutters on Ile à Vache, a small island off the coast of Haiti. The effort proved disastrous. Kock stole colonists' money, gave them inadequate housing, and left them in a state of near starvation. After smallpox swept through the settlement and killed nearly a hundred people, Lincoln gave up on the venture—but not on the idea of colonization.[71]

At the same time his timber scheme was taking shape, Lincoln laid plans for sending African Americans to mine in Panama. Ambrose Thompson of the Chiriqui Improvement Company was slated to head the project. Though warned by Secretary of the Navy Gideon Welles and others that Thompson's scheme was "a swindling speculation," Lincoln lobbied hard to get support for the project. Using backroom political tactics, Lincoln tried to shore up plans for deporting blacks to the Panama mines before word of the effort leaked out.[72]

Word did leak out, and reaction among blacks was predictably hostile. A mass meeting of blacks in Queens County, New York, drafted a letter to Lincoln informing him that "this is our native country; we have a strong attachment naturally to our native hills, valleys, plains, luxuriant forests . . . mighty rivers, and lofty mountains, as any other people." Blacks in Philadelphia were appalled that Lincoln would have them deported simply "to appease the anger and prejudice of the traitors now in arms against the Government."[73] A.P. Smith of New Jersey wrote in an open letter to Lincoln:

> Pray tell us, is our right to a home in this country less than your own, Mr. Lincoln? . . . Are you an American? So are we. Are you a patriot? So are we. Would you spurn all absurd, meddlesome, impudent propositions for your colonization in a foreign country? So do we. . . . But you say: "Coal land is the best thing I know of to begin an enterprise." . . . Coal land, sir! If you please, sir, give McClellan some, give Halleck some, and by all means, save a little strip for yourself. . . . Good sir, if you have any nearer friends than we are, let them have that coal-digging job.[74]

Others criticized Lincoln's plan to compensate slaveholders instead of slaves. At one gathering of angry blacks, John Rock asked the crowd: "Why talk about compensating masters? Compensate them for what? What do you owe them? What does the slave owe them? What does society owe them? Compensate the masters? . . . It is the slave who ought to be compensated." George Williams of North Carolina felt the same way. In a June 1863 letter to the *Christian Recorder*, he insisted that "the country about me, or the Sunny South, is the entailed inheritance of the Americans of African descent, purchased by the invaluable labor of our ancestors, through a life of tears and groans, under the lash and the yoke of tyranny."[75]

Among the most disappointed in Lincoln was Frederick Douglass. "If the black man cannot find peace from the aggressions of the white race on this continent," Douglass pointed out, "he will not be likely to find it permanently on any part of the habitable globe. The same base and selfish lust for dominion which would drive us from this country would hunt us from the world." Though he had hoped for better from Lincoln, this deportation plan made it clear to Douglass that the president was "quite a genuine representative of American prejudice and Negro hatred."[76]

"No Free State Wants Them"

Regardless of Lincoln's feelings, events affecting the role of blacks in the conflict had moved far beyond his control. The pressures blacks had been putting on Union forces in the field demanded an immediate response. The first significant reaction came in May 1861 when General Benjamin Butler, commanding Federal troops in Virginia, realized that it was futile to turn back escaping slaves. They would not stay away. So he declared them "contraband of war" and put them to work building fortifications. Lincoln let the move stand because the slaves were not technically free, just confiscated property. Congress supported that interpretation by passing the First Confiscation Act.

Then, on August 30, the Savannah-born and Charleston-raised General John C. Frémont, commanding the Federal Department of the West, issued the war's first true emancipation proclamation freeing all slaves held by pro-Confederates in Missouri. Lincoln canceled the order and fired Frémont. But blacks kept coming and pressure kept

In 1861, Lincoln said flatly that he had "no purpose, directly or indirectly, to interfere with slavery in the States where it exists." When fugitives began flocking to Union lines, officers issued orders sending them "back to the farm." But they would not stay put. Northern whites came to fear that if slavery were not abolished in the South, the North would soon be "overrun by escaped fugitives." By their own persistence, blacks themselves forced emancipation and made the war a struggle against slavery. (Library of Congress)

building. In April 1862 General David Hunter, headquartered on the South Carolina coast, freed all the slaves in his area of operations and created the war's first black regiment, the 1st South Carolina (later the 33rd South Carolina Regiment, United States Colored Troops). Lincoln rescinded this order too and relieved Hunter of his command.[77]

There was pressure for emancipation on the home front too. Abolitionists had been applying pressure from the war's beginning with little success. But news of black refugees flooding into Union lines sparked a new concern among white northerners. If the war ended with slavery intact, would the slaves go back to their former owners? Yankee troops had already tried—and failed—to force them back. George Boutwell, former governor of Massachusetts, warned in the summer of 1862 that if slavery were not abolished, the North would soon be "overrun by escaped fugitives." A New Bedford editor expressed the same fears in August, telling his readers that, far from encouraging black migration North, emancipation was the "only possible way to *avert* the threatened influx."[78]

His fears seemed to be confirmed a few weeks later when General John A. Dix reported to Secretary of War Stanton that contrabands in Virginia were suffering terribly. Poorly fed and clothed, crowded into broken-down shacks and tents, they were dying "by the hundreds and thousands." The army was simply not equipped to care for them all. So Dix asked permission to contact Governor John Andrew of Massachusetts as well as the governors of other northern states and arrange temporary asylum and employment for the refugees. When word of the plan reached Massachusetts, whites howled in protest. Opposition was especially fierce among Republicans, who accused Dix of saddling their party with the stigma of encouraging black migration North. Governor Andrew took the lead in arguing that black refugees should remain in the South. Within weeks of Dix's request, Andrew was in Washington telling administration officials face to face that Massachusetts would not be a haven for escaped slaves. Silence among white abolitionists confirmed the widespread hostility toward black refugees and went a long way toward defeating Dix's plan to resettle freedom-seeking blacks. "Massachusetts don't want them," declared the editor of Springfield's *Daily Republican*. "No free state wants them."[79]

Pushing for a policy of racial containment, northern whites from a broad range of political stripes pressured Lincoln to keep blacks in the South. Republicans in Congress put pressure on Lincoln as well. They were joined by War Democrats who supported ending slavery as a necessary war measure. Some even argued that escaping slaves ought to be enlisted and put on the front lines. Battle and desertion had depleted Union ranks, and few white volunteers were willing to replace them. In the summer of 1862, Congress forced Lincoln's hand. It passed the Militia Act, authorizing black enlistment under white officers, and the Second Confiscation Act, freeing all slaves owned by pro-Confederate slaveholders. The Second Confiscation Act left in doubt the future of blacks in the United States since it called for their deportation. But it left no doubt that congressional Republicans meant to end slavery among the Rebels and keep black migration to the North in check.[80]

Though the act's intent was clear, its enforcement would be unwieldy. Determining the difference between those slaveholders who had engaged in disloyal acts and those who had not would be almost impossible. Moreover, Lincoln thought that to enforce the act might cause more white soldiers to desert. Forced emancipation might even push the remaining loyal slave states of Missouri, Kentucky, and Maryland out of the Union. "I would do it," Lincoln confessed late that summer, "if I were not afraid that half the officers would fling down their arms and three more states would rise."[81]

"I Never Saw Joy Before"

Lincoln also worried that an emancipation announcement coming after a string of military defeats in the summer of 1862 would make his government look weak and desperate. But the Battle of Antietam changed that. On September 22, just days after the Army of the Potomac turned back a Rebel advance near the western Maryland village of Sharpsburg, Lincoln issued his preliminary Emancipation Proclamation. Effective January 1, 1863, slaves held in areas still in rebellion against the United States would be forever free. The Proclamation was a tentative document that freed only slaves it could not immediately reach; slaves in the "loyal" slaveholding states and parts of Confederate states already under Union control were not affected. It was "a necessary war measure," Lincoln wrote, meant primarily to undermine the rebellion. And it encouraged black "colonization," Lincoln's ultimate solution to the "negro question." But to ease enforcement, it went further than the Second Confiscation Act in promising freedom to all slaves held in rebellious regions, not just those held by rebellious slaveowners. Most important, it turned the Union army into a force for liberation and called for blacks themselves to join that force.[82]

Blacks throughout the country—North and South, free and enslaved—rejoiced as word of the Proclamation spread. Despite the Proclamation's limited nature, Frederick Douglass called it "a moral bombshell" that was more important for its implication than its intent. Whatever Lincoln's view of the matter, blacks themselves would take the document, make it their own, and make it more than it was. Within days of the preliminary announcement of the Proclamation, slaves began escaping to Union lines and claiming their freedom. Even slaves in areas like Kentucky and southern Louisiana, where the document did not apply, nevertheless claimed their freedom. The "freedom train" was rolling on, fueled by the determination of four million Americans who, though born into slavery, would not die enslaved.[33]

On January 1, 1863, at prayer meetings across the South and mass meetings across the North, blacks and their white abolitionist allies celebrated the day of "Jubilee." An appropriately jubilant crowd packed Boston's Music Hall that evening. Among those attending were Henry Wadsworth Longfellow, Oliver Wendell Holmes, Francis Parkman, and Ralph Waldo Emerson. Harriet Beecher Stowe was there too, sitting in the balcony. When the audience called for her, chanting in unison her name, she was so moved that "she could only bow and dab her eyes with her handkerchief." Across town at Tremont Temple, there were three huge meetings that day—morning, afternoon, and evening. At the morning session, William C. Nell spoke of the day as a turning point in the lives of enslaved Americans.

> New Year's day—proverbially known throughout the South as "Heart-Break Day," from the trials and horrors peculiar to sales and separations of parents and children, wives and husbands—by this proclamation is henceforth invested with new significance and imperishable glory in the calendar of time.[84]

Frederick Douglass spoke at Tremont Temple that afternoon and waited there for news from the telegraph office that Lincoln had signed the Proclamation. Evening came and still no word. "We waited on each speaker," Douglass recalled, "keeping our eye on the door." At eleven o'clock, with no news yet, Douglass shouted to the crowd, "We won't go home till morning." Finally, a messenger arrived and read Lincoln's words: "I do order and declare that all persons held as slaves within said designated States, and parts of States, are, and henceforward shall be, free." "I never saw Joy before," said Douglass. "Men, women, young and old, were up; hats and bonnets were in the air."[85]

"Unoffending Negroes Were Brutally Assailed"

Reaction to emancipation among many northern whites could hardly have been less joyous, since they had been told repeatedly by politicians and employers that black migration and job competition—not corruption and profiteering—were the source of low wages. The

Proclamation fed their racist fears. Many were by no means convinced that freedom would keep blacks in the South. It might only free them to migrate north. That became clear shortly after Lincoln announced his intention to issue an Emancipation Proclamation on September 22, 1862. In October, a meeting of white workers in Quincy, Illinois, gave "notice to those engaged in this business of attempting to ride down and crush out the free white workingmen of Illinois, by thus seeking to bring free negro labor into competition with white labor, that we cannot and will not tolerate it; that we will seek our remedy, *first*, under the law; *second*, at the polls; and *third*, if both these fail, we will redress our wrongs in such a manner as shall seem to us most expedient and most practicable."[86]

Democrats tapped into such racist fears and secured significant gains in the fall 1862 elections. When the results came in, a New Jersey soldier took them as a happy sign "that the North is not ruled by a set of infernal fanatics and nigger worshippers." Democratic newspapers continued to fan the flames of racial hatred well into 1863 by touting a series of fictitious or overblown "negro outrages." Accusations ranged from assault to rape and murder, all pointing to the end result of "Black Republican" rule. In fact, it was blacks who were more often the victims of white outrages. That March, as a black man in Detroit was being taken to jail, accused of "an outrage upon a young white girl," angry whites tried to grab him. After being beaten back by police, the rioters—estimated at several thousand—rampaged through the city's black neighborhoods and, wrote one contemporary, "perpetrated the most horrible outrages upon the colored people." Businesses owned by or employing blacks were special targets of the mob. One cooper shop between Fort and Lafayette streets was bombarded with brickbats then set afire. Rioters caught one of the shop's black workers and beat him nearly to death with a shovel. Another they chopped to death with an axe.[87]

Blacks throughout the North felt the weight of an antiemancipation backlash that spring. Failed labor strikes in Boston, Brooklyn, Albany, Cleveland, and Chicago were all blamed on black competition. In Buffalo, white strikers killed three blacks and severely beat twelve more. On March 13, 1863, the *New York Evening Post* reported that Irish longshoremen along the East River had "set out upon a Negro hunt." They went after black workers along the docks, "pommelled them without mercy," then spread out through the ward attacking all the black porters, cartmen, and laborers they could find. In May, violence again broke out on the docks when "a number of unoffending negroes were brutally assailed while quietly pursuing their labors."[88]

Blacks in New York City were even more brutally assailed during the draft riots that summer. In July's nearly week-long rampage, white mobs beat, burned, tortured, and killed as many blacks as they could lay hands on. Three blacks walking home after work on the riot's first evening were attacked on Varick Street in the Eighth Ward. Two got away. The other was beaten several times during a chase that went all the way to Clarkson Street. There the crowd caught sight of an unsuspecting black man named William Jones, who had come out to buy a loaf of bread. The rioters grabbed Jones, hanged him from the nearest tree, then set his still quivering body on fire. William Williams, a black seaman who stopped to ask for directions in the Ninth Ward, was beaten to near unconsciousness. As he lay helpless on the street, some of the rioters threw rocks at him. One rowdy kicked at his eyes. Another picked up a heavy flagstone and slammed it down on Williams's chest. Police finally arrived, put Williams in a cart, and took him to New York Hospital, where he lingered for two hours before death ended his misery.[89]

Most blacks stayed at home, some preparing to defend themselves should the mob try to break in. In a house on Thompson Street, eight women banded together and determined to make their stand in the kitchen. Using several large pots, they brewed a concoction of water, soap and ashes that they called "the King of Pain." A visitor entered and found the defiant women gathered around the boilers with dippers in their hands. "How will you manage if they attempt to come into this room," the visitor asked. "We'll fling hot water on 'em, an' scall dar very harts out," came the reply. The visitor further inquired, "Can you all throw water without injuring each other?" "O yes, honey," they said, "we's been practicin' all day."[90]

"Anything to Beat the South"

These eight women represented blacks by the hundreds of thousands who were ready to fight—on or off the battlefield. Despite opposition from so many of their white countrymen, the Emancipation Proclamation had its intended effect on African American men. They flooded into recruiting offices across the North and flocked to Union lines across the South, tens of thousands of them eager to enlist. Frederick Douglass was among the most enthusiastic supporters of black enlistment. "The iron gate of our prison stands half open," he told African Americans as he urged them to arms. "One gallant rush . . . will fling it wide." Two of Douglass's sons joined that rush along with more than two hundred thousand other black men. Over 80 percent of them were from the southern states. Most had been slaves. But no longer. "Once let the black man get upon his person the brass letters, 'U.S.,'" Douglass proclaimed, "let him get an eagle on his buttons and a musket on his shoulder and bullets in his pocket, and there is no power on earth which can deny that he has earned the right to citizenship." Prince Rivers, a self-emancipated sergeant in the 1st South Carolina Volunteers, made clear what that meant to him: "Now we sogers are men—men de first time in our lives."[91]

Most white men were repulsed at the thought of having to respect the rights of manhood and citizenship for black men. To avoid that eventuality, many whites, especially those in the army, wanted to keep blacks and slavery out of the conflict. One study of letters from Union soldiers showed that prior to emancipation, not three in ten thought that ending slavery should be a war aim. Sergeant William Pippey of Boston thought there were far fewer than that. "I don't believe," he wrote, "there is *one abolitionist* in *one thousand* in the army." The few who held abolitionist views usually keep their opinions to themselves. When Henry Wooten, an enlisted man from New York, spoke up for abolitionism early in the war, one of his fellow soldiers shot him.[92]

Most white soldiers were just as adamant about keeping blacks out of the army. As one Pennsylvania sergeant wrote, "We don't want to fight side and side by the nigger. We think we are too superior a race for that." A corporal of the 16th Michigan insisted that white men were "superior to niggers" and that he did not want "to go through the rough life of A soldier and perhaps get shot, for a d——d nigger." An Indiana private wrote home to his parents: "If old Abe arms them niggers I will quit and go South."[93]

Few soldiers went South, but as Lincoln had feared, tens of thousands did go home. A New York captain wrote that his men were "much dissatisfied" with the Emancipation Proclamation. To them, the conflict had become a "nigger war" and they were all "anxious to return to their homes for it was to preserve the Union that they volunteered." In February 1863 a private of the 66th Indiana wrote from Mississippi that his comrades "will not fite to free the niger . . . there is a Regiment her that say they will never fite untill the proclamation is with drawn there is four of the Capt[ains] in our Regt sent in there Resignations and one of the Liutenants there was nine in Comp. G tride to desert."[94]

Most white soldiers came to abolitionism grudgingly. Some refused to call themselves abolitionists at all. "I am no abolitionist," insisted a 55th Ohio enlistee, "in fact despise the word." But he came to feel that "as long as slavery exists . . . there will be no permanent peace for America. . . . Hence I am in favor of killing slavery." An Indiana sergeant wrote to his wife that although he could not care less for blacks, he would support the Emancipation Proclamation "if it will only bring the war to an end any sooner . . . anything to beat the South."[95]

Jacob Allen, a young abolitionist in the Union army, knew how his comrades felt about blacks and worried that their new antislavery feelings might not last. "Though these men wish to abolish slavery," he wrote to noted abolitionist William Lloyd Garrison, "it is not from any motive outside of their own selfishness; and is there not a possibility that at some not very distant day, these old rank prejudices, that are now lulled to sleep by selfish motives, may again possess these men and work evil?"[96] Frederick Douglass was worried too. What the government could do, it could undo. Might emancipation be in danger if the political winds turned against it? Barely a month after the Proclamation took effect, Douglass voiced his concern before an assembly in New York.

> Much as I value the present apparent hostility to Slavery at the North, I plainly see that it is less the outgrowth of high and intelligent moral conviction against Slavery, as such, than because of the trouble its friends have brought upon the country. I would have Slavery hated for that and more. A man that hates Slavery for what it does to the white man, stands ready to embrace it the moment its injuries are confined to the black man, and he ceases to feel those injuries in his own person.[97]

For the moment, though, the greater threat was the Confederate government. On January 5, 1863, four days after Lincoln signed the Emancipation Proclamation, Jefferson Davis issued an enslavement proclamation under the heading "An Address to the People of the

Free States." White northerners, he charged, had "degraded" themselves by allying with blacks. His government, on the other hand, would maintain white dignity by robbing all blacks of their freedom. As of February 22, 1863, Davis declared, "all free Negroes in the Southern Confederacy shall be placed on the slave status, and deemed to be chattels, they and their issue forever." Any black Union soldiers captured in combat would be subject to enslavement and their white officers subject to execution as leaders of servile insurrection.[98]

That was, of course, assuming that black regiments would ever see combat. So strong was prejudice against their abilities among most Union generals that it seemed as if black soldiers might never be used for any but menial tasks. "I won't trust niggers to fight," insisted General William T. Sherman. "Can they improvise bridges, sorties, flank movements, etc., like the white man?" he asked. "I say no." Blacks should, he said, "be used for some side purposes and not be brigaded with our white men." Many other officers felt the same way. They used black soldiers as a labor force for building fortifications, hauling carts, or digging latrines—anything that might rob them of an opportunity to earn the respect that came with service in combat. In some regiments, the colonel was "Ole Massa." Squads were work "gangs" and their officers "nigger drivers." The soldiers may as well have been slaves.[99]

"Heroic Descendants of Africa"

Still, some commanders of black regiments were committed to earning respect for their men and pushed hard for combat assignments. They made the most of their opportunities when they came. On May 27, 1863, the Louisiana Native Guard, composed for the most part of recently freed blacks, participated in an assault against Confederate fortifications on the Mississippi River at Port Hudson, twenty-five miles north of Baton Rouge. In an after-action report, one of the guard's white lieutenants admitted that he had entertained some fears as to his men's "pluck." "But I have now none," he added. "Valiantly did the heroic descendants of Africa move forward cool as if Marshaled for dress parade, under a most murderous fire from the enemies guns . . . these men did not swerve, or show cowardice. I have been in several engagements, and I never before beheld such coolness

The 107th U.S. Colored Troops at Fort Corcoran in Arlington, Virginia. Though at first opposed to enlisting blacks, Lincoln finally came to realize that he could not do without them. With white enlistments insufficient to win the war, Lincoln had to support emancipation and call on blacks to help achieve it. "Any different policy in regard to the colored man," Lincoln wrote, "deprives us of his help.... Keep it and you can save the Union. Throw it away, and the Union goes with it." (Library of Congress)

and daring. Their gallantry entitles them to a special praise. And I already observe, the sneers of others are being tempered into eulogy."[100]

A few days later on June 7, two regiments of newly freed blacks fended off attacking Rebels at Milliken's Bend, a Federal stronghold on the Mississippi River just north of Vicksburg. "I never more wish to hear the expression, 'the niggers won't fight,' " wrote Union captain M. M. Miller after the battle. One official reported to the War Department that "the sentiment in regard to the employment of negro troops has been revolutionized by the bravery of the blacks in the recent Battle of Milliken's Bend. Prominent officers, who used in private sneer at the idea, are now heartily in favor of it."[101]

The notion that blacks lacked the discipline for soldiering was dealt a further blow on July 16 when the 54th Massachusetts fought off a Rebel charge on James Island just south of Charleston, South Carolina. The regiment suffered nine killed, thirteen wounded, and seventeen missing in action—but it held fast. "It is not for us to blow our own horn," Corporal James Henry Gooding wrote back home to Boston, "but when a regiment of white men gave us three cheers as we were passing them, it shows that we did our duty as men should." An even tougher test came two days later when the 54th spearheaded an assault on Fort Wagner, which guarded the southern approach to Charleston harbor. Gooding later recalled that when the charge sounded,

> we went at it, over the ditch and onto the parapet through a deadly fire; but we could not get into the fort. We met the foe on the parapet of Wagner with the bayonet—we were exposed to a murderous fire from the batteries of the fort, from our Monitors and our land batteries, as they did not cease firing soon enough. . . . The color bearer of the State colors was killed on the parapet. Col. [Robert Gould] Shaw seized the staff when the standard bearer fell, and in less than a minute after, the Colonel fell himself. When the men saw their gallant leader fall, they made a desperate effort to get him out, but they were either shot down, or reeled in the ditch below.

Though the effort to take Wagner failed, it was not from a lack of trying. Six hundred men of the 54th went in on the assault. Forty percent of them were captured, killed, or wounded. One of the most severely injured was Sergeant William Carney, who had retrieved a U.S. flag and carried it back with him despite wounds to his head, chest, right leg, and arm. He became the first of twenty-three black soldiers awarded the Congressional Medal of Honor during the war.[102]

Blacks sometimes received grudging admiration even from Confederates. After the engagement at Milliken's Bend, one Rebel soldier wrote that his black foes fought "with considerable obstinacy, while the white or true Yankee portion ran like whipped curs." Such observations provide evidence that the respect soldiers often displayed across the lines could be displayed toward black soldiers as well. One Yankee wrote of his surprise when Confederates agreed to a picket-line truce with black soldiers facing them. "The rebels and our colored soldiers now converse together on apparently very friendly terms, and exchange such luxuries as apples, tobacco, and hard tack, by throwing them to each other. It was hardly deemed possible that the enemy could be induced to refrain from firing on black troops wherever they could be seen."[103]

But Rebel commanders usually wanted their men to kill as many black troops as possible, at times including those who could have been taken prisoner. Despite the government's official policy that captured blacks were to be enslaved, the unofficial policy of many Confederate officers was that blacks in uniform should be shot on sight—even those trying to surrender. Some rank-and-file Rebels balked at such barbarism. At Milliken's Bend, they took dozens of blacks prisoner rather than murder them in cold blood. One officer recalled hearing his men shout during the battle that surrendering blacks should be spared. When General Edmund Kirby Smith heard that so many blacks had been captured alive, he told one of his commanders: "I hope this may not be so, and that your subordinates who may have been in command of capturing parties may have recognized the propriety of giving no quarter to armed negroes and their officers." Rebel deserters later testified that three days after the battle, they saw black prisoners of war executed.[104]

Such atrocities took place in numerous engagements. In Arkansas at the Battle of Poison Springs, eyewitnesses reported black prisoners of war being "murdered on the spot." The same occurred at the Battle of Saltville in Virginia. When Fort Williams fell to the Rebels in North Carolina, a Union lieutenant recalled that "the negro soldiers who had surrendered were drawn up in line at the breastworks and shot down as they stood." During the Battle of the Crater outside Petersburg, Virginia, attacking Confederates ran their bayonets through wounded black soldiers. After his men slaughtered their surrendered black prisoners at Tennessee's Fort Pillow, an enthused Nathan Bedford Forrest called it a clear demonstration that "negro soldiers cannot cope with Southerners."[105]

After the Battle of Olustee west of Jacksonville, Florida, victorious Confederates roamed among the wounded Federals shooting every black soldier they could find. When William Penniman of the 4th Georgia Cavalry rode up to ask what the men were doing, an officer replied, "Shooting niggers, Sir." Penniman protested that it was shameful to murder wounded prisoners, but the killings continued. One Georgia soldier later recalled: "How our boys did walk into the niggers, they would beg and pray but it did no good." The next day, Penniman rode over the battlefield. "The results," he said, "of the previous night became all to[o] apparent. Negroes, and plenty of them, whom I had seen lying all over the field wounded, and as far as I could see, many of them moving around from place to place, now . . . all were dead. If a negro had a shot in the shin another was sure to be in the head."[106]

Ultimately, the take-no-prisoners policy worked more against Confederates than for them. When word of the murders spread, black soldiers began to fight with a fiery rage that astonished friend and foe alike. The Rebels, recalled one Union officer, "fear them more than they would fear Indians." A white cavalryman from Maine wrote home after one engagement that he saw black troops shooting Confederates who were trying to surrender. "The officers had hard work to stop them from killing all the prisoners," he recalled. "When one of them would beg for his life the niggers would say remember Port Hudson." After a company of black cavalrymen surrounded a band of Confederate guerrillas, someone shouted "Remember Fort Pillow." The blacks captured seventeen prisoners, then shot them dead. A white officer in one black regiment wrote home to his wife that some of his men had killed five captured Confederates. "Had it not been for Ft Pillow," he lamented, "those 5 men might be alive now. . . . It looks hard but we cannot blame these men much."[107]

Indeed, few of their comrades faulted black soldiers for giving no quarter to men that they believed would give them none. The general rule was kill or be killed. Even for those blacks who survived initial captivity, life as a prisoner of war was always brutal and often brief. Private Joseph Howard of the 110th Colored Infantry wrote of his experience: "We were kept at hard labor and inhumanely treated. . . . If we lagged or faltered or misunderstood an order we were whipped and abused. . . . For the slightest causes we were subjected to the lash [and] we were very poorly provided for with food." Medical care for black prisoners was even more poorly provided. Often they could not get any at all. An inmate at Andersonville witnessed the treatment of one black captive who fell into Rebel hands after the Battle of Olustee: "One fellow had a hand shot off and some deranged brutes had cut off his ears and nose. The doctors refused to dress his wounds or even amputate his shattered arm; he was naked in the prison and finally died from his numerous wounds." Blacks held in Confederate prison camps died at a rate of 35 percent, more than twice the average for white captives.[108]

"To the Position of Slaves Again"

The treatment black soldiers got from their own army was hardly better, especially when it came to medical care. Blacks were assigned the least competent doctors and received the least medical attention. An inspector general reported that the surgeon who ran one black hospital "did not evince much knowledge of his duties." Other surgeons attached to black regiments were described as "simpletons" and even "murderers." When one black soldier reported for sick call, the surgeon had him bucked and gagged for faking illness. A day later the soldier was dead. Another surgeon kicked a black patient for leaving his tent without permission. The man had needed to relieve himself. He died that evening. As another dying black soldier lay moaning in pain, a surgeon yelled, "God damn him if he was going to die and don't [make] So much fuss about it." Small wonder that the rate of death from disease for black soldiers was three times that of whites.[109]

If the death rate was higher, basic pay for blacks was lower—ten dollars a month instead of the normal thirteen. And three dollars of black soldiers' pay was withheld for the cost of their uniforms. Still, the need for income among the families of black soldiers was no less. Writing from Union-held Fernandina, Florida, Emma Steward told her husband Solomon that an "administering angel Has Come and borne My Dear Little babe To Join with Them. My babe only Live one day. It was a Little Girl. Her name Is alice Gurtrude steward. I am now sick in bed and have Got nothing To Live on."[110]

The principle of equal pay was as important as its practicality. Black soldiers had fought and died just as whites had. Were their lives worth less? In a letter to President Lincoln, Corporal James Henry Gooding reminded him that "when the war trumpet sounded o'er the land, when men knew not the Friend from the Traitor, the Black man laid his life at the Altar of the Nation,—and he was refused." But when the need for more soldiers became so great that blacks had to be called upon, how did they respond? "Let their dusky forms, rise up, out the mires of James Island, and give the answer. Let the rich mould around Wagners parapets be upturned, and there will be found an Eloquent answer. . . . We have done a Soldiers Duty. Why cant we have a Soldiers pay?"[111]

If they could not have a soldier's pay, many refused to take any at all. In a show of support for their men, neither did some of their officers. Colonel Robert Gould Shaw refused to have anyone in his regiment paid until all his men received equitable pay. Captain A.W. Heasley told his company, "Boys, stand up for your full pay! I am with you, and so are all the officers." Not all officers were so supportive, and mutiny was sometimes the result. After it became apparent that their officers would not petition the government on their behalf, several black units stacked arms and refused to do any service until they got equal pay. When a black artillery company declined to fall out for inspection, all the sergeants and corporals, along with twenty privates, were court-martialed for mutiny. A riot broke out when the court sentenced them to prison.[112]

Most protests over inequitable pay were peaceful but nevertheless determined—even at the risk of life. In March 1864, Sergeant William Walker of the 3rd South Carolina was court-martialed for "leading the company to stack arms before their captain's tent, on the avowed ground that they were released from duty by the refusal of the government to fulfill its share of the contract." Walker was sentenced to death by firing squad. That summer, after more than thirteen months of serving without pay, seventy-four members of Company D, 55th Massachusetts, sent a petition to Lincoln asking for discharge with back pay. "If imediate steps are not takened to Relieve us," they wrote, "we will Resort to more stringent mesures." Whatever measures those might have been, they turned out to be unnecessary. So frequent and intense had such protests become that Congress was finally forced to equalize pay for blacks in June 1864. Still, discrimination was present in the act. Men who had been free before the war got back pay to the time of their enlistment. Those who had been enslaved got back pay only to January 1, 1864.[113]

There was discrimination too in equipping black soldiers. In April 1864, long after the Springfield rifle became standard issue, one officer wrote to the War Department following an inspection of a black field unit: "This Regiment, like most of this class of soldiers, have the old flintlock muskets, altered to percussion, which have been used for a long time. The muskets of this Regiment were condemned once, and have been condemned by an Inspector a second time." Some whites were reluctant to trust blacks with even these antiquated weapons. There were officials who suggested that black soldiers be armed with nothing more than pikes.[114]

Just as discouraging as the abuse they suffered through official channels was the unofficial abuse they suffered from their white counterparts. Despite black soldiers' steadfast combat service, they were continually derided by white soldiers. "Our boys don't think much of them," wrote an Ohio officer. "They still say this is a *White Mans War.*" Blacks were verbally insulted, physically abused, and socially degraded by their white brothers-in-arms. General James S. Brisbin wrote that he witnessed such treatment of black troops just before they were sent into battle at Saltville.

> On the march the Colored Soldiers as well as their white Officers were made the subject of much ridicule and many insulting remarks by the White Troops and in some instances petty outrages such as the pulling off the Caps of Colored Soldiers, stealing their horses etc was practiced by the White Soldiers. These insults as well as the jeers and taunts that they would not fight were borne by the Colored Soldiers patiently or punished with dignity by their Officers but in no instance did I hear Colored soldiers make any reply to insulting language used toward [them] by the White Troops.

Of the four hundred blacks who went into battle that day, over one hundred were killed or wounded. "On the return of the forces," recalled Brisbin, "those who had scoffed at the Colored Troops on the march out were silent."[115]

The most degrading aspect of military life for some black soldiers was the way they were often used as slave labor for white soldiers in the Union army. Colonel James C. Beecher, commanding a regiment of former North Carolina slaves, complained to superiors about his men being "put to work laying out and policing camps of white soldiers. . . . It is a drawback that they are regarded as, and called 'd——d Niggers' by so-called 'gentlemen' in uniform of U.S. Officers, but when they are set to menial work for white regiments what those Regiments are entitled to do for themselves, it simply throws them back where they were before and reduces them to the position of slaves again."[116]

As they had resisted inequitable pay, black soldiers also resisted inequitable treatment—especially treatment that reminded them too much of slavery. When one captain had a soldier tied up, just as a plantation overseer might have done, two of the victim's comrades freed him. Being free had to mean that one could not be bound, else what was the point of being free? One private cut a friend loose and ex-claimed, "No white son of a bitch can tie a man up here." In the 8th Kansas, after a West Point graduate had a black soldier tied up and sus-pended by his thumbs, the troops grabbed their rifles, freed the man, and ran all the officers out of camp. Twenty-six soldiers were soon un-der arrest, but regimental officers wisely let the matter drop.[117]

Most officers were not so generous. Blacks soldiers were charged with mutiny far more often, and punished much more severely, than their white brothers-in-arms. Though blacks accounted for roughly 10 percent of Union servicemen, almost 80 percent of those court-martialed and executed for mutiny were black. And those were the ones who received at least the formality of a hearing. Many did not. Robert Gould Shaw wrote of Colonel James Montgomery, who com-manded another regiment of blacks in the same brigade: "He shoots his men with perfect looseness, for a slight disobedience of orders." So did Lieutenant Francis Bichinel of the 36th U.S. Colored Troops, who shot a black soldier named Silas Holley for nothing more than "alleged stubbornness" and "manifesting a mutinous spirit." Had such traits been capital crimes nearly every soldier, black or white, would have been executed. From the officers' perspective, almost all were guilty of these shortcomings at one time or another.[118]

Poorly as most were treated, it is a testament to their tenacity that the desertion rate among black soldiers was only slightly above aver-age. For those who did desert, the complaint was almost always the same—they had been treated not as soldiers but as slaves. In Septem-ber 1864 Private Spencer Brown of the 5th U.S. Colored Troops de-serted to the Confederates. Prior to the desertion his comrades had heard him remark with disgust "that he was no better treated in the army than he was by his former master." Alfred Dickinson escaped from slavery in 1863 and joined the Union army. He deserted a year later. Confederate troops captured him still wearing his second-hand blue uniform. When asked why he had deserted, Dickinson replied that he had been treated hardly any better by the Yankees than the Rebels.[119]

"Come and Sit by Me"

Still, there were small signs that black soldiers' sacrifices were having at least some impact on white attitudes. Certainly those attitudes remained deeply racist and paternalistic. Many remained downright hostile. In February 1864, white thugs nearly killed a black soldier who walked into a Zanesville, Ohio, barbershop for a haircut. Such violence against blacks, even black soldiers, was fairly common. But there were also scenes that a year before would have been unimaginable. The same month that the Zanesville incident occurred, New York City saw its first black regiment formed, the 20th U.S. Colored Troops. Before it left for the front, supporters insisted on having the 20th parade down streets where blacks had been brutally beaten and murdered just seven months earlier during the draft riots. Now black soldiers marched boldly down those same streets, greeted as one witness recalled with "waving handkerchiefs, flowers [and] acclamation." At Union Square, Charles King, president of Columbia College, addressed the regiment and presented it with a flag along with a parchment scroll signed by those responsible for having the banner made. As King read the names aloud, there was one in particular that caught the attention and tugged at the hearts of everyone in the crowd— Mrs. Robert Gould Shaw. The *New York Times* saw the event as symbolic of a "prodigious revolution which the public mind everywhere is experiencing."[120]

Opposition to using blacks in the army was indeed beginning to crumble during the winter of 1864–65 as Pennsylvania, Ohio, Michigan, Indiana, Illinois, Connecticut, and New York organized black troops by the thousands. In the army too, attitudes were changing. Much as they had resisted it, most white soldiers gradually came to accept emancipation and blacks in the army as a necessary part of the war effort. Some even took pride in it. To one Massachusetts private, there was no question that it was "worth dying to attain . . . the freedom of every human being over whom the stars and stripes wave." Most took a more practical view of blacks in uniform. "I don't care if they are one ½ mile thick in front in every Battel," wrote one soldier. "They will stop Bullets as well as white people."[121] An Irish immigrant put that sentiment to verse.

> Some tell us 'tis a burnin' shame
> To make the naygers fight;
> An' that the thrade of bein' kilt
> Belongs but to the white.

But as for me, upon my soul!
So liberal are we here,
I'll let Sambo be murthered instead of myself
On every day of the year.

On every day in the year, boys,
And in every hour of the day;
The right to be kilt I'll divide wid him,
An' divil a word I'll say.[122]

There were also those white military men whose changing views of black soldiers reflected a more appreciative attitude. One officer from Wayland, Massachusetts, had been described by those who knew him as "a bitter pro-slavery man, violent and vulgar in his talk against abolitionists and 'niggers.'" But after serving with blacks in Louisiana, he was so impressed that he returned home a committed abolitionist. On a train bound for Boston, as a black soldier in uniform stepped onto the car, someone yelled: "*I'm not going to ride with niggers.*" The officer, in full uniform, rose from his seat for all to see and called out: "Come here, my good fellow! I've been fighting along side of people of your color, and glad enough I was to have 'em by my side. Come and sit by me."[123]

"Give Up Slavery and Gain Our Independence"

Confederate officers too were impressed with the effectiveness of black soldiers. It was they and their men, after all, who had been on the receiving end of black fighting skill. After Port Hudson, Milliken's Bend, and Fort Wagner, some Confederates began to imagine what had until then seemed unimaginable—freeing the slaves and arming them. By late 1863 perhaps half the army's men had deserted. Almost none were coming to take their places. If a way could not be found to fill the ranks, the war would be lost. Irish-born General Patrick Cleburne, commanding a division in the Army of Tennessee, was the first high-ranking Confederate to urge filling empty ranks with black troops. In January 1864 he pointed out that "for many years, ever since the agitation of the subject of slavery commenced, the negro has been

dreaming of freedom. . . . To attain it, he will tempt dangers and difficulties not exceeded by the bravest soldiers." Already blacks were
fighting "bravely," as Cleburne stressed, for their freedom in the
Union cause. Why not use that bravery to Confederate advantage?[124]

Southern slaveholders were generally reluctant to place weapons in
the hands of their slaves, but by the winter of 1864–65 the government was running out of options. Two-thirds of the Confederate army
had deserted and over a quarter-million men had been killed. In January 1865 General Robert E. Lee wrote to a friend that although he
considered "the relation of master and slave . . . the best that can exist
between the white and black races while intermingled as at present in
this country," slaves had already been freed and used by Lincoln to
crush the Confederacy. Why should the Confederacy not use them in
its own defense? He urged the Confederate Congress to authorize
slave enlistments immediately and adopt a plan for "gradual and general emancipation" following the war.[125]

Lee's men had mixed views on the matter. A month after the commanding general penned his sentiments, a North Carolina sergeant
wrote that men in his company were deserting over talk of freeing
blacks and putting them in the army. He too was considering it. "I did
not volunteer my services to fight for a free negroes country," he insisted. But a Louisiana sergeant took a more practical view: "If we
continue to lose ground as we have for the last 12 months, we will
soon be defeated, and then slavery will be gone any way, and I think
we should give up slavery and gain our independence." General John
B. Gordon polled his corps outside Petersburg and found that most of
its eighty-six hundred officers and men favored enlisting blacks even if
it meant emancipating them. Howell Cobb suspected that the men
supported black enlistment mainly because they thought it might better their chances of getting a furlough or discharge.[126]

Still there were those who would not support making blacks soldiers for any reason, though they were no less eager to get home.
Grant Taylor wrote home to his wife: "To think we have been fighting
four years to prevent the slaves from being freed, now to turn round
and free them to enable us to carry on the war. The thing is outra-
geous. . . . I say if the worst comes to the worst let it come and stop the
war at once and let us come home."[127] One way or another—with or
without black enlistment, with or without victory—soldiers just
wanted to go home.

On March 13, 1865, at the urging of General Lee and President Davis, the Confederate Congress finally authorized recruitment of up to three hundred thousand slaves. The legislation made no mention of freedom for those who agreed to serve, insisting that both the states and slaveholders must consent to any alteration in the legal standing of slave-soldiers. But in his General Order No. 14 implementing the program, Davis went a step further, stating that "no slave will be accepted as a recruit unless with his own consent and with the approbation of his master by a written instrument conferring . . . the rights of a freedman." It was not quite an emancipation proclamation. But it was a startling statement from the man who had for four years presided over a slaveholders' republic. And it was a frank admission that blacks had long since become, as one southern editor put it, "a sort of balance power in this contest, and that the side which succeeds in enlisting the feelings and in securing the active operation and services of the four millions of blacks, must ultimately triumph."[128]

The observation was true enough, but the Confederacy came to realize it far too late. No more than a few dozen blacks were ever enlisted under its banner. Sixty from Richmond's Jackson Hospital came under fire at Petersburg on March 11, 1865, as members of the Jackson Battalion, composed of three companies of white convalescents and two companies of black hospital workers. That was two days before the Confederate Congress authorized black enlistments. On very rare occasions throughout the war, blacks such as those at Jackson Hospital had been pressed into combat service, often with guns at their backs and their families held hostage in slavery. But no black units ever saw combat as congressionally authorized Confederate soldiers. No regiment of Confederate States Colored Troops was ever formed. By contrast, more than two hundred thousand blacks had joined Union forces by March 1865. Hundreds of thousands more were already free. They needed no favors from a near-dead Confederacy to secure that freedom. They were taking full measure of it themselves, especially black Union soldiers. One spoke with pride about how he had, "for once in his life . . . walked fearlessly and boldly through the streets of [a] southern city! And he did this without being required to take off his cap at every step, or to give all the side-walks to those lordly princes of the sunny south, the planters' sons!"[129]

"A Most Extraordinary Change"

Some took the opportunity their soldiering offered to get their friends and families out of slavery. In September of 1863 members of the 1st Louisiana Native Guards (U.S.) got permission to go on recruiting detail. They had more on their minds than recruiting soldiers. With signed passes in hand, they swept through southern Louisiana freeing slaves and taking them back to New Orleans. When slaveholders protested that they were loyal unionists in Union-held territory and that the Emancipation Proclamation did not apply there, the soldiers leveled their rifles and threatened to shoot anyone who stood in their way. At one plantation in St. Bernard Parish, five soldiers marched on their old master's house and freed their wives.[130]

The slaveholder was fortunate that he suffered only the loss of a few slaves. He might have suffered much more, as some did. William Harris of the 1st U.S. Colored Troops gave his former master a lashing so violent that "blood flew at every stroke." Harris then turned the whip over to three female slaves who "took turns in settling some old scores." Fortunately for slaveholders, such retribution was the exception rather than the rule. Most black soldiers were far more concerned with ending slavery than taking revenge on slaveholders. When slaveholders fell under the control of former slaves, violence rarely came of it.[131]

Major William Holden learned that firsthand, much to his relief. Henry, a former slave of his who had run off to join the Union army after Holden whipped him, came marching back one day leading a dozen more black soldiers. As a young slave who witnessed the homecoming later recalled:

> Now ole Major was sitting in his favorite chair on the porch when he saw Henry coming with those soldiers and he like to fell, he was that scairt. . . . poor ole Major thought Henry remembered that whipping. But Henry drew the men up in front of ole Major and he said, "This is my master, Major Holden. Honor him, men." And the men took off their caps and cheered old Major. And he nearly like to fell again— such a great big burden was off his shoulders then.

The soldiers took their seats at Holden's dining room table, where his wife served them a roast chicken feast. For a former slave to be served at his old master's table, something that would once have seemed impossible, brought a satisfaction that few but those once held in bondage could understand. For Henry, it was an image he would forever hold in his mind as a sign that his freedom was real.[132]

Another way in which former slaves sought to make their freedom real was by becoming literate. Forbidden by law to read or write as slaves, they eagerly embraced literacy as a hallmark of their new status as free people. "Children love the school as white children love a holiday," wrote a teacher at Port Royal, South Carolina. Older blacks loved the school too. One of its pupils was a 105-year-old man who had once served the Revolutionary War general Nathaniel Greene. An elderly black woman was asked why she would want to take the trouble to learn to read at her advanced age. She replied, "Because I want to read de Word of de Lord."[133]

Most of the early black schools were established at the freedpeople's expense, with local black preachers taking a lead role in the undertaking. Soon after slavery was abolished in Washington, the city's black churches turned their basements into free schools. Within weeks of Sherman taking Savannah there were five hundred black children attending schools supported by blacks themselves. In Tallahassee, black ministers established five schools and served as the first teachers. Soon after freedom came to slaves in Texas, there were nearly two thousand black students enrolled in "self-sustaining" schools. And in Little Rock, blacks established the Freedmen's School Society. Its mission was to set up the first free schools for Arkansas's children, black and white. Most poor whites being functionally illiterate at the time, it was efforts such as these that spurred a move toward free public education in the South.[134]

Northern abolitionists too aided the education movement. The New England Freedman's Aid Society and the National Freedmen's Relief Association were among the dozens of organizations that raised money for schools and sent volunteer teachers south. In March 1865, the federal government finally joined the effort with its creation of the Freedman's Bureau. By year's end, the Bureau had constructed 740 buildings for 1,314 teachers and 90,589 students. Between them, the Freedman's Bureau, northern abolitionists, and southern blacks established a system of public education that was unparalleled, even in the North. Daily attendance at New York state's public schools averaged 43 percent in 1865. Average daily attendance at Bureau schools in

Alabama was 79 percent. It was 82 percent in Virginia. One Freed-man's Bureau inspector wrote that no people on earth had ever dis-played "such a passion for education" as the South's former slaves.[135]

Charlotte Forten saw that passion up close. The daughter of es-caped slaves who had fled to Philadelphia years before, Forten volun-teered as a teacher for the Philadelphia Port Royal Relief Association. Soon after she arrived, she wrote to the famed abolitionist William Lloyd Garrison: "I wish some of those persons at the North who say the race is hopelessly and naturally inferior, could see the readiness with which these children, so long oppressed and deprived of every privilege, learn and understand." It was all part of an astounding tran-sformation that had taken place in Union-occupied areas of the south-eastern tidewater. Robert Gould Shaw, who knew Forten and her work well, remarked in a letter home of the former slaves's progress: "Can you imagine anything more wonderful . . . two years ago, their mas-ters were still here, the lords of the soil & of them. Now they all own a little themselves, go to school, to church, and work for wages. It is a most extraordinary change."[136]

Though Shaw may have assumed too little about prewar worship practices among Sea Island slaves, to attend school and be paid wages was certainly a new thing for them. So was owning land, but Shaw's comments on that subject did not tell the whole story. Planters often did move out as the Yankees closed in. When that happened slaves commonly assumed that the land on which their families had lived and worked, sometimes for generations, was now theirs. After Charles Pet-tigrew fled his Bonarva plantation in North Carolina, resident blacks divided the land and livestock among themselves and kept on farming. So did former slaves on nearby Somerset Place. When Yankee troops showed up at the Mississippi plantation of Joseph Davis, the Confed-erate president's brother, Davis was long gone and former slaves were running the place.[137]

They were doing a good job of it too, as were so many other blacks who now considered themselves freeholding farmers as well as free people. "Of all the elements represented in the [Mississippi] Valley," reported General Superintendent of Contrabands John Eaton, "the independent Negro cultivator was without doubt the most successful." Just as impressed was a Union soldier stationed at Plymouth, North Carolina, who went "among the negroes" to see for himself how they were getting along. "They were very intelligent," he wrote, "although they could neither read nor write." His visit also dispelled other myths he had heard so often. "There is no use in repeating that they are not capable of taking care of themselves and that they do not desire their freedom, for it is wholly false."[138]

"Slavery Under a Softer Name"

Unfortunately for former slaves, the notion that they held title to their land was just as false. As far as the federal government was concerned, the plantations were "abandoned" lands subject to federal confiscation and to being sold or leased for nonpayment of taxes. Blacks protested vigorously at the injustice of such a policy. If they had no land, how could they be free? They had worked the land all their lives. The land, they insisted, was theirs by right.

> We has a right to the land where we are located. For why? I tell you. Our wives, our children, our husbands had been sold over and over again to purchase the lands we now locates upon; for that reason we have a divine right to the land. . . . And den didn't we clear the land, and raise de crops ob corn, ob cotton, ob tobacco, ob rice, ob sugar, ob everything. And den didn't dem large cities in de North grow up on de cotton and de sugars and de rice dat we made? . . . I say dey has grown rich and my people is poor.[139]

Such was the reasoning of Virginia freedman Bayley Wyat, though the government was not listening to ex-slaves. In 1863, federal authorities began selling or leasing plantations, usually to favored clients. Most wound up in the hands of northern investors and cotton textile companies. Many went to army officers and government officials. What little was left went to those few freedmen who could afford to buy a little acreage. In South Carolina's Sea Islands auctions, the smallest parcels went to groups of freedmen who pooled their scarce funds for the purchases.[140]

Most plantations in Union-held territory remained in the hands of planters who quickly renounced their Confederate loyalties when the Yankees showed up. Those who had the opportunity to do so before January 1, 1863, when the Emancipation Proclamation went into effect, kept title to their land *and* their slaves. In areas reclaimed for the

Blacks—no longer slaves, but not quite free—working plantation lands in South Carolina. Having worked all their lives without pay, they frequently claimed the land as just compensation. But Lincoln's reconstruction plan returned both land and political power to the planters. Federal troops were used to enforce labor contracts that effectively reenslaved southern blacks. Wendell Phillips complained: "Such reconstruction makes freedom of the negro a sham, and perpetuates Slavery under a softer name." (Planting sweet potatoes, Hopkinson's Plantation, Edisto Island, South Carolina, photograph by H.P. Moore, 1862. Collection of the New-York Historical Society.)

Union after that date, slaves were technically free. But in fact the new "freedom" looked much like the old slavery. Federal policy governing plantations, whether owned or leased, called for keeping blacks on the land as contract laborers or sharecroppers. Though nominally free, nothing was given to them for free. Supplies from plantation stores were doled out on credit, but with markups controlled by the planters. Those markups, which reached as high as 200 percent, were designed to total slightly more than any income workers could produce. Inevitably, when crops were harvested and sold, the workers' profit share rarely covered their debt. At one northern-leased plantation in Louisiana, former slaves ended their first year of freedom with debts ranging from four cents to more than twelve dollars. One of the families showed earnings of $184. Their debt at the plantation store was $190.[141]

Thus freed people were trapped in debt slavery, sometimes called the "new slavery," and it was backed by federal force. Government-sanctioned contracts forbade workers to leave the plantations without their employer's permission. Provost marshals were authorized to round up "vagrant" blacks and to discipline those who resisted the new labor arrangement. It seemed to African Americans and white sympathizers alike, as historian Eric Foner put it, "that the army was acting more like a slave patrol than an agent of emancipation."[142]

Lincoln did little to reassure those who questioned his commitment to slavery's permanent abolition when, in December 1863, he issued his Proclamation of Amnesty and Reconstruction. Under the Constitution's authority granting him power to issue "reprieves and pardons for offences against the United States," Lincoln declared that any Confederate state would be allowed to reestablish a federally recognized state government when a number of its citizens—totaling at least 10 percent of those who had voted in the 1860 presidential election—took an oath of loyalty to the United States and promised to abide by congressional acts and presidential edicts regarding slavery. Any newly formed government applying for recognition must have no provision in its constitution "contravening said oath."[143]

Lincoln's "10 percent plan," as it came to be called, did not quite settle the issue of slavery's future in the succeeded states once they were readmitted. As Lincoln stated in the proclamation itself, all acts and edicts of the federal government in reference to slavery were war measures subject to being "modified or declared void by decision of the Supreme Court." Nor did Lincoln's plan insure any legal protections for newly freed African Americans. Wendell Phillips, a longtime abolitionist from Boston, complained that Lincoln's plan restored "all power into the hands of the unchanged white race." Phillips pointed to the newly reconstructed government in Louisiana where, with Lincoln's backing, General Nathaniel Banks was forcing blacks into labor contracts, and debt slavery, at the point of federal bayonets. "Such reconstruction," wrote Phillips, "makes freedom of the negro a sham, and perpetuates Slavery under a softer name."[144]

Congress worried that to require only 10 percent of the state's voters to swear loyalty to the United States might invite future rebellion. To counter that threat, Congress passed the Wade-Davis bill, requiring 50 percent of the number voting in 1860 to take a loyalty oath before southern state governments could be reorganized. Wade-Davis also contained guarantees of equality under the law for blacks, though there was no reference to black voting rights. Not wanting to repudiate his new Louisiana government reconstructed under the 10 percent plan, Lincoln refused to sign the Wade-Davis bill and let it die by pocket veto. The bill's sponsors responded with a "manifesto" printed in newspapers throughout the country criticizing the president for "dictatorial usurpation."[145]

"I Was Not for Mr. Lincoln"

Among those most upset with Lincoln was Frederick Douglass. He blasted the 10 percent plan as "an entire contradiction of the constitutional idea of the Republican Government." After promising freedom for the slaves and asking them to fight for the Union, Lincoln was now prepared to "hand the Negro back to the political power of his former master, without a single element of strength to shield himself." That fear drove Douglass, along with allies like Wendell Phillips and Elizabeth Cady Stanton, to break with the Republicans and support the newly formed Radical Democratic Party. In May 1864, party delegates met in Cleveland and nominated John C. Frémont as their candidate for president that year. The convention's platform called for equality under the law for all men regardless of race, protection of civil liberties in areas not under martial law, congressional rather than presidential control of reconstruction, distribution of confiscated rebel plantations to soldiers and resident former slaves, and a constitutional amendment abolishing slavery.[146]

Few party members had any real hope that Frémont could win the November election. The more politically astute hoped only that the threat of a radical splinter party might force Republicans either to dump Lincoln at their upcoming convention or at least make their party platform more friendly to blacks. It did neither. When the allied Union Party, comprising Republicans and War Democrats, met on June 7 in Baltimore, Lincoln easily won the delegates' support. As for their platform, the only plank it had in common with Frémont's party was its call for ending slavery by constitutional amendment.[147]

Republicans had long been moving toward support for such an amendment in any case. Some were surely moved at least in part by altruism, but racism and practical politics were the prime motive forces. Large numbers of slaves flooding into Union lines, along with the army's effort to move them on to northern cities, convinced many in Congress that ending slavery was the only way to keep blacks in the South. Constitutional abolition as one element of a racial containment policy was beginning to sway War Democrats as well. Certainly racial containment was viewed as the most palatable way to sell northern voters on the idea of an emancipation amendment. Still, most leading politicians so feared being branded "nigger worshippers" that few were willing to lead a public charge for such an amendment. The main push would come from below.[148]

Organized efforts for statutory emancipation began in the spring of 1863 when Elizabeth Cady Stanton and Susan B. Anthony established the Women's Loyal National League and led it in a petition drive aimed at pressuring Congress for a national emancipation act. They sent out speakers, circulated petitions, and organized League affiliates across the North. The American Anti-Slavery Society soon joined the petition effort, sending speakers of their own far and wide. One of their lecturers was William Andrew Jackson, a former slave who had once belonged to Jefferson Davis.

Though Stanton, Anthony, and their allies at first called only for an abolition act, they quickly shifted their focus after Lincoln announced in December 1863 that the Confiscation Acts and the Emancipation Proclamation were nothing more than war measures that might be voided by the Supreme Court once the war was over. The only way to head off that possibility was with a constitutional amendment abolishing slavery. Within a few weeks, Stanton and Anthony were ready to send Senator Charles Sumner one hundred thousand signatures calling for just that. On February 9, 1864, in a gesture both solemn and symbolic, two black men carried the petitions into the U.S. Senate chamber and laid them on Sumner's desk. Sumner then addressed the Senate. "This petition is signed by one hundred thousand men and women, who unite in this unparalleled manner to support its prayer," he told his colleagues. "They are from all parts of the country and every condition of life. . . . Here they are, a mighty army, one hundred thousand strong, without arms or banners, the advanced guard of a yet larger army." Two months later, on April 8, the Senate passed what would eventually become the Thirteenth Amendment and sent it on to the House of Representatives.[149]

Signatures from the "larger army" of which Sumner spoke poured into House offices over the next few months. By July the list of names totaled nearly four hundred thousand. Lincoln himself, along with the Union Party platform, gave the amendment at least grudging support. Though conservative on granting the rights of full citizenship to blacks, Lincoln knew that he would need the help of the Radicals to win reelection. And he would need the help of blacks to win the war. "Any different policy in regard to the colored man," Lincoln admitted, "deprives us of his help. . . . This is not a question of sentiment or taste, but one of physical force which may be measured and estimated as horse-power and Steam-power are measured and estimated. Keep it and you can save the Union. Throw it away, and the Union goes with it."[150]

Despite backing from Lincoln and the Union Party, the amendment's sponsors could not muster the two-thirds vote in the House necessary to get it passed and sent to the states for ratification. There was too much fear among House Democrats. Many of them had been elected in 1862 on platforms opposing abolition. Now another election year was upon them, and "abolitionist" was still a dirty word among large segments of the northern electorate—so much so that even some of the amendment's backers began calling themselves "emancipationists" as a signal that they supported only nominal freedom, and no more than that, for enslaved blacks. Whatever its implications, the amendment could not threaten white supremacy.[151]

That assurance was not enough to sway House Democrats in the summer of 1864. Nor did it carry much weight with the party as a whole. At their August convention, Democrats refused to support the emancipation amendment. Even their support for maintaining the Union was considerably vague. They adopted a platform promising to halt the fighting, call a convention of all the states, and restore the federal Union. But the question of whether any Confederate state would willingly participate in a convention was left entirely aside. So was the question of slavery, although the Democratic nominee, George McClellan, did say that any state returning to the Union under his administration would receive a full guarantee of its constitutional rights. McClellan's implied message was that the right to hold slaves would be safe.[152]

It was too much for many of the Radicals. Some began encouraging Frémont to drop out of the race. As weak as Lincoln was on anything but nominal freedom for blacks, he did at least seem committed on that point. McClellan, on the other hand, seemed bent on preserving slavery as a constitutional right. That was the last thing Frémont and the Radicals wanted. Lincoln's reelection chances improved with the fall of Atlanta on September 2, 1864, but fear remained that Frémont might still draw enough Radical votes to give McClellan the presidency. After meeting in mid-September with a delegation from the White House, Frémont unconditionally suspended his bid for the presidency and threw his support to Lincoln. "It became evident," Frémont later explained, "that Mr. Lincoln could not be elected if I remained in the field." And he may have been right. After one of the most racist campaigns in U.S. history—with Democrats charging that Lincoln wanted not just freedom but equality as well for blacks, and Republicans denying the accusation at every turn—Lincoln won the popular vote in November by no more than a questionable 10 percent margin.[153]

Stung by Lincoln's colonization plan to send blacks into exile, disgusted by his reconstruction plan that left blacks virtually enslaved, Frederick Douglass and other "Radicals" backed John C. Frémont for president in the summer of 1864. But when it looked as if his candidacy might throw the election to the proslavery McClellan, Frémont withdrew from the race and most Radicals went for Lincoln. "When there was any shadow of a hope," wrote Douglass, "that a man of a more decided anti-slavery conviction and policy could be elected, I was not for Mr. Lincoln." (Library of Congress)

Though they had succeeded in keeping McClellan out of the White House, Radicals were not enthusiastic about giving Lincoln a second term. "When there was any shadow of a hope," wrote Frederick Douglass, "that a man of a more decided anti-slavery conviction and policy could be elected, I was not for Mr. Lincoln." Still, Lincoln did stand by the party platform, at least publicly. A month after his re-election, Lincoln pushed the House to approve the Senate's proposed emancipation amendment. Taking the election's outcome as a referendum, House members finally granted approval in a lame-duck session on January 31, 1865. The proposed Thirteenth Amendment ending slavery went out to the states for ratification with Lincoln's blessing. But that was as far as Lincoln was willing to go. He kept firm control of Reconstruction, stuck to his 10 percent plan, and left the fate of free blacks in the hands of their former masters. What freedom blacks could wrest out of that relationship would be of their own making, not Lincoln's.[154]

From the war's beginning, Lincoln's prime concern had been keeping the South and its cotton wealth in the Union. Even after Congress sent the Thirteenth Amendment out, Lincoln was not beyond backtracking on emancipation if doing so could serve his ends. Lincoln demonstrated that on February 3, 1865, when he and Secretary of State William Seward met with three Confederate officials at Hampton Roads, Virginia, to talk about ending the war. Vice President Alexander Stephens, heading the Confederate delegation, asked for a cease-fire, to be followed by further talks between the two governments. Lincoln replied that such a move was impossible. It would be tantamount to official recognition of the Confederacy. He told Stephens that the Rebels could have an armistice at any time simply by laying down their weapons and acknowledging the Union's supremacy. Seward quickly added that the southern states would still have all their constitutional rights, implying the right to hold slaves. Lincoln, to the Confederates' astonishment, supported Seward's comment by again calling the Emancipation Proclamation a war measure whose application could end with the war. It was hardly less than McClellan had promised during his bid for the presidency. As for the Thirteenth Amendment, though it had been approved by Congress, it had not yet been ratified by the states. Seward pointed out that the southern states could rob the amendment of its required three-fourths approval of the states if they quickly rejoined the Union.[155]

The meeting ended where it began, with Stephens requesting an armistice, leaving the question of union open. Lincoln continued to insist on union as a condition of further talks. But he remained flexible on the question of slavery and was not shy about saying so, at least to close associates. He made clear to Representative James Singleton that "he would be willing to grant peace with an amnesty, and restoration of the union, leaving slavery to abide the decisions of judicial tribunals." A few weeks before the Hampton Roads conference, Lincoln told Orville Browning, a longtime friend and former senator from Illinois, that he "never entertained the purpose of making the abolition of slavery a condition precedent to the termination of the war, and the restoration of the Union."[156] Lincoln's ambiguous attitude toward blacks mirrored that of most northern whites. How former slaves might fare in the war's aftermath was of little concern to them. If, as the price of reunion, southern blacks suffered virtual reenslavement at the hands of a resurgent slavocracy, so be it.

During the war, an enslaved seventy-year-old Georgia grandmother gathered her twenty-two children and grandchildren, loaded them all on a discarded flatboat, and drifted forty hazardous miles down the Savannah River. After a Union vessel brought them on board, the old woman, as one officer recalled, "rose to her full height, with her youngest grandchild in her arms, and said only 'My God! Are we free?' "[157] The answer Lincoln and the country finally gave was "No, not entirely."

7

"Indians Here Have No Fight with the Whites"

Kill them wherever you can find them.[1]

—JAMES H. CARLETON, GENERAL, U.S. ARMY

Nothing lives long, except the earth and the mountains.[2]

—WHITE ANTELOPE, CHIEF, SOUTHERN CHEYENNE

"The National Resources"

That former slaves found themselves not entirely free was disappointing but hardly surprising to those who took careful measure of Lincoln's words and deeds. For an increasing number of freedmen and women, Lincoln seemed less the Great Emancipator and more the Great Equivocator. But then, as Lincoln apologists have stressed for nearly a century and a half, the man was a product of his time and place. Lincoln was indeed that—a product of his time in politics and his place in that social order. His wartime objectives were in perfect accord with those of most northern elites who, from the earliest days of the secession crisis, had insisted on saving the Union with or without regard to slavery. Were the Union to fail, those men stood to lose billions in investments along with ready access to the South's cotton and other resources. Congress controlled interstate commerce and, with their dominance in the House of Representatives, northern business elites controlled Congress. As long as the South remained in the Union, businessmen of the North largely controlled the flow of southern commerce as well. To those who backed Lincoln's war effort politically and financially, the Union was not an abstract ideal to be valued in itself. It was, and had always been, a speculative enterprise serving those with the economic capital and political influence to control raw materials, production, markets, and labor. Resources, including those of the South, served to fuel their money-making machine.

The West too had resources, which both the Union and Confederacy sought to control. Especially important to Confederate officials was the Indian Territory (now Oklahoma), just west and north respectively of the Confederate states of Arkansas and Texas. If the nearly one hundred thousand Indians there could be brought under its control, the Confederacy could use them to shore up its western defenses. The New Mexico Territory too, encompassing the modern states of New Mexico and Arizona, was a prize on which the Confederacy had its eye. If Confederates secured that ground, they could control the newly discovered gold fields of Pinos Altos and threaten southern California. The federal government would have to move quickly to head them off.[3]

Even in those vast stretches of the West where there was no Confederate threat, Federal forces used the war as an excuse to quicken the pace of killing Native Americans and driving the survivors from their homelands. In the eyes of most whites, those lands hardly belonged to the Indians in any case. Lincoln expressed typical imperialist assumptions when he noted that "the national resources . . . are unexhausted, and, as we believe, inexhaustible." Western resources belonged to the nation—Lincoln's nation, not the Indians'—and Lincoln wanted those resources for his war effort. Businessmen wanted them for the profits they could bring. If Indians stood in the way, they were by definition threats to national security and obstacles to "progress." As such, they were subject to extermination.[4]

Elites were backed in their dispossession scheme by hordes of lower-class whites clamoring for western homesteads, though common homesteaders ultimately got only 3.5 percent of western lands.[5] Even so, thousands of them—disinclined to face Confederate battle lines—eagerly slaughtered heathen as well as Christian Indians for

God, for country, or for whatever small plunder might fall their way. Gold and silver strikes in California, Colorado, Nevada, and the Pacific Northwest drove much of the killing. So did the desire for timber, minerals, and transportation routes for mail carriers, stage lines and a proposed transcontinental railroad. Some tribes expressed a willingness to share their lands, realizing only too late that sharing was the last thing whites had in mind. What followed would be but the latest chapter in an old story of indigenous peoples struggling to survive the ravages of an aggressively expansive American empire. Remnants of Indian nations remaining east of the Mississippi River had long and bitter experience with white expansion. Most had been forced off their lands well before the Civil War era. For those remaining, the war posed new challenges in their struggle to adapt and survive.

"Without Our Consent"

Almost every Civil War enthusiast has heard of Ely Parker, the full-blooded Seneca Indian who, as Grant's military secretary, transcribed the terms of Lee's surrender at Appomattox. A grand sachem (hereditary chief) of New York's Iroquois League, Parker worked hard at the study of law and engineering before a chance prewar acquaintance with Grant landed him a position on the general's wartime staff. Parker continued to serve as Grant's aide-de-camp until 1869 when Grant became president. Grant then appointed Parker commissioner of Indian Affairs, the first Native American to hold that office. Parker later played the Wall Street markets with mixed results before taking a civil post in New York.

Though affable, accomplished, and well connected, Parker never had quite the impact on whites that he might have hoped. Far from serving as an ambassador of the common humanity between whites and Indians, he was little more than an out-of-place oddity to all but his closest friends. "To many," wrote one of Parker's biographers, "he was simply 'the Indian,' a quiet curiosity at the headquarters of the army or the salons of New York society."[6] That image has changed little over the past century and a half. Among many Civil War buffs, Parker remains "the Indian"—the only Indian they ever heard of who served in the war.

Far more typical of the twenty thousand Indians in Civil War armies was Austin George, a Connecticut private of Pequot and Mohegan descent. In the 1850s, following an old pattern, Connecticut forcefully confiscated and sold off Pequot lands. What little money the expelled Pequots were due in compensation was siphoned off by corrupt state officials. Some Pequots such as George found employment in the whaling industry but were laid off when whaling declined during the war years. Desperate for income and barred from occupations dominated by white labor, some Pequots enlisted for the state and local bounties they were paid. Austin George became a private with the 31st United States Colored Infantry Regiment, Army of the Potomac. In those days, the term "colored" referred to Indians as well as blacks.[7]

Despite dire economic straits, not all northeastern Indians were ready to risk their lives at the front. Ready or not, though, some whites tried to force them. When state recruiters in Norwich and Montville, Connecticut, tried to conscript Mohegans to meet their enrollment quotas, the Indians fired off an angry protest to the War Department. Reporting that state officials had "taken the liberty to enroll some of the said Mohegan tribe for the present draft without our consent," they reminded Washington that the Constitution barred states from exercising authority over Indian nations. Only the federal government could do that. There is no record of the Mohegans having received a reply.[8]

In the Midwest, those Indians who still had a good deal of land to lose took a different approach. In Michigan especially, growing numbers of whites began crowding lands bordering Ottawa and Ojibwa (Chippewa) territory throughout 1861 and 1862. The Indians knew that demands for more land would soon be coming from Washington. In an ultimately futile attempt to win government favor and save their land, they formed Company K of the 1st Michigan Sharpshooters. Led by Lieutenant Garrett A. Gravaraet, an Indian of Franco-Ottawa descent, this company of mainly Ottawas and Ojibwas, together with representatives from the Delaware, Huron, Oneida, and Potawatomi nations, became the most famous Indian unit to serve the Union.[9]

"Now in a Starving Condition"

Like their northern cousins, scattered Indian peoples remaining in the South weighed their options. In South Carolina's tiny Catawba band, numbering just fifty-five, almost every adult male joined the Confederate army. Long since stripped of their own land, most were day laborers working plantation lands that had once belonged to their ancestors. Impoverished and dependent, the enlistment bounty of fifty dollars was very attractive for these men. They were too few to form a company of their own, and there were no "colored" units for them to join. So they fought alongside their white neighbors in several South Carolina volunteer regiments of the Army of Northern Virginia. These were among the Civil War's few racially integrated units.[10]

Most southern Indians simply tried to stay out of the white man's war. Some were more successful than others. The Florida Seminoles maintained neutrality while allowing both the Union and the Confederacy to court them. In exchange for gifts and supplies, they shrewdly held out the possibility of an alliance without ever committing to either side. The Pamunkeys of Virginia's lower-tidewater region tried to remain neutral as well. Then in the summer of 1862 Union forces invaded their land, stealing much of the Pamunkeys' livestock and forcing some of them to serve as guides and river pilots. When Confederates retook that section of the state, they rounded up Indians suspected of helping the Yankees and sent them to a Richmond prison.[11]

The Lumbees of eastern North Carolina began the war as neutrals but became solidly pro-Union after Confederates began conscripting them to do forced labor. Lumbee guerilla bands took revenge by raiding Confederate supply depots, tearing up rail lines, and doing whatever else they could to disrupt Rebel military operations. Some Indians were conscripted to serve as soldiers, though they proved to be no less resentful than those conscripted for labor. In the spring of 1863, Eastern Choctaws drafted into the 1st Choctaw Battalion, Mississippi Cavalry, deserted en masse to the Federals just before the Vicksburg campaign got underway.[12]

Some North Carolina Cherokees expressed a willingness to serve the Confederacy, but racism nearly kept them out of the ranks. William Thomas, an influential friend of the Cherokees, tried to get a state bill passed authorizing him to raise a Cherokee battalion. The legislature voted it down, citing fears that such a bill might confer citizenship on the Cherokees. In fact, the Cherokees were already citizens of North Carolina, though rarely treated as such, by virtue of previous treaty agreements. One of the bill's leading opponents quipped that he would as soon be seen alongside free blacks at a voting booth as to associate with Cherokees. Undeterred by the setback, Thomas sought Jefferson Davis's permission to enlist Cherokees. Davis readily agreed, giving Thomas a colonel's commission and authorizing him to raise several battalions, one of which was made up entirely of Cherokees. From early 1862 through the war's end, Thomas's Legion of Cherokee Indians and Highlanders—better known simply as Thomas's Legion—ranged through the mountains of western North Carolina and eastern Tennessee enforcing conscription, impressing supplies, and rooting out Union sympathizers.[13]

Many of those Union sympathizers were themselves Cherokee, deserters from Thomas's Legion among them. By 1863, Cherokee soldiers' families were feeling the effects of war. Hunger stalked the Cherokee district as corn meal, flour, and salt became almost impossible to get. In February 1864, Thomas wrote to his superiors that his soldiers' families were "now in a starving condition" and begged assistance for them. None came. Soon the Indians were eating weeds and tree bark to survive. As with so many other Rebel soldiers, hard times turned hundreds of Cherokees against the Confederacy. Some deserted and moved their families out of the region. Others switched sides and joined the Yankees. One group of Cherokees aided Union Colonel George Kirk during his raid through the mountains in June 1864. From then until the war's close, they served in Kirk's 3rd North Carolina Mounted Infantry Volunteers.[14]

"Our Wish Is for Peace"

Further west, peoples of the Indian Territory, often called the Nations since it was occupied by several Indian nations, were also divided in their views about which side to support. Most had no great love for southerners. It was southerners, after all, who now occupied the homelands from which most Indian Territory residents had been removed just a generation earlier. On the other hand, it was the hated government in Washington that had forced their removal from the East. If the Rebels could make good their independence from Washington, perhaps the Indians could too. Supporting the Confederacy might be a first step toward reestablishing sovereign nationhood for themselves. Besides, some of the Nations' most influential chiefs were slaveholders who identified more with the South than the North. Even the territory's majority nonslaveholders, who were inclined to shy away from the Confederacy, had issues with the Federals. Republican leaders, in violation of numerous treaties, had for some time openly supported settling whites in Indian Territory. Now Republicans controlled Washington, and Indians feared a forced removal should they remain in the Union.[15]

The climax came in early 1861 when Washington withheld annuity payments due under treaty obligations for fear that the funds might fall into Rebel hands. Furthermore, to consolidate their forces in the East, Federal troops evacuated their garrisons in the Nations. Without military protection, newly appointed U.S. Indian agents refused to enter the Nations. It seemed to the Indians that Washington had abandoned them. Some feared a Confederate invasion; others thought the time was right to make a bid for independence. Whatever their motives, and most were mixed, the Choctaws were first to act. Their council authorized its chief to assure the seceded states that their "natural affections, education, institutions, and interests" were with the Confederacy. Then the Chickasaw Nation issued its own declaration of independence and made clear its support for Confederate independence as well.[16]

Richmond seized the opportunity and sent Albert Pike, a well-known Arkansas editor and attorney, to negotiate alliance treaties in Indian Territory. By July, the Choctaw and Chickasaw councils were firmly in the Confederate camp. The two nations signed treaties with Pike and organized a mounted rifle regiment for Confederate service. In exchange, they got better terms than they had ever received from the United States. Under the new treaties, Richmond assumed all financial obligations of old agreements with the United States, guaranteed tribal land rights, promised the Nations self-government within their territorial boundaries, and let the Indians send delegates to the new Confederate Congress.[17]

Though Richmond's terms seemed more friendly than Washington's, whites could no more be trusted South than North. Pike had taken pains to portray himself as the Indians' benefactor and the Confederacy as their protector. But in a letter to Jefferson Davis, Pike spoke of the Indian Territory's agricultural fertility, its mineral resources, and how the Confederacy could use them to its advantage with or without Indian consent. The "concessions" made to the Indians, Pike wrote, "are really far more for *our* benefit than for *theirs*; and that it is *we* . . . who are interested to have this country . . . opened to settlement and made into a State"—a state populated, of course, by free whites and enslaved blacks.[18]

The Chickasaws and Choctaws were quickest to be lured in by Pike, largely because of geography. Both nations had lands bordering the Red River, the boundary they shared with Texas, and were more isolated from Union-held Kansas. Other tribes needed more convincing. John Ross, principal chief of the Cherokees, tried for months to steer a neutral course. "I am—the Cherokees are—your friends and the friends of your people," he wrote to Confederate officials, "but we do not wish to be brought into the feuds between yourselves and your Northern Brethren. Our wish is for peace. Peace at home and Peace among you." The Confederacy's Commissioner of Indian Affairs David Hubbard wrote asking Ross to reconsider, arguing that southerners had always been more honorable in their dealings with Indians than had northerners. To that claim Ross replied, "but few Indians now press their feet upon the banks of either the Ohio or Tennessee."[19]

Ross was supported in his bid for neutrality by the Keetowah fac-

CHIEF JOHN ROSS

John Ross, principal chief of the Cherokees, tried to steer a neutral course. "I am—the Cherokees are—your friends," he told Confederate officials, "but we do not wish to be brought into the feuds between yourselves and your Northern Brethren. Our wish is for peace." But Federal withdrawal from Indian Territory (now Oklahoma) in 1861 forced the region's tribes into Confederate alliances. When the Federals tried to return, some Indians switched sides and the territory became a bloody killing ground. (Oklahoma State University)

tion, made up mostly of nonslaveholding full-bloods who advocated traditional Cherokee ways. Also known as Pin Cherokees for the crossed pins they wore as insignia, the Keetowahs generally held mixed-bloods and slavery in low regard, though Ross himself was a mixed-blood slaveholder of only one-eighth Cherokee ancestry. Opposing the Keetowahs were the Knights of the Golden Circle, or the Blue Lodge, composed mainly of slaveholding mixed-bloods. Animosities between the two factions went back to removal days when most full-bloods refused to go voluntarily while the mixed-bloods were more willing to deal with their white cousins. Though the issues were now different, the tale of conflicts among whites driving a wedge between the Indians was a familiar one. Led by Stand Watie (ironically, at only one-quarter short of full blood, more ethnically Cherokee than Ross), the Blue Lodge pressed for a Confederate alliance to help protect them "from the ravages of abolitionists." Already Watie had unofficially raised a force of mixed-blood Cherokee cavalry for Confederate service.[20]

The issue came to a head in August 1861 at a Cherokee national conference. By that time the Rebels had turned back a major Union advance in July at Bull Run. Only days earlier, on August 10, the Union had suffered defeat again at the Battle of Wilson's Creek in Missouri, just across the border from Cherokee lands in Indian Territory. Some of Watie's men, though not Watie himself, had helped beat back the Federals at Wilson's Creek and were credited with a pivotal role in the Rebel victory. It seemed clear that the Confederacy had all but secured its independence, and with the help of Cherokees at that.[21]

To the four thousand Cherokees assembled at Tahlequah, the path of wisdom seemed clear. Washington had abandoned them, and the Confederacy offered better terms. Already Indian Territory was bounded on three sides by the Confederacy. John Ross himself bowed to the inevitable, pointing out that "the Indian Nations about us have severed their connection with the United States and joined the Confederate States. Our general interest is inseparable from theirs and it is not desirable that we should stand alone." His overriding objective, as Ross later explained, was unity among the Cherokees as well as the Nations. "Union is strength," he wrote, "dissension is weakness, misery, ruin." The Keetowahs reluctantly agreed. A few weeks later the Cherokees met with Albert Pike at Tahlequah and bound themselves to the Confederacy. Ross offered the Cherokee home guard regiment, manned by Keetowahs under Ross's ally Colonel John Drew, for Confederate service.[22]

Also signing with the Confederacy at Tahlequah were bands of Osage, Quapaw, Seneca, and Shawnee Indians, all of them previously forced to settle in Indian Territory after expulsion from their eastern homelands. Pike was in high spirits. Already at the Wichita Agency he had secured treaties with most of the Indian Territory's western tribes, among them bands of Tonkawa, Caddo, Waco, Wichita, and Comanche. It seemed that all the Territory Nations, along with their various factions, would soon fall in line and support the Confederacy. The major remaining holdouts were a faction of Creeks together with some of their close cousins, the Seminoles.[23]

"Now the Wolf Has Come"

When the Creeks (or Muskogees in their own language) signed a treaty with Pike on July 10, 1861, and placed a Creek regiment in Confederate service, they had been among the first of the Nations to do so. However, that treaty bore the signatures only of mixed-blood tribal leaders, among them Motey Kennard, Chilly McIntosh, and Daniel McIntosh. No full-bloods had been present. They consistently and passionately refused even to meet with Pike. What divided the mixed- and full-bloods among the Creeks reflected divisions among those of other tribes. And their feud went all the way back to pre-removal days when mixed-bloods, especially the McIntosh, frequently betrayed their own countrymen in favor of the whites. The full-blood Chief Opothleyahola, an old but still energetic man of eighty in 1861, remembered well how the McIntosh and their mixed-blood allies had fought alongside the whites against their brethren during the Creek War of 1813–14. He would never forget how William McIntosh helped General Andrew Jackson slaughter his kinsmen at the Battle of Horseshoe Bend. Nor would he forget how the McIntosh had bargained away Muskogee lands in the East for personal gain.[24]

There were also serious divisions among the Seminoles, most of whom were ethnically Muskogee. Pro-Confederate tribal leaders like John Jumper, an ordained minister, not only signed on with the Confederacy but eagerly recruited Seminoles to enlist with the Creek regiment. But Billy Bowlegs Alligator and others among the more traditionalist chiefs rebuffed Pike's overtures and refused to take sides. They followed the lead of Opothleyahola, who had long counseled Indian neutrality in the coming war between the whites. His heart, recalled a Creek resident of the Nations, "was sad at all the war talk. He visited the homes of his followers or any of the Indians and gave them encouragement to face all these things, but above all things to stay out of the war." At a council of the Nations, Opothleyahola urged his fellow Indians to hold themselves above "this white man's war." It came as a painful blow to Opothleyahola when Ross and the Cherokees sided with the Confederacy. Still the old chief refused to give in.[25]

By September more than seven thousand Indians—women and men, young and old, all forced to accept war or exile—gathered on the Little River near Opothleyahola's lands. Most were Creeks and Seminoles. There were antiwar Indians from other tribes too, among them bands of Chickasaw, Kickapoo, Shawnee, Delaware, Wichita, and Comanche. They were doing well for the moment, but winter was coming and the refugees needed help. That help was due them from the federal government, and Opothleyahola wrote to "the President our Great Father" reminding Lincoln of his treaty obligations.

> You said that in our new homes we should be defended from all interference from any people and that no white people in the whole world should ever molest us . . . the land should be ours as long as the grass grew or waters run, and should we be injured by anybody you would come with your soldiers & punish them . . . now the wolf has come, men who are strangers tread our soil, our children are frightened & the mothers cannot sleep for fear. . . . When we made our Treaty at Washington you assured us that our children would laugh around our houses without fear & we believed you. . . . We do not hear from you & we send a letter, & we pray you to answer. Your children want to hear your word. . . . I well remember the treaty. My ears are open & my memory is good.[26]

Lincoln's ears were not open. Opothleyahola received no reply.

More antiwar Indians joined Opothleyahola over the next few months. November found nearly nine thousand of them encamped on the banks of Little River. There they planned to wait out the war in peace. Though Opothleyahola refused to meet with Confederate officials lest he be suspected of collusion, he did send word that he and his followers posed no danger to the Confederacy. Still, this nonaligned enclave in the heart of Indian Territory worried Confederate officials. Could it become a recruiting ground for the Federals? Already it was a haven for runaway slaves. Might those freedmen arm themselves and spread slave revolt among the Nations? There was no evidence of such a plan. But Colonel Douglas Cooper, commanding Confederate forces in Indian Territory, decided that the risk was too great. He called his Indian troops together for a campaign against the "unionists" on Little River. With his Choctaw-Chickasaw and Creek-Seminole regiments, along with cavalry from Texas, Cooper set out promising either to compel Opothleyahola's submission or drive him and his people from the territory. Mirroring the larger national conflict, Cooper resolved that if unity among the Nations could not be achieved by consensus, it would be imposed at the point of a gun.[27]

Warned of Cooper's planned assault, the old chief and his followers broke camp and struck out for Kansas. It was an arduous journey. Cold and hunger took their toll, but it was the pursuing Confederates that made the trek most deadly. In late November, Cooper caught up with the refugees at Round Mountain just northwest of Tulsa and charged their camp. Opothleyahola's men ambushed the attackers, then set the prairie on fire to cover their retreat as they broke camp and headed north. Cooper stayed in hot pursuit. Reinforced by John Drew's Keetowah regiment, Cooper again sighted his prey on December 8 at Bird Creek. He ordered an assault for the next morning. During the night, though, nearly all the Keetowahs deserted—most of them had never wanted to join the Confederates in the first place. Undeterred by this reduction in force, Cooper stuck to his plan, and on December 9 his remaining troops went in on the assault. Unexpectedly, out on Cooper's right, the Texans began taking heavy fire on their flank. It was a group of the missing Keetowahs, almost four hundred of them, who were now fighting for Opothleyahola and his refugees. The Texans reeled back but refused to break. Fighting continued, neither side giving way, until night made it impossible to tell friend from foe. Reluctantly, Cooper moved his men back to camp five miles from the battle site. Opothleyahola's men broke off as well and continued their flight to Kansas.[28]

Short on supplies, Cooper fell back to Fort Gibson near the Cherokee capital of Tahlequah. There he was met by a force of nearly 1,400

Texas and Arkansas cavalrymen, many of them veterans of Wilson's Creek, commanded by Colonel James McIntosh (no relation to Chilly or Daniel). He and Cooper together laid plans to pursue the refugees. But, still plagued by desertions among the Indians, Cooper's command had to be left behind. On December 22, McIntosh's force set out after Opothleyahola. Four days later McIntosh and his men fell on the refugees at Shoal Creek. Unable to beat back the battle-hardened veterans, the Indians scattered, leaving behind much of their livestock, wagons, and supplies. The Confederates rode after the panicked Indians, cutting down scores of them from behind with sabers or shooting them in the back. Stand Watie and his mixed-blood Cherokees, who had arrived on the field as combat was winding down, joined the pursuit.[29]

About four thousand survivors, less than half the refugees' original number, struggled on in scattered groups toward Kansas. Many had no wagons or livestock. Some were without food, and others walked over frozen ground with bare feet. Old people died. Children died. Babies were born and died of exposure. Warriors died defending their kin as Rebel cavalry continued to hound the fleeing Indians. On December 31, Texas troopers caught up with a small band of Creeks, Osages, and Cherokees. They killed the men and captured their families. What was left of John Drew's regiment attacked a group of their fellow Cherokees, killing one man and taking several prisoners. A detachment led by Colonel Cooper attacked refugee Creeks encamped on the Arkansas River. One warrior was killed. Over twenty women and children were captured. Finally, harsh winds and freezing temperatures forced the Confederates to turn back. The refugees struggled on northward leaving trails of frozen bodies in their wake.[30]

In January 1862 the first of Opothleyahola's remaining followers staggered into Kansas where they were finally able to set up camp in relative safety. But the effort to get there had cost them dearly. Soon after the Indians' arrival, a visiting agent reported on their journey to his superiors.

Their march was undertaken with a scanty supply of clothing, subsistence, and cooking utensils, and entirely without tents, and during their progress they were reduced to such extremity as to be obliged to feed upon their ponies and dogs, while their scanty clothing was reduced to rags, and in some cases absolute nakedness was their condition. Let it be remembered that this retreat was in the midst of a winter of unusual severity for that country, with snow upon the prairie. Many of their ponies died of starvation. The women and children suffered severely from frozen limbs, as did also the men. Women gave birth to their offspring upon the naked snow, without shelter or covering, and in some instances the new-born infants died for want of clothing, and those who survived to reach their present location with broken constitutions and utterly dispirited.

Among those whose health was destroyed by the ordeal was Opothleyahola. Sick with fever as he tried to make arrangements for supplying his people shortly after they got to Kansas, the old chief collapsed and died.[31]

"To Rely upon Themselves"

The campaign to drive out Opothleyahola's people marked the high point of Confederate dominance among the Nations. Within a few weeks Union forces had seized the initiative. On March 6, 1862, Federals heading south clashed with Confederates in Arkansas near Elkhorn Tavern, just east of Indian Territory. In the three-day Battle of Pea Ridge, Indians fought alongside their Confederate allies in a failed attempt to turn back the Federals. After their defeat, Watie's men fell back to Fort Gibson while most of Drew's regiment deserted to the Union side, further widening divisions among the Cherokees.[32]

Meanwhile an expeditionary force of Federal troops and Indians made up of survivors from Opothleyahola's flight was forming in Kansas. That June, it mounted a campaign against Confederate authority in the Nations. On July 3 at Locust Grove the expedition ran into a major Rebel force and sent it flying back to Tahlequah. Panic engulfed the Cherokee capital, and more of Drew's men deserted to the Federals. They assisted with the capture of nearby Fort Gibson and helped occupy Tahlequah itself. John Ross, who felt honor bound to at least appear faithful to his Confederate allies, was declared a paroled prisoner of war and thereby released from any obligations to the Confederacy.

The Federals, ill equipped to follow up on their victory, decided to head back to Kansas. On August 3, Ross and his family, along with one thousand other Cherokees who feared a looming Indian civil war, joined the expeditionary force on its march to Fort Leavenworth. As the refugees had feared, Ross's capture made tensions among the Cherokees even worse. With Ross gone, Cherokee pro-Confederates declared the office of principal chief vacant and elected Stand Watie to fill the post. Ross's men held their own council and not only declared Watie's election illegal but also repudiated their alliance with Richmond. The Cherokee Nation now had two governments contending for legitimacy, though fortunately neither was eager to make war on the other.[33]

Nevertheless, sporadic fighting continued until the summer of 1863 when Federal forces made another major thrust into the Indian Territory. Driving down out of Kansas along the Grand River, Federals and their Indian allies under General James Blunt captured Fort Gibson and made it their base of operations. From there they planned further forays against Confederate-allied Indians. At the same time, a Confederate and Indian force under Colonel Cooper headed out from Fort Smith, Arkansas, to drive the Federals back. Cooper caught up with his quarry at Honey Springs on July 17, but Blunt's superior artillery drove the Confederates back. Sometimes called the "Gettysburg of the West," the Battle of Honey Springs, coming within weeks of both Gettysburg and Vicksburg, was the largest engagement of the war in Indian Territory.[34]

Blunt then turned east to take Fort Smith, driving terrified Confederates before him and leaving devastated Indians in his wake. Those fortunate enough not to be in Blunt's path feared that they soon would be. And they were eager to get out of his way. Blunt's campaign set off a mass migration among pro-Confederate Cherokees, Creeks, and Seminoles that was nearly as brutal as Opothleyahola's flight had been. It became known to the survivors as "the stampede." Most fled south to the unmolested Choctaw-Chickasaw country. Some kept going on into Texas.[35]

Because the previous year's refugees has been mostly anti-Confederate Creeks, the flight of pro-Confederate Creeks now left the Creek Nation almost entirely deserted. Thousands of them filed south in seemingly endless columns of displaced and dejected families.

The Reverend Stephen Foreman, a longtime resident of Indian Territory, witnessed that parade of misery on a stop at the Chickasaw governor's home.

> A great many of the Creeks have also passed, on their way to some better camping place where water and grass are more abundant. Many of them are in a very destitute condition. All that they are with now is a pony, one [or] two pot vessels, and a few old dirty bed clothes and wearing apparel. If they ever had any more it is left behind at the mercy of their enemies. . . . Many who passed I was acquainted with and knew to be in good circumstances having an abundance of everything. Now their all is put into one or two small wagons.[36]

Blunt's campaign was the last major effort either side made to drive their opponents out of Indian Territory. From mid-1863 through the war's end, Federals and Confederates alike kept just enough forces in the region to hold what ground they had. Still the Territory continued to be devastated by a guerrilla war that kept the Nations in turmoil. Much of the violence—such as the sack of Wichita Agency—was driven by old tribal animosities. In that attack, a band of nearly two hundred Union Indians, most of them Kickapoos, fell on their old enemies the Tonkawas and wiped out fully half of the tribe—retribution for earlier cooperation with the Texans against them. Some of the violence sprang from conflicts within tribes, such as Stand Watie's attack on Union-held Tahlequah during which he killed several Union soldiers, burned John Ross's old home, and captured Ross's son and a number of his slaves.[37]

The Nations were also terrorized by bands of outlaws, white and Indian, who flourished in the border regions by raiding Union and Confederate settlements alike. Among these raiders, the most feared in Indian Territory was Colonel Charles C. Quantrill's gang. Quantrill was originally commissioned by Confederate authorities to raise a force of partisans to raid Union border towns and to fight back Union guerilla gangs, or Jayhawkers, from Kansas. But both Quantrill and his Jayhawker counterparts were often just as likely to attack one side as the other. Most partisan bands, regardless of stated allegiance, were in fact raiders for profit who fought each other only when necessary to secure territory for plunder.[38]

Watie took pains to distance himself from such men. The Cherokee leader once wrote of Quantrill that he had "crossed the Arkansas river near the Creek Agency and killed eight men (Creeks) one of them shot a little boy and killed him. I have always been opposed to killing women and children although our enemies have done it." As Watie insisted in a letter to his wife, "I am not a murderer." Watie's efforts usually focused against either his Union-allied opponents, the Keetowah Cherokees, or Union military targets such as store houses and supply lines. Food was especially targeted. So hungry were Watie's men during the winter of 1863–64 that they named their outpost "Camp Starvation."[39]

Watie had long been disillusioned with the government in Richmond for its lack of help with supplies for his troops and their families. Confederate officials had made "no vigorous effort," he complained, to help him drive out the Yankees. Not only that, but the administration was also taking money appropriated by Congress for the Indians and using it elsewhere. He told of one case in which clothing "procured at great trouble and expense, to cover the nakedness of Indian troops" had been given to other Confederate forces. Watie noted that the enemy had "desolated the land and robbed the people, until scarcely a southern family is left east and north of the Arkansas River. . . . The promised protection of the Confederate government, owing, I am compelled to say, to the glaring inefficiency of its subordinate agents, has accomplished nothing; it has been a useless and expensive pageant. . . . the Indians will have at last to rely upon themselves alone in the defense of their country."[40]

Instead of sending help, Confederate authorities made Watie a general, the only Indian to hold that rank on either side during the war. And they gave him even more Indian units that he could not feed. So Watie and his men were indeed forced to rely upon themselves. In June 1864, they captured the Union steamship *J. R. Williams*, loaded with over $100,000 worth of supplies, including 150 barrels of flour and 16,000 pounds of bacon. Many of the Indians, especially the Creeks and Seminoles now under his command, carried the supplies to their refugee families. In September, after defeating a large Union force at the Battle of Cabin Creek deep in Union-held Cherokee territory, Watie took possession of three hundred supply wagons, loaded with food, clothing, blankets, and medicines. Skillfully eluding Union pursuers, Watie and his men made their way with the supplies back to Confederate territory and distributed them to their cold and hungry families in the refugee camps.[41]

"Common Humanity Demands That Something Be Done"

On the other side of the border, refugees in Kansas were faring no better at the hands of Federal agents. A few weeks after they began arriving in January 1862, an army officer wrote of the Indians:

> It is impossible for me to depict the wretchedness of their condition. Their only protection from the snow on which they lie is prairie grass, and from the wind and weather scraps and rags stretched upon switches; some of them had some personal clothing; most had but shreds and rags, which did not conceal their nakedness, and I saw seven, ranging in age from three to fifteen years, without one thread upon their bodies. . . . They greatly need medical assistance; many have their toes frozen off, others have their feet wounded by sharp ice or branches of trees lying on the snow; but few have shoes or moccasins. They suffer with inflammatory diseases of the chest, throat, and eyes. Those who come in the last get sick as soon as they eat. . . . Why the officers of the Indian Department are not doing something for them I cannot understand; common humanity demands that something be done, and done at once, to save them from total destruction.[42]

Frostbite was so rampant that over one hundred Indians had to have limbs amputated immediately.[43]

Three months later, with refugee numbers swollen to 7,600, conditions were little better. In late April, George Collamore, an investigator from the Office of Indian Affairs, was especially struck by the lack of adequate shelter: "Such coverings as I saw were made in the rudest manner, being composed of pieces of cloth, old quilts, handkerchiefs, aprons, etc., stretched upon sticks, and so limited were many of them in size that they were scarcely sufficient to cover the emaciated and dying forms beneath them." Under one of these shelters Collamore found Opothleyahola's daughter "in the last stages of consumption." Nakedness was so common that Collamore was sure many of the men had given up their clothing to provide these crude shelters. And, not surprisingly, frostbite remained rampant. Collamore clearly recalled one "little Creek boy, about eight years old, with both feet taken off near the ankle." There were "others lying upon the ground whose frosted limbs rendered them unable to move."[44]

Food was just as scarce as shelter and just as abysmal. The entire weekly ration for each refugee was a pound of flour, a little salt, and a piece of bacon that Indians and agents alike described as "not fit for a dog to eat." The rancid meat had been shipped to the Indians from Fort Leavenworth after being condemned as "suitable only for soap grease." Those who ate the rotten pork became violently ill.[45]

The passing months brought Washington little closer to meeting its treaty obligations. As the winter of 1862–63 approached, the refugees were still "suffering for clothing and blankets." All they got in the way of shelter were condemned army tents. Archibald Coffin, directing physician for the refugees, complained in September 1863 of poor food leading to gastric disease and poor clothing and shelter leading to pneumonia. "It is no cause of surprise," he wrote, "if we find them falling victim to maladies that otherwise would not be regarded."[46]

Such conditions among the displaced Indians of Kansas were nothing new. In the spring of 1861, William Dole, the U.S. Commissioner of Indian Affairs, sent Augustus Wattles on a tour of Kansas, mainly to report on how the Indians there might side in the upcoming Civil War. Wattles wrote back that Washington had nothing to fear from the Kansas Indians. They were in no condition to fight on either side. The Sac and Fox, driven from their Illinois homes a generation earlier and promised both reservation land and support through cash annuities, were in especially bad shape. "Nearly every family is out of provisions," wrote Wattles, "living scantily on one meal a day Women and children look particularly thin." Most were practically naked. They had no houses, oxen, cows, farming tools, food, or clothing. The disturbed agent reported to Dole: "I have never seen so poor and so miserable a community of people before."[47]

Wattles blamed the destitution on corruption among government-licensed traders and contracted suppliers who had been cheating the Indians, and the taxpayers, for years. When Wattles warned the corrupt businessmen of his planned report, they brushed him off. It was, they told him, an easy matter to buy influence in Washington. His report was no threat to their swindling enterprise. Certainly no report to Commissioner Dole was likely to make a difference. He was one of the chief swindlers.

"If I chose," wrote one of Dole's subordinates, "I could do something more than implicate. I could convict him of enough to dam him forever." Though Dole might have been implicated, conviction was unlikely. Dole, a close friend of Lincoln's, had known the president since their Illinois days. Dole was himself one of the most influential men in Illinois Republican politics. Lincoln had appointed him commissioner of Indian Affairs as a reward for past political favors and now it was payday for Dole and his associates. He gave choice appointments in the Indian system to friends and relatives. He lined his own pockets by speculating in Indian land. During the war, he arranged to cheaply purchase Sac and Fox lands in Kansas that were supposed to be held in trust by the government, then sold them at inflated prices. Other Lincoln appointees, like Secretary of the Interior John Usher and Comptroller of the Currency Hugh McCulloch, also profited from corrupt Indian land deals. So did John G. Nicolay, Lincoln's personal secretary.[48]

Other Washington insiders, including members of Congress, cheated Indians through a kickback scheme called the "Indian Ring." Politicians helped secure appointments for local Indian agents. The agents granted exclusive licenses and contracts for merchants to trade on the reservations. Then the merchants, who held effective monopolies, overcharged the Indians for shoddy goods and sent a portion of their ill-gotten gain back up the line. The overcharges usually ranged anywhere from 100 to 400 percent.

Senator Samuel C. Pomeroy, Republican of Kansas, was among the worst offenders. As financial agent of the New England Emigrant Aid Society in the 1850s, Pomeroy had culled out tens of thousands of acres for himself in Kansas, mostly at the expense of Potawatomies and Kickapoos. Pomeroy sold off most of the land, which made him one the richest men in Kansas. He next entered politics, where he found it easy to continue his swindling ways. In July 1862, Pomeroy wrote to one partner in crime, W.W. Ross, describing a plan to skim annuities even before they went out to Indian agents. Pomeroy had arranged for J.K. Tappan of New York to hold an exclusive trade license with the Potawatomies. Tappan's orders would be charged directly against annuities. "This proceeding is recognized here at the [Interior] Department," Pomeroy assured Ross, "and is all right." Both men would get fully one quarter of the profits. "We have nothing to do, only to take our share of the profits at each payment."[49]

The Pomeroy scheme demonstrated not only how widespread corruption in the Union's Indian system was but also how obvious it was, especially to the Indians. That was a major reason that the Kansas refugees were so eager to get back home. They had had enough of government hospitality. Still, they needed the security Washington promised them under federal treaty. Fifteen hundred members of Opothleyahola's old band had tried to return home with the expeditionary force of 1862, but were forced back to Kansas when the Federals withdrew.

Ross's Cherokees were also eager to go home. Ross himself met with Lincoln in September 1862 to protest lack of federal protection, pointing out that the Cherokees had been forced to sign a treaty with the Confederacy only because Federal forces had withdrawn from the Nations. Despite clear evidence to the contrary, Lincoln refused to admit any failure in protecting the Cherokees. But the president did promise to get them home and secure them there as soon as he could. Finally, in the spring of 1864, Ross and his people were given a federal escort into the Nations. But the escort did not stay, and Lincoln's promised protection never materialized. Constantly harassed by armed raiders, the returning Cherokees were never able to make a crop and suffered from hunger and illness through the rest of the war.[50]

The Kickapoos had had enough of Kansas too, but they did not wait for a federal escort to get out. In September 1864 seven hundred of them broke camp and headed for Mexico. At the war's outset, Mexico had invited the Kickapoos to settle there on condition that they would help defend the country's northern border. It was an attractive offer. To the Kickapoos, an alliance with the Confederacy and their old enemies, the Texans, was out of the question. For years the Texans had pushed them off their traditional hunting grounds. The Kickapoos had sometimes pushed back but to little effect. Some of the Kickapoos accepted Mexico's invitation. Others fled to Kansas, counting on the federal government to meet its treaty obligations. That had been a mistake. Now the survivors were going to join their kinsmen in Mexico.[51]

The refugees first headed west toward the Texas Panhandle before turning south for Mexico. This long looping route would give Texas settlements a wide berth. The Kickapoos wanted no trouble. Despite their best efforts, however, trouble was about to find them. In late December a detachment of about twenty Texas scouts picked up the Kickapoos' trail. At an abandoned camp site they discovered a fresh grave and, over the protests of a few, dug it up to see who they were following. They unearthed the body of a young Kickapoo woman, smartly attired in buckskin and adorned with trinkets. Some scouts

took the trinkets and wore them as souvenirs. Others warned that doing so might bring bad luck.

The scouts immediately sent back word of their find. Soon four
hundred Confederate regulars under Captain Henry Fossett and
Texas militiamen under Captain S. S. Totten were in pursuit. They
caught sight of the Kickapoo encampment at Dove Creek on January
8, 1865. One of Fossett's officers suggested that they talk with the Indians to see if they were friendly. Fossett replied that "he recognized
no friendly Indian on the Texas frontier." Fossett and Totten then ordered their mounted troops on a headlong charge over three miles of
open ground. The surprised Kickapoos quickly rallied. After about
thirty minutes of close fighting, the troopers retreated as quickly as
they had appeared. That night, before the Kickapoos continued on to
Mexico, they buried fifteen warriors. The Texans had suffered twice
that many casualties. As one scout recalled, of those who had plundered the young Kickapoo woman's grave, "every possessor of a trin-
ket met death in the fight."[52]

"Let Them Eat Grass"

Like the Kickapoos of Texas, northern Indians too were being pushed
off their land. And as was so often the case, widespread corruption and
deceit among the whites drove some Indians to push back. In early
1861, the Santee Sioux of Minnesota became special targets of that
corruption and deceit. In 1861, Senator Henry Rice helped engineer a
partial Santee removal, then submitted a claim of $24,000 for his trou-
ble. By 1862, the Santee had nothing left to them in Minnesota except
a reservation ten miles wide, stretching 150 miles along the south bank
of the Minnesota River. Under treaty agreements, annuities in goods,
food, and cash were to be paid to the Santee at two agencies: the Redwood or Lower Agency near what is now Redwood Falls and the Yellow Medicine or Upper Agency near modern-day Granite Falls. Some
of the Santee supplemented that income with annual buffalo hunting
trips. Others, mostly the less traditionally minded "cut-hairs" and
mixed-bloods, took up farming as well.[53]

In fact, the annuities were most often supplemental to the Santee's
own subsistence efforts since most of the payments usually wound up

in the hands of unscrupulous merchants and agents. In January 1862, the Santee agent Thomas Galbraith submitted $52,000 in claims to his immediate superior, Superintendent Clark W. Thompson, a St. Paul banker with a taste for corruption. Galbraith suggested that he and Thompson pad their claims to the Office of Indian Affairs, telling him that "the *biggest* swindle please[s] them best if they but have a *share* in [it]." Galbraith was certain that the assistant commissioner of Indian Affairs, Minnesotan Charles Mix, "would aid you & I think old Mix would easily go in."[54]

Indian traders among the Santee, to whom Galbraith had granted licenses, were just as corrupt as their patron. "The Indians did not think the traders had done right," said Santee Chief Big Eagle. "The Indians bought goods of them on credit, and when the government payments came the traders were on hand with their books, which showed that the Indians owed so much and so much, and as the Indians kept no books they could not deny their accounts, but had to pay them, and sometimes the traders got all their money." Thomas Williamson and Stephen Riggs, two white missionaries among the Santee, confirmed Big Eagle's account in a January 1862 letter to Minnesota's congressional delegation. "The Indians are greatly cheated by the traders," wrote the missionaries, stressing that government agents were in cahoots with the traders. The Santee, some of them on the brink of starvation, were in sore need of their full annuity payments. Williamson and Riggs warned that continued corruption would inevitably result in a "collision with the Indians on our frontiers."[55]

On top of these difficulties, Washington was slow to send out annuity payments in 1861–62. "What in hell is the trouble?" asked one aggravated agent. "Is there any money coming this fall or is Uncle Samuel busted?" Preoccupied with the war, Congress was late in appropriating the funds. Even after it did, distribution was delayed by an extended discussion at the Treasury Department about whether to pay the Indians in paper currency or the usual gold coin. Meanwhile, the Santee were starving. On the poor lands allotted them, the Santee's 1861 fall harvest had failed. What stores they had were gone by the summer of 1862. June came and went, and still no annuity payments. There was plenty of food on hand at the traders' stores, but they refused to extend additional credit. There was food in the government's agency warehouses too, but Galbraith stuck to a policy of not releasing it until the cash annuities arrived. Finally, some of the Santee took matters into their own hands. On July 14, five thousand of them appeared at the Upper Agency and demanded their food. Galbraith relented and distributed just enough to appease them. But it was hardly enough to feed the entire reservation, and Galbraith knew it. Fearing another attempt at the food stores, he asked state officials for help. They responded by sending two companies of the 5th Minnesota Regiment under Lieutenant Timothy J. Sheehan.[56]

As Galbraith had anticipated, the Indians again tried to force the issue. Sheehan's men were no deterrent to the hungry Santee. On August 4, five hundred warriors surrounded the regiment while others broke into a warehouse and began carrying out sacks of flour. Only after Sheehan threatened to fire a howitzer did the Santee stop their looting. With order restored, Sheehan convinced Galbraith not only to distribute a little food to the Indians but also to hold council with the Santee.

On August 6, Galbraith, along with several traders and army officers, met with some Santee chiefs. Speaking on their behalf, Chief Taoyateduta (Little Crow) asked Galbraith to open the agency's storehouses and work out some deal with the traders to open theirs. "We have no food, but here are these stores, filled with food," Little Crow pointed out. "We ask that you, the agent, make some arrangement by which we can get food from the stores, or else we may take our own way to keep ourselves from starving. . . . When men are hungry they help themselves." Galbraith passed the buck. He turned to Andrew Myrick, spokesman for the traders, and said, "Well, it's up to you now. What will you do?" Angered by Little Crow's implied threat, Myrick shot back: "So far as I am concerned, if they are hungry, let them eat grass." Enraged and frustrated at Myrick's reply, the Santee chiefs stormed out.[57]

Frustration was common all across the reservation as the starving Santee asked themselves what to do next. It seemed that one way or another the whites were determined to starve them to death. Then on Sunday, August 17, four young braves returning from an unsuccessful hunt killed five white settlers at Acton Township. After stealing two horses and a wagon, they rushed back to the reservation. That night at a council near the Lower Agency, called to discuss how to proceed in light of the killings, it was clear that most of the attending Santee were ready for war. But Little Crow, who had been to Washington and seen for himself how powerful and numerous the whites were, strongly argued against escalating the violence: "You are like dogs in the hot moon when they run mad and snap at their own shadows. We are only a little herd of buffalo left scattered. . . . The white men are like the locust when they fly so thick the whole sky is a snowstorm. . . . Kill one—two—ten, and ten times ten will come to kill you." In a mock display of the death that awaited his people should they make war on the whites, Little Crow blackened his face and covered himself with a blanket. But the war fever was too hot. When one of the warriors called him a coward, Little Crow threw off his blanket and rose to his feet. "Braves," he told them, "you are little children—you are fools. You cannot see the face of your chief; your eyes are full of smoke. You cannot hear his voice; your ears are full of roaring water. You will die like the rabbits when the hungry wolves hunt them in the Hard Moon. Taoyateduta is not a coward; he will die with you!"[58]

The uprising was on and Little Crow sent messengers to spread the word. Most of the cut-hairs and mixed-bloods decided to stay out of the fight. So did most Santee around the Upper Agency after discussing the matter in council, though some did ride south on their own to join Little Crow. Others broke into the traders' stores, killing one white man in the process and wounding another so badly that he

In 1862, after years of losing lands, being cheated by government agents, and suffering near starvation, the Santee Sioux of Minnesota rose in rebellion. Chief Little Crow (Taoyate-duta) led the uprising but knew it was a futile act of desperation. After arguing against violence and being accused of cowardice, he said: "Braves, you are little children—you are fools. . . . You will die like the rabbits when the hungry wolves hunt them in the Hard Moon. Taoyateduta is not a coward; he will die with you." (Denver Public Library)

later died. But most whites at the Upper Agency, who only a day before had been acting as if they cared little whether the Santee lived or died, were saved by some of those very Santee. When the looting began, one group of Santee herded the whites into a brick warehouse and refused to let the hostiles get at them. After the rampage died down, they escorted the whites on a three-day journey up the Minnesota River and out of the war zone.[59]

Whites at the Lower Agency were not so fortunate. At dawn on August 18, Little Crow and about four hundred Santee overran the agency shouting "Kill the whites! Kill all the whites!" One of the first to die was Andrew Myrick, shot as he fled toward the woods. His killers tore handfuls of grass from the ground and stuffed them into Myrick's dead mouth. Perhaps four hundred whites met the same fate as enraged Santee warriors fanned out from the reservation and attacked settlements in surrounding counties. When a forty-six-man patrol from nearby Fort Ridgely tried to reach the Lower Agency, Santee warriors ambushed it at Redwood River Ferry. Half the soldiers were killed before the patrol could break away. Only one Santee warrior lost his life in the battle.[60]

Over the next few days more Santee joined the fight. Even some of the cut-hairs took off their white-man's clothes, put on war paint, and threw themselves into driving their enemies out of Minnesota. On August 19 about two hundred warriors fell on the town of New Ulm, just down river from the Santee reservation. Townsfolk fought back so stubbornly that the warriors withdrew after a two-hour fire fight. The next day Little Crow led four hundred warriors against Fort Ridgely. The defenders drove the Santee back with cannon blasts. Reinforced overnight by four hundred more warriors from around the Upper Agency, Little Crow attacked Fort Ridgely again on August 21. Again he and his men were held back by artillery fire. On August 22, Little Crow took his force down to New Ulm, and the town faced a second Santee assault. Reinforced itself, New Ulm's defenders beat them back once more.[61]

The setbacks at Fort Ridley and New Ulm emboldened the antiwar Santee, who in open council berated their rash kinsmen for killing the whites. Now retribution from the whites was sure to follow. So heated were the tensions between those who wanted to continue the struggle and those who opposed it that Little Crow feared a civil war might break out among the Santee Sioux. To avoid that possibility, on August 30 Little Crow led his followers and their white captives northwest along the Minnesota River, burning the Upper Agency along the way.[62]

Soon after word of the uprising reached the army, Colonel Henry Sibley was on his way toward the Santee reservation with over sixteen hundred eager volunteers. "It is my purpose," Sibley's commander, General John Pope, wrote him, "utterly to exterminate the Sioux if I have the power to do so and even if it requires a campaign lasting the whole of next year. . . . They are to be treated as maniacs or wild beasts, and by no means as people with whom treaties or compromises can be made." Pope's policy, with which Sibley fully agreed, ignored the fact that their own government's failure to meet treaty obligations had led to the violence. Nor did it give the fleeing warriors much incentive to surrender. On September 23, at what came to be known as the Battle of Wood Lake, Little Crow's Santee tried to turn Sibley and his men back. But heavily outnumbered and outgunned, the Santee had no chance. After two hours of heavy fighting, Little Crow broke off the attack. Leaving over 250 captives behind, his followers and their families headed west to take refuge among their kinsmen in Dakota Territory.[63]

Sibley's men rounded up all the Santee they could find, almost two thousand men, women, and children—full-blood and mixed alike—holding them until the men of fighting age were culled out. Most had surrendered voluntarily, trusting Sibley's word that they would all be fairly dealt with. Sibley then set up a five-man military commission to decide their fate. Its procedure, according to Missionary Stephen Riggs, was "to subject all grown men, with a few exceptions, to an investigation of the commission, trusting that the innocent could make their innocency appear. This was not possible in the case of the majority." In the eyes of the military, these men were guilty until proven innocent simply because they were Santee. None of the defendants were allowed legal council, nor were they permitted to call witnesses to testify on their behalf. By November, the commission had sentenced 307 to death by hanging. Most of them, said Riggs, "were condemned on general principles, without any specific charges proved."[64]

Even as the sentences were being handed down, Henry B. Whipple, the influential Episcopal bishop of Minnesota, mounted a campaign to stop the executions. Well acquainted with corruption in the Indian system, Whipple met with Lincoln and outlined the abuses that had led to violence until Lincoln, as he later said, "felt it down to my boots." In a subsequent letter to the president Whipple insisted, "We cannot hang men by the hundreds. . . . they are prisoners of war. The leaders must be punished but we cannot afford by an wanton cruelty to purchase a long Indian war—nor by injustice in other matters to purchase the anger of God." Another Minnesotan confirmed Whipple's report of corruption, telling Lincoln that the uprising was brought on by "the thievish and dishonest conduct of Government Agents, Officers, [and] Traders." Ironically, corruption in the Indian system played to the condemned men's favor. The prospect of losing so many of the people they cheated for a living, and the precedent it set for the future, was most disturbing to politicians, agents, and traders in the "Indian Ring." Commissioner Dole himself urged Lincoln to intervene on the Santee's behalf.[65]

A little moral suasion and a lot of political pressure convinced Lincoln that he had to act. But there was pressure from the other side too. Newspaper editorials in Minnesota were calling for the executions to go forward. So was Minnesota's entire congressional delegation. Proexecutionists dissuaded Lincoln from commuting all the death sentences, but he did put two of his aides to work reviewing the commission files. What they found was a patchwork record of shoddy and incomplete proceedings. Only thirty-nine case files were in any sense complete. These unlucky few would be the ones to face a hangman's noose. Lincoln justified his action on the grounds that, though no defense witnesses were called, these thirty-nine (later reduced to thirty-eight) might be said to have been guilty of "wonton murder of unarmed citizens" rather than simply being participants in battles. In fact, those Santee most likely to have been guilty of "wonton murder," including the Acton four, had long since fled to Dakota Territory with Little Crow. Lincoln's distinction was politically motivated, not supported by evidence, but it did spare 269 Sioux lives.[66] Still, innocent men would die for the sake of political expediency and indiscriminate revenge. One of the condemned men, Rda-in-yan-ka, wrote to his father-in-law:

> WABASHAW: You have deceived me. You told me that if we followed the advice of General Sibley, and give ourselves up to the whites, all would be well—no innocent man would be injured. I have not killed, wounded, or injured a white man, or any white persons. I have not participated in the plunder of their property; and yet to-day, I am set apart

for execution, and must die in a few days. . . . My wife and children are dear to me. Let them not grieve for me. Let them remember that the brave should be prepared to meet death; and I will do so as becomes a Dacotah.[67]

On December 26, 1862, Rda-in-yank-ka and thirty-seven other Sioux braves were publicly hanged in Mankato. To this day it remains the largest mass execution in American history. A release order for one of the executed Sioux, pardoned for saving a white woman's life, arrived in Mankato a day after the hangings. A short time later, authorities discovered that three other men had been hanged by mistake through a confusion of names.[68]

Little Crow and his band wintered that year near Devil's Lake in Dakota Territory. When spring came, he returned to Minnesota. No one was sure why he went back. Some said he planned to seek permanent refuge in western Canada and went to gather horses for the jour-

On December 26, 1862, after sham trials, thirty-eight Santee were publicly hanged at Mankato, Minnesota, in retaliation for the Sioux uprising. Wrote one condemned man: "I have not killed, wounded, or injured a white man, or any white persons. . . . My wife and children are dear to me. Let them not grieve for me. Let them remember that the brave should be prepared to meet death; and I will do so as becomes a Dacotah.' The Mankato hanging remains the largest mass execution in American history. (*Harper's Weekly*)

ney. Others claimed he wanted only to kill more whites; still others thought he went home to die. If so, he got his wish. On July 1, 1863, while picking berries with his son in the Big Woods, a shot suddenly rang out. Little Crow was dead. The white man who shot him received a $500 bounty. Little Crow's body was taken to Hutchinson where the public was invited to mutilate it. Among other indignities visited on the corpse, firecrackers were set off in the ears and nose to celebrate the Fourth of July. What remained of Little Crow was then dumped into a garbage pit on the edge of town.[69]

"Why Is It the Whites Come to Fight with the Indians?"

By the time of Little Crow's death, Minnesota's Santee Sioux had been herded off to a desolate reservation on Dakota Territory's Crow Creek, where starvation continued to plague them. Accompanying the Sioux were about two thousand Winnebago Indians. Only a few Winnebagos were suspected of participating in the Santee rebellion, but that was all the government needed as justification to force them off their fertile, and valuable, southern Minnesota territory. Lincoln himself signed the order offering up Winnebago land for sale. The Ojibwas were able to avoid removal only because the area they occupied around northern Minnesota's Red Lake was so isolated. After the Ojibwas threatened to kill an agent who was swindling them and firing on an army patrol, instead of forcing them entirely off their land Minnesota negotiated a peaceful settlement involving a partial land cession along the Red River of the North.[70]

Of much greater interest to the white man's government was land in the Idaho and Montana territories where gold fields were attracting thousands of prospectors. To get the miners in and the gold out, travel routes across Dakota Territory had to be secured. Securing those routes would mean disrupting buffalo migrations and driving the natives from their traditional hunting grounds. In 1863, Federal troops rampaged through Dakota Territory east of the Missouri River. What prisoners they took, mostly local Yanktonais Sioux and Santee refugees from Minnesota, were hauled off to the Crow Creek reservation. Those not captured or killed fled west. In 1864, General Alfred Sully and several thousand soldiers struck beyond the Missouri against Western Sioux encampments. The Indians suffered a major blow on

July 28 at the Battle of Killdeer Mountain when, outnumbered and outgunned, they were forced to abandon 400,000 pounds of dried buffalo meat.[71]

The survivors moved further west into the Little Missouri Badlands where they were reinforced by other bands of Western Sioux and Cheyenne traveling north from the Black Hills. The pursuing soldiers caught up with them on August 7 and over the next three days tormented the Indians with small arms and artillery fire. After darkness fell on the last day of fighting, one of Sully's Indian scouts yelled across the lines to ask what Indians were facing them. Thirty-three-year-old Sioux warrior Sitting Bull answered back: "Hunkpapas, San Arcs, Yanktonais, and others. Who are you?" "Some Indians with the soldiers," came the reply. "You have no business with the soldiers," an astonished Sitting Bull told them. That other Indians were fighting against him was not the only thing that bewildered Sitting Bull. "The Indians here have no fight with the whites," he insisted. "Why is it the whites come to fight with the Indians?" We do not know whether Sitting Bull received an answer. If he did, it was probably not one that made any sense to him.[72]

The next day, beaten but not broken, Sitting Bull and his people scattered onto the plains to replenish their supply of buffalo meat. Low on supplies themselves, Sully's men did not follow. Though Sully failed to destroy the Western Sioux, he did establish Fort Rice near present-day Bismarck and permanently garrison two old trading posts further up the Missouri at Forts Berthold and Union. They would serve as bases for what would soon become a brutal and unremitting campaign against the Sioux.[73]

"Indiscriminate Massacre of Indians"

Further west, the natives were already suffering much worse. As the gold rush cranked up and whites flooded into California during the late 1840s and 1850s, they began a war of virtual genocide against the Shasta, Klamath, Yuki, Hoopa, Wiyot, and other Indians. Armed militias and vigilantes drove the natives from their fertile fields and hunting grounds, killing all who resisted. Captives were forced onto unprotected reservations where they were left at the mercy of corrupt agents, swindling traders, and hostile whites who encroached on their land, raided their livestock, raped their women and took them as con-cubines, and kidnaped their children to sell as slaves. Others escaped into the surrounding mountains, forests, and deserts where they faced starvation. Hunger frequently drove them out of their hiding places to hunt game and steal cattle. When whites were killed trying to stop them, armed posses hunted down the refugees with orders to shoot on sight any Indian they found. Local governments offered cash bounties for Indian scalps, friendly or hostile, no questions asked.[74]

Most newspaper editors encouraged the ethnic cleansing, calling repeatedly for the Indians—all Indians—to be utterly wiped out. Few offered any criticism, direct or implied, of the ongoing slaughter. One brave soul who did was twenty-three-year-old Bret Harte, editor of the *Northern Californian* in Union (later renamed Arcata). In February 1860, Harte ran a story entitled "Indiscriminate Massacre of Indians—Women and Children Butchered." It told how a village of sixty friendly Indians on Humboldt Bay had been hacked to death with axes and hatchets. Soon after, the residents of Union threatened Harte's life and ran him out of town.[75]

In 1861 the army stepped in to try to restore order, not by keeping whites from illegally moving onto Indian land but by herding the Indi-ans onto even smaller reservations. From his headquarters at Fort Humboldt, Colonel Francis J. Lippitt sent detachments of the 2nd California Cavalry throughout northern California with orders to give quarter only to those Indians who surrendered voluntarily. The rest were to be slaughtered. By late 1862 hundreds of Indians had been forced onto the Round Valley Reservation, but conditions there were so bad and threats from local whites so ominous that they soon fled back into the mountains. Disgusted by the army's failure to impose a final solution, Governor Leland Stanford unleashed the state militia in what became an outright war of extermination. Led by Lieutenant Colonel Stephen G. Whipple, the militia's 1st Battalion California Mountaineers swept through northern California, killing every Indian they could find. The campaign was so brutal that by the summer of 1864 scattered survivors were begging Whipple to accept their surren-der. With the Indians nearly wiped out in any case, Whipple con-sented to spare, for the time being at least, the few who remained. Their chiefs were hauled off to imprisonment on Alcatraz Island. The rest were forced back onto unguarded reservations, where gangs of marauding whites completed the task of exterminating them.[76]

In southern California's Owens River Valley, Paiutes faced much the same treatment as invading miners and ranchers drove them off their lands. When the Paiutes fought back, detachments of the 2nd California Cavalry were sent after them. At one encampment, the troopers "shot or sabered" every Paiute warrior there. "None escaped," reported the detachment commander, "though many of them fought well with knives, sticks, stones, and clubs."[77]

Paiutes in Nevada Territory were seeing their lands overrun too. A series of gold and silver discoveries between 1861 and 1863 brought settlers in by the thousands. The same was happening in Washington Territory, Idaho Territory, and the new state of Oregon, where miners and other settlers were illegally flooding onto unceded lands of the native Spokan, Snake, Klamath, Modoc, Bannock, Cayuse, and Nez Percé Indians. "To attempt to restrain miners," wrote Washington Territory's superintendent, "would be like attempting to restrain the whirlwind." The government was hardly inclined to try. It was generally viewed as the army's business to kill Indians, not protect them from whites. To use the army against whites in defense of Indians was unthinkable, even if it was whites who were breaking the law.[78]

Still, some tribes, like the Klamath, Modoc, and Nez Percé, were so eager for even the hope of protection that they sought peace at any price. In November 1862, the Nez Percé invited troops to set up Fort Lapwai at the confluence of the Snake and Clearwater rivers, hoping that the army would shield them from white intruders. On the contrary, once the fort was built and the troopers in place, government officials used the implicit threat of force to negotiate a new treaty under which the Nez Percé lost 90 percent of their remaining lands. Miners soon overran even that small tract and nearly wiped out the Nez Percé. The army did not intervene.[79]

Unable to get protection from the government, many of the Indians determined to protect themselves. Snakes and Bannocks were among the first to take direct action against white invaders. They were soon joined by refugees from tribes who had tried and failed to make peace with the whites. Dividing themselves into small bands, they used hit-and-run tactics in attacks on mining camps, farming settlements, isolated ranches, and traveling pack trains. Volunteer cavalry from Oregon and Nevada combed the region trying to catch the raiders but found it impossible to pin them down. "Their stealthy presence is never indicated except by a consummated murder or robbery," wrote a frustrated Senator James Nesmith of Oregon, "while their parties are so small and so perfectly on the alert that pursuit is useless." But during the summers of 1864 and 1865, the army did establish posts throughout the region—McDermit and McGarry in northern Nevada, Bidwell in California, Watson, Alvord, and Logan in Oregon, and Lyon in Idaho. These became base camps from which future campaigns against the Indians would be launched.[80]

"The Carnage . . . Was Horrible"

The Utes, whose lands stretched from western Colorado across parts of Utah and into Nevada, were being overrun as well. In early 1861, Ute chiefs repeatedly asked government officials to expel miners flooding onto their southwestern Colorado lands. The newcomers were setting up permanent settlements and killing off game on which the Utes depended. Typically, Washington's agents refused to use force against the invaders, but the region's Indian superintendent, James Collins, did ask Congress to pay the Utes compensation for their lost hunting grounds. Congress did not respond. To make matters worse, in 1862 the region's Indian superintendency received only half the supplies needed for distribution to the Utes. With whites taking their game and sufficient food not forthcoming from the government, the area's Utes began stealing livestock from ranchers encroaching on their lands. Colorado volunteers responded with a bloody campaign against the Utes, killing many of their warriors and forcing survivors onto a small reservation in the territory's extreme southwest corner.[81]

Further west in the Great Basin of Utah and Nevada, more bands of Utes, along with Pahvants and Gosiutes (a band of Western Shoshonis), were trying to fend off white invaders. They raided mining camps, attacked stagecoaches, and fell on pack trains crossing their land. In the spring of 1863, Federal cavalry chased one party of Utes who had stolen some cattle through the Cedar Mountains and Skull Valley south of the Great Salt Lake. They finally caught up with them at Cedar Fort west of Lake Utah, but the Utes fought off the soldiers and continued on their way. The army attacked them again at Spanish Fork Canyon on April 15. Though thirty warriors were killed, among them a Ute chief, most of the Indians escaped. Unable to defeat the

Indians outright, the army did bring to bear enough pressure to force a treaty. On July 14, under military escort, Utah's governor met with about seven hundred Utes at Spanish Fork Canyon to discuss terms. Under the new treaty, Chiefs Antero, Tabby, Kanosh, and Black Hawk agreed to permit safe passage for whites across their lands. Similar treaties were made with other tribes of the Great Basin. Some gave up portions of their land in exchange for annuity payments and promises of protection from further encroachment. In the years to come those promises, like so many before, would be repeatedly broken.[32]

For the Shoshoni bands of the Wasatch Mountains northeast of the Great Salt Lake, few promises had been given in the first place. Spring of 1860 found hundreds of Mormon wagons rolling into the Cache Valley after a church newspaper called it the best-watered valley in the Wasatch Range. Mormon settlers were also overrunning the Bear River Valley, prime Shoshoni hunting ground for over a thousand years. Robbed of their best food source, hunger began to set in among the Shoshonis. When Utah's Indian superintendent, James Doty, toured the Wasatch Range in 1862 he found Shoshoni bands in a "starving and destitute condition." He tried to supply them as best he could with what little provisions Washington would finance. Some Shoshonis begged food from the settlers, one of whom called the Indians "quite annoying." None of their efforts proved sufficient to meet the need. As far as the Shoshonis could see, the only way to avoid starving to death was to take back their hunting grounds.[83]

The Shoshonis began by denying whites access to their land, attacking wagon trains and stage lines from the Oregon Trail in the north to the Overland Trail in the south. Shutting down those two major east-west roads nearly cut off access to the far West. Postmaster General Montgomery Blair was forced to route all mail to California by sea for the time being. Brigham Young, presiding officer of the Mormon Church, telegraphed Washington that "the militia of Utah are ready and able, as they ever have been, to take care of all the Indians and are able and willing to protect the mail line if called upon to do so."[84]

Without waiting for an answer, Young mobilized Utah militiamen to escort the stage lines. Lincoln did finally authorize a call for volunteers to put down the uprising, and their patrols forced the Shoshonis to cease their raids. But Lincoln did nothing to address the uprising's root cause. In late July 1862, after distributing the little wheat he had to the Shoshonis, Superintendent Doty wrote:

To say they are "destitute" but feeble describes their situation. They took the wheat . . . with the utmost avidity and with hearty thanks; and repeatedly I saw their children, lying on their bellies on the margins of the streams, cropping the young grass. I hope I shall receive the goods from the Dept. in time to clothe their nakedness before the snow falls and winter commences.[85]

The goods never came and starving Shoshonis again went on the warpath. That fall and into the winter they swept through the Wasatch Range, taking what they needed and killing for it when they had to. Regional newspapers carried headlines reading "Indian Murders" and "Murders of Emigrants." All demanded action against the Shoshonis. The army responded by sending a column of California infantry and cavalry regiments under Colonel Patrick Connor, a hot-headed, ill-tempered Irish immigrant. Connor's men fanned out though the Wasatch Mountains with orders from their colonel to "destroy every male Indian whom you may encounter in the vicinity of the late massacres" and "immediately hang them, and leave their bodies thus exposed as an example of what evil doers may expect while I command in this district."[86]

In early December 1862, Connor got word of a large Shoshoni encampment near Bear River Ferry west of Brigham City, where stolen livestock was thought to be held. On December 4, he dispatched mounted troopers from Camp Douglas, just north of Salt Lake City, under Major Edward McGarry to kill or capture the Shoshonis. Arriving the next day, they found that the forewarned Indians had crossed the Malad River, a tributary of the Bear, and cut the ferry rope to prevent their crossing in force. Leaving the horses behind, McGarry's men commandeered a small scow and slowly made their way across the river. Unable to stage a mounted assault, McGarry captured four unwary Shoshoni hostages and sent word to Chief Bear Hunter that they would be killed unless he surrendered. Gambling that McGarry would not murder the prisoners in cold blood, Bear Hunter broke camp and headed his people northward up the Bear River. Though the Shoshonis got away, Bear Hunter had underestimated the white man's propensity for terrorist tactics. McGarry did not hesitate to order the hostages tied up and executed by firing squad. Fifty-one shots rang out before they all died. McGarry's men then threw their bodies into the river.[87]

Most western newspapers applauded McGarry's ruthlessness in dealing with "these human fiends who have too long infested these regions." But one, the *Desert News* of Salt Lake City, feared that murdering the hostages would only make the Shoshonis "more hostile and vindictive." It did. Over the next few weeks, reports of Shoshoni attacks filled the newspapers. Nearly all blamed Bear Hunter's band, though other bands may have been responsible as well. In early January 1863, ten miners traveling south from Idaho to get supplies in Salt Lake City were killed. Soon after, eight men heading to Salt Lake City from the Dakota mines were attacked. Their wagons, and most of their livestock, were lost. One man was killed. On January 14, word reached Colonel Connor that the Shoshonis had killed two expressmen on the Cache Valley Road. Conner quickly put a plan in motion to annihilate Bear Hunter and his people.[88]

Traveling by different routes to confuse Shoshoni lookouts, Conner's men converged on Bear Hunter's winter camp along Bear River in southern Idaho. On the morning of January 29, the village of nearly five hundred Shoshoni men, women, and children became a free-fire zone. Leaving their horses in the rear, Connor's troopers surrounded the Indians and began shooting into their camp. Confusion and terror reigned among the Indians. Warriors rushed out to face their attackers. Women and children took shelter in Beaver Creek, a ravine that flowed through the camp. The overwhelmed warriors too were soon forced back to the ravine as soldiers swept through the camp destroying lodges and food supplies. When they reached the ravine, it quickly became a death trap. "The carnage presented in the ravine was horrible," wrote a reporter who accompanied the troops. "Warrior piled on warrior, horses mangled and wounded in every conceivable form, with here and there a squaw and papoose, who had been accidentally killed." In fact, the killing of women and children was not accidental. It was indiscriminate. The soldiers did not care who they killed as long as the victim was an Indian.[89]

Some Shoshonis tried to escape by swimming the icy waters of Bear River; most were shot before they could get across. Others sought refuge among the willow trees along its banks but were shot down there as well. Only a handful were able to escape, most by scaling the bluffs along Beaver Creek and vanishing into the dense forest. At least 250 Shoshoni men, women, and children died in the assault. One officer put the total killed at close to four hundred.[90] Among the dead was Chief Bear Hunter. The granddaughter of one Shoshoni who survived the massacre later told how he died. Wounded by a gun-shot but still alive, the soldiers

> whipped him, kicked him and tried several means of torture on him. Through all of this the old chief did not utter a word, as crying and carrying on was the sign of a coward. Because he would not die or cry for mercy, the soldiers became very angry. One of the military men took his rifle, stepped to a burning campfire and heated his bayonet until it was glowing red. He then ran the burning hot metal through the chief's ears.[91]

Bear Hunter was not the only one tortured in his final moments. According to several Mormon guides accompanying Connor, in the battle's aftermath some soldiers roamed through the village killing "the wounded by knocking them in the head with an axe and then commenced to ravish the Squaws which was done to the very height of brutality . . . some were used in the act of dying from their wounds." About 160 Shoshoni women and children were finally allowed to sur-render, but Connor left them on the field with little food and no shel-ter to die of exposure or starvation—he did not care which.[92]

After the Bear River Massacre, Connor continued his brutal sweep through the Wasatch Range. By late spring, with many Indians killed and the rest starving, Shoshoni resistance was entirely broken. Nine surviving Shoshoni chiefs met that summer with government officials and signed the Treaty of Box Elder, forcing them onto a small reserva-tion along Idaho's Snake River near what is now Pocatello. Soon after, Utah's governor informed the Overland Mail Company that "all routes of travel through Utah Territory to Nevada and California, and to the Beaver Head and Boise river gold mines, may now be used with safety." Connor reported to his superiors the "happy state of affairs" that his district was now cleared of "savages."[93]

"We Are Men and Braves"

Further south in New Mexico Territory, Confederates were equally as quick to decry the savagery of Indians while ignoring their own be-havior. Lieutenant Colonel John R. Baylor made that clear enough. In 1861, southerners laid claim to what they called the "Confederate

Territory of Arizona," stretching between Texas and California. Baylor, a member of the prominent Baylor family of Texas, was named territorial governor. Soon after his appointment, Baylor established his capital at La Mesilla (now a suburb of Las Cruces) and declared authority over all the territory's inhabitants, Indian nations included. But already the region's Apaches and Navajos were on the warpath. Hunger forced many to turn violent after Federal posts shut down, cutting off annuity payments for land they had been forced to give up. Ranchers occupied their best hunting grounds, and the Indians now had no money to purchase beef cattle. What they could not buy, they were taking by force. Many of the natives, emboldened by the recent withdrawal of so many "blue coats," saw an opportunity to finally drive the whites from their land. They began by shutting down virtually all travel by whites in the territory. It seemed for a time that they might succeed. There appeared to be little either army, Union or Confederate, could do to stop them. Late that year near Fort Stanton, west of modern-day Roswell, a band of Apaches surprised and nearly wiped out a Confederate patrol. Only one man escaped to tell the tale. Troops from Fort Davis, Texas, tracked the Apaches back to their village, but they too were almost all killed. The only man left alive was a Mexican who had served as a guide for the Texans.[94]

Baylor responded with a declaration of extermination against all Indians, friendly or hostile. In an act of chemical warfare, Baylor had a sack of flour poisoned and distributed to local Indians during peace talks. Sixty died an agonizing death after accepting Baylor's gift. When he got word in March 1862 that a band of Apaches had approached the Confederate garrison at Tucson to talk peace, Baylor sent a message to the post commander.

> I learn . . . that the Indians have been to your post for the purpose of making a treaty. The Congress of the Confederate States has passed a law declaring extermination of all hostile Indians. You will therefore use all means to persuade the Apaches or any tribe to come in for the purpose of making peace, and when you get them together, kill all the grown Indians and take the children prisoners and sell them [as slaves] to defray the expense of killing the Indians.[95]

News of Baylor's actions prompted a good deal of controversy in Richmond. No such extermination law had been passed. Baylor defended himself by noting: "If objection is made to that part of my order making the children of the Indians *slaves*, I have only to say that the reasons for making slaves of savage Africans applies to savage Indians, and in my opinion, is the very *method* of *civilizing them*." Though many in Richmond surely agreed, to kill all adult Indians, men and women alike, was hardly Confederate policy. It was not long before Jefferson Davis removed Baylor from office.[96]

It mattered little in any case, for it was not long either before Federal forces drove the Rebels out of what Washington called New Mexico Territory. On March 28, 1862, the Battle of Glorieta Pass just east of Santa Fe left Confederates in control of the field. But Federals in their rear destroyed the entire Rebel wagon train, including 800 draft animals. Their supplies gone, the Confederates had little choice but to fall back. Federal reinforcements continued to flow in, and by June they had pushed the Rebels out of New Mexico for good. There was not much good in it for the Indians, though. The territory's new military commander, General James H. Carleton, was nearly as ruthless as Baylor had been.

Soon after he took charge, Carleton issued orders for Lieutenant Colonel Christopher "Kit" Carson and his 1st New Mexico Regiment to go after the Mescalero Apaches in the mountains of southeastern New Mexico. "All Indian men of that tribe are to be killed whenever and wherever you can find them," Carleton wrote to Carson. "The women and children will not be harmed, but you will take them prisoners. . . . If the Indians send in a flag and desire to treat for peace, say to the bearer that . . . you have no power to make peace; that you are there to kill them wherever you can find them; that if they beg for peace, their chiefs and twenty of their principal men must come to Santa Fe to have talk there; but tell them fairly and frankly that you will keep after their people and slay them until you receive orders to desist from these headquarters."[97]

Carson, who had friends among the Mescaleros, thought the orders far too harsh. He knew that the Mescaleros were an impoverished and poorly armed people living on poor land, and that their raids were driven by a search for food. Carson protested the orders, but carried them out when Carleton refused to amend them—even to the extent of explaining how Indians who were to be shot on sight might safely make it to Santa Fe for peace talks. The inevitable occurred soon after

Carson occupied Fort Stanton and began sending out patrols. One detachment led by Captain James "Paddy" Graydon came across a party of Mescaleros heading for Santa Fe. When one of the chiefs raised his open palm in a sign of peace, Graydon ordered his men to open fire. Twelve Mescaleros fell dead, including two chiefs and at least one woman. As the rest tried to flee, they were ridden down by Graydon's soldiers, who killed five more and wounded several others before the remaining survivors got away.[98]

Profoundly disturbed over the incident, Carson defied Carleton's orders, halted all operations against the Indians, and allowed several Mescalero chiefs to surrender to him personally at Fort Stanton. He then had three of them—Cadete, Chato, and Estrellasent—sent under armed escort to Santa Fe for surrender talks with Carleton. Cadete, speaking for the delegation, maintained a warrior's dignity when he told Carleton:

> You are stronger than we. We have fought you so long as we had rifles and powder; but your weapons are better than ours. Give us weapons and turn us loose, and we will fight you again; but we are worn out; we have no more heart; we have no provisions, no means to live; your troops are everywhere, our springs and waterholes are either occupied or overlooked by your young men. You have driven us from our last and best stronghold, and we have no more heart. Do with us as may seem good to you, but do not forget that we are men and braves.[99]

Carleton dumped the Mescaleros on a desolate eastern New Mexico reservation called Bosque Redondo adjacent to Fort Sumner. By March 1863, over 400 Mescaleros had been force-marched to the post. Another three hundred had already been killed during the campaign. Most of those not killed or captured fled south to Mexico. A few isolated bands remained starving in the mountains. The Mescaleros at Bosque Redondo were hardly better off. Enticed out of the mountains by the promise of food, they were used as slave labor to construct Fort Sumner. When food ran low they tried farming along Bosque Redondo's fifteen-mile stretch of the Pecos River, barely a creek by eastern standards, using its sparse waters for irrigation. But a short growing season and occasional flash floods made their efforts almost useless. Soon the Mescaleros were starving again.[100]

"They Forced My People to Move On"

To make matters worse, Carleton set out to force the more numerous Navajos onto the already overcrowded Bosque Redondo reservation. Recent mineral strikes on Navajo land made Carleton especially eager to move them. Seeing an opportunity to enrich himself, Carleton wrote to Washington in the spring of 1863, requesting funds to build a major road to the Navajo mining country. He told his superiors of "extraordinary discoveries of gold and silver in Arizona Territory," which had been split from New Mexico Territory in February. Carleton even sent gold nuggets to members of Lincoln's cabinet, asking Secretary of the Treasury Salmon P. Chase to "give the largest piece of gold to Mr. Lincoln."[101]

To pave the way for mining operations, Carleton sent Kit Carson's regiment on a brutal scorched-earth campaign against the primarily farming and herding Navajos. Rather than fighting pitched battles, Carleton and Carson planned to starve the Navajos into submission. By fall 1863 Carson's men had destroyed 187 acres of corn and 15 acres of wheat, and had stolen over a thousand animals. Only three Navajos died in the assaults; most fled from the army's onslaught. They were too poorly armed to put up an effective defense. One man tried approaching Fort Canby (formerly and later Fort Defiance) "to have a talk with his white brethren," but was gunned down for his trouble. When he got word that neighboring Zuni tribes were offering refuge to the besieged Navajos, Carleton threatened to capture and kill Zuni hostages if the assistance continued.[102]

In desperation, Navajos began raiding nearby ranches and mining camps searching for food. It was not a lifestyle that could sustain them, nor was it one that they could maintain. "A state of constant warfare was contrary to Navajo nature and totally disruptive of normal Navajo life," wrote historian Frank McNitt. "Stock raisers and farmers could not live as raiding nomads or fugitives." But how could they surrender? As Carson himself later admitted, "they had great fears of being killed on approaching our camp."[103]

Surrender or die; surrender *and* die—whatever the outcome, the Navajos had to surrender. Carson's men drove that point home during a murderous sweep through northeastern Arizona's Canyon de Chelly in January 1863. They struck Navajo winter camps, many of them in cliffside caves, from one end of the canyon to the other. The soldiers took only nineteen women and children captive. Navajo survivors who passed stories on to their descendants vividly remembered what happened during the Canyon de Chelly campaign.

> The firing gradually picked up, and soon it sounded like frying, with bullets hitting all over the cave. This went on nearly all afternoon. Then the firing ceased, but, by that time, nearly all the Navajos were killed. Men, women, children, young men and girls were all killed on the cliffs. Some just slid off the cliffs. . . . only a few survived. Blood could be seen from the top of the cliffs all the way down to the bottom. . . .
>
> The enemies opened rifle fire on the people in the caves, while the people fought back with bows and arrows. Some people were shot; some were falling off the cliff. . . . After more dreadful fighting, dead people were lying here and there, and many wounded were crawling around. Some fell from the cliff, including men, women, children and babies. . . .
>
> Two girls who went into a cave in the cliff were shot down, and they were hanging from the cliff. As my mother's group was running along, there was a woman walking toward them with blood flowing from her hip. She had been shot by the soldiers. . . .
>
> The riders were approaching the woman rapidly and found her where she stood among some tall grass. They rode up close and started circling her on horseback, and they grabbed at her clothes and soon ripped all the clothes off and left her completely nude except for the water jug which still hung from her neck. . . . Then she was shot in the head, slowly fell to the ground and died.[104]

Inevitably, in groups small and large, most of the Navajos began begging for peace terms. "Go to the Bosque Redondo," Carleton instructed his subordinates to tell them, "or we will pursue and destroy you. We will not make peace with you on any other terms." Homeless and starving, the Navajos had little choice but to comply. As the various bands surrendered, they were force-marched nearly four hundred miles to Bosque Redondo during the freezing winter of 1863–64. The Navajos remembered it as the Long Walk. Survivors vividly recalled the brutality.

> Daughter got tired and weak and couldn't keep up with the others or go any farther because of her [pregnancy]. So [we] asked the Army to

hold up for a while and to let the woman give birth. But the soldiers wouldn't do it. They forced my people to move on, saying they were getting the others behind. Not long after [we] moved on, [we] heard a gunshot. . . .

It was horrible the way they treated our people. Some old handicapped people and children couldn't make the journey, were shot on the spot and their bodies left behind for the crows and coyotes.[105]

Suffering from cold, disease, malnutrition, and maltreatment, of the more than eight thousand Navajos who started the journey, three thousand died on the Long Walk.[106]

As Indians continued filtering onto Bosque Redondo, their numbers soon reached nearly ten thousand. It was far more than the arid lands of the reservation could support. By summer the Pecos River was drained nearly dry from overirrigation, and mosquitoes were breeding in the riverbed's stagnant puddles. A resulting plague of malaria swept through the crowded camps, as did dysentery brought on by lack of clean drinking water. So common was it for soldiers to rape Indian captives that syphilis and gonorrhea spread through the camps too. Smallpox, mumps, and other "white man's" diseases added to the Indians' misery.[107]

So many came into Fort Sumner seeking medical help that they

During the freezing winter of 1863–64, U.S. troops force-marched more than eight thousand Navajos to the arid Bosque Redondo reservation in eastern New Mexico. This young mother was among them. Three thousand died on what the Navajos remember to this day as the Long Walk. When a pregnant woman could not keep pace, recalled one Navajo, "[We] asked the Army to hold up for a while and to let the woman give birth. But the soldiers wouldn't do it. They forced my people to move on. . . . Not long after [we] moved on, [we] heard a gunshot." (Library of Congress)

were banished from the post hospital. A nine-room building at a Navajo village just east of the fort was converted to an Indian hospital, though described by one witness as "a regular tumble-down concern." Its rooms were too small. Its cover was a roof in name only. Navajos and Mescaleros alike began to fear the place. "Scarce an Indian comes near their hospital," wrote Dr. George Gwyther, Fort Sumner's post physician. "On some days none at all; yet sickness is plentiful among them. The rattle and song of the medicine men may be heard in many huts. The blackened bodies, close cut hair, destroyed huts—the common signs of sickness and death—are very frequent sights. But the daily report of the steward is: 'No one comes here now, doctor.'" One Navajo interpreter explained why they stayed clear of the hospital: "All who go in never come out."[108]

Soon after their imprisonment, General Carleton congratulated himself on providing the Indians at Bosque Redondo with an opportunity to learn "the art of peace" and "the truths of Christianity."[109]

"I Want Him Dead"

While Carson was rounding up the Mescalero Apaches and Navajos, Carleton also sent troopers after the powerful Chiricahua Apaches of southwestern New Mexico and southeastern Arizona. Gold, silver, and copper had recently been discovered on their lands. Forcing the Chiricahuas to Bosque Redondo would be no easy task, as Carleton had learned early on when his regiments first entered Chiricahua territory. In July 1862, as he and his column were making their way from California to Santa Fe, they were ambushed east of Tucson at Apache Pass by a Chiricahua force led by Cochise and his father-in-law, Mangas Coloradas, chief of an eastern band of Chiricahuas called the Mimbrenos. Though they were unable to turn Carleton back, and Mangas Coloradas was severely wounded, the Chiricahuas made their point. Their land was theirs. No white man would enter it without having a fight on his hands.[110]

Relations between Chiricahuas and whites had not always been so hostile. During the 1850s, Cochise and Mangas habitually granted safe passage to whites on their way to California through Apache territory. Some Apaches established regular trade with stage stations along the Butterfield Overland Mail route. Even after gold was discovered near the Mimbres Mountains in May of 1860, local Chiricahuas tended to treat the white newcomers more as potential trading partners than invaders. Then in the fall of 1860, the elderly but stout Mangas Coloradas, perhaps seventy years of age and well over six feet tall, was visiting the Pinos Altos mining settlement when a group of rowdy miners assaulted him. As one Apache later told it: "The White Eyes bound him to a tree and lashed him with ox goads until his back was striped with deep cuts. He crept away like a wounded animal to let his wounds heal. . . . Never before had anyone struck him, and there is no humiliation worse than that of a whip."[111]

A short time later, Lieutenant George Bascom summoned Cochise to his tent and accused him, falsely as it turned out, of stealing cattle and kidnaping a white child. When Bascom's men tried to arrest him, Cochise drew his knife, slashed his way past the soldiers, cut through the tent wall, and made his escape as bullets whizzed by. Bascom then grabbed five of the chief's relatives who had been waiting outside the tent and held them as hostages. Cochise and his band responded by seizing a Butterfield employee and two hapless travelers near Apache Pass, offering them in exchange for his relatives. Bascom refused to negotiate and both sides ended up killing their hostages.[112]

The incidents with Mangas and Cochise set the Chiricahuas firmly against any further dealings with the whites. They closed down traffic along the Butterfield Road and set out to drive all remaining whites from their land. Ranchers, miners, passersby—none were safe from Apache wrath. By late 1862, even as the Federals were forcing Rebel troops out of the territory, Chiricahua lands had been almost entirely freed of white control.

Still, the best route to southern California passed through the heart of Chiricahua country, and their country held the richest mineral deposits in the southwest. In January 1863, Carleton sent General Joseph West to set up a fort near Pino Altos from which to wage war against the Chiricahuas. As with Carson's campaign against the Mescaleros, there would be no peace talks. Carleton told West that there would be only two options presented to the Chiricahuas—either submit unconditionally or die. But Carleton did not prohibit the promise of peace talks being used as bait to lure the Chiricahuas into a trap, and on January 17, the soldiers did just that. An advanced column, sent out by West to take Mangas dead or alive, hooked up with a group of miners and used them to draw Mangas out. While the soldiers secreted themselves near the Mimbrenos winter camp, the miners sought a parley with Mangas under a white flag of truce. Several of the tribal leaders, Geronimo among them, cautioned Mangas not to trust the whites. But Mangas argued that any chance for peace was worth the risk.

When Mangas came out to talk, the miners leveled their guns, took him prisoner, and delivered him to the soldiers. The next day, West met the column and was delighted to learn that Mangas had been captured. That he had been captured alive, however, was apparently not to West's liking. That night West told the two soldiers guarding Mangas that by morning, "I want him dead."[113]

Daniel Ellis Conner was among the miners camping with the soldiers that night. As he took his turn on watch in the bitter cold, he witnessed the guards torture, then kill, Mangas Coloradas.

> I could see them plainly by the firelight as they were engaged in heating their fixed bayonets in the fire and putting them to the feet and naked legs of Mangas, who was from time to time trying to shield his limbs from the hot steel. When I came up to the fire each time they would become innocent and sleepy and remain so until I departed on my beat again, when they would arouse themselves into the decided spirit of indulging this barbarous pastime. . . . I was about midway of my beat and approaching the firelight. Just then Mangas raised himself upon his left elbow and began to expostulate in a vigorous way by telling the sentinels in Spanish that he was no child to be playing with. But his expostulations were cut short, for he had hardly begun his exclamation when both sentinels promptly brought down their minnie muskets to bear on him and fired, nearly at the same time through his body. The chief fell back off his elbow into the same position in which he had been lying all the forepart of the night. This was quickly followed by two shots through the head by each sentinel's six-shooter, making in all, six shots fired in rapid succession. The old chief died without a struggle in the precise position that he had occupied continuously since dark.[114]

The next day, soldiers threw Mangas's corpse into a shallow grave. His scalp was already gone. Several days later, someone decided that Mangas's skull might make an interesting object of scientific study. They had the body dug up, severed the head, boiled off the soft tissue, then sent the skull to a museum in New York.[115]

More Apaches soon fell prey to the white man's lies. Two days after Mangas's murder, a detachment of California troopers fell on Mangas's winter camp. They killed eleven members of his family who had been told to await his release. Many more were wounded trying to escape. At other Mimbreno camps West's men drew the hungry Apaches out for peace talks with offers of food, then opened fire on them as they ate. Nine were killed. The rest scattered into the hills. Geronimo had been right. Under no circumstances could the whites be trusted.[116]

"The Broad Platform of Extermination"

Over the next few months West's men swept through the region but found it impossible to bring the Apaches to heel. Cochise, Geronimo, and other Chiricahua leaders knew better than to be drawn into "talks" with the whites. In Santa Fe, it became obvious to Carleton that West could not kill or capture the Chiricahuas on his own. So in the spring of 1864 Carlton authorized a vigilante war of genocide against them, calling for "a general rising of both citizens and soldiers" to kill every Apache they could find. Many New Mexico and Arizona whites responded enthusiastically, none more so than a rancher from the Prescott area who signed himself King S. Woolsey.[117]

Woolsey organized a company of vigilantes and, with arms and equipment supplied by army acquaintances, went after the Indians. He targeted not only the Apaches but the Yavapais just east of Prescott whose land he and his friends had coveted for some time. Ranging through eastern Arizona between the Agua Fria, Verde, and Gila rivers, Woolsey and his men terrorized all the Indians they could find, friendly or hostile. At Bloody Tanks, they massacred at least twenty-four Indians after killing six of their chiefs during a duplicitous parley. At Squaw Canyon near the Agua Fria, they bushwhacked an Indian camp, killing fourteen and scattering the survivors. At Quartz Canyon they killed sixteen. Then, near dark on the evening of April 9, 1864, as they paused on a ridge overlooking Big Rump Valley, they sighted a major Indian encampment down below. Woolsey laid plans for a dawn attack the next day, then settled down for a good night's sleep. But he had neglected to give orders prohibiting campfires that night.

At daybreak the wary Indians, having seen smoke up the ridge, were rushing to break camp. By the time Woolsey's men attacked, the Indians had nearly completed their evacuation. A running battle commenced as the vigilantes chased after their quarry, but the Indians quickly vanished into the mountains. Frustrated and enraged, Woolsey turned back to the village and ordered his men to destroy it.[118]

One of the more callous of Woolsey's men, a rogue known only as Sugarfoot Jack, found a baby left behind during the Indians' hasty retreat. He picked it up, tossed it into a burning hut, and watched with apparent delight as the baby roasted alive. Several men tried to pull it out of the flames but were too late to save it. Within minutes, Jack found another unfortunate child. After playing with it for a moment, dancing it on his knee and tickling it under the chin, he took out his revolver, put it to the child's head, and pulled the trigger. Some of the men were so incensed at the killings that they threatened to shoot Jack. The murderer fled before those threats could be carried out. As Jack headed for the hills, Woolsey's men began a heated argument about what type of warfare this was. Some supported Jack, saying all the Indians regardless of sex or age had to be wiped out. Others wanted nothing to do with killing babies, Indians though they were. Woolsey settled the matter by insisting, as he had already told the like-minded General Carleton, that he intended to "fight on the broad platform of extermination." That said, roughly half of Woolsey's company quit in protest and headed home.[119]

The rest continued to follow Woolsey until midsummer, harassing the Indians where they could but doing little more damage. As supplies ran low and the summer heat grew intense, these men too began returning home. So did many of Carleton's soldiers. Despite early success against the Chiricahuas, Carleton and his troopers were never able to root them out of the mountains. With their swift horses and the rifles they bought from Mexican traders, Apache leaders like Cochise and Geronimo became experts at hit-and-run warfare. No sooner could the soldiers respond to one attack before another was reported miles away. If pressed too closely, the Indians simply disappeared into their mountain strongholds. For Carleton's men it was like fighting illusive ghosts. When their enlistments expired in fall 1864, so many of the California troopers mustered out that Carleton had to suspend his Apache campaign.[120]

"Punishing These Treacherous Savages"

Another reason for the failure of Carleton's Apache campaign was his diversion of forces to deal with Comanche and Kiowa to the east. Though their range had been whittled down by the 1860s, their bands still roamed a large area centered on the Texas Panhandle stretching from eastern New Mexico through Indian Territory and up into western Kansas. As Carleton soon learned, though they made their homes mostly on the open plains, they would be no easier to force from their lands than the Apaches had been. For centuries the Comanche and Kiowa had hunted game, mainly buffalo, on the southern plains. Almost a hundred years earlier, the two tribes had combined forces to fight off the Spaniards, then the Anglos. So strong was their alliance that it was frequently said, "As the Comanche goes, so goes the Kiowa."[121]

In August 1861, leaders from nearly every major Comanche-Kiowa band met with Albert Pike at the Indian Territory's Wichita Agency and signed a treaty with the Confederacy. Intentionally drawn up to be vague, Confederate officials chose to interpret the treaty as a cession of lands in Texas and New Mexico. They appropriated nearly $65,000 for cattle and supplies, then set about enticing the Indians to settle down as cow herders just west of the Wichita Agency. The Indians, on the other hand, saw their treaty only as a nonaggression pact and the gifts as a traditional sign of peace. The issue never came to a head since contact between Comanche-Kiowa bands and the Confederacy was cut off after Federally allied Delawares and Shawnees destroyed the Wichita Agency in October 1862.[122]

Soon after, Federal agents approached the Comanche-Kiowa bands with offers of gifts and peace. Though the Indians saw their Confederate peace treaty as still valid, they saw no reason why they could not be on friendly terms with the Federals as well. In April 1863 four Kiowa and two Comanche chiefs, along with several Cheyenne and Arapaho chiefs from Colorado Territory, journeyed to Washington. There they met with President Lincoln at the White House and signed a treaty allowing whites safe passage along the Santa Fe Trail and Cimarron Cutoff. Lincoln then presented the chiefs with peace medals. Under the treaty's terms, the Indians would get a $25,000 annuity for five years in the form of trade goods. The first annuity payment was to be distributed later that year. But the Senate never ratified the treaty. When the Comanche, Kiowa, Cheyenne, and Arapaho showed up to receive their goods at the designated post, nothing was there. Outraged at what they saw as Lincoln's betrayal, they rode off, many vowing to halt travel across their lands until the white man made good on his promise.[123]

Comanche and Kiowa bands were the most aggressive since it was mainly their lands that the Santa Fe Trail and Cimarron Cutoff crossed. Stage lines and mail riders headed for the southwest and California either turned back or were never heard from again. Attacks became so frequent that the trip could not be made without a military escort. Though it might have been less costly simply to pay the promised annuity, by spring of 1864 the Federals determined to force Comanche and Kiowa onto reservations with or without a treaty. Carleton sent out word that all plains Indians in his jurisdiction who did not surrender themselves immediately at the nearest post would be considered hostile. As such, though he had no way of knowing whether all Indians had gotten the word, they were subject to being shot on sight.

To make good on the threat, Carleton sent out Kit Carson and his New Mexico regiments with orders for "punishing these treacherous savages." There were Utes and Jicarilla Apaches with his men as well. Carleton had long feared that these Indians of northern New Mexico might combine forces with the Comanche and Kiowa. Using a common divide-and-conquer tactic, Carleton hired a few Utes and Jicarillas as scouts. Whenever there was a battle, these scouts were to be put out front where they could easily be seen by the Comanche and Kiowa. So incensed would they be that they would never consider an alliance with any bands of Ute or Jicarilla. But for a time it seemed as if there might be no battles. Carson was running into much the same difficulty that the Californians had in going after the Chiricahuas. The Kiowa and Comanche, experts at hit-and-run tactics, were impossible to pin down. It was not until late fall when the Indians began settling in for the winter that Carson had any chance for a major engagement.[124]

Carson's chance came in November 1864 when he got word that a large group of Comanche and Kiowa had set up camp on the Texas Panhandle's Canadian River near the ruins of an old trading post called Adobe Walls. On the evening of November 24, Carson's scouts sighted a Kiowa village of about 170 lodges. Carson's four hundred men attacked at dawn the next day, sending surprised Kiowa fleeing from the camp. Kiowa warriors tried to form a skirmish line behind which the women and children could escape, but found themselves being pushed downriver and losing ground. The two howitzers Carson had were taking out large chunks of the Kiowa line with every blast. About thirty minutes into the fight, just as they were about to be overrun, the embattled Kiowa were joined by over a thousand more Kiowa and Comanche warriors from villages downriver. They had heard the gunfire and were coming to rescue their neighbors. Now hopelessly outnumbered, the hard-pressed soldiers began a retreat back up the Canadian River, stopping occasionally to fire on the pursuing Indians. Had it not been for its howitzers, Carson's force might have been annihilated. His battered expedition limped back to New Mexico, and the Comanche-Kiowa villages were safe for the rest of that winter at least.[125]

"All We Ask Is . . . Peace with the Whites"

A few days after the Battle of Adobe Walls, nearly two hundred miles to the northwest, Cheyenne and Arapaho bands camped on Colorado's Sand Creek were not so fortunate. For them there would be no rescue. On the morning of November 29, 1864, a day that still lives in infamy, troops led by a Methodist minister, Colonel John Chivington, carried out what forever after would be known as the Sand Creek Massacre. With orders from Chivington to take no prisoners, the soldiers slaughtered over 150 Indians, most of them women and children. Only nine of Chivington's men lost their lives, mainly because the Cheyenne and Arapaho braves were not prepared for an attack. There was no reason to think they should expect one. They had already been promised peace by Chivington himself.

Since the Fort Wise Treaty of 1861, many of the Cheyenne and Arapaho had been confined to the Sand Creek Reserve, described by one contemporary as the "most dry and desolate" region in Colorado. The treaty was signed by, among others, Black Kettle and White Antelope for the Cheyenne and Little Raven and Shave-Head for the Arapaho. In exchange for most of eastern Colorado, including prime buffalo hunting ground, the Indians were to be paid annuities. But Sam Colley, the reservation agent, habitually robbed the Indians of their annuity payments. His son Dexter and one other man were licensed to trade at Sand Creek, but often sold the Indians the goods they were supposed to be granted as annuities—that is when Colley allowed the Indians enough money to buy the goods. Starving and disease stricken, most of the Indians left the reservation to join others still hunting buffalo on the open plains. Those who stayed behind frequently drifted off the reservation, compelled by hunger to raid neighboring ranches and rob travelers along the Santa Fe Trail, which ran just south of the Sand Creek Reserve.[126]

In the spring of 1864, Agent H.T. Ketchum investigated conditions among the Cheyenne and Arapaho. He was disgusted by what he found. After visiting one post he wrote to Colorado's territorial governor, John Evans:

> While citizens and soldiers are permitted to enter their villages with whiskey in day time & at night; to make the men drunk & cohabit with the squaws, disseminating venereal diseases among them; while the Commanding Officer at the Post continues to get drunk every day & insult and abuse the leading men of the Tribes, & make prostitutes of their women; you cannot expect to have any permanent peace with these Indians.[127]

As conditions worsened and theft became more rampant among the roving bands, Agent Colley said of the hungry Indians: "I now think a little powder and lead is the best food for them."[128]

Many whites in Colorado agreed. That summer gangs of armed vigilantes and militia units ranged across eastern Colorado killing all the Indians they could find, friendly or hostile, on or off the reservation. Major T.I. McKenney, an army staff officer for the Department of Kansas (which included Colorado Territory), urged his superiors to stop the murders before things got any worse: "I think if great caution is not exercised on our part, there will be a bloody war. It should be our policy to try and conciliate [the Indians], guard our mails and trains well to prevent theft, and stop these [white] scouting parties that are roaming over the country, who do not know one tribe from another and who will shoot anything in the shape of an Indian. It will require only a few more murders on the part of our troops to unite all the warlike tribes."[129]

Far from discouraging the killers, Governor Evans and Colonel Chivington, commanding forces in Colorado Territory, urged them on. Their motives were mixed but seem to have had as much to do with politics as anything else. Colorado residents were scheduled to vote on a request for statehood in September. Evans and Chivington strongly supported the move, sure it would bring them more influence and fortune. They were also sure that to attract investors and immigrants, the Indians would have to be exterminated. But many Colorado voters, fearful that statehood would not only mean higher taxes but would also subject them to the federal draft, blamed Evans and Chivington for stirring up the Indian troubles. As if to confirm that accusation, Evans issued a proclamation "authorizing all citizens of Colorado, either individually or in such parties as they may organize, to go in pursuit of all hostile Indians . . . to kill and destroy, as enemies of the country, wherever they may be found." As an inducement to kill, Evans declared that the property of dead Indians would go to the ones who killed them. He was inviting a vigilante war of wholesale theft and indiscriminate murder. For Evans, Chivington, and their followers, "active extermination" of the "red devils" would be their final solution.[130]

At the same time, in a disingenuous gesture, Evans sent out demands for Cheyenne and Arapaho bands to assemble at specified military posts and surrender themselves—if they could make it there without being shot. Those who failed to comply immediately would be declared "hostile." In fact, as Evans's proclamation guaranteed, there would be no fine distinction between hostile and friendly Indians. It seemed clear to whites and Indians alike that Evans never intended otherwise. Still, so eager were the Indians for peace that some were willing to test yet again whether the white man's word might be trusted. In late August, after considerable debate in council, Black Kettle drafted a letter asking for peace talks. At great risk to themselves, a small band of Indians carried the letter to Fort Lyon just south of the Sand Creek Reserve.[131]

Fortunately for the Indians, the commander at Fort Lyon, Major Edward W. Wynkoop, was at least one white man whose word could be trusted. And he was just as eager for peace as Black Kettle was. After meeting with the Indians, Wynkoop wrote to Governor Evans that he would be escorting Black Kettle, White Antelope, and other Cheyenne and Arapaho chiefs to Denver for peace talks. Neither Evans nor Chivington received the news well. Only days earlier Colorado voters had rejected statehood, and now the two men's final solution to the Indian problem was in jeopardy as well. Could Wynkoop have misunderstood their meaning? They did not want talks with the Indians. They wanted them dead.[132]

At first Evans and Chivington refused a meeting when Wynkoop arrived with the chiefs on September 28. That very day Chivington had received a telegram from his superior, General Samuel R. Curtis, commanding the Department of Kansas from Fort Leavenworth. "I want no peace till the Indians suffer more," wrote Curtis. "No peace must be made without my directions." Though Evans had authority as territorial governor to grant the Indians clemency and thus make peace, he instead deferred to Curtis. Neither he nor Chivington wanted peace. But Wynkoop pointed out that Evans's message to the Indians offered peace to any who would surrender themselves at military posts. Black Kettle and the others had come to Denver in response to that message. How could they now be turned away? After some pleading from Wynkoop, Evans and Chivington, along with Wynkoop, Captain Silas Soule, Lieutenant Joseph Cramer, an interpreter, and a recorder met the chiefs at Fort Weld just outside Denver. Black Kettle, White Antelope, Bull Bear, and One Eye represented the Cheyenne. Neva, Bosse, Heaps-of-Buffalo, and Notanee spoke for the Arapaho.[133]

After a peace pipe was lit and passed around in silence, Black Kettle spoke.

> All we ask is that we may have peace with the whites. We want to hold you by the hand. . . . We have been traveling through a cloud. The sky has been dark ever since this war began. These braves who are with me are all willing to do what I say. We want to take good tidings home to our people, that they may sleep in peace.
>
> I want you to give all these chiefs of the soldiers here to understand that we are for peace, and that we have made peace, that we may not be mistaken by them for their enemies. I have not come here with a little wolf bark, but have come to talk plain with you. We must live near the buffalo or starve. When we came here we came free, without any apprehension, to see you, and when I go home and tell my people that I have taken your hand, and the hands of all the chiefs here in Denver, they will feel well, and so will all the different tribes of Indians on the Plains, after we have eaten and drunk with them.[134]

White Antelope held up the peace medal President Lincoln had given him and said: "I am proud to have seen the chief of all the whites in this country. . . . Ever since I went to Washington and received this medal, I have called all white men my brothers . . . now the soldiers do not shake hands but seek to kill me."[135]

Evans made a few terse remarks about Indian depredations, then Chivington said: "All the soldiers in this country are under my command. My rule of fighting white men or Indians is to fight them until they lay down their arms and submit to military authority. You are nearer to Major Wynkoop [at Fort Lyon] than anyone else, and you can go to him when you get ready to do that." It was all the chiefs needed to hear. Both they and Wynkoop took the remark to mean that peace had been made. According to Chivington, all the Cheyenne and Arapaho had to do was surrender at Fort Lyon, which their chiefs had in fact already done. Unlike Wynkoop, however, Chivington's word could not be trusted. A day after the meeting, Chivington wrote to Agent Sam Colley: "The chiefs brought in by Major Wynkoop have been heard. I have declined to make any peace with them."[136]

By mid-October hundreds of Indians were converging on Fort Lyon to make their surrender official. In accordance with Chivington's instructions at the Fort Weld conference, Wynkoop gladly received them as partners in peace. He distributed food and gifts among the Indians, knowing they would need sustenance until a new treaty could be drawn up and arrangements made with Indian agents to provision the tribes. But on November 4, word reached Fort Lyon that Wynkoop had been relieved of command. His superiors were not happy with the friendly relations he had cultivated with Black Kettle. Replacing him was Major Scott Anthony, who immediately ordered the Indians away from Fort Lyon and back to their old encampments on Sand Creek. There they were to wait until a treaty was ready for their signatures. Black Kettle and the other chiefs were surprised at Anthony's order but readily complied, sure that soldiers would soon come to escort them back to sign a treaty.[137]

The Reverend Colonel Chivington arrived at Fort Lyon on November 28, but he had no treaty with him. Instead he had brought the 3rd Colorado Cavalry Regiment, a rowdy bunch of 100-day volunteers raised in Denver specifically to kill Indians. Their enlistments were about to run out, and they had yet to see any action. Chided in

In September 1864, Major Ned Wynkoop (kneeling, left) escorted Cheyenne and Arapaho chiefs, including Black Kettle (seated third from left), to Denver. There they were promised peace by Colonel John Chivington. This photo was taken just after the conference. Chivington did not pose. On November 29, Chivington led an unprovoked attack on Black Kettle's camp at Sand Creek. White Antelope (thought to be seated second from left) died that day wearing a peace medal given to him by Abraham Lincoln. Captain Silas Soule (kneeling right) refused the order to charge and held his command in check. (Denver Public Library)

Denver newspapers as the "Bloodless Third," these men were eager to get at the Indians. Chivington meant to see that they got their chance. Augmented by troopers at Fort Lyon, he intended to lead an assault against Black Kettle's band at Sand Creek the next day. A few of the officers, Silas Soule and Joseph Cramer among them, strongly protested the plan. Soule and Cramer had both witnessed Chivington's promise of peace at the Fort Weld conference. As Chivington instructed, the Indians had surrendered themselves at Fort Lyon. How could he now order an attack against them? Chivington roared back, "Damn any man who sympathizes with the Indians," adding that it was "honorable to kill Indians under any and all circumstances." He wanted no prisoners taken at Sand Creek.[138]

In the cold gray light of the next morning's dawn, Black Kettle's village of about five hundred Cheyenne and Arapaho awoke to find over seven hundred troopers and four howitzers on the opposing bluffs overlooking the dry bed of Sand Creek. George Bent, a mixed-blood trader living among his mother's people, emerged from his lodge as the soldiers came riding down.

> When I looked toward the chief's lodge, I saw that Black Kettle had a large American flag up on a long lodgepole as a signal to the troops that the camp was friendly. Part of the people were rushing about the camp in great fear. All the time Black Kettle kept calling out not to be frightened; that the camp was under protection and there was no danger. Then suddenly the troops opened fire on this mass of men, women, and children, and all began to scatter and run. At the beginning of the attack Black Kettle, with his wife and White Antelope, took their position before Black Kettle's lodge and remained there after all others had left the camp. At last Black Kettle, seeing that it was useless to stay longer, started to run.[139]

By then most of the Indians were fleeing down the dry bed of Sand Creek trying to find shelter among its pits and gullies. Some of the warriors tried to form a skirmish line to cover the women and children's escape. But the bows, arrows, and few guns they had were no match for the carbines of the charging cavalrymen—some mounted, others dismounted. The warriors were quickly overrun and began fleeing with the rest along Sand Creek. As Black Kettle and his wife turned to follow them, White Antelope ran toward the soldiers, waving his arms and yelling at them in English to stop shooting. It was a useless effort. As bullets flew around them, Black Kettle tried to call him back. But White Antelope ignored his friend. The heartsick chief was tired—tired of seeing his people suffer and die, tired of the white man's lies, tired of fighting, tired of living. He folded his arms over his chest and began chanting his death song: "Nothing lives long, except the earth and the mountains. . . ." Before White Antelope could finish, bullets tore into his chest. When the soldiers reached his body, they found hanging from his neck the peace medal President Lincoln had given him. They scalped him, then sliced off his ears and nose as souvenirs. In a final act of desecration, they removed his scrotum and later used it as a tobacco pouch.[140]

Not all the soldiers were so brutal. Some refused to participate at all, Captain Silas Soule among them. When ordered into the action, he told the men under his command to hold their ground. They did, sitting there on the bluff as they watched the slaughter below.[141] That slaughter was as indiscriminate as it was bloody. As one witness recalled:

> I saw five squaws under a bank for shelter. When the troops came up to them they ran out and showed their persons to let the soldiers know they were squaws and begged for mercy, but the soldiers shot them all. . . . There were some 30 or 40 squaws collected in a hole for protection; they sent out a little girl about six years old with a white flag on a stick; she had not proceeded but a few steps when she was shot and killed. I saw a little girl about five years of age who had been hid in the sand; two soldiers discovered her, drew their pistols, and shot her, and then pulled her out of the sand by the arm. I saw quite a number of infants in arms killed with their mothers.[142]

For many of the soldiers, simply killing their prey was not enough. Mutilation of the living and the dead was common that day, as another witness remembered.

> One old squaw wandered sightless through the carnage. Her entire scalp had been taken, and the skin of her forehead fell down over her eyes to blind her. . . . A group of soldiers paused amid the firing to take turns profaning the body of a comely young squaw, very dead. Indians' fingers were hacked away to get their rings as souvenirs. One soldier trotted about with a heart impaled on a stick. Others carried off the genitals of braves. Someone had the notion that it would be artistic work to slice away the breasts of the Indian women. One breast was worn as a cap, another was seen stretched over the bow of a saddle.[143]

As Chivington had ordered, no prisoners were taken. The few soldiers who tried quickly found that the order was no joke. As several of the men escorted three women and five children back to camp, Lieutenant Harry Richmond of the 3rd Colorado rode up and personally killed and scalped every one of the prisoners while they screamed for mercy. When one officer asked Chivington what to do with Jack Smith, the mixed-blood son of an interpreter captured among the Indians, Chivington shot back, "Don't ask me; you know my orders; I want no prisoners." A short time later, fifteen soldiers entered the lodge where Jack was being held and shot him to death.[144]

Miraculously, over half the Indians at Sand Creek escaped. That was due in large part to a band of warriors who, after digging makeshift rifle pits along the bank and in the creek bed, held off their attackers most of the day. One officer wrote that the Indians there "fought desperately, apparently resolved to die upon that ground, but to injure us as much as possible before they were killed." Had they not tied up so many soldiers, the massacre would surely have been much worse.

Shortly before nightfall, the soldiers finally broke off their attack. Under cover of darkness, the remaining Indians rounded up a few of their scattered horses and gathered all the wounded they could find. Most congregated at a ravine ten miles above their former village and collected grass for fires to keep from freezing. Black Kettle's wife was among the wounded—shot nine times, but still alive. Black Kettle also survived but was the only chief left alive after the massacre. Left Hand, Standing Water, One Eye, War Bonnet, Spotted Crow, Yellow Wolf, Yellow Shield, Bear Man, Two Thighs, and White Antelope—all were dead.[145]

Not satisfied with one massacre, Chivington tried for two. After a day of finishing off wounded Indians left on the field and further mutilating the dead, he turned his men downstream and rode forty miles to the mouth of Sand Creek. There he planned to wipe out Little Raven's band of Arapaho who, like Black Kettle's people, had been told to await word of a formal peace. Word came instead of the Sand Creek Massacre, just ahead of Chivington's column. The Arapaho immediately broke camp and fled south to take refuge among the Kiowa. Finding their village abandoned, Chivington turned around and headed back to Denver. There the Third Colorado Cavalry, hailed now as the "Bloody Thirdsters," rode into town with their plunder on display. For weeks after they could be seen in the streets showing off Indian rings and earrings, some still attached to severed fingers and earlobes. Cheyenne and Arapaho scalps were held up to cheering crowds at Denver theaters. Dozens more were hung over mirrors behind the bars of local saloons. Chivington's report of the attack on Sand Creek praised his men's conduct and closed with the words, "All did nobly."[146]

The Sand Creek survivors limped their way northward, where they were taken in by bands of Northern Cheyenne and Sioux. As word of the massacre spread, outraged Plains Indians banded together in preparation for war. By early January there were 1,500 warriors mobilized along the South Platte River. Four thousand more were gathered at the headwaters of the Republican River. Over the next two months, bands of Cheyenne, Sioux, and Arapaho, along with Kiowa and Comanche warriors, raided all across the central Plains. They destroyed almost every ranch and stage station along the South Platte. They attacked stage lines and supply trains on the Overland Route to Denver. They tore up telegraph lines too, cutting off Denver's communication as well as travel from the East.[147]

Jim Beckwourth, a mulatto who had lived fifty years among the Plains Indians, approached the Cheyenne that winter on behalf of the army and tried to negotiate a peace. Leg-in-the-Water, who had replaced Black Kettle as principal chief, asked Beckwourth:

> What do we have to live for? The white man has taken our country, killed our game; was not satisfied with that, but killed our wives and children. Now no peace. . . . We have now raised the battle-axe until death.[148]

But there were many warriors who still had wives and children. They well knew that to stay and die would mean more suffering for their people. In council, the chiefs decided to break off their attacks, salvage who and what they had, and join with other bands of Cheyenne and Sioux to the north in Dakota Territory. There they would be safe, at least for a time.[149]

8

"Was the War in Vain?"

No man in America rejoiced more than I at the downfall of Negro slavery, but when the shackles fell from the hands of those four millions of blacks, it did not make them *free*; it simply transferred them from one condition of slavery to another; it placed them upon the platform of the white workingmen and made all slaves together.[1]

—WILLIAM H. SYLVIS, LABOR ORGANIZER

As the war for the Union recedes into the misty shadows of the past and the Negro is no longer needed to assault forts and stop rebel bullets, he is . . . of less importance.[2]

—FREDERICK DOUGLASS, AUTHOR, ORATOR, FORMER SLAVE

"What We Want and Need Is Peace"

In the spring of 1864 editor E.H. Grouby of southwest Georgia's *Early County News* wrote: "We cannot help thinking this is the last year of the war. . . . We have now entirely too many little jackass upstarts filling positions in our government." By October, Grouby was sure that those who still backed the Confederacy were mainly speculators who held "fat Government contracts," along with corrupt officials who were "not yet done fleecing the Government." "Their voice," wrote Grouby, "is still for war, war, war!" War supporters were fleecing more than just the government. One Virginia lawyer, who as a member of Congress had called for fighting it out "until the last man fell in the last ditch," was making upwards of $2,000 a day arranging draft exemptions for those who could pay.[3]

During the following winter of 1864–65, citizens held meetings all over the South—at least those parts of the South still unoccupied by Union forces—demanding an end to the war. Nowhere were they more frequent or insistent than in Georgia. A Hart County meeting attended by "a large number" called on Governor Brown to arrange "a speedy peace." Citizens in Lumpkin County did the same. "All most to a man," wrote Lumpkin County resident James Findley, they were eager for peace. When Jackson County residents tried to hold an antiwar meeting, Confederate cavalry broke it up. Undeterred, protestors met again and drafted resolutions urging an end to the "bloody and destructive war." Asserting their "inalienable right of popular assemblage," Jasper County folk met at the courthouse to insist on an end to "the great sufferings of our people." Upson County citizens met at Thomaston and voted "to stop the war on any terms." According to one attendee, "some of the citizens go so far as to say that they will be glad to see Lincoln in possession of the state." One assembly in a rural district of Bibb County was especially aggressive in its demands. A crowd of about sixty voters, all but four of them antiwar men, met to elect local judges. After the balloting, one of the newly elected justices threatened to drive every Confederate official out of Macon and "pledged himself to raise 300 men in twenty-four hours for that purpose if required."[4]

There was at least one prowar meeting in Georgia that winter. In February 1865, the *Augusta Chronicle and Sentinel* editor sarcastically wrote of "the 'great' war meeting—with a slim attendance, recently held in Coweta County." The paper noted that only five of those present had ever been in the army. The rest were exempts "occupying profitable bomb-proof positions—and of course wanted the war to go on." The editor hardly found that surprising. "They want our difficulties settled? Not a bit of it! . . . [T]hey would be obliged to come down to the level of common people. . . . This kind of patriotism is altogether too prevalent." The editor of Georgia's *Columbus Sun* agreed.

It seemed to him that those most likely to advocate "fighting it out" were among the least likely to be in the army. "We know men of this stamp in Columbus."[5]

By the winter of 1865, most common folk were too busy fighting off Confederates to worry about the Yankees. From its inception the Confederacy had been fighting a three-front war: one against the North, another against disaffected white southerners, and yet another against dissident slaves. With deserter and layout gangs, many allied with local blacks, controlling vast stretches of the southern country-side, one southern editor had written in late 1863: "We are fighting each other harder than we ever fought the enemy." By early 1865, the South's inner civil war reached its climax, and anti-Confederate southerners were claiming more and more victories. A February peace meeting in Thomas County, Georgia, turned violent when the assembled antiwar men successfully beat back an assault by pro-Confederates. That same month in Irwin County, local unionists and "a large number of deserters" convened an antiwar meeting at Ir-winville. They adopted several peace resolutions, including one calling for the Confederacy's outright surrender. When a Rebel militia lieu-tenant tried to break up the meeting, Willis Bone, a longtime unionist, knocked him down with a musket and led three cheers for Lincoln. The excited anti-Confederates then drove the lieutenant and every other supporter of the Richmond regime out of town. In effect, Irwin County seceded from the Confederacy that day.[6]

Other Georgia counties were threatening to do the same. Tatnall and Liberty men drew up formal resolutions declaring that they would rejoin the Union whether Georgia did or not. That sort of indepen-dent action had been going on for some time all across the South. Cit-izens of east-central Mississippi's adjoining Newton and Kemper counties met in March 1863 and adopted resolutions expressing their willingness to rejoin the Union. In March 1864 Jackson County, Al-abama, announced its allegiance to the Union and seceded from the Confederacy. A month later huge deserter colonies in Marion County, Mississippi, and Washington Parish, Louisiana, formed "a government of their own in opposition to the Confederate Government." In July, the *Natchez Courier* announced that "the county of Jones, State of Mis-sissippi, has seceded from the State and formed a Government of their own, both military and civil." So did Mississippi's Attala County, de-claring itself "the free state of Attala." In November anti-Confederate

Virginians centered in Montgomery and Floyd counties formed the "State of Southwest Virginia" for which they elected a governor, lieutenant-governor, and "a brigadier-general of deserters."[7]

That fall Jefferson Davis got a disturbing letter from F. Kendall of Greenville, Georgia: "I assure you Sir that if the question were put to the people of this state whether to continue the war or return to the union, a large majority would vote for a return." State governors were getting the same message. In January 1865 one writer who signed herself "A Poor Woman and Children" asked Governor Vance of North Carolina to "try and stop this cruel war." "Here I am without one mouthfull to eat for myself and five children and God only knows where I will get somethin, now you know as well as you have a head that it is impossible to whip they yankees, therefor I beg you for God sake to try and make peace on some terms and let they rest of they poor men come home and try to make somthing to eat, my husband has been kiled, and if they all stay till they are dead, what in they name of God will become of us poor women and children. . . . I believe slavery is doomed to dy out," she insisted. "God is agoing to liberate neggers, and fighting any longer is fighting against God."[8]

Another North Carolinian wrote to Governor Vance reminding him of what had been obvious since state voters rejected secession in 1861: "This never was a war of the majority; with all its horrors it has been forced upon the people contrary to their will and wishes, and it is now perpetuated by the minority against the will of the majority. . . . what we want and need is *peace, blessed peace*." A Randolph County citizen wrote to his local paper asking whether "the people, the bone and sinew of this once great country were ever ligitimately consulted upon the subject of cecession." The implied answer, of course, was "No."[9]

In February 1865, a poignant letter arrived in the office of Georgia's Governor Brown. J.T. Smith of Bibb County had sacrificed as much as anyone for the Confederacy. One son had been killed in battle. Another was maimed for life. Three more were still in the army, and all his property was gone. He pleaded with Brown to "leave the sinking ship." He told the governor that southern newspapers "all state falsehoods when they say that the armies are anxious still to fight. It is not true. The officers with high [salaries] and easy situations . . . get up meetings and pass resolutions to that effect without the knowledge and consent of nine tenths of the privates in the army. . . . They are going home as fast as they can get there. The country is full of deserters and almost every man in the community will feed them and keep them from being arrested. Stop it, my friend, stop it. All the enlightened world is against us, and God himself is against us!"[10]

One might have thought that planters too were against the Confederacy, judging by their lack of material support for it. With the Confederacy starving around them, planters still made sure that cotton dominated much of the South's landscape. In September 1864 alone, at least 440 bales were shipped out of Griffin, Georgia. Other cotton-belt towns reported similar receipts through that fall and into the winter. Sherman's men found about twenty-five thousand cotton bales stockpiled in Savannah after they captured the city in December. When Columbus, Georgia, fell to Yankee troopers the next April, there were one hundred twenty-five thousand bales packed in and around warehouses lining the wharves.[11]

While planters devoted prime farmland to cotton, hundreds of thousands continued to go hungry. In March 1865, a commissary agent wrote from Atlanta that "the suffering for food is absolutely heart rending." Knowing that poor women would break into his commissary and take what they wanted in any case, he had long since opened his doors to them. His office was, he said, "almost constantly thronged with women and children begging for bread. They do not ask for meat, but are satisfied with bread alone. During the late freezing weather, females walked as far as sixteen miles in the mud and ice, for the purpose of getting meal, which they would carry home upon their sholders." It was a pitiful sight, he wrote, to see them come in from the cold with their bonnets and shawls crusted with ice.[12]

Not all southerners were struggling so in the war's closing months. Finer foods were still available for those who could afford them. Blockade runners had long since given up importing basic necessities, preferring instead to smuggle in items they knew would bring top dollar from those who could pay. In December 1864, T.J. MacGare, owner of the Morgan Restaurant in Augusta, Georgia, put an ad in local papers aimed at "lovers of good living and drinking." A city editor who visited the establishment praised its "delicacies and luxuries" as well as its "excellent assortment of the finest kind of liquors." In January 1865, the Rialto Restaurant of Montgomery, Alabama, billed itself as serving "all the luxuries of the season." Another Montgomery establishment advertised the availability of real coffee instead of the cheaper substitutes for "those who consider price no object." As late as

March, only weeks before the war's end, one lady wrote of a meal at the Cook House, a posh Columbus, Georgia, inn, where the table was so heavy with food that it *"actually groaned."* There were sausages, roast pork, cold turkey, biscuits, hot rolls, cornbread, and cake. The next morning at breakfast there was real coffee with milk and sugar.[13]

With Confederate defeat assured and class divisions as sharp as ever, desertion continued to plague the army. Even among those who did not desert, there was little enthusiasm for the war. Most soldiers simply wanted to go home. Requests for discharges and extended furloughs flooded Confederate and state offices. From Randolph County, Georgia, came a petition to have Private B.F. Brooks relieved of duty. His wife, Julia, headed a list of twenty-six names pleading on his behalf. Already at home on leave, Daniel Chessy of Steam Mill in Decatur County asked for an indefinite extension of his furlough. West Sheffield of neighboring Miller County did the same. Most never bothered to ask. "I had permission of my officers to come [home] but didnt return," said Tennessean William Mullins when he applied for a state pension after the war. He walked for many days "through the snow . . . almost barefooted. I found my wife and children in a needy condition and I felt like I ought to stay and support them as the war was almost at a close."[14]

"Don't Think There Is Much Regret for the Loss"

In April 1865, the last major Confederate armies surrendered. On May 10, Yankee troopers captured Jefferson Davis near Irwinville, Georgia, as he fled south in a vain effort to get out of the country and establish a Confederate government-in-exile. Other Rebel officials were soon in custody and the Confederate nation ceased to be. In a way, though, the Confederacy as a nation hardly ever existed at all. Eminent Civil War historian E. Merton Coulter, enamored as he was with the idea of southern nationalism, could still admit that the Confederacy never became an "emotional reality" to most southern whites until long after the war was over. "The Confederacy," Coulter wrote, "was not blessed with a 'one for all and all for one' patriotism with which future generations of sentimental romancers were to endow it. Had it been so, this newborn nation might well have established its independence."[15]

From its beginnings, the Lost Cause lacked support from a majority of southerners. If a house divided against itself cannot stand, then the Confederacy's failure may have been inevitable, especially under the relentless pressures of war. Most white southerners had opposed secession in the first place. Black southerners could hardly feel much enthusiasm for a government that considered slavery their "natural and normal condition." What support the Confederacy did have eroded steadily as the passions of 1861 died away.[16]

In the spring of 1862, conscription only accelerated the decline of support for the war. Devastating as well to the war effort were the attitudes of planters and the privileges granted them by the government. Not only were they exempt from the draft, but they continued to grow too much cotton and tobacco while their poorer neighbors and Confederate soldiers went hungry. In doing so, planters helped starve the Confederacy out of existence. Hunger in the army and hunger at home contributed to a desertion rate that crippled the war effort early on. Robert E. Lee wrote in the fall of 1862 that desertion and straggling were the main reasons for his army's defeat at Antietam. That loss had far-reaching effects. It spurred Lincoln to announce the Emancipation Proclamation, which made diplomatic recognition and aid for the Confederacy by Britain or France impossible. And it drew more than two hundred thousand African Americans, three-fourths of them southerners, into the Union army and navy. Lincoln himself admitted that the war might not have been won without them.[17]

The Union's victory is often attributed to greater northern industry and population. Though it is true that the North had more factories and people than the South, to assume that these were the overriding reasons for Confederate defeat ignores more decisive realities of the battlefield and home front. So successful was the Confederacy's munitions program that never did its forces lose a major battle for lack of war materiel. What they constantly lacked was food; cotton and tobacco production was largely responsible for that. It was equally responsible for home-front food shortages that contributed to inflation, speculation, women rioting, and ultimately to soldiers deserting. Had it not been for the two-thirds of soldiers who were absent by 1864, the Confederacy might well have been able to offset the North's population advantage. As it was, Union armies nearly always held the numerical edge—an edge made even greater by the nearly half-million southerners who wore Union blue. Together with hundreds of thousands more who actively and passively resisted the Confederacy, it was southerners themselves as much as anyone else who were responsible for Confederate defeat.

Those who had not grasped the war's base reality early on came increasingly to view the struggle as little more than a rich man's war. Active support for the war among most plain folk inevitably declined once that realization set in. Thousands refused to serve, and thousands more already in the service abandoned their ranks. In October 1863, Confederate Sergeant G.H. Baughn observed: "The troops are coming to the conclusion that this is a war for the rich men of the South, and they are determined to get out of it." Ultimately, as historian Paul Escott put it, "the decision which common soldiers made with their feet sealed the fate of the Confederacy."[18]

For most soldiers, that decision came much earlier and had its impact much sooner than some historians are willing to acknowledge. They argue that the fall of Atlanta and Sherman's March to the Sea, along with Lincoln's reelection in late 1864, were the key events leading to loss of will and Confederate defeat. It was, they say, military defeat that brought a loss of will and doomed the Confederacy. Certainly defeats on the battlefield sapped the Confederacy's will to fight, but those defeats came largely because so many soldiers had already lost their will and deserted the army.[19] By the time Atlanta was in Union hands, and well before Sherman's March, two-thirds of the Confederate army was absent, "most of them," as Jefferson Davis admitted, "absent without leave." Desertion was at the root of Confederate failures even before the summer 1863 defeats at Gettysburg and Vicksburg, as Robert E. Lee himself wrote just after his September 1862 retreat from Antietam. Soldiers were, in fact, leaving before the war's first year was out, which in large part led to conscription in April 1862.[20]

Some left because the army could not feed them. Some left because their families were not being fed. What little food their families had was often hauled away by impressment companies, made up largely of able-bodied men who preferred to stay safely behind the lines and make war on soldiers' wives and children. Soldiers left because speculators too preyed on their families, often with the backing of corrupt officials. They left because planters grew too much cotton and tobacco—planters who, with government sanction, avoided military service at will. Soldiers left because the Confederacy did little to encourage food production, and its agents lined their pockets with ill-gotten gains. Some left because they had never wanted secession to begin with. Others left because they decided that the cause was not worthy of their families' sacrifice. And, finally, they left because they were tired of fighting a rich man's war.

On April 5, 1865, only days before the war's end, Georgia's *Early County News* concluded:

> This has been "a rich man's war and a poor man's fight." It is true that there are a few wealthy men in the army, but nine tenths of them hold positions, always get out of the way when they think a fight is coming on, and treat the privates like dogs. . . . there seems to be no chance to get this class to carry muskets.[21]

Though the conflict may have been a rich man's war, it was not as much of a poor man's fight as the rich tried to make it. That was true North and South. On both sides, the lowest of the lower classes tended to be as adamant as the rich in their refusal to fight—or refusal to fight for their region's dominant regime. In the South, while most Confederate soldiers were nonslaveholders and poorer than their slaveholding neighbors, southerners even poorer still were more likely to dodge the draft, desert, or serve in the Union army. As for the North, James McPherson in his *Battle Cry of Freedom* presents evidence suggesting that the poorest northerners were among the least likely to serve. It was in fact their resistance to the draft, and northern dissent generally, that goes a long way toward explaining how a Confederacy at war with itself as well as the North was able to survive for as long as it did.[22]

Lincoln's efforts to maintain popular support for the war were never as successful as most postwar popularizers liked to pretend. Shelby Foote, author of a massive three-volume narrative entitled *The Civil War*, recognized the limits of Lincoln's success when he said "the North fought that war with one hand behind its back." But Foote was probably mistaken when he added that the North could simply have "brought that other arm out" if it had needed to. Lincoln and Congress tried repeatedly to do just that with such measures as the Militia Acts of 1862 and the Enrollment Act of 1863. Lincoln's war policies nearly cost him the presidency in 1864 as it was. He had pushed the North as far as it was willing to go in support of the war. That "other arm" simply was not coming out.[23]

In a way, Lincoln's efforts to keep the North's war fever high were arguably even less effective, certainly in terms of recruitment percentages, than Davis's efforts to do the same in the South. Despite the North's population advantage of two to one, only about a million native-born northerners served in the Union military—roughly the same as the number of southerners who served the Confederacy. Nearly a fourth of the Union armed forces were made up of immigrants, and almost another fourth were southerners, black and white. It was immigrants and southerners who gave the Union armies their numerical superiority on the battlefield. In the end, given what support Lincoln was able to muster in the North, it came down to southerners themselves. Had all soldiers *from* the South fought *for* the South, or more precisely for the Richmond regime, the result would have been at least parity on the battlefield and probably victory for the Confederacy.[24]

But that outcome would have required any number of unlikely scenarios: planters forgoing cotton and tobacco in favor of food; speculators reigning themselves in or being reined in by the government; plain folk volunteering to such an extent that no draft was necessary; effective government and planter support for soldiers' families; and the development of a party system to keep dissent safely channeled into the electoral process. Finally, and most unlikely of all, it would have required willing slaves to stay on the plantations or fight for the Confederacy.

Resistance among slaves, up to and including escape, was on the rise well before the war. That resistance itself contributed to slaveholders' push for an independent slavocracy. It is hardly imaginable that slaves would have become less resistant even had the Confederacy survived—especially with free nations to the north, west, and south, and no fugitive slave law to force their return. Resistance and escape would certainly have continued, and most likely would have increased. For the Richmond government to constantly guard every stretch of the Potomac, Ohio, and Rio Grande rivers, not to mention building a Berlin-like wall around the rest of its land border, would hardly have been a workable response. The Confederacy would eventually have had to end slavery or lose much of its black labor force. Ultimately, one way or another, the South's slave-based regime bore the seeds of its own destruction.

As for nonslaveholding whites, shut out as they were from the benefits of a slave economy, it seems unlikely that they would have supported slavery indefinitely. With limited lands and virtually no socioeconomic mobility, many southern whites, three-fourths of them nonslaveholders, were already coming to question slavery by the 1850s. Some, like Hinton Rowan Helper, spoke out forcefully against it. Such resistance on the part of nonelite whites, like resistance among slaves, was a strong force driving slaveholder fears for the future of slavery. And it helped fuel slaveholder demands for a slaveholders' republic.

Then there were issues of white disaffection with the Confederacy. Most southern voters had voiced their displeasure at the polls in 1863 and would surely have done so even more strongly in 1865 had the war not ended when it did. Frank Lawrence Owsley Sr., the leading authority of his generation on the Old South's plain folk, speculated that "the Confederacy, even had it not suffered military defeat at the hands of the North in 1865, would have been defeated in the next state and congressional elections, which would have disintegrated its armies and brought peace."[25]

But the Confederacy did not last that long. By the winter of 1864–65, social and economic disparities among southerners had taken their toll. Lack of food, speculation, cotton and tobacco overproduction, and government corruption, all in the face of hunger and want among the plain folk, ultimately made the war's outcome a matter of indifference to most southerners. It was a rich man's war in any case. Evidence for that seemed clear enough as the war was winding down. In February 1865, one southerner chastised the rich for their continued hypocrisy and callousness.

> That is right. Pile up wealth—no matter whether bread be drawn from the mouth of the soldier's orphan or the one-armed, one limbed hero who hungry walks your streets—take every dollar you can, pay out as little as possible deprive your noble warriors of every comfort and luxury, increase in every way the necesaries of life, make everybody but yourself and non-producers bear the taxes of the war; but be very careful to parade everything you give before the public—talk boldly on the street corners of your love of country, be a grand home general—and, when the war is over, point to your princely palace and its magnificent surroundings and exclaim with pompous swell, "These are the results of my patriotism."[26]

Though most Confederate soldiers abandoned their ranks long before Appomattox, many of those who stayed did so with little enthusiasm for the cause. What loyalty they felt was more for their comrades than the Richmond regime. Sergeant William Andrews, who joined the army in February 1861 and surrendered with Lee at Appomattox, wrote in May 1865: "While it is a bitter pill to have to come back into the Union, don't think there is much regret for the loss of the Confederacy. The treatment the soldiers have received from the government in various ways put them against it." (Courtesy of Longstreet Press, Athens, Georgia)

Patriotism, at least for the Confederacy, was a sentiment long since abandoned by most southerners. Even among those who served to the end, there was little love for the Confederacy. What loyalty they still felt was more for their comrades than for the regime in Richmond. Sergeant William Andrews of the First Georgia Volunteers had joined the army in February 1861 and remained through the entire war. Few could match his service in the cause of southern independence. Still, only a few weeks after his surrender with Robert E. Lee at Appomattox he wrote: "While it is a bitter pill to have to come back into the Union, don't think there is much regret for the loss of the Confederacy. The treatment the soldiers have received from the government in various ways put them against it."[27]

"They Promised to Take Our Land, and They Took It."

Though the Civil War was over, its outcome hardly settled the many other civil wars that still plagued the country. Soldiers home from the battlefield continued their struggle against economic injustice. Women carried on their efforts against social and sexual oppression. And blacks, forced as they were to fight for rights that the postwar Constitution was supposed to have guaranteed, came to feel that Union victory held little but hollow promises for them. "Among the masses of Americans," wrote historian Kenneth Stampp, "there were no victors, only the vanquished."[28]

American Indians too, at least those not already vanquished, had to struggle on for their land and their lives. There were a few successes. Geronimo and his Chiracahua Apaches fought the army to a standstill in the Southwest. So did the Sioux Chief Red Cloud and his people in Dakota Territory. In 1868 they forced the United States to sign a treaty respecting their hunting grounds and closing the Bozeman Trail. In the 1870s, when miners overran the sacred Black Hills in violation of treaty, Sitting Bull and Crazy Horse led the Sioux and Northern Cheyenne off their reservations. Instead of using the army to enforce the treaty and drive out the miners, President Ulysses S. Grant ordered his soldiers after the Indians. Years earlier during the Civil War, northern critics had called Grant a butcher. Now he sent old wartime friends, men like William T. Sherman and Phil Sheridan, to butcher Indians. They did not shy away from the job. "We must act with vindictive earnestness against the Sioux," Sherman said, "even to their extermination, men, women, and children." Sheridan agreed, saying: "The only good Indians I ever saw were dead."[29]

Exterminating the Indians would be no easy task, as another former Civil War commander soon learned. On June 25, 1876, George Custer led his 7th Cavalry against Sitting Bull and Crazy Horse on the Little Big Horn River. He and over two hundred of his men died that day. The Indians escaped. Still the army kept after the Sioux, Cheyenne, and other Plains Indian tribes. But it was starvation, not military might, that finally forced their surrender. In a deliberate attempt to rob the Indians of their primary food source, authorities encouraged the wholesale slaughter of buffalo by the millions. Between 1872 and 1874 alone, 3,700,000 buffalo were killed. Indians were responsible for only 150,000 of those deaths; soldiers killed much of the rest, as did wealthy "sportsmen" from the East. Train passengers also casually shot down buffalo from railcar windows as they rode by. White hunters did most of the damage, killing buffalo only for their hides and leaving the rest to rot on the plains. "[They] have done . . . more to settle the vexed Indian question than the entire regular army," said Sheridan. "They are destroying the Indians' commissary. . . . let them kill, skin, and sell until the buffalo is exterminated." Sheridan almost got his wish. By century's end only a few dozen animals remained.[30]

The Comanche Ten Bears spoke for most Plains Indians when he said at the Medicine Lodge Council:

> I was born upon the prairies, where the wind blew free, and there was nothing to break the light of the sun. I was born where there were no enclosures and where everything drew a free breath. I want to die there, and not within walls. I know every stream and every wood between the Rio Grande and the Arkansas. I have hunted and live over that country. I lived like my fathers before me, and like them, I lived happily.[31]

But the buffalo were gone, and the happy times were gone with them. Indian land was going too. More and more every day was being taken by the whites. "Possession is a disease with them," said Sitting Bull at the Powder River Council. "These people have made many rules that the rich may break but the poor may not. . . . They claim this mother of ours, the earth, for their own." The nation of whites, he said, like a raging river, "overruns its banks and destroys all who are in its path."[32]

Throughout the West, starving and depressed, those who had not already done so had no choice but to surrender and accept confinement on reservations. "Our chiefs are killed. . . . The old men are all dead," said Chief Joseph of the Nez Percé when he gave himself up to the white chiefs, General Oliver O. Howard and Colonel Nelson A. Miles:

> It is cold and, we have no blankets. The little children are freezing to death. My people, some of them, have run away to the hills, and have no blankets, no food. No one knows where they are—perhaps freezing to death. I want to have time to look for my children, and see how many of them I can find. Maybe I shall find them among the dead. Hear me, my chiefs! I am tired. My heart is sick and sad. From where the sun now stands I will fight no more forever.[33]

Geronimo's people too were nearly spent. On the run and handicapped by children who had to be fed, he finally gave in for their sake. So did Sitting Bull after Crazy Horse was killed. But reservation life offered little better for their people. Agents and traders swindled them out of their government food stores. Most Indians could not feed themselves by farming or herding even when they knew how. Lincoln once told a delegation of visiting Indians: "I can see no way in which your race is to become as numerous and prosperous as the white race except by living as they do, by the cultivation of the earth." But, as historian David Nichols points out, "government leaders preached something that their own policies made impossible. . . . ambitious white men were not inclined to permit Indians to have farmland that would permit them 'to become as numerous and prosperous as the white race.' "[34]

"That which you now say we must live on is too small," Ten Bears complained of his people's reservation. "The Texans have taken away the places where the grass grew the thickest and the timber was the best." The only areas usually left for Indians were lands that the whites did not want—lands that would support neither farming nor livestock. Forced to depend on government supplies and seeing those supplies cheated away, Indians frequently wandered off their reservations searching for food. When pressured to go after them, Colonel Ranald S. MacKenzie, the commander at Fort Sill, wrote to General Sheridan: "I am expected to see that Indians behave properly whom the government is starving—and not only that, but starving in flagrant violation of treaty." At the same time, MacKenzie told his subordinate at Fort Reno: "If the Indians from hunger run off contrary to the wishes of the agent to get buffalo, do not attempt to cause their return, or the troops will be placed in the position of assisting in a great wrong."[35]

When the Indians were able to reach their old hunting grounds, most often all they found were buffalo bones scattered as far as the eye could see. Dispirited at such a sight, many lost the will to live. Their way of life, everything they knew, was gone. And there was no hope of its return. What was there to live for? "The white man has the country which we loved," said Ten Bears, "and we only wish to wander on the prairie until we die." But they were usually not allowed even that small dignity. Unlike MacKenzie, most army officers quickly rounded up any Indians found off the reservations, executing them on the spot if they refused to go back.[36]

Hungry and heartsick, desperate for any glimmer of hope, thousands of Indians throughout the West found comfort in the teachings of a Paiute holy man named Wovoka. In the late 1880s, word spread from tribe to tribe of God's promise for their salvation. Hundreds traveled to Nevada to hear the word directly from Wovoka. "I went up to heaven," he told them, "and saw God and all the people who had died a long time ago. God told me to come back and tell my people they must be good and love one another, and not fight, or steal, or lie. He gave me this dance to give my people." The dance, said Wovoka, would bring back the world they had lost. The whites would be gone, the buffalo would return, and so would their dead.

"They danced without rest," one Sioux remembered.[37] Day and night they danced, some for days at a time, chanting their prayers for deliverance. Old Chief Red Cloud later explained:

We were faint with hunger and maddened by despair. We held our dying children, and felt their little bodies tremble as their souls went out and left only a dead weight in our hands. . . . There was no hope on earth, and God seemed to have forgotten us. Some said they saw the Son of God; others did not see Him. . . . The people did not know; they did not care. They snatched at the hope. They screamed like crazy men to Him for mercy. They caught at the promise they heard He had made.[38]

"I suppose the authorities did think they were crazy," a Sioux woman recalled, "but they weren't. They were only terribly unhappy." As they danced themselves to delirium, many reported visions of exactly what Wovoka had foretold. They saw the buffalo again, they saw their loved ones again, all gathered where "there was no sorrow but only joy, where relatives thronged out with happy laughter." Some never returned from that promised land, dancing on until they collapsed and died.[39]

This new Ghost Dance religion, as some called it, sent chills down the spines of whites. They hardly knew what to make of it. In Dakota Territory, word spread among whites that the Ghost Dance was some sort of ceremonial preparation for a Sioux uprising. Authorities ordered the dancing to stop. Now it was the Sioux who were confounded, wondering why their dance so offended the whites. "Our religion seems foolish to you," Sitting Bull told one white man, "but so does yours to me. The Baptists and Methodists and Presbyterians and the Catholics all have a different God. Why cannot we have one of our own? Why does the agent seek to take away our religion? My race is dying. Our God will soon die with us. If this new religion is not true then what matters?"[40]

In December 1890, officials at Standing Rock Agency sent Sioux police on the government payroll to bring in Sitting Bull. He was charged with supporting the Ghost Dance. When several Ghost Dancers tried to stop Sitting Bull's arrest as police were leading the chief out of his lodge, gunfire erupted and the police shot Sitting Bull through the head at point blank range.

The chief's death sent panic through the Hunkpapa Sioux community. About one hundred of them fled to Big Foot's Minneconjou Sioux camp near Cherry Creek, over fifty miles to the southwest. Fearing retribution from the soldiers at Standing Rock, Big Foot led his people toward Pine Ridge, another hundred miles on, to seek safety among the Oglala Sioux under Red Cloud. A few miles short of their destination, Custer's old 7th Cavalry, five hundred strong, caught up with Big Foot's band of about 350 refugees and herded them to an encampment on Wounded Knee Creek. There they surrounded the Sioux, trained four Hotchkiss artillery guns on their camp, and ordered them to surrender. The captives began to do so without resistance, piling their rifles in a heap before the soldiers. But Black Coyote, who was deaf, did not understand the order. When a soldier tried to grab his rifle, the weapon discharged without injuring anyone. But panicked soldiers began shooting indiscriminately into the camp with their rifles and Hotchkiss artillery guns, which fired exploding shells. "An awful noise was heard and I was paralyzed for a time," recalled one young woman who miraculously survived. "Then my head cleared and I saw nearly all the people on the ground bleeding. . . . My father, my mother, my grandmother, my older brother and my younger brother were all killed. My son, who was two years old, was shot in the mouth." The toddler soon died in agony from his wound.[41]

Some of the Sioux men tried to reach their discarded rifles. Most were killed in the attempt. Those who were not tried to set up a makeshift defense for their women and children in a nearby ravine. There they were all shot down—men, women, and children alike. When the soldiers stopped firing, more than 150 Sioux lay dead. Big Foot had been one of the first to die. Over a hundred others scattered across the open prairie where they froze to death. Soldiers loaded the roughly fifty survivors, nearly all of them wounded, into wagons and headed for Pine Ridge. The agency's Episcopal mission opened its doors to the victims when they arrived that night. Pews were cleared out and straw was thrown over the rough wooden floor. It was December 29, four days after Christmas. In the dim candlelight, some could see a banner still hanging over the pulpit which read PEACE ON EARTH, GOOD WILL TO MEN.[42] Eighteen soldiers were awarded the Congressional Medal of Honor for their "valor" at Wounded Knee.[43]

At the time Europeans began their colonization of what would become the United States, the region held an estimated ten million inhabitants. By 1890 there were barely a quarter-million Indians left. They died both of the white man's contagious diseases and of his fixated drive for possession—a disease in itself, as Sitting Bull observed. Not satisfied with the Indians' near-extermination, however, whites set out to destroy their culture too. They took Indian children from their parents, hauled them off to distant schools, and forbade them to dress or speak in their traditional ways. They also attacked the communal structure of Indian society by breaking up reservation lands into individual plots. In 1889, U.S. Commissioner of Indian Affairs Thomas Jefferson Morgan insisted: "The Indians must conform to 'the white man's ways,' peacefully if they will, forcibly if they must. . . . The tribal relations should be broken up, socialism destroyed, and the family and the autonomy of the individual substituted." The white man's motive was not simply ideological. As always, he wanted more land. At Pine Ridge, for example, government agents allotted reservation land to individual Indians and sold the "surplus" land to whites. Doing so reduced the reservation's size from 2.5 million acres in 1904 to less that 150,000 by 1916.[44]

During the twentieth century, Native Americans struggled to maintain what they had and rebuild what they had lost. It was a story filled with both disappointment and perseverance, and with some degree of success as well. Tribal autonomy was restored to some extent, and tribal languages and customs were preserved. Even population numbers rebounded. Today, roughly four million Americans identify themselves as having Indian ancestry in whole or substantial part. Still, Indian voices remain largely ignored and many treaty obligations remain unmet. That would hardy have surprised Red Cloud, who said of the whites in his own time: "They made us many promises, more than I can remember, but they never kept but one; they promised to take our land, and they took it."[45] The struggle goes on.

Chief Red Cloud of the Oglala Sioux struggled all his life to preserve his people's land, their way of life, and their lives. In the end, they were forced onto reservations, cheated by licensed traders, robbed by government agents, and starved by government policies—all in direct violation of treaty agreements. After years of dealing with the whites, the saddened old chief said: "They made us many promises, more than I can remember, but they never kept but one; they promised to take our land, and they took it." (Northwestern University Library)

"Teach Them Their Places"

In the post–Civil War years, even the struggle against slavery, not to mention racial injustice, went on as well. Not long after he passed through the Deep South in the late spring of 1865, General Benjamin Grierson recorded his impressions of the region's people.

> The country was filled with bands of armed marauders, composed mostly of deserters from the late rebel armies, who have returned to find their families suffering from the neglect and persecution of the wealthy leaders, at whose instigation they joined the rebel ranks. The poor people, including the returned Confederate private soldiers, are, as a general thing, now loyal; but the far greater portion of the wealthy classes are still very bitter in their sentiments against the Government, and clutch on to slavery with a lingering hope to save at least a relic of their favorite yet barbarous institution for the future.

Grierson recommended leniency for the poor whites. They had suffered too much already in a war not of their making. But the "spirit of resistance" among slaveholders would have to be broken down completely if former slaves were ever to be truly free.[46]

One Georgia planter spoke for most of his class when he told a Freedmen's Bureau official: "If we cannot whip the Negro, they and I cannot live in the same country." An Alabama woman from Opelika demanded that occupying Federal troops return a young slave girl who had fled to their camp. When told that the girl was now free and could work for wages if she wished, the enraged women replied: "I will not pay her a cent. I will work my hands to the bone first. She belongs to me."[47]

Many former slaveholders were more fearful of having to do physical labor themselves. "I'm no book-keeper," said one planter just after the war. "I never learned a trade; I have no profession. I own these lands, and, if the niggers can be made to work, they'll support me; but there's nothing else I know anything about, except managing a plantation." A former Alabama slave mistress said she could not bear the thought of her daughters working in the fields like common folk. Ann Browder of Eufaula, Alabama, wrote in her diary: "I begin to realize poverty now—last week our cook left." John Horry Dent confided to his journal in the summer of 1865: "Had an ominous dream last night—[I was] pulling fodder."[48]

Underlying planters' lack of a work ethic was the social stigma that labor represented to them. As one northern visitor was repeatedly told, "Work is for 'niggers'—not for white men"—at least not for white men from the old slavocracy.[49] The slavocracy's white women were just as determined to maintain their social standing in relation to blacks. The Reverend Henry McNeal Turner, a black chaplain with the 1st U.S. Colored Infantry, bore witness to that in Smithville, North Carolina, after his regiment occupied the town.[50] During a visit to one of Smithville's leading black women, Turner saw a party of female whites enter the yard and try to take some firewood. Turner's hostess stepped to the door and asked what they were doing with her wood. The women promptly accused her of having stolen it. When she protested that she had gotten it from the Yankees, the whites called her a liar. "I am no more a liar than you are," the woman replied. Turner recalled what happened next.

> This expression, from a negro wench, as they called her, was so intolerable, that the white women grabbed up several clubs, and leaped in the door, using the most filthy language in the vocabulary of indecency. They had not yet observed me as being on the premises. But at this juncture, I rose up, met them at the door and cried out, "Halt!" Said they, "Who are you?" "A United States Officer," was my reply.

"Well, are you going to allow that negro to give us impudence?" "You gave her impudence first," was my reply. "What, we give a negro impudence! We want you to know we are white, and are your superiors. You are our inferior, much less she." "Well," said I, "all of you put together would not make the equal of my wife, and I have yet to hear her claim superiority over me." After that, I don't know what was said, for that remark was received as such an aggravated insult, that I can only compare the noise that followed, to a gang of fice dogs, holding at bay a large cur dog, with a bow-wow-wow-wow.

Turner shortly became "tired of their annoying music" and threatened to arrest the whole gang if they did not get out. The women then marched to regimental headquarters and insisted that the colonel place Turner under arrest. The colonel refused and dismissed the women. "I afterwards learned," Turner wrote, "that they were some of the Southern aristocracy."[51]

Some slaveholders did not even tell their slaves that the war was over and they were free. George Brooks's owner sold him to another man in the fall of 1865. Only later when he escaped to Columbus, Georgia, did Brooks learn he was legally free. It was September before slaves on one Texas plantation got the news. One day a "government man" rode up and "read a paper to the slaves telling them they was free." Recalled the formerly enslaved Susan Merritt: "That's the first we knowed anything about it." Other slaveholders conned their former slaves into making contracts that bound them to service for years after the war.[52]

Slaveholders who held to their old attitudes had a firm friend in the White House. Andrew Johnson, who ascended to the presidency in April 1865 after Lincoln's assassination, was a former slaveholder from Tennessee who was no more committed to civil rights for former slaves than Lincoln had been. Adhering to Lincoln's ten-percent plan, Johnson's only condition for a state's readmission to the Union was the 10 percent loyalty oath and ratification of the Thirteenth Amendment abolishing chattel slavery. Aside from that, Johnson was content to leave southern state governments in the hands of planters and ex-Confederates. They took full advantage of the opportunity. Delegates to the 1865 Georgia constitutional convention reluctantly ratified the Thirteenth Amendment, but defended slavery as "consistent with the dictates of humanity and the strictest principles of morality and religion." And their new constitution, like its 1861 predecessor, left control of the General Assembly in the hands of cotton-belt planters.[53]

Alabama also ratified the Thirteenth Amendment but added that in no way did the action "confer upon Congress the power to legislate upon the political status of freedmen in this State." The former slave states reserved that power for themselves. Said Alabama politician Henry Clayton of the black man: "We are the only people in the world who understand his character, and hence, the only people in the world capable of managing him." And there was only one way to manage the freedmen properly, said Clayton: "Teach them their places, and how to keep them."[54]

One of the first steps in teaching blacks their place came with a series of state laws known as the Black Codes. Under these codes, many of which mirrored the old slave codes, freedom for former slaves became little more than nominal. Blacks could not serve on juries, hold public office, or quit jobs voluntarily. In some states they could not own firearms. Most oppressive were the vagrancy laws. These called for the arrest of blacks found "wandering or strolling about in idleness, who are able to work and who have not property to support them." The state then sold them, usually to large landholders, for the price of their fine. They were supposed to do forced labor only until their new masters were reimbursed. However, with the costs of food, clothing, and shelter added to their debt, blacks convicted of vagrancy would likely remain in bondage the rest of their lives. Since few blacks owned property of any kind, most were in very real danger of being reenslaved under the vagrancy laws.[55]

Those blacks who did find employment were often swindled out of their wages. In one month alone, the Freedmen's Bureau agent in Columbus, Georgia, reported a hundred complaints from area blacks who were not paid their wages or crop shares. Some Bureau agents said that most of their time was spent trying to collect unpaid wages for black workers. In Georgia's Randolph County, only about half the labor contracts were being honored by white employers. That was typical across the South.[56]

Typical also was the violence that kept blacks constantly terrorized. That blacks were no longer their slaves induced a murderous fury in some former slaveholders, especially if freedmen tried to make good on their freedom and leave. "Lots of Negroes was killed

"SELLING A FREEDMAN TO PAY HIS FINE." James E. Taylor, an artist touring the South for *Leslie's Illustrated Newspaper*, sketched this scene in front of the Monticello, Florida, courthouse during the winter of 1866–67. Vagrancy laws throughout the South called for the arrest of blacks found "wandering or strolling about in idleness, who are able to work and who have not property to support them." The state then auctioned them off for the price of their fine. Since most blacks owned no property, they were constantly in danger of being reenslaved.

after freedom," recalled a former Texas slave. "Their owners had them 'bushwhacked,' shot down while they was trying to get away. You could see lots of Negroes hanging to trees in Sabine bottom right after freedom. They would catch them swimming across Sabine River and shoot them."[57]

Some of the violence was more casual, arising from ingrained social attitudes. A black man in New Orleans was shot and killed on the spot for neglecting to remove his hat in front of a white man. Other incidents sprang from the same attitudes coupled with economic envy. Jealous whites sometimes targeted those few blacks fortunate enough to be modestly prosperous in farming or trade. One gang of whites killed blacksmith Abe Lyon for the six hundred dollars in silver he had saved for his daughter's education. The killers riddled his body with thirty-three bullets. Such killings were rarely prosecuted. "Nigger life's cheap now," said one white Tennessean. "Nobody likes 'em enough to have any affair of the sort investigated; and when a white man feels aggrieved at anything a nigger's done, he just shoots him and puts an end to it."[58] It was the most direct way of sending a message to blacks that the war had not changed their place in the social order.

Maintaining the old order meant keeping not only blacks in their places but poor whites too. Members of the old slavocracy repeatedly told one reporter on a postwar tour of the South: "The gentlemen of the country should be the ruling class. . . . Too many vote now, instead of too few." Some suggested educational and property requirements to keep poor whites from voting. But blacks, planters told the reporter, "educated or ignorant, rich or poor . . . must be kept down." Some of the South's newspapermen, many of whom had family or financial ties to the planters, proved ready allies in that effort. The *Argus* of Bainbridge, Georgia, insisted that anyone who supported voting rights for blacks was either "a fool or a knave." Even the poor white man, insisted the paper's editor, had no business meddling in politics: "He has no time to devote to parties or the discussion of political questions which in no way apply to his condition as a pauper."[59]

Allowing ex-Confederates political free reign also jeopardized the lives and livelihoods of southern unionists, most of whom were poor whites. The danger was especially acute where unionists had been in the minority. As a measure of self-protection and political action, they formed Union Leagues, which in some places evolved out of the old antiwar, anti-Confederate peace societies. But the war's end brought little peace for these men. Attacks against them became so frequent and violent in north Alabama that the war hardly seemed to have ended. One Union League activist in the region wrote that they "could no longer do without troops unless you allow the loyal men to kill the traitors out."[60]

To strengthen their position, many Union Leaguers became strong Republicans and allied themselves with blacks in the cause of universal male suffrage. In Tennessee, the state government under its new Republican governor, William Brownlow, enacted black suffrage and became the first ex-Confederate state readmitted to the Union. Republicans in other parts of the South tried to do the same, but with little success. They came close in Louisiana. When Republican Governor James Madison Wells called a constitutional convention in New Orleans to enfranchise blacks, a white mob attacked the assembly. Before federal troops could stop the massacre, three white delegates and thirty-four blacks were dead. Well over a hundred were injured. Local police, most of them ex-Confederates, had joined in the killing. The Johnson administration had been warned of the impending attack, but did nothing to stop it. On the contrary, Johnson had bypassed Governor Wells and sent word to the ex-Confederate mayor of New Orleans that a request to prevent the convention from meeting was approved. It was a license to kill.[61]

If Johnson cared nothing for black voting rights, Congress certainly did. Its Republican majority knew that blacks would vote for Republican candidates if given the opportunity. In 1867 Congress took steps to insure that they got the opportunity. The Reconstruction Act, passed in March over Johnson's veto, divided most of the former Confederacy into five military districts, put military governors in place, and charged them with guaranteeing black voting rights. The next year saw ratification of the Fourteenth Amendment granting citizenship to "all persons born or naturalized in the United States" and promising them "equal protection of the laws." Finally, with the Fifteenth Amendment, the Constitution guaranteed the right to vote for all citizens regardless of race.[62]

Congressional, or Radical, Reconstruction did succeed for a time in extending political rights to southern Republicans, black and white. Blacks voted in large numbers and won seats in the southern state legislatures and even in Congress on the Republican ticket. So did white Republicans, much to the delight of many poor whites. One grateful South Carolinian wrote to the state's new Republican governor:

> I am . . . a native borned S. C. a poor man never owned a Negro in my life. . . . I am hated and despised for nothing else but my loyalty to the mother government. . . . But I rejoice to think that God almighty has given to the poor of S. C. a Gov. to hear to feel to protect the humble poor without distinction to race or color.[63]

But it did not last. Election supervision in most areas was so weak that the planter power structure soon found ways to control both the black vote and the vote of those whites who dared cast Republican ballots. As one planter remarked: "We can control it with little trouble—the only trouble before was that we did not know how to go about it. . . . Every man who voted the Radical [Republican] ticket in this county was watched and his ticket marked and all are now known and they will never cease to regret it, as long as they live."[64]

And they did not. The Ku Klux Klan saw to that. Operating as the terrorist arm of the Democratic Party, bands of hooded night riders terrorized both blacks and whites who openly supported Republicanism. They broke up prayer meetings, burned homes and churches, and beat or killed their unfortunate victims. One particularly vicious Klansman was John Lyons of Lee County, Alabama, widely known for his habit of cutting off body parts. According to the Reverend Wade Owens, a former Lee County slave, Lyons would not hesitate to "cut off a woman's breast and a man's ear or thumb." No one can know how many southern blacks were murdered during the Reconstruction era, but estimates range as high as forty thousand.[65]

Such violence had a direct political purpose—to kill Republicans and intimidate their followers. One evening hooded whites broke into the home of Albert Richardson, a black member of the Georgia legislature, and shot him three times. Another black Georgia legislator, Alan Colby, was dragged from his bed, beaten, and left for dead. Benjamin Randolph, the black chairman of South Carolina's Republican Party was gunned down in broad daylight. White Republicans were targeted too. In Camilla, Georgia, blacks and their white allies were massacred during a Republican rally. George Ashburn, a white Georgian and Republican politician, was killed while on a visit to Columbus. Between one and two o'clock in the morning, a gang of ten to fifteen Klansmen broke into Ashburn's boarding house room and shot him dead. Despite eyewitness testimony, civil authorities concluded that Ashburn was killed by persons unknown. The local military commander intervened and arrested several suspects, some of them leading Columbus Democrats. But when Georgia was readmitted to the Union, the accused men were handed over to officials in Columbus who let the matter drop.[66]

Indeed, by the early 1870s there was a waning commitment by Congress to secure voting rights for southern Republicans, especially blacks. Certainly blacks could provide northern elites with Republican votes, but southern landholders could provide something much more important—the very thing for which they had gone to war in the first place—access to cheap southern resources, especially cotton. All they had to do was give their former adversaries a free hand in dealing with the South's labor force, and riches in the form of lumber, oil, tobacco, and cotton would flow north. This economic alliance with the South's landed gentry was much more valuable to northern industrialists than any political alliance they could ever have with southern blacks. As historian James McPherson writes: "The North's conversion to emancipation and equal rights was primarily a conversion of expediency rather than one of conviction. . . . It became expedient for northern political and business interests to conciliate southern whites, and an end to federal enforcement of Negro equality in the South was the price of that conciliation."[67] Never enthusiastic about a war for emancipation, much less equality, white northerners found the arrangement comfortable. Throughout the early to mid-1870s they withdrew their largely ineffective army of occupation and left the freedmen at the mercy of their former masters.

With planters back in control both politically and economically, they moved to shore up the old order. Southern state governments, like those of the North before them, passed a series of "Jim Crow" laws firmly establishing social segregation. Despite "equal protection of the laws" promised by the Fourteenth Amendment and a congressional Civil Rights Act to back it up, federal courts, including the Supreme Court, refused to declare Jim Crow unconstitutional—all to appease former slaveholders and to ease business relations between northern and southern elites. It was most disheartening to people like Frederick Douglass as they watched the promise of freedom so publicly proclaimed by Lincoln and his party evaporate. "He is a wiser man than I am," Douglass wrote, "who can tell how low the moral sentiment of this republic may yet fall. . . . The Supreme Court has surrendered. . . . It has destroyed the civil rights Bill, and converted the Republican party into a party of money rather than a party of morals." As early as 1867, Douglass had allowed himself to wonder whether the Civil War might "pass into history a miserable failure, barren of permanent results . . . a strife for empire . . . of no value to liberty or civilization." He did not live to see the worst of it.[68]

In 1896, a year after Douglass died, the Supreme Court constitutionally canonized Jim Crow by establishing the "separate but equal" doctrine in its *Plessy v. Ferguson* decision. Segregation, ruled the court majority, was entirely constitutional so long as public facilities provided for blacks were equal to those of whites. The justices well knew that "separate but equal" was a legal and practical fiction, but only one had the integrity to say it. Justice John Marshall Harlan, ironically a former slaveholder, admitted that facilities for blacks were and never would be equal to those of whites if separation were constitutionally sanctioned. The very act of legislated separation, he argued, imposed state-sanctioned inequality—an inequality made unconstitutional by the Fourteenth Amendment. It would be another fifty-eight years before blacks, constantly pushing and prodding for judicial justice, would see the "separate but equal" doctrine overturned in 1954 with the Supreme Court's *Brown v. Board of Education* case.[69]

The intervening decades were a horrific time for African Americans. Legalized segregation, discrimination, and the threat of arbitrary murder, with or without cause, all reflected an ongoing effort to keep blacks "in their place." "When the niggers get so that they are not afraid of being lynched," declared a white Mississippian, "it is time to put the fear in them." It hardly mattered who the victim was. "When there is a row, we feel like killing a nigger whether he has done anything or not," admitted a young white southerner. He was not exaggerating. In 1890, a black man in Augusta, Georgia, was shot repeatedly and left to die in the street. When the body was found, a city resident questioned one of the men he suspected of being involved. "Pat, who killed that nigger?" "Oh, some of the boys," Pat replied with a grin. "What did they do it for?" he was asked. Pat said simply, "Because he was a nigger." To stress how casual the killing had been, Pat added: "And he was the best nigger in town. Why, he would even take his hat off to me."[70]

Whites shot, burned, and lynched blacks with impunity, certain that the law would not touch them. In many cases, the terrorists themselves were law officers as well as law makers. Lynchings were often organized by the Ku Klux Klan, which counted sheriffs, state legislators, and congressmen among its members. Between 1882 and 1968 there were close to five thousand recorded lynchings, almost one a week. Many more, untold thousands, were the victims of sham trials, legal lynchings, and "nigger hunts." Some blacks simply disappeared, carried off and disposed of by "persons unknown." One law officer reported that when a lynch mob broke into his jail, "the first half-a-dozen men standing there were leading citizens—businessmen, leaders of their churches and the community." Few clergymen ever criticized lynching for fear of losing church members. When the Rev. Whitely Langston of Bulloch County, Georgia, expelled several church members for participating in a lynching, he ended up losing a total of twenty-five. Ministers with Langston's integrity were few and far between. Some ministers themselves were members of the Klan. "Our American Christians," observed black editor and antilynching activist Ida B. Wells, "are too busy saving the souls of white Christians from burning in hellfire to save the lives of black ones from present burning in fires kindled by white Christians."[71]

Susie King Taylor, who lived through slavery and its immediate aftermath, read at the turn of the century how the United Daughters of

With southern blacks denied the vote, forcibly segregated, held in tenancy, and lynched with impunity, Susie King Taylor asked in her 1902 *Reminiscences*: "Was the war in vain? Has it brought freedom . . . or has it not made our condition more hopeless?" Taylor had seen the war up close, first as a slave, then a fugitive, and finally in camp with black soldiers. She had seen men struggle and die, and she had struggled herself, to make freedom real. Now the new century dawning promised little better than the old. (Taylor, *Reminiscences*)

the Confederacy had petitioned theaters in Tennessee to ban perfor-
mances of *Uncle Tom's Cabin*. Its portrayal of the slaves' ill treatment,
they claimed, was exaggerated, and it "would have a very bad effect on
the children who might see the drama." Taylor wondered why the
UDC never circulated petitions to "prohibit the atrocious lynchings
and wholesale murdering and torture of the negro? Do you ever hear
of them fearing this would have a bad effect on the children?" Taylor
had seen the war up-close, first as a slave in Savannah, then as a fugitive from slavery, and finally in camp with one of the Union's black
regiments. For years she had seen men struggle and die, and she had
struggled herself, to make freedom real. Now the new century dawning promised little better than the old. "I sometimes ask, 'Was the war
in vain? Has it brought freedom, in the full sense of the word, or has it
not made our condition more hopeless?'" Taylor continued:

> In this "land of the free" we are burned, tortured, and denied a fair
> trial, murdered for any imaginary wrong conceived in the brain of the
> negro-hating white man. There is no redress for us from a government
> which promised to protect all under its flag. It seems a mystery to me.
> They say, "One flag, one nation, one country indivisible." Is this true?
> Can we say this truthfully, when one race is allowed to burn, hang, and
> inflict the most horrible torture weekly, monthly, on another? No, we
> cannot sing, "My country, 'tis of thee, Sweet land of Liberty"! It is a
> hollow mockery.[72]

"The New Slavery"

African Americans of Taylor's day could see little reason to hope for
much better. They could hardly fight back through the political system, barred as they were from voting by such measures as the grandfa-
ther clause, literacy tests, and poll taxes. The latter two worked to keep
many poor whites from voting as well. And, despite lip service to the
idea of a "New South" with a diversified economy modeled after that
of the North, agriculture remained the region's number-one economic activity and cotton was still king. It suited those in power to
keep most southerners, black and white, in poverty.[73]

Continued control of the South's prime farm land was a key element in planters' ability to regain and maintain control. Shortly before

the war's end, many slaves had been guaranteed forty acres and a mule once they became free. It would have been little enough compensation for people who had labored all their lives and never received a cent in pay.[74] But the promise was a hollow one. In December 1865, a former Confederate general offered this unusually candid explanation for continued poverty among southern blacks: "The emancipated slaves own nothing, because nothing but freedom has been given to them."[75]

Planters were backed by their northern allies, who came to their defense whenever the prospect was raised of carving up old plantations and distributing the land to blacks. Never mind that slaveholders had made war on the Union, or that without the aid of southern blacks, the Union might not have survived at all. Blacks had served their purpose and were of no more use to their former allies. "As the war for the Union recedes into the misty shadows of the past," wrote Frederick Douglass, "and the Negro is no longer needed to assault forts and stop rebel bullets, he is . . . of less importance. Peace with the old master class has been war to the Negro. As the one has risen, the other has fallen."[76]

Wealthy northern financiers and industrialists who controlled Congress made war on blacks by making sure that there would be no land redistribution in the South. Such a thing would not only upset business relations with their elite southern partners but would also set a dangerous precedent. An editorial in the *New York Times* insisted that the issue of land redistribution was "a question not of humanity, not of loyalty, but of fundamental relation of industry to capital; and sooner or later, if begun at the South, it will find its way into the cities of the North. . . . An attempt to justify the confiscation of Southern land under the pretense of doing justice to the freedmen, strikes at the root of property rights in both sections. It concerns Massachusetts as much as Mississippi."[77] A threat to men of vast property anywhere was a threat to men of vast property everywhere. The government they controlled and the political parties they owned would protect their property rights.

Men of small property enjoyed no such protection. A growing number of landless whites joined the propertyless freedmen throughout the late nineteenth century. Many had owned no land even before the war. Many others lost their meager holdings to neighboring planters during or after the war for their inability to pay off debts in an inflationary cash-poor economy created by a war not of their making.

Still others moved down from the hill country looking for economic opportunity. They found little or none. With few skills other than agricultural and no land of their own to farm, most blacks and many whites slipped into sharecropping and tenancy, or as many at the time and since called it, "the new slavery."[78]

Ironically, planters as a class lost little as a result the Confederacy's defeat. They retained the labor of blacks and added many thousands of whites to their workforce. Nor did they lose much in terms of wealth. Wealth in the South had always generally been tied to land ownership, and that remained true in the postwar era. Historian Robert McKenzie points out that southern land ownership actually became more concentrated during the 1860s. In western Tennessee, for example, the top 5 percent of white farmers increased their share of real and personal property by nearly one-fourth. By 1870, Tennessee's agricultural elites controlled up to half the state's farm land "while the bottom half of farm households were still virtually landless." Gavin Wright reinforces the point in his work *The Political Economy of the Cotton South*, noting that "despite the decline in average farm size reported in the 1870 census, there was no basic change in the concentration of land ownership. Antebellum holdings were not really broken up in favor of either blacks or white nonslaveholders, and most of the new small farms were tenancies of one kind or another."[79]

Though usually associated with the post–Civil War era, tenant farming and sharecropping were not new at all. In the late 1850s, roughly one in four white farmers in the South worked land owned by someone else. In parts of the South, landless tenants and sharecroppers made up nearly half the rural white population. But tenancy did see a phenomenal growth after the war. By the early twentieth century, two-thirds of farmers, black and white, in the Deep South were tenants. In Alabama's Barbour County alone, the tenancy rate was over 75 percent. Farm tenancy was hardly limited to the South. Nationwide, tenancy rates were well over 25 percent. In Ohio and Indiana, it was nearly 30 percent. New Jersey's rate was just short of 30 percent. In Kansas and Illinois, the tenancy rate was almost 40 percent.[80]

Old or new, North or South, tenant farming was certainly a kind of slavery. Farmers worked for a share of the crop and borrowed against expected earnings. With local landholders and merchants (who were often the same people) keeping the books, tenants' annual incomes almost never covered their previous year's debt. So they were tied to the land until they could pay off what they owed, which was nearly impossible under a system of revolving, ever-increasing indebtedness. Once caught in the cycle of debt, tenants were usually tied to the land and trapped for life, unless, as in slavery times, they managed to slip away.

Even for those farmers who worked their own holdings it was tough to make ends meet. Many were former soldiers with missing limbs or ruined health. When he returned from the war, amputee Joseph Fox learned to do farm work "as best I could with my Left hand." Such debilities inevitably limited farmers' production and their income. Farm income generally was on the decline after the Civil War, largely because small yeoman farmers, like their landless neighbors, were subject to a kind of debt slavery under the oppressive crop-lien system. Farmers were forced to put up their next year's crop as collateral with local planter-merchants in exchange for supplies. But interest rates were so high, ranging up to 100 percent in some cases, that small farmers ended up further in debt than they had been the year before. Many found it impossible to pay off any portion of their debt from one year to the next. These people often fell into tenant farming and lost their land to those who already had large holdings. Tenancy rates continued to rise well into the twentieth century.[81]

"For the Rights of Workingmen"

Debt slavery was also common among industrial laborers, North and South. Workers frequently lived in company housing, worked for company wages, and were often paid not in cash but in company notes, or scrip, that could be spent only at the company store. With the company controlling their salaries, rents, and commodity prices, it is hardly surprising that no matter what their wages were, their cost of living was always higher. The result was that workers constantly owed the company money. Short of becoming fugitives, they could no more escape this urban cycle of debt than could their rural counterparts.

That industrial workers, many of whom had shed blood for the Union, could be so exploited in the wake of a purported war against slavery said much about the conflict's underlying nature. Though Lincoln had rhetorically called the Civil War "a People's contest," Union victory did little for common folk in real terms. "If anybody won the war," said famed Civil War writer Shelby Foote, "it's people like Jay

Gould and Jim Fisk, the robber barons of late in the century"—or, as Kenneth Stampp called them, "the shoddy aristocracy." Using distorted theories of "laissez-faire" capitalism and "social Darwinism,"[82] robber barons argued that the government had no business helping the poor. Those theories, however, did not apply to the robbers themselves. They made sure that government went to work helping them with tariffs that kept prices artificially high, a gold standard that kept the money supply artificially depressed and concentrated, a court system that kept unions at bay, and bought-and-paid-for senators who did their bidding. There were, wrote historians Samuel Eliot Morison and Henry Steele Commager, "Standard Oil Senators, sugar Senators, iron and steel Senators and railroad Senators, men known for their business affiliations rather than for their states." Corporations became more massive, smaller businesses were bought out or driven out, wealth became concentrated in fewer hands, and the gap between rich and poor became ever wider. In 1848, America's single greatest fortune had been 50,000 times greater than the nation's median income. In 1890, it was 370,000 times greater. By that time more than half the nation's wealth was held by just 1 percent of America's super rich. Twenty-nine percent had controlled half the wealth before the Civil War.[83]

The rich man's war was over, and he had won it in more ways than one. The Civil War was a tremendous setback for people's ability to protect their interests through the labor movement. In his study of labor and industry in Lynn, Massachusetts, Alan Dawley wrote that during the war years, "the evils of capitalism seemed to be washed away in the greater sins of slavery, as workers were infused with patriotism for the Union, devotion to its cause, and respect for its leaders and heroes." Of course, this general observation did not apply to all working-class folk across the North. In many areas, workers actively organized to resist Lincoln's war and his draft. But there were enough laborers caught up in the war's patriotic fervor to effectively split the larger labor movement and bring its progress to a halt. Even labor leaders so feared being called "unpatriotic" that they would do whatever it took to avoid the stigma. They and too many of their followers seemed not to grasp that, as Mark Twain later observed with uncommon clarity, "if there is any valuable difference between a monarchist and an American, it lies in the theory that the American can decide for himself what is patriotic and what isn't."[84]

The poor man's fight against corporate enslavement had a long way to go when the Civil War ended. There was no minimum-wage law, and the cost of living in 1865 was roughly 70 percent higher than it had been in 1860. There was no prohibition against abusive child labor, little concern for worker safety, and no workmen's compensation. When a night fire broke out in a mill near Providence, Rhode Island, many of the six hundred workers, women and children among them, jumped to their deaths because doors leading out of the building were locked. There was no compensation for the victims' families. Nor were the mill owners prosecuted. They had broken no laws. Those few state and local laws that gave workers some small protection, like those that restricted working hours to eight or ten a day, were rarely enforced. Not until 1871, when twenty thousand workers marched through the streets of New York City threatening revolution, did authorities begin to pay lip service to the existing eight-hour law. Still, enforcement efforts were uneven at best, conducted only occasionally and more for appearance's sake than anything else. Capitalist bosses owned the politicians and the police, and the bosses wanted no restraints on their treatment of workers.[85]

"Capital is centralizing, organizing and becoming more powerful every day," warned the *Rochester Daily Union and Advertiser* in 1866. "The late war and what has grown out of the war, made Capital stronger. It has made millions all at the expense of the labor of this country, and the capital thus concentrated is to be used in a greater or less degree to defeat the objects sought by the workingmen." If capitalists were organizing against them, laborers had to as well. But labor was at a disadvantage. In the early 1870s when workers marched in Chicago, Omaha, and Cincinnati, they came under police attack. In New York's Tompkins Square, police rode down protesting men, women, and children in what one observer called "an orgy of brutality." During the Great Railroad Strike of 1877, labor's first nationwide uprising, troops killed perhaps fifty protesters in Chicago, twelve in Baltimore, twenty in Pittsburgh, and more in other cities. A Grand Jury found the Pittsburgh shootings to be "wanton killing . . . which the inquest can call by no other name but murder." The same could have been said of the other killings too.[86]

Though the strike failed to gain decent wages, there were hopeful signs for labor. Local militias sympathized with the strikers. One militia company in Buffalo actually joined the strikers. A member of the 69th New York wrote to the *Labor Standard*, "We may be militiamen, but we are workingmen first." Some recalled with pride the sight of "white and colored men standing together, men of all nationalities in one supreme contest for the rights of workingmen." Women stood with them too. The *Baltimore Sun* wrote that "the singular part of the disturbance is in the very active part taken by the women." The Knights of Labor increased its membership, became a national organization, and invited a broad range of workers into its ranks, blacks and women included.[87]

But worker solidarity began a sorry decline in the 1880s. Employers, already skilled at keeping labor divided, began to coopt organized labor itself. In backroom deals with labor leaders, industrialists granted concessions in the form of higher pay and benefits to one group of workers when they agreed to exclude other groups from their unions. Doing so weakened the labor movement in the long run, but the short-term benefits were hard to turn down. Skilled workers temporarily bettered their bargaining position by leaving their unskilled brethren out in the cold. Whites threw their black colleagues to the wolves under similar pressures. Employers still used the courts as well as brute force to break up unions when they could. When they could not, the unions' impact could be limited and more easily controlled by making slight concessions along racial, religious, nativist, and sexual lines. Thus encouraged, Anglo Protestants excluded Irish Catholics, natives shunned immigrants, and men shut women out of their unions.

"Are Women Persons?"

Women and their dependent children were especially vulnerable in the postwar period. As a sympathetic member of the molder's union wrote in an 1866 issue of the *Rochester Union and Advertiser*:

> We all know that many of these working girls and women have lost their husbands, brothers, fathers, and lovers in the late struggle for the life and existence of our common country; and is it not too bad now to see monied corporations—money which they have made, many of them by furnishing the enemies of the government with means to take

the lives of our soldiers—is it not too bad, I say, to see these corporations trying to deprive these widows and orphans, that they have helped to make, of the means to earn an honest living? But corporations, they say, have no souls, and have nothing to answer for.[88]

Corporations were not the only employers lacking souls. Government too, just as responsible for creating widows and orphans, furthered their misery with substandard wages. Faced with callousness on one hand and poverty on the other, women took matters into their own hands. In December 1865, female workers at the Bureau of Printing went on strike for higher wages. They won an 8 percent pay raise, but it was the last they would see for twenty years. And it was still only half what the government paid men in similar positions.[89]

All over the country women were uniting for humane wages and working conditions. Black women in Mississippi formed the state's first labor union, the Washerwomen of Jackson. They informed Jackson's mayor in June 1866:

That on and after the foregoing date, we join in charging a uniform rate for our labor . . . the statement of said price to be made public by printing the same, and any one belonging to the class of washerwomen, violating this, shall be liable to a fine regulated by the class.[90]

In 1869, women at the Cocheco Mills in Dover, New Hampshire, organized and went on strike when the company cut their already dismal wages. Jennie Collins, one of the most active crusaders for workingwomen, called for a boycott against products coming out of the Cocheco Mills. "We working women," she announced, "will wear fig-leaf dresses before we will patronize the Cocheco Company." The strike failed in the end, but Collins was not deterred. She went on to found the Working Women's Club of Boston and was active in the New England Labor Reform League.[91]

Women workers led the way to at least a temporary victory in Fall River, Massachusetts, after a local union of male weavers caved in to pressures for a 10 percent pay cut. In a meeting from which all men except newspaper reporters were banned, the outraged women formed their own union, rejected the pay cut, and developed an effective plan of action. They targeted three mills for strike while accepting pay cuts in other mills "under protest." Workers at the mills still in operation agreed to support the striking workers—3,215 in all—for as long as necessary. When male weavers were told of the plan, they agreed to support it. Less than three months later, the mills gave in.[92]

Women were pressing on the political front too, many hoping that power at the polls would lead to power at the workplace. Time and time again, they ran up against claims that they belonged neither place. Home was where they belonged, so the argument went, ignoring the reality that without jobs many would have no homes. Even if women had to work for wages, antisuffragists argued, they certainly did not have to vote nor should they. Such a thing was seen by many as somehow unnatural. Sidney George Fisher—a Philadelphia lawyer, political essayist, and sometime poet—wrote in 1867 on voting rights for women: "The idea is so absurd & repugnant to all feelings universally received of the true position of women, that it would seem impossible for a scheme so extravagant to be seriously discussed."[93] It was convenient for people like Fisher to deny that women's subordination was a social development, not a natural one. It was a man-made construct. What man can make, man—or woman—can remake.

Some suffragists turned the domesticity argument on its head, insisting that there was no better support for granting women the vote. "We are told that the first duty of woman is a mother, and the highest sphere of woman is the home," wrote one North Carolina suffragist, "and it is that which places upon woman the obligation to enter into the life of her community, and nation, and help to make them a fit home for her child and her family." "It is the right of woman," she insisted, "to use not only the power of persuasion, but the power of the ballot, to protect herself and her children."[94]

The right of women to the ballot was in fact already written into the Constitution. The Fourteenth Amendment made "all persons born or naturalized in the United States . . . citizens of the United States." Under its provisions, no state could "make or enforce any law which shall abridge the privileges or immunities of citizens . . . nor deny to any person within its jurisdiction the equal protection of the laws." "The only question left to be settled now," wrote Susan B. Anthony, "is: Are women persons? And I hardly believe any of our opponents will have the hardihood to say they are not."[95]

To test that assertion, Anthony led a parade of women to the polls during the fall elections of 1872 in her hometown of Rochester, New

York. She expected to be turned back, then planned to bring suit against the state of New York for violating her constitutional rights. To her astonishment, though, the women were all handed ballots and allowed to vote. But it would not be that easy. Two weeks later, a federal marshal knocked on Anthony's door with an arrest warrant charging her with "illegal voting." A judge gave her a $100 fine that she refused to pay. Not wanting to help publicize her cause, the judge declined to give her jail time.[96]

Three years later, in the case of *Minor v. Happersett*, the Supreme Court weighed in on the issue of women's suffrage. Ignoring the supremacy of the U.S. Constitution that they were sworn to uphold, the judges ruled that voting was not a "right" granted by the federal government but a privilege bestowed by individual states. So it was to the states that women went in their quest for the vote. Some had already been pressing on that front. In an effort to attract women to their state, Wyoming legislators became the first in the nation to pass women's suffrage in 1869. Other western states needing women soon followed, and momentum for a national suffrage amendment began to build. Susan B. Anthony herself authored the amendment draft. Finally in 1920, more than a decade after its author's death, the Nineteenth Amendment went into effect.[97]

"Our Democracy Is But a Name"

Though a victory for women's rights, the ballot was no panacea. Deaf and blind as she was, Helen Keller—the Alabama-born author, activist, and affirmed socialist—saw more clearly than most that the struggle for justice was anything but over. She wrote to a fellow suffragist in England:

> Our democracy is but a name. We vote? What does that mean? It means that we choose between two bodies of real, though not avowed, autocrats. We choose between Tweedledum and Tweedledee. . . . You ask for votes for women. What good can votes do when ten-elevenths of the land of Great Britain belongs to 200,000 and only one-eleventh to the rest of the 40,000,000? Have your men with their millions of votes freed themselves from this injustice?[98]

She might have made a similar point about the United States or any other so-called democracy. The social activist Emma Goldman made that point when she wrote: "Our modern fetish is universal suffrage. . . . The women of Australia and New Zealand can vote, and help make laws. Are the labor conditions better there?"[99]

Goldman's point, of course, was that conditions for working folk, male or female, were dismal everywhere whether they had the vote or not. Only united activism could push rights for labor, women, immigrants, poor whites and blacks forward. But divided as those suffering injustice were, pressing forward would be more difficult than it had to be. As always, that was just how elites wanted it. The more divided common folk were, the more afraid they were of each other, the easier they would be to control. As Garrison Keillor recently noted, fear is "the greatest political strategy ever"—at least for those in power.[100]

That fear kept Republicans in power throughout most of the North in the post–Civil War years. And it kept northern Democrats from serving as much of an opposition. Controlled as both parties were by wealthy elites, it mattered little which party held office. Either way, economic elites would frame the debate with veiled and not-so-veiled appeals to racism, nativism, sexism, and religious bigotry. As the party of Union victory in the Civil War, Republicans had an advantage in being able to hold up the figurative "bloody shirt." They made full use of the garment at every opportunity, rhetorically waving it to define patriotism for largely uncritical constituents eager to feel a part of anything larger than themselves. Intimidated northern Democrats rarely offered any significant alternative.

The only political party that did was the Socialist Party. Its four-time presidential candidate, Eugene V. Debs, reminded his audiences that a capitalist controlled two-party system would never represent working-class interests. The two major parties, in the Socialist view, were actually not two parties at all but simply two factions of the clandestine capitalist party that financed them both. Such a system could never be truly democratic, said Debs. "They tell us that we live in a great free republic; that our institutions are democratic; that we are a free and self-governing people. That is too much, even for a joke." Debs sought to offer a real alternative to the capitalist party by calling on voters to "overthrow the capitalist system of private ownership of the tools of labor, abolish wage-slavery and achieve the freedom of the whole working class, and in fact, of all mankind."[101]

It was a message that spoke to the hopes rather than the fears of his listeners. A fellow Socialist once said of Debs: "That old man with the burning eyes actually believes that there can be such a thing as the brotherhood of man. And that's not the funniest part of it. As long as he's around I believe it myself."[102] Far too many people believed it to suit worried elites. Debs was getting more and more votes every time he ran. So during World War I, under the guise of national security, the Socialist Party's treasury was confiscated and its leaders jailed. The peaceful antiwar Debs was hardly a threat to anyone but those who picked the pockets of working folk—which, in the end, was why he was imprisoned. Even from his prison cell, Debs got nearly a million votes. But with "Tweedledum and Tweedledee" dominating the political scene, many potential voters came to feel that the political process held little promise for them. Turnout went into a steady decline from which it has never recovered. Those who did continue to vote were, more often than not, swayed by wedge issues that both parties used to keep nonelites divided.[103]

In the South, too, most poor whites who bothered to vote, or were not prevented from doing so by the poll tax, consistently cast their ballots for the very men who kept them poor. For southerners of the post–Civil War era, the dominant political force was the Democratic Party. Rarely has the United States had a genuine national party system and rarely has any party been truly national. What the "bloody shirt" was to Republicans in the North, it was to Democrats in the South. To vote otherwise, voters were told by the southern Democrats, would mean dishonoring Confederate ancestors and, even worse, white subordination to "negro rule."

Though poor whites had no more love for the planters after than during the war, they were as dedicated as ever to the racist caste system. If nothing else, it gave them an artificial social status that the reality of their impoverishment denied. In 1884, planter John Horry Dent confessed privately in his journal what few planters would say openly: "This is no country for a man who has to start from the bottom rung of the ladder, no room for enterprise."[104] It remained a country whose wealth was tied up in land, and the best land was long since taken. If the South was not a country of economic opportunity for the poor, the planters did at least promise to keep it a white man's country. That promise was enough for most poor whites. Their racist fears kept their families in poverty and the planters in power for generations after the Civil War.

There were those who challenged planter oppression, though not always the caste ideology that supported it. The most serious threat came in the late nineteenth century from the newly formed Populist Party. With its focus on lowering produce transportation costs and reforming the credit and tax systems for common folk, the party attracted yeomen farmers and tenants alike, mainly in the South and West. Of course, the Populist party had no financial backing from economic elites. If they were to have any chance for success, the Populists had to have maximum support from the lower classes to offset the economic advantage of their political opponents. And for that, they needed poor blacks as well as whites.

Georgia Populist Tom Watson was the party's most vocal advocate of black-white cooperation in facing their common economic problems. Time and again, he pointed out "the accident of color can make no difference in the interests of farmers, croppers, and laborers."[105] Watson often spoke to mixed groups of black and white farmers, always hammering home the message of their shared plight. In 1892 Watson told an audience: "You are kept apart that you may be separately fleeced of your earnings. You are made to hate each other because upon that hatred is rested the keystone of the arch of financial despotism which enslaves you both. You are deceived and blinded that you may not see how this race antagonism perpetuates a monetary system which beggars both."[106]

Try as they might, however, the Populists found it impossible to overcome generations of socially ingrained racism. Watson himself recognized the limitations of the Populist approach but could find no way to overcome it. One could get a white farmer's attention, Watson said, with promises to abolish the crop-lien system, provide for more reasonable credit, and reform the regressive tax system. One could demonstrate clearly to him that this was the way out of his poverty. But at the first cry of "Negro rule!" Watson wrote, "the entire fabric of reason and common sense which you had patiently constructed would fall."[107]

Religion also served as a useful tool in promoting the planter agenda. During the congressional campaigns of 1892, a Georgia Democrat branded his Populist opponent an atheist, saying, "He believes neither in Democracy nor in our God." One of the state's most prominent Methodist preachers told voters that a Populist victory would mean no less than "negro supremacy," "mongrelism," and the "destruction of the Saxon womanhood of our wives and daughters." There was economic pressure on voters as well. Merchants frequently refused credit to farmers who would not openly renounce the Populist Party.[108]

And finally, with white supremacy its creed and Robert E. Lee its Christ, the mythological Lost Cause became something of a religion for many white southerners, romanticizing the South's Confederate past and perpetuating its racist future. That Confederate soldiers had "cursed the Southern Confederacy" and small farmers had wished for that "damned Government" to fall apart—that southerners had fought each other "harder than we ever fought the enemy"—all mattered little in the postwar era. What did matter was that the fiction of kind masters, contented farmers, and happy slaves in an idyllic Old South justified the Confederacy, bolstered white supremacy, and fit perfectly with postwar planter politics. Lost Causers went to great lengths to shore up their rosy image of the past. They erected Confederate monuments all over the South. They named towns, counties, parks, and buildings after Confederate heroes. They ennobled and enshrined Confederate icons in novels, in movies, at public events, and on southern state flags. In doing so, they tried to bury the memory of dissent in a divided Civil War South, as one postwar Mississippian put it, "so deep that the hand of time may never resurrect it."[109]

Racism, religion, and the Lost Cause all served to perpetuate a system of class and race oppression that made the New South much like the Old. In fact, it was hardly a "new" South at all. Though the Civil War is still viewed by many as *the* turning point in southern history, providing a convenient line of demarcation between Old South and New, very little actually changed as a result of the war. Planters remained the South's ruling class both politically and economically. Agriculture, particularly cotton agriculture, remained the region's dominant economic force. And while the Civil War did end chattel slavery, most freedmen were simply forced into new forms of social and economic bondage.

Significant change began only in the 1920s after the boll weevil wiped out much of the South's cotton crop. No longer needed to pick cotton, masses of tenant farmers, black and white, were driven off the

Horace Bynum was the oldest living freedman in Russell County, Alabama, when this photo was taken shortly before his death in 1948. For many former slaves, as this photo suggests, the so-called New South was very much like the Old South. Hardly anything had changed for them. They continued to live with cotton, poverty, and virtual slavery for the rest of their days. (Walker, *Russell County in Retrospect*)

land and released from debt slavery. In a way, the tiny boll weevil freed more slaves in a few seasons of pestilence than Lincoln and the Union army did in four years of war. It would take decades more for federal programs from the New Deal on, farm mechanization, expanding educational opportunities, and the civil rights movement to propel the region toward anything like a "new" South.

Southern plain folk realized well before the Civil War ended that the postwar South would hardly be a new one. Their lives would go on much as they always had whether ruled from Richmond or Washington. Neither government had their interests at heart. Cornelia McDonald of Winchester, Virginia, wrote that most common people came to feel "that they would be as well off under one government as another." For one young Confederate soldier, his army's short-lived victory on December 31, 1862, at Murfreesboro, Tennessee, sparked little enthusiasm. "What is gained anyway?" he asked. "It is a rich man's war and a poor man's fight at best."[110]

That realization empowered plain folk across the South to work against the Confederacy. Their actions and attitudes contributed decisively to Confederate defeat, a fact that was well known to southerners at the time. Some had even predicted it. Ben Hill, a soon-to-be Confederate senator, warned before the war began that a divided South could not possibly sustain itself. In the fall of 1862, an Atlanta newspaper put it just as bluntly: "If we are defeated, it will be by the people at home." Of the many epitaphs written for the Confederacy over the years, perhaps the most appropriate is "Died of Class Conflict."[111]

Afterword

The story of common people during the Civil War era is in many ways an inspiring one of how the powerless empowered themselves, collectively and individually, in an ongoing struggle to expand the meaning of freedom and secure its promise for themselves. It was an often heroic struggle in which people took great risks, and in many cases gave their lives, to expand freedom for themselves, their families, their friends, and their posterity.

Yet for all its inspiration and heroism, it is not always an admirable tale. The story is also a tragic one of how common people could be turned against each other, giving in to a culture and politics of fear, bigotry, sexism, and racism, driving them just as strongly to resist expansions of freedom. When people struggled to secure freedom's promise for themselves, it was often only for themselves and for those with whom they most closely identified. And they did it for reasons they believed to be entirely justified. In the name of patriotism, patriarchy, religion, and white supremacy, common people worked against each other, even slaughtered each other by the hundreds of thousands, and felt themselves righteous in doing so. Too often forgotten was the ancient proverb that even the way of a fool is right in his own eyes.

There can be no romantic illusion that the "voice of God" is always found in the will of the people. Still, wisdom is most often found in a multitude of counselors, and to ignore the will of the people is the antithesis of democracy. To ignore that will is to impose oligarchy. Most southerners opposed secession and were ignored. Most northerners opposed war and were ignored. The southern oligarchy wanted secession; the northern oligarchy wanted war in response. Both used their powers of political and public manipulation, driven by baser motives than either openly admitted, and the war came.

The will of the people is never a monolithic thing. Even after the war came and so many common people were diverted from their better human instincts, many others resisted that diversion, separated themselves from it, tried to maintain some degree of humanity through it, or tried to make some greater humanity of it. They did not always succeed to the extent they wished. Often what success they had was superficial at best. But success they did have to some degree, though that success might have come at a lesser price than fratricidal war. Nevertheless, their success did ultimately expand the meaning of freedom, even if it took many more decades of travail for the fruit of their efforts to ripen. The struggle continues to this day. That people-empowered struggle to expand the meaning of freedom, in the end, marks the story of common people in the Civil War era as a hopeful one, one that allows us to know that in all times and places there can be a vein of humanity in the voice of the people which senses, even if it cannot immediately be named, that what we want for ourselves we finally cannot deny to others.

Notes

Introduction: "The People at War"

1. My reference to common people of the Civil War era generally includes classes that have traditionally been underrepresented in centers of governmental and economic authority and whose role in shaping America's past has traditionally been ignored or marginalized. However, those classifications are not entirely rigid. Native Americans, for example, are treated in a single category, recognizing at the same time that some Indian nations contained people who were also partially, even mostly, of European ancestry. Women are treated as a group, recognizing that many were from the wealthy classes as well as laboring classes. Furthermore, such was the nature of their shared difficulties with men of the same categories, female dissenters, black women, and Indian women are treated with other groups in this study. African Americans are treated in a single category, recognizing that black women suffered the double stigma of racial and sexual oppression. Soldiers are treated as a group, recognizing that they were hardly homogeneous. Dissenters are treated as a group, recognizing that dissent by definition marks the group as somewhat uncommon, though dissent became increasingly common, especially in the South, during the course of the war.

Certainly these are not the only ways in which groups cut across racial, gender, and class lines. Race provides perhaps the best example. Blacks were also soldiers (as were several hundred women), and faced all the hardships of their white counterparts. Female African Americans were, of course, women as well. Many slaves and "free persons of color" were as much or more descendants of Europeans as they were of Africans. Nevertheless, African Americans generally shared a set of race-based difficulties that set them apart. Slave or free, North or South, woman or man, soldier or civilian, the pervasive racism of the time imposed a set of obstacles common to blacks regardless of their sex, region, or occupation. It is their efforts to overcome those obstacles in the face of racism and opposition, high and low, that I focus on as their common theme.

2. Fried, *Except to Walk Free*, 30–31. Wright was such an outspoken critic of social, economic, political, and religious repression that any woman who followed suit was condemned for her "Fanny Wrightism." Massachusetts minister Dudley Phelps warned that women who dared lecture to men would inevitably "land on Fanny Wrightism and that such is the fate of all women who venture out of their sphere." Cutter, *Domestic Devils, Battlefield Angels*, 114–15.

3. That support was, however, considerably limited. Historian John Shy, in *A People Numerous and Armed: Reflections on the Military Struggle for American Independence*, estimates that only one-fifth of Americans actively supported the independence movement. Perhaps as many more actively opposed it. The movement's success was made possible mainly by French military intervention. For an overview of common people's role during the era, see Raphael, *People's History of the American Revolution*.

4. Link, *Roots of Secession*, 217; Williams, Williams, and Carlson, *Plain Folk in a Rich Man's War*, 12.

5. For a definitive treatment of the anti-renter movement, see Christman, *Tin Horns and Calico*. For events in Lynn, see Dawley, *Class and Community*.

6. Williams, *Rich Man's War*, 53.

7. Stampp, *Causes of the Civil War*, 68.

8. Formwalt, "Planters and Cotton Production as a Cause of Confederate Defeat," 275.

9. Rable, *Civil Wars*, 126.

10. Fite, *Social and Industrial Conditions in the North*, 9.

11. Williams, *Rich Man's War*, 115.

12. Brooks, *Civil War Medicine*, 9.

13. Watkins, *Co. Aytch*, 194.

14. Martin, *Rich Man's War*, 148; Faust, "Altars of Sacrifice," 1,224.

15. Williams, Williams, and Carlson, *Plain Folk in a Rich Man's War*, 164.

16. Cleveland, *Alexander H. Stephens*, 721; Franklin and Moss, *From Slavery to Freedom*, 188.

17. Williams, Williams, and Carlson, *Plain Folk in a Rich Man's War*, 138.

18. Williams, *Rich Man's War*, 156; Williams, Williams, and Carlson, *Plain Folk in a Rich Man's War*, 134–35; Meyers, "'The Wretch Vickery' and the Brooks County Civil War Slave Conspiracy," 27–38.

19. Ward, *Civil War*, 247.

20. See Jackson, *Century of Dishonor*; Foner, *History of the Labor Movement in the United States*; Owsley, *Plain Folk of the Old South*; Wiley; *Plain People of the Confederacy*; Du Bois, *Black Reconstruction in America*; Aptheker, *American Negro Slave Revolts*; Tatum, *Disloyalty in the Confederacy*.

21. Du Bois, *Black Reconstruction in America*, 722.

22. Some of the most provocative include Bernstein, *New York City Draft Riots*; Shankman, *Pennsylvania Antiwar Movement*; Hauptman, *Between Two Fires*; Clinton, *Other Civil War*; Edwards, *Scarlett Doesn't Live Here Anymore*; Leonard, *Yankee Women*; Jordan, *Tumult and Silence at Second Creek*; Glatthaar, *Forged in Battle*; Robinson, *Bitter Fruits of Bondage*; Weitz, *Higher Duty*; Bynum, *Free State of Jones*; Pickering, *Brush Men and Vigilantes*; Freehling, *South vs. the South*. Such works of the past few decades, along with a number of enduring earlier books, form the basis of this study. Indeed, one of my primary purposes is to highlight material from important works that, in my view, have had less than their deserved impact on our consciousness of Civil War America.

23. Woodworth, Review of *Gods and Generals*, 123–24.

1: "All for the Benefit of the Wealthy"

1. Kibler, "Unionist Sentiment in South Carolina," 358. Aldrich's comment was penned in a private letter to South Carolina planter and U.S. Senator James Henry Hammond on November 25, 1860. After the war, Aldrich became a principal architect of the Black Codes, which sought to keep blacks in virtual slavery. See Wakelyn, *Confederates Against the Confederacy*, 50–51.

2. Reiger, "Secession of Florida," 363.

3. Hannibal Hamlin was Lincoln's vice presidential running mate.

4. Williams, Williams, and Carlson, *Plain Folk in a Rich Man's War*, 13.

5. Foner, *History of the Labor Movement*, 299–300; Reiger, "Secession of Florida," 367; Link, *Roots of Secession*, 225; Williams, Williams, and Carlson, *Plain Folk in a Rich Man's War*, 20.

6. Kibler, "Unionist Sentiment in South Carolina," 358.

7. Williams, Williams, and Carlson, *Plain Folk in a Rich Man's War*, 15.

8. Link, *Roots of Secession*, 226; Bolton, *Poor Whites of the Antebellum South*, 165, 167; Reiger, "Secession of Florida," 360, 363.

9. Phillips, *Wealth and Democracy*, 22; Williams, *Rich Man's War*, 17; Levine, *Half Slave and Half Free*, 37; McKenzie, *One South or Many?*, 68.

10. Planters are usually defined by their ownership of twenty or more slaves. The term "yeoman" refers to small farmers and herdsmen, ranging from those who owned at least three acres of land and no slaves to those who held up to four slaves. Tenants, sharecroppers, and farm laborers—generally referred to (along with unskilled urban workers) as "poor whites"—worked land owned by someone else. The designation "plain folk" or "common folk," when used in reference to the South, generally means yeomen and poor whites, although most often it includes small merchants and skilled artisans (or "mechanics") as well.

Classification of such groups as yeomen, poor whites, and plain folk varies somewhat from one source to another. Steven Hahn, in *Roots of Southern Populism*, tends to view nonslaveholders as a group, as does Grady McWhiney in *Cracker Culture: Celtic Ways in the Old South*. Bill Cecil-Fronsman, in *Common Whites: Class and Culture in Antebellum North Carolina*, treats nonslaveholders and small slaveholders as a group because of their nonelite self-image. In *Masters of Small Worlds*, Stephanie McCurry locates the dividing line between yeomen and planters at ownership of eleven or twelve slaves, the number usually needed to remove a slaveholder from field labor, at least in her South Carolina low-country study region.

Beyond those already mentioned, some of the most insightful works available on the antebellum South's socioeconomic types and their interrelationships are Owsley, *Plain Folk of the Old South*, and Oakes, *Slavery and Freedom*. Two of the very best such studies focusing on particular regions of the South are Harris, *Plain Folk and Gentry in a Slave Society: White Liberty and Black Slavery in Augusta's Hinterlands*, and Bolton, *Poor Whites of the Antebellum South: Tenants and Laborers in Central North Carolina and Northeast Mississippi*.

11. Ware, "Cotton Money," 220; Willoughby, *Fair to Middlin'*, 54, 73.

12. In his study entitled *Poor Whites of the Antebellum South*, Bolton points out that although many poor whites migrated west in search of cheap land, few found any real upward mobility. Bynum's comment is from her review of Bolton's work. See Bynum, Review, 601–2.

13. Aughey, *Iron Furnace*, 226; Oakes, *Slavery and Freedom*, 118; Barney, *Secessionist*

Impulse, 4, 39; Foust, *Yeoman Farmer*, 198. The late antebellum years saw a long-term and accelerating decline in the proportion of slaveholders in the South's free population from 36 percent in 1830 to 31 percent in 1850 and finally to 25 percent by 1860. See Wright, *Political Economy of the Cotton South*, 34.

14. Meriwether, *Slavery in Auburn*, 8–9; Rawick, *American Slave*, ser. 2, vol. 13, pt. 3, p. 1.

15. Stampp, *Peculiar Institution*, 144; Ward, *Civil War*, 9.

16. Clinton, *Harriet Tubman*, 85, 142; Griffler, *Front Line of Freedom*, 95–96; Franklin and Moss, *From Slavery to Freedom*, 188.

17. Williams, *Rich Man's War*, 19; Foner, *History of the Labor Movement*, 252; Franklin and Moss, *From Slavery to Freedom*, 142. A good general discussion of slave resistance can be found in Genovese, *Roll, Jordan, Roll: The World the Slaves Made*, 585–660.

18. Franklin and Moss, *From Slavery to Freedom*, 145.

19. Ibid., 143–45; Aptheker, *American Negro Slave Revolts*, 330; Sellers, *Slavery in Alabama*, 246–47, 248; Douglass, *Narrative*, 81–83.

20. Proctor, "Slavery in Southwest Georgia," 15.

21. Lane, *Rambler in Georgia*, 91; Rawick, *American Slave*, ser. 2, vol. 12, pt. 1, pp. 14–15.

22. Williams, *Rich Man's War*, 20.

23. Rawick, *American Slave*, supp., ser. 1, vol. 3, pt. 1, pp. 6–7, 71.

24. Ibid., ser. 2, vol. 13, pt. 4, p. 124; ibid., supp., ser. 1, vol. 3, pt. 1, pp. 6–7.

25. Oakes, *Slavery and Freedom*, 69. The most thorough treatment of free southern blacks remains Berlin, *Slaves without Masters*.

26. Rawick, *American Slave*, ser. 2, vol. 12, pt. 1, p. 26; ibid., ser. 2, vol. 13, pt. 3, pp. 16, 187; ibid., supp., ser. 1, vol. 4, pt. 2, p. 4.

27. Jordan, *Black Confederates and Afro-Yankees*, 131–32; Craft, *Running a Thousand Miles to Freedom*, 4.

28. Chesnut, *Mary Chesnut's Civil War*, 29, 169.

29. Rable, *Civil Wars*, 36; Craft, *Running a Thousand Miles to Freedom*, 1–2; Breen, "Female Antislavery Petition Campaign," 377–98; Walker, *Backtracking in Barbour County*, 185.

30. Lane, *Rambler in Georgia*, 163.

31. Williams, *Rich Man's War*, 23; Potter, *Impending Crisis*, 398; Rawick, *American Slave*, ser. 2, vol. 13, pt. 3, p. 1; Camp, *Closer to Freedom*, 37–38.

32. Stampp, *Peculiar Institution*, 21–22; Morgan, *American Slavery, American Freedom*, 327.

33. Morgan, *American Slavery, American Freedom*, 250–70, 327. See also Washburn, *Governor and the Rebel: A History of Bacon's Rebellion in Virginia*.

34. Morgan, *American Slavery, American Freedom*, 269–70.

35. Ibid., 334–35, 344; Zinn, *People's History of the United States*, 57.

36. Jefferson borrowed this phrase from the English political philosopher John Locke, but because few people in his American target audience had significant land holdings he replaced Locke's "property" with "pursuit of happiness." See Locke, *Second Treatise of Government*, 70–71.

37. Craven, *Coming of the Civil War*, 119–20, 153–54; Phillips, *Georgia and State Rights*, 158–59; Fleming, *Civil War and Reconstruction in Alabama*, 10. See also Lamb, "James G. Birney and the Road to Abolitionism."

38. Among the best overviews of Indian removal from the South remains

Foreman, *Indian Removal*. For the impact of the southern gold rush on Indian removal, see Williams, *Georgia Gold Rush: Twenty-Niners, Cherokees, and Gold Fever*.

39. Cleveland, *Alexander H. Stephens*, 721.

40. Stampp, *Peculiar Institution*, 21.

41. Freehling and Simpson, *Secession Debated*, 93.

42. Sellers, *Slavery in Alabama*, 347, 346; Cleveland, *Alexander H. Stephens*, 721; Gould, *Mismeasure of Man*, 45.

43. Gould, *Mismeasure of Man*, 70–71. See also Cartwright, "Diseases and Peculiarities of the Negro Race."

44. Cruden, *Many and One*, 204.

45. Daly, *When Slavery Was Called Freedom*, 68, 85; Escott and Goldfield, *Major Problems in the History of the American South*, 430.

46. Antebellum attempts to reconcile scientific evidence with religious belief among scientists, clergy, and laity are reviewed in Hovenkamp, *Science and Religion*.

47. The question of slavery's morality came to a head among the major denominations when the southern wing of the Presbyterian Church split along sectional lines in 1837–38, followed by the Baptists and Methodists in 1845. For an overview of the controversy, see Snay's *Gospel of Disunion: Religion and Separatism in the Antebellum South*.

48. Levine, *Half Slave and Half Free*, 97, 114; Evans, *Born for Liberty*, 108.

49. Harris, *Plain Folk and Gentry*, 75; Williams, *Rich Man's War*, 28.

50. Sellers, *Slavery in Alabama*, 346.

51. The most thorough study of antebellum challenges to academic freedom in the South is Eaton's *Freedom-of-Thought Struggle in the Old South*.

52. Eaton, *Mind of the Old South*, 238, 237.

53. Freehling and Simpson, *Secession Debated*, 93.

54. For good introductions to the role of the yeomen in antebellum southern politics, see Genovese, "Yeomen Farmers in a Slaveholders' Democracy," and Watson, "Conflict and Collaboration: Yeomen, Slaveholders, and Politics in the Antebellum South." See also Thornton, *Politics and Power in a Slave Society: Alabama, 1800–1860*, and Bolton, *Poor Whites of the Antebellum South*.

55. Oakes, *Slavery and Freedom*, 80; Bailey, *Class and Tennessee's Confederate Generation*, 76.

56. Standard, *Columbus in the Confederacy*, 20–21.

57. DeBats, *Elites and Masses*, 425. In *Poor Whites of the Antebellum South*, a study of poor whites in central North Carolina and northeast Mississippi, Bolton draws similar conclusions about the political powerlessness of common folk.

58. Bolton, *Poor Whites of the Antebellum South*, 114; Wallenstein, "Rich Man's War, Rich Man's Fight," 20.

59. Helper, *Impending Crisis*, 42.

60. Bolton, *Poor Whites of the Antebellum South*, 115; Oakes, *Slavery and Freedom*, 76.

61. McKenzie, *One South or Many?*, 68; Bailey, *Class and Tennessee's Confederate Generation*, 58, 60–61; Bolton, *Poor Whites of the Antebellum South*, 131.

62. Williams, Williams, and Carlson, *Plain Folk in a Rich Man's War*, 11; Foner, *History of the Labor Movement*, 263–64.

63. Wells, *Origins of the Southern Middle Class*, 183–91; Foner, *History of the Labor Movement*, 260–62; Shugg, *Origins of Class Struggle*, 116.

64. Simons, *Social Forces in American History*, 227.

65. Hodes, *White Women, Black Men*, 138; Sterling, *We Are Your Sisters*, 29. As Sterling notes: "Records of wills attest to large numbers of stable interracial unions in which genuine affection and loyalty were felt on both sides." She follows with a number of examples. See Sterling, *We Are Your Sisters*, 29–30.

66. Williams, *Rich Man's War*, 31; Griffler, *Front Line of Freedom*, 97.

67. Franklin and Moss, *From Slavery to Freedom*, 146–47; Aptheker, *American Negro Slave Revolts*, 327.

68. Helper, *Impending Crisis*, ix.

69. Ibid., 43.

70. Ibid., 22, 32. For an examination of cotton agriculture's impact on economic progress, see Bolton, *Poor Whites of the Antebellum South*.

71. Williams, *Rich Man's War*, 32.

72. McFeely, *Frederick Douglass*, 62.

73. Range, *Century of Georgia Agriculture*, 28; Helper, *Impending Crisis*, 39, 27. For a modern study of the South's antebellum importation of grain, see Lindstrom, "Southern Dependence Upon Interregional Grain Supplies."

74. Barney, *Secessionist Impulse*, 42; Harris, *Plain Folk and Gentry*, 40; Walker, *Backtracking in Barbour County*, 177; Potter, *Impending Crisis*, 399; Williams, *Rich Man's War*, 33.

75. Shugg, *Origins of Class Struggle*, 76. Soil depletion and a desire to establish slave-state parity in the Senate were additional factors motivating slaveholders to press for slavery's expansion. See Genovese, *Political Economy of Slavery*, 97–98, 247.

76. Genovese, *Political Economy of Slavery*, 266–67, 257–58; Hummel, *Emancipating Slaves, Enslaving Free Men*, 96.

77. Williams, *Rich Man's War*, 218 n. 22. For a discussuon of attempts to spread slavery south of the United Staes, see May, *Southern Dream of a Caribbean Empire*.

78. McFeely, *Frederick Douglass*, 94; Gronowicz, *Race and Politics in New York City Before the Civil War*, 64; Zinn, *Declarations of Independence*, 236; Levine, *Half Slave and Half Free*, 167.

79. Gronowicz, *Race and Politics in New York City Before the Civil War*, xvi, 60–61; Levine, *Half Slave and Half Free*, 167; Rawley, *Race and Politics*, 14.

80. Foner, *History of the Labor Movement*, 268–69; Levine, *Half Slave and Half Free*, 157–58.

81. Phillips, *Wealth and Democracy*, 23; Levine, *Half Slave and Half Free*, 58.

82. Levine, *Half Slave and Half Free*, 55–56; Atack, "Tenants and Yeomen," 20, 22.

83. Craven, *Coming of the Civil War*, 132–33.

84. Foner, *History of the Labor Movement*, 98–99.

85. Levine, *Half Slave and Half Free*, 63, 70; Foner, *History of the Labor Movement*, 220.

86. Foner, *History of the Labor Movement*, 99, 195.

87. Rayback, *History of American Labor*, 94; Foner, *History of the Labor Movement*, 196.

88. Bremner, *Children and Youth*, 574, 617.

89. Rayback, *History of American Labor*, 94.

90. Evans, *Born for Liberty*, 99.

91. Ibid., 93–95; Seidman, "Monstrous Doctrine," 173.

92. Foner, *History of the Labor Movement*, 222; Attie, *Patriotic Toil*, 46; Evans, *Born for Liberty*, 102–03; Badura, "Elizabeth Blackwell," 234.

93. Levine, *Half Slave and Half Free*, 131; Foner, *History of the Labor Movement*, 86, 94, 155, 221–22; Fried, *Except to Walk Free*, 41.

94. Levine, *Half Slave and Half Free*, 133; Rayback, *History of American Labor*, 81–82; Foner *History of the Labor Movement*, 155.

95. Foner, *History of the Labor Movement*, 155–56.

96. Ibid., 156–57.

97. Rayback, *History of American Labor*, 94–95; Foner, *History of the Labor Movement*, 241–45. See also Dawley, *Class and Community: The Industrial Revolution in Lynn*.

98. Hauptman, *Between Two Fires*, 125; Gibson, *American Indian*, 336.

99. Foner, *History of the Labor Movement*, 98–99; Rawley, *Race and Politics*, 12–13; Schwalm, "'Overrun with Free Negroes,'" 151; Voegeli, *Free But Not Equal*, 2; Barney, *Road to Secession*, 66.

100. For a brief description of Indian slavery in California, see Josephy, *500 Nations*, 347.

101. For an overview of the Kansas issue and its national implications, see Gates, *Fifty Million Acres*, and Rawley, *Race and Politics*. Kansas was not admitted to the Union until 1861 after most of the slave states had seceded.

102. Williams, *Rich Man's War*, 39–40.

103. Bolton, *Poor Whites of the Antebellum South*, 162.

104. McPherson, *Struggle for Equality*, 23; Sharkey, *Money, Class, and Party*, 176; Perkins, *Northern Editorials*, 469; Potter, *Impending Crisis*, 443–45.

105. Williams, *Rich Man's War*, 43, 45.

106. DeBats, *Elites and Masses*, 260.

107. Robinson, *Bitter Fruits of Bondage*, 62; DeBats, *Elites and Masses*, 260.

108. Harris, *Plain Folk and Gentry*, 67; Fitzhugh, *Sociology for the South*, 162–63, 225. For a detailed examination of Fitzhugh's thoughts, see Genovese, "The Logical Outcome of the Slaveholder's Philosophy" in Genovese, *World the Slaveholders Made*.

109. Williams, Williams, and Carlson, *Plain Folk in a Rich Man's War*, 11; Foner, *History of the Labor Movement*, 264; Aptheker, *American Negro Slave Revolts*, 345, 347; Wish, "Slave Insurrection Panic of 1856," 211.

110. Holt, *Political Crisis of the 1850s*, 225; Williams, Williams, and Carlson, *Plain Folk in a Rich Man's War*, 12.

111. Aptheker, *American Negro Slave Revolts*, 340, 341–42, 345–46.

112. Williams, "The 'Faithful Slave' Is About Played Out," 90; Robinson, *Bitter Fruits of Bondage*, 42, 43.

113. For apprehension over disunion among larger slaveholders, see Alexander and Duckworth, "Alabama Black Belt Whigs during Secession," and Scarborough, *Masters of the Big House*, 289–90.

114. Baum, *Shattering of Texas Unionism*, 81; Phillips, *Correspondence of Toombs, Stephens, and Cobb*, 527; Freehling and Simpson, *Secession Debated*, 82.

115. Williams, *Rich Man's War*, 49–50.

116. Mallard, "I Had No Comfort to Give the People," 79; Storey, *Loyalty and Loss*, 29.

117. Storey, *Loyalty and Loss*, 29; Aughey, *Iron Furnace*, 50–51.

118. Potter, *Impending Crisis*, 496–97, 507–9; Barney, "Secession," 1379; Davis, *Look Away!*, 264–65; Johnson, *Toward a Patriarchal Republic*, 63. Those who ran in opposition to secession adopted the label of "cooperationists" to indicate their feeling that any southern response to Lincoln's election should be made in cooperation with the slave states as a whole. Beyond that, however, their position was uncertain and ill defined. More likely, their rhetoric represented an attempt to thwart secession by

garnering the undecided vote. For a discussion of the "confused and ambiguous" nature of the cooperationist position, see Johnson, *Toward a Patriarchal Republic*, 26.

119. Bolton, *Poor Whites of the Antebellum South*, 143; Shugg, *Origins of Class Struggle*, 165; Degler, *Other South*, 170; Baum, *Shattering of Texas Unionism*, 47; Potter, *Impending Crisis*, 503–4.

120. Williams, Williams, and Carlson, *Plain Folk in a Rich Man's War*, 15. For a general treatment of the conventions and their composition, see Wooster, *Secession Conventions of the South*.

121. Later that year, the Confederacy did hold a formal presidential election, though the voters were not given much to decide. Davis's name was the only one on the ballot.

122. Williams, *Rich Man's War*, 52; Ash, *Secessionists and Other Scoundrels*, 37–38.

123. Williams, Williams, and Carlson, *Plain Folk in a Rich Man's War*, 14.

124. Bynum, *Free State of Jones*, 98; Reiger, "Secession of Florida," 363; Storey, *Loyalty and Loss*, 18.

125. Shugg, *Origins of Class Struggle*, 163–64; Williams, Williams, and Carlson, *Plain Folk in a Rich Man's War*, 20; Johnson, *Toward a Patriarchal Republic*, 63; Johnson, "A New Look at the Popular Vote for Delegates to the Georgia Secession Convention," 259–75. Though Johnson laid the issue of Georgia's popular vote to rest in the 1970s, Georgia historians are taking their time in catching up to him. The latest edition of Coleman, *A History of Georgia*, the leading history of the state, still cites Governor Brown's fraudulent claim that secessionists won the popular vote by a margin of over thirteen thousand. See Coleman, *History of Georgia*, 150.

126. Baum, *Shattering of Texas Unionism*, 42; Shugg, *Origins of Class Struggle*, 169–70; Potter, *Lincoln and His Party in the Secession Crisis*, 210.

127. Potter, *Lincoln and His Party in the Secession Crisis*, 208. Potter's conclusions are supported by Paul Escott's more recent study, *After Secession: Jefferson Davis and the Failure of Confederate Nationalism*, 23–28, 42–44.

128. Potter, *Impending Crisis*, 473; Williams, Williams, and Carlson, *Plain Folk in a Rich Man's War*, 16.

129. Shankman, *Pennsylvania Antiwar Movement*, 42, 47; Sharkey, *Money, Class, and Party*, 176; Perkins, *Northern Editorials*, 349.

130. Shankman, *Pennsylvania Antiwar Movement*, 51; Perkins, *Northern Editorials*, 331; Williams, *Rich Man's War*, 2; Potter, *Lincoln and His Party in the Secession Crisis*, 52.

131. Stampp, *Causes of the Civil War*, 68; Stampp, *And the War Came*, 127, 244; Foner, *Business and Slavery*, 302; Williams, *Rich Man's War*, 53.

132. Potter, *Lincoln and His Party in the Secession Crisis*, 117, 121.

133. Stampp, *And the War Came*, 130, 140–41, 186; Potter, *Lincoln and His Party in the Secession Crisis*, 157.

134. Bailey, *Probing America's Past*, 369; Foner, *Business and Slavery*, 302; McKay, *Civil War and New York City*, 31.

135. Perkins, *Northern Editorials*, 552–53; Stampp, *And the War Came*, 216.

136. Foner, *Business and Slavery*, 302; Stampp, *And the War Came*, 220–21.

137. Stampp, *And the War Came*, 222; "Lincoln's First Inaugural Address," Heidler and Heidler, *Encyclopedia of the American Civil War*, 5:2287–91; Gienapp, *This Fiery Trial*, 104.

138. Oakes, *Slavery and Freedom*, 183; Perkins, *Northern Editorials*, 365.

139. Perkins, *Northern Editorials*, 679, 377, 687. For an in-depth study of Lincoln's Sumter strategy, see Current, *Lincoln and the First Shot*. See also Ramsdell, "Lincoln and Fort Sumter."

140. "Lincoln's Proclamation," Heidler and Heidler, *Encyclopedia of the American Civil War*, 5: 2300–2301; Perkins, *Northern Editorials*, 738–39, 756; Cochran and Miller, *Age of Enterprise*, 104. The American flag had, in fact, been fired upon on January 9 when the *Star of the West* entered Charleston harbor loaded with supplies and two hundred reinforcements for Fort Sumter. South Carolina artillery opened fire and scored at least one direct hit before the vessel withdrew. There was some editorial consternation in the North, and Buchanan might have used the attack to rouse public outrage, call for volunteers, and commence civil war. But he had no wish to do so and let the incident pass virtually unnoticed. See Stern, *Prologue to Sumter*.

141. Mitchell, *Civil War Soldiers*, 17; Perkins, *Northern Editorials*, 771, 781.

142. Wright, *Conscientious Objectors*, 6; Shankman, *Pennsylvania Antiwar Movement*, 63, 68, 76–77; Sandow, "Limits of Northern Patriotism," 196.

143. Perkins, *Northern Editorials*, 835; "Crittenden-Johnson Resolutions on the Objects of the War," Heidler and Heidler, *Encyclopedia of the American Civil War*, 5:2303; Reardon, "148th Pennsylvania and Home Front Dissension," 5–6.

144. Mitchell, *Civil War Soldiers*, 17; Sandow, "Limits of Northern Patriotism," 186; Hallock, "Role of the Community in Civil War Desertion," 124; Lonn, *Desertion*, 143.

145. Perkins, *Northern Editorials*, 707, 716.

146. Mitchell, *Civil War Soldiers*, 5; McPherson, *What They Fought For*, 52–53; Kruman "Dissent in the Confederacy," 296.

147. Groce, *Mountain Rebels*, 33; Ash, *Secessionists and Other Scoundrels*, 61; Bolton, *Poor Whites of the Antebellum South*, 145, 151–52.

148. Dotson, "Grave and Scandalous Evil," 397; Horst, *Mennonites in the Confederacy*, 26–27.

149. Crofts, *Reluctant Confederates*, 321; Perkins, *Northern Editorials*, 907; Groce, *Mountain Rebels*, 36; Worley, "The Arkansas Peace Society," 445.

150. Shugg, *Origins of Class Struggle*, 172; Williams, *Rich Man's War*, 56–57; Whites, "Civil War as a Crisis in Gender," 14.

151. Bailey, *Class and Tennessee's Confederate Generation*, 80, 77–78.

152. Bolton, *Poor Whites of the Antebellum South*, 158; Shugg, *Origins of Class Struggle*, 171–72.

153. Wiley, *Johnny Reb*, 124; Escott, *After Secession*, 115.

154. Edwards, *Scarlett Doesn't Live Here Anymore*, 87–88; Williams, Williams, and Carlson, *Plain Folk in a Rich Man's War*, 23.

155. Williams, Williams, and Carlson, *Plain Folk in a Rich Man's War*, 21; Dotson, "Grave and Scandalous Evil," 402.

156. Williams, *Rich Man's War*, 58.

157. Escott, *After Secession*, 97–98; Williams, Williams, and Carlson, *Plain Folk in a Rich Man's War*, 18; Storey, *Loyalty and Loss*, 39–40; Current, *Lincoln's Loyalists*, 145.

158. Escott, *After Secession*, 94; Baum, *Shattering of Texas Unionism*, 42; Bailey, "Disloyalty in Early Confederate Alabama," 525.

159. Escott, *After Secession*, 115–16.

160. Bolton, *Poor Whites of the Antebellum South*, 178; Williams, Williams, and Carlson, *Plain Folk in a Rich Man's War*, 19–20.

161. Cecil-Fronsman, *Common Whites*, 205; Tatum, *Disloyalty in the Confederacy*, 144; Bailey, "Disaffection in the Alabama Hill Country, 189; Williams, Williams, and Carlson, *Plain Folk in a Rich Man's War*, 18.

162. Cleveland, *Alexander H. Stephens*, 721; Williams, "The 'Faithful Slave' Is About Played Out," 95–96; Aptheker, *American Negro Slave Revolts*, 360, 363–65.

163. Williams, Williams, and Carlson, *Plain Folk in a Rich Man's War*, 20; Tatum, *Disloyalty in the Confederacy*, viii.

2: "The Brunt Is Thrown upon the Working Classes"

1. Harris, *Plain Folk and Gentry*, 151.

2. Sterling, "Civil War Draft Resistance in the Middle West," 166.

3. Storey, *Loyalty and Loss*, 59–60; Robinson, *Bitter Fruits of Bondage*, 79; Williams, Williams, and Carlson, *Plain Folk in a Rich Man's War*, 18; Baggett, *Scalawags*, 83; Fisher, *War at Every Door*, 42; Ash, *Secessionists and Other Scoundrels*, 115.

4. Williams, Williams, and Carlson, *Plain Folk in a Rich Man's War*, 23–24.

5. Robinson, *Bitter Fruits of Bondage*, 237; Williams, Williams, and Carlson, *Plain Folk in a Rich Man's War*, 21, 22.

6. Williams, Williams, and Carlson, *Plain Folk in a Rich Man's War*, 21.

7. Ibid., 22.

8. Escott, *After Secession*, 63–64; Wiley, *Johnny Reb*, 124–25; Martin, *Rich Man's War*, 75. The most complete discussion of the Confederacy's conscription policy and its impact remains Moore, *Conscription and Conflict*.

9. Williams, Williams, and Carlson, *Plain Folk in a Rich Man's War*, 91–92. Kirkland was fortunate to survive his amputation ordeal. One in four Civil War amputees did not. It is also fortunate for this author that Kirkland survived. He sired six more children after he returned home, one of whom was my great-grandfather.

10. Wiley, *Johnny Reb*, 126; Moore, *Conscription and Conflict*, 29–30; Williams, *Rich Man's War*, 130; Robertson, *Soldiers Blue and Gray*, 38; Martin, *Rich Man's War*, 123. For a discussion of wealthy planters who did serve, see Scarborough, *Masters of the Big House*, 317–72. Scarborough notes that of the Confederacy's 272 largest slaveholders (owning 250 slaves or more), 31 (11.4 percent) saw military service. Four of them (1.5 percent) died on duty. That loss pales in comparison to losses among those not so wealthy. Nearly half the South's military-aged white males served at one time or another. A third of them did not survive the war.

11. Carlson, "Loanly Runagee," 607–08; Moore, *Conscription and Conflict*, 37, 41, 112.

12. Carlson, "Distemper of the Time," 14–21; Davis, *Look Away!*, 237; Escott, *Many Excellent People*, 39; Moore, *Conscription and Conflict*, 56–57; Williams, Williams, and Carlson, *Plain Folk in a Rich Man's War*, 102; Escott, *After Secession*, 116.

13. Watkins, *Co. Aytch*, 69; Escott and Goldfield, *Major Problems in the History of the American South*, 365; Bynum, *Free State of Jones*, 103.

14. E.G. Edwards to C.C. Clay, February 19, 1863, Clay Papers; Williams, Williams, and Carlson, *Plain Folk in a Rich Man's War*, 94–95.

15. Mitchell, *Civil War Soldiers*, 158.

16. Williams, Williams, and Carlson, *Plain Folk in a Rich Man's War*, 94; Rable, *Civil Wars*, 108; Bolton, *Poor Whites of the Antebellum South*, 156.

17. Rable, *Civil Wars*, 76–77; Williams, Williams, and Carlson, *Plain Folk in a Rich Man's War*, 103.

18. Cumming, *Journal*, 243.

19. Williams, *Rich Man's War*, 131–32; Williams, Williams, and Carlson, *Plain Folk in a Rich Man's War*, 100; Escott, *After Secession*, 119; Tatum, *Disloyalty in the Confederacy*, 89.

20. Williams, *Rich Man's War*, 130.

21. Wallenstein, *From Slave South to New South*, 100; Escott, "Cry of the Sufferers," 234.

22. Gates, *Agriculture and the Civil War*, 107; Hill, *State Socialism in the Confederate States*, 4–7.

23. Williams, Williams, and Carlson, *Plain Folk in a Rich Man's War*, 26, 27; Coulter, *Confederate States of America*, 241; Williams, *Rich Man's War*, 99.

24. Robinson, *Bitter Fruits of Bondage*, 202–03.

25. Phillips, *Correspondence of Toombs, Stephens, and Cobb*, 595; Williams, Williams, and Carlson, *Plain Folk in a Rich Man's War*, 28.

26. Williams, *Rich Man's War*, 99–100; Williams, Williams, and Carlson, *Plain Folk in a Rich Man's War*, 34.

27. Gates, *Agriculture and the Civil War*, 30, 33; Williams, *Rich Man's War*, 101; Williams, Williams, and Carlson, *Plain Folk in a Rich Man's War*, 31; Coulter, *Confederate States of America*, 241.

28. Blair, *Virginia's Private War*, 73; Tyler, "Cotton on the Border," 456; Scarborough, *Masters of the Big House*, 352–54; Gates, *Agriculture and the Civil War*, 105.

29. Williams, *Rich Man's War*, 102; Williams, Williams, and Carlson, *Plain Folk in a Rich Man's War*, 32.

30. Williams, Williams, and Carlson, *Plain Folk in a Rich Man's War*, 33.

31. Ibid., 32.

32. Ibid., 31–34; Lebergott, "Why the South Lost," 69; Lebergott, "Through the Blockade," 882–83. Figures rounded to the nearest 100,000 in table 10 of Lebergott's "Through the Blockade" show that of the 6.8 million bales produced in the South during the war, 0.4 were used in the South, 0.5 went to the United Kingdom and Europe, 0.9 went to the North, and 3.8 were destroyed by neglect, the Union army, or southerners themselves. The remaining 1.8 million bales were sold after the war. Cotton production had averaged about 3.5 million bales annually during the late 1850s, reaching just over 3.8 million bales in 1860. See Gray, *History of Agriculture in the Southern United States to 1860*, 2:1026; Wright, *Political Economy of the Cotton South*, 96.

33. Martin, *Rich Man's War*, 133.

34. Robinson, *Bitter Fruits of Bondage*, 149; Williams, *Rich Man's War*, 82–83; Williams, Williams, and Carlson, *Plain Folk in a Rich Man's War*, 34–35.

35. Standard, *Columbus, Georgia, in the Confederacy*, 46; Amos, "All-Absorbing Topics," 19–21; Williams, Williams, and Carlson, *Plain Folk in a Rich Man's War*, 35.

36. Williams, *Rich Man's War*, 84; Williams, Williams, and Carlson, *Plain Folk in a Rich Man's War*, 35.

37. Hill, *State Socialism in the Confederate States*, 8; Gates, *Agriculture and the Civil War*, 34–35; Escott, *After Secession*, 123.

38. DeCredico, *Patriotism for Profit*, 56.

39. Tripp, *Yankee Town, Southern City*, 137; Bynum, *Unruly Women*, 120; Marten, *Texas Divided*, 90; Williams, Williams, and Carlson, *Plain Folk in a Rich Man's War*, 43.

40. Bynum, *Unruly Women*, 126; Williams, *Rich Man's War*, 109.

41. Williams, Williams, and Carlson, *Plain Folk in a Rich Man's War*, 69–70.

42. Ibid., 70; Gates, *Agriculture and the Civil War*, 53; Williams, *Rich Man's War*, 109.

43. Gates, *Agriculture and the Civil War*, 54.

44. Ibid., 68; Williams, *Johnny Reb's War*, 60–61. For a complete treatment of tax-in-kind, see Ball, *Financial Failure and Confederate Defeat*.

45. Williams, Williams, and Carlson, *Plain Folk in a Rich Man's War*, 46, 50, 52; Tatum, *Disloyalty in the Confederacy*, x; Gates, *Agriculture and the Civil War*, 48. James Bush, one of Early County's richest planters, contributed to alienation from the government himself by refusing to accept Confederate currency.

46. Williams, Williams, and Carlson, *Plain Folk in a Rich Man's War*, 48–49, 52; Gates, *Agriculture and the Civil War*, 37.

47. Williams, Williams, and Carlson, *Plain Folk in a Rich Man's War*, 49, 7.

48. Williams, *Rich Man's War*, 85.

49. "An Officer" to C.C. Clay, January 12, 1864, Clay Papers; Williams, *Rich Man's War*, 85.

50. Faust, "Altars of Sacrifice," 1212; Williams, *Rich Man's War*, 81; Hill, *State Socialism in the Confederate States*, 9–10. For the most complete modern study of blockade running, see Wise, *Lifeline of the Confederacy*.

51. Williams, *Johnny Reb's War*, 17.

52. Escott and Goldfield, *Major Problems in the History of the American South*, 365.

53. Escott, "Cry of the Sufferers," 230; Faust, "Altars of Sacrifice," 1212; Blair, *Virginia's Private War*, 108.

54. Williams, Williams, and Carlson, *Plain Folk in a Rich Man's War*, 54–55; Faust, *Mothers of Invention*, 246.

55. Martin, *Rich Man's War*, 129; Williams, *Rich Man's War*, 112–13; Williams, Williams, and Carlson, *Plain Folk in a Rich Man's War*, 65.

56. Cecil-Fronsman, *Common Whites*, 203; Wiley, *Plain People of the Confederacy*, 45–46.

57. Escott, *Many Excellent People*, 40; Williams, *Rich Man's War*, 111–12.

58. Rable, *Civil Wars*, 108; Williams, Williams, and Carlson, *Plain Folk in a Rich Man's War*, 65.

59. Williams, Williams, and Carlson, *Plain Folk in a Rich Man's War*, 58–59.

60. Beringer, Hattaway, Jones, and Still, *Why the South Lost the Civil War*, 13. The Confederate Ordnance Bureau's operation under Josiah Gorgas is most fully explored in Vandiver, *Ploughshares into Swords*. See also Wilson, *Confederate Industry*.

61. Williams, Williams, and Carlson, *Plain Folk in a Rich Man's War*, 59.

62. Ibid., 59.

63. Wilson, *Confederate Industry*, 216; Williams, Williams, and Carlson, *Plain Folk in a Rich Man's War*, 59–60.

64. Coulter, *Confederate States of America*, 236–38; Green, *This Business of Relief*, 78; Tripp, *Yankee Town, Southern City*, 138. For a discussion of the writ of habeas corpus and other civil liberties issues in the Confederacy, see Neely, *Southern Rights: Political Prisoners and the Myth of Confederate Constitutionalism*.

65. Davis, *Look Away!*, 242; Williams, *Rich Man's War*, 143; Williams, Williams, and Carlson, *Plain Folk in a Rich Man's War*, 60, 95.

66. Williams, Williams, and Carlson, *Plain Folk in a Rich Man's War*, 5, 151.

67. Ibid., 94.

68. Baum, *Shattering of Texas Unionism*, 82.

69. Williams, Williams, and Carlson, *Plain Folk in a Rich Man's War*, 152.

70. Harris, *Plain Folk and Gentry in a Slave Society*, 151; Faust, *Creation of Confederate Nationalism*, 37; Williams, Williams, and Carlson, *Plain Folk in a Rich Man's War*, 152–53.

71. Inscoe and McKinney, *Heart of Confederate Appalachia*, 153; Williams, Williams, and Carlson, *Plain Folk in a Rich Man's War*, 152; Lonn, *Desertion*, 70; Bynum, *Free*

State of Jones, 126; Dotson, "Grave and Scandalous Evil," 420; Mallard, "I Had No Comfort to Give the People," 85.

72. Crawford, *Ashe County's Civil War*, 224; Baum, *Shattering of Texas Unionism*, 42, 113–14; Kruman, "Dissent in the Confederacy," 297; Baggett, *Scalawags*, 91; Tatum, *Disloyalty in the Confederacy*, 125; Williams, *Rich Man's War*, 135; Escott, *After Secession*, 155; Fitzgerald, "Poor Man's Fight," 17; Martis, *Historical Atlas*, 82, 83, 84, 87, 118.

73. Williams, *Rich Man's War*, 135–36.

74. Ibid., 136–37. A longer, full-text version of this letter appears in Zinn and Arnove, *Voices of a People's History of the United States*, 202–4.

75. Escott, *After Secession*, 219; Martis, *Historical Atlas*, 111, 113, 118; Moore, *Conscription and Conflict*, 41. See also Alexander and Beringer, *Anatomy of the Confederate Congress*.

76. Owsley, "Defeatism in the Confederacy," 456. Owsley was among the first prominent historians to argue that the causes of Confederate defeat were as much internal as external. In his seminal work, *State Rights in the Confederacy*, Owsley emphasized the concept of state sovereignty written into the Confederate constitution and the weakness it imposed on the central government as a leading factor in the Confederacy's collapse.

77. Neely, *Fate of Liberty*, 106; Lowry, *Story the Soldiers Wouldn't Tell*, 135; Myers, *Great American Fortunes*, 292; Simons, *Social Forces*, 281.

78. Phillips, *Wealth and Democracy*, 39; Myers, *Great American Fortunes*, 295, 403.

79. Jackson, *Twenty Million Yankees*, 76.

80. Myers, *Great American Fortunes*, 403–04, 547–48; Foner, *History of the Labor Movement*, 325.

81. Myers, *Great American Fortunes*, 292–93, 402, 549–52. R. Gordon Wasson, a vice president at J.P. Morgan and Company, attempted to discredit reports of Morgan's culpability in his 1941 book, *The Hall Carbine Affair: A Study in Contemporary Folklore*. Others have come to Morgan's defense, citing improvements that were made on the rifles and pleading that Morgan himself made only a few thousand dollars on the deal. And there has been at least one claim that reports of the rifles being a danger to soldiers were fictitious. See Sinclair, *Corsair*, 18–21; Wheeler, *Pierpont Morgan and Friends*, 74–78; Shenkman, "I Love Paul Revere," 66–68.

82. Attie, *Patriotic Toil*, 130, 142–43, 145, 162; Ginzberg, *Women and the Work of Benevolence*, 167; Marten, "United States Sanitary Commission," 2005. The most complete treatment of the Sanitary Commission remains Maxwell, *Lincoln's Fifth Wheel: The Political History of the United States Sanitary Commission*.

83. Hill, *State Socialism in the Confederate States*, 7–8.

84. Johnson, "Contraband Trade," 637; Myers, *Great American Fortunes*, 542–43.

85. Otto, *Southern Agriculture*, 27–28; Johnson, "Contraband Trade," 636–37.

86. Simons, *Social Forces*, 281–82; Johnson, "Contraband Trade," 641.

87. Simons, *Social Forces*, 282; Cochran and Miller, *Age of Enterprise*, 88.

88. Foner, *History of the Labor Movement*, 326–27; Sharkey, *Money, Class, and Party*, 18; Cochran and Miller, *Age of Enterprise*, 106.

89. Fite, *Social and Industrial Conditions in the North*, 164–65; Cochran and Miller, *Age of Enterprise*, 113–14; Phillips, *Wealth and Democracy*, 36, 39–40.

90. Craig, "Industry, Agriculture, and the Economy," 511. See also Engerman, "Economic Impact of the Civil War," and Gallman, "Commodity Output, 1839–99."

91. Cochran and Miller, *Age of Enterprise*, 107–8, 110; Fite, *Social and Industrial*

Conditions in the North, 13; Myers, *Great American Fortunes*, 406; Foner, *History of the Labor Movement*, 236; Phillips, *Wealth and Democracy*, 41; Lause, "Homestead Act," 992.

92. Shankman, *Pennsylvania Antiwar Movement*, 99–101; McPherson, *Battle Cry of Freedom*, 591; McPherson, *Ordeal by Fire*, 294–95. Republicans did manage a net gain of five seats in the U.S. Senate in 1862, primarily because senators were appointed by 1860-elected and Republican-dominated state legislatures. Only after 1913, with the ratification of the Seventeenth Amerndment, did the Constitution provide for direct election of senators by popular vote.

93. Shankman, *Pennsylvania Antiwar Movement*, 110, 116; Williams, *Rich Man's War*, 162; Ward, *Civil War*, 187.

94. Lonn, *Desertion*, 145, 151; Jimerson, *Private Civil War*, 232; Shankman, *Pennsylvania Antiwar Movement*, 142; Hallock, "Role of the Community in Civil War Desertion," 123.

95. Geary, *We Need Men*, 66; Phillips, *Wealth and Democracy*, 36; Jackson, *Twenty Million Yankees*, 78; Foner, *History of the Labor Movement*, 321; Williams, "Class Conflict, U.S.A.," 448.

96. Johnson, *Abraham Lincoln, Slavery, and the Civil War*, 313.

97. Shankman, *Pennsylvania Antiwar Movement*, 144; Larsen, "Draft Riot in Wisconsin," 423; Sterling, "Civil War Draft Resistance in the Midwest," 482–84; Murdock, *One Million Men*, 30. Statistical evidence of the "striking variations" in the rates of military service according to wealth and social status can be found in Gallman, *North Fights the Civil War*, 71, and Rorabaugh, "Who Fought for the North in the Civil War?" 694–701.

98. Murdock, *One Million Men*, 74, 78; Murdock, *Patriotism Limited*, 57.

99. Massey, *Women in the Civil War*, 214.

100. Lonn, *Foreigners in the Union Army and Navy*, 449, 453, 457–59, 469; Hallock, "Role of the Community in Civil War Desertion," 125–26.

101. Sterling, "Civil War Draft Resistance in the Middle West," 167; Shankman, *Pennsylvania Antiwar Movement*, 141.

102. Palladino, *Another Civil War*, 97; Sterling, "Civil War Draft Resistance in the Middle West," 433. Ironically, though he displayed little concern for the problems of common folk, Wilson was himself of humble origins. See McKay, *Henry Wilson*.

103. Jimerson, *Private Civil War*, 197.

104. Foner, *History of the Labor Movement*, 322; Williams, "Class Conflict, U.S.A.," 448. A more detailed discussion of draft riots can be found in chapter 5. The two most thorough treatments of the riots in New York are Bernstein, *New York City Draft Riots*, and Cook, *Armies of the Streets*.

105. Clark and Hewitt, *Who Built America?*, 625; Fite, *Social and Industrial Conditions in the North*, 184; Foner, *History of the Labor Movement*, 326. Taking 1860 as a base comparison of prices and wages, there was an 18 percent lag of wages behind prices in 1865. Through the efforts of organized labor, wages caught and surpassed prices by 25 percent over the next five years, but that was slight progress considering that the 1860 base represented barely a subsistence standard of living for most workers. For comparison figures, see Sharkey, *Money, Class, and Party*, 457.

106. Cook, *Armies of the Streets*, 28; Paludan, *People's Contest*, 183.

107. Bremner, *Public Good*, 87; Paludan, *People's Contest*, 185.

108. Cook, *Armies of the Streets*, 28.

109. Paludan, *People's Contest*, 154, 155, 185; Gates, *Agriculture and the Civil War*,

223–26, 234, 244–45; Atack and Bateman, "Self-Sufficiency and the Marketable Surplus in the Rural North, 1860," 313.

110. Seidman, "Monstrous Doctrine," 184, 186.

111. Fite, *Social and Industrial Conditions in the North*, 8–9.

112. Paludan, *People's Contest*, 184.

113. Cook, *Armies of the Streets*, 28; Paludan, *People's Contest*, 186; Bremner, *Public Good*, 79.

114. Paludan, *People's Contest*, 185; Bremner, *Public Good*, 76; Fite, *Social and Industrial Conditions in the North*, 200.

115. Palladino, *Another Civil War*, 38; Fite, *Social and Industrial Conditions in the North*, 202; Grossman, *William Sylvis*, 154–55.

116. Paludan, *People's Contest*, 170–71; Sharkey, *Money, Class, and Party*, 177; Montgomery, *Beyond Equality*, 93.

117. Foner, *History of the Labor Movement*, 338–39, 344; Rayback, *History of American Labor*, 111.

118. Commons et al., *History of Labour*, 15–17; Foner, *History of the Labor Movement*, 352; Grossman, *William Sylvis*, 115–19.

119. Commons et al., *History of Labour*, 22–23; Foner, *History of the Labor Movement*, 355–56; Rayback, *History of American Labor*, 111.

120. Commons et al., *History of Labour*, 23; Foner, *History of the Labor Movement*, 356–57; Rayback, *History of American Labor*, 111–12; Fite, *Social and Industrial Conditions in the North*, 210.

121. Paludan, *People's Contest*, 195; Foner, *History of the Labor Movement*, 352, 354; Sharkey, *Money, Class, and Party*, 179; Grossman, *William Sylvis*, 157–65.

122. Clark and Hewitt, *Who Built America?*, 629; Montgomery, *Beyond Equality*, 98–99; Paludan, *People's Contest*, 195; Foner, *History of the Labor Movement*, 352, 354; Rayback, *History of American Labor*, 113; Sharkey, *Money, Class, and Party*, 179.

123. Montgomery, *Beyond Equality*, 98; Clark and Hewitt, *Who Built America?*, 629; Rayback, *History of American Labor*, 109; Fite, *Social and Industrial Conditions in the North*, 189; Paludan, *People's Contest*, 182.

124. Fite, *Social and Industrial Conditions in the North*, 191–92; Cochran and Miller, *Age of Enterprise*, 106–07; Rayback, *History of American Labor*, 109; Sharkey, *Money, Class, and Party*, 179–80; Foner, *History of the Labor Movement*, 327; Grossman, *William Sylvis*, 146–49.

125. Shankman, *Pennsylvania Antiwar Movement*, 97; Miller and Hewitt, *Who Built America?*, 629; Grossman, *William Sylvis*, 51; Montgomery, *Beyond Equality*, 100; Fite, *Social and Industrial Conditions in the North*, 203; Rayback, *History of American Labor*, 110; Sharkey, *Money, Class, and Party*, 178; Foner, *History of the Labor Movement*, 329; Paludan, *People's Contest*, 196.

126. Montgomery, *Beyond Equality*, 100; Palladino, *Another Civil War*, 145; Grossman, *William Sylvis*, 51–52; Sharkey, *Money, Class, and Party*, 178–79; Foner, *History of the Labor Movement*, 328–29; Fite, *Social and Industrial Conditions in the North*, 203; Paludan, *People's Contest*, 196; Rayback, *History of American Labor*, 110. For the complete text of Roscrans's General Order No. 65, see Grossman, *William Sylvis*, 283–84.

127. Palladino, *Another Civil War*, 11; Foner, *History of the Labor Movement*, 353; Paludan, *People's Contest*, 187; Commons et al., *History of Labour*, 11–12; Cochran and Miller, *Age of Enterprise*, 117.

128. Paludan, *People's Contest*, 178; Rayback, *History of American Labor*, 110.

129. Fite, *Social and Industrial Conditions in the North*, 202.

130. Rayback, *History of American Labor*, 110; Paludan, *People's Contest*, 175, 178.

131. Dawley, *Class and Community*, 99, 103–4, 194–95, Palladino, *Another Civil War*, 72–73, 79, 81–82; Rayback, *History of American Labor*, 110; Paludan, *People's Contest*, 175, 178.

132. Long, *Jewel of Liberty*, 203.

133. Ibid., 202.

134. Geary, *We Need Men*, 153–54; Snell, "If They Would Know What I Know," 110–11; Reardon, "We Are All in This War," 27–28.

135. Shankman, *Pennsylvania Antiwar Movement*, 201–2.

136. Ibid.; Smith, "Beyond Politics," 151.

137. Shankman, *Pennsylvania Antiwar Movement*, 201–2; Smith, "Beyond Politics," 152.

3: "The Women Rising"

1. Attie, *Patriotic Toil*, 55.

2. Baker, *Cyclone in Calico*, 11. Bickerdyke eventually became a field agent for the Sanitary Commission.

3. Faust, "Altars of Sacrifice," 1206; Scott, *Southern Lady*, 90.

4. Faust, "Altars of Sacrifice," 1206; Ginzberg, *Women and the Work of Benevolence*, 141; Faust, *Mothers of Invention*, 93–94.

5. Rable, *Civil Wars*, 123, 142; Ginzberg, *Women and the Work of Benevolence*, 144–45.

6. Ginzberg, *Women and the Work of Benevolence*, 141; Attie, *Patriotic Toil*, 55.

7. Ginzberg, *Women and the Work of Benevolence*, 152; Bremner, *Public Good*, 65.

8. Bremner, *Public Good*, 66–68. The most thorough treatments of Clara Barton are Burton, *Clara Barton*; Oates, *Woman of Valor*; and Pryor, *Clara Barton*.

9. Badura, "Elizabeth Blackwell," 232–33; Leonard, *Yankee Women*, 14; Faust, "Altars of Sacrifice," 1215.

10. Faust, *Mothers of Invention*, 102–3; Schultz, *Women at the Front*, 34–37, 83. Schultz's recent work, subtitled *Hospital Workers in Civil War America*, is the most thorough examination of women in health care during the war.

11. Williams, *Rich Man's War*, 78; Gallman, *North Fights the Civil War*, 117–18.

12. Rable, *Civil Wars*, 122–24; Massey, *Women in the Civil War*, 46–47.

13. Massey, *Women in the Civil War*, 52, 63.

14. Faust, *Mothers of Invention*, 98; Williams, *Rich Man's War*, 77; Massey, *Women in the Civil War*, 53; Wood, "War Within," 204–05.

15. Massey, *Women in the Civil War*, 47; Leonard, *Yankee Women*, 30; Wood, "War Within," 207.

16. Massey, *Women in the Civil War*, 49; Baker, *Cyclone in Calico*, 11.

17. Wood, "War Within," 209–10; Massey, *Women in the Civil War*, 49. A monument to Bickerdyke stands on the courthouse square in Galesburg, Illinois.

18. Leonard, *Yankee Women*, 39.

19. Ibid., 123–24.

20. Clinton, *Other Civil War*, 83; Leonard, *Yankee Women*, 134; Massey, *Women in the Civil War*, 62–63. There were, in fact, a few female doctors in the South, such as

Louisa Shepard, who graduated in 1861 from Graefenberg Medical Institute in Dadeville, Alabama, and Elizabeth Cohen, who practiced medicine in New Orleans. See Clinton, *Other Civil War*, 83.

21. Massey, *Women in the Civil War*, 89, 100. Mary Surratt, convicted of complicity in Lincoln's April 1865 assassination, was the only woman to be executed as a result of war-related events.

22. Leonard, *All the Daring of the Soldier*, 24–50; Massey, *Women in the Civil War*, 98. "Far from tormenting her husband to death," writes historian Elizabeth Leonard, "it was Ford herself who died young, possibly as a consequence of her third pregnancy and delivery. In 1871 she left Willard a widower. He never married again."

23. Williams, Williams, and Carlson, *Plain Folk in a Rich Man's War*, 180; Massey, *Women in the Civil War*, 104; Leonard, *All the Daring of the Soldier*, 69.

24. Leonard, *All the Daring of the Soldier*, 57–60; Massey, *Women in the Civil War*, 102; Sizer, "Acting Her Part," 114, 132. Though born in New Orleans and living there at the war's outbreak, Cushman spent much of her childhood in Michigan.

25. Massey, *Women in the Civil War*, 89; Leonard, *All the Daring of the Soldier*, 50–56. See also Ryan, *A Yankee Spy in Richmond: The Civil War Diary of "Crazy Bet" Van Lew*; Varon, *Southern Lady, Yankee Spy*.

26. Blanton and Cook, *They Fought Like Demons*, 9; Sizer, "Acting Her Part," 122–24, 132. Though raised in Michigan, Edmonds was born French Canadian.

27. Blanton and Cook, *They Fought Like Demons*, 6–7; Leonard, *All the Daring of the Soldier*, 220, 239.

28. Massey, *Women in the Civil War*, 81, 84; Leonard, *All the Daring of the Soldier*, 218–20; Wiley, *Billy Yank*, 338.

29. Leonard, *All the Daring of the Soldier*, 202; Blanton and Cook, *They Fought Like Demons*, 27–28, Wiley, *Billy Yank*, 338.

30. Wiley, *Billy Yank*, 338; Leonard, *All the Daring of the Soldier*, 241; Massey, *Women in the Civil War*, 80–81; Wiley, *Johnny Reb*, 334; Blanton and Cook, *They Fought Like Demons*, 36–37, 38, 98, 100. Sarah Wakeman left the only known surviving set of letters from a female Civil War soldier. See Wakeman, *Uncommon Soldier*. As to sexuality, love interests among women in the ranks may not always have been heterosexual. In his memoirs, General Philip Sheridan wrote that an "intimacy had sprung up between" two women who had served as soldiers under his command. See Blanton and Cook, *They Fought Like Demons*, 200-01.

31. Massey, *Women in the Civil War*, 109.

32. Holmes, *Diary of Miss Emma Holmes*, 172; Fox-Genovese, *Within the Plantation Household*, 46; Rable, *Civil Wars*, 130.

33. Taber, *Hard Breathing Days*, 416.

34. Rable, *Civil Wars*, 130; Faust, "Altars of Sacrifice," 1216–17.

35. Rable, *Civil Wars*, 130–31; Massey, *Women in the Civil War*, 113, 118; Faust, *Mothers of Invention*, 88.

36. Massey, *Women in the Civil War*, 132, 139; Faust, *Mothers of Invention*, 88–89.

37. Faust, *Mothers of Invention*, 91.

38. Massey, *Women in the Civil War*, 141.

39. Ibid., 133, 136–38.

40. Fite, *Social and Industrial Conditions in the North*, 187; Foner, *History of the Labor Movement*, 341; Massey, *Women in the Civil War*, 5, 143, 148; Edwards, *Scarlett Doesn't Live Here Anymore*, 92; Faust, *Mothers of Invention*, 90, 278.

41. Foner, *History of the Labor Movement*, 341; Seidman, "Monstrous Doctrine," 178; Wertheimer, *We Were There*, 155, 157; Massey, *Women in the Civil War*, 145; Fite, *Social and Industrial Conditions in the North*, 186.

42. Rogers, *Confederate Home Front*, 81–82; Wertheimer, *We Were There*, 153–54; Paludan, *People's Contest*, 183; Montgomery, *Beyond Equality*, 97; Massey, *Women in the Civil War*, 146.

43. Wertheimer, *We Were There*, 154–56; Foner, *History of the Labor Movement*, 342–43.

44. Foner, *History of the Labor Movement*, 341, 343; Wertheimer, *We Were There*, 152–54.

45. Paludan, *People's Contest*, 183; Foner, *History of the Labor Movement*, 343; Massey, *Women in the Civil War*, 144–45.

46. Williams, Williams, and Carlson, *Plain Folk in a Rich Man's War*, 60; Coulter, *Confederate States of America*, 237; Massey, *Women in the Civil War*, 147.

47. Edwards, *Scarlett Doesn't Live Here Anymore*, 85.

48. Williams, Williams, and Carlson, *Plain Folk in a Rich Man's War*, 71–72.

49. Faust, *Mothers of Invention*, 57, 59–60.

50. Williams, Williams, and Carlson, *Plain Folk in a Rich Man's War*, 72–73.

51. Ibid., 73.

52. Fellman, "Women and Guerrilla Warfare," 158; Edwards, *Scarlett Doesn't Live Here Anymore*, 90–91.

53. Castel, "Dearest Ben," 23; Gates, *Agriculture and the Civil War*, 242; Craig, "Industry, Agriculture, and the Economy," 506; Craig and Weiss, "Agricultural Productivity Growth," 527.

54. Williams, *Rich Man's War*, 113.

55. Wood, "War Within," 199; Castel, "Dearest Ben," 19.

56. Blomquist and Taylor, *This Cruel War*, 87, 99; Gallman, *North Fights the Civil War*, 81.

57. Williams, *Rich Man's War*, 125–26.

58. Castel, "Dearest Ben," 19–20.

59. Blomquist and Taylor, *This Cruel War*, 94, 98.

60. Rable, *Civil Wars*, 61; Faust, *Mothers of Invention*, 124.

61. Lowry, *Story the Soldiers Wouldn't Tell*, 32–33; Fellman, "Women and Guerrilla Warfare," 160–61.

62. Rable, *Civil Wars*, 59–60; Lowry, *Story the Soldiers Wouldn't Tell*, 138.

63. Faust, *Mothers of Invention*, 124.

64. Lowry, *Story the Soldiers Wouldn't Tell*, 97–98. The increased abortion rate during the Civil War years seems to have reflected as much a general trend as any impact the war might have had. According to Lowry, there was one abortion for every thirty live births in 1840. By 1870 the rate was one in five. Over the course of the nineteenth century, the childbearing rate for the average woman in the United States dropped from 7.04 to 3.56. Though urbanization may have been a contributing factor, Lowry concludes that "since there is nothing to suggest a decrease in the incidence of coitus over that century, the best explanation for halving the birth rate is the use of contraception and abortion on a wide and consistent scale."

65. Massey, *Women in the Civil War*, 218–19; Wiley, *Johnny Reb*, 331, 332; Wiley, *Billy Yank*, 298–99; Paludan, *Victims*, 97; Bynum, *Unruly Women*, 135.

66. Massey, *Women in the Civil War*, 68; Williams, *Rich Man's War*, 120–21.

67. Chesnut, *Mary Chesnut's Civil War*, 371.

68. Smith, *Trial By Fire*, 356; Chesnut, *Mary Chesnut's Civil War*, 371; Williams, *Rich Man's War*, 121.

69. Massey, *Women in the Civil War*, 215.

70. Rable, *Civil Wars*, 69.

71. Watkins, *Co. Aytch*, 119–20.

72. Massey, *Women in the Civil War*, 216; Faust, "Altars of Sacrifice," 1221–22.

73. Inscoe and McKinney, *Heart of Confederate Appalachia*, 195; Bynum, *Unruly Women*, 135, 145, 148.

74. McCaslin, *Tainted Breeze*, 57; Fisher, *War At Every Door*, 74.

75. Rable, *Civil Wars*, 161; Lowry, *Story the Soldiers Wouldn't Tell*, 125–26, 137. Rable notes that "at least eighteen Union soldiers were executed for rape during the war, but this statistic says little about the prevalence of the crime" (Rable, *Civil Wars*, 341 n. 25).

76. Massey, *Women in the Civil War*, 230–31.

77. Fellman, "Women and Guerrilla Warfare," 160.

78. Massey, *Women in the Civil War*, 262–64; Lowry, *Story the Soldiers Wouldn't Tell*, 70, 84.

79. Lowry, *Story the Soldiers Wouldn't Tell*, 70, 84; Fellman, "Women and Guerrilla Warfare," 159; Massey, *Women in the Civil War*, 73.

80. Lowry, *Story the Soldiers Wouldn't Tell*, 79–80, 84; Richard, *Busy Hands*, 72.

81. Lowry, *Story the Soldiers Wouldn't Tell*, 64, 147–48; Massey, *Women in the Civil War*, 263.

82. Massey, *Women in the Civil War*, 73–75; Lowry, *Story the Soldiers Wouldn't Tell*, 154–55. As the war was ending, Annie did finally secure her release on one condition—that she would not go "south of the Susquehanna." A short time later, she wrote to Stanton asking that the prohibition be lifted, saying that she wanted to go to New Orleans and serve as a teacher among recently freed blacks: "Mr. Stanton, will you let me go? Give me passage to New Orleans and I will never trouble officials again." There seems to be no record of Stanton's reply, but the Freedmen's Bureau does show an Annie Jones on the payroll at Meridian and Vicksburg, Mississippi, early in 1866. See Massey, *Women in the Civil War*, 75–76.

83. Massey, *Women in the Civil War*, 261-62.

84. Bynum, *Unruly Women*, 119–20; Massey, *Women in the Civil War*, 262; Williams, *Rich Man's War*, 114.

85. Fitzgerald, "Poor Man's Fight," 15; Bynum, *Unruly Women*, 121.

86. Refers to the Battle of Crampton's Gap near Burkittsville, Maryland, September 14, 1862. The battle was part of a larger engagement known as South Mountain during the Maryland campaign of 1862. That campaign reached its climax three days later at the Battle of Sharpsburg, or Antietam.

87. Williams, Williams, and Carlson, *Plain Folk in a Rich Man's War*, 79–80.

88. Rable, *Civil Wars*, 107; Williams, Williams, and Carlson, *Plain Folk in a Rich Man's War*, 27–28.

89. Escott, *After Secession*, 122; Edwards, *Scarlett Doesn't Live Here Anymore*, 89.

90. Wiley, *Plain People of the Confederacy*, 45.

91. Rable, *Civil Wars*, 83.

92. Faust, "Altars of Sacrifice," 1223; Wiley, *Plain People of the Confederacy*, 66; Rable, *Civil Wars*, 73.

93. Williams, *Rich Man's War*, 113–14.

94. Escott, *After Secession*, 122.

95. Massey, *Women in the Civil War*, 171; Williams, Williams, and Carlson, *Plain Folk in a Rich Man's War*, 80; Gates, *Agriculture and the Civil War*, 38–39.

96. Wiley, *Plain People of the Confederacy*, 47–48.

97. Bynum, *Unruly Women*, 133; Gates, *Agriculture and the Civil War*, 39.

98. Cecil-Fronsman, *Common Whites*, 212; Bynum, *Unruly Women*, 134; Thomas, *Confederate Nation*, 204.

99. Friedheim and Jackson, *Freedom's Unfinished Revolution*, 103.

100. Chesson, "Harlots or Heroines?" 131–75; Rable, *Civil Wars*, 108–10; Thomas, *Confederate Nation*, 202–5; Blair, *Virginia's Private War*, 74; Coulter, *Confederate States of America*, 422–23.

101. Amos, "All-Absorbing Topics," 22–23; Gates, *Agriculture and the Civil War*, 39, 40; Coulter, *Confederate States of America*, 241, 243.

102. Williams, Williams, and Carlson, *Plain Folk in a Rich Man's War*, 82–83.

103. *War of the Rebellion*, ser. 4, vol. 2, p. 468; Green, *This Business of Relief*, 78; Williams, *Rich Man's War*, 84.

104. Williams, Williams, and Carlson, *Plain Folk in a Rich Man's War*, 85.

105. Ibid., 85.

106. Ibid., 85–88.

107. Dotson, "Grave and Scandalous Evil," 419; Coulter, *Confederate States of America*, 423; Gates, *Agriculture and the Civil War*, 40; Revels, *Grander in Her Daughters*, 74; Marten, *Texas Divided*, 92.

108. Williams, Williams, and Carlson, *Plain Folk in a Rich Man's War*, 88.

109. Ibid., 88, 83–84.

110. Ibid., 83; Green, *This Business of Relief*, 78.

111. Williams, Williams, and Carlson, *Plain Folk in a Rich Man's War*, 84.

112. Ibid., 83–84, 88.

113. Mitchell, *Civil War Soldiers*, 165.

114. Martin, *Rich Man's War*, 148; Thomas, *History of the Doles-Cook Brigade*, 593–95; Faust, "Altars of Sacrifice," 1224.

115. Wiley, *Billy Yank*, 289–90.

116. Robertson, *Soldiers Blue and Gray*, 135, 244; *War of the Rebellion*, ser. 1, vol. 25, pt. 2, p. 73; Billings, *Hard Tack and Coffee*, 161.

117. Shankman, *Pennsylvania Antiwar Movement*, 147, 143; Palladino, *Another Civil War*, 99, 100; Murdock, *One Million Men*, 48.

118. Gray, *Hidden Civil War*, 138; Cashin, "Deserters, Civilians, and Draft Resistance in the North," 275; Murdock, *One Million Men*, 42.

119. Larsen, "Draft Riot in Wisconsin," 422.

120. Murdock, *One Million Men*, 52–53; Gray, *Hidden Civil War*, 138; Cook, *Armies of the Streets*, 198; Hanna, "Boston Draft Riot," 263–65.

121. Fellman, "Women and Guerrilla Warfare," 156–57.

122. Blakey, Lainhart, and Stephens, *Rose Cottage Chronicles*, 311–12.

123. Williams, *Rich Man's War*, 142; Bynum, *Unruly Women*, 142; Blakey, Lainhart, and Stephens, *Rose Cottage Chronicles*, 311–12.

124. Bynum, *Unruly Women*, 142–44.

125. Williams, Williams, and Carlson, *Plain Folk in a Rich Man's War*, 89.

126. *War of the Rebellion*, ser. 4, vol. 2, p. 721; Andrews, *Footprints of a Regiment*, 39.

127. Andrews, *Footprints of a Regiment*, 39.

4: "We Poor Soldiers"

1. Werner, *Reluctant Witnesses*, 1.

2. Linderman, *Embattled Courage*, 256–57.

3. Smith, *Trial By Fire*, 73–74.

4. In a sampling of 11,000 Confederate infantry privates in 94 regiments from across the South, Bell Wiley identified 5 percent as below age eighteen at enlistment. A similar sampling of over 14,000 Union volunteers showed that 1.6 percent of all enlistees were under eighteen. Taking these samples as representative and using James McPherson's figures of about 2,100,000 and 850,000 troops who served in the Union and Confederate armies, respectively, those under age eighteen at enlistment may have totaled as many as 42,500 for the Confederacy and 33,600 for the Union. Wiley, *Johnny Reb*, 330–31; Wiley, *Billy Yank*, 298–99; McPherson, *Ordeal By Fire*, 184; Linderman, *Embattled Courage*, 26.

5. Dotson, "Grave and Scandalous Evil," 400.

6. Parish, "From Necessary Evil to National Blessing," 61; Murdock, *One Million Men*, 207; Curran, *Soldiers of Peace*, 7. For the importance of Protestant clergy to the Republican agenda, see Howard, *Religion and the Radical Republican Movement*. For the role of Catholics and Jews in the war, see Blied, *Catholics and the Civil War*; Murphy, "The Catholic Church in the United States during the Civil War Period"; Korn, *American Jewry and the Civil War*; and Simonhoff, *Jewish Participants in the Civil War*.

7. Curran, *Soldiers of Peace*, 54, 82.

8. Ibid., 7.

9. Woodworth, *While God Is Marching On*, 178–79. For a discussion of the individual nature of religion in the Old South and how it contrasted with religion in the North, see Wyatt-Brown, *Yankee Saints and Southern Sinners*. See also the introduction to Shattuck, *Shield and Hiding Place*.

10. McPherson, *What They Fought For*, 9, 11, 50.

11. Robinson, *Bitter Fruits of Bondage*, 62; McPherson, *What They Fought For*, 51. The way in which many white southerners viewed slavery as the foundation of white liberty is explored in Harris, *Plain Folk and Gentry in a Slave Society*. See especially chapter 1, "Slavery and Liberty."

12. Wood, "Union and Secession in Mississippi," 141.

13. Balser, *Collected Works of Abraham Lincoln*, 5:423; McPherson, *Ordeal By Fire*, 264; McPherson, *What They Fought For*, 51, 81 n. 14.

14. McPherson, *What They Fought For*, 52–53.

15. Ash, *Secessionists and Other Scoundrels*, 90.

16. McPherson, *What They Fought For*, 53.

17. Cunningham, *Doctors in Gray*, 5; Werner, *Reluctant Witnesses*, 23; Watkins, *Co. Aytch*, 21.

18. Wiley, *Billy Yank*, 288; Williams, *Rich Man's War*, 116.

19. Ward, *Civil War*, 184; Marten, *Children for the Union*, 126; Williams, *Rich Man's War*, 116; Wiley, *Johnny Reb*, 127.

20. Linderman, *Embattled Courage*, 256–57.

21. Woodworth, *While God Is Marching On*, 189.

22. During the latter part of the war, soldiers in the Army of Northern Virginia took to calling themselves "Lee's Miserables" after the 1862 Victor Hugo work *Les Misérables*.

23. Linderman, *Embattled Courage*, 255, 252, 253.

24. Ibid., 253–54.

25. Ibid., 253, 254, 222.

26. Martin, *Rich Man's War*, 122; Cochran and Miller, *Age of Enterprise*, 118; Linderman, *Embattled Courage*, 221.

27. Linderman, *Embattled Courage*, 220–21.

28. Watkins, *Co. Aytch*, 194; Wills, *War Hits Home*, 100; Bennett, *Union Jacks*, 121.

29. Mitchell, *Civil War Soldiers*, 38; Jackson, *So Mourns the Dove*, 35.

30. Wiley, *Johnny Reb*, 136; Marten, *Texas Divided*, 94.

31. Adams, *Doctors in Blue*, 208–9.

32. Ibid., 208; Robertson, *Soldiers Blue and Gray*, 66–67.

33. Bennett, *Union Jacks*, 120.

34. Robertson, *Soldiers Blue and Gray*, 66; Adams, *Doctors in Blue*, 16.

35. Wiley, *Billy Yank*, 230.

36. Billings, *Hardtack and Coffee*, 110.

37. Ibid., 110; Otto, *Southern Agriculture*, 22.

38. Williams, *Rich Man's War*, 233 n. 8.

39. Wiley, *Johnny Reb*, 92; Williams, *Johnny Reb's War*, 17; Mitchell, *Civil War Soldiers*, 163.

40. Andrews, *Footprints of a Regiment*, 151.

41. Wiley, *Johnny Reb*, 134–35; Cunningham, *Doctors in Gray*, 177; Gates, *Agriculture and the Civil War*, 40.

42. Bailey, *Class and Tennessee's Confederate Generation*, 84; Williams, *Johnny Reb's War*, 15.

43. Wiley, *Johnny Reb*, 319; Andrews, *Footprints of a Regiment*, 93–94.

44. Williams, *Johnny Reb's War*, 11; Bernard, *War Talks of Confederate Veterans*, 20; Bailey, *Class and Tennessee's Confederate Generation*, 84.

45. Watkins, *Co. Aytch*, 62.

46. Ibid., 56–57, 60.

47. Wiley, *Billy Yank*, 22, 61.

48. Bailey, *Class and Tennessee's Confederate Generation*, 82–83; Wiley, *Johnny Reb*, 246; Cunningham, *Doctors in Gray*, 202; Robertson, *Soldiers Blue and Gray*, 151.

49. Wiley, *Billy Yank*, 133; Wiley, *Johnny Reb*, 251.

50. Wiley, *Billy Yank*, 124, 126–27; Robertson, *Soldiers Blue and Gray*, 150; Wiley, *Johnny Reb*, 253; Cunningham, *Doctors in Gray*, 187; Williams, "On the Fringes of Hell," 706–7.

51. Lowry, *Story the Soldiers Wouldn't Tell*, 102, 105–8.

52. Robertson, *Soldiers Blue and Gray*, 157, 158; Wiley, *Johnny Reb*, 257–58.

53. Wiley, *Billy Yank*, 130; Robertson, *Soldiers Blue and Gray*, 159.

54. Wiley, *Billy Yank*, 132.

55. Andrews, *Footprints of a Regiment*, 26; Wiley, *Johnny Reb*, 236; Attie, *Patriotic Toil*, 142.

56. Linderman, *Embattled Courage*, 230–31.

57. Cecil-Fronsman, *Common Whites*, 214.

58. Linderman, *Embattled Courage*, 230; Wiley, *Johnny Reb*, 236; Wiley, *Billy Yank*, 198–99.

59. Wiley, *Johnny Reb*, 235, 237.

60. Robertson, *Soldiers Blue and Gray*, 127.

61. Werner, *Reluctant Witnesses*, 37; Freeman, *Lee*, 4:445–46; Marten, *Texas Divided*, 95.

62. Wiley, *Plain People of the Confederacy*, 13–14; Robertson, *Soldiers Blue and Gray*, 129.

63. Linderman, *Embattled Courage*, 52; Robertson, *Soldiers Blue and Gray*, 130.

64. Alotta, *Civil War Justice*, 117, 51, 76; Wiley, *Billy Yank*, 199; Linderman, *Embattled Courage*, 51–52.

65. Upson, *With Sherman to the Sea*, 112; Canney, *Lincoln's Navy*, 127; Alotta, *Civil War Justice*, 47; Wiley, *Billy Yank*, 192–93.

66. Alotta, *Civil War Justice*, 61–63.

67. Blair, *Virginia's Private War*, 65; Casler, *Four Years in the Stonewall Brigade*, 114.

68. Alotta, *Civil War Justice*, 123–25.

69. Billings, *Hardtack and Coffee*, 163.

70. Wiley, *Billy Yank*, 207.

71. Alotta, *Civil War Justice*, 40.

72. Wiley, *Billy Yank*, 194, 197, 206; Billings, *Hardtack and Coffee*, 146; Williams, *Rich Man's War*, 123; Wiley, *Johnny Reb*, 224; Dotson, "Grave and Scandalous Evil," 406. Mainly because of whipping's association with slavery, both the Union and Confederate armies officially abolished it as a punishment for soldiers.

73. Linderman, *Embattled Courage*, 232; Wiley, *Billy Yank*, 212–13.

74. Billings, *Hardtack and Coffee*, 145–46; Wiley, *Billy Yank*, 200.

75. Linderman, *Embattled Courage*, 52–53.

76. Williams, "On the Fringes of Hell," 710.

77. Wiley, *Billy Yank*, 72; Wiley, *Johnny Reb*, 309; Weller, *Civil War Courtship*, 93; Robertson, *Soldiers Blue and Gray*, 142. Euchre is normally a plain-trick card game for four players in fixed partnerships, partners sitting opposite each other.

78. Williams, "On the Fringes of Hell," 711.

79. Dinkins, *Personal Recollections*, 75–76; Newton, *Wisconsin Boy in Dixie*, 72.

80. Robertson, *Soldiers Blue and Gray*, 142.

81. Mitchell, *Civil War Soldiers*, 78–80.

82. Linderman, *Embattled Courage*, 167.

83. Wiley, *Billy Yank*, 86; Wiley, *Johnny Reb*, 83.

84. Wiley, *Billy Yank*, 278, 86; Andrews, *Footprints of a Regiment*, 20.

85. Watkins, *Co. Aytch*, 157.

86. Perman, *Major Problems in the Civil War and Reconstruction*, 207.

87. Marten, "Fatherhood in the Confederacy," 282; Werner, *Reluctant Witnesses*, 31.

88. Linderman, *Embattled Courage*, 22–23; Wiley, *Johnny Reb*, 84.

89. Linderman, *Embattled Courage*, 166–67.

90. Ibid., 167.

91. Wiley, *Johnny Reb*, 80–81; Wiley, *Billy Yank*, 72.

92. Werner, *Reluctant Witnesses*, 35; Robertson, *Soldiers Blue and Gray*, 143; Wiley, *Johnny Reb*, 316. A bronze monument of Richard Kirkland stands on the Fredericksburg battlefield site. In 1996, artist Don Stivers, renowned for his work on the Civil War era, paid tribute to Kirkland in an oil painting entitled *An Act of Compassion*.

93. Williams, "On the Fringes of Hell," 714–15.

94. Williams, *Johnny Reb's War*, 34.

95. Linderman, *Embattled Courage*, 125.

96. Glatthaar, *Forged in Battle*, 25; Wiley, *Billy Yank*, 79; Ward, *Civil War*, 160.

97. Werner, *Reluctant Witnesses*, 25.

98. Bull, *Soldiering*, 231–32.

99. Watkins, *Co. Aytch*, 158; Upson, *With Sherman to the Sea*, 116–17.

100. Wiley, *Johnny Reb*, 75.

101. Upson, *With Sherman to the Sea*, 38.

102. Strong, *Yankee Private's Civil War*, 38–39.

103. Adams, *Doctors in Blue*, 114.

104. Ibid., 126; McCrea, *Dear Belle*, 156.

105. Cunningham, *Doctors in Gray*, 117.

106. Robertson, *Soldiers Blue and Gray*, 163; Williams, *Johnny Reb's War*, 36.

107. Bollet, *Civil War Medicine*, 153.

108. Williams, *Johnny Reb's War*, 35.

109. Adams, *Doctors in Blue*, 118.

110. Cunningham, *Doctors in Gray*, 117.

111. Robertson, *Soldiers Blue and Gray*, 164.

112. Brooks, *Civil War Medicine*, 9.

113. The "three-starred gentry" quote refers to full colonels and general officers in the Confederate Army, all of whom wore three stars on their collars (generals' stars were enclosed by a wreath) regardless of specific rank. Wiley, *Billy Yank*, 142–43; Brooks, *Civil War Medicine*, 9; "An Officer" to C.C. Clay, January 12, 1864, Clay Papers.

114. Imboden, "Confederate Retreat from Gettysburg," 3:424.

115. Jackson, *Twenty Million Yankees*, 94.

116. Bailey, *Class and Tennessee's Confederate Generation*, 81–82.

117. Cunningham, *Doctors in Gray*, 88; Adams, *Doctors in Blue*, 169.

118. Adams, *Doctors in Blue*, 126.

119. Wiley, *Billy Yank*, 148.

120. Adams, *Doctors in Blue*, 139, 141, 144.

121. Ibid., 129. The benefit of using maggots in certain medical procedures had been known during the Napoleonic Wars. It was forgotten until the Civil War, then forgotten again. Its rediscovery during World War I led to the use of maggot therapy in treating osteomyelitis. In the 1930s, research at Johns Hopkins University led to wider use of maggot therapy until the introduction of antibiotics a decade later. Their use has been revived in recent years at wound-care clinics. In January 2004, maggots became the first live animals to receive Food and Drug Administration approval for use as a medical treatment (leeches were approved later that year). "Still 'it takes work to convince people'—including hospital administrators—that 'maggots do work very well,' said Dr. Robert Kirsner, who directs the University of Miami Cedars Wound Center." See "Maggots Make Medical Comeback."

122. Speer, *Portals to Hell*, 16.

123. Ibid., 14.

124. Bailey, *Class and Tennessee's Confederate Generation*, 96.

125. Speer, *Portals to Hell*, 11.

126. Bailey, *Class and Tennessee's Confederate Generation*, 96.

127. Marvel, *Andersonville*, 107; Speer, *Portals to Hell*, 14–15.

128. Horigan, *Elmira*, 168; Bailey, *Class and Tennessee's Confederate Generation*, 96–97; Cunningham, *Doctors in Gray*, 176.

129. Speer, *Portals to Hell*, 16; Linderman, *Embattled Courage*, 236; Bryant, *Cahaba Prison*, 67; Marvel, *Andersonville*, ix, 238–39; Horigan, *Elmira*, 193; Andrews, *War-Time Journal*, 78–79.

130. Gordon, "Surely They Remember Me," 328; Jackson, *So Mourns the Dove*, 32–33; Williams, *Rich Man's War*, 123.

131. Williams, *Rich Man's War*, 123-24; Lindsey, *Reason for the Tears*, 132.

132. Williams, *Rich Man's War*, 124.

133. Ibid., 124.

134. Jones, *Heroines of Dixie*, 183; Jackson, *So Mourns the Dove*, 35; Wiley, *Billy Yank*, 291.

135. Mitchell, *Civil War Soldiers*, 67–68; Paludan, *People's Contest*, 330–31.

136. Edwards, *Scarlett Doesn't Live Here Anymore*, 92–93; Williams, Williams, and Carlson, *Plain Folk in a Rich Man's War*, 161.

137. Wiley, *Billy Yank*, 292; Edwards, *Scarlett Doesn't Live Here Anymore*, 92; Wiley, *Plain People*, 65; Blair, *Virginia's Private War*, 63.

138. Casler, *Four Years in the Stonewall Brigade*, 204–5.

139. Billings, *Hardtack and Coffee*, 100.

140. Wiley, *Billy Yank*, 291.

141. Castel, "Malingering," 29–30; Faust, *Mothers of Invention*, 243.

142. Wiley, *Billy Yank*, 282, 423 n. 18; Blakey, Lainhart, and Stephens, *Rose Cottage Chronicles*, 307; Jimerson, *Private Civil War*, 215; Bynum, *Free State of Jones*, 101, 103.

143. Gates, *Agriculture and the Civil War*, 36; Wiley, *Billy Yank*, 282.

144. Escott, *Many Excellent People*, 43–44.

145. Robinson, *Bitter Fruits of Bondage*, 244; Martin, *Rich Man's War*, 149.

146. Martin, *Rich Man's War*, 127.

147. Geary, *We Need Men*, 45.

148. Faust, *Mothers of Invention*, 243.

149. Martin, *Rich Man's War*, 148; Chesnut, *Mary Chesnut's Civil War*, 773.

150. Lonn, *Desertion*, 234–35; Williams, Williams, and Carlson, *Plain Folk in a Rich Man's War*, 162.

151. Berlin, Favreau, and Miller, *Remembering Slavery*, 228–29.

152. Levine, "Draft Evasion in the North," 819; Neely, *Fate of Liberty*, 131; Wills, *War Hits Home*, 100; Geary, *We Need Men*, 98; Gray, *Hidden Civil War*, 113–14; Linderman, *Embattled Courage*, 232.

153. Escott, *After Secession*, 127; Williams, Williams, and Carlson, *Plain Folk in a Rich Man's War*, 162; Tatum, *Disloyalty in the Confederacy*, 118; Dotson, "Grave and Scandalous Evil," 406–7; Blair, *Virginia's Private War*, 64.

154. Robinson, *Bitter Fruits of Bondage*, 90; Wiley, *Johnny Reb*, 139.

155. Robinson, *Bitter Fruits of Bondage*, 205; Tatum, *Disloyalty in the Confederacy*, 58; Dotson, "Grave and Scandalous Evil," 409; Crawford, *Ashe County's Civil War*, 108; *War of the Rebellion*, ser. 1, vol. 53, 380–81; Escott, *After Secession*, 132.

156. Edwards, *Scarlett Doesn't Live Here Anymore*, 93; Williams, Williams, and Carlson, *Plain Folk in a Rich Man's War*, 182; Lonn, *Desertion*, 69, 70.

157. Cashin, "Deserters, Civilians, and Draft Resistance in the North," 274; Lonn, *Desertion*, 205.

5: "Come In Out of the Draft"

1. Hopper penned these lines on September 9, 1863, to his brother in the Confederate army encouraging him to desert. Davis, *Look Away!*, 233.

2. Pike to Maj. O.A. Mack, Aide-de-Camp and Acting Assistant Provost-Marshal-General, July 22, 1863, *War of the Rebellion*, ser. 3, vol. 3, 565–66.

3. Neely, *Fate of Liberty*, 10; Williams, "Civil Liberties, U.S.A.," 442.

4. Neely, *Fate of Liberty*, 65, 28.

5. Williams, "Civil Liberties, U.S.A.," 442.

6. Neely, *Fate of Liberty*, 28.

7. Ibid., 28.

8. *War of the Rebellion*, ser. 1, vol. 5, 640, 646; Neely, *Fate of Liberty*, 28; Neely, *Union Divided*, 42–44; Curran, *Soldiers of Peace*, 86–87; McPherson, *Battle Cry of Freedom*, 595–96.

9. Sampson, "Charleston (Illinois) Riot," 405–7; Sampson, "Pretty Damned Warm Times," 99–102.

10. Klement, *Limits of Dissent*, 234–35; Williams, "Civil Liberties, U.S.A.," 443.

11. Williams, "Civil Liberties, U.S.A.," 443. See also Klement, *Limits of Dissent*.

12. Neely, *Fate of Liberty*, 109–12; Lonn, *Foreigners in the Union Army and Navy*, 450–51.

13. Murdock, *One Million Men*, 23; Shankman, *Pennsylvania Antiwar Movement*, 151–52; Palladino, *Another Civil War*, 104–5.

14. Wright, *Conscientious Objectors*, 6, 65, 71; Curran, *Soldiers of Peace*, xiii, 66; Murdock, *One Million Men*, 207. For a discussion of the motives of Quakers who served, see chapter 3, "Why Did They Fight?" in Nelson, *Indiana Quakers Confront the Civil War*.

15. Wright, *Conscientious Objectors*, 83.

16. Ibid., 83–84.

17. Curran, *Soldiers of Peace*, 1, 57–58.

18. Ibid., 64.

19. Wright, *Conscientious Objectors*, 165.

20. Ibid., 75–76; Curran, *Soldiers of Peace*, 64–65.

21. Parish, "From Necessary Evil to National Blessing," 64; Andreasen, "Civil War Church Trials," 230–31, 234–35, 220–23.

22. Andreasen, "Civil War Church Trials," 241.

23. Ibid., 220.

24. Shankman, *Pennsylvania Antiwar Movement*, 159.

25. Murdock, *Patriotism Limited*, 54, 58. Married men were not exempt from the Federal draft, but those between the ages of thirty-five and forty-five (the draft's upper age limit) were placed in Class Two and not taken until those in Class One had been drafted.

26. Glass and Singer, *Singing Soldiers*, 136–138.

27. Palladino, *Another Civil War*, 114; Geary, *We Need Men*, 98; Neely, *Fate of Liberty*, 131; Cashin, "Deserters, Civilians, and Draft Resistance," 270; Paludan, *People's Contest*, 168.

28. Lonn, *Desertion*, 140, 155; Gallman, *North Fights the Civil War*, 69; Murdock, *Patriotism Limited*, 54.

29. Murdock, *Patriotism Limited*, 59.

30. Ibid., 78, 147; Gallman, *North Fights the Civil War*, 69; Levine, "Draft Evasion During the Civil War," 819.

31. Murdock, *One Million Men*, 169–72; Murdock, *Patriotism Limited*, 60.

32. Murdock, *One Million Men*, 50–54, 85; Gray, *Hidden Civil War*, 111.

33. Shankman, *Pennsylvania Antiwar Movement*, 146–48; Murdock, *One Million Men*, 47, 58, 41; Foner, *History of the Labor Movement*, 323; Gray, *Hidden Civil War*, 111.

34. Murdock, *One Million Men*, 30, 41.

35. Ibid., 42, 51, 59; Shankman, *Pennsylvania Antiwar Movement*, 147–48.

36. Palladino, *Another Civil War*, 109; Murdock, *One Million Men*, 46, 55, 30.

37. Murdock, *One Million Men,* 46, 48; Gray, *Hidden Civil War,* 137, 138, 154; Paludan, *People's Contest,* 191–92.

38. Foner, *History of the Labor Movement,* 322–23; Cook, *Armies of the Streets,* 139; Paludan, *People's Contest,* 192; Murdock, *One Million Men,* 54, 57, 89; Curran, *Soldiers of Peace,* 85; Williams, "Class Conflict, U.S.A.," 448; Gray, *Hidden Civil War,* 111, 137.

39. Murdock, *One Million Men,* 52–53; Lonn, *Desertion During the Civil War,* 204.

40. Gray, *Hidden Civil War,* 138; Murdock, *One Million Men,* 52–53.

41. Gray, *Hidden Civil War,* 111; Larsen, "Draft Riot in Wisconsin," 422–23.

42. Gray, *Hidden Civil War,* 111–12.

43. Lonn, *Desertion During the Civil War,* 206; Shankman, *Pennsylvania Antiwar Movement,* 148; Palladino, *Another Civil War,* 100–01.

44. Hanna, "Boston Draft Riot," 263–71.

45. Curran, *Soldiers of Peace,* 87, 103 n. 37.

46. Foner, *History of the Labor Movement,* 322; Paludan, *People's Contest,* 190.

47. Bernstein, *New York City Draft Riots,* 18–19, 36; Geary, *We Need Men,* 105; O'Sullivan and Meckler, *Draft and Its Enemies,* 67.

48. Geary, *We Need Men,* 105–6; Williams, "Class Conflict, U.S.A.," 448; Bernstein, *New York City Draft Riots,* 21.

49. Geary, *We Need Men,* 105; Cook, *Armies of the Streets,* 101, 118–19; Bernstein, *New York City Draft Riots,* 36–37; O'Sullivan and Meckler, *Draft and Its Enemies,* 68.

50. Bernstein, *New York City Draft Riots,* 36; Cook, *Armies of the Streets,* 77–81; O'Sullivan and Meckler, *Draft and Its Enemies,* 68. According to Cook, the orphanage housed 237 children at the time of the attack (Cook, *Armies of the Streets,* 77).

51. Cook, *Armies of the Streets,* 194; Paludan, *People's Contest,* 193; Murdock, *One Million Men,* 77; Murdock, *Patriotism Limited,* 60; McPherson, *Battle Cry of Freedom,* 604.

52. Murdock, *One Million Men,* 3–5.

53. Palladino, *Another Civil War,* 104, 106.

54. Lonn, *Desertion,* 206–07; Shankman, *Pennsylvania Antiwar Movement,* 148–49.

55. Murdock, *One Million Men,* 48; Lonn, *Desertion,* 205; Shankman, *Pennsylvania Antiwar Movement,* 154.

56. Murdock, *One Million Men,* 85; *War of the Rebellion,* ser. 3, vol. 3, 565–66.

57. Murdock, *One Million Men,* 55–56, 58, 86; Gray, *Hidden Civil War,* 155; Sterling, "Civil War Draft Resistance in the Middle West," 505–06; *War of the Rebellion,* ser. 3, vol. 3, 632–33.

58. Murdock, *One Million Men,* 51–52, 85–86.

59. Ibid., 54–55, 84–85; Lonn, *Desertion,* 204; Gray, *Hidden Civil War,* 155.

60. Sterling, "Civil War Draft Resistance in the Middle West," 505; Shankman, *Pennsylvania Antiwar Movement,* 157; Murdock, *One Million Men,* 85.

61. *War of the Rebellion* ser. 3, vol. 3, 697.

62. Gray, *Hidden Civil War,* 70–71, 137; Palladino, *Another Civil War,* 106; Klement, *Dark Lanterns,* 132; Milton, *Abraham Lincoln and the Fifth Column,* 246.

63. Klement, *Limits of Dissent,* 263–64; Churchill, "Liberty, Conscription," 295, 296–97.

64. In his 1967 essay "Party Politics and the Union and Confederate War Efforts," Eric McKitrick argued that the North's two-party system helped preserve the Union by discouraging factionalism, as was common in the Confederacy, and by channeling a great deal of dissent into electoral politics. More recently, in his 2002 book *The Union Divided: Party Conflict in the Civil War North,* Mark Neely argues that the two-party system did little to advance the Union's war effort and much to delay victory.

It seems obvious that the work of antiwar Democrats indeed delayed Union victory. By definition, antiwar activity at all levels did. But I tend to agree with McKitrick's conclusion. Had rampant factionalism developed in the North or had violent opposition become more widely organized, which may have occurred without the existence of a loyal opposition party (and which did occur in the Confederacy), the Union war effort would have been even more difficult to sustain.

65. Williams, Williams, and Carlson, *Plain Folk in a Rich Man's War*, 152, 160.

66. Tatum, *Disloyalty in the Confederacy*, 158, 43–44.

67. Julia P. Gwynn to her uncle, July 25, 1863, Lenoir Family Papers; Aughey, *Iron Furnace*, 266; Williams, Williams, and Carlson, *Plain Folk in a Rich Man's War*, 5.

68. "Dobbin" was a colloquialism referring to a farm horse or plodding workhorse.

69. Williams, Williams, and Carlson, *Plain Folk in a Rich Man's War*, 179–80.

70. Wood, "Union and Secession in Mississippi," 146–47; Escott, *After Secession*, 131.

71. Moneyhon, "Disloyalty in Southwestern Arkansas," 233; Escott, *After Secession*, 120.

72. Escott, *After Secession*, 124–25; Wiley, *Plain People of the Confederacy*, 66.

73. Williams, Williams, and Carlson, *Plain Folk in a Rich Man's War*, 188; Davis, *Look Away!*, 271.

74. Bynum, *Unruly Women*, 137; Mallard, "I Had No Comfort to Give the People," 80.

75. Aughey, *Iron Furnace*, 267, 51–52.

76. Dotson, "Grave and Scandalous Evil," 416.

77. Aughey, *Iron Furnace*, 197–98.

78. Williams, *Rich Man's War*, 148.

79. Chesebrough, "Dissenting Clergy in Confederate Mississippi," 119–20; Mallard, "I Had No Comfort to Give the People," 82–83.

80. Mallard, "I Had No Comfort to Give the People," 79–80; Aughey, *Iron Furnace*, 6.

81. Williams, "Civil Liberties, C.S.A.," 441.

82. Chesebrough, "Dissenting Clergy in Confederate Mississippi," 118; Lathrop, "Disaffection in Confederate Louisiana," 309–10.

83. Williams, *Rich Man's War*, 130.

84. Moore, *Conscription and Conflict*, 53; Williams, *Rich Man's War*, 124.

85. Moore, *Conscription and Conflict*, 54–56; Williams, *Rich Man's War*, 133; Baggett, *Scalawags*, 72; Tatum, *Disloyalty in the Confederacy*, 82–83.

86. Williams, *Rich Man's War*, 134; Storey, *Loyalty and Loss*, 69.

87. Moore, *Conscription and Conflict*, 68; Dotson, "Grave and Scandalous Evil," 400, 415.

88. Horst, *Mennonites in the Confederacy*, 80.

89. Ibid., 30, 32–33; Schlabach, *Peace, Faith, Nation*, 190. Though Good entered service on July 8, 1861, nine months before the Confederate draft commenced, he and many others were effectively state draftees. Horst explains: "The prewar militia system of Virginia required all males from eighteen to forty-five years of age to drill several times a year unless exempted. There was no exemption for persons who professed conscientious scruples against military activities. Most Mennonites and Dunkers would not attend these drills but would instead pay a nominal fine of fifty or seventy-five cents. When the war broke out in the spring of 1861, the militia was

called and Mennonites whose names were on the muster rolls found themselves no longer excused by paying muster fines. . . . Most of the men went into the militia under protest, vowing among themselves, to their families, and to the church that they would not use weapons placed in their hands to kill the enemy." Horst, *Mennonites in the Confederacy*, 28–29.

90. Wright, *Conscientious Objectors*, 115–20.

91. Marten, *Texas Divided*, 93–94, 122; Bailey, "Defiant Unionists," 215–18.

92. Moneyhon, "Disloyalty in Southwestern Arkansas," 228–29; Tatum, *Disloyalty in the Confederacy*, 41; Williams, *Rich Man's War*, 132; *War of the Rebellion*, ser. 1, vol. 43, pt. 2, p. 919; Wilse Dial, James Dial, and Calvin Dial to Hunter, July 29, 1863, Dial letter.

93. Inscoe and McKinney, *Heart of Confederate Appalachia*, 193; Lonn, *Desertion*, 69; Dotson, "Grave and Scandalous Evil," 411.

94. Bynum, *Free State of Jones*, 105; conversations with Harold O. Williams, the author's father.

95. Tatum, *Disloyalty in the Confederacy*, 46, 140, 141; Williams, Williams, and Carlson, *Plain Folk in a Rich Man's War*, 171–72.

96. Bohannon, "They Had Determined to Root Us Out," 105; Sarris, "Execution in Lumpkin County," 141–42; Kinsland, "Civil War Comes to Lumpkin County," 23–24; Williams, Williams, and Carlson, *Plain Folk in a Rich Man's War*, 160.

97. Davis, *Look Away!*, 233, 448 n. 25; Blair, *Virginia's Private War*, 66; Tatum, *Disloyalty in the Confederacy*, 115; Williams, Williams, and Carlson, *Plain Folk in a Rich Man's War*, 183; Dotson, "Grave and Scandalous Evil," 416–17.

98. Martin, *Rich Man's War*, 199; Bailey, "Defiant Unionists," 215.

99. Cecil-Fronsman, *Common Whites*, 207; Inscoe and McKinney, *Heart of Confederate Appalachia*, 127.

100. Dotson, "Grave and Scandalous Evil," 427, 416–17.

101. Williams, Williams, and Carlson, *Plain Folk in a Rich Man's War*, 170–71.

102. Paludan, *Victims*, 84–85, 96–98.

103. Tatum, *Disloyalty in the Confederacy*, 90.

104. Aughey, *Iron Furnace*, 192–200.

105. Ibid., 7, 64.

106. Rogers, *Confederate Homefront*, 105–06; Dyer, *Secret Yankees*, 163; Berlin et al., *Free at Last*, 161–64.

107. Tatum, *Disloyalty in the Confederacy*, 24–25, 36; Worley, *Arkansas Peace Society*, 446; Degler, *The Other South*, 171.

108. Smith, "Limits of Dissent and Loyalty in Texas," 137–38; McCaslin, *Tainted Breeze*, 211–12.

109. McCaslin, *Tainted Breeze*, 87–88. Bourland continued his murderous ways long after the hangings, often executing prisoners without even the pretense of a show trial. The murders finally stopped in 1864 only after some of Bourland's own men threatened to call for his court-martial. See Smith, "Limits of Dissent and Loyalty in Texas," 146–47.

110. Marten, *Texas Divided*, 58.

111. Pickering and Falls, *Brushmen and Vigilantes*, 23. Pickering and Falls give the following evidence for their conclusion: "Census records of 1860 for those later indicted in five 1862 hanging deaths show average worth (both real and personal property combined) of $8,605, with the comparable figure for victims being $807. The 1860 census records for those indicted in four 1863 hanging deaths show average worth of

$19,100, with a comparable figure for the victims of $1,269. The difference is such that the vigilantes were wealthier and their victims poorer than the average Texan of that time, whose worth was about $6,000."

112. Fleming, *Civil War and Reconstruction in Alabama*, 138.

113. Williams, *Rich Man's War*, 139–40.

114. Tatum, *Disloyalty in the Confederacy*, 29.

115. Williams, *Rich Man's War*, 140; ibid., 29–30.

116. Longstreet, *From Manassas to Appomattox*, 651; Williams, Williams, and Carlson, *Plain Folk in a Rich Man's War*, 157; Tatum, *Disloyalty in the Confederacy*, 68.

117. Tatum, *Disloyalty in the Confederacy*, 33–34, 123, 157; Noe, "Red String Scare," 316. See also Auman and Scarboro, "Heroes of America in Civil War North Carolina."

118. Tatum, *Disloyalty in the Confederacy*, 120, 154, 158; Dotson, "Grave and Scandalous Evil," 393.

119. Tatum, *Disloyalty in the Confederacy*, 150; Horst, *Mennonites in the Confederacy*, 41–43; Williams, Williams, and Carlson, *Plain Folk in a Rich Man's War*, 163.

120. Williams, *Rich Man's War*, 142; Williams, Williams, and Carlson, *Plain Folk in a Rich Man's War*, 183.

121. Inscoe, "Moving Through Deserter Country," 162.

122. Dyer, *Secret Yankees*, 163; Inscoe and McKinney, *Heart of Confederate Appalachia*, 191–92.

123. Inscoe, "Moving Through Deserter Country," 165.

124. Ibid., 162.

125. Baggett, *Scalawags*, 88–89; Tatum, *Disloyalty in the Confederacy*, 159; Mallard, "I Had No Comfort to Give the People," 83–84.

126. Williams, Williams, and Carlson, *Plain Folk in a Rich Man's War*, 180.

127. Ibid., 180–81.

128. Ibid., 157; Freehling, *South vs. the South*, xiii; Crawford, *Ashe County's Civil War*, 125, 132; Dotson, "Grave and Scandalous Evil," 406; Baggett, *Scalawags*, 78.

129. Bonner, "David R. Snelling," 275–82.

130. Harris, *Plain Folk and Gentry in a Slave Society*, 152; Crawford, *Ashe County's Civil War*, 130; Durrill, *War of Another Kind*, 240; Degler, *Other South*, 170; Glatthaar, *March to the Sea and Beyond*, 147, 150–51.

131. Harris, *Plain Folk and Gentry in a Slave Society*, 151; Marten, *Texas Divided*, 122, 123; Durrill, *War of Another Kind*, 116–17, 133; Mallard, "I Had No Comfort to Give the People," 85.

132. Buker, *Blockaders, Refugees, and Contrabands*, 115–16, 150–51; Baggett, *Scalawags*, 67.

133. McGee, "Confederate Who Switched Sides," 20–28; Williams, *Rich Man's War*, 145–46.

134. Worley, "Arkansas Peace Society," 451; Barnes, "Williams Clan's Civil War," 192, 195, 199–200.

135. Bynum, *Free State of Jones*, 98, 105, 112.

136. Tatum, *Disloyalty in the Confederacy*, 60; Degler, *Other South*, 154–55; Frazier, "Out of Stinking Distance," 163.

137. Davis, *Look Away!*, 247.

138. Tatum, *Disloyalty in the Confederacy*, 45, 50, 51; Davis, *Look Away!*, 264; Marten, *Texas Divided*, 101.

139. Moneyhon, "Disloyalty and Class Consciousness in Southwestern Arkansas," 230; Neely, *Southern Rights*, 105; Fisher, *War at Every Door*, 68–69.

140. Fisher, *War at Every Door*, 85.

141. Tatum, *Disloyalty in the Confederacy*, 137–39; Dotson, "Grave and Scandalous Evil," 410, 416, 422.

142. Bolton, *Poor Whites of the Antebellum South*, 160.

143. Current, *Lincoln's Loyalists*, 137.

144. Ibid., 137–38; Durrill, *War of Another Kind*, 108–09; Auman and Scarboro, "Heroes of America," 345.

145. Carlson, "Loanly Runagee," 600.

146. Williams, Williams, and Carlson, *Plain Folk in a Rich Man's War*, 176–77.

147. Ibid., 164.

148. Ibid., 164–65.

149. Bohannon, "They Had Determined to Root Us Out," 98–106.

150. Williams, Williams, and Carlson, *Plain Folk in a Rich Man's War*, 166–67.

151. Carlson, "Loanly Runagee," 589, Williams, Williams, and Carlson, *Plain Folk in a Rich Man's War*, 174.

152. Turner, *Navy Gray*, 130–31, 325 n. 6.; Tatum, *Disloyalty in the Confederacy*, 87.

153. Buker, *Blockaders, Refugees, and Contrabands*, 98–99, 106–07; Tatum, *Disloyalty in the Confederacy*, 83–84.

154. Aptheker, *American Negro Slave Revolts*, 361; Tatum, *Disloyalty in the Confederacy*, 88.

155. Aptheker, *American Negro Slave Revolts*, 360–61; Escott, *Many Excellent People*, 77; Williams, Williams, and Carlson, *Plain Folk in a Rich Man's War*, 140–41.

156. Williams, *Rich Man's War*, 157; Williams, "The 'Faithful Slave' Is About Played Out," 92–93.

6: "My God! Are We Free?"

1. Williams, Williams, and Carlson, *Plain Folk in a Rich Man's War*, 190.

2. Jordan, *Black Confederates and Afro-Yankees*, 218. The words of slaves, illiterate for the most part, were often necessarily filtered through writers who frequently tried to preserve phonetically the dialects they thought they heard. There was often an element of racism involved as well. It was not uncommon for literate whites to portray blacks as unable to master the rudiments of spoken English despite numerous examples to the contrary. Poor whites and immigrants were often similarly stereotyped.

3. Berlin, Favreau, and Miller, *Remembering Slavery*, 275–76.

4. Williams, *Rich Man's War*, 154.

5. Taylor, *Reminiscences*, 8.

6. Berlin, "The Slaves Were the Primary Force Behind Their Emancipation," 279.

7. Williams, Williams, and Carlson, *Plain Folk in a Rich Man's War*, 138; Williams, "The 'Faithful Slave' Is About Played Out," 97; Marten, *Texas Divided*, 111.

8. Williams, "The 'Faithful Slave' Is About Played Out," 97.

9. Standard, *Columbus in the Confederacy*, 38, 55; Mohr, *On the Threshold of Freedom*, 150; Wilson, *Confederate Industry*, 62; Mohr, "Slavery and Class Tensions," 65.

10. Standard, *Columbus in the Confederacy*, 56.

11. Williams, *Rich Man's War*, 72.

12. Marten, *Texas Divided*, 110; Berlin, Favreau, and Miller, *Remembering Slavery*, 236.

13. Quarles, *Negro in the Civil War,* 37–38; Jordan, *Black Confederates and Afro-Yankees,* 216.

14. Jordan, *Black Confederates and Afro-Yankees,* 229, 217; Cleveland, *Alexander H. Stephens,* 721.

15. Williams, Williams, and Carlson, *Plain Folk in a Rich Man's War,* 190; Quarles, *Negro in the Civil War,* 38.

16. Quarles, *Negro in the Civil War,* 38.

17. Jordan, *Black Confederates and Afro-Yankees,* 218, 177; Williams, "The 'Faithful Slave' Is About Played Out," 86.

18. Faust, "Altars of Sacrifice," 1213; Williams, Williams, and Carlson, *Plain Folk in a Rich Man's War,* 71–72; Williams, "The 'Faithful Slave' Is About Played Out," 96; Aptheker, *American Negro Slave Revolts,* 363.

19. Williams, "The 'Faithful Slave' Is About Played Out," 99.

20. Bryan, *Confederate Georgia,* 124–25; Marten, *Texas Divided,* 111–12.

21. Williams, *Rich Man's War,* 155.

22. Ibid., 155; Sutherland, *Seasons of War,* 73–74; Botkin, *Lay My Burden Down,* 175.

23. Williams, *Rich Man's War,* 156; Marten, *Texas Divided,* 111; Faust, *Mothers of Invention,* 58; Jordan, *Black Confederates and Afro-Yankees,* 177; Robinson, *Bitter Fruits of Bondage,* 180.

24. Crist and Dix, *Papers of Jefferson Davis,* 7:175; Williams, *Rich Man's War,* 158.

25. Mohr, *On the Threshold of Freedom,* 51, 310 n. 86; Bryan, *Confederate Georgia,* 127; Williams, *Rich Man's War,* 158.

26. Aptheker, *American Negro Slave Revolts,* 95, 367; Jordan, *Tumult and Silence at Second Creek,* 5–6.

27. Williams, Williams, and Carlson, *Plain Folk in a Rich Man's War,* 134.

28. Ibid., 134.

29. Ibid., 134–35.

30. Meyers, "'The Wretch Vickery' and the Brooks County Civil War Slave Conspiracy," 27–38; Williams, Williams, and Carlson, *Plain Folk in a Rich Man's War,* 144–50.

31. Williams, Williams, and Carlson, *Plain Folk in a Rich Man's War,* 140; Mitchell, *Civil War Soldiers,* 4; Durrill, *War of Another Kind,* 132–33; Bynum, *Unruly Women,* 123.

32. Quarles, *Negro in the Civil War,* 62–63.

33. Ibid., 62–63; Berlin, Favreau, and Miller, *Remembering Slavery,* 227–28, 264–65; Marten, *Texas Divided,* 110–11.

34. Quarles, *Negro in the Civil War,* 62; Mohr, *On The Threshold of Freedom,* 87–88.

35. Williams, "The 'Faithful Slave' Is About Played Out," 94.

36. Jordan, *Black Confederates and Afro-Yankees,* 69; Aptheker, *American Negro Slave Revolts,* 361–62.

37. Bynum, *Free State of Jones,* 109–10.

38. Storey, *Loyalty and Loss,* 80.

39. Williams, Williams, and Carlson, *Plain Folk in a Rich Man's War,* 131; Berlin et al., *Free at Last,* 124.

40. Inscoe and McKinney, *Heart of Confederate Appalachia,* 228.

41. Taylor, *Reminiscences,* 68.

42. Dyer, *Secret Yankees,* 87–89; Berlin et al., *Free at Last,* 124.

43. Inscoe, "Moving Through Deserter Country," 166, 170.

44. Williams, "The 'Faithful Slave' Is About Played Out," 100.

45. Neely, *Southern Rights*, 135; Quarles, *Negro in the Civil War*, 84.

46. Quarles, *Negro in the Civil War*, 84.

47. Leonard, *All the Daring of the Soldier*, 70, 54–55; Jordan, *Black Confederates and Afro-Yankees*, 284.

48. Wertheimer, *We Were There*, 137–38.

49. Wills, *War Hits Home*, 40.

50. McPherson, *Negro's Civil War*, 154–57. After the war, Smalls served several terms as a congressman from South Carolina in the U.S. House of Representatives. In 1899, he was appointed customs collector for Beaufort and held the position until 1913. Two years later he died of natural causes in the home where he and his mother had once been enslaved. See Uya, *From Slavery to Public Service*.

51. Grant, *Way It Was in the South*, 83; Chesnut, *Mary Chesnut's Civil War*, 407; Quarles, *Negro in the Civil War*, 71; Franklin and Moss, *From Slavery to Freedom*, 209; Escott, "Context of Freedom," 85.

52. Glatthaar, *March to the Sea and Beyond*, 64; Davis, *Sherman's March*, 91–94; Kennett, *Marching Through Georgia*, 290–91.

53. Mitchell, *Civil War Soldiers*, 123; Lowry, *Story the Soldiers Wouldn't Tell*, 124–25.

54. Mitchell, *Civil War Soldiers*, 122–23.

55. Gallman, *North Fights the Civil War*, 139; Clinton, *Harriet Tubman*, 189.

56. Voegeli, "Rejected Alternative," 773; Sterling, *We Are Your Sisters*, 251; Truth, *Narrative*, 140.

57. Schwalm, " 'Overrun with Free Negroes,' " 166.

58. Foner and Lewis, *Black Worker*, 274–75.

59. Ibid., 278–79.

60. Voegeli, *Free But Not Equal*, 2; Gallman, *North Fights the Civil War*, 138.

61. McPherson, *Negro's Civil War*, 248.

62. Voegeli, "Rejected Alternative," 776.

63. Quarles, *Negro in the Civil War*, 26–27; Aptheker, *Documentary History of the Negro People*, 459–60.

64. Quarles, *Negro in the Civil War*, 25–26.

65. Ibid., 29.

66. Balser, *Collected Works of Abraham Lincoln*, 5:423; McPherson, *Ordeal by Fire*, 264.

67. Sterling, *We Are Your Sisters*, 237.

68. Freehling, *South vs. the South*, 96; Quarles, *Negro in the Civil War*, 65.

69. Voegeli, *Free But Not Equal*, 39; Bennett, *Forced into Glory*, 382.

70. Blight, *Frederick Douglass' Civil War*, 122, 137, 138.

71. McPherson, *Struggle for Equality*, 155; McPherson, *Negro's Civil War*, 96–97.

72. Bennett, *Forced into Glory*, 382–83.

73. Blight, *Frederick Douglass' Civil War*, 140.

74. McPherson, *Negro's Civil War*, 92–93.

75. Ibid., 294. The letter refers to General George B. McClellan, commanding the Army of the Potomac, and General Henry H. Halleck, the Union army's general-in-chief.

76. Blight, *Frederick Douglass' Civil War*, 142; Bennett, *Forced into Glory*, 461.

77. Syrett, "Confiscation Acts," 287, 318–19; Gienapp, *This Fiery Trial*, 108; Quarles, *Negro in the Civil War*, 59–61, 109–12; McPherson, *Negro's Civil War*, 46.

78. Voegeli, "Rejected Alternative," 775.

79. Ibid., 766–87.

80. Gallman, *North Fights the Civil War,* 126–27, 130; Quarles, *Negro in the Civil War,* 76.

81. Ward, *Civil War,* 150.

82. *War of the Rebellion,* ser. 1, vol. 15, 621–23, 667–69.

83. Quarles, *Negro in the Civil War,* 164–65.

84. Ibid., 170–71.

85. Ibid., 172; McFeely, *Frederick Douglass,* 215.

86. Gray, *Hidden Civil War,* 100.

87. Jimerson, *Private Civil War,* 39–40; Voegeli, *Free But Not Equal,* 55; Foner and Lewis, *Black Worker,* 281, 284.

88. Foner and Lewis, *Black Worker,* 286–87; Quarles, *Negro in the Civil War,* 236, 238.

89. Cook, *Armies of the Streets,* 82, 97–98.

90. Quarles, *Negro in the Civil War,* 241.

91. Blacks in the Union army totaled 178,895. Figures for those in the Union navy, though less exact, were in the neighborhood of 24,000. Burchard, *One Gallant Rush,* xii; Glatthaar, *Forged in Battle,* x; Urwin, "United States Colored Troops," 2002; Ramold, "African-American Sailors," 14; Ward, *Civil War,* 246; Smith, *Trial By Fire,* 309.

92. McPherson, *What They Fought For,* 56; Jimerson, *Private Civil War,* 41; Mitchell, *Civil War Soldiers,* 14.

93. Jimerson, *Private Civil War,* 93, 95, 41.

94. McPherson, *What They Fought For,* 63.

95. Ibid., 62.

96. McPherson, *Struggle for Equality,* 92.

97. Ibid., 92–93.

98. Quarles, *Negro in the Civil War,* 180; McPherson, *Negro's Civil War,* 174.

99. Voegeli, *Free But Not Equal,* 101; Ward, *Civil War,* 247; Bailey, "The USCT in the Confederate Heartland," 227, 229; Wilson, *Campfires of Freedom,* 39.

100. Berlin et al., *Free at Last,* 440–41.

101. Glatthaar, *Forged in Battle,* 135.

102. Gooding, *On the Altar of Freedom,* 36–39; Burchard, *One Gallant Rush,* 137–141; Glatthaar, *Forged in Battle,* 140.

103. Berlin et al., *Free at Last,* 444; Blackett, *Thomas Morris Chester,* 115.

104. Lowe, "Battle on the Levee," 125; Speer, *Portals to Hell,* 109.

105. Glatthaar, *Forged in Battle,* 156–57; Bailey, "Texas Cavalry Raid," 29; Urwin, "We Cannot Treat Negroes . . . as Prisoners of War," 135–37; Durrill, *War of Another Kind,* 207–08; Suderow, "Battle of the Crater," 203–9; Jordan and Thomas, "Massacre at Plymouth," 190; Current, *Lincoln's Loyalists,* 141. See also Castel, "Fort Pillow Massacre," and Frisby, " 'Remember Fort Pillow!' "

106. Coles, " 'Shooting Niggers Sir,' " 74, 75.

107. Glatthaar, *Forged in Battle,* 155–57.

108. Speer, *Portals to Hell,* 108, 113.

109. Glatthaar, *Forged in Battle,* 190–91; Smith, *Trial By Fire,* 329.

110. Glatthaar, *Forged in Battle,* 170; Sterling, *We Are Your Sisters,* 240–41.

111. Berlin et al., *Free at Last,* 461–62.

112. Ibid., 773; Shaw, *Blued-Eyed Child of Fortune,* 367–68; Taylor, *Reminiscences,* 16; Glatthaar, *Forged in Battle,* 115–16.

113. Franklin and Moss, *From Slavery to Freedom*, 215; Berlin et al., *Free at Last*, 473–75.

114. Quarles, *Negro in the Civil War*, 204–05; Shaw, *Blue-Eyed Child of Fortune*, 368.

115. Jimerson, *Private Civil War*, 103; Berlin et al., *Free at Last*, 489–91.

116. Wilson, *Campfires of Freedom*, 41; Berlin et al., *Free at Last*, 459–60.

117. Glatthaar, *Forged in Battle*, 115, 117.

118. Ibid., 115; Shaw, *Blue-Eyed Child of Fortune*, 369; Blackett, *Thomas Morris Chester*, 115.

119. Lonn, *Desertion During the Civil War*, 149; Blackett, *Thomas Morris Chester*, 115; Jordan, *Black Confederates and Afro-Yankees*, 89–90.

120. McPherson, *Negro's Civil War*, 193–94; Cornish, *Sable Arm*, 253–54.

121. McPherson, *What They Fought For*, 57; Jimerson, *Private Civil War*, 96.

122. Sterling, "Civil War Draft Resistance," 601.

123. Smith, *Trial By Fire*, 331.

124. Freehling, *South vs. the South*, 191.

125. Nolan, *Lee Considered*, 175–77.

126. McPherson, *What They Fought For*, 55; Mohr, *On the Threshold of Freedom*, 278.

127. Blomquist and Taylor, *This Cruel War*, 322–23.

128. Mohr, *On the Threshold of Freedom*, 283–84; Williams, *Rich Man's War*, 174. See also Durden, *Gray and the Black*.

129. Jordan, *Black Confederates and Afro-Yankees*, 222–25, 246–47; Smith, *Trial By Fire*, 327.

130. Berlin et al., *Free at Last*, 111–12.

131. Jordan, *Black Confederates and Afro-Yankees*, 163; Glatthaar, *Forged in Battle*, 202.

132. Berlin, Miller, and Favreau, *Remembering Slavery*, 255–56.

133. Quarles, *Negro in the Civil War*, 292.

134. Ibid., 293–94.

135. Williams, *Self-Taught*, 42, 90–91, 105, 129, Gallman, *North Fights the Civil War*, 135; Quarles, *Negro in the Civil War*, 294.

136. Gallman, *North Fights the Civil War*, 136; Shaw, *Blue-Eyed Child of Fortune*, 373. For an in-depth treatment of what the first few years of the struggle for freedom meant to the former slaves at Port Royal, see Rose, *Rehearsal for Reconstruction*.

137. Durrill, *War of Another Kind*, 141; Foner, *Reconstruction*, 59.

138. Quarles, *Negro in the Civil War*, 248; Durrill, *War of Another Kind*, 144.

139. Foner, *Reconstruction*, 105.

140. Ibid., 52–53.

141. Ibid., 55; Powell, *New Masters*, 90–91.

142. Foner, *Reconstruction*, 55.

143. Johnson, *Abraham Lincoln*, 276–78.

144. Ibid., 277; McPherson, *Struggle for Equality*, 269–70; Foner, *Reconstruction*, 55.

145. Foner, *Reconstruction*, 60–61.

146. Blight, *Frederick Douglass' Civil War*, 182–83; Williams, *Lincoln and the Radicals*, 314–15; McPherson, *Struggle for Equality*, 269–271; Nevins, *War for the Union*, 72–73.

147. Williams, *Lincoln and the Radicals*, 315–16; McPherson, *Struggle for Equality*, 270–71.

148. Jimerson, *Private Civil War*, 39–40.

149. McPherson, *Struggle for Equality*, 125–26.

150. Johnson, *Abraham Lincoln*, 302–03.

151. McPherson, *Struggle for Equality*, 92, 126–27.

152. Sears, *McClellan*, 376; Nevins, *War for the Union*, 102.

153. Nevins, *War for the Union*, 105–06.

154. McFeely, *Frederick Douglass*, 234; Johnson, *Abraham Lincoln*, 308; McPherson, *Struggle for Equality*, 127.

155. Escott, *After Secession*, 222; Davis, *Look Away!*, 408–09; Donald, *Lincoln*, 558–59.

156. Donald, *Lincoln*, 559.

157. Mohr, *On the Threshold of Freedom*, 75.

7: "Indians Here Have No Fight with the Whites"

1. Bailey, *Bosque Redondo*, 66.

2. Berthrong, *Southern Cheyenne*, 219.

3. Gibson, *American Indian*, 366; Hatch, *Blue, the Gray, and the Red*, 86.

4. Nichols, *Lincoln and the Indians*, 164; Gibson, *American Indian*, 366.

5. Lause, "Homestead Act," 992.

6. Armstrong, *Warrior in Two Camps*, x.

7. Hauptman, *Between Two Fires*, x, 147–50.

8. Ibid., 151.

9. Ibid., 126, 133, 143–44.

10. Ibid., 87, 88, 92.

11. Taylor, "Unforgotten Threat," 300–14; Hauptman, *Between Two Fires*, 66; Neely, *Southern Rights*, 134.

12. Finger, *Eastern Band of the Cherokees*, 83; Hauptman, *Between Two Fires*, 66, 87.

13. Finger, *Eastern Band of the Cherokees*, 83, 87, 89; Hauptman, *Between Two Fires*, 103.

14. Finger, *Eastern Band of the Cherokees*, 88, 96–97; Hauptman, *Between Two Fires*, 109.

15. Gibson, *American Indian*, 366; Debo, *History of the Indians*, 169; Nichols, *Lincoln and the Indians*, 26–27.

16. Gibson, *American Indian*, 364, 366–67; Debo, *History of the Indians*, 169–70.

17. Josephy, *Civil War in the American West*, 327–28; Debo, *History of the Indians*, 170–71.

18. Gibson, *American Indian*, 366; Debo, *History of the Indians*, 171.

19. Debo, *History of the Indians*, 169; Moulton, *John Ross*, 169.

20. Franks, *Stand Watie*, 114–15; Josephy, *Civil War in the American West*, 326; Hauptman, *Between Two Fires*, 45–46.

21. Franks, *Stand Watie*, 118–19.

22. Moulton, *John Ross*, 170; Josephy, *Civil War in the American West*, 329.

23. Josephy, *Civil War in the American West*, 228, 330; Gibson, *American Indian*, 367.

24. Hatch, *Blue, the Gray, and the Red*, 4; Josephy, *Civil War in the American West*, 327; White and White, *Now the Wolf Has Come*, 16–17.

25. Josephy, *Civil War in the American West*, 328; White and White, *Now the Wolf Has Come*, 23; Hatch, *Blue, the Gray, and the Red*, 7; Gibson, *American Indian*, 368; Moulton, *John Ross*, 173.

26. Debo, *Road to Disappearance*, 147–48; Warde, "Now the Wolf Has Come," 68–69.

27. McReynolds, *Seminoles*, 294; Debo, *History of the Indians*, 174–75; White and White, *Now the Wolf Has Come*, 35; Banks, "Civil War Refugees from Indian Territory," 286; Hatch, *Blue, the Gray, and the Red*, 7.

28. White and White, *Now the Wolf Has Come*, 100–07; McReynolds, *Seminoles*, 298–300; Josephy, *Civil War in the American West*, 331–32; Gaines, *Confederate Cherokees*, 46–53.

29. Josephy, *Civil War in the American West*, 332; Hatch, *Blue, the Gray, and the Red*, 17–20.

30. McReynolds, *Seminoles*, 302.

31. Ibid., 302–4.

32. Gibson, *American Indian*, 368–69; Hauptman, *Between Two Fires*, 48.

33. Moulton, *John Ross*, 174, 175; Josephy, *Civil War in the American West*, 356–57; Debo, *History of the Indians*, 176–77, 178.

34. Gibson, *American Indian*, 370.

35. Debo, *History of the Indians*, 178; Warde, "Now the Wolf Has Come," 74.

36. Warde, "Now the Wolf Has Come," 76.

37. Hauptman, *Between Two Fires*, 28-29; Franks, *Stand Watie*, 148.

38. Gibson, *American Indian*, 370–71.

39. Debo, *History of the Indians*, 179; Hauptman, *Between Two Fires*, 50; Franks, *Stand Watie*, 154.

40. Franks, *Stand Watie*, 141; Gibson, *American Indian*, 372.

41. Josephy, *Civil War in the American West*, 377; Frank, *Stand Watie*, 162; Gibson, *American Indian*, 371–72.

42. McReynolds, *Seminoles*, 302–03.

43. Debo, *History of the Indians*, 176.

44. Banks, "Civil War Refugees from Indian Territory," 291–92.

45. McReynolds, *Seminoles*, 304–05; Banks, "Civil War Refugees from Indian Territory," 292.

46. Banks, "Civil War Refugees from Indian Territory," 293, 295.

47. Nichols, *Lincoln and the Indians*, 22.

48. Ibid., 21–22.

49. Danziger, *Indians and Bureaucrats*, 7; Nichols, *Lincoln and the Indians*, 13, 14, 15, 18.

50. Debo, *History of the Indians*, 176, 179; Moulton, *John Ross*, 176.

51. Gibson, *American Indian*, 382–83; Gibson, *Kickapoos*, 197–98, 202.

52. Gibson, *Kickapoos*, 202–6.

53. Nichols, *Lincoln and the Indians*, 67–68; Debo, *History of the Indians*, 184. The name Sioux, meaning "snake" or "snakelike enemy," derives from a reference originating with the Ojibwa (Carley, *Sioux Uprising of 1862*, 1). Many Native Americans who identify with the Sioux cultural and ethnic heritage now refer to themselves as Dakota (such as the Santee), Nakota (such as the Yankton), or Lakota (such as the Oglala and Hunkpapa). However, there is a considerable degree of overlap between these groups and none of the respective designations applies to all peoples known as Sioux. Therefore, because Sioux remains the only term common to all these culturally related groups, the term Sioux is used here in for the Dakota, Nakota, and Lakota alike.

54. Nichols, *Lincoln and the Indians*, 68.

55. Anderson and Woolworth, *Through Dakota Eyes*, 24; Nichols, *Lincoln and the Indians*, 75.

56. Nichols, *Lincoln and the Indians*, 67; Carley, *Sioux Uprising*, 5

57. Carley, *Sioux Uprising*, 5–6; Josephy, *Civil War in the American West*, 108–09; Hatch, *Blue, the Gray, and the Red*, 55–56.

58. Clodfelter, *Dakota War*, 35–37; Anderson, *Little Crow*, 132; Meyer, *History of the Santee Sioux*, 114–15; Josephy, *Civil War in the American West*, 111–12.

59. Debo, *History of the Indians*, 186; Josephy, *Civil War in the American West*, 112.

60. Clodfelter, *Dakota War*, 41; Josephy, *Civil War in the American West*, 112.

61. Oehler, *Great Sioux Uprising*, 96–100, 121–38; Clodfelter, *Dakota War*, 41–42.

62. Josephy, *Civil War in the American West*, 127–28; Clodfelter, *Dakota War*, 53.

63. Debo, *History of the Indians*, 187; Nichols, *Lincoln and the Indians*, 87; Jones, *Civil War in the Northwest*, 123–24; Clodfelter, *Dakota War*, 57; Meyer, *History of the Santee Sioux*, 123.

64. Clodfelter, *Dakota War*, 57; Hatch, *Blue, the Gray, and the Red*, 98–99; Josephy, *Civil War in the American West*, 137; Meyer, *History of the Santee Sioux*, 127.

65. Nichols, *Lincoln and the Indians*, 7, 93, 104–5; Clodfelter, *Dakota War*, 58; Hatch, *Blue, the Gray, and the Red*, 101.

66. Nichols, *Lincoln and the Indians*, 108; Meyer, *History of the Santee Sioux*, 124; Hatch, *Blue, the Gray, and the Red*, 97–98, 101, 103; Clodfelter, *Dakota War*, 57; Josephy, *Civil War in the American West*, 137–38.

67. Meyer, *History of the Santee Sioux*, 129.

68. Ibid., 130; Josephy, *Civil War in the American West*, 138.

69. Clodfelter, *Dakota War*, 63–64; Anderson, *Little Crow*, 176–78. Parts of Little Crow's body, including the skull, scalp, and two forearm bones, were salvaged and put on display at the Minnesota State Historical Society in St. Paul. Finally in 1971 those remains were interred at Little Crow's family plot in South Dakota. A grandson of his attended the ceremony.

70. Nichols, *Lincoln and the Indians*, 64, 121, 123; Jones, *Civil War in the Northwest*, 128–29.

71. Hatch, *Blue, the Gray, and the Red*, 161, 162, 164–65; Utley, *Lance and the Shield*, 54–55.

72. Hatch, *Blue, the Gray, and the Red*, 166; Utley, *Lance and the Shield*, 58–59.

73. Hatch, *Blue, the Gray, and the Red*, 166–67; Utley, *Lance and the Shield*, 62, 64.

74. Utley, *Frontiersmen in Blue*, 227–28; Josephy, *Civil War in the American West*, 241–42.

75. Josephy, *Civil War in the American West*, 242.

76. Utley, *Frontiersmen in Blue*, 228–29; Josephy, *Civil War in the American West*, 242–43.

77. Josephy, *Civil War in the American West*, 243.

78. Jackson, *Century of Dishonor*, 117; Gibson, *American Indian*, 376; Nichols, *Lincoln and the Indians*, 23.

79. Danziger, *Indians and Bureaucrats*, 189–90; Utley, *Frontiersmen in Blue*, 226, 227.

80. Josephy, *Civil War in the American West*, 167; Utley, *Frontiersmen in Blue*, 227.

81. Danziger, *Indians and Bureaucrats*, 54–55; Gibson, *American Indian*, 381.

82. Colton, *Civil War in the Western Territories*, 167, 168, 169; Utley, *Frontiersmen in Blue*, 223, Gibson, *American Indian*, 377.

83. Hatch, *Blue, the Gray, and the Red*, 26–27, 30.

84. Utley, *Frontiersmen in Blue*, 223; Hatch, *Blue, the Gray, and the Red*, 30–31.

85. Hatch, *Blue, the Gray, and the Red*, 32.

86. Ibid., 32–33, 35; Josephy, *Civil War in the American West*, 251, 254; *War of the Rebellion*, ser. 1, vol. 50, 144.

87. Madsen, *Shoshoni Frontier and the Bear River Massacre*, 174; Hatch, *Blue, the Gray, and the Red*, 38.

88. Madsen, *Shoshoni Frontier and the Bear River Massacre*, 174; Hatch, *Blue, the Gray, and the Red*, 38.

89. Madsen, *Shoshoni Frontier and the Bear River Massacre*, 185–189.

90. Ibid., 189; Trenholm and Carley, *Shoshonis*, 196; Colton, *Civil War in the Western Territories*, 165.

91. Hatch, *Blue, the Gray, and the Red*, 44; Josephy, *Civil War in the American West*, 259.

92. Josephy, *Civil War in the American West*, 259; Colton, *Civil War in the Western Territories*, 165.

93. Hatch, *Blue, the Gray, and the Red*, 45; Utley, *Frontiersmen in Blue*, 225; *War of the Rebellion*, ser. 1, vol. 50, 659.

94. Colton, *Civil War in the Western Territories*, 122; Frazier, *Blood and Treasure*, 35, 57.

95. Colton, *Civil War in the Western Territories*, 122–23.

96. Neely, *Southern Rights*, 135; Colton, *Civil War in the Western Territories*, 123; Frazier, *Blood and Treasure*, 197.

97. Bailey, *Bosque Redondo*, 66.

98. Thompson, *Desert Tiger*, 52–54.

99. Haley, *Apaches*, 236–37.

100. Josephy, *Civil War in the American West*, 278; Gibson, *American Indian*, 378.

101. Nichols, *Lincoln and the Indians*, 165–66.

102. Colton, *Civil War in the Western Territories*, 137–38, 139, 141; Dunlay, *Kit Carson and the Indians*, 282; Hatch, *Blue, the Gray, and the Red*, 129.

103. McNitt, *Navajo Wars*, 410; Trafzer, *Kit Carson Campaign*, 163.

104. Trafzer, *Kit Carson Campaign*, 154–59; Josephy, *500 Nations*, 353.

105. Josephy, *500 Nations*, 355.

106. Kelly, *Navajo Roundup*, 52; Josephy, *Civil War in the American West*, 286; Hatch, *Blue, the Gray, and the Red*, 136.

107. Bailey, *Bosque Redondo*, 142–43; Gibson, *American Indian*, 379.

108. Bailey, *Bosque Redondo*, 146.

109. Iverson, *Navajo Nation*, 9.

110. Utley, *Indian Frontier*, 66–67; Josephy, *Civil War in the American West*, 274; Sweeney, *Mangas Coloradas*, 438–39.

111. Utley, *Indian Frontier*, 65–66.

112. Ibid., 66.

113. Sweeney, *Mangas Coloradas*, 448–55; Josephy, *Civil War in the American West*, 279–80.

114. Conner, *Joseph Reddeford Walker*, 38–39.

115. Sweeney, *Mangas Coloradas*, 457–58, 460.

116. Josephy, *Civil War in the American West*, 280.

117. Woody, "Woolsey Expeditions," 157.

118. Ibid., 163–64, 166–68; Conner *Joseph Reddeford Walker*, 173–75, 264–66.

119. Conner, *Joseph Reddeford Walker*, 266–68; Utley, *Frontiersmen in Blue*, 256.

120. Josephy, *Civil War in the American West*, 283; Gibson, *American Indian*, 380–81.

121. Hatch, *Blue, the Gray, and the Red*, 169–70.

122. Wallace and Hoebel, *Comanches*, 304–05.

123. Ibid., 305–06; Josephy, *Civil War in the American West*, 288–89.

124. Hatch, *Blue, the Gray, and the Red*, 174; Josephy, *Civil War in the American West*, 289; Mayhall, *Kiowas*, 227.

125. Mayhall, *Kiowas*, 230–31; Wallace and Hoebel, *Comanches*, 306; Colton, *Civil War in the Western Territories*, 146–47; Fehrenbach, *Comanches*, 464–67.

126. Gibson, *American Indian*, 381; Danziger, *Indians and Bureaucrats*, 36.

127. Berthrong, *Southern Cheyenne*, 175.

128. Nichols, *Lincoln and the Indians*, 169.

129. Debo, *History of the Indians*, 192.

130. Josephy, *Civil War in the American West*, 306; Nichols, *Lincoln and the Indians*, 169; *Sand Creek Massacre*, 53; Berthrong, *Southern Cheyenne*, 201.

131. Nichols, *Lincoln and the Indians*, 169; *Sand Creek Massacre*, 53; Utley, *Indian Frontier*, 89.

132. Utley, *Indian Frontier*, 89–90.

133. Brown, *Bury My Heart at Wounded Knee*, 78–79; Schultz, *Month of the Freezing Moon*, 109; Berthrong, *Southern Cheyenne*, 212.

134. Schultz, *Month of the Freezing Moon*, 109–10.

135. Ibid., 111.

136. Ibid., 113; Utley, *Indian Frontier*, 91.

137. Josephy, *Civil War in the American West*, 307–8; Schultz, *Month of the Freezing Moon*, 118.

138. Berthrong, *Southern Cheyenne*, 220; Hoig, *Sand Creek Massacre*, 140–41; West, *Contested Plains*, 301.

139. Other reports noted that a white flag of truce was tied to the pole as well just below the United States flag. Hoig, *Sand Creek Massacre*, 150.

140. Berthrong, *Southern Cheyenne*, 219; Schultz, *Month of the Freezing Moon*, 135; Hoig, *Sand Creek Massacre*, 153.

141. Hoig, *Sand Creek Massacre*, 151.

142. Schultz, *Month of the Freezing Moon*, 138.

143. Ibid., 138.

144. Ibid., 139, 141; Berthrong, *Southern Cheyenne*, 221.

145. Berthrong, *Southern Cheyenne*, 219; Schultz, *Month of the Freezing Moon*, 141. In October 2000 Congress passed legislation to create a memorial area encompassing over twelve thousand acres on the site of the Sand Creek Massacre. The legislation was sponsored by Colorado Senator Ben Nighthorse Campbell, whose ancestors were among those killed at Sand Creek. The bill, said Campbell, serves as "acknowledgment by Americans that we are better than our past." See "Congress Passes Bill to Set Up First Site in Memory of Indian Massacre."

146. Hatch, *Blue, the Gray, and the Red*, 212; Josephy, *Civil War in the American West*, 311–12; Danziger, *Indians and Bureaucrats*, 44.

147. Colton, *Civil War in the Western Territories*, 159–60; Berthrong, *Southern Cheyenne*, 227; Utley, *Indian Frontier*, 93–94.

148. Berthrong, *Southern Cheyenne*, 224.

149. Utley, *Indian Frontier*, 94.

8: "Was the War in Vain?"

1. Foner, *History of the Labor Movement*, 394–95.

2. McPherson, *Struggle for Equality*, 431.

3. Williams, Williams, and Carlson, *Plain Folk in a Rich Man's War*, 178; Martin, *Rich Man's War*, 123.

4. Williams, Williams, and Carlson, *Plain Folk in a Rich Man's War*, 185–86.

5. Ibid., 186.

6. Tatum, *Disloyalty in the Confederacy*, xii–xiii; Williams, Williams, and Carlson, *Plain Folk in a Rich Man's War*, 183–84, 186.

7. Williams, Williams, and Carlson, *Plain Folk in a Rich Man's War*, 186; Tatum, *Disloyalty in the Confederacy*, xiii, 106, 163; Lonn, *Desertion During the Civil War*, 70; *War of the Rebellion*, ser. 1, vol. 32, pt. 3, 755; Bynum, *Free State of Jones*, 126; Wood, "Union and Secession in Mississippi," 145; *War of the Rebellion*, ser. 4, vol. 3, 802–4, 812–14; Dotson, "Grave and Scandalous Evil," 424.

8. Berlin et al., *Free at Last*, 151; Wiley, *Plain People of the Confederacy*, 67; Edwards, *Scarlett Doesn't Live Here Anymore*, 85.

9. Davis, *Look Away!*, 246; Bynum, *Unruly Women*, 149.

10. Williams, Williams, and Carlson, *Plain Folk in a Rich Man's War*, 182.

11. Ibid., 187.

12. Ibid., 188.

13. Rogers, *Confederate Home Front*, 131; Williams, Williams, and Carlson, *Plain Folk in a Rich Man's War*, 188.

14. Williams, *Rich Man's War*, 173; Bailey, *Class and Tennessee's Confederate Generation*, 102–3. Mullins's pension request was rejected.

15. Coulter, *Confederate States of America*, 105, 374.

16. Cleveland, *Alexander H. Stephens*, 721.

17. Johnson, *Abraham Lincoln*, 302–03.

18. *War of the Rebellion*, ser. 1, vol. 30, pt. 4, 180; Escott, *After Secession*, 128.

19. Mark Weitz makes this point as well in response to historians James McPherson and Gary Gallagher. See Weitz, *Higher Duty*, 118–19; McPherson, *Drawn with the Sword*, 129; Gallagher, *Confederate War*, chapter 3.

20. Escott, *After Secession*, 219; *War of the Rebellion*, ser. 1, vol. 19, pt. 2, p. 622.

21. Williams, *Rich Man's War*, vii.

22. Harris, *Plain Folk and Gentry in a Slave Society*, 152; Crawford, *Ashe County's Civil War*, 130; Durrill, *War of Another Kind*, 240; Degler, *Other South*, 170; Glatthaar, *March to the Sea and Beyond*, 147, 150–51; McPherson, *Battle Cry of Freedom*, 608.

23. Foote made his comments during an interview with Ken Burns for the PBS special *The Civil War*. Quoted in Ward, *Civil War*, 272.

24. Lonn, *Foreigners in the Union Army and Navy*, 582.

25. Owsley, "Defeatism in the Confederacy," 456.

26. Williams, Williams, and Carlson, *Plain Folk in a Rich Man's War*, 193–94.

27. Andrews, *Footprints of a Regiment*, 184.

28. Stampp, *And the War Came*, 298.

29. Debo, *History of the Indians*, 234; Brown, *Bury My Heart at Wounded Knee*, 170.

30. Gibson, *American Indian*, 415; Brown, *Bury My Heart at Wounded Knee*, 265; Josephy, *500 Nations*, 375.

31. Gibson, *American Indian*, 408–9; Brown, *Bury My Heart at Wounded Knee*, 241–42.

32. Ibid., 392.

33. Josephy, *500 Nations*, 416.

34. Ibid., 407, 429; Nichols, *Lincoln and the Indians*, 187–88.

35. Brown, *Bury My Heart at Wounded Knee*, 242, 336.

36. Ibid., 242.

37. Josephy, *500 Nations*, 437; Gibson, *American Indian*, 478.

38. Brown, *Bury My Heart at Wounded Knee*, 439; Josephy, *500 Nations*, 438.

39. Josephy, *500 Nations*, 437–38; Gibson, *American Indian*, 478.

40. Gibson, *American Indian*, 464.

41. Brown, *Bury My Heart at Wounded Knee*, 439–40, 442–43; Josephy, *500 Nations*, 440–41.

42. Brown, *Bury My Heart at Wounded Knee*, 444–45; Josephy, *500 Nations*, 441.

43. "Medal of Honor Recipients. Indian Wars Period."

44. Josephy, *500 Nations*, 430, 431.

45. Brown, *Bury My Heart at Wounded Knee*, 450.

46. *War of the Rebellion*, ser. 1, vol. 49, pt. 1, p. 301.

47. Williams, *Rich Man's War*, 187.

48. Smith, *Trial by Fire*, 638; Williams, *Rich Man's War*, 187.

49. Smith, *Trial by Fire*, 638.

50. Smithville, located in Brunswick County at the mouth of the Cape Fear River, changed its name to Southport in 1886.

51. McPherson, *Negro's Civil War*, 210–11.

52. Williams, *Rich Man's War*, 187–88; Escott, "Context of Freedom," 99; Berlin, Favreau, and Miller, *Remembering Slavery*, 270.

53. Wynne, *Continuity of Cotton*, 2–4.

54. Williams, *Rich Man's War*, 188.

55. Grant, *Way It Was in the South*, 95–96; Williams, *Rich Man's War*, 189; Flynn, *White Land, Black Labor*, 35–37; Drago, *Black Politicians and Reconstruction in Georgia*, 103.

56. Grant, *Way It Was in the South*, 117, 99.

57. Berlin, Favreau, and Miller, *Remembering Slavery*, 270.

58. Smith, *Trial by Fire*, 637, 846, 847, 659.

59. Ibid., 661; Williams, *Rich Man's War*, 188.

60. Fitzgerald, "Poor Man's Fight," 17. See also Fitzgerald, *Union League Movement in the Deep South*.

61. Fitzgerald, "Poor Man's Fight," 17; Foner, *Reconstruction*, 262–63; McPherson, *Ordeal by Fire*, 516.

62. Both federal and state courts interpreted the amendment as applying only to males. Voting rights for women were not guaranteed by constitutional amendment until 1920.

63. Foner, *Reconstruction*, 345.

64. Drago, *Black Politicians and Reconstruction in Georgia*, 148.

65. Escott, *Many Excellent People*, 156; Rawick, *American Slave*, ser. 1, vol. 6, 308; Smith, *Trial by Fire*, 855.

66. Foner, *Reconstruction*, 351, 548; Smith, *Trial by Fire*, 845–46; Formwalt, "Camilla Massacre," 399–426; Conway, *Reconstruction of Georgia*, 158–60; Drago, *Black Politicians and Reconstruction in Georgia*, 145–46; Daniell, "Ashburn Murder Case," 296–312.

67. McPherson, *Struggle for Equality*, 430–31.

68. McFeely, *Frederick Douglass*, 380, 255.

69. For a legal and historical treatment, see Lofgren, *The "Plessy" Case*.

70. Litwak, "Hellhounds," 26, 27.

71. Ibid., 12, 21. For an overview of Klan activities in the early twentieth century, see MacLean, *Behind the Mask of Chivalry*.

72. Taylor, *Reminiscences*, 61–62, 65–66.

73. Two of the best overviews of how planters regained power in the South are Lewis Nicholas Wynne's *Continuity of Cotton* and Jonathan Wiener's *Social Origins of the New South*.

74. Well into the twentieth century there were former slaves who still felt the injustice of working without pay. In 1936, Mary Carpenter of Harris County, Georgia, asked one special favor of the person interviewing her for the Federal Writers Project: "All us old slave-time darkies oughta be pensioned, and I wish you'd tell Governor [Eugene] Talmadge that I said that." Rawick, *American Slave*, supp., ser. 1, vol. 3, pt. 1, p. 145.

75. Foner, *Nothing But Freedom*, 6.

76. McPherson, *Struggle for Equality*, 431.

77. Friedheim and Jackson, *Freedom's Unfinished Revolution*, 255.

78. Grant, *Way It Was in the South*, 137.

79. McKenzie, *One South or Many?*, 98, 100; Wright, *Political Economy of the Cotton South*, 160–64. For an excellent study making many of the same points, see Formwalt, "Planter Persistence in Southwest Georgia, 1850–1870."

80. Williams, *Rich Man's War*, 192; Coleman, *History of Georgia*, 259; Atack, "Tenants and Yeomen in the Nineteenth Century," 6, 21.

81. Bailey, *Class and Tennessee's Confederate Generation*, 90; Phillips, *Wealth and Democracy*, 37–38; Wright, *Political Economy of the Cotton South*, 174; Coleman, *History of Georgia*, 259.

82. Darwin himself never intended that his observations of nature be used to justify social oppression. See Browne, *Charles Darwin*, 313–14.

83. Gienapp, *This Fiery Trial*, 105; Ward, *Civil War*, 273; Stampp, *And the War Came*, 298; Cochran and Miller, *Age of Enterprise*, 106, 116, 165; Phillips, *Wealth and Democracy*, 38, 42, 43, 46.

84. Dawley, *Class and Community*, 195; "Directory of Mark Twain's Maxims, Quotations, and Various Opinions."

85. Craig, "Industry, Agriculture, and the Economy," 509; Wertheimer, *We Were There*, 174; Foner, *History of the Labor Movement*, 381.

86. Foner, *History of the Labor Movement*, 370, 468, 471; Wertheimer, *We Were There*, 177–78.

87. Foner, *History of the Labor Movement*, 469, 473; Wertheimer, *We Were There*, 178–79.

88. Foner, *History of the Labor Movement*, 383.

89. Massey, *Women in the Civil War*, 135.

90. Wertheimer, *We Were There*, 176.

91. Ibid., 174–75.

92. Ibid., 175–76.

93. Smith, *Trial by Fire*, 870.

94. Edwards, *Scarlett Doesn't Live Here Anymore*, 184.

95. Young, *Dissent in America*, 291.

96. Clinton, *Other Civil War*, 95; Young, *Dissent in America*, 287.

97. Clinton, *Other Civil War*, 95; Young, *Dissent in America*, 287–88.

98. Zinn, *Twentieth Century*, 48.

99. Ibid.

100. Keillor, "We're Not in Lake Wobegon Anymore."

101. Zinn, *Twentieth Century*, 69, 43.

102. Ibid., 43.

103. Even in the 2004 presidential election, which saw the highest voter turnout in thirty-six years, more than 40 percent of eligible voters did not vote. Without some basic restructuring of the electoral process, voter turnout will likely remain relatively unchanged. For a percentage listing of voter turnout in presidential elections, see Brinkley, *Unfinished Nation*, A26–A32.

104. Flynn, *White Land, Black Labor*, 150.

105. Woodward, *Tom Watson*, 190.

106. Ibid. Watson later adopted an "if you can't beat them, join them" strategy, becoming one of the most racist campaigners in U.S. political history. It worked. In 1920, Watson was elected to the U.S. Senate.

107. Ibid., 191.

108. Ibid., 195. Politically motivated economic intimidation is hardly a thing of the past. On September 9, 2004, forty-one-year-old Lynne Gobell, who operated a bagging machine at a production plant in Moulton, Alabama, was fired by her Republican boss because she refused to remove a Kerry/Edwards sticker from her car. A few days later, John Kerry called to offer her a job on his campaign staff. She accepted. Rothschild, "You're Fired," 28–29.

109. Watkins, *"Co. Aytch,"* 69; *War of the Rebellion*, ser. 4, vol. 3, 413; Williams, Williams, and Carlson, *Plain Folk in a Rich Man's War*, 164; Bynum, *Free State of Jones*, 135. Two excellent treatments of the Lost Cause ideology are Foster, *Ghosts of the Confederacy*, and Goldfield, *Still Fighting the Civil War*.

110. Faust, *Mothers of Invention*, 246; Rutledge, "Civil War Journal," 108.

111. Williams, Williams, and Carlson, *Plain Folk in a Rich Man's War*, 7; Robinson, *Bitter Fruits of Bondage*, 283.

Bibliography

Adams, George Worthington. *Doctors in Blue: The Medical History of the Union Army in the Civil War*. Baton Rouge: Louisiana State University Press, 1996.

Alexander, Thomas B., and Richard E. Beringer. *The Anatomy of the Confederate Congress: A Study of the Influences of Members Characteristics on Legislative Voting Behavior, 1861–1865*. Nashville, TN: Vanderbilt University Press, 1972.

Alexander, Thomas B., and Peggy J. Duckworth. "Alabama Black Belt Whigs during Secession: A New Viewpoint." *Alabama Review* 17 (1964): 181–97.

Alotta, Robert I. *Civil War Justice: Union Army Executions Under Lincoln*. Shippensburg, PA: White Mane Publishing, 1989.

Amos, Harriet E. "'All-Absorbing Topics': Food and Clothing in Confederate Mobile." *Atlanta Historical Society Journal* 22 (1978): 17–28.

Anderson, Gary Clayton. *Little Crow: Spokesman for the Sioux*. St. Paul: Minnesota Historical Society, 1986.

Anderson, Gary Clayton, and Alan R. Woolworth, eds. *Through Dakota Eyes: Narrative Accounts of the Minnesota Indian War of 1862*. St. Paul: Minnesota Historical Society Press, 1988.

Andreasen, Bryon C. "Civil War Church Trials: Repressing Dissent on the Northern Home Front." In Cimbala and Miller, *Uncommon Time*.

Andrews, Eliza Frances. *The War-Time Journal of a Georgia Girl, 1864–1865*. Edited by Spencer Bidwell King, Jr. 1908. Reprint, Atlanta: Cherokee Publishing Co., 1976.

Andrews, William H. *Footprints of a Regiment: A Recollection of the First Georgia Regulars, 1861–1865*. Introduction by Richard M. McMurry. Atlanta: Longstreet Press, 1992.

Aptheker, Herbert. *American Negro Slave Revolts*. 1943. Millwood, NY: Kraus Reprint Co., 1977.

———, ed. *A Documentary History of the Negro People in the United States*. Vol. 1. New York: Citadel Press, 1951.

Armstrong, William H. *Warrior in Two Camps: Ely S. Parker, Union General and Seneca Chief*. Syracuse, NY: Syracuse University Press, 1978.

Ash, Stephen V., ed. *Secessionists and Other Scoundrels: Selections from Parson Brownlow's Book*. Baton Rouge: Louisiana State University Press, 1999.

Atack, Jeremy. "Tenants and Yeomen in the Nineteenth Century." *Agricultural History* 62 (1988): 6–32.

Atack, Jeremy, and Fred Bateman. "Self-Sufficiency and the Marketable Surplus in the Rural North, 1860." *Agricultural History* 58 (1984): 296–313.

Attie, Jeanie. *Patriotic Toil: Northern Women and the American Civil War*. Ithaca, NY: Cornell University Press, 1998.

Aughey, John H. *The Iron Furnace: or, Slavery and Secession*. 1865. Reprint, New York: Negro Universities Press, 1969.

Auman, William T., and David D. Scarboro. "The Heroes of America in Civil War North Carolina." *North Carolina Historical Review* 58 (1981): 327–63.

Badura, Catherine O. "Elizabeth Blackwell." In Heidler and Heidler, *Encyclopedia of the American Civil War*.

Baggett, James Alex. *The Scalawags: Southern Dissenters in the Civil War and Reconstruction*. Baton Rouge: Louisiana State University Press, 2003.

Bailey, Anne J. "Defiant Unionists: Militant Germans in Confederate Texas." In Inscoe and Kenzer, *Enemies of the Country*.

———. "A Texas Cavalry Raid: Reaction to Black Soldiers and Contrabands." In Urwin, *Black Flag Over Dixie*.

———. "The USCT in the Confederate Heartland, 1864." In Smith, *Black Soldiers in Blue*.

Bailey, Fred Arthur. *Class and Tennessee's Confederate Generation*. Chapel Hill: University of North Carolina Press, 1987.

Bailey, Hugh C. "Disaffection in the Alabama Hill Country, 1861." *Civil War History* 4 (1958): 183–93.

———. "Disloyalty in Early Confederate Alabama." *Journal of Southern History* 23 (1957): 522–28.

Bailey, Lynn R. *Bosque Redondo: The Navajo Internment at Fort Sumner, New Mexico, 1863–1868*. Tucson, AZ: Westernlore Press, 1998.

Bailey, Thomas A. *Probing America's Past: A Critical Examination of Major Myths and Misconceptions*. Vol. 1. Lexington, MA: D.C. Heath, 1972.

Baker, Nina Brown. *Cyclone in Calico: The Story of Mary Ann Bickerdyke*. Boston: Little, Brown, 1952.

Ball, Douglas B. *Financial Failure and Confederate Defeat*. Urbana: University of Illinois Press, 1991.

Balser, Roy P., ed. *The Collected Works of Abraham Lincoln*. 9 vols. New Brunswick, NJ: Rutgers University Press, 1953–55.

Banks, Dean. "Civil War Refugees from Indian Territory in the North, 1861–1864." *Chronicles of Oklahoma* 41 (1963): 286–98.

Barnes, Kenneth C. "The Williams Clan's Civil War: How an Arkansas Farm Family Became a Guerrilla Band." In Inscoe and Kenzer, *Enemies of the Country*.

Barney, William L. *The Road to Secession: A New Perspective on the Old South*. New York: Praeger Publishers, 1972.

———. "Secession." *Encyclopedia of the Confederacy*, edited by Richard N. Current. New York: Simon & Schuster, 1993.

———. *The Secessionist Impulse: Alabama and Mississippi in 1860*. Princeton, NJ: Princeton University Press, 1974.

Baum, Dale. *The Shattering of Texas Unionism: Politics in the Lone Star State During the Civil War Era*. Baton Rouge: Louisiana State University Press, 1998.

Bennett, Lerone, Jr. *Forced into Glory: Abraham Lincoln's White Dream*. Chicago: Johnson Publishing, 2000.

Bennett, Michael J. *Union Jacks: Yankee Sailors in the Civil War*. Chapel Hill: University of North Carolina Press, 2004.

Beringer, Richard E., Herman Hattaway, Archer Jones, and William N. Still. *Why the South Lost the Civil War*. Athens: University of Georgia Press, 1986.

Berlin, Ira. "The Slaves Were the Primary Force Behind Their Emancipation." *The Civil War: Opposing Viewpoints*, edited by William Dudley. San Diego, CA: Greenhaven Press, 1995.

———. *Slaves Without Masters: The Free Negro in the Antebellum North*. New York: The New Press, 1974.

Berlin, Ira, Marc Favreau, and Steven F. Miller, eds. *Remembering Slavery: African Americans Talk About Their Personal Experiences of Slavery and Freedom*. New York: The New Press, 1998.

Berlin, Ira, Barbara J. Fields, Steven F. Miller, Joseph P. Reidy, and Leslie S. Rowland, eds. *Free at Last: A Documentary History of Slavery, Freedom, and the Civil War*. New York: The New Press, 1992.

Bernard, George S., ed. *War Talks of Confederate Veterans*. Petersburg, VA: Fenn and Owen, 1892.

Bernstein, Iver. *The New York City Draft Riots: Their Significance for American Society and Politics in the Age of the Civil War*. New York: Oxford University Press, 1990.

Berthrong, Donald J. *The Southern Cheyennes*. Norman: University of Oklahoma Press, 1963.

Billings, John D. *Hardtack and Coffee*. 1887. Reprint, Williamstown, MA: Corner House, 1987.

Blackett, R.J.M., ed. *Thomas Morris Chester, Black Civil War Correspondent*. Baton Rouge: Louisiana State University Press, 1989.

Blair, William. *Virginia's Private War: Feeding Body and Soul in the Confederacy, 1861–1865*. New York: Oxford University Press, 1998.

Blakey, Arch Fredric, Ann Smith Lainhart, and Winston Bryant Stephens Jr., eds. *Rose Cottage Chronicles: Civil War Letters of the Bryant-Stephens Families of North Florida*. Gainesville: University Press of Florida, 1998.

Blanton, DeAnne, and Lauren M. Cook. *They Fought Like Demons: Women Soldiers in the American Civil War*. Baton Rouge: Louisiana State University Press, 2002.

Blied, Benjamin J. *Catholics and the Civil War: Essays*. Milwaukee, WI: n.p., 1945.

Blight, David W. *Frederick Douglass' Civil War: Keeping Faith in Jubilee*. Baton Rouge: Louisiana State University Press, 1989.

Blomquist, Ann K., and Robert A. Taylor. *This Cruel War: The Civil War Letters of Grant and Malinda Taylor, 1862–1865*. Macon, GA: Mercer University Press, 2000.

Bohannon, Keith S. " 'They Had Determined to Root Us Out': Dual Memoirs by a Unionist Couple in Blue Ridge, Georgia." In Inscoe and Kenzer, *Enemies of the Country*.

Bollet, Alfred Jay. *Civil War Medicine: Challenges and Triumphs*. Tucson, AZ: Galen Press, 2002.

Bolton, Charles C. *Poor Whites of the Antebellum South: Tenants and Laborers in Central North Carolina and Northeast Mississippi*. Durham, NC: Duke University Press, 1994.

Bonner, James C. "David R. Snelling: A Story of Desertion and Defection in the Civil War." *Georgia Review* 10 (1956): 275–82.

Botkin, B.A., ed. *Lay My Burden Down: A Folk History of Slavery*. Athens: University of Georgia Press, 1989.

Breen, Patrick H. "The Female Antislavery Petition Campaign of 1831–32." *Virginia Magazine of History and Biography* 110 (2002): 377–98.

Bremner, Robert H. *The Public Good: Philanthropy and Welfare in the Civil War Era*. New York: Alfred A. Knopf, 1980.

———, ed. *Children and Youth in America: A Documentary History*. Vol. 1. Cambridge: Harvard University Press, 1970.

Brinkley, Alan. *The Unfinished Nation: A Concise History of the American People*. Vol. 1. 4th ed. Boston: McGraw-Hill, 2004.

Brooks, Stewart. *Civil War Medicine*. Springfield, IL: Charles C. Thomas, 1966.

Brown, Dee. *Bury My Heart at Wounded Knee: An Indian History of the American West*. New York: Holt, Rinehart, Winston, 1970.

Browne, Janet. *Charles Darwin: The Power of Place*. New York: Alfred A. Knopf, 2002.

Browne, Junius Henri. *Four Years in Secessia: Adventures Within and Beyond the Union Lines*. Hartford, CT: O.D. Case, 1865.

Bryan, T. Conn. *Confederate Georgia*. Athens: University of Georgia Press, 1953.

Bryant, William O. *Cahaba Prison and the Sultana Disaster*. Tuscaloosa: University of Alabama Press, 1990.

Buker, George, E. *Blockaders, Refugees, and Contrabands: Civil War on Florida's Gulf Coast, 1861–1865*. Tuscaloosa: University of Alabama Press, 1993.

Bull, Rice C. *Soldiering: The Civil War Diary of Rice C. Bull*. K. Jack Bauer, ed. Novato, CA: Presidio, 1977.

Burchard, Peter. *One Gallant Rush: Robert Gould Shaw and His Brave Black Regiment*. New York: St. Martin's, 1965.

Burton, David H. *Clara Barton: In the Service of Humanity*. Westport, CT: Greenwood Press, 1995.

Bynum, Victoria E. *The Free State of Jones: Mississippi's Longest Civil War*. Chapel Hill: University of North Carolina Press, 2001.

———. Review of *Poor Whites of the Antebellum South*, by Charles C. Bolton. *Journal of Southern History* 61 (1995): 601–02.

———. "Telling and Retelling the Legend of the 'Free State of Jones.'" In Sutherland, *Guerrillas, Unionists, and Violence on the Confederate Home Front*.

———. *Unruly Women: The Politics of Social and Sexual Control in the Old South*. Chapel Hill: University of North Carolina Press, 1992.

Camp, Stephanie M.H. *Closer to Freedom: Enslaved Women in Everyday Resistance in the Plantation South*. Chapel Hill: University of North Carolina Press, 2004.

Canney, Donald L. *Lincoln's Navy: The Ships, Men and Organization, 1861–65*. Annapolis: Naval Institute Press, 1998.

Carley, Kenneth. *The Sioux Uprising of 1862*. St. Paul: Minnesota Historical Society, 1976.

Carlson, David. "'The Distemper of the Time': Conscription, the Courts, and Planter Privilege in Civil War South Georgia." *Journal of Southwest Georgia History* 14 (1999): 1–24.

———. "The 'Loanly Runagee': Draft Evaders in Confederate South Georgia." *Georgia Historical Quarterly* 84 (2000): 589–615.

Cartwright, Samuel A. "Diseases and Peculiarities of the Negro Race." In *The Cause of the South: Selections from* De Bow's Review, *1846–1867*, edited by Paul R. Paskoff and Daniel J. Wilson. Baton Rouge: Louisiana State University Press, 1982.

Cashin, Joan E. "Deserters, Civilians, and Draft Resistance in the North." In *The War Was You and Me: Civilians in the American Civil War*, edited by Joan E. Cashin. Princeton, NJ: Princeton University Press, 2002.

Casler, John O. *Four Years in the Stonewall Brigade*. 4th ed. Dayton, OH: Morningside Bookshop, 1982.

Castel, Albert. "Dearest Ben: Letters from a Civil War Soldier's Wife." *Michigan History* 71 (1987): 18–23.

———. "The Fort Pillow Massacre." In Urwin, *Black Flag Over Dixie*.

———, ed. "Malingering: 'Many . . . diseases are . . . feigned.'" *Civil War Times Illustrated* 16 (1977): 29–32.

Catton, Bruce. *Reflections on the Civil War*. New York: Berkley Books, 1982.

Cecil-Fronsman, Bill. *Common Whites: Class and Culture in Antebellum North Carolina*. Lexington: University Press of Kentucky, 1992.

Chesebrough, David B. "Dissenting Clergy in Confederate Mississippi." *Journal of Mississippi History* 55 (1993): 115–31.

Chesnut, Mary. *Mary Chesnut's Civil War*. Edited by C. Vann Woodward. New Haven, CT: Yale University Press, 1981.

Chesson, Michael B. "Harlots or Heroines? A New Look at the Richmond Bread Riot." *Virginia Magazine of History and Biography* 92 (1984): 131–75.

Christman, Henry. *Tin Horns and Calico: A Decisive Episode in the Emergence of Democracy*. New York: Holt, 1945.

Churchill, Robert. "Liberty, Conscription, and a Party Divided: The Sons of Liberty Conspiracy, 1863–1864." *Prologue* 30 (1998): 295–303.

Cimbala, Paul A. and Randall M. Miller, eds. *An Uncommon Time: The Civil War and the Northern Home Front*. New York: Fordham University Press, 2002.

———, eds. *Union Soldiers and the Northern Home Front: Wartime Experiences, Postwar Adjustments*. New York: Fordham University Press, 2002.

Clark, Christopher, and Nancy A. Hewitt. *Who Built America?: Working People and the Nation's Economy, Politics, Culture, and Society*. Vol. 1. American Social History Project. New York: Worth Publishers, 2000.

Clay, C.C., Papers, 1811–1925. Rare Book, Manuscript, and Special Collections Library, William R. Perkins Library, Duke University.

Cleveland, Henry. *Alexander H. Stephens in Public and Private*. Philadelphia: National Publishing, 1866.

Clinton, Catherine. *Harriet Tubman: The Road to Freedom*. New York: Little, Brown, 2004.

———. *The Other Civil War: American Women in the Nineteenth Century*. New York: Hill and Wang, 1984.

Clinton, Catherine, and Nina Silber, eds. *Divided Houses: Gender and the Civil War*. New York: Oxford University Press, 1992.

Clodfelter, Micheal. *The Dakota War: The United States Army Versus the Sioux, 1862–1865*. Jefferson, NC: McFarland, 1998.

Cochran, Thomas C., and William Miller. *The Age of Enterprise: A Social History of Industrial America*. New York: Macmillan, 1942.

Coleman, Kenneth, ed. *A History of Georgia*. 2nd ed. Athens: University of Georgia Press, 1991.

Coles, David J. "'Shooting Niggers Sir': Confederate Mistreatment of Union Black Soldiers at the Battle of Olustee." In Urwin, *Black Flag Over Dixie*.

Colton, Ray C. *The Civil War in the Western Territories*. Norman: University of Oklahoma Press, 1959.

Commons, John R., David J. Saposs, Henlen L. Sumner, E.B. Mittelman, H.E. Hoagland, John B. Andrews, and Selig Perlman. *History of Labour in the United States*. Vol. 2. New York: Macmillan, 1918.

"Congress Passes Bill to Set Up First Site in Memory of Indian Massacre." Associated Press, October 24, 2000, www.cnn.com/2000/ALLPOLITICS/stories/10/24/sand creekmassacre.ap/.

Conner, Daniel Ellis. *Joseph Reddeford Walker and the Arizona Adventure*. Norman: University of Oklahoma Press, 1956.

Conway, Alan. *The Reconstruction of Georgia*. Minneapolis: University of Minnesota Press, 1966.

Cook, Adrian. *The Armies of the Streets: The New York City Draft Riots of 1863*. Lexington: University Press of Kentucky, 1974.

Cornish, Dudley Taylor. *The Sable Arm: Black Troops in the Union Army, 1861–1865*. Lawrence: University Press of Kansas, 1987.

Coulter, E. Merton. *The Confederate States of America, 1861–1865*. Baton Rouge: Louisiana State University Press, 1950.

Craft, William. *Running a Thousand Miles for Freedom: The Escape of William and Ellen Craft from Slavery*. 1860. Reprint, with foreword and biographical essay by R.J.M. Blackett. Baton Rouge: Louisiana State University Press, 1999.

Craig, Lee A. "Industry, Agriculture, and the Economy." In *The American Civil War: A Handbook of Literature and Research*, edited by Steven E. Woodworth. Westport, CT: Greenwood Press, 1996.

Craig, Lee A., and Thomas Weiss. "Agricultural Productivity Growth During the Decade of the Civil War." *Journal of Economic History* 53 (1993): 527–48.

Craven, Avery O. *The Coming of the Civil War*. Chicago: University of Chicago Press, 1957.

Crawford, Martin. *Ashe County's Civil War: Community and Society in the Appalachian South*. Charlottesville: University Press of Virginia, 2001.

Crist, Lynda Lasswell, and Mary Seaton Dix, eds. *The Papers of Jefferson Davis*. Vol. 7. Baton Rouge: Louisiana State University Press, 1992.

Crofts, Daniel W. *Reluctant Confederates: Upper South Unionists in the Secession Crisis*. Chapel Hill: University of North Carolina Press, 1989.

Cruden, Robert. *Many and One: A Social History of the United States*. Englewood Cliffs, NJ: Prentice-Hall, 1980.

Cumming, Kate. *Gleanings from Southland: Sketches of Life and Manners of the People of the South Before, During, and After the War of Secession*. Birmingham, AL: Roberts and Son, 1895.

———. *The Journal of Kate Cumming—Confederate Nurse*. Edited by Richard Harwell. Savannah, GA: Beehive Press, 1975.

Cunningham, H.H. *Doctors in Gray: The Confederate Medical Service*. Baton Rouge: Louisiana State University Press, 1958.

Curran, Thomas F. *Soldiers of Peace: Civil War Pacifism and the Postwar Radical Peace Movement*. New York: Fordham University Press, 2003.

Current, Richard Nelson. *Lincoln and the First Shot*. Prospect Heights, IL: Waveland Press, 1990.

————. *Lincoln's Loyalists: Union Soldiers from the Confederacy*. New York: Oxford University Press, 1994.

Cutter, Barbara. *Domestic Devils, Battlefield Angels: The Radicalism of American Womanhood, 1830–1865*. Dekalb: Northern Illinois University Press, 2003.

Daly, John Patrick. *When Slavery Was Called Freedom: Evangelicalism, Proslavery, and the Causes of the Civil War*. Lexington: University of Kentucky Press, 2002.

Daniell, Elizabeth Otto. "The Ashburn Murder Case in Georgia Reconstruction, 1868." *Georgia Historical Quarterly* 59 (1975): 296–312.

Danziger, Edmund Jefferson, Jr. *Indians and Bureaucrats: Administering the Reservation Policy during the Civil War*. Urbana: University of Illinois Press, 1974.

Davis, Burke. *Sherman's March*. New York: Random House, 1980.

Davis, William C. *Look Away!: A History of the Confederate States of America*. New York: Free Press, 2002.

Dawley, Alan. *Class and Community: The Industrial Revolution in Lynn*. Cambridge: Harvard University Press, 1976.

DeBats, Donald A. *Elites and Masses: Political Structure, Communication, and Behavior in Ante-Bellum Georgia*. New York: Garland Publishing, 1990.

Debo, Angie. *A History of the Indians of the United States*. Norman: University of Oklahoma Press, 1986.

————. *The Road to Disappearance: A History of the Creek Indians*. Norman: University of Oklahoma Press, 1941.

DeCredico, Mary A. *Patriotism for Profit: Georgia's Urban Entrepreneurs and the Confederate War Effort*. Chapel Hill: University of North Carolina Press, 1990.

Degler, Carl N. *The Other South: Southern Dissenters in the Nineteenth Century*. Boston: Northeastern University Press, 1982.

Devens, R.M. *The Pictorial Book of Anecdotes and Incidents of the War of the Rebellion*. Toledo, OH: W.E. Bliss, 1873.

Dial Letter. Letter no. 3143. Southern Historical Collection, University of North Carolina at Chapel Hill.

Dinkins, James. *Personal Recollections and Experiences in the Confederate Army*. 1897. Reprint, Dayton, OH: Morningside Bookshop, 1975.

"Directory of Mark Twain's Maxims, Quotations, and Various Opinions." www.twainquotes.com/Vote.html.

Donald, David Herbert. *Lincoln*. New York: Simon & Schuster, 1995.

Dotson, Rand. " 'The Grave and Scandalous Evil Infected to Your People': The Erosion of Confederate Loyalty in Floyd County, Virginia." *Virginia Magazine of History and Biography* 108 (2000): 393–434.

Douglass, Frederick. *Narrative of the Life of Frederick Douglass*. 1845. Reprint, New York: Signet, 1968.

Drago, Edmund L. *Black Politicians and Reconstruction in Georgia: A Splendid Failure*. Baton Rouge: Louisiana State University Press, 1982.

Drake, J. Madison. *Fast and Loose in Dixie: An Unprejudiced Narrative of Personal Experience as a Prisoner of War*. New York: Authors' Publishing Company, 1880.

Du Bois, W.E.B. *Black Reconstruction in America, 1860–1880*. New York: Harcourt, Brace, 1935.

Dunlay, Tom. *Kit Carson and the Indians*. Lincoln: University of Nebraska Press, 2000.

Durden, Robert F. *The Gray and the Black: The Confederate Debate on Emancipation*. Baton Rouge: Louisiana State University Press, 1972.

Durrill, Wayne K. *War of Another Kind: A Southern Community in the Great Rebellion.* New York: Oxford University Press, 1990.

Dyer, Thomas G. *Secret Yankees: The Union Circle in Confederate Atlanta.* Baltimore: Johns Hopkins University Press, 1999.

Eaton, Clement. *The Freedom-of-Thought Struggle in the Old South.* New York: Harper and Row, 1964.

———. *The Mind of the Old South.* Baton Rouge: Louisiana State University Press, 1964.

Edwards, Laura F. *Scarlett Doesn't Live Here Anymore: Southern Women in the Civil War Era.* Urbana: University of Illinois Press, 2000.

Engerman, Stanley. "The Economic Impact of the Civil War." *Explorations in Economic History* 3 (1966): 176–99.

Escott, Paul D. *After Secession: Jefferson Davis and the Failure of Confederate Nationalism.* Baton Rouge: Louisiana State University Press, 1978.

———. "The Context of Freedom: Georgia's Slaves during the Civil War." *Georgia Historical Quarterly* 58 (1974): 79–104.

———. " 'The Cry of the Sufferers': The Problem of Welfare in the Confederacy." *Civil War History* 23 (1977): 228–40.

———. *Many Excellent People: Power and Privilege in North Carolina, 1850–1900.* Chapel Hill: University of North Carolina Press, 1985.

Escott, Paul D., and David R. Goldfield, eds. *Major Problems in the History of the American South.* Vol. 1. Lexington, MA: D.C. Heath, 1990.

Evans, Sara M. *Born for Liberty: A History of Women in America.* New York: Free Press, 1989.

Faust, Drew Gilpin. "Altars of Sacrifice: Confederate Women and the Narratives of War." *Journal of American History* 76 (1990): 1200–28.

———. *Mothers of Invention: Women of the Slaveholding South in the American Civil War.* Chapel Hill: University of North Carolina Press, 1996.

Fehrenbach, T.R. *Comanches: A History, 1706–1875.* New York: Alfred A. Knopf, 1974.

Fellman, Michael. "Women and Guerrilla Warfare." In Clinton and Silber, *Divided Houses.*

Finger, John R. *The Eastern Band of the Cherokees, 1819–1900.* Knoxville: University of Tennessee Press, 1984.

Fisher, Noel C. *War at Every Door: Partisan Politics and Guerrilla Violence in East Tennessee, 1860-1869.* Chapel Hill: University of North Carolina Press, 1997.

Fite, Emerson David. *Social and Industrial Conditions in the North During the Civil War.* 1910. Reprint, Williamstown, MA: Corner House, 1976.

Fitzgerald, Michael W. "Poor Man's Fight." *Southern Exposure* 18 (spring 1990): 14–17.

———. *The Union League Movement in the Deep South: Politics and Agricultural Change During Reconstruction.* Baton Rouge: Louisiana State University Press, 1989.

Fitzhugh, George. *Sociology for the South; or, The Failure of Free Society.* New York: Burt Franklin, 1854.

Fleming, Walter L. *Civil War and Reconstruction in Alabama.* New York: Columbia University Press, 1905.

Flynn, Charles L., Jr. *White Land, Black Labor: Caste and Class in Late Nineteenth-Century Georgia.* Baton Rouge: Louisiana State University Press, 1983.

Foner, Eric. *Reconstruction: America's Unfinished Revolution, 1863–1877.* New York: Harper and Row, 1988.

Foner, Philip S. *Business and Slavery: The New York Merchants and the Irrepressible Conflict.* New York: Russell and Russell, 1968.

———. *History of the Labor Movement in the United States from Colonial Times to the Founding of the American Federation of Labor*. New York: International Publishers, 1947.

Foner, Philip S., and Ronald L. Lewis, eds. *The Black Worker: A Documentary History from Colonial Times to the Present; Volume 1: The Black Worker to 1869*. Philadelphia: Temple University Press, 1978.

Foreman, Grant. *Indian Removal*. Norman: University of Oklahoma Press, 1932.

Formwalt, Lee W. "The Camilla Massacre of 1868: Racial Violence as Political Propaganda." *Georgia Historical Quarterly* 71 (1987): 399–426.

———. "Planter Persistence in Southwest Georgia, 1850–1870." *Journal of Southwest Georgia History* 2 (1984): 40–58.

———. "Planters and Cotton Production as a Cause of Confederate Defeat: The Evidence from Southwest Georgia." *Georgia Historical Quarterly* 74 (1990): 269–76.

Foster, Gaines M. *Ghosts of the Confederacy: Defeat, the Lost Cause, and the Emergence of the New South, 1865–1913*. New York: Oxford University Press, 1987.

Foust, James Donald. *The Yeoman Farmer and Westward Expansion of U.S. Cotton Production*. Chapel Hill: University of North Carolina Press, 1967.

Fox-Genovese, Elizabeth. *Within the Plantation Household: Black and White Women of the Old South*. Chapel Hill: University of North Carolina Press, 1988.

Franklin, John Hope, and Alfred A. Moss Jr. *From Slavery to Freedom: A History of African Americans*. 7th ed. New York: McGraw-Hill, 1994.

Franks, Kenny A. *Stand Watie and the Agony of the Cherokee Nation*. Memphis, TN: Memphis State University Press, 1979.

Frazier, Donald S. *Blood and Treasure: Confederate Empire in the Southwest*. College Station: Texas A&M University Press, 1995.

———. "'Out of Sinking Distance': The Guerrilla War in Arkansas." In Sutherland, *Guerrillas, Unionists, and Violence on the Confederate Home Front*.

Freehling, William W. *The South vs. the South: How Anti-Confederate Southerners Shaped the Course of the Civil War*. New York: Oxford University Press, 2001.

Freehling, William W., and Craig M. Simpson, eds. *Secession Debated: Georgia's Showdown in 1860*. New York: Oxford University Press, 1992.

Freeman, Douglas Southall. *R.E. Lee: A Biography*. 4 vols. New York: Charles Scribner's Sons, 1934–35.

Fried, Albert, ed. *Except to Walk Free: Documents and Notes in the History of American Labor*. Garden City, NY: Anchor Books, 1974.

Friedheim, William, with Ronald Jackson. *Freedom's Unfinished Revolution: An Inquiry into the Civil War and Reconstruction*. American Social History Project. New York: The New Press, 1996.

Frisby, Derek W. "'Remember Fort Pillow.'" In Urwin, *Black Flag Over Dixie*.

Gaines, W. Craig. *The Confederate Cherokees: John Drew's Regiment of Mounted Rifles*. Baton Rouge: Louisiana State University Press, 1989.

Gallagher, Gary W. *The Confederate War*. Cambridge: Harvard University Press, 1997.

Gallman, J. Matthew. *The North Fights the Civil War: The Home Front*. Chicago: Ivan R. Dee, 1994.

Gallman, Robert. "Commodity Output, 1839–99." In *Trends in the American Economy in the Nineteenth Century*, edited by William Parker. Princeton, NJ: Princeton University Press, 1960.

Gates, Paul W. *Agriculture and the Civil War*. New York: Alfred A. Knopf, 1965.

———. *Fifty Million Acres: Conflicts Over Kansas Land Policy, 1854–1890*. Ithaca, NY: Cornell University Press, 1954.

Geary, James W. *We Need Men: The Union Draft and the Civil War*. DeKalb: Northern Illinois University Press, 1991.

Genovese, Eugene D. *The Political Economy of Slavery: Studies in the Economy and Society of the Slave South*. New York: Vintage Books, 1967.

———. *Roll, Jordan, Roll: The World the Slaves Made*. New York: Vintage Books, 1976.

———. "Yeomen Farmers in a Slaveholders' Democracy." *Agricultural History* 49 (1975): 331–42.

Gibson, Arrell Morgan. *The American Indian: Prehistory to the Present*. Lexington, MA: D. C. Heath, 1980.

———. *The Kickapoos: Lords of the Middle Border*. Norman: University of Oklahoma Press, 1963.

Gienapp, William E., ed. *This Fiery Trial: The Speeches and Writings of Abraham Lincoln*. New York: Oxford University Press, 2002.

Ginzberg, Lori D. *Women and the Work of Benevolence: Morality, Politics, and Class in the Nineteenth-Century United States*. New Haven, CT: Yale University Press, 1990.

Glass, Paul, and Louis C. Singer. *Singing Soldiers: A History of the Civil War in Song*. Foreword by John Hope Franklin. New York: Da Capo Press, 1975.

Glatthaar, Joseph T. *Forged in Battle: The Civil War Alliance of Black Soldiers and White Officers*. New York: Free Press, 1990.

———. *The March to the Sea and Beyond: Sherman's Troops in the Savannah and Carolinas Campaigns*. New York: New York University Press, 1985.

Goldfield, David. *Still Fighting the Civil War*. Baton Rouge: Louisiana State University Press, 2002.

Gooding, James Henry. *On the Altar of Freedom: A Black Soldier's Civil War Letters from the Front*. Edited by Virginia Matzke Adams. Amherst: University of Massachusetts Press, 1991.

Gordon, Lesley J. "'Surely They Remember Me': The 16th Connecticut in War, Captivity, and Public Memory." In Cimbala and Miller, *Union Soldiers and the Northern Home Front*.

Gould, Stephen Jay. *The Mismeasure of Man*. New York: W.W. Norton, 1981.

Grant, Donald L. *The Way It Was in the South: The Black Experience in Georgia*. Edited with introduction by Jonathan Grant. New York: Birch Lane Press, 1993.

Gray, Lewis Cecil. *History of Agriculture in the Southern United States to 1860*. Vol. 2. Gloucester, MA: Peter Smith, 1958.

Gray, Wood. *The Hidden Civil War: The Story of the Copperheads*. New York: Viking Press, 1942.

Green, Elna C. *The Business of Relief: Confronting Poverty in a Southern City, 1740–1940*. Athens: University of Georgia Press, 2003.

Griffler, Keith P. *Front Line of Freedom: African Americans and the Forging of the Underground Railroad in the Ohio Valley*. Lexington: Unversity of Kentucky Press, 2004.

Groce, W. Todd. *Mountain Rebels: East Tennessee and the Civil War, 1860–1870*. Knoxville: University of Tennessee Press, 1999.

Gronowicz, Anthony. *Race and Class Politics in New York City Before the Civil War*. Boston: Northeastern University Press, 1998.

Grossman, Jonathan Philip. *William Sylvis, Pioneer of American Labor*. New York: Columbia University Press, 1945.

Hahn, Steven. *The Roots of Southern Populism: Yeoman Farmers and the Transformation of the Georgia Upcountry, 1850–1890*. New York: Oxford University Press, 1983.

Haley, James L. *Apaches: A History and Culture Portrait*. Norman: University of Oklahoma, 1981.

Hallock, Judith Lee. "The Role of the Community in Civil War Desertion." *Civil War History* 29 (1983): 123–34.

Hanna, William F. "The Boston Draft Riot." *Civil War History* 36 (1990): 262–73.

Harris, J. William. *Plain Folk and Gentry in a Slave Society: White Liberty and Black Slavery in Augusta's Hinterlands*. Middletown, CT: Wesleyan University Press, 1985.

Hatch, Thom. *The Blue, the Gray, and the Red: Indian Campaigns of the Civil War*. Mechanicsburg, PA: Stackpole Books, 2003.

Hauptman, Laurence M. *Between Two Fires: American Indians and the Civil War*. New York: Free Press, 1995.

———. *The Iroquois in the Civil War*. Syracuse, NY: Syracuse University Press, 1993.

Heidler, David S., and Jeanne T. Heidler, eds. *Encyclopedia of the American Civil War*. 5 vols. Santa Barbara, CA: ABC-CLIO, 2000.

Helper, Hinton Rowan. *Impending Crisis of the South*. 1857. Reprint, Cambridge: Harvard University Press, 1968.

Hill, Louise B. *State Socialism in the Confederate States of America*. Charlottesville, VA: Historical Publishing Co., 1936.

Hodes, Martha. *White Women, Black Men: Illicit Sex in the Nineteenth-Century South*. New Haven, CT: Yale University Press, 1997.

Hoig, Stan. *The Sand Creek Massacre*. Norman: University of Oklahoma Press, 1961.

Holmes, Emma. *The Diary of Miss Emma Holmes, 1861–1866*. Edited by John F. Marsalek. Baton Rouge: Louisiana State University Press, 1979.

Holt, Michael F. *The Political Crisis of the 1850s*. New York: W.W. Norton, 1978.

Horigan, Michael. *Elmira: Death Camp of the North*. Mechanicsburg, PA: Stackpole Books, 2002.

Horst, Samuel. *Mennonites in the Confederacy: A Study in Civil War Pacifism*. Scottsdale, PA: Herald Press, 1967.

Hovencamp, Herbert. *Science and Religion in America, 1800–1860*. Philadelphia: University of Pennsylvania Press, 1978.

Howard, Victor B. *Religion and the Radical Republican Movement, 1860–1870*. Lexington: University Press of Kentucky, 1990.

Hummel, Jeffrey Rogers. *Emancipating Slaves, Enslaving Free Men: A History of the American Civil War*. Chicago: Open Court Publishing, 1996.

Imboden, John W. "The Confederate Retreat from Gettysburg." In *Battles and Leaders of the Civil War*, edited by Clarence C. Buel and Robert U. Johnson. 4 vols. New York: Century, 1887–88.

Inscoe, John C. "Moving Through Deserter Country: Fugitive Accounts of the Inner Civil War in Southern Appalachia." In Noe and Wilson, *Civil War in Appalachia*.

Inscoe, John C., and Robert C. Kenzer, eds. *Enemies of the Country: New Perspectives on Unionists in the Civil War South*. Athens: University of Georgia Press, 2001.

Inscoe, John C., and Gordon B. McKinney. *The Heart of Confederate Appalachia: Western North Carolina in the Civil War*. Chapel Hill: University of North Carolina Press, 2000.

Iverson, Peter. *The Navajo Nation*. Westport, CT: Greenwood Press, 1981.

Jackson, Alto Loftin, ed. *So Mourns the Dove: Letters of a Confederate Infantryman and His Family*. New York: Exposition Press, 1965.

Jackson, Donald Dale. *Twenty Million Yankees: The Northern Home Front*. Alexandria, VA: Time-Life Books, 1985.

Jackson, Helen Hunt. *A Century of Dishonor.* 1881. Reprint, New York: Harper Torch-books, 1965.

Jimerson, Randall C. *The Private Civil War: Popular Thought During the Sectional Conflict.* Baton Rouge: Louisiana State University Press, 1988.

Johnson, Ludwell H. "Contraband Trade During the Last Year of the Civil War." *Mississippi Valley Historical Review* 49 (1962–63): 635–52.

Johnson, Michael P., ed. *Abraham Lincoln, Slavery, and the Civil War: Selected Writings and Speeches.* Boston and New York: Bedford/St. Martin's, 2001.

———. "A New Look at the Popular Vote for Delegates to the Georgia Secession Convention." *Georgia Historical Quarterly* 56 (1972): 259–75.

———. *Toward a Patriarchal Republic: The Secession of Georgia.* Baton Rouge: Louisiana State University Press, 1977.

Jones, Katherine M., ed. *Heroines of Dixie: Spring of High Hopes.* St. Simons Island, GA: Mockingbird Books, 1983.

Jones, Robert Huhn. *The Civil War in the Northwest.* Norman: University of Oklahoma Press, 1960.

Jordan, Ervin L., Jr. *Black Confederates and Afro-Yankees in Civil War Virginia.* Charlottesville: University of Virginia Press, 1995.

Jordan, Weymouth T., Jr., and Gerald W. Thomas. "Massacre at Plymouth." In Urwin, *Black Flag Over Dixie.*

Jordan, Winthrop D. *Tumult and Silence at Second Creek: An Inquiry into a Civil War Slave Conspiracy.* Baton Rouge: Louisiana State University Press, 1993.

Josephy, Alvin M., Jr. *The Civil War in the American West.* New York: Alfred A. Knopf, 1992.

———. *500 Nations: An Illustrated History of North American Indians.* New York: Alfred A. Knopf, 1994.

Keillor, Garrison. "We're Not in Lake Wobegon Anymore." *In These Times,* August 26, 2004. www.inthesetimes.com/site/main/article/979/.

Kelly, Lawrence. *Navajo Roundup: Selected Correspondence of Kit Carson's Expedition against the Navajo, 1863–1865.* Boulder, CO: Pruett Publishing Co., 1970.

Kennett, Lee. *Marching Through Georgia: The Story of Soldiers and Civilians during Sherman's Campaign.* New York: Harper Collins, 1995.

Kibler, Lillian A. "Unionist Sentiment in South Carolina." *Journal of Southern History* 4 (1938): 346–66.

Kinsland, William S. "The Civil War Comes to Lumpkin County." *North Georgia Journal* 1 (summer 1984): 21–26.

Klement, Frank L. *Dark Lanterns: Secret Political Societies, Conspiracies, and Treason Trials in the Civil War.* Baton Rouge: Louisiana State University Press, 1984.

———. *The Limits of Dissent: Clement L. Vallandingham and the Civil War.* Lexington: University Press of Kentucky, 1970.

Korn, Bertram Wallace. *American Jewry and the Civil War.* 1951. Reprint, Philadelphia: Jewish Publication Society of America, 2001.

Kruman, Marc W. "Dissent in the Confederacy: The North Carolina Experience." *Civil War History* 27 (1981): 294–313.

Lamb, Robert Paul. "James G. Birney and the Road to Abolitionism." *Alabama Review* 47 (1994): 83–134.

Lane, Mills, ed. *The Rambler in Georgia.* Savannah, GA: Beehive Press, 1973.

Larsen, Lawrence H. "Draft Riot in Wisconsin, 1862." *Civil War History* 7 (1961): 421–27.

Lathrop, Barnes F. "Disaffection in Confederate Louisiana: The Case of William Hyman." *Journal of Southern History* 24 (1958): 308–18.

Lause, Mark A. "Homestead Act." In Heidler and Heidler, *Encyclopedia of the American Civil War.*

Lebergott, Stanley. "Through the Blockade: The Profitability and Extent of Cotton Smuggling, 1861–1865." *Journal of Economic History* 41 (1981): 867–88.

———. "Why the South Lost: Commercial Purpose in the Confederacy." *Journal of American History* 70 (1983): 58–74.

Lenoir Family Papers. Personal correspondence, 1861–1865. Inventory number 426, Manuscripts Department, Southern Historical Collection, University of North Carolina at Chapel Hill.

Leonard, Elizabeth D. *All the Daring of the Soldier: Women of the Civil War Armies.* New York: Penguin Books, 1999.

———. *Yankee Women: Gender Battles in the Civil War.* New York: W.W. Norton, 1994.

Levine, Bruce. *Half Slave and Half Free: The Roots of Civil War.* New York: Hill and Wang, 1992.

Levine, Peter. "Draft Evasion in the North During the Civil War, 1863–1865." *Journal of American History* 67 (1981): 816–34.

Linderman, Gerald F. *Embattled Courage: The Experience of Combat in the American Civil War.* New York: Free Press, 1987.

Lindsey, Bobby L. *The Reason for the Tears: A History of Chambers County, Alabama, 1832–1900.* West Point, GA: Hester Printing Co., 1971.

Lindstrom, Diane. "Southern Dependence Upon Interregional Grain Supplies: A Review of the Trade Flows, 1840–1860." *Agricultural History* 44 (1970): 101–13.

Link, William A. *Roots of Secession: Slavery and Politics in Antebellum Virginia.* Chapel Hill: University of North Carolina Press, 2003.

Litwak, Leon F. "Hellhounds." In *Without Sanctuary: Lynching Photography in America*, by James Allen, Hilton Als, Congressman John Lewis, and Leon F. Litwak. Santa Fe, NM: Twin Palms Publishers, 2000.

Locke, John. *The Second Treatise of Government.* Indianapolis, IN: Bobbs-Merrill, 1979.

Lofgren, Charles A. *The "Plessy" Case: A Legal-Historical Interpretation.* New York: Oxford University Press, 1987.

Long, David E. *The Jewel of Liberty: Abraham Lincoln's Re-election and the End of Slavery.* New York: Da Capo Press, 1997.

Longstreet, James, *From Manassas to Appomattox: Memoirs of the Civil War in America.* Philadelphia: J.B. Lippincott Co., 1896.

Lonn, Ella. *Desertion During the Civil War.* 1928. Reprint, with introduction by William Blair, Lincoln: University of Nebraska Press, 1998.

———. *Foreigners in the Union Army and Navy.* New York: Greenwood, 1969.

Lowe, Richard. "Battle on the Levee: The Fight at Milliken's Bend." In Smith, *Black Soldiers in Blue.*

Lowry, Thomas P. *The Story the Soldiers Wouldn't Tell: Sex in the Civil War.* Mechanicsburg, PA: Stackpole Books, 1994.

MacLean, Nancy. *Behind the Mask of Chivalry: The Making of the Second Ku Klux Klan.* New York: Oxford, 1994.

Madsen, Brigham D. *The Shoshoni Frontier and the Bear River Massacre.* Salt Lake City: University of Utah Press, 1985.

"Maggots Make Medical Comeback." Associated Press, August 3, 2004, www.cnn.com/2004/HEALTH/08/02/maggot.medicine.ap/index.html.

Mallard, M. Shannon. "'I Had No Comfort to Give the People': Opposition to the Confederacy in Civil War Mississippi." *North & South* 6 (May 2003): 78–86.

Marten, James. *Children for the Union: The War Spirit on the Northern Home Front.* Chicago: Ivan R. Dee, 2004.

———. "Fatherhood in the Confederacy: Southern Soldiers and their Children." *Journal of Southern History* 63 (1997): 269–92.

———. *Texas Divided: Loyalty and Dissent in the Lone Star State, 1856–1874.* Lexington: University Press of Kentucky, 1990.

———. "United States Sanitary Commission." In Heidler and Heidler, *Encyclopedia of the American Civil War.*

Martin, Bessie. *A Rich Man's War, A Poor Man's Fight: Desertion of Alabama Troops from the Confederate Army.* 1932. Reprint, with new introduction by Mark A. Weitz, Tuscaloosa: University of Alabama Press, 2003.

Martis, Kenneth C. *The Historical Atlas of the Congresses of the Confederate States of America, 1861–1865.* Gyula Pauer, cartographer. B. Reed Durbin, research assistant. New York: Simon & Schuster, 1994.

Marvel, William. *Andersonville: The Last Depot.* Chapel Hill: University of North Carolina Press, 1994.

Massey, Mary Elizabeth. *Women in the Civil War.* Lincoln: University of Nebraska Press, 1994.

Maxwell, William Quentin. *Lincoln's Fifth Wheel: The Political History of the United States Sanitary Commission.* New York: Longmans, Green, 1956.

May, Robert E. *The Southern Dream of a Caribbean Empire, 1854–1861.* Baton Rouge: Louisiana State University Press, 1973.

Mayhall, Mildred P. *The Kiowas.* 2nd ed. Norman: University of Oklahoma Press, 1971.

McCaslin, Richard B. *Tainted Breeze: The Great Hanging at Gainesville, Texas, 1862.* Baton Rouge: Louisiana State University Press, 1994.

McCrea, Tully. *Dear Belle: Letters From a Cadet and Officer to His Sweetheart, 1858–1865.* Edited by Catherine S. Crary. Middletown, CT: Weslyan University Press, 1965.

McCurry, Stephanie. *Masters of Small Worlds: Yeoman Households, Gender Relations, and the Political Culture of the Antebellum South Carolina Low Country.* New York: Oxford University Press, 1995.

McFeely, William S. *Frederick Douglass.* New York: W.W. Norton, 1991.

McGee, Val L. "The Confederate Who Switched Sides: The Saga of Captain Joseph G. Sanders." *Alabama Review* 47 (1994): 20–28.

McKay, Ernest A. *The Civil War and New York City.* Syracuse, NY: Syracuse University Press, 1990.

———. *Henry Wilson: Practical Radical; A Portrait of a Politician.* Port Washington, NY: Kennikat Press, 1971.

McKenzie, Robert Tracy. *One South or Many?: Plantation Belt and Upcountry in Civil War–Era Tennessee.* Cambridge: Cambridge University Press, 1994.

McKitrick, Eric. "Party Politics and the Union and Confederate War Efforts." *The American Party Systems: Stages of Political Development,* edited by William N. Chambers and Walter Dean Burnham. New York: Oxford University Press, 1967.

McNitt, Frank. *Navajo Wars: Military Campaigns, Slave Raids, and Reprisals.* Albuquerque: University of New Mexico Press, 1972.

McPherson, James M. *Battle Cry of Freedom.* New York: Oxford University Press, 1988.

———. *Drawn with the Sword.* New York: Oxford University Press, 1996.

———. *The Negro's Civil War*. Urbana: University of Illinois Press, 1982.

———. *Ordeal by Fire: The Civil War and Reconstruction*. 2nd ed. New York: McGraw Hill, 1992.

———. *The Struggle for Equality: Abolitionists and the Negro in the Civil War and Reconstruction*. Princeton, NJ: Princeton University Press, 1964.

———. *What They Fought For, 1861–1865*. Baton Rouge: Louisiana State University Press, 1994.

McReynolds, Edwin C. *The Seminoles*. Norman: University of Oklahoma Press, 1957.

McWhiney, Grady. *Cracker Culture: Celtic Ways in the Old South*. Tuscaloosa: University of Alabama Press, 1988.

"Medal of Honor Recipients. Indian Wars Period." www.army.mil/cmh-pg/mohind.htm.

Meriwether, Harvey. *Slavery in Auburn, Alabama*. Auburn: Alabama Polytechnic Institute Historical Studies, 1907.

Meyer, Roy W. *History of the Santee Sioux: United States Indian Policy on Trial*. Lincoln: University of Nebraska Press, 1967.

Meyers, Christopher C. "'The Wretch Vickery' and the Brooks County Civil War Slave Conspiracy." *Journal of Southwest Georgia History* 12 (1997): 27–38.

Milton, George Fort. *Abraham Lincoln and the Fifth Column*. New York: Vanguard Press, 1942.

Mitchell, Reid. *Civil War Soldiers*. New York: Viking, 1988.

Mohr, Clarence L. *On the Threshold of Freedom: Masters and Slaves in Civil War Georgia*. Athens: University of Georgia Press, 1986.

———. "Slavery and Class Tensions in Confederate Georgia." *Gulf Coast Historical Review* 4 (1989): 58–72.

Moneyhon, Carl. "Disloyalty and Class Consciousness in Southwestern Arkansas, 1862–1865." *Arkansas Historical Quarterly* 52 (1993): 223–43.

Montgomery, David. *Beyond Equality: Labor and the Radical Republicans, 1862–1872*. New York: Alfred A. Knopf, 1967.

Moore, Albert Burton. *Conscription and Conflict in the Confederacy*. New York: Hillary House, 1963.

Morgan, Edmund S. *American Slavery, American Freedom: The Ordeal of Colonial Virginia*. New York: W.W. Norton, 1975.

Moulton, Gary E. *John Ross: Cherokee Chief*. Athens: University of Georgia Press, 1978.

Murdock, Eugene C. *One Million Men: The Civil War Draft in the North*. Madison: State Historical Society of Wisconsin, 1971.

———. *Patriotism Limited, 1862–1865: The Civil War Draft and the Bounty System*. Kent, OH: Kent State University Press, 1967.

Murphy, Robert Joseph. "The Catholic Church in the United States during the Civil War Period, 1852–1866." *Records of the American Catholic Historical Society* 39 (1928): 271–346.

Myers, Gustavus. *History of the Great American Fortunes*. New York: Modern Library, 1937.

Neely, Mark E., Jr. *The Fate of Liberty: Abraham Lincoln and Civil Liberties*. New York: Oxford University Press, 1991.

———. *Southern Rights: Political Prisoners and the Myth of Confederate Constitutionalism*. Charlottesville: University Press of Virginia, 1999.

———. *The Union Divided: Party Conflict in the Civil War North*. Cambridge: Harvard University Press, 2002.

Nelson, Jacquelyn S. *Indiana Quakers Confront the Civil War*. Indianapolis: Indiana Historical Society, 1991.

Nevins, Allan. *The War for the Union: The Organized War to Victory, 1864–65*. New York: Charles Scribner's Sons, 1971.

Nichols, David A. *Lincoln and the Indians: Civil War Policy and Politics*. Columbia: University of Missouri Press, 1978.

Noe, Kenneth W. "Red String Scare: Civil War Southwest Virginia and the Heroes of America." *North Carolina Historical Review* 69 (1992): 301–22.

Noe, Kenneth W., and Shannon H. Wilson, eds. *The Civil War in Appalachia: Collected Essays*. Knoxville: University of Tennessee Press, 1997.

Nolan, Alan T. *Lee Considered: General Robert E. Lee and Civil War History*. Chapel Hill: University of North Carolina Press, 1991.

Noyes, Edward. "White Opposition to Black Migration into Civil-War Wisconsin." *Lincoln Herald* 73 (1971): 181–91.

Oakes, James. *Slavery and Freedom: An Interpretation of the Old South*. New York: Vintage Books, 1990.

Oates, Stephen. *A Woman of Valor: Clara Barton and the Civil War*. New York: Free Press, 1994.

Oehler, C.M. *The Great Sioux Uprising*. New York: Oxford University Press, 1959.

O'Sullivan, John, and Alan M. Meckler, eds. *The Draft and Its Enemies: A Documentary History*. Urbana: University of Illinois Press, 1974.

Otto, John Solomon. *Southern Agriculture During the Civil War Era, 1860–1880*. Westport, CT: Greenwood Press, 1994.

Owsley, Frank Lawrence. "Defeatism in the Confederacy." *North Carolina Historical Review* 3 (1926): 446–56.

———. *Plain Folk of the Old South*. Baton Rouge: Louisiana State University Press, 1949.

———. *State Rights in the Confederacy*. 1925. Reprint, Gloucester, MA: Peter Smith, 1961.

Palladino, Grace. *Another Civil War: Labor, Capital, and the State in the Anthracite Regions of Pennsylvania, 1840–68*. Urbana: University of Illinois Press, 1990.

Paludan, Phillip Shaw. *A People's Contest: The Union and the Civil War, 1861–1865*. New York: Harper and Row, 1988.

———. *Victims: A True Story of the Civil War*. Knoxville: University of Tennessee Press, 1981.

Parish, Peter J. "From Necessary Evil to National Blessing: The Northern Protestant Clergy Interpret the Civil War." In Cimbala and Miller, *Uncommon Time*.

Perkins, Howard Cecil, ed. *Northern Editorials on Secession*. Gloucester, MA: Peter Smith, 1964.

Perman, Michael, ed. *Major Problems in the Civil War and Reconstruction*. Lexington, MA: D.C. Heath, 1991.

Pickering, David, and Judy Falls. *Brush Men and Vigilantes: Civil War Dissent in Texas*. College Station: Texas A&M University Press, 2000.

Phillips, Kevin. *Wealth and Democracy: A Political History of the American Rich*. New York: Broadway Books, 2002.

Phillips, Ulrich B., ed. *The Correspondence of Robert Toombs, Alexander H. Stephens, and Howell Cobb*. Washington, DC: Government Printing Office, 1913.

———. *Georgia and State Rights*. Washington, DC: Government Printing Office, 1902.

Potter, David M. *The Impending Crisis, 1848–1861*. Completed and edited by Don E. Fehrenbacher. New York: Harper and Row, 1976.

————. *Lincoln and His Party in the Secession Crisis*. Introduction by Daniel Crofts. Baton Rouge: Louisiana State University Press, 1995.

Powell, Lawrence N. *New Masters: Northern Planters During the Civil War and Reconstruction*. New Haven, CT: Yale University Press, 1980.

Proctor, William G., Jr. "Slavery in Southwest Georgia." *Georgia Historical Quarterly* 49 (1965): 1–22.

Pryor, Elizabeth Brown. *Clara Barton, Professional Angel*. Philadelphia: University of Pennsylvania Press, 1987.

Quarles, Benjamin. *The Negro in the Civil War*. 1953. Reprint, with introduction by William S. McFeely, New York: Da Capo, 1989.

Rable, George C. *Civil Wars: Women and the Crisis of Southern Nationalism*. Urbana: University of Illinois Press, 1989.

Ramold, Steven J. "African-American Sailors." In Heidler and Heidler, *Encyclopedia of the American Civil War.*

Ramsdell, Charles W. "Lincoln and Fort Sumter." *Journal of Southern History* 3 (1937): 259–288.

Range, Willard. *A Century of Georgia Agriculture: 1850–1950*. Athens: University of Georgia Press, 1954.

Raphael, Ray. *A People's History of the American Revolution*. New York: The New Press, 2001.

Rawick, George P., ed. *The American Slave: A Composite Autobiography*. Ser. 1 and 2, 19 vols. Supplement, ser. 1, 12 vols. Westport, CT: Greenwood Press, 1972 and 1977.

Rawley, James A. *Race and Politics: "Bleeding Kansas" and the Coming of the Civil War*. Philadelphia: J. B. Lippincott, 1969.

Rayback, Joseph G. *A History of American Labor*. New York: Macmillan, 1961.

Reardon, Carol. " 'We Are All in This War': The 148th Pennsylvania and Home Front Dissension in Centre County during the Civil War." In Cimbala and Miller, *Union Soldiers and the Northern Home Front.*

Reiger, John F. "Secession of Florida from the Union—A Minority Decision?" *Florida Historical Quarterly* 48 (1969–70): 358–68.

Revels, Tracy J. *Grander in Her Daughters: Florida's Women During the Civil War*. Columbia: University of South Carolina Press, 2004.

Richard, Patricia L. *Busy Hands: Images of the Family in the Northern Civil War Effort*. New York: Fordham University Press, 2003.

Robertson, James I. *Soldiers Blue and Gray*. Columbia: University of South Carolina Press, 1988.

Robinson, Armstead L. *Bitter Fruits of Bondage: The Demise of Slavery and the Collapse of the Confederacy, 1861–1865*. Charlottesville: University of Virginia Press, 2005.

Rogers, William Warren, Jr. *Confederate Home Front: Montgomery During the Civil War*. Tuscaloosa: University of Alabama Press, 1999.

Rorabaugh, W.J. "Who Fought for the North in the Civil War?: Concord, Massachusetts, Enlistments." *Journal of American History* 73 (1986): 694–701.

Rose, Willie Lee. *Rehearsal for Reconstruction: The Port Royal Experiment*. New York: Vintage Books, 1964.

Rothschild, Matthew. "You're Fired!" *The Progressive* (November 2004): 28–29.

Rutledge, Stephen W. "Stephen W. Rutledge: His Autobiography and Civil War Journal." *East Tennessee Roots* 6 (fall 1989): 101–12.

Ryan, David D. *A Yankee Spy in Richmond: The Civil War Diary of "Crazy Bet" Van Lew*. Mechanicsburg, PA: Stackpole, 1996.

Sampson, Robert D. "Charleston (Illinois) Riot." In Heidler and Heidler, *Encyclopedia of the American Civil War.*

———. "'Pretty Damned Warm Times': The 1864 Charleston [Ill.] Riot and the 'Inalienable Right of Revolution.'" *Illinois Historical Journal* 89 (1996): 99–116.

Sand Creek Massacre: A Documentary History. Introduction by John M. Carroll. New York: Sol Lewis, 1973.

Sandow, Robert M. "The Limits of Northern Patriotism: Early War Mobilization in Pennsylvania." *Pennsylvania History* 70 (2003): 175–203.

Sarris, Jonathan D. "An Execution in Lumpkin County: Local Loyalties in North Georgia's Civil War." In Noe and Wilson, *The Civil War in Appalachia.*

Scarborough, William Kauffman. *Masters of the Big House: Elite Slaveholders of the Mid-Nineteenth-Century South.* Baton Rouge: Louisiana State University Press, 2003.

Schlabach, Theron F. *Peace, Faith, Nation: Mennonites and Amish in Nineteenth-Century America.* Scottsdale, PA: Herald Press, 1988.

Schultz, Duane. *Month of the Freezing Moon: The Sand Creek Massacre.* New York: St. Martin's Press, 1990.

Schultz, Jane. *Women at the Front: Hospital Workers in Civil War America.* Chapel Hill: University of North Carolina Press, 2004.

Schwalm, Leslie A. "'Overrun with Free Negroes': Emancipation and Wartime Migration in the Upper Midwest." *Civil War History* 50 (2004): 145–74.

Scott, Anne Firor. *The Southern Lady from Pedestal to Politics, 1830–1930.* 1970. Reprint, Charlottesville: University Press of Virginia, 1995.

Sears, Stephen W. *George B. McClellan: The Young Napoleon.* New York: Ticknor and Fields, 1988.

Seidman, Rachel Filene. "A Monstrous Doctrine?: Northern Women on Dependency during the Civil War." In Cimbala and Miller, *Uncommon Time.*

Sellers, James Benson. *Slavery in Alabama.* 2d ed. Tuscaloosa: University of Alabama Press, 1964.

Shankman, Arnold. *The Pennsylvania Antiwar Movement, 1861–1865.* Rutherford, NJ: Fairleigh Dickinson University Press, 1980.

Sharkey, Robert P. *Money, Class, and Party: An Economic Study of Civil War and Reconstruction.* Baltimore: Johns Hopkins University Press, 1959.

Shattuck, Gardiner H. *A Shield and Hiding Place: The Religious Life of the Civil War Armies.* Macon, GA: Mercer University Press, 1987.

Shaw, Robert Gould. *Blue-Eyed Child of Fortune: The Civil War Letters of Colonel Robert Gould Shaw.* Edited by Russell Duncan. Athens: University of Georgia Press, 1992.

Shenkman, Richard. *I Love Paul Revere, Whether He Rode or Not.* New York: Harper Perennial, 1991.

Shugg, Roger W. *Origins of Class Struggle in Louisiana: A Social History of White Farmers and Laborers during Slavery and After, 1840–1875.* Baton Rouge: Louisiana State University Press, 1939.

Shy, John. *A People Numerous and Armed: Reflections on the Military Struggle for American Independence.* New York: Oxford University Press, 1976.

Simonhoff, Harry. *Jewish Participants in the Civil War.* New York: Arco Publishing Co., 1963.

Simons, A.M. *Social Forces in American History.* New York: International Publishers, 1926.

Sinclair, Andrew. *Corsair: The Life of J. Pierpont Morgan.* Boston: Little, Brown, 1981.

Sizer, Lyde Cullen. "Acting Her Part: Narratives of Union Women Spies." In Clinton and Silber, *Divided Houses.*

Smith, Adam I.P. "Beyond Politics: Patriotism and Partisanship on the Northern Home Front." In Cimbala and Miller, *Uncommon Time.*

Smith, David P. "The Limits of Dissent and Loyalty in Texas." In Sutherland, *Guerrillas, Unionists, and Violence on the Confederate Home Front.*

Smith, John David. *Black Soldiers in Blue: African American Troops in the Civil War Era.* Chapel Hill: University of North Carolina Press, 2002.

Smith, Page. *Trial By Fire: A People's History of the Civil War and Reconstruction.* New York: McGraw-Hill, 1982.

Snay, Mitchell. *Gospel of Disunion: Religion and Separatism in the Antebellum South.* New York: Cambridge University Press, 1993.

Snell, Mark A. " 'If They Would Know What I Know It Would Be Pretty Hard to Raise One Company in York': Recruiting, the Draft, and Society's Response in York County, Pennsylvania, 1861–1865." In Cimbala and Miller, *Union Soldiers and the Northern Home Front.*

Speer, Lonnie R. *Portals to Hell: Military Prisons of the Civil War.* Mechanicsburg, PA: Stackpole Books, 1997.

Stampp, Kenneth M. *And the War Came: The North and the Secession Crisis, 1860–61.* Chicago: University of Chicago Press, 1950.

———, ed. *The Causes of the Civil War.* Englewood Cliffs, NJ: Prentice-Hall, 1974.

———. *The Peculiar Institution: Slavery in the Ante-Bellum South.* New York: Vintage Books, 1956.

Standard, Diffie William. *Columbus, Georgia, in the Confederacy: The Social and Industrial Life of the Chattahoochee River Port.* New York: William-Frederick Press, 1954.

Sterling, Dorothy, ed. *We Are Your Sisters: Black Women in the Nineteenth Century.* New York: W.W. Norton, 1984.

Sterling, Robert. "Civil War Draft Resistance in the Middle West." Ph.D. diss., Northern Illinois University, 1974.

Stern, Philip Van Doren. *Prologue to Sumter.* Bloomington: Indiana University Press, 1961.

Still, William. *The Underground Rail Road.* Philadelphia: Porter and Coates, 1872.

Storey, Margaret M. *Loyalty and Loss: Alabama's Unionists in the Civil War and Reconstruction.* Baton Rouge: Louisiana State University Press, 2004.

Strong, Robert Hale. *A Yankee Private's Civil War.* Edited by Ashley Halsey. Chicago: H. Regnery Co., 1961.

Suderow, Bryce A. "The Battle of the Crater." In Urwin, *Black Flag Over Dixie.*

Sutherland, Daniel E. *Guerrillas, Unionists, and Violence on the Confederate Home Front.* Fayetteville: University of Arkansas Press, 1999.

———. *Seasons of War: The Ordeal of a Confederate Community, 1861–1865.* Baton Rouge: Louisiana State University Press, 1995.

Sweeney, Edwin R. *Mangas Coloradas: Chief of the Chiracahua Apaches.* Norman: University of Oklahoma Press, 1998.

Syrett, John. "The Confiscation Acts: The North Strikes Back." In Cimbala and Miller, *Uncommon Time.*

Taber, Thomas R., ed. *Hard Breathing Days: The Civil War Letters of Cora Beach Benton.* Albion, NY: Almeron Press, 2003.

Tatum, Georgia Lee. *Disloyalty in the Confederacy.* 1934. Reprint, with new introduction by David Williams, Lincoln: University of Nebraska Press, 2000.

Taylor, Robert A. "Unforgotten Threat: Florida Seminoles in the Civil War." *Florida Historical Quarterly* 69 (1991): 300–314.

Taylor, Susie King. *Reminiscences of My Life in Camp*. 1902. Reprint, with introduction by James M. McPherson, New York: Arno Press and the New York Times, 1968.

Thomas, Emory M. *The Confederate Nation, 1861–1865*. New York: Harper and Row, 1979.

Thomas, Henry W. *History of the Doles-Cook Brigade, Army of Northern Virginia, C.S.A.* Atlanta: Franklin Publishing, 1903.

Thompson, Jerry D. *Desert Tiger: Captain Paddy Graydon and the Civil War in the Far Southwest*. El Paso: Texas Western Press, 1992.

Thornton, J. Mills, III. *Politics and Power in a Slave Society: Alabama, 1800–1860*. Baton Rouge: Louisiana State University Press, 1978.

Trafzer, Clifford E. *The Kit Carson Campaign: The Last Great Navajo War*. Norman: University of Oklahoma Press, 1982.

Trenholm, Virginia Cole, and Maurine Carley. *The Shoshonis: Sentinels of the Rockies*. Norman: University of Oklahoma Press, 1964.

Tripp, Steven Elliott. *Yankee Town, Southern City: Race and Class Relations in Civil War Lynchburg*. New York: New York University Press, 1997.

Truth, Sojourner. *Narrative of Sojourner Truth*. 1878. Reprint, with introduction by Jeffrey C. Stewart, New York: Oxford University Press, 1991.

Turner, Maxine. *Navy Gray: A Story of the Confederate Navy on the Chattahoochee and Apalachicola Rivers*. Tuscaloosa: University of Alabama Press, 1988.

Tyler, Ronnie C. "Cotton on the Border, 1861–1865." *Southwestern Historical Quarterly* 73 (1970): 456–77.

Upson, Theodore F. *With Sherman to the Sea: The Civil War Diaries and Reminiscences of Theodore F. Upson*. Edited by Oscar Osburn Winther. Millwood, NY: Kraus Reprint Co., 1943.

Urwin, Gregory J.W., ed. *Black Flag Over Dixie: Racial Atrocities and Reprisals in the Civil War*. Carbondale: Southern Illinois University Press, 2004.

———. "United States Colored Troops." In Heidler and Heidler, *Encyclopedia of the American Civil War*.

———. "We Cannot Treat Negroes . . . as Prisoners of War." In Urwin, *Black Flag Over Dixie*.

Utley, Robert M. *Frontiersmen in Blue: The United States Army and the Indian, 1848–1865*. New York: Macmillan, 1967.

———. *The Indian Frontier of the American West, 1846–1890*. Albuquerque: University of New Mexico Press, 1984.

———. *The Lance and the Shield: The Life and Times of Sitting Bull*. New York: Ballantine Books, 1993.

Uya, Okon Edet. *From Slavery to Public Service: Robert Smalls, 1830–1913*. New York: Oxford University Press, 1971.

Vandiver, Frank E. *Ploughshares into Swords: Josiah Gorgas and Confederate Ordnance*. Austin: University of Texas Press, 1952.

Varon, Elizabeth. *Southern Lady, Yankee Spy: The True Story of Elizabeth Van Lew, A Union Agent in the Heart of the Confederacy*. New York: Oxford University Press, 2003.

Voegeli, V. Jacque. *Free But Not Equal: The Midwest and the Negro During the Civil War*. Chicago: University of Chicago Press, 1967.

———. "A Rejected Alternative: Union Policy and the Relocation of Southern 'Contrabands' at the Dawn of Emancipation." *Journal of Southern History* 69 (2003): 765–90.

Wakelyn, Jon L. *Confederates Against the Confederacy*. Westport, CT: Praeger, 2002.

Wakeman, Sarah Rossetta. *Uncommon Soldier: The Civil War Letters of Sarah Rosetta*

Wakeman, Alias Private Lyons Wakeman, 153rd Regiment, New York State Volunteers. Edited by Lauren Cook Burgess. New York: Oxford University Press, 1996.

Walker, Anne Kendrick. *Backtracking in Barbour County: A Narrative of the Last Alabama Frontier.* 1941. Reprint, Eufaula, AL: Eufaula Heritage Association, 1967.

———. *Russell County in Retrospect.* Richmond, VA: Dietz Press, 1950.

Wallace, Ernest, and E. Adamson Hoebel. *The Comanches: Lords of the South Plains.* Norman: University of Oklahoma Press, 1952.

Wallenstein, Peter. "Rich Man's War, Rich Man's Fight: Civil War and the Transformation of Public Finance in Georgia." *Journal of Southern History* 50 (1984): 15–42.

———. *From Slave South to New South: Public Policy in Nineteenth-Century Georgia.* Chapel Hill: University of North Carolina Press, 1987.

War of the Rebellion: A Compilation of the Official Records of the Union and Confederate Armies. 128 parts in 70 vols. and atlas. Washington, DC: Government Printing Office, 1880–1901.

Ward, Geoffrey C. *The Civil War.* New York: Alfred A. Knopf, 1992.

Warde, Mary Jane. "Now the Wolf Has Come: The Civilian Civil War in the Indian Territory." *Chronicles of Oklahoma* 71 (1993): 64–87.

Ware, Lynn Willoughby. "Cotton Money: Antebellum Currency Conditions in the Apalachicola/Chattahoochee River Valley." *Georgia Historical Quarterly* 74 (1990): 215–33.

Washburn, Wilcomb E. *The Governor and the Rebel: A History of Bacon's Rebellion in Virginia.* Chapel Hill: University of North Carolina Press, 1957.

Wasson, R. Gordon. *The Hall Carbine Affair: A Study in Contemporary Folklore.* New York: Pandick Press, 1941.

Watkins, Sam R. *Co. Aytch: Maury Grays, First Tennessee Regiment.* 1882. Reprint, Wilmington, NC: Broadfoot Publishing, 1987.

Watson, Harry L. "Conflict and Collaboration: Yeomen, Slaveholders, and Politics in the Antebellum South." *Social History* 10 (1985): 273–98.

Weitz, Mark A. *A Higher Duty: Desertion among Georgia Troops during the Civil War.* Lincoln: University of Nebraska Press, 2000.

Weller, Edwin. *A Civil War Courtship: The Letters of Edwin Weller from Antietam to Atlanta.* Edited by William Walton. Garden City, NY: Doubleday, 1980.

Wells, Jonathan Daniel. *The Origins of the Southern Middle Class, 1800–1861.* Chapel Hill: University of North Carolina Press, 2004.

Werner, Emmy E. *Reluctant Witnesses: Children's Voices from the Civil War.* New York: Westview Press, 1998.

Wertheimer, Barbara Mayer. *We Were There: The Story of Working Women in America.* New York: Pantheon Books, 1977.

West, Elliott. *The Contested Plains: Indians, Goldseekers, and the Rush to Colorado.* Lawrence: University Press of Kansas, 1998.

Wheeler, George. *Pierpont Morgan and Friends: The Anatomy of a Myth.* Englewood Cliffs, NJ: Prentice Hall, 1973.

White, Christine Schultz, and Benton R. White. *Now the Wolf Has Come: The Creek Nation in the Civil War.* College Station: Texas A&M University Press, 1996.

Whites, LeeAnn. "The Civil War as a Crisis in Gender." In Clinton and Silber, *Divided Houses.*

Wiener, Jonathan M. *Social Origins of the New South: Alabama, 1860–1885.* Baton Rouge: Louisiana State University Press, 1978.

Wiley, Bell I. *The Life of Billy Yank: The Common Soldier of the Union.* Baton Rouge: Louisiana State University Press, 1971.

———. *The Life of Johnny Reb: The Common Soldier of the Confederacy.* Baton Rouge: Louisiana State University Press, 1978.

———. *The Plain People of the Confederacy.* 1943. Reprint, with new introduction by Paul D. Escott, Columbia: University of South Carolina Press, 2000.

Williams, David. "Civil Liberties, C.S.A." In Heidler and Heidler, *Encyclopedia of the American Civil War.*

———. "Civil Liberties, U.S.A." In Heidler and Heidler, *Encyclopedia of the American Civil War.*

———. "Class Conflict, C.S.A." In Heidler and Heidler, *Encyclopedia of the American Civil War.*

———. "Class Conflict, U.S.A." In Heidler and Heidler, *Encyclopedia of the American Civil War.*

———. " 'The "Faithful Slave" Is About Played Out': Civil War Slave Resistance in the Lower Chattahoochee Valley." *Alabama Review* 52 (1999): 83–104.

———. *The Georgia Gold Rush: Twenty-Niners, Cherokees, and Gold Fever.* Columbia: University of South Carolina Press, 1993.

———. *Johnny Reb's War: Battlefield and Homefront.* Abilene, TX: McWhiney Foundation Press, 2000.

———. " 'On the Fringes of Hell': Billy Yank and Johnny Reb at the Siege of Kennesaw Mountain." *Georgia Historical Quarterly* 70 (1986): 703–16.

———. *Rich Man's War: Class, Caste, and Confederate Defeat in the Lower Chattahoochee Valley.* Athens: University of Georgia Press, 1998.

Williams, David, Teresa Crisp Williams, and David Carlson. *Plain Folk in a Rich Man's War: Class and Dissent in Confederate Georgia.* Gainesville: University Press of Florida, 2002.

Williams, Heather Andrea. *Self-Taught: African American Education in Slavery and Freedom.* Chapel Hill: University of North Carolina Press, 2005.

Williams, T. Harry. *Lincoln and the Radicals.* Madison: University of Wisconsin Press, 1941.

Willoughby, Lynn. *Fair to Middlin': The Antebellum Cotton Trade of the Apalachicola/Chattahoochee River Valley.* Tuscaloosa: University of Alabama Press, 1993.

Wills, Brian Steel. *The War Hits Home: The Civil War in Southeastern Virginia.* Charlottesville: University Press of Virginia, 2001.

Wilson, Harold S. *Confederate Industry: Manufacturers and Quartermasters in the Civil War.* Jackson: University Press of Mississippi, 2002.

Wilson, Keith P. *Campfires of Freedom: The Camp Life of Black Soldiers during the Civil War.* Kent, OH: Kent State University Press, 2002.

Wise, Stephen R. *Lifeline of the Confederacy: Blockade Running during the Civil War.* Columbia: University of South Carolina Press, 1988.

Wish, Harvey. "The Slave Insurrection Panic of 1856." *Journal of Southern History* 5 (1939): 206–22.

Wood, Ann Douglas. "The War Within: Women Nurses in the Union Army." *Civil War History* 28 (1972): 197–212.

Wood, John W. "Union and Secession in Mississippi." In *Southern Unionist Pamphlets and the Civil War,* edited by John L. Wakelyn. Columbia: University of Missouri Press, 1999.

Woodward, C. Vann. *Tom Watson.* 2d ed. Savannah, GA: Beehive Press, 1973.

Woodworth, Steven E. Review of *Gods and Generals*. *Journal of American History* 90 (2003): 123–24.

———. *While God Is Marching On: The Religious World of Civil War Soldiers*. Lawrence: University Press of Kansas, 2001.

Woody, Clara T., ed. "The Woolsey Expeditions of 1864." *Arizona and the West* 4 (summer 1962): 157–76.

Wooster, Ralph. *The Secession Conventions of the South*. Princeton, NJ: Princeton University Press, 1962.

Worley, Ted R. "The Arkansas Peace Society of 1861: A Study in Mountain Unionism." *Journal of Southern History* 24 (1958): 445–56.

Wright, Edward Needles. *Conscientious Objectors in the Civil War*. New York: A.S. Barnes, 1961.

Wright, Gavin. *The Political Economy of the Cotton South: Households, Markets, and Wealth in the Nineteenth Century*. New York: W.W. Norton, 1978.

Wyatt-Brown, Bertram. *Yankee Saints and Southern Sinners*. Baton Rouge: Louisiana State University Press, 1985.

Wynne, Lewis Nicholas. *The Continuity of Cotton: Planter Politics in Georgia, 1865–1892*. Macon, GA: Mercer University Press, 1986.

Young, Ralph F. *Dissent in America*. Vol. 1. New York: Pearson Longman, 2005.

Zinn, Howard. *Declarations of Independence: Cross-Examining American Ideology*. New York: Harper Perennial, 1990.

———. *A People's History of the United States*. New York: Harper and Row, 1980.

———. *The Twentieth Century: A People's History*. New York: Harper and Row, 1984.

Zinn, Howard, and Anthony Arnove. *Voices of a People's History of the United States*. New York: Seven Stories Press, 2004.

Index

abolitionists and abolitionism: and black refugees, 356; as "dirty word," 384; and Emancipation Proclamation, 358; William Lloyd Garrison, 38–40, 362, 378; Grimké sisters, 30; Rowan Hinton Helper on, 36–37; in Kansas, 47; and labor movement, 39; in the military, 361, 362; in the North, 38; portrayal of northerners as, 195; and start of the war, 65; women, 42–43; worries in South about, 3
abortion, 158
Acors, Almira, 170–71
Adair, J.B., 88
Adobe Walls, Battle of, 439–40
African Americans (blacks), 1, 453; and "10 percent plan," 381; and anti-Confederates, 338–43; backlash against, 359–60; changes in situation of, 376–79; and Confederate army, 153–54, 329, 365–67, 373–75; deportation of, 352–53; and draft riots, 277; W.E.B. Du Bois, 8, 10, 11, 344; employment of southern, 328–29; and enslavement proclamation, 362–63, 366; and labor movement, 486; Robert E. Lee on, 374, 375; Abraham Lincoln's attitude towards, 352–53; lynching of, 277, 478, 480; military

service of, 349–52; and Populist Party, 492; post–Civil War treatment of, 469–80; rebellion of, 71–72; Susie King Taylor, 326–27, 340, 479, 480; treatment of in the North, 38, 346–49; Sojourner Truth, 346, 347; Harriet Tubman, 17–18, 342, 346; and Union army, 341–45, 457; and Union victory, 462; and voting, 475–77, 480. *See also* black soldiers; Douglass, Frederick; Emancipation Proclamation; free blacks; rebellion; slavery; slave(s)
Africans, 27
Agassiz, Louis, 27
"the age of shoddy," 104, 105
Alabama, 55–57, 70, 71, 174–75, 472
"Albert Cashier," 143
Albright, Jacob, 70
alcohol, 210
Alcorn, James, 82
Alcott, Louisa May, 234
Aldrich, Alfred P., 13, 14
Allen, A.M., 204
Allen, Jacob, 362
Allen, W.B., 20
Allen, William, 34
Alligator, Billy Bowlegs, 398–99
"Amazonian warriors," 175